THE
DEVIANT'S
WAR

———

THE

DEVIANT'S

WAR

THE HOMOSEXUAL

VS.

THE UNITED STATES

OF AMERICA

ERIC CERVINI

FARRAR, STRAUS AND GIROUX

NEW YORK

Farrar, Straus and Giroux
120 Broadway, New York 10271

Owing to limitations of space, illustration credits can be found on pages 495–496.

Library of Congress Control Number: 2020003415
ISBN: 978-0-374-13979-7

Designed by Gretchen Achilles

Our books may be purchased in bulk for promotional, educational,
or business use. Please contact your local bookseller or the Macmillan
Corporate and Premium Sales Department at 1–800-221-7945, extension 5442,
or by e-mail at MacmillanSpecialMarkets@macmillan.com.

www.fsgbooks.com
www.twitter.com/fsgbooks • www.facebook.com/fsgbooks

1   3   5   7   9   10   8   6   4   2

To the teachers in my life,
the most important of whom is my mother, Lynn

Vice is a monster of so frightful mien,
As, to be hated, needs but to be seen;
Yet seen too oft, familiar with her face,
We first endure, then pity, then embrace.

—ALEXANDER POPE, 1733

Displayed on the wall of a police headquarters
in a large American city, 1965

CONTENTS

THE
DEVIANT'S
WAR

———

THE RITUAL

It began, as usual, in a public restroom. For ten years, Laud Humphreys of Oklahoma had been an Episcopal priest, but now he watched the silent choreography of the men. As always, the ritual of a men's room, or "tearoom," functioned somewhat like a game: positioning, signaling, contracting, payoff. Standing, looking, touching, fellatio.

"Like the smell of urine, fear pervades the atmosphere of the tearooms, making furtive every stage of the interaction," Humphreys later wrote. But if all went well, the ritual concluded with an adjustment of the pants and a zip of the fly. A shoulder pat, a hand wave, or a quiet "Thanks." Nobody hurt, nobody offended.

In 1966, as a doctoral student in sociology at Washington University in St. Louis, Humphreys had initiated his research in the city's public park restrooms. Married with two children, he developed a novel method to conceal his identity as a researcher and earn the trust of the "sexual deviants." He adopted the role of the "watch-queen," or a "voyeur-lookout" who guarded the men from nonparticipants and police officers. If someone approached, he coughed; if the coast was clear, he nodded.

"By passing as a deviant, I had observed their sexual behavior without disturbing it," explained the sociologist. Over the course of two years, he observed hundreds of sexual acts, taking notes with a hidden tape recorder.

The next step in his methodology contributed most to the controversy that surrounded the publication of his findings. Humphreys also followed the men to their cars, recorded their license plate numbers, and then carried that information to a police station. There, after Humphreys claimed to be performing "market research," friendly officers gave him the names and addresses of the men.

He waited a year, then changed his dress, hairstyle, and car. He traveled to the men's homes, rang their doorbells, and said he was a social health researcher. While sitting in their living rooms or drinking beer on their patios, he asked the men about their lives.

Over half of them, he learned, were married to women. The rest, even if they identified as gay, saw tearooms as safe havens. After all, where else could they go to meet others like themselves? In midcentury America, gay bars were perilous places. The police could raid them at any moment. Patrons risked being identified by coworkers, neighbors, or even the Federal Bureau of Investigation. At home, roommates or landlords were watching. Sometimes, police officers used telephoto lenses or high-powered binoculars to catch acts of sodomy or lewd conduct.

The names, addresses, and occupations of those arrested for homosexual activity often appeared in the next day's newspaper, which exposed their deviancy to families and employers. "Six Arrested in Perversion Case Here," read one typical headline. A seaman, twenty-five, of McAllister Street; an auto agency clerk, twenty-seven, of Clay Street; a musician, thirty-six, of Taylor Street; a drama coach, twenty-three, of Seventh Avenue; a photo refinisher, forty-three, of Laurel Street.

After World War II, homosexual arrests—including those for sodomy, dancing, kissing, or holding hands—occurred at the rate of one every ten minutes, each hour, each day, for fifteen years. In sum, one million citizens found themselves persecuted by the American state for sexual deviation.

Men unable to risk identification had only the public restroom, a space both public and private. When an intruder—a policeman or an unsuspecting passerby—interrupted the ritual, participants could claim to be using the restroom for its intended purpose. They simply performed "huge elaborate disinterest" until the threat washed his hands and disappeared.

Laud Humphreys ultimately concluded that police departments, by criminalizing sexual activity in public restrooms, created crime from a harmless activity, stigmatizing homosexuality and incentivizing blackmailers.

He estimated that 5 percent of St. Louis's adult male population engaged in the ritual of the tearoom. "What the covert deviant needs is a sexual machine—collapsible to hip-pocket size, silent in operation," he wrote. "In tearoom sex he has the closest thing to such a device."

The sociologist also noticed something curious about the men he observed. When interviewed in their homes, those who visited tearooms tended to project a high level of morality. A "breastplate of righteousness," Humphreys called it. Compared to a control group, tearoom participants lived in clean homes, drove nice cars, went to church, and supported the efforts of the local Vice Squad. They were conservative; they did not attend civil rights demonstrations. By embracing respectability, Humphreys concluded, these men shielded themselves—and others—from the humiliation of the tearoom.

With the publication of Humphreys's research, journalists and fellow sociologists leapt to denounce the former priest. He had deceived the tearoom-goers and made them vulnerable to prosecution, they argued. Washington University's chancellor, upset that Humphreys had not reported the men to the police, revoked his research grant and teaching contract.

Humphreys eventually repudiated the dishonest elements of his methodology, and at a 1974 sociology conference, while his wife sat in the audience, he announced that he was a gay man.

Sociology professors now teach Humphreys's book *Tearoom Trade* as an example of unethical research, ignoring his findings about the men who exited the tearoom before enshrouding themselves in cloaks of propriety. Meanwhile, stories of gay liberation in America often begin with a June 1969 uprising, instantaneous and transformative, outside a bar in Greenwich Village.

A 1950s tearoom, however, is where this book, a tale of sexual deviants versus their government, begins. The path to equality exists not only because of a riot, but also because of a battle that began in a public restroom. Today, LGBTQ+ Americans march because a scientist named Dr. Frank Kameny once entered a tearoom. A young Harvard-educated astronomer, Kameny listened to classical music and wore three-piece suits. He never liked to talk about his participation in the ritual.

That summer evening, as Kameny stood before a urinal, two police officers hid above him, watching from behind a ventilation grill in the ceiling. They arrested him as he exited the restroom, triggering his personal ruin and the strange series of events that led him and his country to gay liberation.

Pride emerged, slowly yet irrevocably, from a regime of secrecy and shame.

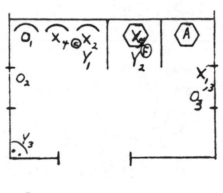

(F) = Fellatio performed

(C) = Contract made

Field notes from a tearoom encounter

1.

THE ASTRONOMER

As a teenager, Franklin Edward Kameny easily observed the problem. "I was well aware of the quite unequivocal direction of my masturbation fantasies," he later recalled. And unlike many adolescents growing up in the 1930s, he even had a word for it. He knew the definition of *homosexuality*.

But to make the next logical step, to conclude that his attraction to other boys made him a homosexual, would have represented the height of illogic. Indeed, since his birth on May 21, 1925, his world had been one of symmetry, rules, and rationality. Even in the chaos of New York City and the despair of the Depression, life seemed essentially linear. Sensible.

His father, Emil Kameny, had followed the path of the American dream, becoming an electrical engineer after emigrating from Poland. Rae Beck Kameny, whose parents emigrated from Austria-Hungary, grew up on the Lower East Side and worked as a high-ranking secretary. After marrying Emil in 1922, she became a housewife, the strong-willed head of a home comfortably situated in the Jewish-American middle class. Franklin and his younger sister, Edna, grew up in a handsome, semi-attached brick house in Richmond Hill, a German and Irish neighborhood in southeastern Queens.

Franklin's parents quickly recognized the unique nature of his mind. He taught himself to read by the age of four, and he used this new skill to systematically plan the rest of his life. When his grandmother gave him *The Book of Knowledge*, a World War I–era children's encyclopedia, he read it cover to cover. The science sections fascinated him the most, so the four-year-old decided to become a scientist. By the age of six, he narrowed

his chosen profession down to a specialty. He would become an astronomer, learning the secrets of the heavens.

"And," as he often said when concluding stories from his life, "that
was that."

The short, hazel-eyed Franklin—he had a mischievous, captivating
smile—was precocious but shy. His mother knew that if she reasoned
with her son, if she explained the logic behind a decision or rule, he would
obey. In school, he mostly kept his thoughts to himself. When he inevitably noticed teachers' errors, he remained quiet. He entered high school
at the age of twelve.

A rational boy striving toward the stars in a straight, structured world,
Franklin could not possibly conclude he was a homosexual. But because
he accepted the existence of his desires—they were objectively *there*, after
all—Franklin searched for an alternative, more acceptable explanation for
them, and he found one. As a quiet, awkward student surrounded by significantly older classmates, Franklin saw himself still maturing, both
physically and socially. His desires, he told himself, were symptoms of an
unfortunate but universal phase through which his peers had already progressed. The sexual attraction he felt for boys would, as he matured, be
replaced by an attraction to girls.

As the years passed, though, Franklin remained trapped in a state that
felt alarmingly less temporary with each nighttime fantasy. He confronted the possibility that his theory was wrong, and reevaluated his
position. If he had desires for other boys, and if those desires hurt nobody,
how could they possibly be in error? If his condition—however long it
lasted—conflicted with society, and if rejecting himself was ipso facto illogical, then he had no choice but to reject society itself.

If society and I differ on something, the fifteen-year-old Franklin
concluded, I'm right and society is wrong. And if society rejected him?
"Why, society can," as he later described the realization. "They'll lose
more than I will."

The next year, increasingly confident in the power of his nonconforming mind, Kameny implemented a systematic investigation of his religious beliefs. At the end of that process, he concluded that God did not
exist. He became an atheist, and that was that.

At Richmond Hill High School, Franklin remained quiet, alone among his thoughts. He had absolutely no interest in sports. He claimed to have a small circle of friends, but his mother could never recall meeting them. He went on a date or two with a girl, but nothing came of his half-hearted efforts.

So Franklin threw himself into the skies. He founded an astronomy club and became its president. He frequently visited the New York City planetarium. His mother bought him a telescope, and he spent countless nights studying the stars, alone. "His work in that class was as near 100% perfect as I ever hope to see," his physics teacher later wrote. "I sometimes thought his greatest fault was in taking his work too seriously."

He felt at home in the isolated, regimented universe of summer camp, attending coed Nokomis Camps, an hour's drive north of the city, every year since he was a young boy. In high school, he became a counselor, taking pride in coordinating astronomical activities for the younger campers. One year, Franklin sexually experimented with a fellow male counselor. Describing the experience later in life, Franklin remained reticent; the boy had been a close friend who never identified as gay. "There was ferment there, but nothing at all real," he explained. Franklin was not a homosexual, after all, and the camp never discovered his transgression. "He has a fine character," the Nokomis director wrote, "and his background and family are symbols of true Americanism."

Frank Kameny enrolled at Queens College, just up the road from his family home, in September 1941. The sixteen-year-old had been a freshman for only a few weeks when hundreds of Japanese warplanes flew toward the Hawaiian island of Oahu on the morning of December 7, 1941.

WHEN AMERICA ENTERED World War II, the draft's minimum age was twenty-one. Five years too young, Kameny continued his studies, commuting to Queens College from his home in Richmond Hill. He majored in physics, and his decade-long path to becoming an astronomer looked as if it would continue unbroken. But in November 1942, Congress lowered the draft's minimum age to eighteen. Kameny would become eligible for the draft in six months.

His family scrambled to keep the patently nonathletic, budding young scientist away from the front lines. In December 1942, the military announced the creation of the Army Specialized Training Program (ASTP), designed to provide a constant stream of technically trained young specialists during wartime. Instead of fighting on a battlefield, Kameny would remain in a university classroom, along with 150,000 other scientists, engineers, medics, and linguists in training.

The ASTP required men to formally enlist and begin basic training before they could enroll in courses. So on May 18, 1943, three days before his eighteenth birthday, Kameny joined the army.

At the induction station, a secretary handed him a pencil and a questionnaire. As he completed the form, he saw the question: "Is the opposite sex unpleasant to you?" Kameny, along with nearly eighteen million other inductees, had to prove he was a stable heterosexual with "the ability to accept the male pattern of our society," as psychiatrists put it. Since early 1942, army examiners had searched for the appearance-based warning signs in inductees, among them "feminine bodily characteristics," "effeminacy in dress and manner," and a "patulous rectum." But as examiners became overwhelmed by the number of men they had to interview, they increasingly relied on a questionnaire to identify inductees who "failed" and required a more extensive examination by a professional psychiatrist.

Like the vast majority of other gay men confronted by the question, Kameny checked "no."

At basic training in Fort Benning, Georgia, Kameny spent three months learning to fire rifles and machine guns. The army then shipped Kameny to the University of Illinois at Urbana-Champaign to study mechanical engineering. Sharing a room with other trainee-soldiers in the Sigma Chi fraternity house, Kameny was grateful to be safe in America during that frigid Midwest winter of early 1944.

In February, only six weeks after the beginning of Kameny's program, General George Marshall informed the secretary of war that the impending invasion of France required an additional 134,000 men who had already completed basic training. He recommended withdrawing all but thirty thousand participants from the ASTP.

"The rug was just pulled out from under us," Kameny recalled.

He found himself sleeping on a sodden field in Camp Polk, Louisiana. He became an infantry private, the lowest rank in the army, tasked with operating an eighty-one-millimeter mortar.

In November 1944, he set sail for Europe on a Cunard White Star luxury liner converted for the war; rows of hammocks lined its decks. Rae Beck Kameny had been volunteering for the Red Cross and shrewdly learned her son's time of departure. When Kameny arrived at the Hudson Piers, wearing his heavy knapsack, he saw his mother there, too, distributing doughnuts to the terrified men.

The ASTP fiasco represented, as one historian put it, a "series of disillusionments" for Kameny and thousands of trainees like him. The military had repeatedly claimed that it needed the technical skills of high-achieving young men, but as the Kamenys saw it, now it was discarding his prodigious mind onto the battlefield. Kameny had placed his life in the care of the United States government, and as his mother put it, "he got a dirty deal."

KAMENY'S SHIP slowly approached England, dropping depth charges and zigzagging to avoid German submarines. After three weeks, Kameny landed in Southampton, and the army sent him to a tent camp a few miles away from Stonehenge. Not yet in the fog of war, he waited. Kameny had Christmas dinner in a sympathetic local's unheated mansion, shivering beneath blankets. He visited London, and from Hyde Park, he saw V-2 rockets—the Nazi "vengeance" missiles—fall upon the city. Looking upward, above the terror and destruction that surrounded him, Kameny marveled at the weapons, the first man-made objects to travel into space. They looked like meteors, soaring across the sky.

By the time Kameny's unit reached France, the Battle of the Bulge had finished. He spent most of January 1945 waiting in Alsace-Lorraine's silent, eerie cold. The Americans had retrieved their dead, but the Germans had not. Kameny wandered the endless, bitterly frozen farmland, still spotted with foxholes. As the ground began to melt, Kameny saw boot tips sticking up from the snow.

In the Netherlands, he fought. As part of a mortar crew, Kameny could not see where his shells landed. He did not know how many German soldiers he killed. But he also carried a semiautomatic carbine, which he occasionally fired at closer range. He took prisoners. When he found himself under heavy artillery fire, fearing for his life, he often took shelter in locals' basements, where, if he found canned jars of food, he would feast.

"We lost quite a number of men," he remembered decades later. "I could easily enough . . ." He stopped himself midsentence, looked away, and changed the subject.

Kameny was in the medieval German town of Duderstadt on May 8, when the Nazis surrendered. With the fighting over, Kameny used his German skills to serve as an interpreter for his unit. It was a warm spring of wary optimism. On his twentieth birthday, two weeks after the Allied victory, Kameny received a package. Sent by his mother in New York, the box had miraculously arrived in time. It contained a birthday cake. The package had been in the mail for a month, so when Kameny opened it, he found the cake covered in the most brilliantly colorful array of mold he had ever seen.

On March 24, 1946, the army discharged Kameny, and he returned home to Richmond Hill. After two years away, he did not discuss the war. He tried not to think about it. He pushed his memories—the shells, his carbine, the prisoners—to a compartmentalized corner of his mind, a simple task for a young man long accustomed to relegating so much of himself to a dark part of his consciousness.

Historians have described World War II as a "nationwide coming out experience" that forced young gay men out of their small towns and into confined same-sex environments, where they could finally encounter others like themselves in training, in port, and in battle.

Kameny, however, ignored the opportunities for homosexual experiences. "Oh," he sighed in the final years of his life, while recalling the missed chances for sex during his army years, "there were so many."

But that was that.

KAMENY RETURNED to Queens College, where he received the lowest grades of his academic career, but Harvard accepted him nonetheless. He moved to Cambridge, Massachusetts, in early 1948 to begin the PhD program in astronomy.

During Kameny's first year at Harvard, someone invited him to a Boston gay bar. He wanted to go, and he knew he would likely enjoy it. And if he enjoyed it, he would likely return. And if he kept returning, if he found himself voluntarily trapped in Boston's gay world, that would indicate that he was a homosexual, which he was not. The "tissue paper barrier," as he later described it, still existed between his urges and his acceptance of those urges. He was not ready to tear down that thin wall. So he declined the invitation, explaining he did not care for beer. A perfectly honest excuse, he assured himself, since he in fact did not like beer, not yet.

The skies kept him distracted from the truth. By 1949, he earned his master's degree, and during the summers of 1950 and 1951, he managed Harvard's prodigious Oak Ridge astronomical observatory. It contained the largest optical telescope on the East Coast, a cylindrical behemoth containing a five-foot mirror, housed under a protective dome and perpetually pointed at celestial bodies trillions of miles away. Every few years, reflecting telescopes need their fragile, flawless mirrors re-coated with aluminum. After studying a new technique for accomplishing this feat, Kameny perfected it. He repaired Harvard's 120-cubic-foot aluminization tank, then carefully placed a giant sheet of glass inside, ensuring not a single piece of dust occupied the chamber. He used a vacuum to remove every molecule of air within it, then heated the aluminum until it evaporated. Individual aluminum molecules flew through the emptiness of the tank until they collided, with perfect smoothness, onto the glass. Not only did Kameny master this complicated process, but he also became its national authority. He wrote a 171-page telescope aluminization manual, which, to this day, is still available for reference at Harvard's astronomy library.

He taught Harvard College students, wielding considerable power over the sons of America's elite: Ted Kennedy and Adlai Stevenson III were undergraduates at the time. Kameny kept himself permanently busy, teaching navigation and other astronomical courses, running public observatory nights, and traveling to New Haven, where he taught astronomy to the men of Yale.

As Kameny became an authority in Cambridge, he grew to despise the town. "I hate cold weather," Kameny later explained. "I *loathe* it." The constant presence of clouds, moreover, made data collection via telescope nearly impossible. So when he attended a conference on his specialty of photoelectric spectroscopy in Flagstaff, Arizona, he visited the University of Arizona's Steward Observatory in Tucson, 250 miles south. It had a desert climate, a decent telescope, and plenty of access to offer. A man preoccupied with logic and order, Kameny noticed that the rains occurred at pleasingly predictable intervals, from two until four each afternoon. He quickly arranged to spend a year there.

In Tucson, Kameny befriended an undergraduate physics student who recognized a compatriot in Kameny and hesitantly came out to him. Kameny told him that he, too, felt the same way about men. Together, they dipped their toes into the vibrant gay underground world of Tucson, where Kameny met Keith.

On Kameny's twenty-ninth birthday, May 21, 1954, they became lovers. He and Keith drove to the middle of the desert a few miles north of Tucson, and on a warm night, they lay under a clear sky, a full moon. It was, as Kameny observed with Keith in his arms, perfect. How could something so beautiful, so objectively full of joy, be any less natural, any less right, than the infinite stars above him?

That summer, the couple drove to California—Kameny's first trip to the West Coast—where, in Los Angeles and San Francisco, he learned the rules and rituals of America's gay underground. Kameny and his lover returned to conquer the gay world of Tucson, where the astronomer found a home. "I took to gay life," he later explained, "like a duck to water, as if it had been made for me, or I for it. And that was it."

After a year in Tucson, Kameny received a position at Armagh Observatory in Northern Ireland, and in September 1954, he sailed for Europe once again. He explored the small, covert gay world of Belfast, where he learned to enjoy beer. Whispers spread through the gay underground of Northern Ireland about the American in Armagh, and more than once, the astronomer had to escort a visitor—unknown, unannounced, and hopeful to meet the foreigner—away from the observatory.

Kameny and Keith exchanged letters between Armagh and Tucson, and when Kameny returned to Boston, they called each other every few weeks. After a while, though, their lives continued down separate paths. Later, in several interviews before his death, Kameny would never reveal Keith's last name.

But he described one last interaction: twenty years after leaving Tucson, Kameny received an old, yellowed news clipping in the mail. It was an article from an Arizona newspaper, written about a local astronomer leaving for Northern Ireland. It came from Keith, the first object of Kameny's love, who had held on to it for two decades.

KAMENY RETURNED to Harvard in the fall of 1955 and immersed himself in both the stars and gay Boston. Bars that attracted a gay clientele—they could not label themselves gay bars for fear of the police—proliferated rapidly after World War II, and Boston had nearly two dozen of them in the 1950s. Scollay Square had sailor-filled bars, like the Lighthouse and the Silver Dollar. The crowded, more obviously gay bars were in Park Square: Punch Bowl, Playland, Jacques. The theater district was home to an elegant, dimly lit, stained-glass-paneled former speakeasy called the Napoleon Club, with its baby grand piano, suit-and-tie requirement, and visitors like Liberace and Judy Garland. Then, only a few blocks from Harvard Square was the new, romantic, mural-covered Casablanca, housed below the Brattle Theater. Though most gay Harvard students preferred the anonymity of the downtown bars, as one historian explains, "many a Harvard gay found his future lover on its barstools, where only men foregathered."

Faced with such a vibrant gay world, Kameny spent the last year of his PhD dividing his energies, precisely fifty-fifty, between writing his thesis and cruising, even finding a way to do both simultaneously. He always carried, as he would for the rest of his life, a pencil and paper to gay bars. While flirting with a man, he sometimes whipped out his pencil and paper to write down a thought about his dissertation. By the end of the evening, he would have a long list of notes to himself, and the next morning, by the time he said farewell to that night's conquest, his day of astronomy was already planned.

He also cruised Boston's public spaces: Cambridge Common, Arlington Street, and the bank of the Charles River in front of Harvard. That summer, for the first time, he went to Provincetown, the gay-friendly town on the tip of Cape Cod, which, as Kameny would later say with a knowing laugh, needed no elaboration.

Kameny completed and defended his thesis, "A Photoelectric Study of Some RV Tauri and Yellow Semiregular Variables," in 1956. He received his doctorate in astronomy, after fifteen years of higher education and military service, that June. The junior senator from Massachusetts John F. Kennedy spoke at his commencement, arguing for the "need for greater cooperation and understanding between politicians and intellectuals."

Kameny planned to enter academia that fall, teaching and researching at Georgetown University in Washington, D.C. Finally, he could sign his letters "Dr. Franklin E. Kameny, PhD."

After dreaming about it for twenty years, he was an astronomer.

ON THE EVENING of Tuesday, August 28, 1956, Kameny attended the closing banquet of the American Astronomical Society's ninety-fifth annual meeting at the University of California, Berkeley, only a few minutes' ride from San Francisco's East Bay train terminal.

It had been a long conference: 5 days, 105 papers, and a trip 2 hours south to the Lick Observatory. Kameny presented an abstract of his research, which *The Astronomical Journal* had accepted for publication. At the banquet, a National Science Foundation official presented a "very optimistic view" of astronomy-related funding from the United States federal government. Kameny had reason to feel good.

Within a few hours, by 12:45 a.m., he was in jail.

"We observed KAMENY in the place for half hour," reported the police officers, who had caught Kameny in the public lavatory of the downtown train terminal.

From behind the ventilation grille, the officers had seen another man arrive and stand, waiting, before a urinal. Robert Pier was twenty-seven, nearly six foot two, with brown hair and blue eyes. He worked in a public relations company.

The police, still watching Kameny, "then observed him stand alongside of PIER at the urinal. PIER then reached over and touched the private parts of KAMENY."

The police's description of the crime ends there. Kameny later claimed the man touched him for less than five seconds. Perhaps Kameny became nervous and fled, or perhaps the encounter lasted longer than that. He never liked to discuss the incident.

"When questioned both admin [*sic*] the act," concluded the officers.

Kameny spent the night behind bars, faced with charges of lewd conduct and loitering.

The next morning, Kameny went before the city's municipal court. The judge threw out the loitering charge, and the remaining lewdness charge left Kameny with two choices. He could plead not guilty, remaining in San Francisco for an undefined number of days until the case concluded, or he could plead guilty, pay a fifty-dollar fine, and receive just six months of probation. His new job at Georgetown began in just a few days, so Kameny made the logical choice. He pleaded guilty and paid the fine. Just like a speeding ticket, he reasoned.

A few minutes after the trial, Kameny visited the probation office, where he learned a piece of reassuring news. If he complied with the conditions of his probation, California law permitted "setting aside a verdict of guilty and dismissal of the accusations," releasing him from "all penalties and disabilities resulting from the offense." He would be able to apply for jobs—and testify under oath—with the knowledge that the final disposition of his arrest had been "Not Guilty, Case Dismissed."

And that, Kameny thought, would be that.

Franklin Edward Kameny, circa 1945

2 .

———

THE LETTER

In 1916, Dr. Alfred C. Kinsey entered Harvard with a secret. Despite his homosexual desires, the zoologist never entered the gay world of Boston. He remained quiet and conservative, a "shy and lonely young man who had avidly pursued gall wasps instead of girls," as a colleague later described him.

The blue-eyed, bow-tied scientist did not intend to spark a sexual revolution. In 1938, after eighteen years as a biology professor at the University of Indiana, the institution selected him to lead its new marriage course. Scientists, Kinsey observed, knew less about human sexual behavior than they did about farm animals. When he began a survey of his students' sexual practices, it grew to include a national sample. He paid no heed to social norms. Just as he had collected gall wasps, he collected "sexual histories" in every part of the country, from every locale imaginable, including—for methodological reasons only—bars for homosexuals. He analyzed only the results for white men.

Sexual Behavior in the Human Male hit American bookshelves in 1948, the year Frank Kameny entered Harvard. It contained eight hundred pages of bland scientific prose and cost six dollars and fifty cents (nearly seventy in today's dollars). Its publisher expected to sell only five thousand copies. *The New York Times* refused to review or advertise it, but the tome quickly reached number two on its bestseller list, selling over half a million copies.

Kinsey admitted he was "totally unprepared" for what he had discovered.

No matter how he recalculated the data, his findings remained the same: homosexuals existed everywhere. Fifty percent of all males admitted to having an erotic response to other males, and 13 percent engaged in primarily homosexual behavior for three years or more. Homosexual activity took place "in every age group, in every social level, in every conceivable occupation, in cities and on farms, and in the most remote areas of the country." In a society that deemed homosexuality either immoral, a sickness, or both, *Sexual Behavior in the Human Male* provided evidence that gay sex was, in fact, objectively normal.

Kinsey also found that *all* men, not just gay men, broke America's codes of morality. Fifty percent of husbands cheated on their wives. In achieving orgasm—through sodomy, adultery, or fornication, for example—an estimated 95 percent of American males had broken at least one state or federal law that regulated sexual activity.

His downfall began in 1953, when he published a sequel, *Sexual Behavior in the Human Female*. Lesbians tended to achieve orgasms more frequently than straight women, he concluded, since the penis was not so important to female pleasure. Accused of "hurling the insult of the century against our mothers, wives, daughters and sisters," Kinsey lost his funding. By 1956, Kinsey feared losing his Institute for Sex Research.

The guardians of morality could not undo Kinsey's impact on American public life. "No single event," *TIME* explained, "did more for open discussion of sex than the Kinsey Report, which got such matters as homosexuality, masturbation, coitus and orgasm into most papers and family magazines."

In 1950, a graduate student at Northwestern University wrote an essay lauding Kinsey for illustrating that "hypocrisy has been legislated into the statutes of the various states." The student, Hugh Hefner, published the first issue of *Playboy* three years later.

On August 25, 1956, at 8:00 a.m. Eastern Time, Dr. Alfred Kinsey, age sixty-two, died of heart complications. Only four hours later, at 9:00 a.m. Pacific Time, Dr. Frank Kameny attended the opening session of the American Astronomical Society's ninety-fifth annual meeting at the University of California, Berkeley. Because of the recently departed Kinsey,

Frank Kameny could guess the statistical probability that any given man in the audience had once achieved an orgasm from homosexual activity: 37 percent.

He also knew there existed a significant likelihood that he could encounter one of those men, later that night, in a public restroom.

KAMENY ARRIVED in Washington without knowing any homosexuals in that city, so he remedied the problem systematically. "I simply proceeded to go to gay bars every single night, seven nights a week," he later explained. He researched the locations of the city's gay bars and began collecting data on the foreign world of gay Washington. He concluded it was most efficient to meet people in quantity, not quality. Then, after a year or so, he would have the raw material to build a social life of his own.

The nucleus of gay Washington had long been Lafayette Square, the public park immediately adjacent to the White House. In the early nineteenth century, the square contained slave pens, and in 1885, after the city decided to keep the park open all night, men began appearing there for sex. It was a logical location: downtown, dark, and with plenty of trees for cover. By the early twentieth century, men of all backgrounds knew where to go for a sexual encounter with other men.

Washington did not become a truly gay city, however, until the New Deal. As the federal bureaucracy expanded in response to the Depression, young men streamed into the District for jobs. The trend continued during World War II, and the population of the Washington area doubled from 700,000 to 1.4 million between 1930 and 1950. The city scrambled to accommodate its population boom by building rooming houses and apartments, which further removed men and women from the watchful eye of their families and placed them in spaces dominated by other young, single tenants. There, parties could be private. Many young men had roommates, and nobody asked questions about two men living together.

The gay bars of 1950s Washington were peculiar places. After Prohibition ended, Congress, which directly controlled the capital's laws, technically outlawed *all* bars, and only restaurants could attain liquor licenses in the District of Columbia. The law also required patrons to remain seated as they consumed alcohol. If patrons wanted to change seats, a server would move their drinks for them. All such establishments closed at midnight on Saturdays and Sundays.

The gay bars for white men opened downtown, not far from Lafayette Square. The Chicken Hut was the most popular of them all, less than a block from the square. During the day, it served as a lunchtime cafeteria, attracting straight government workers. But at night, a pianist dominated the space, regaling the audience with show tunes and camped versions of ballads. As midnight approached, the Hut often filled to capacity. The patrons joined in the Hut's theme song, the Whiffenpoof Song, and raised their beer glasses to sing, "Doomed from here to eternity / God have mercy on such as we."

On the next block stood the staid Derby Room, with a maître d' who welcomed newcomers at the door before ushering them down the staircase to their seats—as the rest of the patrons watched their entrance. If one stood on the sidewalk between the Chicken Hut and the Derby Room, groups of gay men seemed to be everywhere.

Though Washington did not enact its own Jim Crow laws, de facto segregation reigned in the establishments that constituted the gay scene. The Chicken Hut did not serve Black customers until a 1953 Supreme Court decision, and even then, it placed RESERVED signs on tables to tell African Americans that there was no room for them.

In total, by the time Kameny arrived in 1956, Washington had no fewer than seventeen bars that primarily catered to homosexuals, including the two bars open to gay Black men, located in the Columbia Heights and Shaw neighborhoods. White men like Kameny, however, did not venture there. His world, the world of the downtown gay bars, was white.

Fear of persecution seeped into each of the establishments. The policing of gay Washington began as early as the 1890s, when officials installed lighting around monuments and increased overnight officer patrols "in the interest of morality." In 1946, the U.S. Park Police established an investigative unit, which included six plainclothesmen who secretly monitored public restrooms. Washington's Metropolitan Police established a Morals Division with four undercover policemen, tasked solely with finding and arresting homosexuals.

"Never a week went by," one gay Washington resident remembered, "where you didn't read *The Washington Post* and it would come out with somebody who was picked up in one of the parks for soliciting." Police arrested one victim per day during the "Sex Perversion Elimination Program" of 1947.

The Washington police in the 1950s commonly assaulted or arrested those who cross-dressed, especially drag queens of color. (Drag shows primarily took place in straight bars, rather than gay bars, which did not dare draw attention to themselves.) As one Black drag queen later remembered, the police "liked to just jump out on you and [making thumping sound] do you any way—tear your clothes off, take your wig off." After repeatedly resisting police brutality, she eventually left Washington, fearing that the police, if she fought back once more, would kill her.

But the authorities tolerated the white bars of downtown gay Washington. As long as their patrons followed the rules—no standing, no dancing, no drag—they could exist in the spaces they had created for themselves, a world in the shadow of the White House.

Kameny felt safe in this world, and in time, he felt powerful, too. As he visited the bars each night, the astronomer gathered an immense quantity of social data, and with so much information on gay Washington, he became its expert.

Saturdays at midnight, gay men and women flooded out of the closing bars and into private homes, bringing their own beer and, ideally, dates. Kameny estimated that he went to fifty-two of these late-night parties during his first year in Washington. He became a clearinghouse of information on social events, and bar goers began asking him the same question each Saturday: where was that night's party? His phone rang endlessly. "I just sat home as the gatherer and dispenser of information until I decided to pick myself up and go to one of them," he later recalled.

Kameny's network expanded across the East Coast. During his first year in Washington, he discovered the gay summer resort of Cherry Grove on New York's Fire Island. He began inviting his growing Washington network, and his vacation group snowballed to include thirty homosexuals—from Washington, Philadelphia, and New York—in two mammoth cottages.

Acting as a travel agent for the group, he made airplane reservations, which inevitably resulted in very gay flights. Kameny once convinced an airline captain to allow his party, which filled the entire plane, to consume the liquor they had brought on board—in blatant violation of FAA regulations. At the end of the journey, one passenger snatched the bewildered flight attendant's hat from her head. The group began passing it around the plane. Each passenger placed a donation into it, thanking her for serving their raucous group. "I don't think the hostess will ever forget us," Kameny later remarked.

Hundreds, perhaps thousands, learned the astronomer's name. Kameny explained his manic party-going and social organizing as an attempt to compensate for the experiences he missed during his time in the closet. "Lost time syndrome," he called it. And though Kameny provided an undeniable service to his community, he did not mind the clout, the feeling of being *the* undeniable expert on gay Washington, that came with it.

Georgetown University did not invite Kameny to return for the fall semester of 1957. The decision apparently had nothing to do with his robust gay life. "I personally feel my tenure was not extended primarily because on my application I stated that I had no professed religion," Kameny later told investigators.

That same year, the United States government realized it desperately needed him.

BEFORE FEAR, there was awe. On the night of October 4, 1957, America learned that a foreign object—emitting an ominous beeping sound—was orbiting the planet. "Listen now," announced an NBC Radio host, "for the sound that forevermore separates the old from the new."

"Red 'Moon' Flies 18,000 M.P.H.," announced *The Washington Star* on its front page. "Soviets Fire Earth Satellite into Space," proclaimed *The New York Times*, featuring an illustration of the sphere's path across the Atlantic Ocean. The military rushed to track Earth's new moon, and Americans looked skyward with wonder, squinting and straining to see *Sputnik* with their own eyes.

In the days that followed, a cloud of existential dread settled upon the nation. "Russia had beaten the United States in the satellite race," the

Star wrote. Not only did the United States lack its own functioning satellite, but *Sputnik* weighed eight times more than the American device still in development. The public contemplated the profoundly unsettling fact that America was no longer the most technologically superior nation on Earth. When Senate majority leader Lyndon Johnson gazed at the stars from his Texas ranch, as he later wrote, "the sky seemed almost alien." Indeed, if the Soviets controlled the sky, what now could rain down from it? The Central Intelligence Agency warned that the country faced "a period of grave national emergency." Politicians from both parties demanded a reevaluation of everything that had allowed the fiasco to occur.

Technology and its creators represented the country's only hope. "We must change our public attitude toward science and scientists," concluded *LIFE* magazine. If America wanted to reassert its technological superiority, it needed knowledge of the heavens. Almost overnight, astronomers found themselves among the country's most important citizens.

Frank Kameny had long hypothesized man would someday leave Earth's atmosphere, and he dreamed of experiencing the peace of weightlessness for himself. With the launch of the Space Race, a year before the creation of NASA, the astronomer stood a remarkably good chance of someday achieving that feat. In July, after leaving Georgetown, Kameny began working for the federal government, using astronomical measurements to create incredibly precise maps for the Army Map Service (AMS).

To send a rocket containing a human—or an atomic bomb—to space, one must know exactly where it will land. If the Americans or the Soviets wanted to send manned rockets or intercontinental ballistic missiles into space, those machines needed to land on a specific target many thousands of miles away. Slightly imprecise calculations meant catastrophe, so the Army Map Service hired scientists like Kameny.

He explained his job to nonastronomers—in his nasal, staccato voice—with the clarity of a university lecturer. "As the moon appears to move across the sky, in its path it appears to eclipse a great many stars, quite aside from the Sun. And these are known as occultations. And in general these are quite instantaneous . . . the star is there [Kameny snapped his fingers] and it's gone. And then it reappears [snap] like that, when it comes out from the other side of the moon." By measuring the length of these occultations at different points on Earth—in Washington and Moscow, for example—Kameny could calculate the precise distance between them. The army could then calibrate an intercontinental ballistic missile to travel exactly that distance.

The astronomer's trajectory pointed upward, and in those early days of the Space Race, his terrestrial limits disappeared by the day. Nine days after *Sputnik*, *The Washington Star* predicted that humanity would soon reach the moon, likely after the construction of a space station. And after that? "There will be flights to other planets, like Mars and Venus," wrote the *Star*. "Then there will be interstellar flights—visits to stars many thousands of light years away."

Kameny already worked for the organization best equipped for space travel, the United States Army. Dr. Wernher von Braun, the army scientist responsible for America's only successful ballistic missiles, had been publicly pressing for a manned mission to the moon, a mission that would depend on missile technology, since 1952. In the final days of October 1957, he and other army officials lobbied Eisenhower to send their rockets higher and farther. "Missiles are the soldier's best friend," one general told the *Star*.

When America created its space agency, Kameny planned to join it along with Dr. von Braun and his fellow scientists. When the government started recruiting astronauts for missions to the unknown, journeys of uncertainty and danger but of crucial importance to America and the human race, Frank Kameny would be among the first to volunteer.

THE LETTER ARRIVED in late October, while Kameny was supervising a team of AMS scientists on the Big Island of Hawaii.

"It is necessary that you return at once to the Army Map Service in connection with certain administrative requirements," it said. "You should plan to leave Hawaii at your earliest convenience, and in any event within 48 hours of receiving this letter."

The summons came not from Kameny's immediate superior, but from the AMS's civilian personnel officer, the man in charge of hiring and classifying employees. A mistake had been made, Kameny told himself.

"It is hoped that the interruption of your work will be only temporary," wrote the personnel officer.

Kameny flew back to Washington, where he waited for an explanation. But with each passing week, as his employer remained silent, Kameny felt history leaving him behind. He watched the Soviets launch the *Sputnik II* satellite, which held a television camera, a life-support system, and a dog named Laika. Russian manned spaceflight was imminent.

On November 7, President Dwight D. Eisenhower appeared on television to reassure the nation, announcing the development of a continental defense system and the creation of a new position, the special assistant to the president for science and technology. "What the world needs today, even more than a giant leap into outer space, is a giant step toward peace," said Eisenhower.

On Tuesday, November 26, Kameny arrived at the understated brick headquarters of the Army Map Service in Brookmont, Maryland, just north of Washington. He sat across from two Civil Service Commission investigators.

"Mr. Kameny," began one of them, "your voluntary appearance here today has been requested in order to afford you an opportunity to answer questions concerning information which has been received by the U.S. Civil Service Commission relative to your application." The astronomer's appointment had been temporary and subject to investigation, they reminded him. They were recording his responses.

Kameny swore to tell the truth, and then the question came. "Information has come to the attention of the U.S. Civil Service Commission that you are a homosexual. What comment, if any, do you care to make?"

FOUR MONTHS EARLIER, when Kameny applied to the Army Map Service, he noticed an alarming question on the federal job application, known as Form 57. "Have you ever been arrested, charged, or held by Federal, State, or other law enforcement authorities?"

Kameny admitted his San Francisco arrest and provided the required details. "August 1956; Disorderly Conduct; San Francisco; Not Guilty;

Charge Dismissed." Despite his disclosure, the Army Map Service hired him three days later. His San Francisco arrest, as the probation officer had promised him, truly meant nothing.

"I do not recall the exact charge," Kameny now explained at his interrogation, more than a year later. "I had let a man whose name was not known to me touch me on the penis for a few seconds. He just reached over and touched me." There had been no solicitation, no erection, and Kameny had pushed the man's hand away after a few seconds. "I was only curious as to what he was going to do," he explained. "I had no intention of engaging in any homosexual act, nor did I."

Then, the allegation he was a homosexual.

Kameny had two responses prepared. "Under the laws of this country," he began, "any sexual activity whatever, of any description at all is illegal on the part of an unmarried person," said Kameny. Indeed, all premarital sexual activity, gay or straight, remained illegal in the District of Columbia. As Kinsey had revealed, nearly all Americans were guilty of violating *some* sexual regulation—fornication, sodomy, adultery.

Second, added Kameny, "as a matter of principle one's private life is his own."

The investigators wanted specifics. "What and when was the last activity in which you participated?"

Kameny repeated himself. "Under the laws of our country—"

With that, the interview ended.

ON DECEMBER 6, America launched its answer to *Sputnik*, the Vanguard rocket, which traveled four feet off the ground before exploding in a nationally televised inferno. By then, Kameny had hired an attorney and sat through another interview, defending his "not only satisfactory, but excellent" work for the AMS.

"Dr. Kameny," asked the investigators, "have you engaged actively or passively in any oral act of coition, anal intercourse or mutual masturbation with another person of the same sex?"

Kameny dodged the question. Legislating morality was "the province of the USSR, not the USA," he argued.

Four days after the Vanguard explosion, the Army Map Service informed Kameny that it planned to terminate him on December 20, pending an appeal. The AMS's official reason appeared to have nothing to do with homosexuality. According to the AMS personnel officer, Kameny had falsified an official government document. When he answered "August 1956; Disorderly Conduct; San Francisco; Not Guilty; Charge Dismissed" on his Form 57, that response had been technically false. Kameny had not been arrested for disorderly conduct, but rather for loitering and "lewd, indecent, or obscene" conduct. According to the AMS, Kameny "failed to furnish a completely truthful answer," and for that reason, it terminated him.

The separation letter gave Kameny three days to respond.

"I wish to commence by stating that as a matter of firm personal principle, morality and ethics, I do not knowingly and/or intentionally make, and have not made misstatements of fact, of any sort, whether formally, officially, in writing, and/or under oath, or casually, informally, and unofficially," wrote Kameny. He claimed that his response to the arrest question on Form 57 was correct "to the best of my knowledge and belief at the time the form was filled in." It was all a mistake. "I have neither the experience nor the legal background—I was hired as a scientist, not as a lawyer—to know all of the ins and outs of legal terminology and nomenclature involving such charges."

Kameny argued that his arrest, long dismissed, was irrelevant, "not of great importance as far as competent service to the government is concerned." Kameny submitted the appeal, certain the matter would be cleared up in due time. "I was very naive and expected that all you need is a nice, rational appeal," he later remembered. "And of course that wasn't all you needed."

Four days after Kameny wrote his appeal, the army scientist Dr. Wernher von Braun called for the creation of a national space agency while testifying before Lyndon Johnson's Senate subcommittee on satellite and missile programs. *The New York Times* declared the "blond, broad-shouldered and square-jawed" scientist a "hit."

Kameny, an avid consumer of newspapers, likely did not miss the irony of the two scientists' respective situations. Kameny faced a government purge and the loss of his career after a single personal indiscretion.

Von Braun, meanwhile, was leading the creation of America's national space program, his public demons long forgiven by the federal government. While Kameny had fought for the Americans during World War II, von Braun had worked tirelessly for the Nazis, leading the design of the slave-manufactured V-2 "vengeance" missiles that nineteen-year-old Kameny had witnessed, standing in Hyde Park during the final months of the war, falling upon the city of London.

The AMS formally dismissed Kameny on December 20, 1957. Never again would he work for the United States government.

Lafayette Square and its public restrooms

―――――

3

THE PANIC

According to the Russians, Colonel Alfred Redl of the Austro-Hungarian Empire had slightly graying blond hair and a "greasy" outward appearance. He spoke "sugar-sweetly, softly."

Beginning in 1901, Redl worked as a high official in Austria's Evidenzbureau, where he single-handedly built its counterespionage program. He had more access to classified information than perhaps anyone else in the empire.

In Vienna, Redl's homosexuality was an open secret. He often appeared at society events with his longtime "nephew," and he maintained several other affairs. He had no reason to be fearful of exposure, since even the emperor's brother enjoyed cross-dressing and the occasional army officer.

Redl closely guarded his work as a double agent, however. During his service in the Evidenzbureau, he offered Austrian war plans to the Italian military attaché in exchange for cash. An Italian intelligence officer later recalled it "required no effort" to recruit him. Redl simply mailed envelopes full of Austrian secrets and received thousands of kronen in return.

He then began sending military plans to the Russians, too. Redl became fabulously wealthy, lavishing gifts on his lovers and driving two of the empire's most expensive automobiles. For years, no one seemed to question how he afforded such extravagances on his government salary.

In May 1913, after Austrian counterintelligence officials intercepted a Russian letter containing six thousand kronen, they staked out the Vienna post office to identify its recipient. They were appalled to discover Redl.

The army wanted to keep the matter quiet, since public knowledge of treachery at such a high level would have been a profound humiliation. After following him to his hotel, Redl's own protégé handed him a pistol. Army officials always maintained that Redl voluntarily took his life.

News of the colonel leaked, fact became intertwined with fiction, and the myth of the homosexual traitor came into being. A Berlin newspaper described Redl's "homosexual pleasure palace, filled with perversities." The Austrian Army needed a scapegoat for the 1.3 million casualties in that first year of World War I, so it blamed Redl and the larger, more insidious "homosexual organization" that protected him within the military.

Three years later, when a young Allen Dulles, the future CIA director, arrived in Vienna to work at the U.S. embassy, he found everyone still whispering about the homosexual spy who had lost the First World War for the empire.

By the end of World War II, America had become a more open place for homosexuals, but they also confronted novel threats conjured by a political coalition that exploited the uncertainty of the new world order. In 1945, only months before President Roosevelt died, Republicans and Southern Democrats formed the House Un-American Activities Committee (HUAC). In the 1946 midterm election, after Republicans pledged to "ferret out" threats to the "American way of life," they won the first congressional majority in sixteen years.

In March 1947, President Truman established the Federal Employee Loyalty Program, and the government began investigating its employees to determine their loyalty. Three months later, the Democrat-controlled Senate Committee on Appropriations warned about "the extensive employment in highly classified positions of admitted homosexuals, who are historically known to be security risks." The committee empowered the secretary of state with "absolute discretion" to purge employees, including homosexuals, who threatened national security.

In September 1949, America learned that the Soviet Union had detonated its first nuclear weapon. In October, eleven Communist leaders were convicted for advocating a violent revolution in America, and in December, China fell to the Communists.

On January 21, 1950, a jury convicted suspected spy Alger Hiss of perjury.

On February 3, authorities arrested physicist Klaus Fuchs for nuclear espionage.

And on February 9, junior senator Joe McCarthy stood before a women's club in Wheeling, West Virginia, and announced, "I have here in my hand a list of 205—a list of names that were made known to the Secretary of State as being members of the Communist Party and who nevertheless are still working and shaping policy in the State Department."

Nobody else had seen the list. When reporters caught him at an airport and demanded to see it, he offered to show them—then realized he had left it in his baggage. His number of alleged Communists soon changed from 205 to 57. "Rarely," *The Washington Post* declared, "has a man in public life crawled and squirmed so abjectly."

On the evening of February 20, McCarthy arrived on the Senate floor with an overstuffed briefcase that purportedly contained his list of Communist-linked security risks in the State Department. For six hours, he provided a warped summary of eighty-one cases, relying on unproven allegations from a three-year-old congressional investigation. "In short, the speech was a lie," concluded historian Robert Griffith.

Two of the cases involved alleged homosexuals, who were "rather easy blackmail victims," explained McCarthy. It was a shrewd maneuver: what editorial board or politician would dare argue that sexual deviants belonged in the federal government?

McCarthy would later recuse himself from hearings on the issue of homosexuals in the government. At forty-one, the senator was unmarried, and the issue raised questions about his own sexuality.

Other Republicans took the lead. A week after McCarthy's Senate speech, his colleagues coerced Deputy Undersecretary of State John Peurifoy, a security official testifying in defense of his department, into making a startling admission. In only three years, he admitted, ninety-one homosexual employees had resigned upon investigation under Truman's loyalty program.

And with that, as the *New York Post* referred to it, the "Panic on the Potomac" began. Conservative newspapers leapt upon the admission. Congress scheduled hearings. Homosexuality, observed a columnist on *Meet the Press*, became "a new type of political weapon" that could "wreck the Administration." The chief of the Washington Vice Squad testified there were "3,750 perverts employed by government agencies." Republican senator Kenneth Wherry alleged the Soviets were using a list of American homosexuals—originally compiled by Hitler—to blackmail federal employees for government secrets. Washington, he said, faced an "emergency condition."

The Senate committee tasked with solving the homosexual problem, led by Democrat Clyde Hoey of North Carolina, began closed hearings in July. Admiral Roscoe Hillenkoetter, the director of the government's new Central Intelligence Agency, testified first. He arrived with a thirty-eight-page statement, and ten of those pages chronicled a "classic" case, one "known all through intelligence circles," an example that would leave "no doubt as to the fact that perversion presents a very definite security risk."

Of all the intelligence available to the CIA, its director chose to rest his case against homosexuals on the forty-year-old story of Colonel Redl. In Hillenkoetter's retelling, Redl had been an "honest" man who found himself in an imperial army with unforgiving policies against homosexuality. The Russians hired a young newsboy, who "became very intimate" with Redl. Next, they broke into the colonel's room and caught him in an "act of perversion." After threatening to expose him, the Russians gained copies of the Austrian war plans prior to the outbreak of violence.

And so a single urban legend, the telling of which was almost entirely, verifiably inaccurate (in fact, a 1907 Russian diplomatic cable had falsely labeled Redl "a lover of women") became the primary piece of evidence that guided federal employment policy toward homosexuals for decades to come.

The CIA director then explained the "general theory as to why we should not employ homosexuals or other moral perverts in positions of trust." He gave thirteen reasons to the senators.

1. Homosexuals experience emotions "as strong and in fact actually stronger" than heterosexual emotions.
2. Homosexuals are susceptible "to domination by aggressive personalities."
3. Homosexuals have "psychopathic tendencies which affect the soundness of their judgment, physical cowardice, susceptibility

to pressure, and general instability, thus making a pervert vulnerable in many ways."

4. Homosexuals "invariably express considerable concern" about concealing their condition.

5. Homosexuals are "promiscuous" and often visit "various hangouts of his brethren," marking "a definite similarity to other illegal groups such as criminals, smugglers, black-marketeers, dope addicts, and so forth."

6. Homosexuals with "outward characteristics of femininity—or lesbians with male characteristics—are often difficult to employ because of the effect on their co-workers, officials of other agencies, and the public in general."

7. Homosexuals who think they are discreet are, in reality, "actually quite indiscrete [sic]. They are too stupid to realize it, or else due to inflation of their ego or through not letting themselves realize the truth, they are usually the center of gossip, rumor, derision, and so forth."

8. Homosexuals who try "to drop the 'gay' life and go 'straight' . . . eventually revert to type."

9. Homosexuals are "extremely vulnerable to seduction by another pervert employed for that purpose by a foreign power."

10. Homosexuals are "extremely defiant in their attitude toward society," which could lead to disloyalty.

11. "Homosexuals usually seem to be extremely gullible."

12. Homosexuals, including "even the most brazen perverts," are constantly suppressing their instincts, which causes "considerable tension."

13. Homosexuals employed by the government "lead to the concept of a 'government within a government.' That is so noteworthy. One pervert brings other perverts. They belong to the lodge, the fraternity. One pervert brings other perverts into an agency . . . and advance them usually in the interest of furthering the romance of the moment."

The testimony of subsequent intelligence officials echoed that of the CIA director, and the Hoey committee's final report primarily drew from the testimony of its lead witness, sometimes verbatim. As the Hoey report concluded, homosexuals were ipso facto security risks. Colonel Redl remained its only example.

Hillenkoetter's thirteen principles became official government doctrine. The government incorporated the Hoey report into its security manuals, forwarded it to embassies, and shared it with its foreign allies. "The notion that homosexuals threatened national security," explains historian David Johnson, "received the imprimatur of the U.S. Congress and became accepted as official fact." When the federal government needed to justify its homosexual purges, it simply pointed to the Hoey report.

Dwight D. Eisenhower won the presidency in 1952 with the help of the slogan "Let's Clean House" and whispers that his opponent, Adlai Stevenson, had homosexual tendencies. Three months after his inauguration, Eisenhower signed Executive Order 10450, which expanded the government's purging authority—originally given to the State Department—to all federal agencies. Any employee who exhibited "criminal, infamous, dishonest, immoral, or notoriously disgraceful conduct" had no place in the federal bureaucracy. With a Republican in the White House, the purges became less of a spectacle and more of a quiet, well-oiled machine. In Eisenhower's 1954 State of the Union, he boasted of removing 2,200 security risks in only a year.

McCarthy's downfall came later that year, but the purges remained alive, as did the rumors that always seemed to saturate America's capital. After two Republican senators learned that the son of Senator Lester Hunt of Wyoming, a Democrat, had been arrested in Lafayette Park, they gave Hunt a choice. He could withdraw from his 1954 reelection campaign or face the publicity of his son's homosexual arrest. The Senate was virtually tied. If Hunt resigned, he risked shifting power to the Republicans.

On the morning of June 19, 1954, Senator Hunt, a straight victim of antigay political blackmail, entered his Capitol office and shot himself with a .22-caliber rifle.

TWO DAYS BEFORE Christmas 1957, Frank Kameny once again appeared at the understated brick headquarters of the Army Map Service in Maryland. He demanded a hearing.

The AMS officials gave Kameny twenty minutes to prepare.

Kameny then sat before the commanding officer of the AMS and its chief personnel officer, the same two men responsible for his dismissal.

Kameny presented his case, and as the officials responded with their reasoning for his dismissal, he noticed something odd. The officials did not seem to care about the alleged falsification of his application. A man arrested for homosexual activity, they explained, was not reliable enough to be granted a security clearance.

The officials clarified that they did not, of course, actually believe Kameny to be a security risk. He was no more of a risk than *they* were. But, unfortunately, regulations forced them to act otherwise. Their hands were tied.

Kameny realized he needed a more comprehensive defense, one that took into account not just the falsification charge, but also the real issue at hand: his alleged homosexuality. The AMS officials permitted Kameny to supplement the hearing with a written appeal, and he spent the final days of 1957 compiling a final, unimpeachable defense.

First, he wrote several Harvard friends and colleagues to ask for affidavits that attested to his "morality & truthfulness." Yale professor Harlan Smith wrote that he had "the highest confidence in Dr. Kameny's character, veracity and truthfulness." The former director of the Harvard observatory, Harlow Shapley, wrote that Kameny was a "citizen loyal and upright;—a man of good character." An army friend attached his affidavit with a note. "How important your field has become in the last few months. I suppose recent events may have brought about quite a considerable change in your plans."

A typical man in Kameny's position, if he did not resign quietly, would have vehemently denied any insinuations of homosexuality and explained why the arrest was a misunderstanding, the falsification an innocent mistake. Yet Kameny's twelve-page written appeal contained not a single denial of his homosexuality. Rather, the document represented the first iteration of a philosophical and practical critique of the federal government's sexual conformity program, the first draft of an argument that would dominate the rest of his life.

He toed the line of admitting guilt in San Francisco, but he did not cross it. "In the case of the act in question, even if it were repeated (as it has not been and will not be) there still exists no logical, rational connection with reliability, or with the ability to preserve proper security or to adhere to security regulations."

Kameny demanded that the officials evaluate him as an individual. "I have formulated a personal moral and ethical code of my own," he wrote. "I observe this code in my daily life, rigorously and strictly, without departure or deviation." His work at the AMS had been excellent—the best his supervisors had ever seen—and to consider arbitrary regulations above these individual characteristics verged on totalitarianism.

He twisted the knife, one which only a scientist so necessary to the Space Race could wield. If the government stopped wasting its time and money with investigations, he wrote, "perhaps a few of the artificial satellites to go up in coming years will be American ones."

Kameny's statement accompanied a final, critical item in his defense package, a document he would never talk about later in his life: a letter from a psychiatrist.

IN THE LATE NINETEENTH CENTURY, doctors argued about the nature of homosexuality. Was it a vice of the weak? A type of insanity? Or a congenital problem, a lapse in evolution?

In 1909, Dr. Sigmund Freud visited America, and with his rise, sexual deviance became a problem of the mind. Though Freud identified homosexuality as a benign condition, most of his followers came to label it a sickness, including Dr. Benjamin Karpman of Washington, D.C.

The "burly, gruff, bearded Freudian," as friends described him, emigrated from the Russian Empire as a nineteen-year-old in 1907. He joined the staff of America's first federally funded mental institution, St. Elizabeths Hospital in Southeast Washington, in 1920.

Karpman believed that criminals—including homosexuals—belonged not in jails, but under the care of psychiatrists. He formulated the ideal of the "normal pervert," who, like a physically disabled person, managed to lead an otherwise normal life. A homosexual cure was possible, Karpman concluded, but the patient had to "earnestly and sincerely" desire it. Even in the case of the "sexual psychopath"—a pervert who compulsively engaged in "socially prohibited or unacceptable sexual aggressiveness"—the proper treatment involved therapy, not incarceration.

Karpman predicted a sexual revolution within weeks of World War II's end. "Definite changes in sexual freedom were observed in the wake of World War I," he told an interviewer, "and this war, more global in character and involving many more people, is likely to bring in its wake far greater changes in sexual behavior." He foresaw that America would have more divorces, men would demand virgin brides less often, and pre-marital sex would become more common. He made these arguments with unprecedented authority; psychiatrists had screened over eighteen million inductees during the war, thrusting the field into the conscious-ness of the nation.

Dr. Karpman became the chief psychotherapist of St. Elizabeths in 1948, the same year as the publication of *Sexual Behavior in the Human Male* (a local synagogue invited Karpman to answer the congregation's questions about the report). During that year's cultural upheaval, Con-gress wrote Washington's sexual psychopath law.

Republican congressman Arthur Miller of Nebraska, himself a doctor, sponsored legislation to strengthen the penalties for sexual crimes against children. It created a system for psychiatrists to diagnose and commit "sexual psychopaths" to St. Elizabeths. The Miller Act became Washing-ton's first sodomy law. It prohibited taking "into his or her mouth or anus the sexual organ of any other person or animal," in addition to the recip-rocal act. "Any penetration, however slight" was sufficient to complete the crime.

In February 1948, Karpman testified in favor of Miller's bill, and President Truman signed it in June. Authorities arrested the first two sodomy offenders—an interracial duo caught on the National Mall—that summer. They arrested forty people, including three women, for sod-omy by the end of 1949. And by 1950, psychiatrists committed fifteen men to St. Elizabeths with their new authority under the Miller Act. Some of those offenders did not have criminal records beyond a charge of solicitation.

Twenty-nine states enacted or revised their own sexual psychopath laws between 1946 and 1957. In only a decade, homosexuals had gradu-ated from criminals—merely incarcerated after homosexual activity—to *mentally ill* criminals subject to psychiatric remedies, which included shock therapy, castration, and lobotomies.

Despite his involvement in the rise of America's sexual psychopath laws, Karpman still felt compelled to defend homosexuals. In the middle of the 1950 panic, he told an audience that the homosexual purges represented a "witch hunt." When Congressman Miller, also on the panel, cited Nazi efforts to blackmail homosexuals in Washington, Karpman retorted that adulterous heterosexual men could be blackmailed in exactly the same way.

Karpman retired from St. Elizabeths in 1957, but he continued to lecture and practice privately. He appeared on the radio, released a new book, and came to the attention of Frank Kameny.

One morning in January, Kameny appeared in Karpman's office. They had four sessions together, and Karpman did something extraordinary. He asked Kameny to draft a letter that the psychiatrist could then send, on the astronomer's behalf, to the Army Map Service. The sympathetic psychiatrist would help Kameny fight the witch hunt.

Kameny, with the help of the attorney he had retained in December, assumed the voice and authority of Dr. Benjamin Karpman. "I have examined Dr. Franklin E. Kameny in regard to the significance of the act involved in connection with his arrest in San Francisco in August, 1956, in relation to his entire personality and orientation," he wrote. "Perhaps the one characteristic which all scientists hold in common is that of curiosity—a curiosity about all things; a curiosity which transcends most boundaries. Dr. Kameny shares in this to a very high degree. I have no reason to believe that his motivation in this case was other than curiosity, having observed someone very obviously loitering, to see what was going to happen."

Yes, Kameny had sexually experimented in recent years, but "his personal relationships, until rather recently, were entirely heterosexual," he claimed. "I would not consider his actions as immoral, and I would not feel justified in considering Dr. Kameny as a homosexual."

When Karpman read the draft at a subsequent session, he requested only one addition, a more detailed explanation of what had happened in San Francisco. The astronomer returned to his typewriter. "Dr. Kameny entered the lavatory for legitimate purposes," he wrote. When he noticed the man "peering over the top of the partition between two stalls, Dr. Kameny's curiosity was aroused, and he remained somewhat longer than was absolutely necessary, in order to see what would occur." When the man moved to the urinal and then reached for Kameny, the astronomer experienced "a moment's immobility" before he "firmly removed the man's hand" and exited.

During their sessions together, the psychiatrist continued asking the astronomer about his life. At one of their final sessions, as they discussed sexual relationships in Kameny's past, Karpman asked the thirty-two-year-old about his thoughts on marriage.

Kameny froze. He felt "on the defensive," as he wrote to Karpman later that day. "My mind tends to close down and withdraw, and I find that, under such circumstances, I frequently give answers which, in retrospect, are incomplete, often with glaring omissions, as in this case."

Perhaps worried that he had betrayed his homosexuality, he wrote with new information for the psychiatrist. Kameny had forgotten to tell Karpman about his love interest, a twenty-five-year-old woman. They had been seeing "a great deal of one another," almost every day. "I would be pleased to marry her, altho [sic] I'm not sure of her feelings—if she is. We're not by any means engaged, but she has no objection to my telling people, as I've told a number, in recent months, that we're considering the possibility of becoming engaged." Kameny suggested that Karpman use this fact as "a possible item which you may care to work into any letter you write, or use as background for any comments or verdicts you make."

Kameny lied in an effort to keep his job, but he could only bring himself to do so through a proxy, the psychiatrist. He drafted one of his letters to Karpman on a piece of scrap paper that also contained a doting birthday note to Keith, his first lover from Tucson. "Always remember," he told Keith, "that I'm cheering you in all your successes, rejoicing with you in all your happiness, sympathizing with you in your failures, grieving with you in your miseries."

The letter that Karpman ultimately signed contained a defense of the astronomer even more compelling than Kameny's own draft. "I went carefully into his past life," wrote Karpman. The astronomer had experienced a normal upbringing, without "any odd, peculiar behaviors either in childhood or adolescence which sometimes are signs and symptoms of the deviation yet to come."

Kameny's adult sex life, wrote Karpman, was normal. There had been experimentation, "of course," but Kameny was "at present courting a young woman with serious intentions," explained the psychiatrist. "There is little doubt that he will marry and assume a normal life as so many do." Kameny was "entirely marriageable."

As for the San Francisco incident, it had been a misunderstanding. "I find nothing wrong with his behavior. That he did not act quite as the policemen thought he should act, does not mean that he did not act normally. Normal people react in many different ways to the same situation."

"These lavatories are used so often by sexual deviates," he concluded, "that any normal person cannot enter them without running the risk of being involved in something or other. Sincerely yours, Benjamin Karpman, M.D."

To Keith, Kameny signed, "as ever and always, with the deepest of affection and fondness, Frank."

IN JANUARY, while Kameny sent the components of his defense package to the AMS, his fight became more complicated. On January 18, he received notice from the Civil Service Commission that it was barring him from working in *any* federal agency for three years. It did so not because of his falsification of Form 57, but because he had refused to answer questions about his "moral conduct." Kameny now faced a two-front war. Not only did he need to persuade the AMS to reinstate him, but he now needed to persuade the CSC to allow the AMS to do so.

His interrogators, responded Kameny, had refused to provide any specific charges against him. "In the American tradition you must prove me guilty. You have not done so. You have not even begun to do so," he wrote. "The firing of one single government Astronomer deprives the government of between 2% and 4% of all the Astronomers it has at the moment, to the best of my knowledge," he added.

Once again, Kameny did not claim to be straight. Karpman's letter, which he forwarded to the CSC, told the lie for him.

After reviewing Kameny's defense package, the AMS officially rejected his appeal on March 12, an unsurprising outcome. As Kameny saw it, the same two AMS officials acted as the plaintiffs, prosecutors, judges, jury, and appeals court.

Their reasoning, however, had since changed. No longer citing the falsification charge, they dismissed Kameny "to better promote the efficiency of the Federal Service," a reference to the federal law that permitted the CSC to dismiss homosexuals.

Kameny soon appeared at the office of the army's chief of engineers—and then at the secretary of the army's office—to discuss his rejection. He found the officials there pleasant, sympathetic, even. But as long as the CSC debarment stood, they explained, their hands were tied.

On March 27, after learning the CSC had *also* rejected his appeal, Kameny arrived at the CSC's headquarters. He insisted on speaking to somebody in the Investigations Division. He demanded that this official retrieve his record. Upon what, he asked, did the CSC base its charge of immoral conduct?

This information cannot be revealed, the official responded. The commission has to protect its informants.

Kameny persisted. Who is the official's boss? Where is his office? Kameny marched to the superior's office while the lower official nervously followed the enraged astronomer.

"This procedure was repeated—and again—and again—and again, until I had worked myself up almost to the top of the Investigations Division," Kameny later recalled.

At last, Kameny reached the chief of the Adjudication Division in the CSC's Bureau of Personnel Investigations. The official admitted that his record contained nothing except the San Francisco incident and, in Kameny's paraphrasing, the "tone and tenor, but not the gist of substance" of his remarks to the CSC interrogators.

Kameny had finally confirmed that the CSC had no concrete evidence against him. It had simply interpreted his refusals to cooperate during his November and December interrogations as admissions of guilt.

On March 30, Kameny appealed to the CSC's chairman, Harris Ellsworth. Six weeks later, after receiving Ellsworth's rejection, the astronomer promptly departed for the CSC headquarters.

No, you are not able to speak to the chairman, explained Ellsworth's assistant, Helen Castle. Yes, I am familiar with your file.

Is it true, asked Kameny, that it contains nothing more than the San Francisco incident and the "tone and tenor" of my interrogation?

Yes, responded Castle.

The astronomer returned home and wrote a second appeal to Ellsworth. His AMS supervisor "almost desperately" wanted him back, he wrote. Only the day earlier, he explained, Dr. von Braun had stated that the government needed to make the fullest possible use of scientists if it was to achieve parity with the Russians. Kameny simply wanted to work for his country.

On June 12, Ellsworth rejected this final appeal.

Kameny's father, a man who had been harsh on young Franklin and whom he rarely discussed, died exactly two weeks later.

AT THE BEGINNING of his ordeal, Kameny had assumed the matter would be resolved quickly. He survived on meager savings and unemployment compensation, but he was often unable to pay his bills.

In late spring, as the AMS and CSC rejections carved away at Kameny's optimism, he began searching for work. If he could not work in the government, he would turn to academia and private industry. But in a post-*Sputnik* world, those institutions—even universities—only hired astronomers for space projects. And because outer space involved the federal government and national security, astronomy jobs necessitated a security clearance.

Kameny knew that his CSC file would inevitably materialize in any clearance investigation. He had perhaps the most in-demand job training in America—an astronomer at the beginning of the Space Age—yet no company would hire him. "I was flown in luxury for interviews all over the country—Los Angeles, San Francisco, Boston, elsewhere—and treated with great deference, and 'wooed' with great care, until the security question came up each time," he later wrote.

If Kameny wanted to work as an astronomer, he had no choice but to clear his name. And if Harris Ellsworth would not do it, then he would proceed up the hierarchy to the man who had appointed the CSC chairman: Dwight D. Eisenhower.

The CSC was attempting to "utterly and permanently destroy an Astronomer" who merely wanted to help his country, wrote Kameny to the president.

"They did not dare to raise a finger in my behalf," he later recalled of the White House.

After Eisenhower, Kameny then turned to Congress. He wrote to his own congressman from New York, Albert Bosch, and to the chairs of the relevant House and Senate committees, including Civil Service, District of Columbia, Manpower Utilization, and Senator Johnson's Space Committee.

At least two of the elected officials, Albert Bosch and Lyndon Johnson, contacted Ellsworth for an explanation.

Kameny understood "all of the circumstances of his case," responded Ellsworth. If Kameny was *truly* in earnest about pursuing the matter, perhaps the astronomer would share his CSC interview transcripts with the elected officials, he wrote.

After Ellsworth's insinuations, the politicians did no more for the astronomer. Kameny had appealed to the highest levels of the American government. It marked the end of the road.

On September 28, two weeks after Ellsworth's damning letter to Bosch and Johnson, police officers arrested Kameny in Lafayette Park.

The officers never charged him, but Kameny knew that the arrest would remain on his record. He could no longer claim that the San Francisco incident had been a fluke. Karpman's letter became laughable, Kameny's fate sealed.

He wrote to the CSC chairman on October 2, only four days after his arrest, with new, colorful fury. He accused Ellsworth of lying to Bosch, Johnson, and the White House. "I am NOT aware of any reasons for which I should be barred from Federal civil service employment, and I grant none. I am NOT aware of all of the circumstances of my case. Despite my best efforts—and I have tried hard—I have been able to be presented only with vague, indefinite, broad—and totally unsubstantiated and unproven—allegations, insinuations, and suggestions of the most general and non-specific nature."

His CSC interrogations, "which smack of the Gestapo," had proven that Kameny was *not* the immoral one. "You, Mr. Ellsworth, and your commission, not I, are guilty of gross immorality and grossly unethical conduct."

He also made a new argument, a legal one. "By what right does the CSC—or anyone else in the Government—dare to tell a citizen what is and is not moral?" Because morality was a "matter of individual and personal opinion and religious belief," the CSC's allegations represented "a clear breach of the guarantee of freedom of religion under the first amendment to the Constitution."

The purges were dysfunctional, and homosexuals—though he did not dare to use that word—worked in all levels of the government. "Are you truly unaware that your efforts are no more likely to succeed than an attempt to empty the ocean with a teaspoon?" Kameny asked. "Are you aware that your Civil Service is over-run with the 'tainted' (in the sense that I am falsely accused of being tainted)?" The "sacred" Pentagon? The "super-super-secret" CIA? The Washington police? Public school teachers? Postal workers? Yes, even "my dear old Army Map Service?" And the military, "so full of 'tainted' individuals, at all ranks from the lowest on up to high ranking officers, that were all discovered and discharged simultaneously, our whole military establishment would collapse in utter chaos?"

The commission, wrote Ellsworth in a curt response, would not take any further action in Kameny's case.

Johns Hopkins University rejected Kameny's job application two weeks later. Kameny's unemployment compensation would expire in December, and he had no job prospects. He contacted Ellsworth one last time.

"I demand to have justified to me your action in 'killing off' one already-trained scientist on superficial, trivial, irrelevant, immaterial grounds," he wrote. "What justification does the CSC have for its overall policy toward those who evince some evidence of sexual or other irregularity in their personal, private backgrounds? On what grounds, and by what logical, rational chain of reasoning does the CSC deduce that these people are unfit for, or unsuitable for government employment? I demand a clear rigidly logical answer to the last two questions."

"In two weeks, Mr. Ellsworth, my Unemployment Compensation will run out," he said. "Largely through your actions, I have no prospect of a suitable job. My financial resources are completely exhausted. At [that] time, therefore, I plan simply to cease eating entirely, and to starve to death. As you enjoy your Christmas dinner, you might keep in mind that, through your actions, one of your fellow human beings will be about to die. I hope you enjoy the role of an executioner."

Throughout Kameny's ordeal, one option had dangled above the scientist, the ultimate realization of the self-fulfilling prophecies made by McCarthy, Hillenkoetter, and Hoey. Kameny had never dared to mention this option until now, after he had already lost everything. "There is only one alternative to complete starvation, which I have thus far been able to discover," he warned Ellsworth. He found this option "repugnant and distasteful," but he saw no other choice, especially since his own government had declared him persona non grata. He could begin working for another government.

"I must confess that a stomach which has only occasionally been properly filled in the past eight months, and which has before it only the prospect of total and permanent emptiness, is a powerful incentive toward overcoming even such formidable obstacles as learning the Russian or some other language," he wrote.

The Soviets, after all, needed astronomers like him.

The Threat of the Sexual Psychopath, June 1947

4

THE UNION

Former schoolteacher Byron N. Scott entered Congress in 1935, but he proved to be a disappointing politician. An American Civil Liberties Union (ACLU) official called the young, handsome congressman from Long Beach "liberal though unimportant." After Scott faced charges of drunk driving, he lost his campaign for reelection in 1938.

He decided to go to law school. Scott joined the District of Columbia Bar in 1949, and Senator McCarthy made his infamous speech the following February. Amidst the uproar, Scott began to defend the victims of McCarthyism.

First, at the request of the ACLU, the calm, slow-speaking Scott defended a Berkeley scientist who had refused to testify before HUAC. Scott successfully cleared the scientist of sixteen contempt of Congress charges after emphasizing his constitutional right to avoid self-incrimination.

In 1955, William Henry Taylor—an International Monetary Fund official accused of Communist espionage—described his Kafkaesque nightmare to the press. "Not once have I been confronted with an accuser or informer; not once have I been allowed to cross-examine. The charges against me have always been somewhat elusive in that they lack precision as to date, manner, form, and content." For eight years, Taylor had quietly rebutted the charges, including those made by the U.S. attorney general, with affidavits or in closed sessions of Congress.

Byron Scott began representing Taylor, and his trial became public. Scott held a news conference to demand that Congress allow Taylor to cross-examine his accusers. Scott mounted a "tremendous counterattack," as one legal scholar called it, and the following year, the International Organizations Employees Loyalty Board cleared Taylor of all charges. Scott publicly demanded an apology from the attorney general.

Scott continued taking the cases of embattled government employees, and press conferences became his signature tactic. Determined that America should know what the federal government was doing to its citizens, he perfected the art of crusading against the crusades.

On April 12, 1959, Scott held another press conference prior to an especially important hearing. He was about to argue before the Supreme Court on behalf of two federal employees. Oral arguments took place on April 20, and after that date, Scott had the time to take some pro bono work.

He took on the case of an astronomer in despair.

KAMENY HAD CHOSEN to starve. His unemployment compensation and savings evaporated by the end of 1958, and he borrowed only the absolute minimum necessary to keep himself alive. He divided that money into a daily allowance of twenty cents per day, enough for two or three frankfurters and half a pot of mashed potatoes. Sometimes he splurged on margarine, and he often went several days without eating anything at all.

Only Kameny and his government knew of his starvation. It was a matter of principle and pride, a hunger strike without the publicity. He had spent half his life preparing to be an astronomer, and an astronomer he would be. "I was determined that while I would compromise up to a point on the type of work I would do, I was NOT going to throw away my training and abilities on some menial job, even if I starved first," he wrote.

But he told nobody else. His mother did not know the depths of his situation, and she certainly did not know of his homosexuality. Kameny's vast social network may have been spread too thin. Years later, when asked whether the gay community could have helped him, he denied there had even *existed* a gay community in Washington. His Saturday-night social connections "were on a different kind of a basis," he opaquely explained. The astronomer could not bring himself to ask for money.

Taking a menial job would have implied defeat, but Kameny had identified one last option to continue fighting.

On December 15, 1958, Kameny contacted Penelope Wright, an executive assistant at the ACLU's Washington office. It was unlikely that the ACLU would help the astronomer, since the organization did not believe homosexuals had civil liberties that needed protection. In a policy statement released the year prior, the ACLU had concluded it was "not within the province of the Union to evaluate the social validity of laws aimed at the suppression or elimination of homosexuals."

As for the government's gay purges, the ACLU gave its stamp of approval. "Homosexuality is a valid consideration in evaluating the security risk factor in sensitive positions," it declared. Homosexuals had rights, of course, but they were the same rights accorded to any other American citizen—those of due process.

Shortly after the Union's adoption of that statement, when a group of New York homosexuals asked the ACLU to participate in a panel about "minority problems," the Union's response was cordial but clear. "While we appreciate your kind invitation to address your group, we must decline," wrote its assistant director. "The civil liberties aspects of the question of sexual deviation is so small that we do not devote major attention to this issue."

The Washington ACLU office, meanwhile, was especially unlikely to take Kameny's case. Not only did it primarily focus on legislative lobbying, but throughout the 1950s, its officials regularly funneled lists of suspected Communists to the FBI, hoping to build "goodwill" and proactively rebut charges of its own subversion. The office had a clean, patriotic image to maintain.

Yet the Union took pity on Kameny, and its Washington office referred him to a sympathetic ACLU-affiliated attorney, Byron Scott. In April 1959, Scott agreed to represent the astronomer on a contingent fee basis, so Kameny would only pay if he won. With an attorney well practiced in grinding the bureaucratic gears of McCarthyism to a halt, he at last had reason to be optimistic.

THAT SAME MONTH, Kameny's landlord tried to evict him. The astronomer appeared before a judge to explain his situation, and the judge, rather than evicting him, referred Kameny to the Salvation Army for food assistance. The astronomer received eleven dollars' worth of food. "A feast," he called it.

Kameny contacted an employment agency to find a temporary job, but the National Employment Service failed to place him anywhere. Its employees also took pity on him, so the agency itself hired him as a temporary worker. After sixteen months of unemployment and four months of near starvation, Kameny took the position. He finally had an income, albeit a tenuous one, and he persuaded a bank to give him a loan. His short-term prospects looked brighter.

Kameny's largest source of hope remained in Byron N. Scott. Aside from his own legal successes, Scott also had reason to be optimistic about Kameny's case. The country's politics, culture, and laws were changing at an accelerating rate.

McCarthy, after all, was dead. With the senator's fall, America asked itself if the paranoia had gone too far. Democrats regained control of Congress in 1954 and began holding hearings on Eisenhower's security program. "Michelangelo might not be able to get a job under such terms," joked Senator Hubert Humphrey. Dr. Karpman's views of the purges became more common among his peers. The Group for the Advancement of Psychiatry warned of the "injustice" caused by the "inflexible application" of rules against homosexuals in the government.

On the legal front, in May 1955, the prestigious American Law Institute decided that private, consensual sexual behavior—including sodomy and adultery—did not truly harm others. "This area of private morals," it concluded, "is the distinctive concern of spiritual authorities." The ALI acknowledged that sex laws diminished police resources and actually *promoted* blackmail by enabling criminals to threaten disclosure of sexual violations to authorities. "The age-old problem of using the law to enforce moral behavior, after slumbering Vesuvius-like for many years, once more seems ready to erupt," concluded the *Star* in its coverage of the ALI vote.

In 1957, the Supreme Court ruled that only material dealing "with sex in a manner appealing to prurient interest" could be labeled obscene. Anything "having even the slightest redeeming social importance" was permissible. And in January 1958, without even hearing oral arguments, the court declared that homosexual magazines were not obscene; they could be sent in the mail.

The Supreme Court had not yet decided that homosexuals were suitable for government service, but it was beginning to move—albeit modestly—to rein in the federal government's purges of loyalty and security risks.

One case involved William Greene, an aeronautical engineer, who designed flight simulators and rocket launchers for the navy. He had a top secret security clearance until the Defense Department revoked it. The Pentagon had found evidence of Communist associations, so Greene lost his job.

Not once did the government provide witnesses for cross-examination. It based its accusations on confidential reports, but Greene could not view those, either. He sued the secretary of defense, and his attorneys argued before the Supreme Court on April 1, 1959.

Five days later, Kameny wrote to the chief justice of the Supreme Court, Earl Warren. Still without food or income, Kameny described the "startling parallel" between the government's treatment of homosexuals and the "treatment, in Germany, by Nazis, of the Jews." The main difference, he concluded, was "that the US has not resorted to crematory ovens for this minority—yet!"

"Anything which you can do by your decisions to weaken the security program," he added, "will be much to the good."

KAMENY LOST his temporary job at the National Employment Service after only six weeks. It no longer needed him.

After his experiences interviewing at private companies, Kameny hypothesized that their security offices refused to authorize his hiring because they assumed he would fail to receive a security clearance from the Department of Defense. With no chance of acquiring a clearance, Kameny had become a marked man.

On June 1, Kameny wrote directly to Neil McElroy, the secretary of defense, to ask for a meeting. Perhaps officials would be more understanding, he reasoned, if the bureaucrats had to justify the astronomer's exclusion to his face. The next day, Kameny received a call from the Pentagon. An official in the Office of Security Policy, R. L. Applegate, invited him to the Pentagon to discuss the matter.

On June 3, the astronomer walked into an office on the fourth floor of the United States military's mammoth headquarters. Applegate and two of his colleagues listened to Kameny for over an hour.

Applegate explained that companies often had their *own* security policies. He could only promise to look into Kameny's case, and the astronomer left the meeting with hope. "I wanted action, and I wanted it promptly," he wrote. "I got it!"

On June 17, Byron Scott filed Kameny's complaint against the secretary of the army, Wilber M. Brucker, in district court. First and foremost, Scott argued, Kameny had no intent to deceive in his Form 57. Second, Kameny's exclusion was based on mere suspicion of homosexuality, and the government had no concrete facts to substantiate the suspicion. Third, the government had never afforded Kameny the opportunity to rebut any specific claims, thus depriving him of procedural due process.

The complaint raised another issue that Kameny had been contemplating since he had secured Scott as his attorney. Because nobody had ever sued the government for its gay purges, the complaint was a newsworthy event. Newspapers could easily learn about it and report the details of Kameny's case, including his arrest and even his street address. In the midst of another job search, publicity would only make matters worse.

Kameny mentioned his concerns to Scott. Was it possible to remain anonymous?

It was. His case could be styled either *Anonymous v. Brucker* or *Kameny v. Brucker*. Kameny had a month to think about it while Scott prepared the papers.

"Whatever the problems might be in facing the world," he later explained, "there were much worse problems in facing myself."

The lawsuit became *Kameny v. Brucker*.

To his relief, the newspapers ignored his lawsuit. Kameny could only wait for the government's response and, eventually, a hearing.

On June 29, the Supreme Court ruled in favor of aeronautical engineer William Greene. A clearance holder, it found, could not "be deprived of the right to follow his chosen profession without full hearings where accusers may be confronted and cross-examined."

The next day, R. L. Applegate—writing from the same office that had denied Greene a clearance—sent another letter to Kameny. No company had yet requested a security clearance for the astronomer because they had all assumed he would not receive one. "An arrest record, in and of itself, does not necessarily disqualify a person for a security clearance," added Applegate. "It is not unusual for persons with unfortunate or regrettable incidents in their past to be found by the Department of Defense to be sufficiently trustworthy and reliable to be granted a security clearance."

Kameny, disappointed that he did not receive a direct promise of a clearance, appeared at the Pentagon once again.

Applegate admitted that Kameny's lawsuit represented the best route to a security clearance. He wished him luck. To Kameny's surprise, Applegate then asked the astronomer a question: what do *you* think of the department's homosexual policies?

They are unduly and unnecessarily harsh, responded Kameny. The blanket denial of a clearance to all homosexuals is quite unwarranted.

No such blanket denial exists, responded Applegate.

Is it really possible, Kameny dubiously asked, for a known, currently active, overt homosexual to obtain or to retain a clearance?

Yes, said Applegate.

Kameny, shocked by the admission, repeated his question two more times, and then once more as he exited Applegate's office. Each time, he received the same clear response.

Kameny now had something invaluable, a security official's assertion—both in person and in writing—that neither an arrest nor homosexuality per se made him ineligible for a clearance. With Applegate's letter in hand, Kameny held the Pentagon official to his word. He applied for several astronomy-related jobs, and when employers asked for references that would attest to his suitability, Kameny did not only list his usual Harvard and Georgetown references. He now listed R. L. Applegate of the Department of Defense.

He wrote to Johns Hopkins, which had rejected him in 1958, asking to be reconsidered for a position. "I have in my possession a letter from Mr. Applegate," he wrote, that indicated "there would probably be no great obstacle to my being granted a clearance once formal application had been made for one."

At least one company phoned the Pentagon to verify the astronomer's claims. "The Defense Department will interpose no objections to Dr. Kameny's being hired for work involving access to classified information," the security office replied.

Kameny's analysis of the larger homosexual issue had also evolved. "I have done a great deal of thinking, since our second meeting, upon the matters you brought up and which we discussed, in somewhat veiled terms, during the last third of our conversation," he told Applegate. The Pentagon official had asserted that a homosexual without anything to fear, or anything to hide from blackmailers, would have no problem acquiring a security clearance. Thus, the root of the problem lay not in society, but rather in the homosexual's view of himself. "It is not society's attitude toward these people which is important, or even relevant," Kameny wrote, "but the attitude of these people toward society and toward themselves."

Yes, society was becoming "notably and increasingly more tolerant," but more important, "these people" were gaining self-respect. (In his letter to Applegate, not once did he use the word *homosexual*.)

Kameny began to hear back from potential employers. A military research group at the Massachusetts Institute of Technology made its position clear. "It would appear that there exists a reasonable chance of a clearance being granted for you if we were to request it," but there was also "an administrative policy aspect" that would "preclude our offering you employment irrespective of any security problems."

NASA, formed only months earlier, also rejected the astronomer.

In early September 1959, however, Kameny found a job as a scientist. The Gardner Laboratory manufactured testing devices for paint and other coating materials, and because it sold those devices to the general public, the position did not require a security clearance. Kameny could finally eat, and with Byron Scott, he prepared for the first hearing in his case.

STANDING BEFORE Judge Burnita Matthews, a government attorney explained that Kameny's three-year debarment from the civil service provided "a necessary period of rehabilitation." As Kameny later put it, the CSC argued that it had followed "the necessary forms, rites, rituals and ceremonies," and the court did not have the authority to question the dismissal.

While Kameny waited for a decision, he tested an expansion of the extralegal tactic that had worked so well with Applegate and his job search. He would demand meetings with authorities and then capture their denials of homosexual discrimination on the record.

Because homosexuals could not dance in Washington's gay bars, a group had established a private club in a large rented house near Dupont Circle. There, men could dance with men.

One night in November, the police raided the house. Kameny wrote to the police commissioner and promised to do everything in his power to oppose increases in police funding unless the commissioner could explain its raid. Soon thereafter, Kameny received a call from a man with a slow, deep voice. This is Chief Blick. Come to my office at nine o'clock tomorrow morning.

Roy Blick was the chief of the Metropolitan Police Department's Morals Division. Kameny could have made that appointment, but he wanted to assert his authority. Kameny told Blick that he was unavailable.

Well, I can phone your employer and take care of it for you, the chief responded.

Kameny refused, then offered to come at 2:00 p.m., a few days later.

On that date, the astronomer arrived at the police headquarters and met Blick, an intimidating figure. Having been on the force for nearly thirty years, Blick had helped organize the sex squad in 1940. Early in his career, a tear gas shell had exploded in his face during a raid, leaving him with only one eye. As Kameny sat down, Blick began asking questions: Where do you work? Where do you live?

Kameny ignored the questions and began scolding the chief of the Washington Vice Squad. The raids were "perfectly illegal" and a waste of police resources, he argued. Moreover, why was there a prohibition of dancing in public places?

The chief explained that the police had no objections to such behavior as long as nothing indecent occurred.

That answer is too vague, the astronomer replied. What does *indecent* mean?

People groping each other, responded Blick.

"And with that in hand," Kameny later recalled, "I began to push for dances in gay bars."

On December 22, 1959, Judge Matthews granted the federal government's motion to dismiss Kameny's case. He had lost the first round. Byron Scott appealed, hoping to convince the court of appeals to remand the case back to the district court for a full trial. Scott simply had to prove that valid issues were at stake, and the more substantive arguments would come later. As Scott explained to Kameny, the appeal would take "just a small bite." Scott filed the appeal on April 8, 1960, and again, the government argued that the AMS and CSC actions were not subject to review by the court. Unlike aeronautical engineer William Greene, Kameny had received an opportunity to rebut the allegations.

"My attorney says that they have no valid argument there," explained Kameny.

On May 5, Kameny wrote to an organization of homosexuals in New York. "This will be a very long letter," he warned.

He explained his saga and gave insight into his relationship with Scott. "My attorney and I have worked closely together on this—I have not been just a passive participant; many of our arguments originated with me." Though they were currently arguing that his case should merely be heard, they also had a set of arguments "in reserve, ready to be used."

Kameny had done a great deal of thinking since his productive conversation with R. L. Applegate at the Pentagon. When it came to security clearances, Kameny had concluded that "a homosexual who is willing, should the necessity arise, to stand up on his own two legs before the world, as he is, and to defend his right to live his life as he chooses, can get and retain a clearance."

Though the civil service barred homosexuals because of their "immoral conduct" rather than their risk to national security, the CSC never defined what constituted immoral conduct. Morality, after all, was an arbitrary concept. If Kameny could persuade the government—and other homosexuals—that deviant sexual behavior was not immoral, then the law would not apply. "By Unwritten rule only, of long standing, homosexuality is considered immoral," he explained. Just as recent decisions were "slapping down equally vague definitions of obscenity," Kameny could force the government to "define terms of this sort clearly, explicitly, and in writing."

Kameny and Scott thus prepared to make the unprecedented legal argument that homosexuality was morally good. "We assert, flatly, and without compromise," Kameny wrote, "that homosexuality whether by act or by mere inclination, is not immoral, and, in fact, that it can be cogently argued that for those so inclined, it is moral in a positive sense."

Emboldened with a job, Kameny was not the same man who had lied about a nonexistent future fiancée. For the first time, he could envision a future in which he had to sacrifice neither his principles nor his livelihood. "The past 2½ years have not been easy ones," he wrote. "I am, perhaps, just beginning to 'see the light' after an extended period of darkness." So he would fight, and he would fight as a homosexual who saw his condition as a positive, moral trait.

"I am not a belligerent person, nor do I seek wars," Kameny explained, "but having been forced into battle, I am determined that this thing will be fought."

AFTER A COURT OF APPEALS HEARING on May 18, 1960, Kameny wrote back to MIT, shaming the institution for its "ultra-conservative personnel policies."

"Unconventional, and in some ways a nonconformist I may well be, but there is nothing in my life of which I am ashamed, nor of which I feel guilty, nor, in regard to which, I cannot 'look anyone squarely in the eye,'" he wrote. His case was "being vigorously fought through the courts," he explained. "I expect to win."

On June 6, a three-judge panel of the U.S. court of appeals unanimously affirmed the dismissal of Kameny's case. The AMS had given "specific details" for his removal and accorded "all procedural prerogatives," so any consideration of the CSC's decision-making was therefore "unnecessary."

Scott and Kameny requested a rehearing, and at this point, they introduced their "reserve" arguments. Their petition represented a Hail Mary; perhaps the court, like Applegate, would take pity on an astronomer willing to fight openly as a homosexual.

"My attorney informs me," wrote Kameny, "that the case has created a considerable stir at the Court of Appeals, since this represents the first time anyone has ever challenged the Government's policies on these matters—particularly on constitutional rather than procedural or mere factual grounds."

The court of appeals should rehear his case, his petition argued, because the government discharged Kameny "solely because he was suspected of homosexuality." The fact that his "sex life may be different from other citizens bears no reasonable relation to the objective of bettering the efficiency of the Federal Service." Above all, Kameny had a "federally guaranteed right to be free from discrimination which, he submits, is no less illegal than discrimination based on religious or racial grounds."

It was no coincidence that Kameny first made the comparison between homosexual and racial discrimination in the summer of 1960. The Greensboro sit-ins were coming to a successful end. Segregationists, gripping the mantle of moral authority, had long argued that the mixing of the races would weaken the country and aid the Communists. But then the young Black demonstrators at Greensboro—well dressed, silent, and thoroughly nonviolent—attempted to order hamburgers at a Woolworth's lunch counter. Americans watched white retaliators—"ducktailed sideburned swaggerers, the rednecked hatemongers, the Ku Klux Klan," as *TIME* described them—repeatedly attack the stoic protesters. Afterward, how could Southern whites possibly claim civility and moral authority?

In August, Washington's municipal court of appeals ruled that "lewd, obscene, or indecent" sexual acts—the same charge Kameny faced in San Francisco—were legal when "done privately in the presence of only one other person who solicited or consented to the act."

The decision "rendered a service to common sense and common decency," wrote *The Washington Post*. The police, it wrote, were the ones behaving immorally by resorting to the entrapment of homosexuals. "There is no better word for this than disgusting."

To win his case, Kameny only had to convince two or three judges that his case had nothing to do with falsification, with security, or with efficiency, that it had everything to do with his status as a homosexual citizen. Perhaps, like in Greensboro, the scales of morality would tip in favor of the persecuted once more.

On August 31, 1960, the court of appeals denied Kameny's petition

for a rehearing. Kameny had lost once again, leaving only the Supreme
Court.

SIX DAYS LATER, a disaster unfolded for both Kameny and the American
government. On September 6, William Martin and Bernon Mitchell—
"clean-cut fellows who looked like typical all-American boys," as one
magazine described them—sat on an elevated stage in Moscow's House
of Journalists, flanked by blue velvet drapes. The hall was crowded with
journalists, and the duo stared at rows of television cameras. The defec-
tors, formerly code clerks in the hypersecretive National Security Agency,
began divulging America's darkest secrets—surveillance flights, over-
throwing regimes, spying on allies.

"Investigators also have learned that Mitchell was hired by the National Security Agency despite a bad security report, alleging homosexual
activity in his youth," reported columnist Jack Anderson. "Both men were
entrusted with vital information on how we crack secret Soviet codes.
Their disappearance is considered the worst security breach since World
War II."

Congress planned hearings, and the next day, Eisenhower called for a
reexamination of the government's entire security program. The NSA investigated and purged twenty-six alleged homosexuals in a matter of
weeks. "Nothing has stirred Washington quite so much since Sputnik I
went into outer space," wrote one columnist.

Despite the duo's claims, nobody seemed to believe Martin and
Mitchell had defected for political or ideological reasons. "One of them
was mentally sick, and both were obviously confused," explained the Pentagon. Mitchell's own father alluded to blackmail. "This thing was not
voluntary," he said.

After thirteen months, two thousand hours of investigation, and sixteen executive session hearings, HUAC ultimately concluded that homosexuality caused their defection. "Never once," historian James Bamford
concluded, "did the committee bother to look into what might have been
the deeper reasons for the defection."

"Is it not time to face the question of homosexuals frankly and coura-
geously?" asked conservative columnist George Sokolsky. "In a time of

total war when everything becomes a weapon, the homosexual has proved himself to be an easy tool in the hands of the Russians who have no scruples using them to betray their own country."

"The Reds are using a new tactic in recruiting spies and traitors, and it's working," wrote *Top Secret*, a gossip magazine. "The new tactic is to gain access to American secrets by using—homosexuals!"

That fall, Byron Scott declined to take *Kameny v. Brucker* to the Supreme Court. The attorney, after fighting for Kameny nearly two years without pay, could not identify a path to a favorable decision. If Kameny wanted to plead his case before the nation's highest court, he would have to do it alone.

"IF I'D GONE THAT FAR, I simply wanted to go on," Kameny later explained. Scott gave him a Supreme Court rule book and examples of a petition for writ of certiorari, the document that would attempt to persuade the court to take his case. The attorney helped him draft a request for a time extension, and Kameny then received a letter—on blue stationery, signed by Earl Warren, as he later boasted—granting him sixty additional days to submit a brief.

With the petition, Kameny faced a much greater likelihood that the media would report on his case, and that his employers, his family, and the public would learn of his situation. "Thus far it has received no newspaper publicity," wrote Kameny in August. "But that, unfortunately, may end."

As Kameny began working on his brief, he received encouragement in the form of another man interested in the plight of his kind.

Jack Nichols was twenty-two years old, six foot three, and had short, dark hair. One night in late 1960, he sat on a sofa at one of gay Washington's weekend house parties. Nichols heard a commanding voice explaining how author Donald Webster Cory had made an excellent case for the rights of homosexuals. In the aftermath of the Kinsey report, Cory had identified homosexuals as a minority group. "We are a minority, not only numerically, but also as a result of our caste-like status in society," Cory had written. Jack Nichols, like Kameny and countless other homosexuals, had read Cory's book.

Nichols stood from the sofa and walked to the group of men standing by a window. "The man who spoke was animated by a peculiar intensity," Nichols later wrote, "each of his words clipped, authoritative and academic in tone. As I approached he looked at me appreciatively, stepping back to make room in the semi-circle."

By the end of the night, Nichols learned the details of Kameny's case, and Kameny promised to call him, since the astronomer still could not afford a telephone of his own.

A few days later, Nichols climbed the stairs to Kameny's small, gloomy apartment in Adams Morgan. They became friends, meeting regularly for the rest of 1960 to discuss developments in Kameny's case, the civil rights movement, and the homosexual organizations in other cities. The astronomer had found an ally, a gay one, to replace Scott.

As Kameny worked on his brief, he also noticed signs of change. In November, America elected as its president the young Catholic senator who had spoken at Kameny's Harvard commencement only four years earlier.

Despite the Martin and Mitchell case and the continuance of the purges, cracks seemed to be growing in the foundation of moral authority that enabled the local policing of gay Washington. That month, the *Post* reported on a recent moment of absurdity. One evening, a uniformed Park Police officer was patrolling Lafayette Park when he saw three men lingering by the lavatory.

What are you men doing? asked the officer, a Black man.

Mind your own business, responded one of the men.

The officer arrested the man and led him, struggling, to a call station. The detainee called for help, and the two other loitering men ran toward the officer. According to the *Post*, the officer "promptly and efficiently, employing his judo training for the purpose, flipped all three of them onto their backs and into the park shrubbery."

The officer then recognized one of them as a member of the Metropolitan Police Morals Division. All three had been undercover police officers, waiting to catch homosexuals in the park restroom; not once had they identified themselves. The Park Police gave its officer a fifteen-day suspension, without a hearing, for his "inability to work harmoniously with the Metropolitan Policemen."

"In a town where crime is rampant and on the increase," editorialized the *Post*, "why should three (3) detectives of the Metropolitan Police be stationed in Lafayette Park? And why should they be out of uniform?" it asked. "The whole process borders on provocation and entrapment. Why should the simple job of policing Lafayette Park not be done by ordinary policemen—in uniform?"

The *real* moral actor was the Black Park Police officer, punished for doing his job. "He showed simply a considerable skill at judo and a highly developed sense of decency," concluded the *Post*.

President Kennedy swore his oath of office on January 20, 1961, and Kameny read his speech in the *Star*. The new president had promised "renewal as well as change" and warned of "destruction unleashed by science." When the astronomer noticed the immortal line—"my fellow Americans: ask not what your country can do for you—ask what you can do for your country"—he reached for his pen, drew brackets around that phrase, and saved it for the rest of his life.

One week later, Frank Kameny submitted the first Supreme Court petition ever written against the federal government's gay purges. It was a modest proposal, explained Kameny in the document's preamble. "This court is asked, merely, to affirm that issues and questions of sufficient validity and gravity exist to warrant the granting of a full court hearing to the case in all of its aspects."

Kameny wrote for a minority that composed "10% of our population at the very least—perhaps, at least some 15,000,000. This is a group comparable in size to the Negro minority in our country, and of roughly the same order of magnitude as the Catholic minority; a group of some 2½ times the size of the country's Jewish minority and comparable to the world's Jewish population." He had been "branded, publicly and (if they are not reversed) permanently, by the majesty of the United States Government, as a dishonest person, and as an immoral person, neither of which he is. And he has been so branded without a shred of fact to bear out the accusations, and, more important, without a chance to defend himself in an impartial hearing."

Kameny also wrote the petition to teach the court about the problem of the homosexual. Both the executive and judicial branches, he explained, needed to be "instructed in regard to certain factual, sociological, and other realities which the government stubbornly ignores, and of which the Court, certainly in a formal sense, through an almost total lack of previous cases, arguments, decisions, and precedents, is uninformed."

For sixty pages, the astronomer detailed his arguments. He began with the overriding fact that no immoral behavior had occurred in San Francisco. Unlike his early appeals, his brief did not deny homosexual activity. Instead, he denied the immorality of what had occurred. "Illegal conduct (not an issue here) may conceivably have occurred," he admitted, "but not immoral conduct."

The Civil Service Commission, he continued, had refused to provide specific evidence to substantiate its allegations of immoral conduct. Its ban on immoral behavior was "far too vague to be implemented," and it imposed "an odious conformity" on government employees. The CSC's decisions were therefore "punitive, and, therefore, arbitrary and capricious."

Plus, argued Kameny, regulating morality at all was unconstitutional. Morals were "a matter of a citizen's personal opinion and his individual religious belief," so by "establishing a tyranny over the mind of the citizen," CSC regulations violated "the provisions, stipulations, spirit, and intent" of the First Amendment.

He called upon the government to act ahead of public opinion, just as it had acted in the confrontations of the 1950s civil rights movement. "There will be no riots in the streets if homosexuals are no longer fired from the government service; no government buildings will be blown up; there will be no need to call out troops to protect Federal employees; there will be no mass resignations or boycotts of the Federal service, or any other signs of protest analogous to those occurring in the South in regard to racial integration."

Just like the cases against Jim Crow, his case was a matter of morality, wrote Kameny. "The government's regulations, policies, practices and procedures, as applied in the instant case to petitioner specifically, and as applied to homosexuals generally, are a stench in the nostrils of decent people, an offense against morality, an abandonment of reason, an affront to human dignity, an improper restraint upon proper freedom and liberty, a disgrace to any civilized society, and a violation of all that this nation stands for."

And if the government's behavior was so clearly immoral, what did that mean about his own behavior? Indeed, asked Kameny, "what is immoral conduct?" He answered with an amplified version of what he had declared the previous summer. "Petitioner asserts, flatly, unequivocally, and absolutely uncompromisingly, that homosexuality, whether by mere inclination or by overt act, is not only not immoral, but that for those choosing voluntarily to engage in homosexual acts, such acts are moral in a real and positive sense, and are good, right, and desirable, socially and personally."

For Kameny, it was merely a logical argument, a tactical maneuver to prove the arbitrary nature of the government's reliance on a moral code. The government argued homosexuality was immoral, so he would argue it was moral. Who could argue otherwise, other than a misinformed society and a God who, in the eyes of an atheistic Kameny, did not exist?

By submitting the brief with his true name, fully aware of the likelihood that the media would report on the circumstances of his case, Kameny made this claim of morality with openness. Kameny did not explicitly identify as a homosexual in his brief, but neither did he deny engaging in homosexual activity. Instead, he denied engaging in *immoral* activity, and he allowed the court to label him as a homosexual on its own. Now, if the Defense Department claimed he was susceptible to blackmail, he could simply point to his brief, for it meant he had nothing to hide.

Though Kameny did not have a term for it yet, by exposing the arbitrary logic of the purges with his own, contrary logic, he formulated gay pride as a political tool of resistance, a weapon to be wielded, for now, only in the courts. He saw growing evidence that a minority group could claim morality for itself in a rapidly changing legal and cultural landscape, and he crafted a manifesto that would forever guide his activist strategy and ideology of pride. The Kameny brief marked a declaration of war by a new political entity: the proud plaintiff.

"In World War II," wrote Kameny, "petitioner did not hesitate to fight the Germans, with bullets, in order to help preserve his rights and freedoms and liberties, and those of others. In 1960, it is ironically necessary that he fight the Americans, with words, in order to preserve, against a tyrannical government, some of those same rights, freedoms and liberties, for himself and for others. He asks this court, by its granting a writ of certiorari, to allow him to engage in that battle."

On March 21, Kameny received another blue piece of paper signed by Chief Justice Earl Warren. The Supreme Court of the United States had unanimously rejected his petition.

Top Secret *magazine, February 1961*

5.

THE MATTACHINE

In 153 B.C., Ancient Rome fixed January 1 as the inauguration day of its consuls, and that date became the beginning of a new year. On that day, the two new chief magistrates sacrificed bulls to Jupiter, and in later centuries, they swore an oath to the emperor. Romans celebrated the occasion, known as the kalends, with impressive festivity: they exchanged so many gifts that package deliveries congested roads across the empire. Citizens ate and drank to excess at lavish banquets, and the rules that defined Roman society were temporarily loosened. Masters even played dice with their slaves.

The early Christians denounced the kalends as pagan devil worship, but the festival's traditions only grew in popularity. When the empire banned the consuls' bull sacrifice in 399 A.D., a new tradition grew in its place. The kalends became an occasion to mock the regime. Revelers, often wearing animal masks, traveled from door to door, harassing public officials in the middle of the night. Soldiers in Amasea elected a mock emperor, and many of them dressed as women to join his "harem." During the kalends, as one sixth-century church official complained, a man "*se frangit in feminam*," or weakens himself into a woman.

By the thirteenth century, the new year's tradition of mockery had seeped into French and Italian churches as the Feast of Fools, a celebration of the Bible's proclamation that "God chose what is foolish in the world to shame the wise." For one day, low-ranking clergy and choirboys assumed the positions of bishops or cantors. They elected a Bishop of Fools, wore masks, and dressed as women.

The church banned the practice in 1435, but the foolery had already spread to the townsfolk. In France, associations of young men called Sociétés Joyeuses—devoted to satire, music, and comedy—began to multiply. One of the most important societies, a legally recognized organization with hundreds of members, was led by the Mère Folle, or the Mother Fool, a man in drag. On Mardi Gras, she paraded down the streets of Dijon on a chariot behind her dominion of hundreds of colorfully uniformed, scepter-wielding men. On moving stages, actors criticized the immoral and the corrupt behind the comedy of their satire and the anonymity of their masks.

One of their routines involved a comedic, choreographed sword fight timed to music, known as *les matassins*, or the mattachine. The name, derived from either the Italian *matta* (fool) or the Spanish *matar* (to kill), was telling in either sense; the dancers wore bells on their knees and feigned a dramatic combat to the death. Though the Sociétés Joyeuses disappeared with the absolute monarchy of Louis XIV, *les matassins* survived. Spanish colonists brought their own version, *la danza de mattachines*, to the Americas, where it fused with native analogues over the centuries. To this day, men in parts of Mexico dance *los mattachines* with masks and colorful headdresses while a *viejo*—often dressed as a woman—mocks and scares the audience.

Harry Hay discovered the dance of the mattachine while teaching his class, "Music, Barometer of the Struggle," at the People's Education Center of Los Angeles in the late 1940s. Hay was six foot three, a handsome yet struggling actor, and an unyielding believer in the revolution of the proletariat.

Hay was married to a woman, a fellow Communist, and had two children, but he frequently sought restroom encounters with men in a nearby park. He often attended homosexual house parties.

In 1948, Kinsey's findings of rampant homosexuality gave Hay a revolutionary idea. Perhaps homosexuals were just like workers according to Marxist theory, an oppressed minority unaware of its own existence and potential power. Homosexuals could pool money to protect victims of police entrapment and the government's purges, Hay imagined. They could even organize to wield political power within the Democratic Party.

One night, he drunkenly composed a manifesto for a new organization that would do just that.

The idea died until 1950, when Hay fell in love with an angular, twenty-eight-year-old fashion designer named Rudi Gernreich. The Jewish former dancer had arrived to America in 1938 as a teenager fleeing from the Third Reich. Hay's prospectus for a gay organization enthralled Gernreich, but only five years after Hitler's fall, the refugee urged caution. The Nazis, Gernreich told Hay, had used the records of Berlin's Institute for Sex Research to identify homosexuals and send them to death camps. McCarthy was rounding up alleged Communists and homosexuals, and who knew what could happen to the members of a gay organization with Marxist foundations?

The couple proceeded carefully. Over the next few months, Hay and Gernreich quietly recruited five more Communists and fellow travelers, all white men. By mid-1951, the group had agreed on the organization's purposes: to unify homosexuals "isolated from their own kind," to educate others in response to the "woefully meager and inconclusive" research on homosexuality, and to lead "the whole mass of social deviates" as they created a "highly ethical homosexual culture." Political action was "imperative."

When Hay taught about the Sociétés Joyeuses in his class, he speculated that the all-male groups—dedicated to music, dance, and satirical whimsy—were full of homosexuals. So the men chose the "Society of Fools" as the organization's interim name before settling on the more severe-sounding "Mattachine Society." And because the word *homosexual* was so commonly used by psychiatrists to describe a sickness, they searched for an alternative word, one that sounded more benign and less clinical, a word they could claim as their own. They settled on *homophile*.

The Mattachine Society's structure became a pyramid of five hierarchical "orders," each with increasing responsibility, prestige, and secrecy as a member climbed them. Open discussion groups served as recruiting grounds for potential Society members, who were then invited to join a "guild" of the secretive First Order. Because of its cell-like structure, the Society allowed members to remain anonymous, yet still a member of a brotherhood.

As the discussion groups multiplied, the Society began holding dances in private homes. Hay once caught a gay coworker standing in a doorway with tears running down his face.

He had never seen so many men dancing together and looking so beautiful, his coworker explained.

In February 1952, Hay received a telephone call in the middle of the night. Dale Jennings, a slim, bespectacled Fifth Order member, was in jail. He had been in a park restroom when a "big, rough-looking character" began following him home. A witness saw the stranger forcefully enter Jennings's front door, and Jennings soon found his hand being forced down the front of the man's trousers. Seconds later, Jennings was in handcuffs. The man had been a police officer.

The next morning, after Hay posted bail, he and Jennings decided to fight the blatant case of entrapment. That night, at an emergency meeting, the Fifth Order agreed to utilize the case to publicize and dramatize the oppression of homosexuals. They found a lawyer and developed a risky defense strategy.

To publicize the case without revealing the existence of the Society, the Fifth Order created a Citizens Committee to Outlaw Entrapment. They circulated leaflets—"NOW Is The Time To Fight. The issue is CIVIL RIGHTS."—in public restrooms and on park benches, at the gay beaches of Santa Monica, and in the gay-owned shops of West Hollywood.

Yes, Dale Jennings was a homosexual, his attorney told the jury. But there was a difference between *being* a homosexual and engaging in lewd conduct. "The only true pervert in the courtroom," he argued, "is the arresting officer." After thirty-six hours of deliberation, eleven out of twelve jurors voted to acquit Jennings. The judge dismissed the case.

The Citizens Committee declared victory. Never before had an admitted homosexual walked away from a lewd conduct case in the state of California. If the Mattachine could convince eleven straight jurors that a homosexual was the victim of injustice, the founders asked, could they convince the world of the same?

"Were heterosexuals to realize that these violations of our rights threaten theirs equally, a vast reform might even come within our lifetime," wrote Jennings a few months later. "This is no more a dream than trying to win a case after admitting homosexuality."

Because of the Jennings case, the Mattachine exploded in size. Discussion groups multiplied across Southern California and into the Bay Area, where gay women, too, joined in large numbers. By May 1953, the Fifth Order estimated that it had nearly a hundred discussion groups and more than two thousand participants. One group created a magazine, and Dale Jennings became its first editor. *ONE* magazine's inaugural issue, released in January 1953, featured his case as its cover story, and it was soon selling thousands of copies per month. Finally, a gay movement existed in America.

The Mattachine continued fighting additional entrapment cases, and it moved into the realm of political action that Hay had, from the beginning, identified as so crucial. In 1953, the organization sent a political questionnaire to candidates for mayor and city council. Should the city continue Vice Squad arrest quotas? Should police decoys continue entrapping homosexuals?

The questionnaire marked the beginning of Hay's downfall. *Los Angeles Mirror* columnist Paul Coates learned of the survey and began an investigation into the homosexual group supposedly fighting to live "with pride and without fear." When Coates called the state Division of Corporations, it had no record of the Mattachine. The columnist acknowledged homosexuals "might swing tremendous political power," but he warned a "well-trained subversive" could easily take control of a homosexual group, turning it into a "dangerous political weapon" against America. "If I belonged to that club," wrote Coates, "I'd worry."

It was, after all, a time of fear. McCarthy ruled Washington, and HUAC had just arrived in Los Angeles to conduct hearings on the Communist subversion of Hollywood. Discussion groups across the state began clamoring for transparency and a voice in Mattachine decision-making. Some rejected the existence of a homosexual minority, and others were horrified by the foundation's political activism. One Mattachine group called for an American loyalty oath.

On May 23, 1953, Marilyn Rieger, a lesbian businesswoman, circulated a rousing letter to the delegates of a Mattachine convention in Los Angeles. What use was pride—or minority status—if homosexuals still moved "underground, in secrecy and with fear"? It was only by "coming out into the open," she wrote, "by declaring ourselves, by integrating, not as homosexuals, but as people, as men and women whose homosexuality is irrelevant to our ideals, our principles, our hopes and aspirations, that we will rid the world of its misconcepts of homosexuality and homosexuals."

The next day, all seven founders, including Harry Hay, stepped onto the stage and removed their masks of anonymity. Before a shocked and murmuring audience, they announced themselves as the elusive Fifth Order, then declared that they would resign from the organization they had founded. Despite the cries of "oh, no, no," that arose from the audience, Rieger and her openness faction declared victory. They became the leaders of a new, democratic Mattachine Society.

After resigning from the organization he founded, Hay fell into a deep depression and considered ending his life. His dreams of a militant, politically active, and proud homosexual minority were over.

ACCORDING TO the Mattachine's new leadership, the group's name no longer referred to a masked society of fools, but rather to court jesters who "lived and moved in the circles of the nobility."

Talk of a gay minority or a clandestine brotherhood disappeared. The homosexual became "no different from anyone else except in the object of his sexual expression." Rather than working to develop a new minority ethic and culture, the new Mattachine would assimilate, encouraging behavior "acceptable to society in general." It would organize blood drives and hospital fund-raisers to present an image of an upstanding group of citizens who only happened to be homosexual. In its effort to change society, the unmasked Mattachine decided not to speak to the public, but instead to the nobility of the midtwentieth century: the psychiatrists, attorneys, and religious figures who had the ability to shape America's perception of the sexual deviant.

No longer would the homosexuals fight in court, and political action in the aftermath of the candidate questionnaire fiasco became unthinkable. "We do not wish to speak out the truth 'no matter what the consequences'—we believe that the consequences matter very much indeed," explained the Mattachine's new chairman to *ONE*'s Dale Jennings. "To keep quiet is not necessarily to deny the truth."

The new Mattachine shrank dramatically in size. In the immediate aftermath of the reorganization, discussion group leaders resigned en masse. Women, especially, felt alienated by the new leadership, and Marilyn Rieger resigned from the Mattachine only six months after her openness campaign. At the May 1955 Mattachine convention, only thirty-one delegates attended, and twenty-nine were men.

One of the delegates was thirty-six-year-old Buell Dwight Huggins. Originally from Illinois, Huggins had been expelled from the state university after making a sexual advance in a university men's room.

After the Mattachine conference, Huggins moved to the District of Columbia. Perhaps motivated by the convention, he decided to create the capital's first organization of homosexuals.

On June 28, 1956, not long after Frank Kameny attended his Harvard commencement, B. D. Huggins rented a post office box for the Washington chapter of the Mattachine Society. He penned a newsletter, which promised to fight antihomosexual laws and attempted to combat local homosexuals' fears of the new organization. "The risks that you will assume with us," wrote Huggins, "are far less than the risks many take in their daily and nocturnal rounds of the parks, theatres, and bars."

An official in the New York Mattachine, founded only a year earlier, admonished Huggins to restrict his activities to research and education. Hal Call, of the national Mattachine, which had recently moved its headquarters to San Francisco, concurred. "Discretion here is certainly the better part of valor," he wrote.

The Washington Mattachine, after acquiring a maximum of sixteen newsletter subscribers and thirteen members, never became a functional membership organization. Kameny never joined the group. And within three years, the organization—prohibited from political activism and inhibited by fear—had disappeared. Indeed, a ten-dollar membership fee (roughly eighty-five in today's dollars) merely paid for a magazine, a newsletter, and the many risks associated with joining an organization of homosexuals.

The dangers, after all, remained real. Before the 1959 national Mattachine conference in Denver, the host chapter persuaded Mattachine headquarters to allow publicity. Its officers sent out press releases and even held a press conference. They used their real names, and *The Denver*

Post wrote about the convention fairly and extensively. The publicity led to a large convention crowd and a growth in membership, but at the convention itself, the delegates noticed two large men at the opening proceedings.

They were morals officers. One month later, the Denver Police raided the homes of three Mattachine members. In the home of the chapter's librarian, officers found Society mailing lists and photographs of naked men. The librarian spent sixty days in jail, and at least two members lost their jobs. As the chapter newsletter described it, a "wave of fear" gripped gay Denver, and local homosexuals avoided the once-promising chapter for the rest of its existence.

The national Mattachine, meanwhile, faced rebellion. The New York Mattachine had become the largest chapter, yet its members still sent their dues to San Francisco. At the September 1960 convention, the New York delegation arrived with allegations of financial impropriety. What was the Mattachine headquarters doing with all its money?

On March 15, 1961, the national Mattachine disintegrated. In a five-to-two decision, its board of directors revoked the charters of all out-of-state chapters, citing irreconcilable budgetary problems. Only the San Francisco group, shrinking to focus on local issues, was permitted to continue using the Mattachine name. Chapters across the country heard the news with shock and confusion. The Boston and Denver groups evaporated altogether.

Five days after the implosion of the national Mattachine, Frank Kameny received his rejection letter from the Supreme Court of the United States.

THE ASTRONOMER HAD been prepared for the court's denial. The same day Kameny received Justice Warren's rejection, he wrote to the Civil Service Commission's new equality-minded commissioner, John Macy Jr., to request reemployment. He then sent a copy of his Supreme Court brief to President Kennedy, demanding "some action from the New Frontier!"

He heard only silence from the president, so he wrote again to the CSC chairman. "The winds of change are blowing, Mr. Macy. These fifteen or more million Americans are not going to stand, indefinitely, for the type of discrimination, persecution, suppression, and oppression which they have been receiving at the hands of your commission and other constituted authority, any more than the Negroes have been willing to. The homosexual in this country is in the position that the Negro was in about 1925, when he first began to fight, in a coordinated fashion, for his proper rights."

Meanwhile, the renegade Mattachine Society of New York (MSNY) wanted to expand. Since 1960, Kameny had been exchanging letters with Albert de Dion, its chairman. De Dion and his lover, Curtis Dewees, dressed ruggedly, wore crew cuts, and stood at five foot eight. Most New Yorkers assumed they were brothers, not a couple.

Since the disappearance of the Washington chapter, de Dion and Dewees had planned to reestablish an area council in the nation's capital. In the middle of these discussions with the national Mattachine, de Dion received a letter from Frank Kameny, requesting a donation for his legal battle. The officers' fifty-dollar contribution represented an extraordinary investment in a man they had never met. By the end of the month, the MSNY had only eighty-eight dollars in its bank account.

With the 1961 collapse of the national Mattachine, the New York chapter found itself unleashed. On March 27, the same day it decided to keep the Mattachine name, the new MSNY decided to "lay the ground work" for a new, less-centralized "federation or alliance of independent organizations whose major interests lie in the area of human-sexuality-and-society."

Kameny wanted to meet the man who had sent him the fifty-dollar check, and de Dion wanted to meet a potential founder of a new allied group in Washington. "Sometime this summer or early fall," wrote de Dion in May, "my roommate and I may visit Washington to talk up the Mattachine among those on our mailing list and former members." He asked Kameny to find "an inexpensive meeting place, centrally located" and to tell his friends—and their friends—so they would have "promise of a decent beginning."

On the night of May 20, Louis Fochett attended a drag show. In high school, Fochett had planned to become a professional dancer, and now, for the third time in a week, he watched a troupe of three female impersonators. In the middle of their performance, Fochett stood—along with five other officers from the Washington Vice Squad—and arrested the tall brunettes for an indecent performance.

On June 22, CSC chairman John Macy Jr. responded to Kameny's appeal. "The Commission's policy," Macy informed him, "based on impartial consideration of many cases involving all aspects of human behavior, is that homosexuals or sexual perverts are not suitable for Federal employment."

Gardner Laboratories laid off Kameny that month. He responded to Macy by accusing him of perpetuating a homosexual "genocide through permanent unemployment."

Earlier that year, Kameny had braced for his own name to appear in print while he waited for the Supreme Court's decision. Washington papers regularly reported on cases that the court turned down, and there was every likelihood that they would report on the unprecedented homosexual suit. The Supreme Court did appear on the front page of the *Star* on the day it rejected Kameny's case, but the article covered a different discrimination case: the appeal of three Black students jailed for participating in Louisiana lunch counter sit-ins.

To his relief, neither Kameny's employer nor his mother learned of his case, but on July 10, the unemployed Kameny received an unsettling letter. A subscriber of *ONE* magazine wanted a copy of his petition. Kameny had sent copies of the brief to *ONE* and the Mattachine, but he had requested anonymity. How, he wondered, had this man learned his name and his address? Who else now knew his identity?

Kameny wrote immediately to *ONE*, and its editor reassured him. The magazine had kept his name anonymous, and it had only reported on his case in its May 1961 newsletter, *ONE Confidential*, intended only for its most committed supporters. It had referred to him only as "PETITIONER." The correspondent had found Kameny's name—and then his address—by searching through *The United States Law Week*.

The magazine had marveled at the astronomer's "almost incalculable courage." It chronicled his entire saga, from his administrative nightmare to when he "drew a deep breath" and appealed to the Supreme Court. For six paragraphs, it quoted his brief, including his claim that homosexual acts were "good, right, and desirable." It lauded the astronomer's "carefully-planned and logically-reasoned" exposition of the homosexual's "basic rights" and his unprecedented legal declaration that homosexual behavior was morally good.

Kameny sent a copy of his brief to the man who had written him. "You may, of course, show it to anyone whom you please. If it will cause others to stand up for their rights before any level of government, then it will have served its purpose." Until now, his battle had simply been a logical progression of events in the life of a single, nonconforming man. Kameny was right; the government was wrong. The courts needed an education; he would provide it. But by the summer of 1961, Kameny understood that his struggle represented something much larger. It represented hope for a minority that, despite the efforts of Harry Hay, did not yet know its power.

THE LAST WEEK OF JULY, homosexuals in the Washington area received an invitation. "Dear Friend," began de Dion's letter, "What will you be doing next Tuesday, August 1st? If you are interested in being part of an exciting social movement, then plan to attend a meeting of the Mattachine Society at the Manger Hay-Adams Hotel. Representatives of the Society will be on hand to discuss plans for forming a Mattachine group in Washington.

"Recent progress in educating the public about sexual deviation will be reviewed. It is our purpose to show that the mutual cooperation of both laymen and professional members of the public can focus attention on the need for further research and open discussion of sex behavioral problems in your community."

On August 1, at 8:30 p.m., fifteen men walked past the Italian Renaissance–style columns of the Hay-Adams hotel, through its opulent wood-paneled lobby, and into its executive meeting room. Immediately across the street was Lafayette Park, the site of their sexual fantasies, their criminal nightmares, and the center of their world. From the hotel entrance, if the men squinted, looking past the trees and the public restroom, they could see the illuminated White House.

De Dion and Dewees were explaining the history and purposes of the

Mattachine when a sixteenth man, a friend of Kameny's named Ron Balin, arrived late. Balin surveyed the room and leaned over to whisper in Kameny's ear. He needed to speak with him in the hallway.

Balin pointed to a handsome, dark-haired man sitting immediately next to Kameny's empty chair. That's Sergeant Fochett, said Balin, referring to the same Vice Squad detective known for arresting gay men in Lafayette Park and, earlier that summer, the three drag performers.

Kameny was skeptical, but it did seem as if the man had been taking a lot of notes. Though Kameny—like everyone in gay Washington—knew of Fochett by name, he did not know his face.

Are you sure? asked Kameny.

Absolutely sure, said Balin.

After Kameny returned to the meeting room, he looked covertly behind the alleged detective. He looked again, and finally, he saw it: a holstered gun under the man's jacket.

The astronomer knew the law. The sixteen men were doing nothing illegal, so Kameny remained quiet until the end of the meeting.

While I may be mistaken, announced Kameny, I understand we have a member of the Morals Division here with us this evening. Would he care to say anything?

Fochett, understandably, was startled. No, no, he said. Chief Blick of the Morals Division had received an invitation to the meeting—he had been on the MSNY's mailing list—and I'm here simply to observe and take notes. Moreover, he said, I'm very much impressed by the high level at which your group is operating.

Kameny and the other attendees left the Hay-Adams with the knowledge that the Vice Squad would learn about their meeting within hours or even minutes. When they went to bed that night, they could not have been entirely certain whether they would find their names, occupations, and addresses in the Washington papers—or whether they would find themselves in jail—the next morning.

The magazine of the San Francisco
Mattachine, May/June 1955

6.

THE BUREAU

In 1933, a few months after the attorney general appointed him director of the new Division of Investigation in the Department of Justice, J. Edgar Hoover read an appalling description of himself in *Collier's* magazine. Hoover, the leader of America's "secret federal police system," was "short, fat, businesslike," and walked with a "rather mincing step, almost feminine." It marked the first time anyone had put the rumors in print. The thirty-eight-year-old, unmarried Hoover still lived with his mother, and he had never been seen with a woman. The Bureau responded quickly, planting a story in *Liberty* magazine—the same publication delivered by a young Franklin Kameny in Queens—that described him as "170 pounds of live, virile masculinity."

Despite the rumors, America's growing preoccupation with sexual deviance helped Hoover grow his personal empire of surveillance, which would ultimately last forty-eight years and eight presidents. In 1935, the division became the Federal Bureau of Investigation, and its director began throwing fuel onto America's concern about sex crimes. The "sex fiend, most loathsome of all the vast army of crime, has become a sinister threat to the safety of American childhood and Womanhood," warned Hoover in 1937. His Bureau opened a Sex Offenders file, and across the country, police roundups of sexual deviants became the norm. The director's "War on the Sex Criminal," meanwhile, helped him justify a larger, better-funded Federal Bureau of Investigation.

On April 10, 1950, two months after Senator McCarthy's Wheeling speech, a special messenger arrived at the White House to deliver a confidential letter to one of President Truman's top advisors. The FBI, wrote Hoover, had obtained a list of 393 federal employees who had been arrested on charges of "sexual irregularities." Within days, the FBI's "Sex Deviates" program came into being. From then on, when the Metropolitan Police made a homosexual arrest, the department automatically forwarded the deviant's fingerprints to the Bureau, which checked them against its files. The FBI then forwarded its information to the Civil Service Commission or the employee's federal agency, which promptly purged the homosexual from its ranks.

Hoover's Sex Deviates program grew from a simple clearinghouse of arrest information to a mammoth apparatus of homosexual surveillance. In June 1951, the director ordered his subordinates to begin forwarding not only arrests, but also mere *allegations* of homosexuality to the CSC. If federal employees had suspicions about a coworker's sexuality, they could simply inform the FBI. The suspected homosexual would be in an interrogation room—and often without a job—within days.

The Bureau kept track of Washington's homosexuals through a simple, elegant system. If a Bureau supervisor noticed an allegation of homosexuality in a file, the director held him "personally responsible" for underlining the deviant's name with a green pencil. The Records section, when it saw the green underline, indexed the name accordingly, and Hoover gained one more homosexual for his vast collection of secrets.

Hoover also used the purges to strengthen his reign. To ensure that the Eisenhower-Nixon ticket won the 1952 election, he leaked allegations—that Democratic candidate Adlai Stevenson had twice been arrested for homosexual activity—to Nixon, McCarthy, and the press. Sometimes, if the Bureau learned that a public official was closeted, the FBI refrained from telling that official's agency. Instead, the Bureau stayed quiet if the official agreed to become a "listening post" for Hoover, giving the director one more set of ears to spy on political adversaries within the government. By maintaining this regime of blackmail, Hoover did not need further proof that homosexuals threatened national security. Indeed, if it was so easy for him to blackmail homosexuals, why would the Soviets not blackmail them, too?

When Hoover learned of the Mattachine Society in 1953, he ordered an investigation of the homosexual organization. The investigation yielded an extensive report, which relied upon twenty-one different informants and ultimately concluded that Communists did *not* control the Mattachine. But the Bureau's list of homosexuals grew. After the Society organized its blood drive to demonstrate the upstanding nature of homosexuals, the FBI easily acquired the names of those who had donated. Over the next five years, the Bureau forwarded its fifty-three-page Mattachine report—and the names contained within—to at least ten federal agencies, which could then appropriately administer their own purges.

On July 28, 1961, two FBI agents appeared at the offices of the San Francisco Mattachine to speak with Hal Call, the organization's chairman. Call had dissolved the Society's national structure only weeks earlier, partially because of the rumormongering Mattachine chapter in New York. He had been in the Mattachine since the days of the Fifth Order, and he had joined Marilyn Rieger's openness faction in 1953.

Call agreed to hand over information about other homophile activists if it would be of interest to the police. He agreed to add the Bureau to the *Mattachine Review*'s mailing list. And yes, Call told the special agents, the San Francisco Mattachine "would be willing to cooperate with the FBI in assisting and locating homosexuals whether they are members of the Society or not."

Four days later, on August 1, sixteen men prepared to congregate in the Washington Hay-Adams hotel to create a homophile organization of their own. They planned to purloin the Mattachine name, which Hal Call claimed as the sole property of the San Francisco chapter.

Hours before the meeting, Washington's Metropolitan Police received an anonymous call. It likely came from within the staff of the Hay-Adams hotel, since the caller provided not only the time and location of that evening's Mattachine Society gathering, but also the name and address of the New York man who had reserved the meeting room.

Deputy Chief Roy Blick of the Morals Division immediately reported the information to the Federal Bureau of Investigation. Blick thought he knew what the homosexuals would discuss: why Martin and Mitchell, the homosexual traitors, had defected to Russia. Perhaps these homosexuals were also government workers, and maybe they planned to defect, too.

The FBI's Washington Field Office scrambled to search Bureau records for information on the Mattachine Society, and it found alarming information. In 1959, the Office of Naval Intelligence had concluded that 60 percent of Mattachine officers were both homosexuals *and* Communists. When an FBI special agent informed Marshall Jones, the manager of the Hay-Adams, about the nature of that evening's reservation, Jones agreed to spy on the homosexuals.

During the meeting, while Sergeant Fochett listened from inside the meeting room, Jones walked past the entrance of meeting room 120. He noticed that the door was ajar, so he walked past it again. The men inside, he noticed, were well dressed. They had ordered only sixteen coffees.

When he strained to hear what they were discussing, Jones only managed to catch two words: *bylaws* and *resolutions*.

The next day, when he informed a special agent of these facts, Jones admitted that they had been a "very well behaved group."

On August 8, a report on the Washington homosexuals' first meeting arrived at the desk of J. Edgar Hoover, only a few blocks away.

AL DE DION did not seem concerned about the attendance of Sergeant Fochett at the Hay-Adams meeting, but was worried about another matter. Something had been missing, he told Kameny. "This was urgency. The urgent call to do something that had to be done. It seems that at the present time a group in Washington does not feasible [*sic*] and I will therefore call it out." He promised to send a letter to the MSNY's Washington members informing them of the decision to abort. "I'm sure you understand," he wrote.

But why did Kameny need the permission of the MSNY, an organization that itself had gone rogue, to create his own Mattachine in Washington? If Kameny promised to avoid causing any problems of his own, why would de Dion not want a friendly organization that would be indebted to him?

Kameny argued his case, and on November 7, only three days after de Dion rejected the concept of a Washington Mattachine, the MSNY chairman sent another letter to his members in the capital area. "Dear

Friend: It has been a long time since you have heard from us in regards to the Mattachine group in Washington. But now we have scheduled another meeting."

On Wednesday, November 15, 1961, in a second-floor apartment on a tree-lined Mt. Pleasant street, across the creek from the National Zoo, a small group of men created the Mattachine Society of Washington. The attendees voted to call themselves the Mattachine for the simple reason that homosexuals and experts across the country already knew and respected that name.

The MSNY's articles of incorporation, ratified only two months earlier, provided a helpful, publicity-conscious template for the MSW, an organization already under threat from the Morals Division. The MSNY existed to "sponsor, supervise, and conduct scientific research," to generate public and professional interest in "sex behavioral problems," to aid in the "adjustment to society of any person with sex behavioral problems," to protect them from discrimination, and to publicize their activities. It was taciturn and defensive, begging for legitimacy in a world that recoiled from nonconformity and spat upon deviance. It never once mentioned the word *homosexual*.

Over the next few weeks, as Kameny and the local recruits developed their own constitution, it became clear that the astronomer's organization would resemble neither the MSNY nor any other homophile group since the days of the Fifth Order. Unlike the other groups, Kameny's Mattachine would fight.

"It is the purpose of this organization to act by any lawful means," the MSW's constitution declared, "(a) To secure for homosexuals the right to life, liberty, and the pursuit of happiness," (b) to "equalize" homosexuals and heterosexuals "by eliminating adverse prejudice, both private and official," (c) "to secure for the homosexual the right, as a human being, to develop and achieve his full potential and dignity," (d) to "inform and enlighten the public about homosexuals," and (e) to "assist, protect, and counsel the homosexual in need." The MSW would be a civil liberties organization, and it had no interest in scientific research. As Kameny argued, what was the purpose of studying homosexuality or its causes when they already knew discrimination existed?

The Society's constitution also made clear what the organization was *not.* "It is not a purpose of this organization to act as a social group, or as an agency for personal introductions," said the constitution. Now, if dubious heterosexuals accused them of being an organization for illicit purposes, they could simply point to the MSW constitution.

The attendees agreed upon another purpose to the Society, a purpose which caused some disagreement in the weekly apartment meetings that continued through November. The young Jack Nichols, who had been a keen supporter of Kameny's legal fight and subsequent organizing, argued that the MSW needed to ally with other civil rights groups. Though Kameny initially spoke against mixing causes, he eventually acquiesced. The MSW, its constitution declared, "will cooperate with other minority organizations which are striving for the realization of full civil rights and liberties for all."

Otherwise, the Mattachine Society of Washington operated like any other, straight civic organization. There would be an executive board, elected every January, and meetings each month. Kameny himself would serve as president until the following election. The constitution mandated the use of Robert's Rules of Order—including its provisions for motions, seconds, and points of order—to enforce fair, democratic decision-making in Society meetings.

As a homosexual organization, it established measures to protect its members. The Society required prospective members to find two existing members to sponsor them, and even then, the applicants would receive only provisional memberships. After a three-month probationary period, they became eligible for permanent membership. Meanwhile, the Society maintained only two sets of membership records, available only to its officers. "Under no circumstances whatsoever," stated the MSW constitution, "shall the membership records or any information therein be disclosed or communicated to, or be available to anyone else." If a member was found to "not subscribe to or conform to the purposes of the organization," that member faced expulsion after a written notice, a hearing, and a final vote by two-thirds of the membership.

On November 29, the MSW membership approved its constitution and bylaws, and Kameny began publicizing his new organization within gay Washington. Just as he had brought his astrophysics notebook to gay bars during his Harvard days, he now brought a stack of MSW literature to the gay bars of Washington.

Although gay Washington was vibrant, it was fearful. Its world over-lapped with—but could never touch—the world of the federal government, and its inhabitants could not avoid the miasma of the purges. Those with the most to gain from the Society, federal workers who needed protection, also had the most to lose. So despite Kameny's efforts, the Society grew slowly. It had only seventeen members by the spring of 1962.

The MSW's board also attempted to improve the recruitment efforts—and the security—of the Society. On February 5, it created a publicity committee, which researched the possibility of newspaper advertisements. The board voted to establish "permanent pseudonyms" for each Society officer. Board member Paul Kuntzler became Paul Lemay, and Jack Nichols became Warren Adkins—both named after former lovers.

Kameny himself did not adopt a pseudonym. He saw it as a matter of principle. In a just society, he should not need a pseudonym, and that was that. But he also recognized a practical concern: he still intended to acquire a security clearance, and if he used a false name, he could no longer claim to be a publicly avowed homosexual immunized against blackmail.

Frank Kameny, president of the fledgling Mattachine Society of Washington, therefore became the easiest member for Captain Blick, Sergeant Fochett, and J. Edgar Hoover to identify and locate.

IF SOMETHING WENT WRONG—if the Society's lists were taken or its members were purged or its officers were arrested—there existed another Washington-based organization, founded within days of the MSW, that may have been willing to help. This group was not only a sibling of the Mattachine, but nearly a twin. In November 1961, a group of attorneys met to create the National Capital Area Civil Liberties Union (NCACLU), a semiautonomous affiliate of the national ACLU. Kameny had scheduled the first meeting of the Mattachine Society of Washington for exactly the same day as the NCACLU's own formation meeting.

Kameny did not want to miss the formative meeting of what he expected would become the staunchest defender of civil liberties in the Washington area, and he recognized an important possibility. Perhaps this new group of civil libertarian attorneys, as they started with a clean slate and an empty case docket, would adopt the cause of the homosexual American citizen. So Kameny postponed the first meeting of the Mattachine for one week, until November 15, so that he could become a charter member of the NCACLU.

Kameny entered that first NCACLU meeting as the first openly gay man to petition the Supreme Court, and he expected a degree of respect for that feat. He faced an uphill battle establishing legitimacy within the NCACLU, however. When Kameny asked an NCACLU's executive secretary to read his brief, explaining that it was an effort to educate the court on principles that "needed saying," the official responded dubiously. "In honesty, I cannot say that it is a good legal job and if its contents 'needed saying,'" wrote the secretary. "I cannot bring myself to think that you chose a very good forum or medium for saying them. I do not mean to say that I disagree with the arguments, but that they seem to me poorly tailored to fit a court context."

For the professional attorneys volunteering in the NCACLU, constitutional test cases needed to be winnable. The Kameny brief, however, emphasized his own principles and logic—often evident only to himself— over pragmatic, proven legal maneuvering. Worst of all, he had already appealed it to the highest court in America. If Kameny was going to win the NCACLU as an ally, he had to persuade its attorneys to adopt test cases other than his own. To do that, he would need to find victims of the purges who were, like him, willing to take the federal government to court.

BRUCE SCOTT WAS a clean-cut, forty-nine-year-old man with a deep voice and a slow, Midwestern cadence. Scott, working as a Department of Labor analyst in 1947, had been arrested for loitering in Lafayette Park. As the purges grew, he knew his day would eventually come.

In February 1956, Scott's personnel officer informed him that the Department of Labor had conducted a security review of its employees. Now, said the official, might be a good time for him to resign.

For five years, Scott floated between menial jobs, often living on no more than fifty cents per day. In May 1961, he was working in a warehouse when he read a feature in *ONE* magazine's *Confidential* newsletter about an

unnamed Washington man who had sued the government. He wrote to
ONE for Kameny's name, then trekked up the steps of the Supreme Court
to find the astronomer's address. Scott frantically wrote Kameny a letter.

Six weeks later, the two disgraced federal employees met. The moment
was serendipitous for them both. Scott, at his wits' end, already wanted to
sue the Department of Labor, and Kameny was about to form his Society.
When the pair learned of the inaugural NCACLU meeting, Kameny and
Scott attended it together. A week later, Scott became a founding member of the MSW. As an executive board member, he became known as
"Bruce Schuyler."

Scott immediately began moving to reclaim his job in the federal government. In October, he passed the CSC's Federal Administrative and
Management Examination, and on April 27, 1962, the inevitable interrogation occurred.

"The Civil Service Commission has information indicating that you
are a homosexual," stated the CSC investigator. "Do you wish to comment on this matter?"

"No," he responded. "I do not believe the question is pertinent insofar
as job performance is concerned."

And that was that.

Kameny's second legal ally, Richard Schlegel, had been known as the
"most flaming queer in all of Penn State."

On July 31, 1961, the day before the Washington Hay-Adams meeting, Schlegel's nightmare began. In a carbon copy of Kameny's own fiasco,
the army dismissed him from his civilian job—three marines claimed he
had made sexual advances toward them—and the CSC duly barred him
from federal employment. Schlegel appealed his dismissal, and when that
failed, he decided to sue the government.

In October 1961, after writing to *ONE* for assistance in his case, he
was surprised to learn of a man in Washington who had already fought
the purges. A few weeks later, Schlegel also attended the MSW's first
meeting. Kameny became his legal advisor.

Kameny later denied that the MSW revolved around his own personal fight against the federal government, but *Kameny v. Brucker* un-
questionably defined his new organization. His moral logic guided the
MSW's ideology, his reliance on the courts and civil libertarian attorneys

determined its strategy, and his target—the federal government itself—provided its purpose. Most important, the Kameny brief served as a recruitment tool, a magnet that pulled the victims of the purges, drifting in the void of unemployment and starvation, into Kameny's war.

Under the all-seeing eye of J. Edgar Hoover, the astronomer could expect more of those victims—homosexuals with little left to lose.

ON SUNDAY, MAY 27, at 6:15 p.m., a clerk at the FBI headquarters received a call from a man with information for the Bureau.

A new organization had formed in Washington, said the caller. He had *thought* the group was merely a society of homosexuals, but, in reality, the group was full of Communists. He worried for the country's security, since two of the organization's members had secret government clearances. One of them had applied to work for the CIA. There would be another meeting in four days, and the caller wanted to talk to the FBI, in person, before then. He had more information.

The clerk advised the caller to contact the Bureau's Washington Field Office (WFO), located in the old post office, a few blocks away. The clerk asked for the caller's name.

Warren Scarberry, said the caller.

And the name of the organization?

The clerk hurriedly wrote its ominous name, "THE MANAGING SOCIETY."

Scarberry arrived at the WFO two days later. A nineteen-year-old from Akron, Ohio, Scarberry was blond, of average height, and slightly heavy. Family friends remembered him as friendly and polite. But he liked to tell stories, and sometimes, he lied.

At the Bureau, Scarberry told a special agent that he was a member of this new organization, in fact called the Mattachine Society. As the agent later summarized the meeting, Scarberry wanted to provide "a couple of names of members who are government employees."

Why was he voluntarily providing this information?

"SCARBERRY stated that he was angry with the homosexual element in this town and that this is his way of getting even with them."

Scarberry immediately identified Kameny as the president of the

Society, and the rest of his information focused on another member whom he seemed to know particularly well: Ronald Brass, Scarberry's roommate and alleged lover. Brass, a Department of Commerce employee, had brought Scarberry to a Society meeting. Brass had recently told Scarberry "that he had had an affair with [REDACTED]." The CIA, said Scarberry, had also recently interviewed Brass for a position there.

Scarberry knew of another government employee in the Society, but he did not know his true name. "The Mattachine Society," he told the Agent, "considers themselves to be a select group of homosexuals and that most of them are very careful about divulging their true names and consequently they usually use code names at the meetings and when they receive mail from the Society." But Scarberry guessed that "numerous" other federal employees participated in the Society.

Yes, said Scarberry, there existed a membership list. In fact, the Society's secretary maintained a "complete list of all the members, their addresses and their assigned code names." Yes, he could acquire a copy of this list at the Society's next meeting, scheduled for two days later. It would likely be an easy task, especially since, as the special agent put it, "the secretary has taken a like to him."

The MSW meeting took place the following Thursday evening, in a member's apartment on Sixteenth Street Northwest. Scarberry attended with Brass. That night, Scarberry called the FBI special agent. Unfortunately, he had been unable to obtain the Society's membership list. But he could provide something even better: a list of eighty-five homosexuals in the Washington area, including their names and addresses. Most of them, he claimed, were government employees. Within hours, the special agent met with Scarberry to acquire it.

Scarberry still believed he could deliver more names, including those on the MSW's membership list. He would call back in a month, he promised, after the next meeting of the Society.

SIX DAYS AFTER Scarberry offered his list to the Bureau, two agents appeared at the headquarters of the United States Department of Commerce. They were looking for Ronald B. Brass, an employee of the department since 1958.

The agents showed their badges and took Brass to room 5010, in the Department's Office of Security. They wanted to talk to him, explained the agents, to investigate allegations of homosexuality. Their source was confidential.

Are you a member of the Mattachine Society of Washington?

Yes, he admitted.

Is it really full of homosexuals?

Yes.

Brass feared losing his job, but he feared lying to the FBI even more. Yes, he had "homosexual tendencies." He looked at "some males in the same manner as a man would look at females." He admitted to visiting gay bars and associating with the "gay crowd."

The Department of Commerce now had enough information to purge him, and at this point, the agents returned to the topic of the MSW.

Do you have a copy of the Society's membership list?

No, said Brass.

Would you procure a copy and give it to us?

Brass explained that the list was only available to the organization's officers.

Well, could you draft a list of members whom you know by name?

No, said Brass, because I do not know the other members' names.

One of the agents made a proposition. The FBI wanted Brass to perform a service, which entailed continued participation in the Society. Brass would simply learn the other members' names and then report them to the FBI.

Brass wanted to make sure he understood their offer. Are you suggesting, he asked, that my tenure at the Department of Commerce depends upon compliance with this request?

No, no, said the agents. The department makes its own decisions, and the FBI simply investigates and reports its findings.

Brass declined the agents' request. He left room 5010 confident in his refusal to divulge his fellow MSW members' names but resigned to his fate.

THE BUREAU FOLLOWED through on its implied threat, and it informed the Department of Commerce of the homosexual within its ranks.

When Brass told Kameny about the interrogations, the MSW leader demanded that Brass keep his lips sealed from that point forward. It was not too late to salvage his job, Kameny assured him, perhaps with the help of the ACLU.

The FBI agents' brazen attempt to infiltrate the MSW had disturbed Kameny, so on June 28, Kameny wrote to Attorney General Robert Kennedy. The FBI's interrogations of MSW members—he did not mention Brass by name—were "grossly improper and offensive," a form of "harassment of intimidation." He had discussed the matter with the ACLU, which agreed with him. He requested that inquiries into membership of the Society, a fully legal organization, "be brought to a halt immediately." He enclosed the MSW's statement of purposes.

Kameny never received a response from Robert Kennedy, and Warren Scarberry continued working to acquire more information for his FBI handlers. By August 1962, the Bureau had upgraded his status from potential confidential informant (PCI) to a trusted confidential informant (CI).

The FBI destroyed the files of its Sex Deviates program in 1978, and the vast majority of informants' names in its Mattachine file have been thoroughly redacted. But on August 16, 1962, a confidential informant "who has furnished reliable information in the past" called the Bureau to request a meeting. The next day, the informant behaved remarkably like Warren Scarberry; he mentioned the member who had introduced him to the group, he was eager to provide information, and he had something tangible to hand over—a copy of the Society's constitution.

The Bureau already had a copy, so the special agent probed him for other, more helpful information. A postal inspector had recently asked the Bureau if it knew anything about a "club made up of colored homosexuals called CC." Do you know of that club?

Yes, said the informant. It's the Cozy Corner, indeed a "hangout for colored homosexuals." In fact, he continued, there is another such "hangout" called Van Dyke's. He offered the names of "three colored homosexuals" whom he knew congregated at that bar.

The Bureau duly forwarded this information to the United States Postal Service, but it seemed more concerned about the informant's final piece of intelligence.

The Mattachine Society of Washington, claimed the informant, planned to send letters to every member of the Senate and the House of Representatives, "complaining about the alleged mistreatment of homosexuals." The person in charge of this effort was Frank Kameny.

After meeting with the informant, the FBI special agent called Deputy Chief Roy Blick of the Morals Division. Do you have any information about Kameny?

Yes, I do, said Blick. Back in 1959, after the department had raided a private homosexual club in Washington, a man named Frank Kameny had written to the police chief, "complaining bitterly" about the raid. Blick and Kameny had even met to discuss the matter. In fact, said the deputy chief, I have a photograph of this man. Would the Bureau like it?

Within a few hours, the special agent acquired the image of the astronomer.

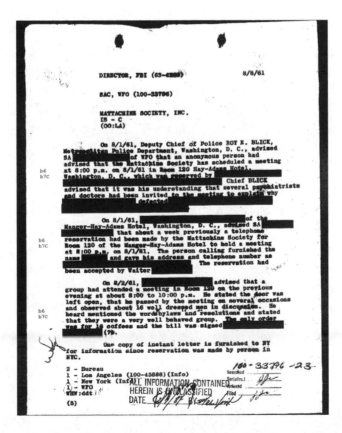

The Hay-Adams meeting, August 1961

7

THE CRUSADER

Charlie Hayden wanted to be the president of the United States, but he also wanted to have sex with men. By January 1959, the twenty-year-old already looked like a politician—his hair perfectly parted, his eyes an earnest gray blue, his suits well fitted. Yes, he enjoyed picking up men in gay bars, but as a college student, he prioritized achieving power for himself. Indeed, he understood that students accused of homosexuality at the University of Texas faced three options: withdraw with a clean record immediately, get expelled after a week, or take a lie detector test administered by the Texas State Police.

When Charlie returned to Austin for the spring semester of his junior year, he learned that campus newsstands had stopped selling *Playboy* and other adult magazines. Distributors had bowed to pressure from an anti-obscenity committee of the local Parent-Teacher Association.

Charlie drafted a petition labeling the extralegal censorship a "violation of our right to freedom of the press," and three days later, he had acquired more than 1,700 supporters, including a significant number of faculty members and local figures. The PTA retreated, and *Playboy* returned to the students' newsstands.

The student's crusade turned him into a university hero, and he planned to harness his fame into political power on campus. He turned to an issue that he thought would galvanize all students: rising tuition costs.

"Hayden plans Capitol March to Protest House 'Fees Bill,'" read the front page headline of the May 6, 1959, *Daily Texan*. Students had not marched for fifteen years, and Charlie planned the march against the wishes of the student body president, who called the walk "irresponsible." Why risk alienating legislators?

At one o'clock that hot Texas day, a crowd of hundreds began gathering at the university's Littlefield Fountain, which stood on a hill above the state Capitol. Uninterested in the protest itself, they began heckling Charlie. "Then," as a student magazine described the scene, "a small group of fun-loving boys broke from the sidelines, dashed out onto the esplanade, seized Hayden, and dunked him, wash 'n wear suit, button-down shirt, regimental tie and all, in the fountain."

Cognizant of the live audience and the rolling television cameras, Charlie smiled throughout the ordeal. "Well, we came for a riot, now we've had one!" he stood and yelled, dripping from the edge of the fountain. Everyone laughed.

"March Fails: Hayden's Attack on Fees Bill Finishes with Fountain Fiasco," declared *The Daily Texan*. But the humiliation at the fountain ensured that the entire university learned about an issue that had, until then, been ignored. "We sought to stir this complacent and apathetic campus to speak out for its own interests," argued one of Charlie's allies, "and in this we claim success."

Newspapers across the state reported on the lighthearted tale, and as a result, something remarkable happened. Readers, drawn to the whimsical drama, found themselves alarmed by the possibility of a tuition increase at all of Texas's state colleges. They wrote to their legislators en masse, and the bill stalled.

"You are a radical. Your methods of accomplishing things are most unorthodox; nonetheless you are a true nonconformist," a group of supporters wrote to Charlie after the embarrassment. "So to you—Fearless Charlie . . . CRAZY CHARLIE, we say onward and upward!"

Charlie spent the summer of 1959 working as a hustler on Hollywood Boulevard in Los Angeles. He wanted to get away from Texas for a while, and why not hang out with the other pretty queens, making money from an activity he already enjoyed? After eight weeks of standing on a street corner, eyes burning from the soot, Charlie eventually concluded that the profession was not for him. One man in a Corvette gave him only two dollars for a parking lot blowjob. He returned to

Austin with a craving for an office job and a redefined notion of what constituted hard work.

But he still wanted power. In March 1960, he ran for president of the University of Texas's student government. Charlie campaigned vigorously, speaking against tuition increases and, more controversially, for racial integration of the university.

He heard the rumors, of course. CHARLIE HAYDEN IS A QUEER, said the graffiti in bathroom stalls. And shortly before the election, Charlie received the dreaded summons to the office of the dean. After Charlie vehemently denied the homosexual allegations and refused to drop out of the race, the university allowed him to stay enrolled. He was too well-known, and the administration wanted to avoid a public scandal.

On election day, out of nearly five thousand votes cast, Charlie missed assured victory in a runoff election by only thirty votes. Five months later, the university permitted him to graduate, but the rumors had extinguished his desire to enter American politics. If seeking the presidency of the University of Texas's student government had nearly derailed his life, then he was able to imagine the ruin that would befall him if he ever ran for a real political office.

His battles, however, gave him an addictive taste of the spectacle. Conjuring headlines was easy, he realized, even if his critics questioned his motives. "Is Hayden a sincerely idealistic reformer, or mainly a rabble-rouser out to raise hell and make a name for himself?" asked a student magazine (a combination of both, it concluded).

Because of Charlie, for once, undergraduates were actually talking about student politics. For once, *The Daily Texan* had become interesting. And for once, someone had persuasively argued that students, if properly organized, could become a loud, indomitable force against the status quo. "Hayden's most useful service," the *Ranger* concluded, had been "troubling the placid waters wherein dwells the traditional ruling elite," a service that had, in the end, "gained him so many enemies."

CHARLIE HAD ANOTHER NAME. Five years earlier, while visiting his father in New Jersey, he had discovered the Mattachine. In 1958, he had lied about his age—the MSNY enforced a twenty-one-year-old minimum—to become one of its first twenty members. His father, after reading Charlie's diary, accepted his son's homosexuality, and when Charlie disclosed his Mattachine activities, Mr. Hayden did not object. But his father did have one request: use a name other than Hayden. From then on, in New York's gay world, Charlie called himself Randolfe Wicker. First name Randolfe, because it seemed classy and unique. Last name Wicker, because it sounded awfully similar to "wicked."

On visits to New York during college breaks, as the teenager became a regular at the Village's gay bars, Wicker realized he had been wrong about homosexuals. They were not, as he had gathered from newspapers during his childhood, all drag queens, child molesters, or Communists. In fact, they were just as diverse, just as *normal*, as heterosexuals. How, the young Wicker wondered, could the world be so wrong about homosexuals?

He moved to New York in 1961, the year of Kennedy's inauguration. After finding a low-paying job in a building demolition company, Wicker began developing grandiose plans for Mattachine's relationship with the public. And in April 1962, he heard an opportunity to combat the stereotypes. On New York's WBAI radio channel, a panel of psychiatrists claimed that they could cure homosexuals with just eight hours of therapy. Wicker promptly marched into the WBAI office with a business card. WBAI had featured a biased, one-sided panel, argued Wicker, and now it owed the homosexual minority—the only real experts on the issue—equal time to respond.

The station acquiesced, and a few weeks later, on a humid summer night, Wicker sat on the floor of a Village apartment with seven other homosexuals. An Ampex 600 recorded everything they said.

When WBAI started publicizing the broadcast, the station received a bad omen. A critic at the *New York Journal-American* declared that WBAI had caved to an "arrogant card-carrying swish" by agreeing to produce the program. He advised WBAI to change its call letters to "WSICK."

On July 15, at 7:00 p.m., the recording hit the airwaves. "So why don't we begin at the beginning with an obvious question," began the straight moderator. "What is the Mattachine Society?"

Wicker had a soft-spoken voice with a hint of a Texan drawl. After explaining the Mattachine's focus on research and education, he posed a revealing question of his own. "Everyone's heard of it. How many people are really familiar with its program? Anyone? Nope. No one. I'm the only one."

"My God," said the moderator. "Well, I guess that answers that question."

For the next hour and a half, the homosexuals talked frankly among themselves—about their minority, about society, and about sex. No, they explained, the homosexual's life was not primarily "concerned with seduction," as the moderator put it. "Generally," said one participant, "the homosexual has a very strong moral fiber and a very definite set of rules."

How should the "straight world" approach homosexuals?

"Well, I'd sum it up in a phrase," responded Wicker. "I'd say, just: 'Live and let live.'"

"I think we all have skeletons in our closets, and the less stones thrown the better," said another homosexual.

With that, the program, titled "Live and Let Live," ended. To experience the momentous occasion, homosexuals hosted listening parties across the city. Gay men had never simply talked to one another, as gay men, on the air.

The next day, *The New York Times* featured two separate articles on the "unusual" program. "The contemporary public seems ready to accept almost any subject matter so long as it is presented thoughtfully," concluded its media critic. Stations rebroadcast the program in San Francisco and Los Angeles. Alternative and adult magazines clamored to print the program's transcript.

Reveling in the media circus, Wicker consolidated his position as America's homosexual spokesman. On August 5, when he spoke to the New York chapter of the American Humanist Association, the hall overflowed with more than a hundred attendees, the chapter's largest crowd to date.

Wicker's efforts sent shock waves through the national homophile movement, still scarred by the persecution that invariably followed homophile news-making. Wicker had "startled" the MSNY, wrote one of its members. "We survive because we are dull and plodding."

To de Dion and Dewees of the MSNY, Wicker's publicity efforts seemed disorganized and tactless. *ONE* magazine, meanwhile, saw danger in the WBAI program's candidness. "No homosexual, no matter how well trained, should ever allow himself to speak extemporaneously upon the subject," it wrote.

Wicker still sent news of the program and offered a tape of the broadcast—for a steep six dollars—to the handful of homophile organizations that existed in July 1962.

Frank Kameny, president of Washington's new Mattachine Society, quickly responded with six dollars attached. He asked "to discuss matters of mutual interest" with the country's first publicist for gay rights.

IN AUGUST 1962, an FBI special agent received a piece of information from his contact in air force intelligence. The San Francisco Mattachine planned to hold a convention "to formulate plans for an all out homosexual assault" against the government's security programs. The Mattachine, he warned, would encourage test cases against the government, and the homosexuals planned "to charge, in the press and in court, that their acts are no more inimical to good security than a general officer who can be compromised for living with, say, a Japanese prostitute."

The Bureau deployed five special agents to investigate the convention. It acquired a recording of the proceedings, which captured a combative speech by Richard Schlegel, one of the founding members of the Mattachine Society of Washington.

Schlegel spoke as part of a panel titled "A Decade of Progress in the Homophile Movement." The United States Department of Defense, he began, was the country's "repository of greatest organized bigotry." If homosexuals could change the policies of the Pentagon, he argued, the rest of the government would follow suit. The idea that the American government could decide what constituted morality was patently unconstitutional, he asserted. Yes, there had been legal challenges against the government's role as moral arbiter, including *Kameny v. Brucker*, but they fell short. "The petition was denied—properly, I have to admit grudgingly—for Kameny's presentation, brilliant as it was, was long on emotion but short on law."

The FBI, after analyzing the recording of Schlegel's speech, concluded that Schlegel planned to take his own case against the army—a case nearly identical to that of Frank Kameny—to the Supreme Court, if necessary.

After the "fiery" speech, as *ONE* referred to it, attendees agreed it was "perhaps the most 'radical' and challenging paper ever presented before an American homophile organization." Schlegel's legal call to arms echoed across the national homophile movement in the months that followed. Two homophile publications featured Schlegel's speech, and as a result, hundreds of homosexuals learned about Kameny's legal war.

The remnants of the original Mattachine, still led by Hal Call, threatened Kameny and Schlegel's crusade. After nearly two years, Call remained preoccupied by the unauthorized use of the Mattachine name. Call warned Kameny that the naming disagreement was "a cause of confusion and distress" that harmed the entire movement. "Unfortunately," he concluded, "we cannot force the change through court action—our organization does not have the money for that."

Kameny refused to change his organization's name, but if he had known the truth about Call, he may have given more weight to the threat. Only days before Call wrote Kameny, the San Francisco activist met with an FBI special agent. Call gave the agent three copies of Richard Schlegel's convention speech, which outlined the MSW's plans to wage a legal assault on the United States Department of Defense.

IN THE SUMMER OF 1962, inspired by Wicker's successes, Kameny and his executive board developed a plan. First, the Society decided to target the media. They would purchase newspaper ads to offer information on the Mattachine, and they would disseminate news releases to announce the Society's existence to the world. With media coverage and therefore legitimacy, the homosexuals would lobby the United States Congress for reform.

"A formation of a new social action group in the greater Washington, D.C. area is announced," began the MSW's news release. It planned to target the three pillars of government persecution: the CSC, the military, and the security clearance system.

The Society sent out its release in mid-August, and as Kameny waited for the media coverage, he cultivated his alliance with Randy Wicker. "I

HOPE TO MEET WITH YOU IN THE VERY NEAR FUTURE," wrote Wicker. "I HOPE THAT YOU DON'T AVOID PERSONAL CONTACT WITH OFFICIALS IN HIGH PLACES."

"Dear Mr. Wicker—or should I call you Mr. Hayden, or Randolfe, or Charlie?" began Kameny on August 21. "No, I haven't been avoiding contacts with officials in high or low places," he explained. The Society had already sent its advertisement requests and press releases to Washington newspapers, but they had refused to print the Society's ad. No articles materialized from the press release.

Kameny remained optimistic about the Society's upcoming congressional lobbying campaign. "If we can get even one mildly sympathetic reply," he wrote, "we will have broken a hitherto impenetrable wall, and will have gained immeasurably." Also, did Wicker want to join him on Fire Island for Labor Day weekend? Was it true that New York's Everard Turkish Baths had *closed*?

On August 28, 1962, the Mattachine Society of Washington commenced the largest political action ever undertaken by a group of homosexuals. The Society made itself known to nearly every high official, elected or appointed, in all three branches of the United States federal government. Letters arrived in the offices of President Kennedy, Vice President Johnson, and the entire presidential cabinet; all 535 senators and congressmen; every justice of the Supreme Court and an array of lower court judges; and every commissioner of the District of Columbia. Each official learned the name of the Society's unemployed president, Franklin E. Kameny.

The Society had borrowed a Robotype machine, a mammoth apparatus that typed form letters like a player piano, to send customized letters to each official. In each envelope, the Society's board enclosed the group's statement of purposes and its press release. And in each letter, Kameny attacked the government's antihomosexual policies as "archaic, unrealistic, and inconsistent with basic American principles." He extended a request to meet with each recipient.

Because of Warren Scarberry, the FBI had prepared itself for the Society's letter-writing campaign. On August 20, three days after Scarberry's tip and a full week before the mailing, J. Edgar Hoover received five copies of a memorandum that summarized the Bureau's information on

Kameny and his Society. Though the Mattachine had, in reality, only a couple dozen members, the memo warned that it contained as many as three hundred homosexuals. With the memorandum, if members of Congress flocked to J. Edgar Hoover for information about the Society, the Bureau would be prepared.

In the weeks following the mailing of the letters, however, only two congressmen forwarded their letters to the Bureau. One cautious congressman, Joe M. Kilgore of Texas, wrote to Hoover inquiring about Kameny's assertion that thousands of homosexuals worked in the federal government. Was there any truth in that claim? He asked about the steps "being taken to remove such described types."

The vast majority of officials ignored Kameny for a simple reason. "On its face," admitted Kilgore, the Society's materials "appear to be a hoax." The Department of Defense planned no action because—as one Pentagon official told his neighbor, an FBI agent—it considered the letters the "works of a crank."

Within the Civil Service Commission, officials quietly investigated Kameny's letter. The CSC's chairman, John W. Macy, requested an internal review of its "legal implications." L. V. Meloy, the CSC's general counsel, unearthed Kameny's Supreme Court brief and forwarded it to Macy. The Court "was not impressed" by Kameny's argument, Meloy advised. "I think we can dispose of the constitutional question rather quickly."

Chairman Macy responded to the MSW on September 28. "It is the established policy of the Civil Service Commission that homosexuals are not suitable for appointment to or retention in positions in the Federal service," he wrote. "There would be no useful purpose served in meeting with representatives of your Society."

From members of Congress, at first, the MSW only heard disgust. "Your letter of August 28 has been received," responded Republican congressman Charles E. Chamberlain of Michigan, "and in reply may I state unequivocally that in all my six years of service in the United States Congress I have not received such a revolting communication." Democratic congressman Paul C. Jones of Missouri returned Kameny's letter with a handwritten note in its margin. "I am unalterably opposed to your proposal and cannot see how any person in his right mind can condone the practices which you would justify," he wrote. "Please do not contaminate my mail with such filthy trash."

On September 8, Kameny received a one-sentence letter. "In answer to your letter of August 28, 1962, you may see me at my office at 9:30 on Wednesday, September 12th. Yours very truly, ROBERT N. C. NIX, M.C."

Congressman Nix of Philadelphia, a Democrat, was Pennsylvania's first Black U.S. representative and the sixty-four-year-old son of a former slave. In 1962, by agreeing to meet with the Society, Nix became America's first member of Congress to speak to homosexual activists. He did so within weeks of an election.

Kameny walked into the imposing Cannon House Office Building, through its light-filled, marble rotunda, and sat with the congressman. Nix told Kameny he was willing to help the Society in any way possible, and he even suggested they meet again once Kameny had specific ideas for how his office could help the MSW. Kameny quickly wrote to a Philadelphia-based homophile organization to urge its members to vote for Congressman Nix in the upcoming election.

Two days after Nix's letter, the Society's president received a response from Congressman William Fitts Ryan, a first-term Democrat from New York's Upper West Side. The tall, forty-year-old Princeton man was glad to hear of the Society's formation. "I hope that you will continue to keep me informed of the views of your group," he said.

By the end of the week, Kameny had secured a meeting with Ryan's administrative assistant. Yes, Ryan was willing to help his homosexual constituents in need, said the staffer. Yes, he would speak on the Mattachine's behalf and even present specific legislation. No, he had not been aware that there existed a Mattachine Society of New York. And no, said Ryan's assistant, the congressman would not be embarrassed by a show of support from homosexuals in the upcoming election. Kameny immediately wrote to MSNY, urging the New Yorkers to establish relations with their congressman.

For the first time, homosexuals had committed allies in the legislative branch of the federal government, and they immediately utilized the relationship. In September, the House of Representatives debated H.R. 11363, a bill that strengthened the Department of Defense's security clearance program in the aftermath of *Greene v. McElroy.* The legislation permitted the Department of Defense to deny a clearance holder's right to cross-examination if it threatened "the national security."

Kameny wrote to Nix and Ryan to urge them, "on behalf of 15,000,000 American homosexuals," to vote against the security clearance bill. It would, he warned, cause "a 'purge' of homosexuals, in large numbers, from jobs in government and in private industry."

On September 19, both Nix and Ryan voted against H.R. 11363, which ultimately failed by only six votes. Yes, Congressman Ryan told Kameny, he had voted in accord with Washington's first homosexual lobby.

ON SEPTEMBER 5, one week after he announced the Society's existence to the federal government, Kameny received a letter from the District's chief of the Department of Licenses and Inspections, enforcement branch.

The department had, for undisclosed reasons, initiated a "review" of the Society's application for a charitable solicitation license. Kameny had failed to include two items: first, the addresses of the Society's other officers, and second, the names of the members who would be issued solicitation cards, meant to reassure citizens of a charity's legitimacy.

On September 10, Kameny arrived to room 112A of the District Building. There, he saw a familiar face: Deputy Chief Roy E. Blick of the Morals Division. The District's government, collaborating with the police (which, in turn, collaborated with the FBI) wanted the names of the Society's homosexuals.

Kameny asked the presiding official, the assistant superintendent of licenses and permits, to remove Blick from the conference room. Why, asked Kameny, are the police involved in a simple licensing matter? The official refused, and Blick stayed. A representative from the enforcement branch then made his case against the Society. The Mattachine had been operating with an improperly granted license, which should therefore be revoked.

First, the Society had not solicited anything at all, argued Kameny. Second, he was willing to provide the missing information, in the form of pseudonyms and PO boxes, which the District had hitherto ignored. On what grounds, he demanded, could the District possibly revoke the Society's license?

The assistant superintendent had no choice but to agree with Kameny.

"Group Aiding Deviates Issued Charity License" announced the *Star's* September 16 article. The media, which had previously ignored the Mattachine, finally had a story, a scandal.

The superintendent of licenses and permits, C. T. Nottingham, spoke to the *Star* angrily, enthusiastically, and on the record. Nottingham had no authority to deny a license to any organization that properly filled out an application, he complained. "The license chief," wrote the *Star*, "added that if the group solicits 'as much as one dollar,' he would order them to open their books and records for examination."

The Society had not solicited any funds, Kameny had explained to the *Star* reporter. He provided the origin of the name "Mattachine" but refused to disclose the number of members in his Society. Wary of media coverage that he had not expected—and over which he had no control—he requested that the *Star* not print his name. The newspaper complied.

Unlike Wicker, Kameny did not attempt to turn his organization's first press exposure into more publicity. The press was not only out of his control, but also secondary in purpose. Kameny focused on gaining entrée with those who had *real* power, like members of Congress and officials in the federal bureaucracy. If anything, publicity threatened his aims. Nix and Ryan could, after all, easily read the *Star* article and decide that the Society was nothing more than a political liability, a controversy in the making.

Wicker and Kameny had become, through different routes, America's homosexual authorities. Though the press ignored Kameny's press releases, his outreach to federal officials seemed to be working. And because direct lobbying seemed to be so effective, Kameny saw publicity more as a threat than an opportunity. The congressional meetings, he warned Hal Call on October 15, "are matters of subtle and carefully handling [*sic*], which can be badly upset should a publicized report of them get back to some of the officials involved."

As Kameny's authority rose in Washington, he had more to lose. The same day he wrote to Hal Call, Kameny received a letter from the

Department of Defense. The Pentagon wanted to meet with a delegation of homosexuals from the Mattachine Society of Washington.

FOR THREE MONTHS, the Society had been attempting to coerce the Pentagon into scheduling a meeting with a Mattachine delegation. Kameny felt confident about that possibility since, in 1959, one Pentagon official—R. L. Applegate—had been willing to discuss his situation. Applegate had even given Kameny reason to believe that admitted homosexuals could, in theory, receive security clearances.

In July 1962, as companies continued to reject the unemployable astronomer, he reached out to the Pentagon once again. "I cannot get a job unless I get a clearance, and I cannot get a clearance, under your regulations, until I get a job," he told the deputy assistant secretary of defense for security policy.

Miraculously, two days after writing to the Pentagon, Kameny found a job. He would work as a physics consultant at a private thermal electro-optical systems laboratory. Though it would pay him on a week-to-week basis—and offer only a fraction of other, similarly qualified physicists' salaries—Kameny no longer worried about starvation. He still needed to apply for a clearance, but the progressive-minded president of the company, fully aware of his predicament, promised to help him through the process.

When Bruce Scott, writing as "Bruce Schuyler," requested a meeting with the Pentagon, twice the Pentagon responded by explaining that a meeting would not be productive. Twice Scott wrote back to ask for a conference. After he castigated Applegate for "seeking studiously to avoid discussion of the particular issues," the Pentagon official finally agreed.

Kameny had been living with a roommate, a twenty-two-year-old Washington native named Allen Duncan. The young man's father worked as a prominent builder in the area, and his mother, Marie, was an exquisite baker. Pillsbury featured her chocolate nut-butter cookies in its 1951 recipe book.

On October 23, 1962, Marie Duncan, mother of five, walked into the headquarters of the American military with three homosexual men. Kameny had understood the significance of the Pentagon meeting, the first between Department of Defense officials and representatives of the gay minority, and he wanted it recorded. When she volunteered to lend her typing skills for the meeting, Mrs. Duncan of Bethesda, Maryland, became America's first stenographer for an organization of homosexuals.

"Tell us exactly what you have in mind," began Applegate. Herbert Lewis, director of the Industrial Personnel Access Authorization Review Division, sat next to him. Across from the officials—next to Mrs. Duncan—sat Kameny, Bruce Scott, and Ron Balin, the MSW member who had identified Sergeant Fochett at the Hay-Adams meeting.

The security clearance program, Kameny argued, had not been successful. Because homosexual clearance holders lived "in constant fear of being discovered" by the Pentagon, and because they could not report blackmail attempts without also exposing themselves, blackmailers had free rein. Pentagon policies were therefore *increasing* the risk of blackmail. And if 10 percent of America's three million security clearance holders—

"I don't believe it would be that high," interjected Applegate.

"We feel that it is," responded Kameny.

"You are in a better position to have the figures than I," admitted Applegate.

Bruce Scott then offered a simple solution to the problem. "Each person wants to know that he can go to his employer and say, 'I have been approached by the Communists who are trying to pressure me because I am homosexual' without losing his job." The government could pursue the Communist blackmailer, and the homosexual could keep his job.

But this solution was impossible, according to Applegate's collcague, Herbert Lewis, because homosexuals were mentally ill. "A homosexual is disturbed primarily," he said. "The overt homosexual whose mode of conduct leads to a possibility of arrest on criminal charges is subject to pressures."

"Are you going to castrate everyone to grant clearances?" responded Kameny.

Throughout the discussion, especially when the MSW delegation made a particularly persuasive point, the officials returned the discussion to the pathological nature of homosexuality. "Do you look upon this as a mental illness? Not any at all?" Lewis incredulously asked.

"No," said Kameny. "A certain number are mentally ill, but they are not the majority."

"I am saying that all homosexuals are unstable," said Lewis.

"Do you say all negroes are dirty and stupid? You are doing that to the homosexual," responded Kameny.

"A homosexual is unstable because psychiatrists say so," explained Lewis.

Halfway through the conference, Applegate noted that, surprisingly, no one had mentioned morality.

First, responded Kameny, morality was not the concern of the federal government. But if they *were* going to discuss the morality of homosexuality, he had his own revolutionary ideas on the matter. "It is not only not immoral," declared Kameny in a forceful echo of his Supreme Court brief, "but it is moral and good and right."

What mattered, Kameny argued, was not how society viewed homosexuality, but rather how the *homosexual* viewed homosexuality. If the gay security clearance holder embraced his sexual orientation—if he knew it was right and proclaimed it before the world—then how could he possibly be the victim of blackmail?

"What the maniac thinks he is doing is right," responded Lewis. "We are talking about something that goes back to the beginning of time. Get Pope John to endorse homosexuality."

The officials argued that the homosexuals needed to target society itself. "Society," said Lewis, "for the past 1900 years might be all wrong. And you have a good job cut out to change it."

"This is not the place to start. Start with society," added Applegate.

"The lead has to come from the government," responded Kameny.

"We suggest you start this by the administration," said Applegate. Indeed, the Pentagon was simply following an executive order of the president.

"You are saying concentrate on the White House," said Scott.

"That is right," said Applegate.

When Balin argued that the Pentagon still had some "leeway" on how it administered the executive order, Lewis dismissed the concept. "These arguments have been made constantly by members of your minority group over the years. And the board has not accepted it," he said.

"On what do you base it on?" asked Kameny.

"On the basis of . . ." Lewis hesitated. "Blind unthinking prejudice." He laughed.

"On what do you base it on?" asked Kameny again, unamused.

"History of 1900 years' society," responded Lewis.

But what *evidence* do you have, asked Kameny, "that individual homosexuals are not reliable? Then it becomes a matter of blind prejudice if—"

"We are not servants of the people," Applegate interrupted. The Pentagon simply carried out the laws of Congress and the policies of the Kennedy administration. Homosexuals needed to go to the White House, to the Capitol—not the Pentagon.

"I suggest that if you want to change, your proper place is go to the president," said Applegate, hoping to wrap up the meeting.

After all, he said, the officials were just trying to help.

DURING THE THREE-HOUR MEETING, the officials did not recommend that the Society sue the Pentagon. A week after the conference, Bruce Scott wrote Applegate and Lewis to thank them for the meeting. Though the MSW preferred negotiation, he wrote, "we are now rounding up cases to challenge your criteria and policies, administratively, at first, and then in the courts, up to the US Supreme Court, if need be." The legal challenge would not just come from the Society, he warned, since the organization was "strongly suggesting to our brother organizations" that they tell their members to fight.

Kameny followed through with the threat. He wrote to Wicker, to the Mattachine Societies in New York and San Francisco, and to smaller organizations across the country. Homosexuals facing the revocation of their security clearances should not just deny the allegations, Kameny told these organizations. Rather, they should challenge the security system itself. "Please do your best to encourage anyone having such difficulties to fight the matter fully, and please publicize such encouragement as widely as possible," he advised.

On the West Coast, homophile activists were already eyeing the concept of a legal assault. Randy Wicker worked as the New York news correspondent for Guy Strait and José Sarria's League for Civil Education, which had gained several hundred members in San Francisco. On October 15, in the same *LCE News* issue that contained Wicker's report on the MSW's congressional meetings, the front page declared a legal war—"WE MUST FIGHT NOW"—on the police harassment of San Francisco's gay bars. "Yes, there is war," wrote Strait, "a fight in the courts of our country to regain rights. Let those who will, join in the fight. Let those of faint heart stand by or at least stand aside." Two weeks later, the LCE announced plans to send its complaints to "each and every member of Congress."

In Washington, the local National Capital Area Civil Liberties Union chapter had autonomy. It could choose the cases it sponsored, and it still had an empty docket. When Ronald Brass, the first victim of FBI informant Warren Scarberry, found himself being purged from his Department of Commerce position, Kameny turned to the NCACLU. A Union board member agreed to take Brass's case, and with his representation, Brass managed to keep his job.

The MSW also infiltrated the NCACLU's operations. After Kameny and Bruce Scott attended the Union's first meeting, they kept returning. And as the NCACLU grew, it needed help in its office. Scott, still hoping to sue the Civil Service Commission, was especially interested in the NCACLU's work, so when he lost his warehouse job and learned of the Union's clerical needs, he applied to work there. Bruce Scott, secretary and founding member of the Mattachine Society of Washington, became an administrative secretary of the ACLU's Washington chapter.

Kameny, meanwhile, worked to ensure that the NCACLU embraced gay rights as one of its causes. He did so quietly, strategically, and with cunning. He, or an MSW representative, attended each and every committee meeting relevant to the homosexual citizen, like the Police Practices Committee and the Security and Loyalty Committee. In the fall of 1962, when the Union announced the first meeting of its Committee on Discrimination and Segregation, Kameny called its chairman. What type of discrimination, he asked, is the committee planning to fight?

Oh, well, wherever discrimination exists—the usual groups, Kameny later recalled him saying.

What about homosexuals?

Well, that's up to the members of the committee.

Kameny arrived to the committee's first meeting and sat in a circle with twenty-five attorneys. Each attendee gave his name, address, and special areas of interest in the legal field of discrimination. Kameny explained he was interested in discrimination against homosexuals. But for the next hour and a half, the attorneys discussed only discrimination against Black Americans.

After a while, though, they reached a quandary. Other legal groups were already fighting for Black civil rights, they concluded. What more could the NCACLU contribute?

Well, we have a gentleman here who is interested in discrimination against homosexuals, said the chairman. Let's discuss that.

For twenty minutes, the attorneys examined the plight of the homosexual. Kameny very consciously kept quiet, supplying statistics only when it seemed necessary. Well, this is something that we clearly don't know anything about, concluded the chairman, before turning to Kameny. Will you talk to us about it?

Kameny drafted the press release. His speech to the NCACLU would take place on the evening of December 3, in the second-floor boardroom of the Philip Murray Building, a modern glass-covered structure in downtown Washington. The Soviet flag flew just a few feet from the boardroom's large windows, since the U.S.S.R.'s embassy stood immediately across the street. As Kameny entered the Philip Murray Building at 8:00 p.m. that night, he likely did so with the knowledge of an open secret in Washington: FBI agents were in the building, too, photographing everyone who entered or exited the Beaux-Arts Russian compound only a few feet away.

"First, the number of homosexuals," began the gay astronomer, standing before a room of straight attorneys. He cited Kinsey to support his "conservative" and "handy" 10 percent figure. Yes, the homosexual was indeed a minority, he contended, "several times the size of the Jewish minority." The Mattachine Society of Washington was, he explained, exactly "what the NAACP or CORE are for the Negro." But unlike African Americans, homosexuals had no explicit protection in the Constitution, nothing to which they could even point.

Kameny's speech was, at its core, a cry for help. He described the vast scale of America's gay purges, taking place not just in the government, but in private industry, too. "Virtually all homosexuals work, at all times, with the sword of immediate summary dismissal hanging over their heads," he explained. But there existed no greater danger than in the federal bureaucracy, where the CSC's efforts to uncover homosexuals "remind one of the Nazis hunting down Jews."

Kameny admitted that he had no idea where to begin. The media had ignored his press releases and rejected his ads. The government, engaging in "a vast conspiracy of official silence," had ignored his letters. While "the Negro community," he argued, were "experienced professionals in these matters," homosexuals and his Society were "but amateurs."

He pleaded for assistance from both African Americans and from the ACLU. "We call upon them," he concluded, "and upon the ACLU with their long experiences in these areas, to assist us in a battle which, for us, has just begun."

As he waited for the attorneys' reaction, Kameny understood the high stakes of his speech. At best, the Union could become the Society's sister organization, a permanent ally, and even the legal arm of the homophile movement. At worst, his provocative claims that homosexuals actually represented a threatened minority—not to mention his references to the Holocaust—could forever alienate the ACLU's heterosexual members.

Kameny knew he could not afford to lose the attorneys' help. Three weeks earlier, Warren Scarberry had relayed alarming information to Ronald Brass. CSC investigators, Scarberry claimed, had visited Brass's apartment, asked about Brass's political beliefs, and made a list of all of Brass's books.

The investigators had threatened Scarberry, claimed the FBI informant. They had said they could prove Brass was a Communist.

And, Scarberry added, "Kameny is in serious trouble."

KAMENY DID NOT YET KNOW about the other, more powerful forces within the American government that were simultaneously mobilizing against him.

Two months earlier, on October 10, the United States House of Representatives convened at noon. The missile situation in Cuba was nearly a crisis. Congressman Paul Rogers of Florida discussed the Greeks' decision to halt shipping to Fidel Castro's Communist nation. Why had the British not joined the embargo?

A Democratic congressman from Athens, Texas, then took the floor. "Mr. Speaker, the matter about which I shall speak has nothing to do with foreign affairs," he began. "However, a few days ago there was an article which appeared in the local press relating to the fact that under the District of Columbia Charitable Solicitation Act permission had been granted to a society of homosexuals to solicit charitable contributions in the District of Columbia.

"Mr. Speaker, the Superintendent of Licenses and Permits said that his office had no authority to deny a solicitation permit under the law to these people.

"Mr. Speaker, the acts of these people are banned under the laws of God, the laws of nature, and they are against the laws of man.

"Mr. Speaker, I have today introduced a bill to correct this situation."

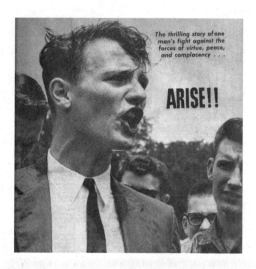

Randy Wicker at the University of Texas, May 1959

8

THE ALLIANCE

B ut where were all the lesbians?

In the late 1940s, Del Martin stood in a San Francisco lesbian bar. A sturdy, black-haired woman, she stared, trying to figure out the small groups of women speaking to one another, ignoring her. They seemed suspicious of strangers like her. This was it? Where were the *rest* of the female homosexuals?

She had married a man and given birth to a daughter. As World War II came to an end, she had fallen in love with a female neighbor, acknowledged her homosexuality, and left her husband.

Martin understood that she would be forever stigmatized; she contemplated suicide. When her ex-husband remarried, he approached Martin with an irrefutable argument. Their daughter needed a mother *and* a father, he said. She needed to be raised by a normal, stable couple.

Martin allowed the heterosexual couple to take her only child.

In 1949, she moved to Seattle for a new job at a trade journal, the *Daily Construction Report*. Soon after her arrival, a female coworker noticed her. Like the men, Martin carried a briefcase.

Phyllis Lyon had also come from San Francisco, and her life as a heterosexual had been relatively painless. Fun, even. She had been engaged and disengaged; she had experimented with boys; she wore long hair and lipstick.

After two years as friends, Lyon invited Martin to her apartment for dinner, and later that evening, as they sat together on a divan, Martin leaned toward Lyon. Lyon did the same. The two women became lovers, creating a relationship that would last for fifty-six years, interrupted only by death.

In 1953, the couple moved back to San Francisco, where Martin was again—this time with a companion—an outsider in a lesbian bar. She and Lyon wanted homosexual friends, but the patrons did not trust new faces. The police could raid the bars at any moment, and heterosexual tourists often intruded, staring at the lesbians as if they were zoo animals.

On September 21, 1955, Martin and Lyon joined three other couples to form a secret society, America's first known lesbian organization. They called themselves the Daughters of Bilitis, an obscure reference to the fictional Ancient Greek woman who, in the 1894 poetry of Pierre Louÿs, loved both men and women. The name sounded like any traditional organization of female heterosexuals, something like the Daughters of the American Revolution. Who, other than scholars of nineteenth-century poetry, would guess that the DOB was really an organization of sexual deviants?

The eight women elected Del Martin as the first president of the DOB, and Lyon became its secretary. The couple had finally found a lesbian community. "We were just happy we met six more lesbians," Lyon later recalled.

A year later, the DOB had fifteen members and a magazine, *The Ladder*, which referred to the lesbian's duty to climb the ladder of social acceptance. Society made lesbians fearful, and so the organization remained small. Martin and Lyon understood that lesbians not only risked losing everything, but they were also *women* who risked losing everything. If a lesbian managed to find a job in a profoundly sexist society, or if she was financially dependent on her family, or if she was a single mother dependent on the government, how could she possibly risk alienating her boss, her loved ones, the government?

Martin and Lyon attempted to combat this fear, and they did so with the help of the overwhelmingly male Mattachine Society. The DOB's first public discussion, cosponsored with the Mattachine, simply tried to reassure lesbians; Martin and Lyon brought attorneys and psychiatrists to combat myths and inform the attendees that they should not be afraid of their own identities. By recruiting women at Mattachine and *ONE* magazine conventions, the DOB leaders slowly grew their organization, first by creating a Los Angeles chapter, and then, in 1958, a New York chapter.

Their alliance with the male-dominated organizations came at a cost. Although those groups shared their lesbian contacts, their strategies, and their materials, they rarely took the lesbians—or their unique concerns—seriously. When DOB members attended Mattachine events, the discussion topics remained the same. Delegates talked about how promiscuous males, seeking illicit sex in public spaces, were the victims of police entrapment, how male gay bars were raided and its patrons harassed, and how male employees had lost their jobs. They never talked about the plight of the lesbian.

At the 1959 Mattachine Convention in Denver, Del Martin lost her patience. "At every one of these conventions I attend, year after year, I find I must defend the Daughters of Bilitis as a separate and distinct women's organization," she declared. "What do you men know about Lesbians?"

The next year, when the DOB updated its constitution, it prohibited chapters from joining other organizations, and it required them to maintain physically separate headquarters and mailing addresses. As one DOB official put it, the amendments sent a clear message to the men of the Mattachine. "Up yours."

DAUGHTERS OF BILITIS? What the hell kind of name is that?

Barbara Gittings sat in a San Francisco living room with fifteen lesbians, who seemed pleasant. They drank refreshments. The twenty-four-year-old Gittings looked and sounded like a youthful librarian—short hair, large glasses, and a clear, refined voice. Though she had just met them, Gittings had no scruples about offending the older women in the apartment. The name of the organization, Gittings told her hosts, was too complicated, too long. How did you spell it, or even pronounce it? (Buh-lee-tis.) And, to top it off, wasn't Bilitis a *fictional* bisexual, not even a real human being? What were they doing with such an absurd name?

As a child, Gittings had wanted to become a nun. Steeped in her family's Catholicism and wealth, she glided between Mass and white-gloved debutante teas. While studying theater at Northwestern, she excavated written materials on homosexuality beneath the imposing stone buttresses and stained glass of the university's neo-Gothic library. The books she found were anything but reassuring. Pathology, disturbance, maladaptation, arrested development, they said. The studies compared the measurements of various body parts—earlobes, fingernails, hips—of homosexuals and heterosexuals. They analyzed homosexuals' favorite color (green). And, overwhelmingly, they discussed only men.

Her obsession with understanding herself took precedence over everything else in her life, including her studies. She stopped going to class and failed her freshman year.

Gittings moved to a Philadelphia rooming house, and on weekends, she dressed as a boy—was that not what all lesbians did?—and hitchhiked up Route 1 to New York. The truck drivers never bothered the bespectacled girl in male drag. When she reached New York's lesbian bars, she found that nobody wanted to discuss literature or hostel trips or baroque music. Alone, Gittings stood in the bars, holding a cup of ice water, pretending it was gin on the rocks.

In the summer of 1956, after learning about the Daughters of Bilitis from *ONE* magazine, Gittings traveled to San Francisco with a rucksack on her back. In the DOB, despite her dislike of the organization's name, Gittings found a home. By 1958, Barbara Gittings had become the founding president of the New York chapter of the Daughters of Bilitis. While working as a mimeograph operator in an architectural firm, she spent nearly every weekend commuting from Philadelphia to New York, where she built the East Coast's first lesbian organization. In this pre-Wicker era, *The Village Voice* would not take her ads, and only a handful of women—culled from *The Ladder*'s subscriber list—attended the first meeting. But by 1961, her mailing list contained almost three hundred names. Lesbians could meet one another in a safe setting, and for Gittings, that was enough.

In February 1963, when Del Martin retired after six years as editor of *The Ladder*, Gittings began serving as her interim replacement. For her first issue, she featured a story about a lesbian wedding.

That same month, as a representative of the Daughters of Bilitis, she attended a meeting to discuss the possibility of creating America's first alliance of homosexual organizations. It took place in the Washington home of a man named Frank Kameny.

THE MSW'S UNPRECEDENTED contacts with members of Congress had made it *the* group to emulate. When Kameny sent news of the meetings to the organization formerly known as the Mattachine Society of Philadelphia—it renamed itself "The Janus Society" after the national Mattachine's collapse—the group asked not only to print the news, but also for a copy of the MSW's constitution, to be used as a template for its own organizing document.

ONE invited Kameny to speak about his "struggles with officialdom" at its 1963 Midwinter Institute that coming January. "I didn't suspect," admitted one MSNY officer, "that you would get the kind of response you did from your mailings to Congressmen."

In December 1962, a group of MSNY and MSW officers congregated in Kameny's home. If the West Coast had its *ONE* and Mattachine conventions, they asked themselves in that informal meeting, why not establish a convention for homophile organizations on the East Coast? Why not use that convention to promote an alliance among the groups, providing them with the opportunity to exchange ideas and coordinate activities?

Representatives of four groups—MSW, MSNY, the Janus Society, and DOB—formally met in Philadelphia on January 26, 1963, and they decided to hold a conference that summer. At a second meeting on February 23, they met in Kameny's home and formalized the planning committee's name: the East Coast Homophile Organizations (ECHO). Barbara Gittings took notes on the plans for the conference. They would invite psychiatrists, clergy, lawyers, government officials, and artists, she wrote.

At first, Gittings remained uncertain about ECHO. Was it "a springboard for a formal re-affiliation of those 3 Mattachine-spawned groups," having invited DOB only for its "money and energy," or was it a "marvelous opportunity" for publicity and professional contacts? But later in her life, Gittings had only one vivid memory about meeting Kameny. For the first time, she had met someone who had "firm, uncompromising positions about homosexuality and homosexuals' right to be considered fully on par with heterosexuals."

At the March meeting, held in New York, Frank Kameny finally met Randy Wicker. As Wicker complained to Gittings, the MSNY officials had attempted "to keep Kameny away from me the entire weekend," but, in the militant activist's words, "I do what I damn please."

"Thank yo ufo a thoroly [*sic*] pleasant evening (and morning)," Kameny later wrote Wicker, "including the night's accommodations. I had wanted to get to know you for quite some time, and I feel that I did, to a considerable extend [*sic*], and most pleasurably so." They had discussed Kameny's Supreme Court brief, Wicker's publicity efforts, and the legal ambitions of the MSW. "You, as a personality, are a large morsel to swallow all at once," added Kameny, "and I am still digesting and assimilating all that I acquired during the 15 hours that we were together."

KAMENY HAD TAKEN Warren Scarberry's claims seriously. According to the FBI informant, Kameny faced a federal investigation because authorities believed that his housemate, twenty-two-year-old Allen Duncan (whose mother had recorded the Pentagon meeting for the Society), was only fourteen years old.

Was Scarberry lying, continuing to wreak havoc on Washington's "homosexual element," or telling the truth, all the while concealing his complicity in Brass's nightmare? Kameny himself knew Scarberry to be erratic, but his claims about the CSC investigators *sounded* accurate.

Kameny turned to the NCACLU, which agreed to defend Kameny against such "slander." The MSW president's speech had been a resounding success, and with the Union's intervention, Ronald Brass still had his job. Scarberry's warnings, it became clear, had been empty.

The relationship between the NCACLU and the MSW continued to grow. In March 1963, Kameny wrote to Curtis Dewees. The NCACLU, "entirely at THEIR own initiative," he breathlessly reported, "has TENTATIVELY AND PROVISIONALLY decided to put out a 'white paper' on employment discrimination against the homosexual."

Kameny's greatest NCACLU coup, however, came in the form of Bruce Scott, secretary of the Mattachine Society of Washington. Since his CSC interrogation in April 1962, when Scott had refused to answer questions about his sexuality, he had been fighting the same administrative battle that Kameny had fought four years earlier.

After Scott lost his administrative appeals and turned to the courts, he faced a choice. He could copy Byron Scott's initial legal strategy for Kameny's case, maintaining he had been denied procedural due process, or he could force the issue of homosexual exclusion by admitting his sexuality, dooming his chances of a successful appeal, and daring the commission to exclude him.

In September 1962, he chose the latter option. "Let me for this particular appeal," he wrote to CSC chairman Macy, "assume that I have engaged in 'homosexual conduct.'" He just wanted a clear answer to a very simple question: did the government have the power to arbitrarily exclude homosexuals from federal employment?

In December, only weeks after Kameny's speech, the NCACLU agreed to take the case of Bruce Scott, a logical choice for the attorneys' first homosexual plaintiff. As the NCACLU's secretary, they already knew him. They understood that he was an upstanding man, undeserving of the underemployment he had experienced for years.

In March, Scott and Kameny learned that David Carliner, the chairman of the NCACLU, had agreed to represent Scott. Carliner, a good-humored attorney with a strong jaw and hazel eyes, would fight the case not just on the technicalities of Scott's dismissal but, as Kameny put it, "on an initial admission, by all concerned, of the fundamental fact." Carliner would not deny that Scott was a sexual deviant, and he would directly confront the constitutionality of the purges.

On April 23, Carliner submitted Scott's lawsuit against Chairman Macy of the Civil Service Commission. First and foremost, Carliner argued, the CSC never demonstrated any specific immoral conduct. What, exactly, did Scott *do*? Moreover, not only did the government have no legal authority to disqualify job applicants because of their alleged immoral conduct, but such behavior had no relationship to their jobs in the first place. To argue that homosexual conduct automatically made one unsuitable was arbitrary, capricious, and discriminatory, denying the plaintiff due process. Finally, to label homosexual conduct *itself* as immoral was arbitrary. Indeed, what right did the government have to decide what was moral or immoral?

According to *The Washington Star*, Bruce Scott hoped to become a "symbol" that would force the government to reevaluate its policies. The newspaper listed his full name and his street address in Virginia.

SCOTT'S LAWSUIT REPRESENTED an act of bravery, since gay Washington remained an unsafe place. On the night of Saturday, May 25, 1963, Walter William Goldstein walked into the Gayety Buffet. The restaurant, located halfway between the White House and the Capitol, had been a gay bar since 1952, attracting a working-class, "rough trade" clientele. Goldstein wore makeup.

Washington still required bar patrons to sit as they consumed alcohol, so Goldstein and three friends sat, talking, at a booth. He soon noticed four men standing in the restaurant. Within seconds, they began grabbing patrons from their booths, seemingly at random, and instructed them to stand.

One of the men, wearing a dirty white T-shirt and dark trousers, pointed at Goldstein. You, he said, come here.

Why? For what reason? said Goldstein.

The man in the white T-shirt reached across the booth and pulled Goldstein from the booth. Why me? he asked the man. What did I do?

Because you're under arrest, said the man.

Goldstein soon found himself at the First Precinct station with five other scared, confused men. The police refused to tell them the nature of their arrests, despite Goldstein's demands.

We know you're a queer, said the officer. Everyone at the Gayety was a queer.

But you were there, too, retorted Goldstein.

The punches came in three rapid blows to the side of Goldstein's rib cage. He fell to the floor.

You're in my office now, don't fall on my floor, said the officer. Goldstein slipped into unconsciousness.

Kameny vaulted to action, beginning with a fact-finding mission. He hunted down Goldstein and the other five victims. Predictably, the police had informed the employer of one of the men, who immediately lost his job. Meanwhile, Kameny found a Gayety waitress who was willing to testify that there had been no disorderly conduct in her establishment.

In only a few weeks, and with the NCACLU's assistance, Kameny persuaded three men to write and notarize affidavits that chronicled the raid and the subsequent police harassment. By the end of the month, both Goldstein and another victim had filed official complaints drafted by Kameny.

The MSW president wrote to Police Chief Robert Murray. Not only did the men have the "full support and backing" of the NCACLU, he warned, but the Society threatened to take matters into its own hands. "We have no wish unnecessarily to embarrass the Police Department, or to cause difficulties for you," Kameny threatened. "Therefore we shall not—at this time—create any publicity in these matters." He demanded a meeting.

Chief Murray promptly delegated the matter to Deputy Chief Blick, who then traveled to the Gayety to interview its staff about the incident. Blick ultimately agreed to a conference with Kameny and Society officials, where Kameny reiterated what he had written to Chief Murray. The Mattachine Society of Washington would not tolerate harassment or "contempt, derision, and ridicule" directed toward homosexuals. In the future, the Society would strike back with publicity, turning to the media and causing certain embarrassment for the police department.

THREE WEEKS AFTER the Gayety raid, Kameny received a summons in the mail. The letter, titled "SUSPENSION AND REMOVAL OF RONALD BERTRAM BRASS," came from John H. Harmon III, an NCACLU attorney.

"You are hereby requested to make yourself available for the purpose of giving testimony in the above matter," it said. The hearing was to take place at 10:00 a.m., Tuesday, June 18, 1963, at the Department of Commerce headquarters.

The ax had fallen in March. Despite the efforts of the NCACLU, the Department of Commerce—nine months after Warren Scarberry's revelations—suspended Brass without pay from his job as an international economist. One month later, Brass received a list of charges. From December 1961 to October 1962, wrote the Department of Commerce, "you engaged in homosexual conduct, activities, and relationship with one Warren Scarberry."

The department had a strong case. Not only did it have Scarberry's information, but it also had Brass's own confessions from his first, pre-Kameny interrogation. It knew about his membership in the Mattachine and his pseudonym, "Russell Brenner." Worst of all, said the department, "by your own admission you have frequented places attended exclusively or almost exclusively by homosexuals; you have, by such associations permitted yourself to be accosted and 'propositioned' by homosexuals for the purposes of committing immoral acts." Because Brass had falsely denied committing such acts, he was "not reliable or trustworthy," and thus subject to "coercion, influence, or pressure."

First, the NCACLU tried to save Brass's job. His attorney, John H. Harmon III, decided not to not deny Brass's homosexuality, his participation in perverted acts, or his membership in the Mattachine. Instead, he would dismantle the blackmail rationale by arguing exactly what Kameny had theorized three years earlier. By living *publicly* as a homosexual, a federal employee could become immune to coercion. To prove this case, Harmon solicited statements from the most open homosexuals in the country, including Frank Kameny and the other Mattachine presidents. As Brass himself explained to Kameny, "He hopes these statements to be in the form of an answer to the question: Do you feel that your homosexual activities, including membership and participation in the Mattachine Society, can subject you to coercion, influence, pressure, or blackmail?"

Kameny wrote to Curtis Dewees of MSNY and Hal Call of Mattachine San Francisco to request the statements, "needed very PROMPTLY."

Armed with these letters, on June 18, Kameny arrived at the Department of Commerce. Three men sat before him on a panel, and the chairman reminded Kameny of his oath to tell the truth.

"Fine," said Kameny. "Before we start, would it be possible for me to have the name and official address of each person here?"

The panel introduced themselves: first, the chairman, an attorney from the Department of State; then, an official from a housing agency; and, finally, Robert H. Fuchs of the Central Intelligence Agency.

"Excuse me?" asked Kameny, startled.

"Central Intelligence Agency," repeated Fuchs.

"Now, Doctor, before we start these proceedings—" began the chairman.

"Just a minute—" Kameny interjected.

"Mr. Harmon, please proceed," said the chairman, ignoring him.

"Dr. Kameny, does the name, the Mattachine Society of Washington, D.C., strike you with familiarity?"

Kameny explained the purposes of the organization. No, it did not appear on the Department of Justice's list of proscribed organizations. No, it did not encourage the commission of homosexuality in public places. And no, the MSW never attempted to "coerce, influence or pressure" Ronald Brass.

"Do you, Dr. Kameny, as president of the Mattachine Society, swear allegiance to the United States of America?"

"Yes, certainly," said Kameny.

The Society, he explained, was a professional organization legally advocating for a minority group. Its members had never been subject to blackmail, and it was open to heterosexuals, too.

"Dr. Kameny," asked Harmon, "do you personally know one Warren Scarberry?"

"I do."

Kameny would not reveal Scarberry's sexual orientation, but when pressed by the chairman, he admitted, "I have met him in surroundings where there were other homosexuals present. That is all I can say."

"What is Warren Scarberry's reputation in the homosexual community of Washington?" asked Harmon.

Scarberry was a "somewhat erratic, somewhat unstable person who cannot always be taken at face value," said Kameny.

"What do you mean by the word 'erratic'?" asked the chairman.

"You can't always count on the truth of what he says," said Kameny. Scarberry was unreliable, always on the move, with a new passion each day. "He is in Washington today, Baltimore tomorrow, Ohio the next day."

Harmon had no further questions.

"Dr. Kameny," began the department's attorney, "have you ever been convicted of any sexual offense within the United States?"

Kameny admitted his San Francisco arrest, clarifying that he had not been convicted.

"Do you regard yourself as a homosexual, Doctor?"

"I look upon that question as improper, as if you ask me my religion or political beliefs."

"Is Warren Scarberry well known among the homosexuals?"

"He is known to a large number of homosexuals that I know, yes."

"Did he ever attend any of the Mattachine Society meetings?"

Kameny refused to answer.

"Doctor, you mentioned Mr. Scarberry had a reputation among the homosexuals," said the department attorney. "Who are those persons?"

"You want names?"

"Yes."

"Considering current unfortunate Federal Government policies on this, I couldn't possibly give a name. I would not have a night's sleep for the rest of my life if I gave anybody's name," said Kameny.

When he returned to his car, Kameny found a parking ticket waiting for him. He promptly mailed it to the Department of Commerce attorney who had cross-examined him, requesting that the official pay it.

ON JUNE 5, 1963, two weeks before the Brass hearing, FBI director J. Edgar Hoover received an invitation to a public lecture, featuring *The Homosexual in America* author Donald Webster Cory, to be held at the Gramercy Hotel the next day. The MSW's event was titled "THE HOMO- SEXUAL ... Minority Rights, Civil Rights, Human Rights." Though the Society charged $1.50 for admission, the director's ticket had COM- PLIMENTARY scrawled across it.

The Society had become frustrated, and as a result, it had become bold. Despite the letter-writing campaign, the congressional meetings, and the Pentagon conference, the purges remained intact. Kameny still did not have a security clearance.

"I have watched all too much of my recent life dribble wastefully and uselessly down the drain, with my training and abilities largely unused, simply because I did not have a clearance," he told R. L. Applegate at the Pentagon. Why, he began to wonder, should he continue tiptoeing around these supposedly sympathetic federal officials, remaining cautious not to alienate them, if doing so would get him nowhere?

Kameny still understood that publicity came with dangers. He and other Society members had jobs to maintain, and direct exposure in the press promised to raise questions among their current and future employers. So when the Society released its first newsletter, the *Gazette*, in May 1963, its masthead included only pseudonyms. It did not mention Kameny's name.

The first issue of the *Gazette* summarized the Society's accomplishments to date, celebrated Randy Wicker's work in New York, and explored a question that had been preoccupying the Society. How could their organization grow without threatening the safety and livelihood of its members? Having closed meetings—requiring a sponsor and board approval for each new member—made expansion difficult. But, in a catch-22, few members would join without security measures in place. Meetings thus consisted of only a few men meeting privately in apartments, discussing Kameny's legal crusade and other topics like "The Homosexual and His Family" and "Religion and the Homosexual."

The answer to the growth-security conundrum, MSW members eventually concluded, lay in carefully curated public events, a strategy both Del Martin and Harry Hay had implemented in their own organizations. Donald Webster Cory agreed to give a public lecture for the MSW, and in April, Kameny began looking for a venue. George Washington University, several churches, and a Jewish Community Center turned him down. When one board member attempted to advertise the event in *The Washington Post*, the publication refused.

The Society eventually found a venue, the Gramercy Hotel, and on June 4, while Kameny investigated the Gayety raid, "Bruce Schuyler" sent the invitations. He provided complimentary tickets to proven allies like Congressmen Nix and Ryan; to potentially sympathetic officials like Robert Kennedy, Lyndon Johnson, and Supreme Court justice William Douglas; and to those most responsible for the maintenance of the purges, like R. L. Applegate, CSC chairman John Macy, and J. Edgar Hoover.

Within hours of Hoover's receipt of the complimentary ticket, one of his special agents began investigating the lecture. By now, in addition to Warren Scarberry, the Bureau had found a *second* source within the Society, a potential confidential informant (PCI) who confirmed the date and time of the lecture.

On June 7, a top FBI official reminded Hoover of the Society's mission to create a "highly ethical homosexual culture," quoting from Harry Hay's outdated constitution. Once again, the official recommended that the director not respond.

"Right," scrawled Hoover.

Three days later, at 8:00 p.m. on June 11, a *TIME* reporter arrived to the Scott Room of the Gramercy Inn, located halfway between Dupont Circle and the White House. *The Washington Post*, after refusing to advertise the event, also sent a reporter. The Pentagon sent two officials.

In the audience of fifty to seventy-five attendees sat two FBI informants. Warren Scarberry arrived late, giving him only a few minutes to pick up a copy of the literature available for the audience—the *Gazette*, the MSNY's newsletter, and a couple pamphlets. He recognized approximately twenty-five homosexuals in the audience, and he thought the rest looked like homosexuals, too. Two weeks later, when Scarberry briefed his FBI handler on the event, he reported that Cory had merely followed the "party line" of the homophile movement.

No, he had not been in contact with other homosexuals in the MSW. But yes, he would "have further meetings with them," and yes, he promised to "advise of their full identity."

Five weeks after the lecture, the Bureau's second informant provided a forty-seven-page transcript of the entire event, created by the Society for homosexuals either unable or too fearful to attend. The special agent in charge of the Washington Field Office sent two copies directly to Hoover on July 22.

The FBI director may have noticed something peculiar about the transcript. The man who called the meeting to order was not Frank Kameny, but rather "Frank Lockwood, President, presiding."

Despite all his letters and meetings, threats and lawsuits, Kameny's fear of seeing his name in the press remained intact. He could claim to be an open and proud homosexual for the sake of legal argumentation, but he could not yet bring himself to live that assertion. In 1961, despite his willingness to publicly file his lawsuit, he celebrated the lack of news coverage surrounding *Kameny v. Brucker;* in 1962, he requested anonymity in his *Star* interview; in 1963, the *Gazette*'s masthead lacked his name; and now, in the aftermath of the Society's first public event, he used a pseudonym. Perhaps he did so because of his job, always precarious, or because of his family. Rae Beck Kameny still did not know the truth about her son.

By the time Hoover received the Cory transcript, however, the director seemed more concerned by a homosexual threat that was, according to informant number two, imminent.

In August 1963, warned the informant, fifty homosexuals would picket the White House to protest government discrimination of homosexuals. In a copy of a memorandum sent to Hoover, the Bureau later redacted the name of the man who planned to lead this group.

In another copy, however, FBI censors failed to redact his name. The leader audacious enough to picket the White House on behalf of homosexuals, Hoover learned, was named "RANDY."

"JACKSON, MISS.—The Justice Department has been asked to investigate the rape of three girls and sexual abuses against several others who were jailed in freedom demonstrations here," began a story on the June 11, 1963, front page of *The Washington Afro-American.*

The National Association for the Advancement of Colored People (NAACP) had been protesting Mississippi's segregation and disenfranchisement of African Americans throughout the year. It had organized pickets, a boycott of white businesses, and a voting rights campaign, which triggered a white backlash of arrests, sexual assault, and other nightly horrors.

If *Washington Afro-American* readers finished that day's article, making it past the trauma of the arrests, the rapes, the shootings, and the legal battles, they may have noticed an advertisement immediately below it, located halfway down the sixth page of their newspaper:

TONITE

DONALD WEBSTER CORY

author of *The Homosexual in America*

in a public lecture

THE HOMOSEXUAL . . .
MINORITY RIGHTS, CIVIL RIGHTS, HUMAN RIGHTS

THE SCOTT ROOM
GRAMERCY INN

Though *The Washington Post* refused the Society's ad, the *Afro-American* gladly accepted $10.80 for it. After the event, the Washington edition of the *Afro-American*, a Baltimore-based national newspaper founded by a former slave, also reported on it. "Homosexual's Civil Rights Discussed in Lecture Here," it announced. Cory had "demonstrated that the problem under consideration is part of the overall problem of minority-majority relations in the United States." He had argued that without addressing the homosexual problem, "one cannot treat other minority problems."

Much of that *Afro-American* issue covered the assassination of Medgar Evers, an NAACP official in Mississippi. An FBI employee nevertheless located the *Afro-American*'s Cory article, a slight but unprecedented step toward an alliance between the Black freedom movement and the overwhelmingly white homophile movement. The employee scissored out the news item and carefully placed it in the Society's file.

Randy Wicker, meanwhile, wanted to replicate the civil rights movement. He, along with the rest of America, had watched Martin Luther King Jr.'s Birmingham campaign with admiration and dismay. In early May, he saw the children—the girls wearing dresses and the boys wearing tucked shirts—bravely marching, gleefully waving from the school buses that Bull Connor's police then used to transport them, hundreds of adolescents, to jail. He saw the public outcry, and on May 10, he saw the city of Birmingham surrender. That same day, he saw Black labor leader A. Philip Randolph announce plans for a one-hundred-thousand-person march on Washington, intended to "wake up Negro America to the job crisis now upon it."

A month later, on June 11, the day of the Cory lecture and the *Afro-American* advertisement, Wicker saw President Kennedy's speech, a response to the breathtaking spectacle of Birmingham, Governor Wallace's defiance, and King's warnings of an impending march on Washington.

America faced "a moral crisis," said Kennedy. "A great change is at hand, and our task, our obligation, is to make that revolution, that change, peaceful and constructive for all." The president pledged to sign a comprehensive civil rights bill.

Wicker had already achieved much of what he wanted, transforming the whispered topic of homosexuality into an issue discussed widely and frankly in the media, thereby combatting the negative stereotypes of homosexuals so firmly entrenched in American life.

By June, while Kameny cautiously planned his Society's first public event, Wicker reveled in new heights of fame. That month, the *New York Post Magazine* introduced Wicker, a young man with the appearance of "a blond-haired, college-boy cheerleader" and afflicted with an "undetectable" homosexual condition. Wicker, "like most of his group, enjoys 'cruising'—the homosexual equivalent of a boy-girl pickup," wrote Levin.

That month, the men's magazine *Nugget* published an entire profile, "The Gay Crusader," on Wicker and his crusade against the "corporate image" of the homophile movement. "We must ask ourselves: Is this crusade an upstaging of the more conservative homophile organizations?" asked a DOB reviewer in Barbara Gittings's *Ladder*. "What is our answer to Randolfe Wicker's truth-telling publicity campaign?"

Wicker seemed to be leaving the homophile movement behind. "All embattled minority groups must eventually have a spokesman; the Negroes have Martin Luther King," explained the *Nugget* article. "Now, at long last, the homosexuals have Randolfe Wicker."

Yet Wicker was no King. The latter, in direct communication with President Kennedy, also had the ears of the media and the allegiance of thousands of Black citizens willing to step onto the forbidden streets of the South. They marched and organized despite the murderous realities of

Jim Crow, resulting in the televised spectacles and haunting images—the dogs, the water, the children—that shook the nation to its core.

In the ten weeks after the Birmingham settlement, America witnessed 758 racial demonstrations—and 14,733 subsequent arrests—in 186 cities. A. Philip Randolph's vision of one hundred thousand protesters descending upon Washington became more real by the day. Why, asked Wicker, were homosexuals not marching, too?

The FBI learned of his plans from informant number two on June 6, the same day it confirmed the time and place of the Cory lecture. "RANDY," wrote the special agent, "told PCI he was bringing approximately fifty homosexuals to Washington, D.C., in August, 1963, to picket the White House and they were planning to carry placards inscribed with slogans criticizing the government for discriminating against homosexuals in government employment."

"RANDY," said the informant, was hoping to "solicit the aid of homosexuals in Washington, D.C., to help him in this demonstration." The informant had promised he would assist with the demonstration.

The informant told the special agent he would "immediately notify him when he heard from 'RANDY.'"

On June 12, the day after President Kennedy's televised speech on civil rights, his Secret Service received a memorandum from the FBI. "HOMOSEXUALS PLANNING TO PICKET WHITE HOUSE," it said. The Bureau, after summarizing its informant's information, promised to keep the Secret Service updated.

The Bureau only heard silence. Informant #2 never learned more about Wicker's plans.

"I haven't died," Wicker told Kameny in July. First, he wanted to write a book, but doing so was proving to be "a pain in the ass."

"Quite honestly I am in a quiet period so far as organizational activity is concerned," he said. "My next major effort will be picketing the White House this fall—so far I have 12 to 20 pickets; heterosexuals included—could be a bombshell!"

But for now, wrote Wicker, "I have just been screwing around and having fun."

Kameny was not prepared to picket, either. "The homosexual community will not put on as spectacular a display as the Negro community is now putting," he told Kennedy advisor Ted Sorensen in late June. But homosexuals were "near the breaking point," he warned. "The lessons being taught by the Negro are being learned elsewhere."

That month, the only information the Bureau received about a homosexual demonstration came from Warren Scarberry, who had recently protested not for homosexual equality, but for racial equality. On June 14, Scarberry marched from Lafayette Park to the Department of Justice as one of three thousand marchers participating in "March on Washington Now," a protest organized by the Congress of Racial Equality. Scarberry, though unaffiliated with the group, was "sympathetic to the plight of the Negro in Washington," as he explained to the special agent.

According to an FBI file titled "SEXUAL PERVERTS, WASHINGTON, D.C., AREA," Scarberry described his experience in the march. "He stated upon arrival at Lafayette Park, he noticed a Negro male carrying a sign," wrote the special agent. "He asked the Negro to let him carry the sign, the Negro agreed, and he carried the sign in the parade." The placard, written by the Black marcher but carried by the white Scarberry, an FBI informant responsible for the ruined career of at least one homosexual, said EQUALITY FOR ALL.

IN LATE 1962, Kameny began renting a house, a two-story brick Colonial Revival built seven years earlier. Surrounded by spacious lawns, the elegant home stood in the leafy, residential Palisades neighborhood of northwest Washington. With income from Quanta Laboratories, Kameny could afford rent, but not furniture. Most of the house remained bare in that first half of 1963.

When Jack Nichols, the young charter member of the MSW, mentioned that he and his lover were looking for a new home, Kameny offered to rent them the sofa bed in his living room.

"His scientism was evident even in the kitchen," Nichols later remembered. "He kept foods belonging in one category with their kind, while others were separated by variety with equal exactness." The radio was perpetually tuned to classical music. On car journeys, Kameny whipped out a map and calculated the *exact* time it would take to reach their destination; he had timed the District's stoplights.

Kameny lost his job by the end of June, and the house remained empty. His laboratory had made cutbacks, and as a consultant without a security clearance, he was one of the first dismissed. Kameny began collecting unemployment compensation and applying to jobs once more.

On July 5, Congressman John Dowdy of Texas again rose on the floor of the United States House of Representatives.

"Mr. Speaker, it came to my attention last fall that the District of Columbia government had granted a society of homosexuals a license to solicit charitable contributions in the District of Columbia.

"I introduced a bill in the last Congress to correct this situation, but it was too late to receive action at that time. Earlier this year, I introduced the bill again, as H.R. 5990, with the earnest hope that it will receive the approval of this Congress.

"I would call attention to the fact that I believe all of us received a letter from the President of the Mattachine Society of Washington, in August of last year, in which he enclosed an excerpt from the constitution of his society, and a news release which he had just issued. To refresh memory, I include those matters with my remarks.

"The Mattachine Society is admittedly a group of homosexuals. The acts of these people are banned under the laws of God, the laws of nature, and are in violation of the laws of man. I think a situation which requires them to be permitted a license to solicit charitable funds for the promotion of their sexual deviations is a bad law, and should be changed forthwith."

Dowdy's proposed bill amended the District of Columbia Charitable Solicitation Act, which regulated the activities of nonprofit organizations in Washington. The first section of the bill forced the District to distribute charitable licenses only to groups that promoted the "health, welfare, and the morals of the District of Columbia."

In its second section, the real purpose of the bill became clear. "Notwithstanding the District of Columbia Charitable Solicitation Act or any other provision of law, the certificate of registration heretofore issued to the Mattachine Society of Washington under such Act is revoked."

Kameny had not learned about Dowdy's bill in 1962. Now, with the bill under consideration, it took only five days for Kameny to receive the news. On July 10, he frantically wrote to David Carliner of the NCACLU. Is the bill likely to pass in the House? The Senate? Will there be hearings? Is there a chance President Kennedy would actually sign it? If it passes, should we take it to court? Has the ACLU ever *seen* a bill like this?

"This is, of course, just the type of harassing legislation which has been directed, at a state and local level, against the NAACP in the South," he wrote. "We are rank novices at this sort of thing. Can you offer any suggestions."

At an emergency meeting, the MSW board drafted a letter to the District's board of commissioners. "As an organization lawfully operating in the District of Columbia, for lawful purposes, we wish to express our strong opposition to this bill," wrote the board.

Frank Kameny also contemplated whether to defend his organization before Congress, a choice he knew could destroy him. He understood that doing so would attract the harsh lights of the media, risk the anonymity and security held so dear by his organization, and expose him, a jobless man, to potential employers, his family, and the public.

Kameny also recognized the opportunity to become the first gay man to testify on behalf of homosexuals before the United States Congress, an arena untested even by Randy Wicker. Who else would be willing to protect his organization? Most important, who else would be objectively more qualified to speak for him, his organization, or his minority?

The MSW president, only weeks after hiding his name in the Cory transcript, made his decision. On July 31, he sent twenty-four letters, one to each member of the House Committee on the District of Columbia, to "respectfully request that hearings be held prior to the reporting out of this legislation, and that representatives of this Society be given an opportunity to testify."

On August 6, Kameny received a letter from the clerk of the House's Committee on the District of Columbia. Hearings would take place at the Cannon House Office Building on August 8, in two days. "You are hereby invited to testify," the clerk told Kameny, "if you so desire."

Barbara Gittings in the early 1960s

9

THE CONGRESSMAN

Congressman John Vernard Dowdy saw the world of God crumbling around him. A stout, bespectacled fifty-one-year-old with a ruddy complexion, Dowdy was a self-made man in the truest sense, the Texan sense. Born to a poor family, he grew up only a few miles from the Louisiana border. He worked as a court reporter, and for eight years, he taught himself the law. In 1940, he received the highest bar exam score in the state.

In 1944, though Dowdy had never practiced law, he ran for district attorney. The ambitious court reporter won that race, and for eight years he served as an earnest, methodical, church-attending prosecutor. Often willing to cut a deal for a guilty plea, Dowdy still found aggression to be especially necessary for some defendants. "This Negro is a lustful animal," he told one jury, "because he lacks the very elements of mankind." That defendant received the death sentence, and in 1952, Dowdy won a seat in the House of Representatives.

A few months after Dowdy swore his oath of office, the first issue of *Playboy* appeared on American newsstands. The development troubled Dowdy; his time as a district attorney had convinced him that pornography caused sex crimes. "Almost invariably, sex-offenders told me they were excited by such matter prior to the commission of their offenses," he later wrote.

Appointed to the House Post Office and Civil Service Committee, Dowdy gained the power to fight Hugh Hefner and the forces of perversion, so he initiated his crusade. In March 1956, Dowdy introduced legislation that allowed the postmaster general to temporarily detain obscene mail until a court could decide the material's mail-worthiness. Only four months later, the Senate unanimously approved Dowdy's bill, and on July 27, President Eisenhower signed it into law.

But what did *obscene* mean? The Supreme Court, eleven months after the enactment of Dowdy's bill, opened the floodgates with its 1957 *Roth* decision. How could Dowdy and his allies protect American children from pornography when its protectors merely had to claim it had "redeeming social importance"? The decision marked the beginning of a "sudden revolution," as the President's Commission on Obscenity and Pornography later described it, in what Americans could legally enjoy.

Dowdy doubled his efforts. Democratic leadership moved him to the District of Columbia Committee, so the third-term congressman shifted his crusade to the morality of the nation's capital. In March 1958, he introduced a new bill to punish the creation or distribution of publications dedicated to "scandals/whoring, lechery, assignations, intrigues between men and women, and immoral conduct of persons" with fines up to five hundred dollars and a yearlong jail sentence.

For five years, Dowdy attempted to guide various forms of this bill through Congress. And for five years, despite the support of numerous religious groups, he faced defeat. He watched *Playboy*'s circulation grow and America's sinners become emboldened by a Supreme Court that continuously whittled away at the moral fabric of America, first allowing homosexual publications, then adultery-ridden films, and finally, in 1962, homosexual pornography itself.

That year, Dowdy nearly lost his seat. In the Democratic primary that May, he ran against a thirty-year-old lawyer, Benton Musslewhite. The attorney, a former star quarterback at Southern Methodist University, ran a pro-Kennedy campaign and ultimately lost to Dowdy by a mere forty-one votes.

If Dowdy wanted to secure his renomination in 1964, he needed a victory, and only five months after his primary scare, he came close to acquiring one. On October 3, ten days before Congress adjourned for the midterm elections, a House-Senate conference committee approved Dowdy's obscenity bill, which then headed to President Kennedy's desk.

Less than a week before Dowdy returned to Texas for his reelection campaign, he learned Kennedy planned to veto the bill. So he went on the offensive, initiating two other battles. First, he announced his opposition to the use of federal marshals in the racial integration of the University of Mississippi. The following day, three days before the Eighty-Eighth Congress adjourned, Dowdy began his second battle, introducing a bill against the Mattachine Society of Washington.

"Of course, no action will be possible on the proposal until next session, but I wanted to put my colleagues on notice that action was impending," he explained to a constituent.

Kennedy indeed vetoed Dowdy's obscenity bill, citing "grave" constitutional concerns, but the congressman's district forgave him for the failure. Dowdy won reelection with 87 percent of the vote.

The next year, Dowdy reintroduced two bills. First, in May, his obscenity bill, and in July, H.R. 5990, a piece of legislation that would, as he promised a constituent, "take the wind out of the sails of the so-called Mattachine Society of homosexuals." This time, with such an easy target, the congressman knew he would win.

As one Texan politician described Dowdy's strategy, "He's against Negroes and queers—and down here that's unbeatable."

ON THE MORNING of August 8, Kameny awoke to thrilling news. Despite *The Washington Post*'s refusal to publish his advertisements, on page fourteen, below an editorial protesting a Virginia judge's injunction against African American civil rights demonstrations, lay an editorial titled "Unpopular Causes."

"A House District subcommittee is to hold a hearing this morning on an unfortunate bill introduced by Rep. Dowdy of Texas," it began. The paper quoted the Society's "unconventional" constitution (the *Post*, Kameny learned, had kept his materials from the mail-writing campaign) and explained that the group did not "promote homosexual activity."

Not only did Dowdy's bill violate the First Amendment by requiring government approval of an educational organization's morality, *Post* readers learned, but by revoking the Society's license, it operated as a bill of attainder, or a law that punishes without a trial, something forbidden by the Constitution.

The editorial did not mention Kameny's name. So although he had a new ally, Kameny walked into the Cannon House Office Building—the same imposing structure in which he had met Congressman Nix—still awaiting his imminent exposure.

At 10:25 a.m., the hearing began. While Kameny sat in the audience, seven congressmen faced the room: four Democrats, including Dowdy, and three Republicans. "The first witness on our list," began Dowdy, "is Robert F. Kneipp, Esq., from the Corporation Counsel's Office."

Kneipp sat at the witness table with a copy of a letter signed by the District commissioners, the three appointed officials who governed Washington. Next to him sat another representative of the District of Columbia's government, C. T. Nottingham, the license and permits official who had angrily spoken to the *Star* about his inability to block the licensing of the Society.

"The Commissioners," said Kneipp, "object to the enactment of H.R. 5990 for two principal reasons." First, to require that *all* charitable organizations promoted the District's "health, welfare, and the morals" would impose "a heavy and difficult burden" on Washington's government, he began.

The District of Columbia, to Dowdy's dismay, was defending the homosexuals. Kneipp explained that the bill would require the District to hold hearings for *each* charitable organization in the District, more than 163 per year.

"You are permitting them to solicit contributions for the promotion of perversions and immorality," accused Dowdy.

Kneipp explained that the Society, in fact, had an educational purpose. He then explained the second problem with the bill: its explicit revocation of the Society's charitable solicitation license. The commissioners had "grave" concerns about the bill's constitutionality, echoing President Kennedy's own word choice in his veto of Dowdy's obscenity bill.

C. T. Nottingham, the superintendent of licenses and permits, testified that he, for one, wanted the right to deny licenses. As the law stood, he would be forced to grant licenses to Communists, too.

"As far as I know, all of the security risks that have deserted the United States and gone over to the Communists have been these homosexuals," said Dowdy.

"I have another descriptive term that I don't think would be polite to use," added Nottingham.

"**WE HAVE THE PRESIDENT** of the Mattachine Society here who wanted to testify," said Dowdy. "You are not going to have long now, Kameny, if you will come around we will hear what you have to say."

Kameny sat at the witness table. "Mr. Chairman, members of the committee, I appear here today as president of the Mattachine Society of Washington," he began, reading from his meticulously organized, three-part statement.

"Let me interrupt you. You have been a governmental employee, have you?"

"I have been, at one time."

The delegitimization of the witness began. What branch of the government? Were you discharged as a security risk? Why were you discharged? Did you admit immoral conduct? Do you admit immoral conduct now?

"I do not."

"Very well. Proceed."

Kameny explained that his society was a civil liberties organization, not a social one. It attempted to change laws and educate the public. It was entirely legal. The definition of "revolting," as Dowdy had put it, was a matter of personal taste—like different types of food.

"Let me ask a question," said Dowdy. "Isn't it true that your society is devoted to convincing the public that homosexuality or homosexual activity is normal, moral, and worthy of equal status with heterosexual marriage when two homosexuals form an indefinite time alliance for homosexual purposes?"

Kameny had not considered gay marriage before, and the Society did not even have a position in it. "If two individuals wish to enter into such a relationship it is certainly their right to do so as they choose; yes, sir."

"And you want that in spite of everything that is in the laws of the various States and the Bible, both the Old and New Testaments? You oppose all of that?"

"We will refer to those matters in a moment. We do—"

A bell rang.

"We are going to have to adjourn," said Dowdy. "That is the second bell." They would reconvene the next morning.

"D.C. FIGHTS BILL CUTTING HELP FOR HOMOSEXUALS," announced *The Washington Evening Star.*

In the article's penultimate paragraph, the *Star* printed his name. "The president of the Mattachine Society of Washington, Franklin E. Kameny, began to read a prepared statement but was cut off when the subcommittee was forced to close the hearing after the House went into session," it reported.

Kameny, unemployed and still closeted back home, had been exposed.

AT 10:10 THE NEXT MORNING, Kameny resumed his seat at the witness table.

"Now, do you consider yourselves to be a separate race from ordinary people?" began Dowdy.

No, said Kameny.

Well, the American Constitution only protects citizens from discrimination based on race, creed, color, or previous servitude, said Dowdy. "So it must be a religion that you are practicing."

"No."

"A perversion in pornography, and so on."

"We have nothing to do with pornography or obscenity."

"I have looked at some of your books. Actually, I consider them pornography."

"Well, the Postmaster General allows them to go through the mail," said Kameny. He introduced a copy of the Society's *Gazette.*

Dowdy then commenced a line of questioning based on information that could have only come from one of two individuals: J. Edgar Hoover or Deputy Chief Blick of the Metropolitan Police. Indeed, at that very moment, Blick sat in the audience, listening to Kameny's every word.

"Are you part of this national Mattachine Society?" asked Dowdy.

Kameny explained the national Mattachine no longer existed.

"Let me ask you this. Didn't the Philadelphia branch, and the New York branch, come down here to help you organize this last time?"

"Members of"—Kameny stumbled—"two members of the New York group came down for our—we didn't exist as a group then."

Is your Society the same that was active in Washington in 1958? Why did you dissolve the first group? Why was it dissolved?

His strategy became clearer. "Do you have a charter from that society to use its name?"

"No, we do not."

"Then what is your legal authority to use a copyrighted and registered organizational name?"

Within the first few minutes of the hearing, the congressman had already identified the import of the Society's naming dispute with Hal Call. Dowdy wanted something to destroy the homosexual organization. With a revoked license, he could return to Texas in a few weeks with a tangible victory, at last, over immorality.

"Their name is not copyrighted or registered," said Kameny.

"They didn't register it out in California?" asked Dowdy, skeptically, before moving on to his next topic: blackmail.

"I have here one of the *Mattachine Reviews*, which is published, I take it, by your national society," said Dowdy. He held up a copy of an April 1960 edition.

"I emphasize they are not part of us nor we of them," said Kameny.

Dowdy pointed to an article titled "Never Pay Blackmail" and began reading from it. "'Between paying him and killing him, then killing him is the wiser alternative.' Do you teach that, also?"

"We tell our members to go to the police department where any matter of blackmailing will be properly handled," said Kameny. "I have yet to meet the homosexual who has actually been subject to blackmail."

"How large a chapter do you have?"

"It is smaller than we would like it to be, growing rapidly. We have approximately 30 to 40 people," said Kameny.

"And, of course, it is your purpose that you would like to be larger," said Dowdy, "to promote your perversion so that you have more people in your—"

Kameny explained it was impossible to recruit homosexuals. There were, in fact, heterosexuals in the MSW, too.

"Can you name one of them?" asked Dowdy.

"I am sorry. I am strictly prohibited by the constitution of my society from disclosing any identities."

"Mr. Chairman, will you yield at that point?" interjected Congressman Frank Horton, a Republican from New York. Is the Mattachine a secret organization?

Kameny asked for a definition of the word *secret*.

Do you refuse to answer the question? asked Horton. Are the members known?

"No, they are not."

How often does it meet? Are the meetings public? asked Horton.

How does the Mattachine publicize the meetings? asked Dowdy. How many invitations does it send? Only fifty? But don't you claim to have a quarter of a million homosexuals in Washington? Of those, how many work for the government?

What exactly *is* a homosexual? asked Horton.

What is the name of the Society's publication? asked Dowdy. The *Gazette*? Is it monthly? Sent through the mail? What is its circulation?

Only 250 subscribers, answered Kameny.

What about a homosexual cure? interjected Congressman B. F. Sisk of California.

"We certainly would not oppose it," said Kameny. But homosexuals are not sick, and the Society does not concern itself with a cure. "The NAACP does not try to see what can be done about bleaching the Negro."

"You do condone the homosexual act, do you not?" asked Congressman Horton.

"We feel that it should not be made criminal."

"You do condone the homosexual act, do you not?"

"My statement stands. We feel that it should not be a matter of criminal law."

How does the Society publicize? Radio? Have you put these programs on the air? Do you have a treasury? A treasurer? Who is the treasurer? ("Earl Goldring," answered Kameny.) Do you have a secretary? What is his name? ("Bruce Schuyler.") Do you have a vice president? Who is he? ("Ellen Keene.") Is she a homosexual? ("To the best of my knowledge, she is not.") Do you have any other officers? ("No, we do not.") How much money do you have in your treasury? How many contributions has the Society received?

"Some twenty or so," said Kameny.

The number surprised Horton. Only thirty to forty members and twenty contributions *total*? Does the Society even have a bank? A checking account? A savings account? Stock?

"When we are wealthy enough to have stocks we will consider ourselves most fortunate," replied Kameny.

"If you are completely open and aboveboard, why must the membership be secret?" asked Dowdy.

"An unemployed and starving member of the Mattachine Society or of any other group is a rather ineffective member," said Kameny. "As long as people are thrown out of jobs irrationally for being homosexuals we are not going knowingly to lead to their losing their jobs."

"Could the witness answer now, do you refuse to make available to the District a list of your membership?" asked Horton.

Yes, said Kameny, he refused. Horton asked again, and then a third time.

"With all due respect, speaking for the society, your request must be declined." Kameny quoted from the Society's constitution, which allowed for only two copies of a membership list. He had provided all necessary information about the Society's officers, including their names, to the District's licenses office.

Dowdy smelled blood. "Is that their true names?"

"That is their names," said Nottingham, the District licensing official.

"I am asking the witness here, is that their true names?"

"Those are the names with which they are registered in the society," said Kameny. "I know of no others, as president of the society."

"So that isn't their names. You have got dummies registered with the District as officers of your society?"

Kameny repeated himself.

"And that is not their true names?"

"They may or they may not be."

"You are unwilling to tell us that that is their true names, that those are their true names?"

Dowdy asked four more times, and each time, Kameny refused to answer.

"But as far as you know they may be aliases or completely fictitious?" asked Congressman George Huddleston Jr., a Democrat from Alabama.

"It is not impossible but I have no reason to think that they were adopted for purposes of fraud."

Kameny had said the word himself. "I think the very filing of the application for charter with fictitious names on it ipso facto is fraud," said Huddleston. He read from the Charitable Solicitation Act, which punished false or fraudulent statements with a jail sentence. "I think maybe this ought to be looked into," said Huddleston.

"With full knowledge that they are fictitious names," added Dowdy.

A man rose from the audience. He handed Kameny a note, from which Kameny read. "I might point out that it is not unlawful to adopt a pseudonym in the District of Columbia," said the witness.

"Who was that that just gave you that note?" asked Dowdy.

"I do not know," said Kameny.

"Identify yourself," said Dowdy to the man.

"My name is Monroe Freedman, sir. I am the next witness."

"Are you a member of this society?"

"I am not here in any capacity other than as chairman of the Freedom of Communications Committee of the National Capital Area Civil Liberties Union."

Twice more Freedman refused to answer whether he was a member of the Society.

"What is your occupation?"

"I am a member of the bar and a law professor at George Washington University."

"Can we assume from your refusal to answer that you are a member of this society?"

"You may assume anything you choose, sir. I refuse to answer the question. My private associations are not germane to this proceeding."

"We will get to you after we get through with this witness," said

Dowdy. He turned back to Kameny. "Now you said some of the members of your society were not homosexuals. Name me one of them."

Three times, Kameny refused to answer. Upon the fourth repetition of Dowdy's question, the witness made an admission. "We have one of our members in the audience who is not a homosexual."

A woman stood.

"What is your name?"

"My name is Ellen Keene."

"Are you the secretary?"

"No, I am not."

"The vice president?"

"Yes."

"Are you a homosexual?"

"No," said Keene.

Kameny interrupted. "I am afraid that is not relevant to H.R. 5990."

Dowdy turned to Kameny. "Have you ever performed the homosexual act?"

Kameny refused to answer.

At this point, Dowdy, the former district attorney, began prosecuting Kameny for fraud. "You signed the application, did you not, to the District of Columbia for the registration under the Charitable Solicitation Act?"

"I did."

You listed Ellen Keene, Bruce Schuyler, and Earl Goldring?

Yes.

Horton jumped in. You read the application? You signed it? You swore the facts to be true? Before a notary public? On July 29, 1963? Did you know the name "Bruce Schuyler" was a "pseudonym or it was an adopted name or it was not the real name of the individual involved?"

"I have not granted yet that any of those statements you made are true," said Kameny.

But you *did* know a Bruce Schuyler? Where does he live? Is he in the phone directory? Is he married? Again, where does Schuyler live? Is it an adopted name? What about Earl Goldring and the other officers? Do they have other names?

"You have asked me this some five times and I have indicated as many times that I cannot disclose this," said Kameny.

"But you do of your own knowledge know they have other names?"

"For the sixth time, no. I cannot answer the question."

Horton continued probing him for information on Earl Goldring, and almost endlessly, on everything else, including the Society's meetings, its newsletter, its educational activities, its finances, and its fund-raising activities.

"As the president of this organization what is your definition of the homosexual act?" asked Horton.

Kameny explained it included *any* act between two members of the same sex. "It even includes shaking hands, as far as that goes."

"What is another act, homosexual act, in your definition?"

Two men dancing together, said Kameny.

Horton wanted another (dancing), another (kissing), and another.

"Any of a large, possible, number of varieties of genital contact and activity," answered Kameny, at last.

Horton wanted to know the different varieties. He wanted to know exactly what Kameny wanted legalized, he explained.

He asked Kameny to read from the sodomy law.

"Every person who shall be convicted of taking into his or her mouth or anus the sexual organ of any other person or animal," read Kameny, "shall be convicted of having carnal copulation in an opening of the body except sexual parts."

This is the law, asked Horton, that you want repealed? This is what your Society is educating the public about? You are in favor of *bestiality*?

Kameny said he wanted to omit discussion of animals, but Horton— and then Huddleston, too—repeatedly pressed him on the issue.

Kameny fell into the trap. He admitted he was not personally opposed to bestiality. It was a "matter of an individual preference."

"In other words, then, it doesn't shock your morals," said Huddleston.

"No," answered Kameny. He tried to steer the discussion back to homosexuality, returning to his statement. "Those who find homosexuality revolting are free not to engage in it. But under our system, this does not require that all conform," he read.

Dowdy interrupted. Is the Society an "amoral organization?"

Kameny admitted his Society had not taken a "specific stand" on the morality of homosexuality. "I will state for myself," he added, "that I feel that homosexuality whether by mere inclination or by overt act is not only not immoral but when homosexual acts—when performed voluntarily by consenting adults—are moral in a positive and real sense and are good and are right and are desirable both for the individuals performing them and for the society around them."

Dowdy referred Kameny to the Scripture. "The Lord was emphatic in regard to the sin of abomination," he explained. "He excused neither the active nor the passive participant in the homosexual act in these words: 'If a man also lie with mankind as he lieth with a woman both of them have committed an abomination. They shall surely be put to death. Their blood shall be upon them.' I cannot see how you can interpret that as you have, or that there could even be a difference of opinion in regard to what that says."

"I will point out," responded Kameny, "that the eating of cooked food, the wearing of clothes, and the meeting of this committee this morning in a cooled room on a hot summer day can all be considered to be in violation of the laws of nature." Illinois recently repealed its sodomy laws, he added. The Mattachine Society wanted the same done in the District of Columbia.

What about bestiality? asked Huddleston.

What about homosexual activity among more than two people? asked Horton. Should gay *group* sex be legal, too?

"This is an interesting point," conceded Kameny. "My organization has taken no particular stand on that."

"I mean, you are making a recommendation to a committee of Congress now for proposed legislation," chided Horton. If sodomy were legal, would there be a limit to the number of people allowed to engage in it?

"As long as there is no public disorder involved," answered Kameny.

"All right," said Horton. "Now, how many people do you believe could be involved?"

Kameny explained it was impossible to set a specific limit.

"Would you permit ten?" asked Horton, repeatedly. What about twenty?

"Certainly. You can have a dinner party for two and have a dinner party for fifty as long as it is carried out in an orderly fashion. I fail to see a difference."

Kameny's comparison reminded Congressman Dowdy of something he had read. "I saw a so-called newsletter," he said, "put out by some bunch of perverts which mentioned the fact that somebody was gaining weight on a dict of semen. Is that the kind of dinner party you are talking about?"

"No, it is not," said Kameny. "I was referring to an ordinary, conventional dinner party of the type that you or Mr. Horton might attend."

"We don't go to the kind of parties you are talking about," retorted Dowdy.

The questioning continued ad nauseam, designed entirely to embarrass and entrap the homosexual witness. Dowdy interrogated Kameny about his positions on gay marriage and prostitution, fornication and adultery, incest and national security, the origin of the term *homophile* and Kameny's attempts to compare homosexuals to the African American minority. "Are you trying to pull them down to your moral level or trying to elevate yourselves?"

In total, Kameny testified for three and a half hours. As Dowdy concluded his questioning, he turned back to Nottingham. "You will then, Mr. Nottingham, check to see if these are real persons or fictitious names?"

"Yes, I will."

"And look into the suspension of this license."

"I certainly will look at it and apply those penalties that are available, yes."

Dowdy still wanted to interrogate the other members of the MSW executive board. "Can you get in touch with them as soon as you are excused, and ask them if they will be here at 2:30 to testify on this matter?"

Kameny promised he would try to reach them.

For one hour, he could breathe.

"MR. KAMENY, will you come around, please," began Dowdy after the recess. "Were you able to contact either one of your—"

"No, I was not," interrupted Kameny. "Not on this short notice."

Dowdy had one last question. "Are you the same Franklin Edward Kameny who was involved in a lawsuit that was cited in the *Federal Reporter*, second series, volume 282 at page 823, in which you were suing Wilbur M. Brucker, Secretary of the Army?"

"And the Civil Service Commissioners, yes," said Kameny. "That went to the Supreme Court."

"What were the charges brought against you which were involved in this lawsuit?"

"The charges were two: one was alleged, but unproven, falsification of form 57." Dowdy, it seemed, wanted to establish that Kameny had a history of falsifying government documents.

"What was the false statement you made in form 57 as alleged?"

"I don't feel that this information is relevant to H.R. 5990."

"We can get it of course," said Dowdy.

"Of course you can."

Dowdy instead decided to try his luck with the woman in the room, the vice president of the Mattachine Society of Washington, "Mrs. Ellen Keene."

"We will call Mrs. Keene next," he said.

"Will Mrs. Keene please come around," said Huddleston.

Her real name, according to surviving members of the Society, was Eleanor McCormick. Some remembered her as a heterosexual wife of a Mattachine member. Others remembered her as a lesbian, the widow of a gay man who had committed suicide.

"Are you married?" began Congressman Horton. "What is your husband's name?"

"I can't tell you," said Keene. "I do not wish to tell you."

"Where do you live, Mrs. Keene?"

"I do not wish to tell you."

Keene confirmed she had been the Society's vice president since February.

Horton wanted details: how many members were at the election?

Twenty people, she guessed.

"Where was the meeting held?"

A private home, she answered.

"Were these men and women or was it mostly men?"

"There was at least one other woman there at the time."

Keene had learned about the Society from friends, she explained. Meetings lasted approximately two hours.

What do they *do* at the meetings? asked Horton.

"We discuss what problems there are to be faced with respect to—"

"Let's talk about one of those problems. Give us specifically one of those problems."

Employment discrimination against homosexuals, answered Keene.

"Are refreshments served at these meetings?"

"Usually at the end we have punch and cookies, 15 minutes or so."

"Have you ever seen or participated in any homosexual acts either during the course of these meetings or subsequent thereto in the private homes?" asked Horton. Do you discuss homosexual acts?

"No. I might say that my observation has been that any attempt to discuss it would be very much frowned on."

Is Keene your real name? asked Dowdy.

She refused to answer.

Are you a member of the Daughters of the Bilitis?

No, said Keene.

Where do you work? Where does your husband work? Is he a member?

"No."

"Does he know you are a member of the society?"

"Yes."

"He approves of it?"

"I assume so, yes."

Dowdy dismissed her and called the next witness, Professor Monroe H. Freedman.

FREEDMAN INTRODUCED HIMSELF as a professor at George Washington University Law School. An alumnus of Harvard College and Harvard Law School, he chaired the NCACLU's freedom of communications committee. He refused to disclose whether he was a member of the Society, but yes, he admitted, Freedman was his true name.

No, he was not an attorney for the Society. He only represented the

NCACLU, which had a mission to protect the Constitution of the United States. "I might say, sir, that the bill is rather remarkable in the amount of unconstitutionality that it has been [*sic*] managed to pack into two short paragraphs," Freedman added.

First, he explained, the NCACLU opposed H.R. 5990's "unconstitutionally vague qualification on freedom of speech." The issue, he told the congressmen, was "not whether we agree or disagree with Mr. Kameny or the Mattachine Society, but whether we are going to interfere with their expressions to the public."

He treated Dowdy like a law student. If H.R. 5990 were passed, asked Freedman, would it be legal to raise money for mothers of illegitimate children? "Is this a moral thing to do?"

"That is a charitable purpose," answered Dowdy.

"I see," said the professor. "But is it moral? It is a vague standard."

Second, the bill was "as clear a case of a bill of attainder and denial of equal protection of the laws and denial of due process of law as one could conceive of."

"It is not that at all," answered Dowdy, now on the defensive. "It is just removing a permit, not a license, a permit that they have to—"

"But what is the justification for doing this?" asked Freedman

"They are collecting funds for the promotion of an illegal enterprise," answered Dowdy.

It is the right of any American, explained Freedman, "to propagandize any crazy idea he has." The protection of morality was no excuse: "There are so many things that are immoral that we should not draw legislative lines around; the most deadly of the sins that we know, hatred, lust, greed, covetousness, we do not have legislation against those things."

Horton wanted a specific recommendation. What should Congress do instead?

"My recommendation to you, sir, is to tear up this bill and forget about it."

DOWDY WANTED to conclude the hearing.

"You say you teach law at Georgetown University?" he asked Freedman.

"George Washington University."

"Are they aware of your activities in behalf of this Mattachine Society?"

"Not to my knowledge; I am sure they will be shortly."

Dowdy turned to Kameny, still sitting in the audience, to ask for a list of those who had donated to the MSW. Kameny refused.

"They are concerned," explained Freedman, "about the kind of harassment that many of them apparently have already suffered and which, I think, was implicit in your own question to me, Does my university know that I am testifying here on behalf of the Mattachine Society? Why would you ask such a question—"

"I wanted to know," interrupted Dowdy.

"—if it were not implicit in the question that this might do me some professional harm?"

"I just wanted to know if they knew or approved of it," said Dowdy.

"I think the record will be quite clear," said Freedman.

"I think you are sensitive to the question," added Congressman Horton.

"I am sensitive on the issue; yes. I certainly am, because I do not think that one should suffer, nor do I expect to, frankly, in his job, because of his ideas that have nothing to do with his performance of his job."

"I believe that is all," said Dowdy. He turned back to Kameny. "Mr. Kameny, you are going to let us know after you have contacted your two officers?" He wanted them to testify, too.

"Yes," said Kameny.

At 4:20 p.m., Dowdy recessed his subcommittee's hearing, to reconvene at the congressman's pleasure.

And that was that.

ON AUGUST 15, Dowdy wrote to the president of the District of Columbia board of commissioners. "This organization of homosexuals is a 'secret' society," he wrote. The officers' names were "obviously fictitious." The organization's president, moreover, had been dismissed from his job at the Department of Defense because of a "homosexual morals offense committed in a public rest-room in San Francisco."

"I and other members of our Subcommittee feel strongly that the

dignity of the District of Columbia should not be loaned to such a group."
Dowdy formally requested a permanent revocation of the Society's
permit.

The congressman may have had help determining that the names
were indeed false, since another man in the federal government, one
deeply concerned with the moral decline of America, was simultaneously
investigating the Society.

The same day Kameny began his testimony, J. Edgar Hoover received
a copy of a Society document titled "Discrimination Against the Employment of Homosexuals." And as the hearings continued, the FBI
combed Washington's newspapers for news about the Mattachine. It
clipped two articles for its Mattachine file, including "Group Defends
Fund Collecting Role" from the *Daily News* and "Bill on Homosexuals
Held Unconstitutional" from the *Star*.

Four days after Kameny finished testifying, an FBI special agent interviewed a confidential informant about two individuals—censors later
redacted their names—connected to the Mattachine.

That same day, at 11:00 a.m., the special agent delivered an envelope
to the Identification Division of the FBI. It contained the constitution of
the Mattachine Society of Washington.

In less than five hours, by 3:45 p.m., the Identification Division uncovered three latent fingerprints on the Society's envelope and constitution. The analysts then cross-referenced those prints with the two names.

The next day, Hoover himself wrote to the Washington Field Office
with the results of the analysis. The fingerprints did *not* match those of
anyone with those two names.

In all likelihood, the names were "Bruce Schuyler" and "Earl Goldring,"
and the informant was Warren Scarberry.

The District of Columbia's licensing office began investigating the
Society, attempting to determine whether its president, in applying for a
charitable solicitation license, had committed fraud.

John Vernard Dowdy

10.

THE MARCH

On August 13, the same day J. Edgar Hoover reviewed the fingerprint analysis of the homosexual constitution, Senator Strom Thurmond of South Carolina stood on the floor of the United States Senate.

Thurmond, a vehement segregationist, had information that would wreak havoc upon—and perhaps even collapse—the Black freedom movement's upcoming March on Washington, scheduled for August 28. Armed with ample evidence, the senator announced that the chief architect of the March was a sexual pervert.

Bayard Rustin had many strikes against his name: Black, gay, socialist, pacifist. In 1944, while the Quaker-influenced Pennsylvanian was in jail for refusing to fight in World War II, a prison psychiatrist described him as "a classical picture of a constitutional homo—the invert type, the high voice, the extravagant mannerisms, the tremendous conceit, the general unmanliness."

Over the next two decades, authorities arrested Rustin more than twenty times for his nonviolent, Gandhi-inspired activism, but one of his arrests haunted him for the rest of his life, ensuring that his name remained in the shadows of history.

On January 21, 1953, Rustin spoke about African decolonialization in Pasadena, California, on behalf of the Fellowship of Reconciliation (FOR), a peace organization. By then, he was on the path to becoming an American Gandhi. In 1947, he had codirected the country's first Freedom Ride, designed to test the Supreme Court's desegregation of interstate transportation. By 1953, he was speaking to captive audiences across the United States.

After Rustin's Pasadena speech, at 3:00 a.m. that night, police officers arrested Rustin for performing oral sex on two men in the back of a car. A judge sentenced him to sixty days in jail.

One gay FOR member, upon hearing the news, wrote to Harry Hay's Los Angeles Mattachine Society. Was there any way he could be saved?

The Mattachine could do nothing, and Rustin served the full sixty days.

Civil rights leaders began to see him as a liability. When Rosa Parks's bus boycott began in Montgomery, Alabama, FOR officials warned that Rustin's involvement would "set back the whole cause."

Undaunted, in February 1956, Rustin drove to Montgomery. When he arrived, the young Martin Luther King Jr. had not entirely embraced nonviolence. Floodlights surrounded his house, which had been bombed by white terrorists only days earlier. Armed guards protected his home, which also contained loaded guns.

Civil rights leaders must give up all arms, Rustin explained to King, if they were to inspire nonviolence among their followers, exposing a regime that relied upon arrests, bombs, and fear.

Montgomery's reporters became suspicious of Rustin, who spoke with a peculiar accent and claimed to be a foreign reporter. King had him smuggled out of Montgomery in the back of a car, and the movement attempted to hide the secret of the gay pacifist.

But because of Rustin, who continued strategizing for the minister from New York, the guns and floodlights disappeared. King became America's beacon of nonviolent protest.

In December 1962, as the centennial of the Emancipation Proclamation approached, Rustin and labor leader A. Philip Randolph developed a plan for a March on Washington for Jobs and Freedom. Rustin wrote the official proposal for the March and decided its message, "the economic subordination of the American Negro."

Other organizations, including the NAACP and King's Southern Christian Leadership Conference (SCLC), faced a choice. They could sponsor the homosexual-planned event or be excluded from a historic moment altogether.

In May, King's SCLC became a March cosponsor, and that summer, Senator Thurmond learned the secret of the March. He had proof, courtesy of J. Edgar Hoover. Standing before the Senate, Thurmond pointed to Rustin's Pasadena police record and declared that "Mr. March-on-Washington himself" had been guilty of "sex perversion."

Rustin prepared for the worst. At a press conference that day, A. Philip Randolph stood before reporters with a prepared statement. "I speak for the combined Negro leadership," he began, "in voicing my complete confidence in Bayard Rustin's character."

"My task is to see that 100,000 people called to Washington reach Washington, they make their protest non-violently and that they return home safely," explained Rustin himself.

No fewer than two hundred thousand marchers attended Rustin's March.

Frank Kameny marched with them. He organized a group of seven Mattachine members, including Jack Nichols, who knew homosexual marches would come, but not yet. For now, the homosexuals marched only for another minority, dreaming that perhaps, someday, they would march for themselves.

The marchers decided against carrying signs that announced their presence as part of a homosexual organization. "We reasoned that it would be impolite," recalled Nichols.

RANDY WICKER'S THREATENED MARCH had never materialized. But at 7:55 p.m. on August 30, two days after the March on Washington, the FBI's Washington Field Office received an anonymous phone call. The caller, according to a memo for J. Edgar Hoover, was a "male, apparently a Caucasian, who indicated he had received information that homosexuals may picket the Department of Justice, Friday, 9/6/63. He inferred they would protest that the FBI was discriminating against homosexuals."

The caller refused to identify himself or provide the names of any participants.

A special agent rushed to confirm the information, and four days later, the Bureau heard from a "reliable" informant. The informant, likely Warren Scarberry, indicated that the anonymous caller had faulty information. Approximately one hundred MSNY members indeed planned to protest in Washington, he said, but they planned to target not the Department of

Justice, but the White House. Yes, said the informant, the MSW planned to join them.

Hoover warned Robert Kennedy of the homosexuals' plans and forwarded a copy of the information to the White House.

The Secret Service again prepared itself for Randy Wicker and the country's first homosexual demonstration.

AFTER THE DOWDY HEARINGS, Kameny felt emboldened. The "hostile" subcommittee, wrote Kameny to other homophile organizations, had "attempted, without success, to badger, browbeat, embarrass, and intimidate the witnesses." Even if the bill passed, Kameny knew the NCACLU would sue, and the Society would have the *Post* as an ally.

The Dowdy affair pushed Kameny into the public eye, but it also taught him the importance of performing *respectable* homosexuality, a tactic he increasingly began to enforce. The August edition of *ONE* included a pencil sketch of a sailor, sitting on a toilet, penis exposed, and the MSW made its opinion known. After Kameny and Keene had "done much to dispel some of the popular misconceptions of homosexuals," complained Bruce Scott on behalf of the Society, "now along comes your magazine with a drawing which Congressman Dowdy can wave at his colleagues in the House of Representatives and shout: 'What did I tell you? These unnatural people are not interested in educating others except to their own unnatural lusts!'"

As for picketing, Kameny's experiences with Dowdy had also taught him, as he explained to Wicker, that "the off-the-cuff-ness and spontaneity must go." If homosexuals *were* to picket, the event needed to be perfectly choreographed. "The general advisability of this must be considered, first. Then EVERY step and EVERY detail must be planned and thought out," he wrote.

Thus, while Wicker schemed, Kameny focused on planning the inaugural ECHO conference, to be held in Philadelphia over Labor Day weekend.

Only days before the opening gavel, the Drake Hotel tried to cancel. The manager explained that he did not want people talking about sex in his hotel. After ECHO officials threatened to sue for breach of contract, however, the hotel capitulated.

The organizers, including Kameny in Washington and Clark Polak in Philadelphia, meticulously planned the publicity efforts of the conference. They informed the Philadelphia newspapers and printed hundreds of invitations for members of the American Psychological Association, which was holding its annual meeting in the same hotel.

On Friday evening, the ECHO organizers held a press conference and cocktail reception for members of the media. Not a single newspaper appeared, and only one freelance reporter attended.

"He loved us all," reported Barbara Gittings's ECHO correspondent in *The Ladder*. "He even stayed up late and helped to fold the convention programs. It was during this interlude that a delegate from Washington Mattachine made his classic remark: 'Now you can say that you participated in a homosexual brochure-folding orgy!'"

"Deadly respectability was the keynote," the reporter would later write. "Everyone was conservatively dressed, the men mostly in Ivy League fashion, the women in dresses or suits. No bottled-in-blond men, limp wrists or lisping here, thank you."

Donald Webster Cory, author of the seminal *The Homosexual in America*, spoke first on the matter of image. Yes, there had been progress, he told the audience of one hundred delegates. But why were so few homosexuals involved in the movement? Attachment to the image of a respectable homosexual resulted in "puritanism," warned Cory.

In the next speech, R. E. L. Masters acknowledged that effeminate homosexuals were likely to be "seriously disturbed" and harmful to the movement. But, as he concluded, "Can your movement retain its good conscience when it rejects those who are rejected by every other quarter?"

The conference only became more uncomfortable. A minister defended the church's evaluation of homosexuality as a sin, and a panel discussed the problem of homosexual psychologists.

The Saturday-night banquet featured keynote speaker Dr. Albert Ellis, a psychologist and author of *Sex Without Guilt*. The ballroom filled with delegates, their guests, and curious psychologists from the APA conference. The hotel set up extra tables to accommodate the attendees.

As Ellis began speaking, it became clear that the conference organizers had made a grave mistake. The "fixed or exclusive homosexual," he told the audience, "is wrong, meaning inefficient, self-defeating and emotionally disturbed."

Though the homosexual had the right to be wrong, he was "fetishistically deviated," Ellis continued. A "well-adjusted" homosexual did not exist. Homosexuals were "short range hedonists; and also take the easy way in their non-sexual life." Most homosexuals were "borderline or outright psychotics," and only suicidal patients were sicker than the homosexual.

For an "interminable" hour, as *The Ladder* later put it, the audience—including Frank Kameny—sat in silence. At the end of his speech, a lesbian attendee rose. "Any homosexual who would come to you for treatment, Dr. Ellis, would *have* to be a psychopath," she said.

The applause was deafening.

The next day, Kameny spoke about "The Homosexual and the United States Government." He detailed his Society's battles against the Pentagon and the CSC, but at the end of his talk, the delegates all wanted to hear the same story. What about *Dowdy?*

Kameny regaled the audience with the tale of his confrontation with the congressman.

"Dear Mr. Dowdy," wrote Kameny on September 6. "In view of the interest indicated by you and your Subcommittee in the activities of the Mattachine Society of Washington, we enclose, herewith, a copy of the program of our recent convention in Philadelphia."

Four days later, Kameny received a notice from the District of Columbia's Department of Licenses and Inspections. The Society's application, the District alleged, "contains false information; to wit, the names of the vice president, secretary, and treasurer." It ordered the MSW to show cause why its certificate of registration should not be revoked.

For the second time, Kameny faced an allegation of falsifying a government document. The first time, he had lost his career. Now, if the District stripped the Society of its ability to raise funds, Kameny would lose his organization, all he had left.

AFTER NCACLU ATTORNEY Monroe Freedman testified at the Dowdy hearing, he donated one dollar to the MSW. He requested the creation of a John V. Dowdy charitable fund to support "the psychiatric treatment of Members of Congress who have pronounced lewd, lascivious, and obscene tendencies."

That same day, Kameny received the notice of the District's proposal to revoke his Society's charitable solicitation license. Monroe Freedman, a sympathetic NCACLU lawyer who understood the intricacies of the Society's battle, became the Mattachine Society of Washington's first attorney.

The District's Department of Licenses and Inspections scheduled a hearing for September 24, and as Freedman began investigating, he found a loophole. The Charitable Solicitation Act only required an organization to acquire a certificate if it raised $1,500 or more in any given year, yet the Society had raised only $125 in 1962.

Freedman met with Robert Kneipp at the Corporation Counsel's office to confirm his theory. Did the homosexuals even *need* a license?

"Mattachine Unit Loses Its Permit to Solicit Funds," announced the *Star* on October 4. The Society "surrendered" its license, and the District canceled the hearing.

One week later, board of commissioners president Walter Tobriner wrote to Congressman Dowdy. The homosexuals were indeed exempt from the charitable solicitation law, he advised, but the District was now preparing amendments to *remove* that exemption and "make it as difficult as possible for secret organizations such as the Mattachine Society to be registered under the act and the regulations."

The District scheduled a public hearing on these amendments for November 8, and twenty-seven-year-old attorney Zona Hostetler, arguing on behalf of the NCACLU, defended the homosexuals. The District's proposed amendments were prepared for "no other apparent reason than to harass the Mattachine Society," she argued. The new District regulations represented a targeted infringement of the Society's First Amendment rights and were no less unconstitutional than Dowdy's bill.

The Society then waited for the final decisions of the District commissioners and the House Committee on the District of Columbia. But for now, under current regulations, the Society was safe.

Monroe Freedman charged two hundred dollars for his services. To pay that bill, the Society initiated a fund-raising drive. "Perhaps you have a friend, a relative, or a business acquaintance who is a homosexual, or perhaps you are one yourself," said its fund-raising letter. "Our goal is $1499.99."

SINCE THE ANONYMOUS PHONE CALL in August, the Bureau had heard nothing about the homosexuals' upcoming march in Washington. On October 18, an FBI employee noticed an article on page twenty-eight of *The New York Times*. "Homosexual Group Asks Understanding," it reported. The name of a public relations director who spoke before 350 students at City College, according to the article, looked familiar: Randolfe Wicker. The employee underlined his name.

Four days later, the New York Field Office updated Hoover on Wicker's proposed march. The Bureau had contacted "confidential sources familiar with certain phases of homosexual activities within the Greater New York City area," and they knew nothing about the demonstration.

According to another informant, "the idea of the society members marching to Washington never got out of the idea stage, and was merely brought up at a meeting by one of the members because of the publicity being given to the Negro march on Washington at that time." Wicker had failed to mobilize the New York Mattachine.

Yet the Bureau had evidence that Kameny, though unwilling to picket, was finally following Wicker's media-focused lead. On October 24, Hoover learned that Kameny planned to appear on the Steve Allison radio show.

"This is the first time that a Washington radio station has devoted a full program to the controversial subject of homosexuality," announced a Society press release. He made these appearances using his own name.

"It is with very sincere regret that we have been forced to withdraw our offer of employment," wrote one company to Kameny on November 11. The Atomic Energy Commission, explained the personnel manager, "refused to authorize our hiring you as a Geophysicist."

President Kennedy was shot eleven days later.

On December 15, less than a week after the Bureau completed its five-volume report on the assassination—containing "totally inconclusive" information, Earl Warren complained—the FBI acquired a copy of the MSW's fund-raising letter.

As summarized in a memorandum circulated among at least ten top FBI officials, the Society "exerted pressure on the Civil Service Commission to discontinue its policy of excluding homosexuals from government."

J. Edgar Hoover noticed that line, buried in the middle of the memorandum, underlined it, and scrawled beneath it: "Has Civil Service done this?"

In reply, an FBI official summarized a year-old letter from CSC chairman John W. Macy Jr. to "Bruce Schuyler." Homosexuals were "not suitable for appointment" to the Civil Service, Macy had written.

"Someone should re-check with CSC," Hoover responded on December 23.

Officials rushed to confirm the policy with the CSC. Within twenty-four hours, a CSC official confirmed that the "CSC has, in fact, been under considerable pressure from captioned society during recent months, but has not changed its basic policy excluding all homosexuals from Government service."

Hoover received the reassuring news on Christmas Eve, 1963. "They should stick to it," he wrote.

BRUCE SCOTT HAD moved back to Chicago, where he was unemployed, living with his sister, and becoming increasingly depressed. "Since I arrived here, my being completely dependent upon others, when I used to be so independent and able to do for others, has really begun to weigh on me, and the temptation to take the easiest way out and so cease being a burden, is becoming greater and greater," he wrote Kameny. "My court case, and the fact that I would be letting a lot of people down by not fighting it through, is about all that is causing me to hesitate."

On January 15, 1964, Judge George L. Hart of the district court announced his decision in *Scott v. Macy*. "Homosexual conduct is immoral under present mores of our society and abhorrent to the majority of the people," Hart ruled. "Maybe it shouldn't be, but it is." Judge Hart agreed with the U.S. attorney: because homosexuals repulsed their heterosexual coworkers, they thus harmed the "efficiency of the service."

Despite David Carliner's arguments—that under the government's standard, "an office full of white supremacists could force the firing of a Negro"—Scott had lost the first round.

The next week, in an editorial titled "Misplaced Morality," *The Washington Post* criticized Judge Hart's decision. Yes, homosexuality was "undoubtedly" abhorrent, but some homosexuals led "thoroughly useful, successful and apparently normal lives," wrote the paper. "To deny such persons all chance to work for their government is wholly arbitrary and unjust."

"The editorial in *The Washington Post* has made me feel that the case has now been worthwhile, if it accomplishes nothing further," said Scott.

Kameny, meanwhile, wrote his own letter to Judge Hart, urging his "most careful re-consideration."

IN JANUARY 1964, after six months without a job, Kameny found employment. An electronics company in Virginia hired him as a physicist. Kameny caught up on his rent payments and paid off his commercial debt. With less stress, he started gardening. Rosebushes, vegetables, and flowers appeared at his house on Cathedral Avenue.

"It is good also that you have income once again," wrote Bruce Scott. "Just do not endanger it by taking too much time for Mattachine."

But Kameny grew preoccupied with the MSW's plans to host that year's ECHO conference, and after the debacle of Dr. Ellis, the MSW president was determined to shape it into an event that emphasized the morality and encouraged the militancy of the homosexual. On February 8, at an ECHO planning meeting, Kameny suggested a theme for the conference: "Homosexuality: Civil Liberties and Social Rights." The delegates unanimously approved his motion.

Kameny also amplified his efforts to teach the heterosexual public that homosexuals were neither sick nor immoral. The previous December, Kameny had delivered his first public speech, a lecture to a Jewish audience at Temple Sinai's Sunday discussion series. In March 1964, he contacted *LIFE* magazine. "At the suggestion of Mr. Randolfe Wicker, of the Homosexual League of New York, we are sending, herewith, copies of various items put out by, or in connection with the Mattachine Society of Washington," he wrote.

In April, he traveled to Chicago to appear on the television show *Off the Cuff*, in a panel organized by Wicker and featuring a priest, a psychiatrist, and Del Shearer, the president of the DOB's Chicago chapter. Homosexuals are not sick, explained Kameny and Shearer.

"Yes, it is possible to be a happy homosexual!" said Shearer.

"Homosexual acts on the part of consenting adults are moral in a positive sense, and are good and are right for the individual and for society," added Kameny.

Their claims sparked resistance. In May, *The New York Times* carried an article on its front page, "Deviants Proud, Doctors Report." The New York Academy of Medicine had released a report in response to homosexuals' new claims that "their deviancy is 'a desirable, noble, preferable way of life,'" reported the *Times*. As the academy's report concluded, "homosexuality is indeed an illness."

The *LIFE* feature, "Homosexuality in America," appeared in June. It featured dark, blurred photographs of gay men in the shadows. Yes, the gay world was "sad and often sordid," but some homosexuals, it admitted, were "discarding their furtive ways and openly admitting, even flaunting, their deviation."

Kameny himself had been arguing against the concept of homosexuality as a sickness since early 1963. That October, after the nightmare of Dr. Ellis, Society member Jack Nichols had written to the MSW's executive board to urge an official policy statement on the sickness question.

Homosexuals needed "bolstering and self-confidence," wrote Nichols. "When members of that community ask us: Are we sick?—and when we answer: 'SORRY—WE DO NOT TAKE A POSITION ON THAT SUBJECT,' we are going to be able to do very little in the way of making their self-image rise."

How could homosexuals ever expect to follow in the footsteps of the Black freedom movement, marching in the streets of Washington, if they thought they were sick? "The Question: AM I SICK? is not an academic drawing-room inquiry," concluded Nichols. "It is an agonizing cry."

Kameny pressed their case in the March 1964 edition of the Society's *Gazette*. "If nothing else was made plain at our recent ECHO convention, the abysmally poor quality and lack of validity of virtually the entire body of psychiatric and psychological research on this question became clearly evident."

Homosexuals needed to make one fact abundantly clear, he argued. They were *not* sick. And if evidence suggested otherwise? "I shall give serious thought to leaving the movement. I do not anticipate that I shall ever need to do so."

If homosexuals were not sick, still others labeled them sinners. After Kameny's Temple Sinai speech, Jack Nichols initiated his own religious outreach effort. Nichols, a Unitarian, sent copies of Donald Webster Cory's *The Homosexual in America* to seven Unitarian ministers in the Washington area, urging them to learn about the plight of the homosexual minority.

"The happy result occurred yesterday morning," Nichols wrote Cory in February. "The first clergyman in the Washington area, Reverend Robert J. Lewis, preached the first words ever heard from a Washington pulpit on the subject of homosexuality. He was standing 100% on your book."

In two subsequent discussion groups led by Kameny and Nichols, the River Road Unitarian Universalist Congregation in Bethesda discussed how it might "erase prejudice against homosexuals," as Nichols described it.

"The churches may prove to be strong allies," he predicted.

By April, the Mattachine Society of Washington had created a new Committee on Religious Concerns, and Jack Nichols became its first chairman.

On July 22, 1964, Kameny appeared as the MSNY's one hundredth monthly speaker, delivering a lecture titled "Civil Liberties: A Progress Report."

He outlined his organization's strategy, which was still unique within the movement. While the DOB emphasized social services for its members and the MSNY emphasized the education of the public, the MSW emphasized civil liberties and social action.

"Any movement which relies solely upon an intellectually-directed program of information and education, no matter how extensive, to change well-entrenched, emotionally-based attitudes, is doomed to disappointment," he told his audience. "The Negro tried for 90 years to achieve his purposes by a program of information and education," and his accomplishments during that time were "nothing compared to those of the past 10 years, when he tried a vigorous civil liberties, social action approach and gained his goals thereby."

Federal policies and public opinion interacted "strongly and circularly," and homosexuals needed to attack them both: through publicity and lawsuits, outreach to religious leaders, and alliances with attorneys. Homosexuality was no sickness. It was not immoral. The movement needed to embrace those facts if it intended to defeat the forces of discrimination.

"We are dealing with an opposition which manifests itself," Kameny explained, "as a ruthless, unscrupulous foe who will give no quarter and to whom any standards of fair play are meaningless."

Homosexuals needed to fight accordingly.

TWO WEEKS LATER, Kameny received a phone call from the FBI.

The homosexuals had upset J. Edgar Hoover. On July 16, 1964, the FBI director received a copy of the spring 1964 edition of the Society's *Gazette*, which chronicled the fight against Congressman Dowdy and Kameny's statement on the sickness question.

"The above Society has apparently added the Director to its mailing list to receive its 'Gazette,' a newsletter for homosexuals," wrote a Bureau official. "This material is disgusting and offensive and it is believed a vigorous objection to the addition of the Director to its mailing list should be made."

He made a heavy-handed recommendation that "two Agents from the Crime Records Division contact the president of this group to advise him in strong terms that Mr. Hoover objects to receiving this material and his name should immediately be removed from their mailing list."

"Right," said Hoover.

Next to the director's approval, in a handwritten note undetected by FBI censors, the Bureau identified its target. "Kameny, 5020 Cathedral Ave."

At first, the agents could not find him. Kameny was away from Washington that weekend, delivering his MSNY speech. At last, on August 6, a special agent reached Kameny by telephone. The FBI hoped to speak with him, the agent explained. Could an agent or two come to visit?

No, answered Kameny. As a matter of principle, he did not allow federal investigators or FBI agents into his home. However, he was available during his lunch hour at 12:30 p.m. the next day, and he would be happy to speak to the Bureau at its headquarters in the Department of Justice. ("The FBI doesn't like to be reminded they work for the Justice Department," he later explained.)

Kameny arrived at the FBI offices with *Gazette* editor Robert Belanger—or "Robert King"—five minutes late. The two homosexuals sat across from two FBI agents.

A memorandum, circulated among five top Bureau officials, summarized the meeting. "Kameny and King were informed that the presence of Mr. Hoover's name on their mailing list is considered offensive and they were requested to delete his name from this list," it said.

Kameny and Belanger explained that *other* officials besides Hoover received the newsletter, including President Kennedy, the attorney general, and cabinet members. The Society merely hoped to influence them and promote sympathy for the homosexual minority.

But Congress makes the laws and the attorney general determines Department of Justice policies, responded the special agents. "Therefore, there would appear to be no need to forward such material to the FBI."

The Mattachine Society of Washington had a right to communicate with the government officials of its choice, responded Kameny.

That said, added Belanger, they did not wish to "antagonize" officials if they "strongly resented" the material. The homosexuals promised to bring the Bureau's request before the Society's board of directors, and after only eight minutes, the meeting, "conducted in a calm and dispassionate manner," ended.

On the way out, Belanger offered an olive branch. "King mentioned that the Mattachine Society would be holding a convention in Washington, D.C., in October and, somewhat facetiously, added that Mr. Hoover is most cordially invited to attend," reported the FBI memorandum.

"This invitation was emphatically and immediately declined."

IN LATE JULY, Kameny learned that the House would vote imminently on Dowdy's bill, and he turned to the NCACLU. "ACLU Asks Solicitation Bill's Defeat," announced the *Post*. "It is no business of the Government to pass judgment on the objectives of organizations of private citizens," explained David Carliner, the NCACLU chairman.

On August 11, Congressman Dowdy stood on the floor of the House of Representatives. "Mr. Speaker, by direction of the Committee on the District of Columbia, I call up the bill (H.R. 5990) to amend the District of Columbia Charitable Solicitation Act to require certain findings before the issuance of a solicitation permit thereunder, and for other purposes."

Dowdy had made a last-minute change to the bill. The legislation no longer specifically targeted the MSW, and it now required organizations to prove that they would "benefit or assist in promoting the public health or welfare and will not offend the public morals." It simply allowed the commissioners to revoke a certificate—or, if interpreted properly, the exemption—of an immoral organization. The congressman had resolved his legislation's chief problems, and the bill, despite its ambiguous language, became passable.

William F. Ryan of New York, the congressman who had pledged his support of the Mattachine two years earlier, rose to speak. "Mr. Speaker," he began, "I oppose this bill with or without the amendment. The issue really before the House is whether or not the District of Columbia Commissioners are to be set up as judges of public morality in the District of Columbia."

Congressman Gene Snyder, a Republican from Kentucky, interrupted Ryan. "Mr. Speaker, will the gentleman yield?"

"I yield."

"Mr. Speaker, I want to see if I understand the gentleman correctly," said Snyder. "Do I understand that the gentleman condones what this Mattachine Society has been doing?"

"The purpose of that society is not before the House at all. If the committee wants to legislate against a particular group, let it bring such legislation before the House."

"Does the gentleman refuse to say that he does not condone what they are doing?"

"That is not the issue," said Ryan.

No, explained a Ryan ally, the opponents of the bill did not condone the Mattachine Society of Washington.

"I would suggest that the Members who are opposing this bill, and being misled by these queer ideas should get a copy of the hearings and read it," responded Dowdy. "This Kameny fellow claims ten percent of the employees in all the departments of Government are qualified for membership in his society. I had statements made to me that nothing could or would be done about this problem because of the power of the homosexuals in Washington."

The debate lasted over an hour, and afterward, the members of Congress decided whether to vote on behalf of morality or on behalf of the supposedly powerful homosexual lobby of Washington.

One by one, the House of Representatives voted on Dowdy's bill. Congressmen Ryan and Nix voted against it. Congressman Dowdy and three hundred other representatives, however, voted in favor. With a final vote of 301–81, Dowdy's bill won in a landslide.

If the bill passed the Senate, and if President Lyndon Johnson, another Democrat from Texas, signed it, H.R. 5990 would become law, potentially stripping the Society of its exemption and outlawing its ability to raise any funds for its activities. If the District of Columbia enforced Dowdy's bill as per his wishes, the MSW would cease to exist.

But the following day, buried in the Washington *Daily News*'s extensive coverage of the vote, a single line provided immeasurable relief to Kameny and the members of his Society. "The bill now goes to the Senate District Committee where no further action is anticipated," the paper reported. Congress was scheduled to adjourn on October 3, and the District of Columbia committees still had other business to prioritize above a bill with dubious effectiveness and constitutionality. Plus, Dowdy could still return home and claim that he had passed a bill against homosexuals in the House of Representatives.

"The whole thing so far seems to have had been nothing but publicity," wrote one MSW member, summarizing Dowdy's crusade. "Anyway, the bill has not become law and is dead, dead, dead."

IN NEW YORK, Randy Wicker had grown sick of the Mattachine. Despite his planning, his urging, and his long record of publicity success, the MSNY refused to join him in a picketing demonstration at the White House—or *anywhere*—for homosexual rights. The organization was stagnating, he realized. Worst of all, New York's homosexuals at large were unwilling to join the movement. They remained complacent in their underground world of parks, restrooms, and Mafia-controlled gay bars, which banned him from distributing MSNY literature. Their patrons mockingly referred to him as "Miss Mattachine."

Wicker walked away from the movement and resolved to fight on behalf of the entire sexual revolution, instead. In early 1964, Wicker joined the League for Sexual Freedom, a new organization formed by Jefferson Poland, a twenty-one-year-old "free love" advocate.

At weekly meetings in Greenwich Village, the dozen-member league discussed the meaning and limits of sexual freedom: pornography, homosexuality, prostitution, bestiality, pedophilia. By March, to Wicker's delight, the League was marching. Its members marched against obscenity statutes and, later that summer, outside the Women's House of Detention, calling for the legalization of sex work. "Most of the demonstrators were bearded young men," reported the *Daily News*.

The League did not "want to get in a rut" by continuing to picket for the same issue, so at each of its meetings, the League asked: Which facet of American puritanism would they attack next?

On the League for Sexual Freedom's advisory committee was Dr. Franklin E. Kameny, a Wicker recruit. Though Kameny remained unwilling to organize his own MSW march, he did not oppose the idea per se. Undertaken by others with less to lose, a march might work, he reasoned. He even developed an idea for the League's next target.

As 1964 progressed, Kameny had noticed a problem faced by more and more young homosexuals, one reminiscent of his own dilemma two decades earlier. The conflict in Vietnam was increasingly ensnaring America, and 16,263 U.S. military advisors were already deployed there by the end of 1963. The military, as it evaluated men for service, confronted a new generation of Americans who, unlike the seventeen-year-old Kameny, were willing to admit their homosexuality to the United States government.

As Kameny's public appearances multiplied, and as he became known as the government authority within the homophile movement, homosexual service members started turning to him. "I hope that you may have some time to discuss the situation with me in the hopes that I may be guided to the reinstatement of my commission or at the very least, an honorable discharge," wrote one member of the air force, referred to Kameny by *ONE*, in May 1964.

In early 1964, Kameny suggested that the League for Sexual Freedom picket the institution responsible for making the "dirty deal" that threw him into the battlefields of World War II: the United States Army.

"The boy who is in charge of the League for Sexual Freedom called to-day and he wants to picket," Wicker wrote Kameny in the summer of 1964. "I suggested we picket the Army as you suggested." Wicker needed more information about army policies for the picket, tentatively scheduled for September. "PLEASE SEND ME ALL THIS INFORMATION. . . . SUCINCTLY [*sic*] STATED AND WELL DOCUMENTED," he wrote.

Kameny drafted letters for Wicker to send to the secretaries of defense and the army, plus a flyer that protested the "outright bigotry" of the army.

Wicker adopted Kameny's letter to the army secretary, adding a warning of future demonstrations in Times Square, and almost all of the flyer, adding his own large, handwritten title, THE ARMY VERSUS SEX.

On September 16, Wicker announced his plans at an MSNY meeting. That coming Saturday, the League would picket the army's downtown induction center on Whitehall Street.

For most MSNY members, it was a terrifying, absurd prospect. Never before had a homophile organization demonstrated in America, and for good reason. If the press arrived, picketers risked their faces appearing on television or their names in newspapers, to be scanned and recorded by the FBI. Many MSNY members were not out to their families—Wicker and Kameny had not told their mothers, yet—and certainly not out to their employers. If the federal government, the very target of the League's demonstration, learned of the demonstrators' identities, they would face a lifetime ban from federal employment. To march as a homosexual, like a tearoom arrest, meant risking permanent exposure as a sexual deviant.

On that rainy afternoon of Saturday, September 19, only three other MSNY members joined Wicker at the Army Induction Center: Craig Rodwell—a twenty-three-year-old, wholesome looking former ballet dancer—and two young lesbian members of the MSNY and DOB, Renee Cafiero and Nancy Garden. Wicker brought his lover, Peter Ogren, and then there were the League's members: music critic Jack Diether, LSF president Jefferson Poland, and his girlfriend, who brought her infant child. The total number of attendees at America's first homosexual picket, child included, was nine.

The cameras and reporters never came. On a Saturday, the induction center was closed, and only one guard stood in the door, observing the homosexuals as they silently marched in a circle. The men wore suits and the women wore skirts "to look as normal as possible," recalled Nancy Garden.

ARMY INVADES SEXUAL PRIVACY, said the sign held in one hand by Randy Wicker, while his other hand clutched a sheaf of Kameny's leaflets. HOMOSEXUALS DIED FOR U.S. TOO, said Cafiero's sign. LOVE AND LET LOVE, said Jack Diether's.

Afterward, the wet marchers warmed themselves in a Bickford's cafeteria. "We felt a little let down because it had been so uneventful," remembered Garden.

"Dr. Kameny—Demonstration was not successful," wrote Jefferson Poland later that month. "Rain, about 7 pickets, no press."

Despite the gloom, the demonstrators felt relieved, even triumphant; they had marched without harassment or injury. For the first time in history, a group of homosexuals had picketed against the U.S. federal government and emerged unscathed.

Wicker resolved to plan another demonstration, a larger one.

IN OCTOBER 1964, Gail Johnson, a straight woman from Boston, served as the MSW's secretary. Only twenty-one years old, Johnson had approached Kameny and Nichols during their February question-and-answer session at the River Road Unitarian church in Bethesda.

I believe homosexuals deserve equal treatment, she told them. I'm willing to work toward that end. Does your Mattachine Society allow heterosexuals as members?

Equal rights for straight folks, you mean? Nichols laughed.

Johnson attended every subsequent Society meeting, and after she was elected secretary, it became her duty to send the Society's official response to J. Edgar Hoover, who was still waiting to be removed from the homosexual mailing list.

The executive board had made a perceptive observation about the FBI affair. Nowhere in the *Gazette* did it list Kameny's phone number, his address, or even his name. Yet, somehow, the special agents knew to contact him.

"The conclusion is thus unavoidable that the F.B.I. maintains some sort of file on the Mattachine Society of Washington," wrote Johnson, on October 1, to one of the special agents who had interviewed Kameny and Belanger.

The homosexuals were willing to make a deal. "We will remove Mr. Hoover's name from our list," promised Johnson, "if we can have a letter, signed by Mr. Hoover personally, assuring us (a) that any files on the Mattachine Society of Washington, maintained by the Federal Bureau of Investigation, have been destroyed; and (b) that all references to The Mattachine Society of Washington in any individual citizen's file or other record maintained by the Federal Bureau of Investigation have been deleted, and (c) that this situation will remain so."

To whom at the FBI, asked Johnson, could the Society send its materials, instead?

"This letter is a blatant attempt to open a controversy with the Bureau," observed an FBI official in an internal memorandum. "Any further contact with them will be exploited to the Bureau's disadvantage. It is apparent they are attempting to involve government officials in their program for recognition and any further contact by the Bureau will only serve their ulterior motives."

The official made two recommendations: first, that Gail Johnson's letter not be acknowledged, and second, that the FBI ignore all future correspondence from the Mattachine Society.

"I concur," wrote Hoover.

BARBARA GITTINGS DID NOT PLAN to attend the ECHO 1964 convention until she learned that Frank Kameny would criticize the DOB philosophy in a debate. He intended to argue against the lesbian organization's focus on enlightening the homosexual, instead advocating for direct action via lobbying and lawsuits. "Wonderful!" wrote Gittings. "The movement needs to do some soul-searching."

Despite Gittings's enthusiasm, the DOB board remained suspicious of the male, Mattachine-dominated ECHO conference. Now, a man wanted to use the event, partially funded with DOB dues, to attack their organization's mission. "A public debate would seem to me nothing short of idiotic," wrote DOB board member Agatha Mathys. "I don't want any outsider telling me how to run my business."

The debate stayed on the program, especially since the organizers faced larger problems. First, three separate Washington hotels canceled on the homosexuals—the last one, the Manger-Hamilton, only ten days before the conference. Miraculously, the MSW found a hotel available and willing to host the homophile conference, the Sheraton-Park Hotel, a mammoth, historic Colonial Revival structure in Northwest Washington. Meanwhile, attorney Monroe Freedman threatened to sue the Manger-Hamilton Hotel, negotiations commenced, and ECHO walked away with a five-hundred-dollar out-of-court settlement.

Next came the neo-Nazis. They may have learned about the conference from an ad in *The Village Voice*. "Homosexuality: Social Rights and Civil Liberties," it announced, promising speakers like David Carliner of the NCACLU, Rabbi Eugene Lipman of Washington's Temple Sinai, and Franklin E. Kameny, PhD. The ad provided a phone number.

Followers of George Lincoln Rockwell, modern-day Hitler supporter and founder of the American Nazi Party, picked up the phone. Nazis would be attending the conference, they warned. The MSW notified the police, and the ECHO organizers developed an emergency plan in case the Nazis actually appeared.

On the morning of Friday, October 9, 1964, delegates began arriving. EAST COAST HEMOPHILE ORGANIZATIONS, announced the signs in the elevators, posted by a confused Sheraton employee. Randy Wicker could not attend, but for the delegates, he sent hundreds of lavender lapel buttons proclaiming EQUALITY FOR HOMOSEXUALS (Kameny detested their unprofessional color. "People will see these and say 'well, what more can you expect from a bunch of fairies,'" he admonished Wicker).

The attendees included Robert Graham, a handsome man in a tweed jacket. An MSW member recognized him as part of the Metropolitan Police Department's Morals Division. News of the officer's presence spread. "Why was he there, if not to memorize faces?" asked *The Ladder*. Despite his presence, the attendees, numbering less than a hundred, seemed electrified. "There's a different mood," one attendee noted. Indeed, the MSW had orchestrated a militant event. Robert Belanger, speaking as "Robert King," opened the conference with a call to arms. "I stand here in the fear that someone I know from the world of the heterosexual may walk in that door and I will be discovered," said the bespectacled, dark-haired ECHO coordinator, a thirty-three-year-old originally from Massachusetts.

"We want to live in a world where this constant fear of discovery does not exist because it does not matter, and this world will come," Belanger declared.

"We are asking for the rights, and all the rights, afforded the heterosexual. We are still in the asking stage. We will soon reach the demanding stage," he warned. "A dormant army is beginning to stir."

Julian Hodges, the newly elected MSNY president, inspired by Kameny's speech earlier that summer, offered political strategy. "Let us learn a lesson from the Negro civil rights movement," he said. "Since they started involving themselves in the practical workings of everyday politics, we have seen vividly and dramatically what can be done by a movement seeking fulfillment of rights.

"Are we really so naive as to believe that we can exist, and continue to exist, unless we involve ourselves in politics?"

Next came a parade of NCACLU attorneys with a message very different from that of the psychiatrists at the 1963 conference. Homosexuals, said the lawyers, needed to fight for themselves. Monroe Freedman spoke first, chronicling the Dowdy saga and applauding Kameny's defense of his Society. The congressman was the "world's leading authority" on homosexual publications, he joked. "He has a large stack—I understand a closetful."

At 3:15 p.m., Kameny moderated a legal panel featuring six attorneys from the NCACLU, including its chairman, David Carliner. The attorneys encouraged the audience to attack discrimination not just through the courts, but through the public, too. "To lay the basis for getting favorable decisions, a lot has to be done in the country to affect the climate," they concluded.

At that night's banquet, DOB's Marge McCann, the conference's mistress of ceremonies, opened the evening with awards, including an official citation for the public official who had most helped the homophile movement in the year 1964, the Honorable John Dowdy of Texas. By introducing H.R. 5990, Dowdy had "provided the homosexual community with the use of the Congress of the United States as a forum in which to plead its case," she announced. For that, the homosexual community was grateful.

The next afternoon, Dr. Frank Kameny debated Dr. Kurt Konietzko, a Philadelphia sociologist, about whether homosexuals should focus on educating the public or changing the laws. The two men quickly agreed on a major principle, however: homosexuals should prioritize legal battles.

Yes, the movement also needed to educate the country about homosexuality, conceded Kameny, but the teachers should be the homosexuals themselves. "We had better start educating the public to the fact that when they want reliable information on homosexuals and homosexuality, they come not to the psychiatrists, not to the ministers, and not to all the rest—they come to us." The audience applauded.

By 3:00 p.m. Sunday, the last day of the conference, there had been no neo-Nazis, no Vice Squad arrests. Jack Nichols had organized a discussion among religious leaders, including Rabbi Lipman of Temple Sinai, Reverend Lewis of River Road Unitarian church, and four other ministers.

The audience of one hundred people, including visitors from a Methodist Church convention also in town, waited for the panel to begin. Three men entered the hotel and approached the door to the meeting room. One of them, a young, blond, well-dressed man, carried a massive, pink, gift-wrapped box labeled QUEER CONVENTION.

The man walked into the meeting room, and a DOB member flipped the switch of her tape recorder.

"Would somebody call Rabbi Lipman, please?" asked the man, speaking in a Southern accent. "Is Rabbi Lipman in the house?"

The room fell silent. As the Nazi approached the religious panel, the leaders of ECHO's four homosexual organizations—MSW, MSNY, Janus Society, and DOB—initiated their emergency plan. Unaware of the man's intentions or the box's contents, they stood, linked arms, and created a human barricade between the intruder and the religious leaders.

"I've got twenty-four quarts of Vaseline here to deliver to Rabbi Eugene Lipman," said the man. "I believe all you queers will be able to make use of it."

More of the audience joined the line of homosexuals, which inched forward. The man pushed against them. "Would you quit pushing me, you queers," he said.

"You must either pay an admission or get out," warned Robert Belanger, the conference coordinator.

"Sir, you are trespassing," said Father John F. Harvey, a Catholic theologian.

"You are being asked to leave," added Frank Kameny.

During the scuffle, the Nazi stepped on the foot of Shirley Willer, the president of the DOB's New York chapter. "Sir, you're stepping on my foot. Would you please move," she told him.

"I believe you're trying to kick me, aren't you, lesbian?" he said, with an eerie smile.

Willer repeated herself, louder.

At that moment, Officer Graham of Washington's Metropolitan Police finally appeared. He arrested the Nazi. The room could breathe, and later, even joke about the incident. "Knowing Shirley," Jack Nichols later said of the brusque DOB leader, "I had visions of the DOB chasing Nazis down Connecticut Avenue."

As Officer Graham led the intruder out of the room, the audience clapped, unaware that their Vice Squad savior had provoked the largest gay scandal in American history, a saga that had begun only three days earlier.

Renee Cafiero at the Whitehall Induction Center, September 19, 1964

11

THE BOUQUET

On the evening of Wednesday, October 7, 1964, while the MSW distributed press releases for its upcoming ECHO conference, *Newsweek* magazine celebrated the opening of its new twelfth-floor headquarters, one block from the White House. Hosted by publisher Katharine Graham, the glamorous party welcomed six members of President Johnson's cabinet, numerous foreign diplomats, and other top administration officials.

The guest list included Walter Jenkins, a forty-six-year-old White House staffer with a flushed face and gray hair. Catholic, married with six children, and from rural Texas, Jenkins had been at President Johnson's side for twenty-five years. By 1964, he was Johnson's most reliable aide and confidant, an indefatigable assistant in the president's aggressive politics, secretive personal life, and dubious finances. "If Lyndon Johnson owed everything to one human being other than Lady Bird, he owed it to Walter Jenkins," recalled Johnson aide Bill Moyers. The last staffer to leave the White House each night, Jenkins knew the administration's most classified secrets.

Three weeks before the 1964 presidential election, Jenkins's boss was about to win. "Nothing, it had seemed, could conceivably stand in the way of Democrat Lyndon Johnson's inexorable march back to the White House," wrote *TIME*.

Jenkins arrived at the *Newsweek* party at 7:15 p.m. After meeting his wife there, Jenkins had three or four drinks. At 8:00 p.m., he brought his wife downstairs to a car, which took her to another party. Jenkins told her he would return to the *Newsweek* office for one more drink before finishing work at the White House.

Near 8:30 p.m., Jenkins left the party, turned the corner, and entered the YMCA. He walked downstairs to the men's restroom, a dark, nine-by-eleven-foot space with the stench of disinfectant and stale tobacco. The restroom had two toilet stalls and four narrow steps that led to the door of a shower room, which had been padlocked for a decade.

Officer Robert Graham, the Morals Division officer assigned to monitor the ECHO conference that weekend, had the key to the padlock. When Jenkins entered the restroom, Graham was hiding in the abandoned shower room, watching from one of two peepholes in the door. A second Morals Division officer stood next to him.

The officers saw Jenkins encounter another man, an older Hungarian immigrant. Without saying a word, Jenkins entered a stall with him. The officers' elevated position allowed them to look over the partition between the two rooms, and watch.

"Who was supposed to have been workin' on who?" an intrigued President Johnson, in a recorded telephone conversation, later asked a top FBI official.

"Walter was supposed to be the active one, Mr. President. In other words, this 62-year-old man was letting Walter have it and Walter was taking it."

Officer Graham and his colleague arrested the two men. At 10:10 p.m., Jenkins paid fifty dollars in bond, left jail, and worked at the White House until midnight.

One week later, on October 14, Jenkins received the first call from a *Star* reporter, who had received an anonymous tip. The White House aide called Abe Fortas, President Johnson's longtime attorney and fixer. "A terrible thing has happened," he told Fortas.

Jenkins arrived, distraught and incoherent, at Fortas's home. Jenkins had destroyed the president, he told Fortas. He threatened to shoot himself. Fortas took him to George Washington University Hospital for "high blood pressure and nervous exhaustion," and the hospital put the heavily sedated Jenkins on twenty-four-hour suicide watch.

At 8:09 p.m., United Press International broke the story, and newspapers flocked to print the unprecedented scandal.

Walter Jenkins became the country's most infamous sexual deviant. By the election, according to one poll, 87 percent of Americans knew his name.

Johnson requested and received Jenkins's resignation on the fifteenth, and he ordered J. Edgar Hoover to conduct an investigation. Was Jenkins entrapped by Communists (or Republicans)? Was he a victim of blackmail? Had Jenkins, and Johnson by employing him, threatened national security?

Television stations described the affair as "sad and sordid," the same two adjectives used by *LIFE* magazine to describe the gay underground in its "Homosexuality in America" article, published less than four months earlier. "Mr. Jenkins is now in the care of his physician and his many friends will join in praying for his early recovery," announced the president.

Johnson's opponent, Senator Barry Goldwater, refused to add to Jenkins's "private sorrow" by campaigning on the scandal. "As for Mr. Jenkins and his family, there can be only compassion," wrote *The New York Times*.

To the media's surprise, America shrugged its shoulders about the possibility of a sick homosexual in the White House. "The voters we talked to," concluded columnists Rowland Evans and Robert Novak, "simply didn't care."

As the election approached, the FBI concluded a mammoth nine-day investigation, which involved dozens of special agents and interviews with more than five hundred people connected to Jenkins, including peers from his Texas primary school. The YMCA arrest had not been an isolated incident, the Bureau learned. Jenkins had first engaged in homosexual activity as a child. Even worse, he had been arrested in the same YMCA bathroom in 1959, two years before the FBI cleared him for his position at the White House.

The information put Hoover in an uncomfortable position. As the man responsible for the day-to-day operation of the gay purges, he could maintain that Jenkins had, in fact, represented a security risk, an admission that would suggest his own Bureau had failed to detect him. Alternatively, if he exonerated Jenkins, Hoover would imply that a homosexual did not *necessarily* represent a security risk.

On October 22, the Bureau concluded that Jenkins had not "compromised the security or interests of the United States in any manner." Jenkins may have been a homosexual, but he was not a threat.

"The FBI report was by any accounting a curious one," reported *TIME* on October 30, only four days before Johnson beat Goldwater in one of the largest electoral landslides in American history. "It seemed all the more curious in the light of an episode that took place the very day President Johnson ordered the investigation."

Soon after Walter Jenkins arrived at George Washington University Hospital, while guarded by private attendants and held behind a DO NOT DISTURB sign, the disgraced White House staffer received a bouquet of mixed fall flowers.

It arrived with a card signed "J. Edgar Hoover and Associates."

"THE JENKINS AFFAIR has had marvelous results here," wrote MSNY board member Dick Leitsch at the end of October. The scandal had increased the organization's membership and its authority; newspapers now turned to homosexuals for their own analysis of the incident. The affair, added Leitsch, "certainly has pointed out to any number of New Yorkers the stupidity of the hiring policies in the government."

After the FBI released its report, Kameny wrote Washington's three major newspapers to highlight Jenkins's "clean bill of health" on security matters. "If there is anyone in this country who is now totally invulnerable to threats of blackmail and other improper coercion, and who obviously fully deserves a security clearance at the highest level, it is Walter Jenkins," he wrote. Kameny called for President Johnson to reappoint Jenkins to his post, and to do so with haste.

Moreover, what were police officers doing in public restrooms? In attempting to catch homosexuals, did the police invade the privacy of straight toilet users, too? In the aftermath of the scandal, for the first time, the Washington press began an extensive discussion of the topic. On December 7, the *Star* reported on the use of two-way mirrors and

0

video cameras in an Ohio public restroom. A few days later, dozens of papers across the country reported on the postmaster general's decision to remove peepholes in five thousand post office restrooms. They were, he said, "an unfortunate invasion of privacy."

On December 23, the NCACLU, likely spurred by Kameny, released a "STATEMENT ON JENKINS CASE" that decried the surveillance of restrooms. "D.C. Asked to Bar Use of Police Peepholes," reported the *Post*. It marked only the beginning of that paper's newfound fascination with Washington's gay world, for the Jenkins affair had given readers only a tantalizing glimpse.

WHILE KAMENY BASKED in the publicity sparked by Walter Jenkins, Barbara Gittings embraced lesbian pride. The 1964 ECHO conference had inspired her, and she resolved to use her editorship of the staid, eight-year-old *Ladder* to promote Kameny's brand of homosexual militancy.

Gittings quit her job, turned full-time to *The Ladder*, and began articulating lesbian defiance. *Ladder* covers had always featured drawn illustrations or silhouettes of unidentifiable women, but Gittings's November 1964 issue featured a photograph of Ger van Braam, a lesbian from Indonesia, on its cover. "Tell the world that we are happy being ourselves and no distorted convention-victims anymore," wrote van Braam.

"I do think our world is getting to be 'more gay,'" wrote a Mississippi reader the next month. "I am a lesbian and rather proud of it. I believe it's right and wonderful."

In New York, meanwhile, Randy Wicker could not completely tear himself from the homophile movement. On December 2, he and three other picketers stationed themselves at entrances to the lecture hall at Cooper Union in Greenwich Village, where a psychiatrist was giving a lecture titled "Homosexuality, A Disease."

WE REQUEST 10 MINUTES REBUTTAL TIME, said their signs.

The lecture's organizers gave Wicker his ten minutes, and from a microphone in the audience, he attacked the concept of homosexuality as an illness. The "so-called experts" disagreed about the theory, often contradicting one another, he argued. Plus, studies almost always relied upon "unhappy, ill-adjusted homosexuals who were patients undergoing therapy." What about the well-adjusted homosexual?

"Applause for the challenger topped applause for the lecturer, who appeared stunned for a moment by the reaction of the audience," reported *The Ladder*.

"I just tore them apart," remembered Wicker fifty years later.

The day after Christmas, Wicker wrote Kameny with a piece of news. "It might upset you," he warned. Wicker had adopted yet another "way-out cause," one that would "no doubt cause a convulsion from the bottom of the homophile movement to the very top. However, I am sticking to my guns as an individual and as a radical."

REPEAL MARIHUANA PROHIBITION!!! said the flyers, distributed by Wicker on December 27. As the public relations director for LeMar, Legalize Marijuana, Wicker distributed literature while twenty-two other protesters marched around Tompkins Square.

"For three hours in a misty drizzle the pickets marched with placards reading, 'Smoke pot, it's cheaper and healthier than liquor,'" reported *The New York Times*. "The poet Allen Ginsberg led the group for a while in a Hindu chant that he describes as a magical invocation to Shiva, the god of yoga and marijuana."

The Village Voice mentioned Wicker's Mattachine activism and described the buttons on his chest: LET'S LEGALIZE POT, I'M FOR SEXUAL FREEDOM, LEGALIZE NARCOTICS FOR ADDICTS, and REPLACE J. EDGAR HOOVER.

Ronald Brass, upon reading the article, grew appalled by the soiling of the Mattachine name. "I've reached the conclusion," he told Kameny, "that Randy Wicker is an idiot."

IN JANUARY OF EACH YEAR, the MSW elected its president. Since the beginning, Kameny had faced challengers. In 1963, Bruce Scott, and in 1964, Ron Balin.

Kameny had won each time, but his opponents raised valid complaints. Because the Society's constitution required the use of Robert's Rules of Order—the rigid, complex procedures for debate and decision-making—Kameny insisted upon the use of them in meetings. He memorized the rules, totaling hundreds of pages of intricate guidelines, and used them to his advantage. Board members found themselves listening to Kameny's own interminable speeches yet unable to make their own dissenting points. They inevitably ran out of time to discuss their own agenda items. Those were the *rules*, Kameny explained. "Frank was impossible," remembered one Mattachine member. "You just gave up." And for a while, his filibuster strategy worked. Who else, besides Kameny, would master the complex debate procedures so thoroughly?

Then the Society's membership had begun to stagnate. Meetings were dry, business-only, and dominated by Kameny. He refused to allow social events that might attract or retain new members. "How many brunches does the ACLU give? The NAACP?" he asked.

In December 1964, Kameny faced a mutiny. That month, the Society's membership received a letter signed by eleven members, including four board members. "Don't you honestly think it is time for a change—after three years under one and the same authoritarian regime?"

The signatories urged members to write in "Robert K," the pseudonym of *Gazette* editor and ECHO coordinator Robert Belanger, on their ballots. "He will be the voice of the members rather than a solitary leader who goes against the general consensus and insists that he is ALWAYS right." The Society would become an organization "SUPPORTED and ENJOYED by the members by exchanging its status as a one-man organization for that of a unified effort."

"DON'T LET FRANK PUT HIS CLAMP AND STAMP ON THE SOCIETY FOR ONE MORE YEAR."

"BREAK UP KAMENY HALL."

Kameny's allies struck back in a letter signed by charter member Jack Nichols, former secretary Gail Johnson, and five others. To witness true leadership, one needed to look only at the transcript of the Dowdy hearings or the policy positions of the NCACLU, they argued.

"ALL THE WAY WITH FRANKLIN K."

"CIVIL LIBERTIES AND SOCIAL RIGHTS? HAVE F.E.K. TO LEAD YOUR FIGHTS."

When MSNY board member Dick Leitsch learned of the campaign, he wrote to Belanger in defense of Kameny. "He is the only person I know of in this movement who will stand up before the public, before newspapermen, before the world and say 'I'm Franklin E. Kameny, a homosexual, and I represent the homosexual minority. We want such and such done.' Would you do this? I don't know, but I do know you hide behind a pseudonym, which is something of a hint."

"To remove him from office would be a victory for the Dowdys, the N.Y. Academy of Medicine and the Bull Conners [*sic*] of the world," Leitsch warned one pro-Belanger MSW member.

In January, by a margin of one vote, Frank Kameny lost the presidency of the organization he had founded.

"I never told Frank this, but I cast the deciding vote," admitted MSW member Paul Kuntzler, forty-five years later. "Frank thought I was going to vote for him."

"Allow me to extend my deepest sympathy," wrote Ronald Brass, days after the election. "There is some speculation that this may mean the end of the Washington Mattachine Society."

"THIS SERIES OF ARTICLES would not have been written five years ago," began Jean M. White's January 31, 1965, article, the first of five, on the front page of *The Washington Post*'s Outlook section. White, a World War II navy veteran, had covered Rustin's March on Washington, and one year later, she had attended the 1964 conference of the East Coast Homophile Organizations.

White's first article introduced readers to the multilayered world of gay Washington. Not *all* homosexuals were "'flaming faggots' who swish along the street," she explained. There were middle-class men, too, like one "former Government astronomer with a doctor's degree from Harvard," a man who "deplores the perverts and 'queens' and points out that heterosexuals also have their rapists, child molesters, sadists and neurotics."

"He has sought a lasting relationship without success," she added.

Her second article, and each one following it, appeared on the front page of the paper: "Scientists Disagree on Basic Nature of Homosexuality, Chance of Cure," then "Homosexuals Are in All Kinds of Jobs, Find Place in Many Levels of Society."

The "obviously sick" stereotypes, "the transvestite 'queens,' the compulsive sex psychopaths, and the 'sadie-mashies,'" she wrote, "are as unwelcome in polite 'gay' society as child molesters and rapists are in straight heterosexual society." As for the well-adjusted homosexuals like Franklin E. Kameny, they simply wanted equality.

"The public response to the Jenkins arrest has been encouraging of a more enlightened public attitude," concluded White's series. "But today society offers no place, no help, and no hope to the homosexual. Laws are harsh on him; his existence is precarious; exposure brings ruin and social ostracism.

"Yet society has to deal with the homosexual in its midst."

The series represented a "major breakthrough," as Kameny put it, and not only because it informed the *Post*'s straight audience about the sheer number of homosexuals, their plight, and the existence of a diverse, sometimes even normal homosexual world. Jean White's articles also informed the paper's *homosexual* readers of those same facts.

"Congratulations to you and the Mattachine Society for the fantastic series of articles currently running," wrote one Washington resident. "I wouldn't have believed such unbiased reporting was possible if I hadn't seen it with my own eyes."

The series rippled across the country. The *Providence Sunday Journal* reprinted it, and *The Denver Post* published its own six-part series on the new "Militant Minority."

Not since the Kinsey report had the American press discussed the plight of the homosexual with so much vigor. Walter Jenkins, like Alfred Kinsey, unwittingly catalyzed a revolution in pressrooms across the country. Hugh Hefner's *Playboy*, for one, mentioned homosexuality at least twice per issue for an entire six months after the Jenkins affair. Kameny finally had evidence to suggest the time had come for a more aggressive strategy, one that would produce even more attention for his minority.

THE MSW'S NEW LEADERS had no plans to exile the founder of their organization. "Do you really think we would be stupid and ungrateful enough to let a man like that go to waste and thereby deny the value of all his achievements??" responded one MSW member to Dick Leitsch. "He who is THE expert on the homophile movement??"

For no less than two years, Kameny had argued that homosexuals were perfectly healthy, but he did not prioritize the issue until Jean White. While writing her series, the *Post* reporter had researched the opinions of psychiatrists, who promised cures and asserted that homosexuals were, in fact, sick. She also turned to Frank Kameny. What was the position of the Mattachine Society of Washington?

The homosexuals, Kameny realized, did not have an official policy on the matter. Just as Congressman Dowdy forced Kameny to articulate a position on gay marriage, White forced him to articulate one on the sickness question.

"The statement," Kameny told White in mid-January, "which I promised to whip into shape for you is:

"'In the absence of valid evidence to the contrary, homosexuality must be considered neither a sickness, a disturbance, neurosis, psychosis, or other pathology, nor as a malfunction or maladjustment of any sort, but as a preference, liking, or propensity, fully on par with, and not different in kind from, heterosexuality.'"

The matter grew more urgent. On January 31, the same day as White's first article, *The New York Times* ran its own story on the findings of a University of Pennsylvania psychotherapist. "THERAPY IS FOUND CURING DEVIATES," it announced.

Though Kameny had given White a statement that summarized his personal beliefs on the matter, the MSW had not yet adopted an official position on the sickness debate. Now, with a policy statement drafted, Kameny brought it to his Society for a vote. On March 4, 1965, the MSW's entire membership debated whether homosexuality was a disease. Nichols, Kameny, and their allies arrived well prepared. At the meeting, attended by nearly the entire Society membership, they brought medical and sociological books with key passages highlighted.

Well, I know a lot of people who are sick, argued MSW president Robert Belanger. Others asserted that the Society needed to present *both* sides of the debate. The medical experts, after all, disagreed with one another.

"We cannot play the role of a passive battlefield, across which the 'authorities' fight out the question of our sickness," responded the statement's supporters. "In the last analysis, WE are the authorities, and it is up to us to take an active role in determining our own status and our own fate."

On March 4, in a 27–5 vote, the Mattachine Society of Washington adopted the official position that homosexuals were healthy. Kameny experienced his first victory since his electoral defeat, though the membership had condensed his original statement, deleting four of his synonyms for "sickness."

"With his passion for scientific precision he'd erred, some of us felt, on the side of wordiness," Nichols remembered.

"Why use 100 words when 200 will do?" Kameny joked.

WHILE THE MSW FOUGHT against the concept of homosexuality as a sickness, it also fought against homosexuality as a sin. On February 14, 1965, Reverend David H. Cole of the Unitarian church of Rockville, Maryland, delivered a sermon titled "The Strangers Among Us."

"The bar to Federal employment of homosexuals is a scandal which no civilized government should tolerate," he said, urging his congregation "to join with the ACLU to demand civil rights, full rights, and opportunities for homosexual citizens." After the service, Kameny joined eleven other MSW members in a discussion group with the congregation. Homosexuals are always welcome in our church, said the straight congregants.

On March 22, five Society members and an ecumenical group of eleven religious figures met to discuss remedies to the "alienation and estrangement" that existed between homosexuals and the religious community.

The sympathetic Unitarian minister, Reverend Cole, could not attend. After his homosexuality sermon, he left for Selma, Alabama, as one of forty Washington-area Unitarians who planned to march with Dr. King.

WITHOUT THE PRESIDENCY, Frank Kameny had less to lose. No longer the sole representative of the homosexual's interests in Washington, he could take risks. And with more time on his hands, he could expand his influence beyond Washington.

In October 1964, the leader of the Philadelphia-based Janus Society,

Clark Polak, created a new homophile publication, titled *Drum*. The magazine, modeled after *Playboy*, interspersed serious reporting with photographs of shirtless men. Kameny agreed to serve on the staff of the magazine, and for *Drum*'s first issue, he wrote an article on the Dowdy saga. His name appeared on the issue's masthead. *Drum*'s male models, after all, were still 50 percent clothed.

In the December 1964 issue, the men suddenly became fully nude—nothing revealed, but naked nonetheless. (It appealed to the "giddy faggots,"wrote Dick Leitsch at the time,whereas the new joint MSW-MSNY magazine, the *Eastern Mattachine Magazine*, appealed "to the thinking homosexual.")

That issue represented "the last straw," wrote Kameny. After the Dowdy affair, and amidst so much media attention after Jenkins, how could a homosexual organization align itself with a semipornographic publication?

By February, ECHO expelled the Janus Society from its ranks. Kameny's name disappeared from *Drum*'s masthead. And in Janus's place, four Philadelphia women created the Mattachine Society of Philadelphia.

Kameny, no longer required to receive the MSW board's approval before contacting the government, also unleashed a flood of letters upon the federal government.

Even before the MSW election, Kameny had lost his patience. On November 24, 1964, he noticed an article buried on page thirty of *The New York Times*. "An official of the Office of Economic Opportunity [OEO] said here yesterday that boys with police records or homosexual tendencies would not be accepted for youth camps planned in the Federal antipoverty campaign," it began.

Kameny had long argued that if homosexuals were to picket, they first needed a specific reason, ideally a response to a concrete, illustrative injustice, something like the 1955 case of Rosa Parks. They needed a catalyzing moment that would cause the public and the media to agree with the protesters, something to make the public say, "Yes, that *is* wrong."

The exclusion of homosexuals from President Johnson's celebrated antipoverty program represented the perfect injustice. "Genocide is an ugly word, but when you systematically exclude all relevant members of a large class of the citizenry from a chance to raise themselves from a starvation level, genocide is the word that must be used," he told OEO director Sargent Shriver.

If the OEO did not change its policy, threatened Kameny, he would refuse to file a tax return for 1964, and the MSW would demonstrate. "I have available to me the services of a number of people who will picket on these questions," he wrote. "I have been responsible for two instances of picketing in New York on other sociological questions, involving basic rights. There will be picketing in New York, and possibly in Washington and elsewhere."

Over the next few weeks, Kameny considered whether he would actually stage an act of civil disobedience. As he looked around him, in those first few months of 1965, *everyone* seemed to be discarding the arbitrary rule of law in the pursuit of justice. On February 1, Selma authorities arrested Martin Luther King Jr. and three hundred demonstrators for marching to demand the right to vote.

Five days later, the NYPD arrested Randy Wicker for peddling copies of LeMar's *Marijuana Newsletter* on a Greenwich Village sidewalk.

On February 18, Alabama state troopers shot and killed Jimmie Lee Jackson, a twenty-six-year-old Black demonstrator in Selma, as he attempted to shield his mother from a police club. King and his colleagues planned a march from Selma to Montgomery, Alabama's capital, in his honor.

On Sunday, March 6, at 9:30 p.m., ABC screened the film *Judgment at Nuremberg*, an Academy Award–winning exploration of the German public's complicity in the Holocaust.

"Hitler did some good things," said one of the characters, a German servant. "But the *other* things, we know nothing about that. Very few Germans did."

"And if we *did* know," said another character, "what could we do?"

Suddenly, an ABC correspondent interrupted the film with breaking news. Forty-eight million Americans, wrenched from postwar Germany, found themselves staring at fifteen minutes of footage from Selma, shot only hours earlier. They saw the Alabama troopers' flying nightsticks, the blinding tear gas, and the demonstrators' broken limbs.

Five days later, white segregationists murdered Unitarian minister

James Reeb, a friend and colleague of Rockville Unitarian's Reverend Cole, in Selma.

On March 15, in a speech later reprinted in the *Eastern Mattachine Magazine*, President Johnson stood before Congress and called for a voting rights bill. "What happened in Selma is part of a far larger movement which reaches into every section and State of America," said Johnson. "The time of justice has now come. No force can hold it back."

On March 17, Reverend Cole, only a month after urging his congregation to fight the government's gay purges, was arrested in Selma for attempting to picket the mayor's house without a permit.

The next day, Frank Kameny made his decision. He wrote to Sargent Shriver, IRS commissioner Sheldon Cohen, and President Johnson. "When my government has resolutely closed to us all channels of communication, when it has left open to us no channels and avenues of recourse and redress; when it offends us by refusal even to talk with us; when it degrades and insults and humiliates us, and denies to us our dignity as human beings and citizens—and when it perpetrates upon us one outrage after another—then civil disobedience remains the only course left to us by our government."

For now, he would avoid publicity in case Shriver and the OEO decided to negotiate. If not, there would be lawsuits, pickets, and press releases, he warned.

The IRS responded three weeks later. "Severe penalties can be and are invoked in any case of willful failure to file and pay income tax when due."

Kameny buckled within three days. "Upon careful consideration of strategy and tactics," he responded, "I have decided to devote the coming year—along with, and with the assistance of others—to a vigorous and effective program of action and agitation, public and private."

He would therefore defer nonpayment of his taxes—"for one year only." He enclosed a check for $575.95.

ON APRIL 1, 1965, after nearly two years of false alarms, J. Edgar Hoover learned of yet another plan for a homosexual picket at the White House.

Warren Scarberry had called Washington's Metropolitan Police earlier that day to inform an officer that he, alone, planned to demonstrate at the White House. He would do so on April 3, from 12:00 to 1:00 p.m.

The FBI again warned the Secret Service, and Hoover himself notified the attorney general.

That Saturday, for one hour, Scarberry held a sign that read STOP DISCRIMINATION AGAINST HOMOSEXUALS outside the White House.

An officer from the Third Precinct asked him if he was a homosexual.

Are *you* a homosexual? responded Scarberry.

Two hours after the young man finished picketing, at 2:50 p.m., Kameny presided over a Washington meeting of seven women and four men as they planned the second annual ECHO convention.

On April 7, Dick Leitsch wrote Kameny with a request. "Frank, you and Bob [Belanger] said that guy who picketed the White House was a kook, but handled himself well, and did a good job. You also said you know him. Could you make arrangements with him for Craig [Rodwell], some others, and myself to come to Washington some Saturday afternoon and picket with him? We'd like to very much, unless you know of some reason why we shouldn't."

Warren Scarberry, the FBI informant who had handed eighty-five homosexuals to J. Edgar Hoover, was about to lead the country's first organized homosexual picket of the White House, a feat Kameny wanted for himself.

ON APRIL 15, 1965, Cuba's state-run newspaper, *El Mundo*, announced that Fidel Castro's Communist government intended to impose "revolutionary social hygiene" to address the "rampant" and "abominable" vice of homosexuality. The next day, on April 16, *The New York Times* carried the news. "This was understood," it concluded, "as a warning that homosexuals would be rounded up and sent to labor camps."

That night, Kameny received two phone calls. First, from Dick Leitsch. In two days, on Easter Sunday, New York homosexuals would gather at the United Nations to protest the Castro regime's announcement, said Leitsch.

Then, a call from Jack Nichols in Washington. This is the moment, the precipitating event to galvanize both homosexuals and the American public, Nichols argued. It was time for the Mattachine Society of Washington to march.

Kameny first reacted with skepticism. Homosexuals have long been persecuted all over the world, he answered. Why protest Cuba? Moreover, the logical place to picket is the Cuban Embassy, which does not exist, he explained. Diplomatic communications traveled through Switzerland.

Then let's make it a White House matter, Nichols argued. The U.S. government persecutes us, and so does the Cuban government.

Nichols had struck a chord. For eight years, since his second 1957 interview with CSC investigators, the former astronomer had labeled American antihomosexual policies "the province of the USSR."

"'We could,' admitted Kameny, the first signs of sly humor now creeping into his tones," Nichols later wrote. "I knew I'd convinced him."

The Society would picket the White House, in Washington's first organized demonstration of homosexuals, the following day.

Call everyone, ordered Kameny.

Walter Jenkins with President Lyndon Johnson, early 1960s

THE PICKET

Lilli Vincenz picked up the telephone on the evening of Friday, April 16, and agreed to become the first lesbian to march at the White House for homosexual equality.

Born in Nazi Germany, Vincenz immigrated to New Jersey in 1949, at the age of eleven. A short-haired brunette with striking blue eyes, she attempted to date men through college, and she did not kiss a woman until she studied abroad at the University of Munich. "It just blew me out of the water," she later remembered.

When she began a PhD program in comparative literature at Columbia University, she felt alone, unaware of New York's gay world, and depressed. After contemplating suicide, she dropped out of school within weeks.

In 1962, she entered Women's Army Corps (WAC) training in Fort McClellan, Alabama, where she lived in a hall with forty other women. Her officers seemed suspicious. They knew she had a master's degree. Why had she enlisted in the army?

In the spring of 1963, Vincenz began a new position as a neuropsychiatric technician at the Walter Reed National Military Medical Center in Washington. Vincenz soon met another lesbian, who introduced her to the female side of gay Washington. While Vincenz completed training at Walter Reed, the two women drove to a lesbian bar, located in the basement of a Russian restaurant, holding hands. It represented the extent of Vincenz's homosexual activity.

Her straight roommate, after noticing the two women together, drew conclusions and reported her. Vincenz had lasted just one week. Her commanding officer gave her two options. She could either face a court-martial or sign a statement admitting her homosexuality, resulting in an immediate discharge from the army. Faced with the decision, Vincenz began sobbing.

Oh, you'll cry a lot more during the court-martial, said the major.

Vincenz signed the statement. Yes, she admitted, she was a homosexual. But as she walked out of the WAC office, having lost her military career, she felt free. "What I had always dreaded, exposure, was more a relief than a disaster," she later explained.

"Dear Mr. Kameny," she wrote on August 30, 1963, three weeks after the Dowdy hearings. "As someone who has recently moved to this area, I am very interested in the program of the Mattachine Society of Washington and would like to be acquainted with it."

She worked evenings as a waitress at Mrs. K's Toll House in Silver Spring, Maryland, but still found time to interview with the Society's board.

"Upon their recommendation, the Executive Board invites you to attend the meetings of the organization and to join us," wrote Bruce Scott on November 1. Lilli Vincenz thus became the Society's first lesbian member.

Within four months, she was serving as the MSW's secretary and lobbying congressmen against H.R. 5990. Though she grew frustrated with Kameny's autocratic leadership style, supporting Belanger in his electoral coup, she allied with the Society's founder in the sickness debate.

In April 1965, she had grown unhappy with her job and wanted to quit. The government already knew of her sexuality, so she had nothing to lose. Vincenz agreed to march.

That Friday night, seven others agreed to join Vincenz, Kameny, and Nichols. Judith Kuch, a bisexual woman, and Gail Johnson, the straight secretary who succeeded Vincenz in the role, brought the female tally to three. Jon Swanson, Paul Kuntzler, and two men with security clearances—Perrin Shaffer and Otto Ulrich—also agreed to march. Jack Nichols brought his coworker Gene Kleeberg. The Society's president, Robert Belanger, did not attend.

Kameny disseminated the rules that night, which he summarized later that month for San Francisco's Guy Strait. "By strict instruction, the pickets were conservatively dressed—the men in suits, ties, white shirts; the women in dresses; all well groomed." He permitted the marchers to make their own signs, which, "of course, were cleared in advance." Kameny's reasoning for the dress code was simple. If you're asking for equal employment rights, he told Nichols, look employable.

With only hours before the demonstration, Kameny contacted the Washington papers, inviting them to cover the first demonstration by a group of homosexuals at the White House.

"THE DEMONSTRATION STARTED shortly after 8 a.m. when the first picket appeared outside the White House," reported the front page of *The Washington Post*. "By noon, Deputy Chief Albert Embry estimated their number at 15,000."

END THE WAR IN VIETNAM, said their signs.

In February, Johnson had authorized the first American air strikes. On March 8, one week before the president's Selma speech, the first 3,500 American marines landed at Da Nang. On April 17, the day of the march, sixty-three air force and navy fighter jets bombed two major North Vietnamese highways. Some 320,000 leaflets, calling for unconditional peace talks, fell onto the city of Donghoi. Each featured an autographed portrait of President Johnson.

That day's "March on Washington to End the War in Viet Nam," organized by the Students for a Democratic Society, marked the largest peace demonstration in American history.

Pacifists like Bayard Rustin had called for civil disobedience, but at the time of the march, there were not yet sit-ins, no burned draft cards. One of only four arrests occurred when a neo-Nazi tackled a twenty-two-year-old student who had been sitting in Lafayette Park, listening to Bob Dylan's "Subterranean Homesick Blues" on a portable record player.

The Vietnam marchers had disappeared by 4:00 p.m., when the ten Mattachine marchers arrived to Lafayette Park. On that warm and sunny day, approximately fifty thousand tourists visited the National Mall, viewing Washington's cherry blossoms in their fullest bloom. Late that afternoon, many were still passing by the White House.

Lige Clarke drove a borrowed convertible to drop off his boyfriend, Jack Nichols, at Lafayette Park. He then continued to the Pentagon for an afternoon shift in the Office of the Army Chief of Staff. Gail Johnson, tense and wearing high heels, arrived on the back of her boyfriend's motorcycle. Perrin Shaffer and Otto Ulrich, the security clearance holders, arrived wearing sunglasses to conceal their identity from the press and federal investigators.

Kameny immediately began choreographing the event. The marchers would silently walk in a circle before the White House, he explained. They agreed that Jack Nichols would lead the procession. "I was tall and an all-American sort," Nichols later explained. Kameny would follow him.

The former astronomer ensured that the signs were logically ordered. First, Nichols carried the group's thesis.

FIFTEEN MILLION U.S. HOMOSEXUALS PROTEST
FEDERAL TREATMENT

Next, the connection to current events.

CUBA'S GOVERNMENT PERSECUTES HOMOSEXUALS,
U.S. GOVERNMENT BEAT THEM TO IT

Then, the homosexuals' demands.

WE WANT: FEDERAL EMPLOYMENT; HONORABLE
DISCHARGES; SECURITY CLEARANCES

GOVERNOR WALLACE MET WITH NEGROES;
OUR GOVERNMENT WON'T MEET WITH US

JEWS TO CONCENTRATION CAMPS UNDER NAZIS;
HOMOSEXUALS TO WORK CAMPS UNDER CASTRO

IS THE U.S. MUCH BETTER?

At 4:20 p.m., the marchers moved to a portion of the sidewalk, allocated by the police, in front of the White House fence. Tourists seemed to be everywhere. What if Nazis or regular, outraged Americans attacked the marchers? What if the police officers arrested them once they saw the messages on their signs? And the Secret Service?

For an hour, until exactly 5:20 p.m., the Mattachine Society of Washington marched in silence.

"Only a very few hostile remarks were passed by the throngs of tourists flocking and driving by," wrote Kameny in a press release. "Much interest was shown; many pictures of signs and demonstrators were taken." The police's behavior was "fully satisfactory," he continued. The Nazis never appeared.

One newspaper reported on the picket. *The Washington Afro-American*, on page eighteen of its April 20 issue, cited the "Governor Wallace" sign and concluded with a quote from the group's founder. "We're being just as much discriminated against as the colored citizen has been," said Kameny.

Nothing had happened, and for the marchers, that was enough.

"HISTORY IN THE MAKING," Kameny told Gittings. "I'm writing this, very very wearily, and very very contentedly, after returning home following a 10-person picketing." Yes, Scarberry had picketed the White House first, he admitted, but that day's march constituted Washington's first demonstration by a homosexual organization.

They pledged to picket again, and next time, the marchers would be "immunized against fear," as Jack Nichols later put it.

"We were going to change the world," remembered Vincenz.

Gail Green, the straight marcher who had been especially nervous, similarly felt her fears dissipate with the indifference of the world around them. As she explained to Kameny, marching had brought her to a major conclusion: one should never picket in high heels.

"AMERICANS! CIVIL LIBERTARIANS! HOMOSEXUALS!" began Randy Wicker's leaflets.

After mimeographing thousands of copies, he thrust them into the hands of Greenwich Village pedestrians on Friday and Saturday evenings. "This Easter Sunday you have the opportunity of joining fellow Americans in protesting the Cuban Government's deplorable policies regarding homosexuals," they said.

On a cloudy, frigid Sunday afternoon, twenty-nine picketers—including Wicker, Leitsch, and poet Allen Ginsberg—met at the MSNY offices. They walked up Fifth Avenue to Forty-Second Street, weaving through the Easter parade crowds, and continued north to a roped-off area in Hammarskjöld Plaza, a park adjacent to the United Nations headquarters. For two hours, they marched, with signs proclaiming: LABOR CAMPS TODAY—OVENS TOMORROW? INDIVIDUAL FREEDOM— SI! PERSECUTION—NO! SEX IN ANY FORM IS GOOD.

"Let all good men of good will join forces," said their flyers, "to turn back the ugly tide of totalitarianism whose stained flag now drips with the blood of its defenseless homosexual victims."

In New York, too, the spectators and the press left the homosexual demonstrators alone. "Both demonstrations and their effects can probably best be summed up by a remark overheard at Hammerskjold Plaza," reported the *Eastern Mattachine Magazine*, "when one woman in a mink stole and an Easter bonnet stood watching the demonstration with another middle-aged lady, then turned and said: 'You know, when you're as disliked as homosexuals, it takes a lot of guts to stand up for your rights.' They folded their handbills into their purses and walked away."

In silence, the floodgates of homosexual protest had opened.

KAMENY RECEIVED Warren Scarberry's panicked phone call at 3:30 a.m. Thursday morning, three days after the New York picket. Scarberry had been arrested by two police officers in Washington's Fox Lounge. He claimed they had threatened to beat him. "He broke down quite completely on the phone," Kameny told Ronald Brass.

Two days later, Scarberry stood in front of the Tenth Precinct police station, holding a sign, STOP POLICE HARASSMENT OF HOMOSEXUALS. When Ronald Brass later admonished Scarberry for "shaking things up," threatening the Society's cordial relationship with the police, and "making a fool of himself," the former FBI informant acquiesced. He agreed to stop picketing.

"He is under the impression that the demonstration by MSW was a direct consequence of his actions," Brass informed Kameny.

Plus, "the mere act of picketing is undignified," added Brass.

Despite Brass's objections, by the end of the month, Kameny had become chairman of the MSW's new Committee on Picketing and Other Lawful Demonstrations. With a new tool in his arsenal, Kameny turned to his original foe, the Civil Service Commission. He wrote—and Belanger signed—a letter to Chairman Macy reiterating his 1962 request for a meeting and threatening to picket.

"No useful purpose would be served by meeting with representatives of your society," responded Macy.

In the aftermath of the demonstrations, the Society felt emboldened. The first weekend of May, the group met to create pamphlet holders from manila folders, labeled TAKE ONE.

In each folder, they placed ten copies of a pamphlet drafted by Kameny, titled "How to Handle a Federal Interrogation."

"On matters having in any way to do with homosexuality," the flyer advised, "say NOTHING; 'no-thing' means NO thing; and 'no' means NONE AT ALL, with NO exceptions. It does NOT mean 'just a little.'"

The TAKE ONE folders materialized across Washington. Lige Clarke, despite the risk of losing his security clearance, placed seven in the halls of the Pentagon. Two appeared in the Department of Commerce, one in the State Department.

Over the next two months, military officials inundated the FBI with reports of the document's appearance across the country. In May, an investigator forwarded one that had been discovered in a Fort Monmouth, New Jersey, telephone booth. By June, the Bureau had received copies from investigators in Fort Campbell, Kentucky; Fort McPherson, Georgia; Fort McClellan, Alabama; and Fort Bragg, North Carolina.

In a July memorandum to the attorney general, J. Edgar Hoover summarized the Society's instructions to outline its "obstructive tactics." The memorandum discussed the MSW alongside the Communist Party, the American Nazi Party, and the Ku Klux Klan.

Meanwhile, in May, Kameny prepared for a second picket attempt, this time, with proper publicity. "HOMOSEXUALS TO PICKET WHITE HOUSE," announced his release.

On the afternoon of Thursday, May 27, Jack Nichols traveled to the offices of Washington's news outlets to deliver the press release in person. He described the scene for Dick Leitsch a few days later. "Girls, sitting around in their offices chatting—took it from me—and as the door closed, I could hear their screams all the way down the hall. Some of them followed me and asked questions—and others came running out to get drinks of water so that they could have a peek at a real live faggot," wrote Nichols. "I loved every minute of it."

That Saturday, from 12:00 to 2:00 p.m., ten men and three women picketed the White House. Jack Nichols led the march with his FIFTEEN MILLION U.S. HOMOSEXUALS PROTEST FEDERAL TREATMENT sign, and new all-American placards replaced the Cuba signs.

GOVERNMENT POLICY CREATES SECURITY RISKS

DISCRIMINATION AGAINST HOMOSEXUALS IS AS IMMORAL
AS DISCRIMINATION AGAINST NEGROES, JEWS

WHITE HOUSE REFUSES REPLIES TO OUR LETTERS.
AFRAID OF US?

The Associated Press, UPI, Reuters, the French News Agency, the *New York World-Telegram*, and ABC-TV sent reporters, photographers, and television cameras.

"We were told that it made a most impressively good-looking picket line," Kameny told Gittings the next day.

Larry Littlejohn of San Francisco wrote Kameny as soon as he saw the homosexual marchers on television. "Many congratulations," he wrote. "This is a real contribution toward breaking the conspiracy of silence."

The rest of the country learned of the picket the next day, reading the UPI and AP stories in papers across America. "Protest Subject Is Deviants," announced the *Press & Sun-Bulletin* of Binghamton, New York. At least a dozen other papers—in Minneapolis, Akron, San Bernardino, Fort Myers, Des Moines, and Tampa, to name a few—covered the march. "The neatly dressed dozen paced silently within pavement bounds set by watchful police," reported the AP. The "well dressed and well behaved" homosexuals staged a "quiet, orderly" demonstration, wrote the UPI. To Kameny, the descriptions proved that his dress code worked exactly as he had intended.

That Sunday, the *Chicago Sun-Times* reprinted Jean White's homosexuality series. Four months earlier, *The Washington Post* had published White's piece alongside an image of a blurred silhouette of a man walking alone in the snow, without a name or face. But in the *Sun-Times*'s May 30 reprint, readers saw the clear, stoic faces of Jack Nichols, Frank Kameny, and Lilli Vincenz.

IN MAY, David Carliner of the NCACLU argued Scott's case before the United States Court of Appeals for the District of Columbia Circuit. Before three judges, Carliner explained that one's private sexual behavior did not affect the efficiency of the civil service. The logic of the purges not only contradicted the Kinsey report and medical experts, argued Carliner, but also was "at war with a wide range of constitutional principles."

On June 7, 1965, in *Griswold v. Connecticut*, the Supreme Court ruled that states could not outlaw birth control. For the first time in history, the court explicitly acknowledged a constitutional right to privacy, implied throughout the Bill of Rights. Because the decision suggested that *other* immoral acts—adultery, fornication, and homosexuality—could soon fall under the protected realm of morality and privacy, it gave the homophile movement "a renewed sense of hope and optimism," as the *Eastern Mattachine Magazine* reported.

Nine days later, the court of appeals released its decision in *Scott v. Macy*. The Civil Service Commission, wrote Chief Judge David Bazelon, "may not rely on a determination of 'immoral conduct,' based only on such vague labels as 'homosexual' and 'homosexual conduct,' as a ground for disqualifying appellant for Government employment." Because the government had not told Scott *exactly* what he had done, he could not refute the charges, a denial of due process.

Scott had won, but the purges remained intact. "In my view," concluded Bazelon, "this does not preclude the Commission from excluding appellant from eligibility for employment for some ground other than the vague finding of 'immoral conduct' here."

"The walls of Jericho have been shaken, but they have not yet come tumbling down," wrote Kameny in a press release. "No Federal court has gone as far as this opinion in strongly suggesting that homosexual conduct may not be an absolute disqualification," reported the next day's *Post*.

The day after the decision, Bruce Scott awoke to a story in the *Chicago Sun-Times*—it did not include his name—and a telegram from Don Slater of *ONE* magazine: "CONGRATULATIONS ON YOUR SUCCESSFUL APPEAL YOU HAVE DONE US ALL A GREAT SERVICE." *Drum* magazine began advertising copies of the *Scott* decision, for one dollar each, to its circulation of thousands.

The MSW, meanwhile, had planned to picket the CSC before the decision, and now its board asked whether it was still appropriate to demonstrate, especially while the government considered whether to appeal *Scott* to the Supreme Court.

A picket risked Kameny's own livelihood, for once again, he found himself unemployed. Now, in a post-*Scott*, post-Jenkins America, he believed there existed a chance—albeit a slim one—that the government would hire him. Two days after the *Scott* decision, Kameny wrote to John Macy to request the expungement of his debarment. The CSC had never provided him the specifics of *his* homosexual activity, either, he complained.

Bruce Scott favored a CSC picket. "Perhaps the picketing coupled with the Circuit Court's decision in my case will focus the attention of the press and public on the authoritarian procedures," he told Kameny.

On June 21, Kameny sent Chairman Macy a threat. The homosexuals would picket in four days unless the CSC agreed to meet, he warned. If not, they would distribute a predrafted press release, enclosed.

"We consider that no useful purpose would be served by such a meeting," responded Macy.

The press releases arrived at newsrooms across Washington, and on June 26, ten days after the Society's first legal victory over the gay purges, twenty-five picketers—eighteen men and seven women—demonstrated at the headquarters of the Civil Service Commission.

CIVIL SERVICE COMMISSION REFUSES TO CONFER WITH
HOMOSEXUALS. AFRAID?

CHAIRMAN MACY IS GUILTY OF IMMORAL CONDUCT

CHAIRMAN MACY IS WASHINGTON'S GOVERNOR WALLACE

The picketers saw a man in a car approach the entrance of the CSC headquarters, stop, and watch the demonstrators before driving onward. Kameny later swore it was Chairman Macy himself.

WHILE KAMENY and his Society picketed in Washington, twenty-eight-year-old Clark Polak became the homosexual Hugh Hefner of Philadelphia. For two years, Polak had supported and emulated Kameny. He donated one hundred dollars—nearly eight hundred in today's dollars—to the MSW to help it survive the Dowdy affair; the two leaders appeared together at lectures in Washington and Philadelphia; and Polak sent an endorsement to Kameny in his failed 1965 Mattachine campaign. "I would bow to Frank's leadership," he wrote.

Polak's magazine, however, increasingly conflicted with the image Kameny hoped to project in his demonstrations. After Janus's expulsion from ECHO, *Drum*'s content became even more explicit. In April, Polak published a "Guide to Cruising," and in his July issue, he planned to depict an uncensored male buttocks—a "physique photograph," as they were called.

Kameny could not forget Dowdy's attempt to tarnish his respectable Society with the crass words and images of other homosexuals. He feared his opponents would use *Drum*'s semipornographic material to discredit his suit-and-tie society. *This* is the type of material your movement is publishing?

On June 3, Kameny persuaded the members of the MSW to adopt an official policy statement. "The publication of physique photographs bears no relevance to its conception of the nature of the homophile movement and that therefore, no such photographs will appear in the Society's publications, and no material officially issued by the Mattachine Society of Washington will be released to any publications in which such photographs appear on a regular basis."

The statement represented a proactive defense measure, a cleansing of the Society's hands. Now, if government officials or congressmen held up a copy of *Drum*, Kameny could simply point to the MSW's official policy.

As the pickets continued, Kameny's dress code became more specific. In May, he finalized the official regulations of his picketing committee. "Picketing is not an occasion for an assertion of personality, individuality, ego, rebellion, generalized non-conformity or anti-conformity," he wrote.

Onlookers, he explained, were more likely to accept controversial ideas if picketers bore "the symbols of acceptability, conventionality, and respectability, as arbitrary as those symbols may be." Kameny, a man who had long rejected conformity, nevertheless recognized the trappings of conformity as a political tool.

History provided evidence that the tactic worked. Before the Civil War, mothers of young enslaved African Americans, for instance, taught them Victorian standards of speech and behavior, as historians have put it, "to humanize themselves in white eyes, perhaps even securing a minimal measure of personal safety." In the mid-twentieth century, the tactic manifested itself in the Black freedom movement's deployment of a white middle-class image. "Dress modestly, neatly . . . as if you were going to church," Black organizers told marchers.

Kameny thus required male marchers to wear suits, female marchers to wear dresses. He required men to have recent haircuts and fresh shaves; he discouraged beards. He approved all signs in advance; they needed neat and clear lettering. He required marchers to carry the signs assigned to them and to maintain their correct, logical ordering. He prohibited picketers from talking among themselves; he did not allow them to smoke or to take refreshment. He permitted them to leave the picket line only when *absolutely* necessary.

"I'm all in favor of well-groomed pickets," remarked Ronald Brass, "but isn't it going a little too far to require suits in summer?"

The temperature reached nearly ninety degrees Fahrenheit on the

Fourth of July, 1965, when thirty-nine picketers—thirty-two men and seven women—appeared at Philadelphia's Independence Hall.

Their signs spoke to the tourists visiting the birthplace of the Declaration of Independence and the Constitution on the country's birthday.

AN INALIENABLE RIGHT; THE PURSUIT OF HAPPINESS;
FOR HOMOSEXUALS TOO?

STOP CRUEL AND UNUSUAL PUNISHMENT
FOR HOMOSEXUALS

To Kameny's dismay, two MSNY members arrived at Independence Hall wearing informal summer attire. Kameny explained that although they had traveled nearly a hundred miles to demonstrate, the rules were clear. Unfortunately, he could not permit the pair to participate.

"Frank, since I became an admirer of yours, I knew the day would come when a fundamental difference of opinion would come," wrote MSNY's Dick Leitsch the next day. "That point has been reached."

"The more I think of . . . your anti-muscle book policy, your dedication to conservatism and middle-class values, the more I am at odds with the Washington Mattachine," Leitsch continued. "It appears that you are making the same mistakes that were made in New York years ago—an effort to form an 'elite,' based on 'high moral principles.' In other words, to out middle-class the middle-class."

Kameny refused to apologize. "First, I will bitterly resist seeing the homophile movement become broadened into the conformophobe movement," he began. "Much of my life has been devoted to fighting conformity, to going my own way. . . . BUT that applies to MY life as an individual." When it came to the movement, homosexuals needed to prioritize strategy and tactics above all else. "We would not meet with Mr. Macy wearing open-necked shirts and chino pants!! We can't expect a picket line so dressed to get a meeting with him—or with LBJ!!"

"Grubbiness," Kameny concluded, "has never, to your knowledge, been a stereotype of a homosexual. Do our pickets your way, and it will soon become so."

And that was that.

ON FRIDAY, JULY 30, five hundred copies of a flyer materialized in the hallways of the Pentagon. A group of homosexuals planned to protest the United States armed forces, it announced.

Since May, Kameny had been writing the secretaries of the military's four branches to request a meeting and threaten a demonstration. The Pentagon ignored his letters, but once the flyers appeared, the Joint Chiefs of Staff directed an officer in the army's Criminal Investigations Department (CID) to photograph and then identify the homosexual picketers.

Shortly before 2:00 p.m. on the thirty-first, a CID investigator stationed himself outside the River Entrance of the Pentagon. He began photographing the sixteen arriving picketers—twelve men and four women—with his telephoto lens.

Kameny arrived in his 1956 Chevrolet two-door. "Another white male, age 34, 5' 9" with crew-cut, weighing approximately 155 pounds was operating a 1962 or 1963 Volkswagen bearing [REDACTED] with a Congressional Staff license plate attached." The CID officer captured three other license plates and the face of each picketer.

IF YOU DON'T WANT A MAN, LET HIM GO, said their signs. DON'T RUIN HIS ENTIRE LIFE IN THE PROCESS.

HOMOSEXUALS DIED FOR THEIR
COUNTRY TOO

STOP WASTING TAXPAYERS' MONEY ON HUNTS
FOR HOMOSEXUALS

On one sign, a demonstrator stapled his air force honorable discharge and Military Police brassard.

Three weeks later, the CID investigator contacted the FBI. The picketers may work in the government, he said. The Bureau may want to investigate.

The FBI immediately identified Frank Kameny (it later failed to redact the "PHD" after his name). As for the picketer with the government license plate, the FBI promised "to identify the above described individual and furnish the information to the appropriate Government agency."

Around this time, MSW member Otto Ulrich learned that investigators were circulating a photograph of him among his former colleagues at the Library of Congress, asking if anyone knew his identity.

IN *THE LADDER*, Barbara Gittings gave Frank Kameny a platform to speak directly to the Daughters of Bilitis. "We ARE right; those who oppose us are both factually and morally wrong," he wrote in a May 1965 feature on homosexual scientific research.

Meanwhile, the DOB's national governing board grew preoccupied by the dangers of Kameny's pickets. At a June 5 ECHO planning meeting in New York, Kameny moved that ECHO officially sponsor the upcoming CSC and July 4 pickets, and the delegates adopted his motion in a 9–3 vote.

The DOB delegates voted against the motion, since DOB policies prohibited them from participating in political actions. When the DOB delegates informed their national governing board in San Francisco of the picketing plans, the board's response was, according to the ECHO meeting minutes, "immediate, adamant, and horrified."

The DOB saw no choice but to withdraw from the alliance of homosexual organizations. "Unilateral picketing by the homosexual community alone would be detrimental to the homophile movement," explained the DOB in an official statement. Direct action, the lesbian group believed, was simply too risky—it would almost certainly spark a backlash—until homosexuals had "sufficient support and involvement from the larger community."

Gittings urged the DOB to support ECHO's "well-considered and well-planned picketing project," and Kameny himself wrote to the DOB national headquarters. To wait for more acceptance by the public before picketing was "arrant nonsense," he said. "'Uncle Tomism' in our movement is on its way toward becoming as discredited as it is in the Negro movement."

"With the kindest of feelings toward you, I will say that if you do not keep up with the movement, I predict that DOB will go 'down the drain' as a meaningful organization—not by overt act of anyone else in the movement, but because that's just the way movements evolve," he continued.

"We do not want to write DOB off. But we cannot allow DOB to hold back our progress; there is too much at stake."

On August 8, Kameny attended a meeting of the New York DOB in the organization's basement office. Shirley Willer was presiding. Willer, as Lilli Vincenz later explained, "did not want men, even if they were gay, to interfere with, invalidate, or ignore the perspectives of lesbians." Yet here she faced a loud gay man attempting to control the actions of a lesbian organization. During the meeting, Willer and Kameny began arguing about attorney fees from the 1964 ECHO conference, and Kameny's voice reached a "pitch of the high C," as Lilli Vincenz described it. "Suddenly I had the sinking feeling that he was about to lose his mind," she recalled.

Willer asked Kameny to leave. When he refused, she grabbed Kameny by the collar and pushed him toward the door. Kameny pushed back, then carefully removed Willer's glasses. Willer again pushed Kameny toward the door, and he kicked her in the stomach. Another DOB member tackled Kameny from behind, and he finally departed, apologizing to the other women in the room.

Rumors of the altercation spread throughout the movement. "Well, the various versions I heard of the Willer-Kameny embroiglio (sp?) were as follows," wrote DOB member Jody Shotwell to Kameny a few days later. "When Shirley tried to eject you, bodily, you punched her in the jaw. Another version . . . that you slapped her."

Kameny sent Willer a lengthy letter and, in a rare moment of contrition, apologized to the New York DOB leader. "I wish, hereby, to tender my sincerest apologies to you."

Barbara Gittings, meanwhile, continued a quieter, more subtle campaign to promote militancy among the Daughters of Bilitis. Her October 1965 issue of *The Ladder* featured a smiling Lilli Vincenz leading three men—one with a clergyman's collar, two in business suits—in the June picket outside the Civil Service Commission.

Gittings believed that if the rest of the DOB saw that the demonstrators were not "wild-eyed, dungareed radicals," as one *Ladder* reader put it, the lesbians would change their minds about the act of protest.

In Washington, Vincenz began contemplating how to manage Kameny, a tempestuous astronomer who suffered from clear "symptoms of emotional disturbance."

He threatened the public image of the entire movement, she warned another activist. Another "stroke of emotional outburst" had the potential to ruin everything.

SECRETARY OF STATE Dean Rusk received the question during his press conference on August 27, 1965. Most of the briefing had been about Vietnam. The Communists, said Rusk, were "determined to take over South Viet Nam and control its future by force, and we are determined to see that this does not happen."

"Mr. Secretary," began a reporter, "perhaps you are aware that this Department is to be picketed between 2:00 and 4:00 tomorrow by a self-described 'minority group.' If you are aware of the particular circumstances, is there anything that you would care to say at this point about the personnel policies at issue?"

"Well, you have been very gentle," answered Rusk. "I understand that we are being picketed by a group of homosexuals."

The reporters laughed.

"The policy of the department," continued Rusk, "is that we do not employ homosexuals knowingly, and that if we discover homosexuals in our department, we discharge them."

Kameny was ecstatic. Not only did Rusk's answer offer advance publicity for the picket, but it also proved that the secretary of state, fourth in line to the presidency, *knew* about their demonstrations.

The next day, CBS-TV arrived to the Diplomatic Entrance of the State Department building to film the twelve picketers.

STATE DEPARTMENT POLICY ON HOMOSEXUALS CREATES SECURITY RISKS. MCCARTHYISM IS DEAD; LET'S BURY IT.

The CBS reporters interviewed Kameny, who spoke in his emphatic, clipped tones while looking downward, too consumed by his thought process for any semblance of charisma. "Every American citizen has the *right* to be considered by his government on the basis of his—own—personal—merit—as an individual."

While Kameny talked to the television reporter, a member of the Metropolitan Police's Special Investigations Squad stood a few feet away, taking photographs of the marchers. Earlier, the officer had asked for a list of the picketers' names, and Kameny had refused to provide it.

"Those picketing were orderly, and no unusual incidents took place," summarized an FBI memorandum, which arrived at the offices of the Secret Service and local intelligence agencies—and landed on the desk of J. Edgar Hoover—within a week. Hoover may have noticed that the picketers looked especially content during this particular demonstration. In one surveillance photograph, a marcher in sunglasses stares directly at the camera, grinning. The picketers had good reason to be in high spirits. Before they started marching on that hot, humid day, Kameny had delivered the news. Only hours earlier, exactly three years after the Society had first requested a conference with the Civil Service Commission, its top officials agreed to meet with the MSW.

The homosexuals thus marched with satisfaction and, with their first picketing victory, just the slightest taste of power.

MSW surveillance photograph, August 28, 1965

13.

THE STUDENT

In December 1964, J. Edgar Hoover received a handwritten letter from Robert Martin Jr., a high school student in New Jersey. "Dear Mr. Hoover, Could you please tell me if the organization 'Young Americans for Freedom, Inc.' is a communist front organization, communist subverted, or in danger of becoming either?"

Hoover responded by applauding Martin's concern, but he could not comment on the content of FBI files, which indicated that YAF was, in fact, an anti-Communist organization. The director instead provided Martin several pieces of literature on the subject, including "Faith in God—Our Answer to Communism," and promptly opened a file on Martin.

The son of a retired navy commander, Martin had brown curly hair, a cherubic face, and a gifted mind. He graduated valedictorian of his class in 1965 and gained admission to Columbia University in New York. A conservative youth, Martin had served as the local chairman of Youth for Goldwater until the Arizona senator's devastating loss the previous year. The student planned to become a United States senator someday, ideally representing a small state. Delaware, perhaps.

Martin was attracted to both men and women, and as an intelligent adolescent in a post-Jenkins America, he easily diagnosed himself as a homosexual. ("I was and am actually bisexual, but orientational dualism was even stronger then than it is now," he later explained.)

During the summer of 1965, his mother caught him with a man and grew outraged. Martin ran away from home and arrived in New York, homeless. As he entered the city's vast gay world, he stumbled upon the Mattachine Society of New York and its president, Julian Hodges. When Hodges learned of Martin's predicament, the MSNY president offered him a place in his Greenwich Village apartment.

MSNY planned to host ECHO that year, and that August, Hodges held a series of preparatory meetings in his apartment. At one of those meetings, Hodges's young houseguest met one of the ECHO planners, an astronomer.

That fall, Martin began his freshman year at Columbia, and for an entire year, he met no other gay students. But he kept in touch with Kameny, and Martin mentioned his hopes of interning on Capitol Hill. Martin needed to travel to Washington for interviews, he explained.

Kameny responded that he had a spare room in his Northwest Washington house. Martin was welcome to stay with him, as his guest, the following January.

ON THE EVENING OF September 8, five MSW members—including Frank Kameny, Lilli Vincenz, and Gail Johnson—walked across the plaza of the Civil Service Commission headquarters, the site of their demonstration less than three months earlier. They had returned to meet with L. V. Meloy, the CSC's general counsel, and Kimbell Johnson, the director of the Bureau of Personnel Investigations.

The homosexuals did not bring a stenographer, but in the immediate aftermath of the meeting, Lilli Vincenz drafted a scathing five-page letter addressed to the CSC officials. "You told us that all the homosexuals with which you had come in contact had been sent by the police because of violation of the law. They had been solicitors and child molesters. You said, 'What I can't stand is those people that take a youngster home, get him drunk and then seduce him.' You seemed surprised that our organization in no way condones these activities nor attempts to make them legal," wrote Vincenz. "Mr. M, you assume that every homosexual is ashamed and guilty.

"'Is that all you people want?' Mr. M, you asked, when we said we only wanted to plead for the rights of consenting <u>adults</u> to lead their private lives as they see fit without being persecuted and disqualified from job [*sic*]. IS THAT ALL?"

The officials requested a formal statement of the Society's position, and they promised a reply from the commissioners themselves. The MSW immediately began work on what ultimately became a fully foot-noted, sixteen-page manifesto proclaiming the "moral right" to be homosexual and decrying the "morally indefensible" purges.

Then, only days after the conference, the MSW learned that the CSC did not intend to appeal the *Scott v. Macy* decision. In early October, the CSC deemed Bruce Scott officially eligible for federal employment.

"And so ends *Scott v. Macy*, after 3½ years, with complete vindication of Scott," wrote Kameny. His dual strategy of lawsuits and demonstrations seemed to be functioning just as he intended.

LILLI VINCENZ HAD GROWN disappointed in Robert Belanger, the MSW's second president. Not only did he fail to appear at their pickets, but the Society seemed to be stagnating once more.

In the summer of 1965, Belanger resigned, citing personal reasons. "The whole thing is still very mysterious," Kameny told Gittings. "I keep getting the feeling that there's more going on behind the scenes here than I know about."

The membership replaced Belanger not with Kameny, but with Jon Swanson, or "John Marshall," an angular, bespectacled man who had marched in the first White House picket.

Restrained from power once again, Kameny developed an idea to reassert his authority in the national homophile movement. He wanted to transform ECHO into a national organization that emulated the structure of the ACLU. It would have a central headquarters and semiautonomous regional affiliates across the country. Quietly, Kameny began propagating his proposal to activists in other states.

When the MSW's executive board learned of the idea, they took measures to protect their autonomy from their dictatorial ex-president. Six MSW board members—including Marshall, Nichols, Vincenz, and Johnson—sent a letter to the entire membership. "There are several people who are moving swiftly behind the scenes, without your knowledge, to make ECHO an organization which would <u>direct</u> rather than <u>coordinate</u> the activities of member organizations," they wrote. "A SUPER organization would necessarily lead to the enthronement of a HOMOPHILE CAESAR called a President or an Executive Director."

Despite the suspicions of the MSW's board members, they still planned to attend the 1965 ECHO conference, to be held at New York's Biltmore Hotel on September 24. Ten days before the convention, an anonymous caller telephoned the NYPD, promising to break up the "queer convention." The hotel learned of the threat and used it as an opportunity to cancel, and the homosexuals again scrambled to find a venue. At last, the stylish Barbizon-Plaza agreed to accommodate them.

The Friday night before the conference, two officers—one from disturbance control and another from the Vice Squad—visited the ECHO suite at the hotel. They were there to protect the homosexuals, they explained.

The next morning, Dick Leitsch of the MSNY welcomed more than two hundred delegates, representing twelve organizations and including visitors from San Francisco.

In Kameny's address to the attendees, he recounted the history of his Society's direct action campaign and pressed for the adoption of picketing. He showed a color film of the Independence Day picket and alluded to the demonstrations' success. "Doors have been opened to us that were not opened by any other method over years of trying," he explained. When Kameny finished, he received a standing ovation and shouts of "bravo," the most enthusiastic audience response of the convention.

Before that night's banquet, a CBS television crew arrived to set up its lights for a documentary on homosexuality. Under the lights, Paul Goodman, the bisexual anarchist writer and psychotherapist, gave his keynote address. "Look, your homophile organizations are now using techniques picked up from the Negro civil rights movement," he told the overwhelmingly white audience. "I hope therefore that you have the decency to support them on their picket lines." Just as King had come out against the Vietnam War, homosexuals needed to come out against other American injustices. "The answer has to be what is humanly right," he explained. "And in the end, you'll go further that way."

After the banquet, representatives from twelve organizations packed into the ECHO suite to discuss, in a spur-of-the-moment meeting, the movement's "mutual problems, objectives, and techniques," as the *Eastern Mattachine Magazine* reported. There had been a lack of communication within the national homophile movement, they concluded. West Coast activists had no idea what the East Coast did, and vice versa. Perhaps a *national* homophile conference would allow for the exchange of ideas, they decided. Geographically, they would have to compromise. The Midwest? The South? In a formal vote, the delegates decided to hold a national meeting of homophile groups in Kansas City. America's first national meeting of independent homophile organizations would take place in February 1966.

In the December issue of *Drum*, Clark Polak, still exiled from ECHO, described the convention as an "almost criminal waste of time, talent and money."

BRUCE SCOTT RECEIVED a letter from William J. Scruggs, chief of the CSC's Professional Examining Section, on October 21, less than a week after he learned of his renewed eligibility for federal employment. Yes, wrote Scruggs, pursuant to the district court's order, Scott was now eligible for federal employment. "However, we are compelled by information available to us to initiate action to determine your suitability for employment."

The CSC had renewed its battle. By first rating him eligible, it avoided the Supreme Court *and* delayed any change in policy. Now it simply planned to purge him yet again. "I was naive enough to think that my trial was over," Scott told Kameny. "I am right back where I was four years ago and the entire fight is to begin all over again."

David Carliner and the NCACLU began drafting another lawsuit.

WHEN ERNESTINE EPPENGER moved to New York, her college best friend came out to her. Ernestine, do you know that I'm gay? he asked. Do you know the term *gay*?

"All of a sudden, things began to click," she later explained. She knew others like her existed. As a Black lesbian woman, she reasoned there must also exist a movement for homosexuals, something like the Black freedom movement.

She had already left the NAACP in favor of the more militant, demonstration-friendly Congress of Racial Equality. "I always had the impression that the NAACP's chief aim was to create a sort of pad for outstanding Negroes that they could get ahead," she admitted to Barbara Gittings for a *Ladder* interview. It did not seem to care about the Black man or woman on the street.

Eppenger soon found the DOB and joined it immediately, choosing "Ernestine Eckstein" as her pseudonym. But the DOB, she soon realized, cared too much about the individual lesbian, focusing only on social and educational events. The group had a ridiculous name, and it even eschewed picketing, which she believed to be a relatively conservative activity. After growing frustrated, Eppenger even considered starting her own lesbian organization.

But she had faith that the DOB would evolve. Someday, the DOB would embrace picketing and legal battles. Then, once all homosexuals were fighting properly for themselves, they could turn to "the question of transvestites," as she explained to Gittings.

"I'm surprised you threw that in," responded Gittings. "The transvestites. You mean we should think about their right to dress as they please without discrimination?"

"The homophile movement is only part of a much larger movement of the erasure of labels," explained Eppenger. "And I think the right of a person to dress as he chooses must necessarily follow when we expand our own philosophy of bringing about change for the homosexual."

When Eppenger learned of a homosexual picket in Philadelphia on Independence Day, she agreed to march, thus becoming the first lesbian of color to march in a homophile demonstration. In October, when she learned the MSW planned to host a final picket of the White House, she agreed to march there, too.

It marked the final march of 1965. After the inconclusive CSC meeting and the Bruce Scott legal disaster, it became clear the demonstrations—attracting only dozens, at most—had failed to effect immediate change. "The walls didn't come crumbling down," as Kameny later put it. Press interest seemed to be dwindling, and it was becoming increasingly clear that the MSW needed a change in tactics.

On October 16, ten thousand demonstrators marched on New York's Fifth Avenue, three thousand marched in Berkeley, and over one hundred other cities marched against American intervention in Vietnam.

On October 23, only forty-five homophile picketers—thirty men and fifteen women—marched in a large oval outside the White House, stepping on the fallen autumn leaves. Eppenger arrived from New York wearing chic white sunglasses. DENIAL OF EQUALITY OF OPPORTUNITY IS IMMORAL, said her sign. Gittings, wearing aviators, arrived from Philadelphia and carried her sign: SEXUAL PREFERENCE IS IRRELEVANT TO FEDERAL EMPLOYMENT.

CBS, still shooting its documentary on homosexuality, attended the picket, as did two FBI agents. And, for the first time, the picketers encountered a counterdemonstration. Two teenaged males, separated from the homosexuals by the police, carried their own signs:

ARE YOU KIDDING?

GET SERIOUS

After the march, the picketers walked one block to the Chicken Hut, where they ate in the restaurant/bar's upstairs section. They discussed tactics, gossiped about the upcoming national conference, and drank.

The next month, Ernestine Eppenger won the vice presidency of the DOB's New York chapter, gaining office as part of a militant, pro-picketing ticket. She immediately invited Kameny and Gittings to speak to the DOB-NY's members, with the hope of getting "these people to realize there is such a thing as the homophile movement."

IN NOVEMBER, after eight months, Kameny remained unemployed. He continued applying for astronomy jobs (including one at NASA's Goddard Space Flight Center), but without his presidency of his Society—

and now, with no more pickets—he had additional time on his hands. So he began an effort to become the national spokesperson for the homosexual.

The new Mattachine Midwest flew him to Chicago to take part in a panel on a popular late-night ABC television show hosted by gossip columnist Irv Kupcinet. Later, before a large crowd of Chicago homophile activists, he showed picketing videos on a projector.

The MSW, on the other hand, became less and less Frank Kameny's organization. Jon Swanson, the Society's new president, decided that the MSW needed an office, and it therefore needed to fund-raise. On November 20, to celebrate its fourth anniversary, the Society hosted a cocktail party at the Golden Calf, a gay bar. Not only did the fund-raiser contradict the MSW's constitutional policy against social events, but it also had a casual dress code.

In December, Kameny campaigned for the MSW's presidency, hoping to reclaim the reins of the organization he saw as his own. Marshall's "personal popularity" was not enough, he wrote to the Society's members. Their organization needed "intellectual consistency, ideological purity, and long-range strategy."

In January, the members of his organization again kept the "homophile Caesar" away from the presidency.

That month, Kameny approached ten months of unemployment. ("We cannot fill any positions that would best suit your previous experience," said NASA.) Then, on Wednesday, January 26, a nineteen-year-old Columbia student named Bob Martin arrived at Kameny's door.

It had been a terrible month for Martin, too. His roommates, upon discovering his homosexual activities, informed the college dean. "I'm quite surprised and upset, as they mean an awful lot to me," Martin wrote in his diary. "Feel persecuted and followed."

He moved out on January 25, and the next day, he traveled to Washington to interview for internships on Capitol Hill. He arrived at Kameny's home on 5020 Cathedral Avenue that night.

"Leave on Greyhound bus through snow, 1 hour late," wrote Martin. "To Frank Kameny's after waiting—and freezing—for hours. Have sex."

By the end of his five-day visit, Martin had received internship offers from three different congressmen. He made plans to live with Frank Kameny during the summer of 1966, five months later.

WASHINGTON'S FIRST HOMOSEXUAL OFFICE, a two-room suite on the eighth floor of a grungy building at 1319 F Street NW, three blocks from the White House, opened in January. It contained a library of books related to the homosexual, the Society's files, and, most important, a staffed telephone. Each weeknight, Washington's homosexuals could call the Society's new number for information, advice, or, if facing trouble, help.

That month, Lilli Vincenz published the first edition of the Society's new publication, *The Homosexual Citizen*. The issue featured a picketing report by Kameny, a national news report by Jack Nichols, and an ad by the Golden Calf. Kameny worried that these developments represented a turn inward, a symptom of stagnation. Indeed, how did an office or a magazine help the American homosexual citizen at large?

On January 21, *TIME* published an unprecedented feature on "The Homosexual in America." Kameny had spoken extensively to the *TIME* reporter in the final months of 1965. "Hopefully an enlightened public will prove more compassionate than days past," the reporter had told him. "We mean to do a good piece."

Homosexuality, *TIME* concluded, "is a pathetic little second-rate substitute for reality, a pitiable flight from life. As such it deserves fairness, compassion, understanding and, when possible, treatment. But it deserves no encouragement, no glamorization, no rationalization, no fake status as minority martyrdom, no sophistry about simple differences in taste—and, above all, no pretense that it is anything but a pernicious sickness."

The homophile movement, MSW president Jon Swanson wrote in *The Homosexual Citizen*, needed to consider the potential of a heterosexual backlash. "If a reactionary period is on the distant horizon—or even closer—it is best that we 'make hay while the sun shines,'" he wrote. They needed to press for change with even more vigor.

Only days after the *TIME* essay, evidence of an intransigent, reactionary government appeared within the halls of the FBI. On February 6, the Washington Field Office received a phone call from a man in Florida. One of the FBI's employees, the man claimed, had a son who was a member of the Mattachine Society of Washington.

Special agent J. Richard Nichols, an eighteen-year veteran of the FBI, had received a commendation from J. Edgar Hoover—for his "sincere devotion to duty"—only one week earlier. But four days after the call from Florida, he admitted his transgressions. His son, MSW charter member Jack Nichols, had come out to him in 1954, yet Nichols Sr. had never informed the Bureau. Worse, the special agent had known that his son was an officer of a homosexual organization.

Agent Nichols requested clemency from the Bureau. "If asked to do so by the Bureau, he will stop seeing his son," reported an internal memorandum.

The FBI's administration division concluded that the Special Agent had failed to report a potential "source of embarrassment to the Bureau," and his deception was "inexcusable."

Despite Nichols Sr.'s offer to excommunicate his son, Hoover nevertheless censured him, placed him on probation, and transferred him to Milwaukee for the rest of his career. Jack Nichols never heard from his father again.

ON TUESDAY, FEBRUARY 15, Kameny left Washington for the Kansas City meeting of America's homophile organizations. He took a train to Philadelphia, where he met Barbara Gittings and her lover, Kay Tobin Lahusen. In a Volkswagen, they drove west through a snowstorm. Late Thursday night, they arrived to the State Hotel in Kansas City.

"The 'gathering of the clans' started on Friday, with people beginning to arrive from all directions, for the meeting," Kameny told Bob Martin. Jack Nichols and Jon Swanson represented the MSW, and in sum, thirty-eight delegates arrived to represent fourteen organizations.

The meeting began the next morning in the State Hotel's Crystal Room. The delegates elected a straight minister, Clay Colwell of San Francisco's Council on Religion and the Homosexual, as their chairman.

Clark Polak of the Janus Society stood and called for a homosexual

Bill of Rights, which had been drafted, at least in part, by Kameny. It included legal reform, the MSW's sickness statement, and the "moral right to be homosexual."

The West Coast groups, especially the Society for Individual Rights (SIR), objected. Why were the delegates debating abstract principles and *ideology*? Did it even matter? Why not *plan* something instead?

The delegates agreed on the legalization of homosexual activity and their opposition to the purges, but the sickness statement sowed discord. The views of psychiatrists, argued West Coast activists, were irrelevant to the homophile movement.

Kameny responded that the sickness question was, in fact, the "most important single question facing our Movement today," the root of *many* of the homosexuals' problems, including their exclusion from the military, their lack of self-esteem, and the negative perceptions held by the straight public.

Only four of the fourteen organizations voted in favor of a declaration that homosexuals were healthy. The motion failed.

"The meeting was, to me, a great disappointment," Kameny told Martin. "The Saturday session was, I felt, a total victory of mass intellectual mediocrity."

By the end of the conference, the delegates had tabled the sickness question and whether they had the "moral right to be homosexual." They had no time to consider the creation of a national affiliation or organizational "superstructure."

There *had* been tangible successes, however. Despite Kameny's warnings about mixing causes, the delegates adopted a plan, introduced by the DOB's Phyllis Lyon, to organize a national series of meetings on Armed Forces Day, where they would discuss the problem of the homosexual and the draft. They decided on a name for their convention, the "National Planning Conference of Homophile Organizations," and agreed on an August date for their second meeting, to take place in San Francisco.

Kameny and Gittings drove back east, and en route, they met Clark Polak at the Kinsey Institute at Indiana University, Bloomington. Kameny had been in correspondence with the researchers there, who invited the homophile delegation for a visit. "We were given the 'red carpet' treatment," gloated Kameny.

That night, Dr. William Simon, a Kinsey Institute researcher, took Kameny and Polak to a Bloomington gay bar. Both Kameny and Polak wore Randy Wicker's lapel buttons, one a lavender equal sign, the other EQUALITY FOR HOMOSEXUALS. As the bar's patrons crowded around them, staring at the subversive buttons in awe, a bartender stuck one high up on the wall, for all future patrons to see. He asked Kameny to send a dozen more.

"The upshot," Kameny told Martin, "was that Clark and I each went home with someone."

The next morning, Kameny lectured about homosexuality to Dr. Simon's class, his first time teaching students in a decade. He cruised the YMCA in Columbus, Ohio, stopped at a Philadelphia bathhouse, and arrived back in Washington on Friday morning, February 25. That day, CSC chairman John Macy sent his official response to the demands of the Mattachine Society of Washington.

HOMOSEXUALS, SAID MACY, did not exist. "We do not subscribe to the view, which indeed is the rock upon which the Mattachine Society is founded, that 'homosexual' is a proper metonym for an individual," he wrote. It was merely an *adjective* to describe overt behaviors. By denying the existence of homosexual Americans, the commission could also deny that it discriminated against a minority group.

Macy claimed that the CSC cared only about the employee's impact on the efficiency of the civil service. Homosexuals had no place in the federal workforce because they caused "apprehension" and "revulsion" in their coworkers, not to mention "the unavoidable subjection of the sexual deviate to erotic stimulation through on-the-job use of common toilet, shower, and living facilities."

"We reject categorically," added Macy, "the assertion that the Commission pries into the private sex life of those seeking Federal employment, or that it discriminates in ferreting out homosexual conduct." The CSC did not proactively investigate and purge homosexuals; if homosexual behavior remained "truly private," then employees would be safe.

"In point of fact," responded Kameny, "you do grant the validity of the use of the word 'homosexual' as a noun, and are actually so using and thinking in terms of it." Plus, Macy had already used *homosexual* as a noun in previous correspondence. Worst of all, Macy had merely identified the problems and prejudices of *heterosexuals*, not homosexuals. "The government of Nazi Germany seized upon and reinforced an endemic anti-Semitism of long-standing, which was part of the mores of the Germany of that day," Kameny wrote.

Macy's letter had a silver lining. At last, the government found itself defending the rationale behind its purges in a tangible document for public consumption. If this rationale later changed, or if the government acted in a manner inconsistent with the letter's claims, Kameny would be able to leap upon it, taking advantage, as he wrote in *The Ladder*, of the CSC's "masterful stroke of illogic."

KAMENY APPROACHED a full year of unemployment. He had been relying on loans from friends, including at least one from Clark Polak (who had even offered him a job at *Drum* magazine). He was several months behind on rent. In early March, Kameny wrote to the NCACLU explaining his situation, a repeat of his late-1950s nightmare. Every astronomy job required a clearance, and personnel officers—who talked among themselves, he suspected—knew he was unlikely to receive one from the Department of Defense. NASA, Johns Hopkins University Applied Physics Laboratory, IBM, and Fairchild Hiller Space Systems all said they had no jobs suitable for the astronomer.

"It thus seems necessary to force the Department of Defense to act on a clearance for me, without my having a job," Kameny explained. Would the NCACLU take his case?

At this moment, Kameny's mother, Rae, learned of her son's homosexuality. He had told his sister, Edna, the year prior, and she subsequently told their mother.

Rae sent her son a letter. She wished Franklin had revealed himself earlier, she wrote. She and her husband may have been able to do something about his condition. She felt responsible, sorrowful.

"You need have no sense of guilt," responded Kameny. "I don't think that you made me as I am in this context. I see nothing to blame you about, if you did—you also made me a human and sensitive person; one with a brilliant and trained mind; one with an extraordinary personality (in every good sense), and many other things."

"If you DID make me as I am—I thank you for it."

Plus, to be gay was no sickness, he added. It was just like being Jewish.

"I wish that I could go along with you all the way, but my sorrow and grief and sense of guilt are still very, very great," responded Rae Beck Kameny. "How can I help feeling sorrow at the thought of a man who, as you say yourself, is brilliant, sensitive, with a marvellous personality, who can't bring all these characteristics out in the open and make the most of them? Because you are all these things is precisely why I suffer so."

She urged Franklin to leave Washington for a "fresh start" in a city not dominated by the federal government.

"I hope to hear very soon that you have a marvellous job, where your talents will be fully appreciated."

"All my love, always."

KAMENY RECEIVED the good news only three weeks later. "Calloo, Callay, oh frabjous day—!!! I have a job," he told Bob Martin.

A member of the NCACLU had referred Kameny to a small optics firm in Silver Spring, where he would work as a consultant. If all went well, he would eventually become a regular employee. Kameny had been honest about the circumstances of his government dismissal, and the company promised to support his efforts for a security clearance.

"I will have been out of work for EXACTLY one year," he informed Gittings. "I just wonder————..."

He asked Clark Polak for a six-hundred-dollar loan to support him until his first paycheck.

After sending the letters of good news to his friends and colleagues, Kameny traveled straight to David Carliner's office for an update on the Bruce Scott case.

"The daffodil buds are getting ready to open, the tulip buds are forming," he told Martin. "I have much to do, since, shortly, I'll no longer be a gentleman of leisure."

On Armed Forces Day, though he had originally opposed the plan for a demonstration, Kameny organized his Washington contingent in earnest, but on his own terms. For one, he enforced his dress code. "You may be disturbed to learn that at none of our public demonstrations are we going to insist on a particular mode of dress," Don Slater of Los Angeles told him. "Our Committee insists that the public will have to take us as we are: both the bizarre and the ordinary. If we want to be accepted, we must fully accept in turn."

At 3:00 p.m. on May 21, 1966, Kameny led a four-mile march of approximately twenty people from the White House to the Pentagon. "We don't dodge the draft; the draft dodges us," said their signs. After picketing from 4:00 to 4:30 at the Pentagon, Kameny left immediately for the airport, where he boarded a flight to New York.

There, he spoke at a public protest rally hosted by Ernestine Eppenger's newly militant chapter of the Daughters of Bilitis. Even Kameny's DOB foe, Shirley Willer, participated in the event.

Only West Coast newspapers covered the demonstrations, a novel phenomenon on that side of the country. Three hundred homosexuals recited the pledge of allegiance in front of the Federal Building in San Francisco, and a motorcade of thirteen cars, emblazoned with large signs, paraded down the streets of Los Angeles.

Kameny's war against the federal government had spread first to New York and now to California. At the end of the month, the MSNY board voted to honor both Kameny and Gittings with honorary memberships in the MSNY. "If the homophile movement, as an active, effective weapon for social change, can claim a father," Dick Leitsch told Kameny, "it would certainly be you."

But in Washington, Kameny's fight remained in a stalemate. In the White House, the CSC, and the Pentagon, nothing had changed.

One week after Armed Forces Day, Bob Martin, the bisexual, Goldwater-supporting Columbia student, moved into the newly employed astronomer's home.

Barbara Gittings, front, and Ernestine Eppenger
at the White House, October 23, 1965

14.

THE ILLUSTRATOR

On October 18, 1965, three months after twenty-eight-year-old Donald Lee Crawford picketed in front of the Pentagon, he sat before two special investigators from the Office of Naval Intelligence. A short, slender man with brown hair, brown eyes, and glasses, Crawford already had an honorable discharge from the navy. He worked as an illustrator for the Research Analyst Corporation, and he did not see the harm in telling the investigators the truth. He agreed to sign a statement.

Six months later, in April 1966, Crawford received a notice from Walter T. Skallerup Jr., deputy assistant secretary of defense for security policy at the Pentagon. "<u>NOTICE OF SUSPENSION OF ACCESS AUTHORIZATION</u>," it said. Until that moment, Crawford had held a top secret security clearance, which permitted him to work on classified government projects contracted to his employer. The Pentagon had reason to believe he engaged in "criminal, immoral and notoriously disgraceful conduct," specifically "acts of sexual perversion with numerous males." These acts reflected "such poor judgment and instability as to suggest that [he] might disclose classified information to unauthorized persons." Crawford could, therefore, be subjected to "coercion, influence, or pressure which may be likely to cause [him] to act contrary to the national interest."

In May, the Pentagon received Crawford's response. "I know of no such acts of sexual perversion," it began. And, before Crawford could respond to the allegations, he had some questions. How did the Pentagon define the term *sexual perversion*? What about *immoral*? *Disgraceful*?

Notoriety? He wanted the "entire chain of reasoning" relating acts of sexual perversion to eligibility for security clearance. He demanded to know which criminal statutes he had violated in "<u>each</u> particular, individual instance." He requested "copies of the relevant published papers or other documents of professional authority (psychological, psychiatric, sociological, medical, or other)" that characterized homosexual activity as a security risk. Specifically:

1. Behavior
2. Activities
3. Associations
4. Reliability
5. Untrustworthiness

Frank Kameny, financially stable, lacking a focus in his fight against the government, and stripped of his presidential powers in the MSW, had agreed to represent Donald Crawford. As his cocounsel, Kameny chose Barbara Gittings of Philadelphia.

AFTER THEIR FIRST EVENING in Washington, the sexual tension between Bob Martin and Frank Kameny became more intense with each subsequent conversation. "I must confess that I found you most tempting and tantalizing, last night," Kameny wrote the Columbia freshman in February 1966, following a visit to New York. "I didn't want to take any kind of initiative, however (as sorely tempted as I was to do so), unless you were receptive to such attentions (were you??)."

Martin kept Kameny abreast of his own sexual exploits, including orgies and hustling at the St. Marks Baths. "I decided to play the innocent straight and boy, what a ball I had," he wrote. "5 orgasms and $10 in the process."

Their correspondence became increasingly platonic, however, and eventually burgeoned into a friendship. "Guess what?" asked Martin in April. "I'm taking Astronomy next year! (Or is it astrology??)"

That summer, Martin arrived to Washington for an internship in the office of Congressman Howard "Bo" Callaway, a Republican from Georgia.

Almost immediately, he began creating shock waves within Kameny's gay world. On July 2, Martin met White House marcher Perrin Shaffer—"have him 7 times! Quite compatible"—and, on July 4, founding MSW member Dick Schlegel, who treated Martin to brunch and dinner at the Chicken Hut. "He's hypnotized by me," wrote the undergraduate on July 4.

Kameny was in Philadelphia that Independence Day, picketing in the first annual "Reminder Day" demonstration, the brainchild of MSNY's Craig Rodwell. The New Yorker, galvanized by Kameny's pickets, had wanted to continue demonstrating even after the conclusion of the 1965 picketing campaign. Although dwarfed by the burgeoning Vietnam protests, the gay Independence Day pickets would serve as an annual reminder of the homosexual citizens' existence, something like a holiday of resistance, to be held on the day of America's birth.

"Let me assure you," said Rodwell, "that if anyone does show up at the bus dressed in sneakers, bluejeans, or outlandish clothing, we will promptly return their $5.00 and remind them that participants in such a demonstration are not there to assert their individual egos, but rather as representatives of millions of homosexual citizens."

The young organizer invited the attendees, drafted the signs, and placed advertisements. Kameny edited Rodwell's signs ("Omit sign 3—they aren't killing us off—yet") and informed Philadelphia authorities of the march, to take place between 2:00 and 4:00 p.m.

On the Fourth—at 103 degrees, Philadelphia's hottest on record—five hundred demonstrators appeared for an antiwar rally. They burned army discharges and an officer's commission, and thirty-seven demonstrators were arrested.

Rodwell's bus left from New York to Philadelphia at 11:00 a.m. On the journey, they sang the "Homophile Freedom Song," written by a MSNY member and sung to the tune of "The Battle Hymn of the Republic."

> *Mine eyes have seen the struggles of the Negroes and the Jews,*
> *I have seen the counties trampled where the laws of men abuse,*
> *But you crush the homosexual with anything you choose,*
> *Now we are marching on.*

A visibly sweating Wicker marched behind Gittings, who held her sign: HOMOSEXUALS SHOULD BE JUDGED AS INDIVIDUALS. Another man carried an American flag as the homosexuals walked in silence behind a police barricade.

The press ignored them.

Kameny returned to Washington, where Martin was wreaking havoc.

July 5—"Decide against going out with Schlegel."

July 11—"Take Jon Sturm, Perrin, and one other home for mild orgy."

July 17—"Dispute with Frank on serving dinner."

July 18—"Fight with Frank over party guests."

For Martin's birthday on July 27, Kameny gifted him a trip to Fire Island, but their fights continued.

Aug 14—"Crisis with Frank, who is sexually frustrated about me."

Aug 16—"Have long talk with Frank, and crisis seems to be smoothing out. Have cold, suspect something wrong with rectum, maybe gonorrhea."

Martin recovered by Labor Day weekend, when the pair arrived at the Beach Hotel and Club in Cherry Grove. After a series of police raids, the MSNY had posted blue mimeograph posters all over Cherry Grove, listing Kameny's recommendations for arrested homosexuals.

Kameny and Martin remained safe from the police, and at Fire Island, for the first time, Martin met another gay Columbia student. James Millham knew several other gay Columbia students, he told Martin. When Martin returned to campus in a few days, he would have a community of homosexuals, a family.

FOR TWO YEARS, Barbara Gittings had worked full-time in the movement, surviving on a modest inheritance. By the summer of 1966, *The Ladder* looked little like the publication she had begun editing three years prior. She gave the magazine a subtitle, "A Lesbian Review," which became larger and larger beneath *The Ladder* until the title and subtitle were exactly the same size. Gittings had featured three more lesbian faces on *The Ladder*'s cover during her editorship, including a smiling Lilli Vincenz marching at the CSC, another close-up of Vincenz, and a close-up of Ernestine Eppenger in June 1966.

That same month, the DOB's governing board fired Gittings. Her magazine had become too militant, too pro-picketing, too provocative for the education and information-focused Daughters of Bilitis. For the first time in nearly a decade, she was cut loose from the DOB, free to take projects of her choosing. Ernestine Eppenger, frustrated in her efforts to bring militancy to the DOB chapter in New York, quit that month, too.

Randy Wicker, equally exasperated by the MSNY, channeled his energies elsewhere. "I spent ten years of my life trying to save the world," the twenty-eight-year-old told *The Washington Post*. "I just got fed up and decided it was time to save myself." Recognizing a business opportunity in his homemade lapel buttons—they were always a hit at Village parties—he invested three thousand dollars to open a store, Underground Uplift Unlimited. There, he sold buttons that appealed to all sides of the political spectrum, but the sex-related buttons sold best.

BATMAN LOVES ROBIN

FORNICATION IS FUN

LET'S FACE IT—WE'RE ALL QUEER

By August 1966, he was selling thousands of buttons per month. He attributed his success to an increasing desire among Americans "to be noticed, to stand out from the crowd." Conformity and respectability, Wicker understood, were dead.

ON THURSDAY MORNING, August 25, 1966, sixty-eight homosexuals and allies arrived at the Bellevue, an elegant Beaux-Arts hotel in San Francisco. They passed the lobby's gold-and-marble grand staircase and entered the conference room, where—because of its poor acoustics and sound system—they strained to hear the proceedings of that year's second meeting of the National Planning Conference of Homophile Organizations.

The delegates elected Clay Colwell, the straight minister, as the chair of the conference. An irritated Kameny spoke shortly thereafter, criticizing the movement's hesitancy to speak for itself. Look no further than their last conference in Kansas City, he argued. "Who spoke for us to the newspapers—an avowed HETEROsexual! Ridiculous! And a bit sad!" What the movement really needed, he argued, was a "clear, consistent, coordinated, positive philosophy and ideology, vigorously and actively propounded publicly at every opportunity."

Shirley Willer, recently elected the president of the national DOB, also criticized the delegates. "The lesbian," she explained, "is discriminated against not only because she is a lesbian, but because she is a woman." Female homosexuals faced problems of job security, career advancement, and, for many women, families from previous marriages. "We suspect that should the male homosexual achieve his particular objectives in regard to his homosexuality he may possibly become a more adamant foe of women's rights than the heterosexual male has ever been," concluded Willer. She called for the delegates to affirm that as homosexuals fighting for gay rights, they cared about women's rights, too. The call from the "booming" DOB president, as *ONE* magazine later referred to Willer, went ignored by the rest of the delegates.

The delegates spent the rest of the day bickering over procedural technicalities, including the voting power of delegations, the use of Robert's Rules of Order, and the allowance of outside guests. "Everyone wants to be a champion of the movement—a Martin Luther King of homosexuality," explained one delegate. It was "a very ungentlemanly (unladylike?) bitch-fight," as another attendee put it.

On Saturday, the delegates called for the creation of a national legal defense fund, which would operate like the NAACP's own Legal Defense Fund, founded nearly three decades earlier. The delegates voted against including *homosexual* in the fund's name, however. Who, they asked, would write a check to an organization with that word in the title?

The most spirited discussion occurred after a Mattachine Midwest motion to create a confederation of homophile organizations, an umbrella organization with a centralized ACLU structure envisioned by Kameny. Vanguard, an organization of young hustlers based in San Francisco, came out against the idea. "The various types of homosexuals are so far apart that a union of them would seem no less than a miracle," argued Vanguard's president, complaining of the "middle class" control of the other organizations. The delegates defeated the motion in a 35–23 vote.

On Sunday, the Tavern Guild, a coalition of San Francisco gay bars, instructed the delegates to meet at a sleazy north-end bar at 10:00 a.m. A carpool then took them forty miles east, to a plot of land in a hidden valley.

Surrounded by six hundred homosexuals, the sophisticated Foster Gunnison of Connecticut stood in awe. The Sunday picnic featured a swimming pool, a dance floor imported from a go-go club, and a softball field ("you haven't seen ANYTHING till you've watched 18 homos playing a game of soft-ball," he wrote). A cook grilled steaks while wearing a bonnet and a dress.

Homosexuals were "scrambling around, sometimes aimlessly, searching for identity," concluded Gunnison. "I am struck by how much preoccupation is shown with clothes (often offbeat) as symbols in this respect."

Two delegates, for example, arrived to represent the Circle of Loving Companions, a new organization. Both had long, flowing hair and said they were married to each other. They wore elaborate costumes— either fourteenth-century forester or eighteenth-century hermitage, guessed Gunnison—and handmade amber amulets that depicted a halo around an upright penis. The older of the two was the fifty-four-year-old Harry Hay, the founder of the original Mattachine Society, the man who had envisioned the creation of a unique homosexual ethic and culture seventeen years earlier.

A MONTH LATER, on September 27, Bob Martin told his new gay friend at Columbia, James Millham, about the homophile movement. While he spoke, the idea came to him. Columbia needed a Mattachine Society of its own.

On October 2, Kameny sent Martin copies of nearly all literature ever produced by the MSW, and Gittings sent copies of *The Ladder*. "If we'd been sensible and foresighted, you'd have done all this reading all summer long, and taken this stuff up to NY with you," Kameny admonished.

Kameny had become a father figure. "Dear friend, son, companion, fellow homophile leader—Bob," he wrote in October. "Got my telephone bill today (actually, yesterday)—almost $85, of which about $25 is calls to or from you."

With Kameny and Gittings's guidance, Martin replicated the Mattachine Society of Washington. The Episcopal chaplain of the university agreed to sponsor the new organization, and Martin joined the local ACLU to ask for its cooperation. For his pseudonym, Martin chose "Stephen Donaldson."

On October 27, a Columbia dean received a call from an attorney representing the MSNY, urging the university to reject the new campus group. MSNY president Dick Leitsch believed that Martin was treading on the MSNY's territory, causing confusion over who *truly* represented New York's homosexuals. If Martin's group caused controversy or embarrassment, reasoned Leitsch, it would risk all the connections and respect the MSNY had worked so hard to build.

In November, Martin agreed to change his group's name to the Student Homophile League, but the university itself raised another obstacle. To gain recognition from Columbia, a student organization needed to submit a list of its members. Martin, who had sworn anonymity to his network of Columbia homosexuals, requested an exemption. To be on a list of homosexuals on campus, he explained to the university, was unthinkable to gay students, especially if that list wound up in the wrong hands.

Until Columbia relaxed its rules, or until the members of the Student Homophile League were willing to be known, the group could only exist underground. Martin and his gay friends therefore met secretly. Together, they experimented with LSD, or, on a typical Saturday, began at Julius' bar, watched a drag show in the Bowery, and then ended the night at the Stonewall Inn, dancing.

Kameny, proud of his knowledge of New York's gay landscape, was unfamiliar with the last venue. "What is the Stonewall, at which you danced?"

ON OCTOBER 7, 1966, Bruce Scott's case returned to court.

This time, the CSC had provided Scott with four pages of evidence. "In view of the information which has been cited above," asked the CSC, "do you now deny that you have engaged in homosexual acts?"

David Carliner of the NCACLU responded in April, accusing the CSC of failing to provide any specific evidence of *immoral* conduct. In October, he filed suit against Chairman Macy once again.

Meanwhile, Kameny's arguments against the purges were becoming the national policy of the ACLU. The national Union still technically adhered to its 1957 policy approving of the purges, but beginning in the spring of 1966, the national Due Process Committee began reconsidering the question. After examining the NCACLU's new policy, Macy's letter to the MSW, and the *Scott* decision, the committee made its recommendation in November. "Homosexuality per se should not bar from government employment persons who are presently practicing homosexuals in their private lives," it concluded.

On January 6, 1967, Judge George Hart, the same district court judge who had ruled against Scott in 1965, released his decision in *Scott II*. An active homosexual, he decided, should not be permitted to work for the government.

"Every civil rights group seems to have its Scott," reported the MSNY newsletter. "The Negroes had Dred Scott and we have Bruce."

TWO WEEKS LATER, David H. Henretta Jr., an Industrial Personnel Security Clearance Office examiner assigned to the case of Donald Crawford, received a package from Kameny and Gittings. Inside, he found a gift and an accompanying letter. "We formally request, hereby, that before the Field Board Hearing in the above-captioned case, you have read the enclosed book: *The Trial*, by Franz Kafka."

For months, Kameny and Gittings had prepared to represent Crawford in his upcoming Department of Defense hearing, which would determine whether Crawford could retain his top secret clearance. The duo planned to represent him only until they appealed to the highest levels of the military. Then they would hand Crawford's case—and later, others like his—to the NCACLU. "We are hopeful, through this and other means, of eliciting well-based test cases, in large number, utterly to destroy" the purges, explained Kameny.

As amateur attorneys, they knew they were unlikely to win at the administrative level. But just as Kameny had hoped to educate the Supreme Court with his 1961 brief, perhaps they could educate the Pentagon officials in the process. Hence, the Kafka.

"We are busily honing our already-razor-sharp intellectual claws," they warned.

In 1918, the United States Armed Forces had erected two monstrous, wood-and-concrete, warehouse-like structures next to the reflecting pool of the Lincoln Memorial, close to where the Vietnam Memorial now stands. Intended to provide temporary offices for thousands of military personnel during World War I, the buildings had stood for more than fifty years. By 1967, they were dilapidated and structurally unsound, their hallways crooked.

At 10:00 a.m., on Thursday, February 24, Frank Kameny, Barbara Gittings, and Donald Crawford walked into the Munitions Building, the temporary structure closest to the Lincoln Memorial. They proceeded to room 4245, where the homosexuals met three attorneys for the Department of Defense; the examiner, David Henretta; and a stenographer, there to transcribe the entire proceeding.

"All letters, motions, and related correspondence in the applicant's case, with the exception of the book entitled 'The Trial,' by Franz Kafka, have been made a part of the record," began Henretta.

One of the Pentagon attorneys asked to hear, for the record, that Crawford actually wanted Kameny, never trained as an attorney, to represent him.

Yes, said Crawford.

In his opening statement, Kameny introduced Gittings as an expert on homosexuality. "To my right is the hero of the drama, Mr. Donald Lee Crawford, the applicant," he continued.

The security clearance system was an "exercise in the subtle, and often the flagrant and shameless, imposition of conformity and the suppression of dissent in matters of conduct, ideas, morality," he explained. Because the Department of Defense based its policies on morality and religious precepts, they were unconstitutional. By appealing to reason and common sense, he would prove that the Department of Defense had no choice but to reinstate the security clearance of Donald Crawford.

Thomas Nugent, assistant counsel for the Department of Defense, then presented the government's first witness.

Robert Kain, a special agent for the Office for Naval Intelligence, testified that Crawford had voluntarily confessed his homosexual activity.

The department lawyers then called Donald Crawford to testify.

Yes, he admitted, I wrote my confession in my own hand.

"Did you engage in acts of mutual masturbation?"

Kameny objected, and the examiner overruled him.

Nugent repeated the question.

"You can assume, yes, I do partake in that practice of today," responded Crawford.

"Do you engage in other acts of other homosexual activity other than mutual masturbation?"

Objection; overruled.

"I have engaged in other acts, yes."

"Do you engage in acts of fellatio, either upon your person or upon some other person?"

"Yes."

"Do you engage in anal sodomy upon another person or allow it to be done upon your person?"

"Yes."

"Do you continue to have homosexual associations with strangers?"

"No."

"All of the activity took place in Washington, D.C. Is that correct?"

"Yes."

"I have no further questions."

They recessed for lunch.

"I WOULD LIKE to present Dr. Charles W. Socarides of New York City," began Rowland A. Morrow, another Pentagon attorney. A Harvard College graduate, the forty-five-year-old Socarides had begun his psychiatric training twenty years earlier as an intern at St. Elizabeths Hospital in Washington. He had just completed the manuscript of a four-hundred-page volume tentatively titled *The Homosexual: A Psychoanalytic Study*.

There were two types of homosexuals, explained Socarides. First, there were "obligatory homosexuals" who, after "the terror of childhood," needed homosexual relief "no matter the price, the danger." Second, there were "non-obligatory homosexuals," those who temporarily experimented with homosexuality only in confined environments, like prisons and concentration camps.

Is the obligatory homosexual a diagnosable pathological condition?

"I certainly consider it a pathological condition," answered Socarides. "It certainly is diagnosable."

"Doctor, I would like you to look at a booklet entitled 'The Diagnostic and Statistical Manual of Mental Disorders,'" said Morrow. "I see you have a copy of it. I will ask you to tell the Board where it is that sexual deviation is classified."

Homosexuality, read Socarides, is classified by the American Psychiatric Association's manual under "personality disorders, sociopathic type."

Is mutual masturbation between two males a form of sexual perversion?

Yes, said Socarides. "In homosexuality, ironically enough, a homosexual is seeking his lost masculinity. He is not seeking femininity; he is seeking to become a man because the very roots of his identity as a man were so hampered and so impaired and crippled in early childhood that he must, through joining with the men, identify with the men, taking his penis to become a man. This is the irony of homosexuality."

"Doctor, do you consider that a person who is an obligatory homosexual is sick?"

"Yes, very sick."

So an obligatory homosexual suffers from a disorder or compulsion?

"Yes; homosexuality is a reparative move against the tremendous damage that is going on inside a man's mind," said Socarides. "As the addict would tell you, he has to get his shot, and so does the homosexual."

"Under such conditions of psychic disequilibrium, this diagnosed obligatory homosexual would react in a reckless manner, in your opinion?"

"Anything can happen if pain and fear, rage and guilt are of sufficient intensity with anyone."

Morrow handed Socarides to Kameny for cross-examination.

"You have referred repeatedly to homosexuals and your experience with them," began Kameny. "Where do you see these homosexuals?"

"I see these homosexuals in my office; I see them at conferences at medical schools; I see them and discuss them with the residents I supervise who treat homosexuals."

"In short, all of these homosexuals you see are under what can slightly be broadly termed clinical circumstances?"

"Yes."

"In other words, you are seeing a thoroughly skewed sampling."

For three additional hours, Kameny struggled with his line of questioning.

How do you define pathology? he asked.

A disease that causes suffering and impaired normal functioning, answered Socarides.

"For people in this country with Black skin, their skin brings pain and suffering. Do you call that a disease?"

Objection; sustained. "That is going a little bit too far," said the examiner. It was getting late, he reminded Kameny.

They recessed at 5:45 p.m., after nearly eight hours in the crumbling Munitions Building.

KAMENY AND GITTINGS were shell-shocked. Not only had they never heard of Socarides, but he seemed to represent the human manifestation of all the discriminatory logic that they had long fought. "We wonder," Kameny later said, "whether the Department has not, for months, been collecting little bits and pieces of all our enemies and assembling them into one exaggerated creature of the civilized anti-homosexual labeled Dr. Socarides."

They had prepared a counterattack, however. Five months earlier, eminent psychiatrists across the country had received a letter from Barbara Gittings. Will you write a statement, she had asked, about whether a homosexual is *always* a security risk?

At 2:00 p.m. on the second day of the hearing, Gittings began introducing the psychiatrists' responses.

First, Dr. Leon Salzman, a psychiatry professor at the Georgetown School of Medicine.

Next, Dr. Evelyn Hooker of UCLA, a groundbreaking psychologist.

Dr. Joseph N. De Luca of Greystone Park State Hospital.

Professor Gordon Allport, an eminent Harvard psychologist.

Dr. Wardell Pomeroy, a coauthor of the Kinsey report.

Dr. Thomas Szasz, a famous critic of the psychiatric field.

In sum, Gittings presented letters from sixteen psychiatrists. Each contradicted the government's sole expert witness and directly refuted the Department of Defense's psychiatric rationale for its refusal to grant security clearances to homosexuals. "It is indeed possible for a homosexual to be emotionally stable and to present no danger when entrusted with secret information," said Evelyn Hooker's letter.

At 3:10 p.m., after nearly two full days of testimony, the hearing concluded. Though Kameny and Gittings would have to wait several months for a decision, they felt confident.

After that day, the Department of Defense never cited the pathology of homosexuality in front of the two amateur attorneys. Dr. Socarides disappeared from the halls of the Pentagon.

Before Kameny and Gittings departed, one of the Pentagon attorneys, James A. Cronin, turned to them. Do you still think the Pentagon is staging a Kafkaesque show trial? he asked. Did the hearing seem unfair?

No, they admitted. It seemed fair.

Frank Kameny and Bob Martin on Fire Island, September 1966

15.

THE FLOOR PLAN

In a debate over the 1964 Civil Rights Act, Senator Sam J. Ervin Jr. of North Carolina denounced it as "the most monstrous blueprint for governmental tyranny ever presented to Congress." Yes, of course he favored civil rights for African Americans, claimed the affable, bulbous-nosed sixty-seven-year-old. But not at the expense of whites' civil liberties.

After the bill's passage, Ervin shifted his focus to the law's implementation, fighting the Johnson administration's efforts to enforce school desegregation in the South. Almost simultaneously, Ervin's Senate Subcommittee on Constitutional Rights began receiving complaints from federal workers. The Civil Service Commission had begun sending them questionnaires to ask about their race, they told him.

Chairman Macy claimed that the questionnaires were intended merely to detect discrimination within the government, calculated anonymously, for the first time, by computers. But for Ervin, they raised the more disturbing possibility of minority quotas or affirmative action. The senator scheduled hearings, beginning a crusade against the federal government that appeared to have nothing to do with white supremacy. Instead, he could claim to be protecting federal employees' right to privacy.

In December, Ervin released the "shocking" results of his inquiry. Not only did the federal government ask about race, but it asked about other personal topics, too—religion, drinking, love, and sex. Such questions were "appropriate to totalitarian countries and Gestapo states," he claimed.

After the Supreme Court declared the existence of a constitutional right to privacy in its 1965 *Griswold* decision, Ervin doubled his efforts. Indeed, if Americans now had the right to be left alone, did they not have the right to be left alone as they discriminated against African Americans?

On February 21, 1967, Ervin stood on the Senate floor once again to speak not as an embattled Southerner decrying a civil rights bill, but as a civil libertarian in favor of a federal employee bill of rights.

To support his case, Ervin presented seventy-two articles from North Carolina and across the country. "Criticism Greets CSC Proposal to keep Dossier on Every Employee," announced the *Star*. "Homosexual Query Asked in State Department," reported the *Post*. His most recent article came from *The Nation*, a liberal magazine, published only the day prior. It chronicled a litany of offensive questions asked by federal investigators and concluded with the "considerable courage" of Bruce Scott. How, asked the *Nation* article, could Chairman Macy have the audacity to tell the Mattachine Society of Washington that the CSC did not pry into the private lives of federal employees, then tell Bruce Scott it had evidence he had engaged in homosexual conduct?

The senator from North Carolina left the Senate floor with an astonishing fifty-two cosponsors for his bill of rights. Ervin, who would spend much of 1967 fighting against fair housing legislation and the confirmation of America's first Black Supreme Court justice, had become the homosexual minority's most powerful ally within the federal government.

IN JANUARY 1967, Kameny again lost his campaign for president to Jon Swanson. The MSW's founder remained on the board and faithfully attended its meetings, but other homophile groups began to wonder: why was nothing happening in Washington?

The world seemed to be moving forward while Kameny acted alone and his organization watched. On March 7, CBS aired its long-awaited television documentary on homosexuality. It opened with an interview with MSW's Jack Nichols and included footage of the 1965 Washington pickets. Though it also introduced Dr. Socarides and his theories, the MSW's *Homosexual Citizen* applauded CBS for its "courageous intentions," especially since it ran the feature without a corporate sponsor.

That same week, Jack Nichols organized a meeting of the MSW's religious spin-off organization, the Washington Area Council on Religion and the Homosexual, the first meeting after a year of dormancy. Afterward, Nichols planned an official tour of gay Washington for May 18, allowing the ministers to see the Chicken Hut for themselves.

By July, the Society was holding its meetings in a new permanent location, the basement of St. Mark's Episcopal Church in Capitol Hill. To reach the space, members traveled down a flight of stairs, crossed the dirt floor of a furnace room, and entered a small room without windows. It was a grim venue, but as Kameny argued, at least it protected attendees from police and FBI surveillance.

In New York, Bob Martin balanced his Columbia schoolwork with hustling on Third Avenue, working with the Young Republicans, and gaining university recognition of his new Student Homophile League (SHL). The university refused to grant an exemption for its membership list rule, so Martin responded with an inspired plan. He approached straight students sympathetic to his dilemma and asked them to sign their names, pro forma, as members of the SHL, thus shielding the homosexuals in the group.

In April, the SHL became the first university-recognized gay student organization in America. Martin distributed a press release announcing the news and his plans to expand the SHL across the country.

"Columbia Charters Homosexual Group," announced the front page of *The New York Times*. The article chronicled Martin's roommate fiasco, the need for a gay student group on campus, and the gay organizer's victory over the university.

Outraged calls flooded into the university, horrifying the fund-raising office and the alumni association. The dean of the university, David B. Truman, "expressed regret over the formation of the group," reported the *Spectator*. As for the university's fund-raising campaign, the SHL "sure as hell won't help," said the dean.

Administration officials initiated efforts to revoke the university's recognition of Martin's organization. Columbia's lawyers began investigating whether the group had violated sodomy laws.

The most vociferous response came from MSNY's Dick Leitsch, up-set that the SHL controversy threatened alliances with New York politi-cians. "I was speaking at Ohio University when I first heard of the chartering of the Columbia faggot group," he told Kameny. "I just got back late last week, and walked into the biggest fuckin mess I ever had on my hands. Boy, when you and Barbara meddle and interfere, you cer-tainly do a good job of it!

"New York's homosexuals spoke with one voice: Mattachine," he wrote. "Soon it'll be like the Negro movement. The caphony [*sic*] will be so loud you won't be able to hear any voices at all, just a meaningless roar.

"Organize New Orleans or something, but, for god's sake, stay out of New York."

A few weeks later, Martin returned to Kameny's guest bedroom for another summer with the astronomer.

ON JULY 4, Eugenie Anderson, a government representative to the United Nations and the official speaker for the Independence Day celebrations in Philadelphia, spoke before a crowd of five thousand outside Indepen-dence Hall.

Nearly half a million American troops were on the ground in Viet-nam. As she spoke, three hundred protesters stood behind wooden barri-cades, chanting "bring the troops home now." Another twenty-five had their own protest section. They carried a Viet Cong banner and yelled support for the North Vietnamese.

By 3:30 p.m., the crowds disappeared, rain clouds gathered, and police officers were carrying away the barricades.

"You're sure we won't need these?" said one.

"Not with this group," said another. "They never give us any trouble"

Kameny organized his thirty protesters—seventeen women, thirteen men—slowly and systematically, a well-oiled machine in a gray suit. "Pick up the signs in numerical order," he ordered. "Don't talk to passersby. We quit at 5 P.M. sharp."

As they marched, tourists emerged from viewing the Liberty Bell, glanced at the signs, and stopped in their tracks. A few marchers handed out flyers to the crowd, which continued staring in disbelief, and the tourists took them without a smile.

"Are those people all—"

"I mean, they look okay."

Kameny wore a SPOKESMAN badge, speaking to reporters and encouraging the demonstrators as they marched for an hour and a half.

"All we can do is bring our problem to the public and see what happens," he explained to *The Philadelphia Inquirer*.

Six days later, Kameny received the decision of Examiner Henretta in the case of Donald Crawford. Henretta began with a definition from Webster's dictionary. "*Sexual perversion*—n: activity (as sodomy, fellatio, bestiality) leading to complete gratification that is preferred by an adult to heterosexual coitus," it said.

Crawford, wrote Henretta, had admitted to sexual perversion. He had broken Washington's sodomy law. Though his acts may not have been notorious, they were certainly disgraceful and immoral. Crawford's greatest sin, however, was the fact that he *continued* engaging in homosexual activity despite "the overwhelming adverse effect his homosexual activities may have on all facets of his life." Because he acted as a homosexual while knowing that doing so would harm him, Crawford demonstrated "extremely poor judgment over a long period of time from which would logically flow an interference of unreliability and untrustworthiness."

It was not consistent with the interest of the United States to grant Crawford a security clearance, ruled Henretta. The illustrator's security clearance remained suspended.

"What a shabby, shoddy performance!" responded Kameny in his apoplectic demand for an appeal hearing. Henretta's assertion about poor judgment was "tantamount to saying that the Jews in Germany, who were fed to ovens and gas chambers, were merely reaping the just consequences of the revelation of their extremely poor judgment over a long period of time engaging in Jewish conduct and activity (such as going to Synagogue on Saturday) which, after all, they KNEW—for over 10 years—was against prevailing German mores and official governmental policy, and would have an 'overwhelming adverse effect—on all aspects of (their) life.'"

Similarly, he continued, "for a Negro not to make maximum use of available skin-lightening creams and hair-straightening devices, and not to do his best to 'pass' as a white 'does indicate extremely poor judgment over a long period of time.'" What, asked Kameny, was the difference in the case of Donald Crawford?

The hearing had been a farce, concluded Kameny, nothing more than a charade with a foregone conclusion. The government had performed its ceremonies and rites. It had followed the script. But ultimately, the trial had been devoid of meaning.

AT 3:45 A.M. on the night of July 22, an undercover police officer entered an unlicensed after-hours club in Detroit's Economy Printing building. He ordered a beer, the signal to the rest of the Vice Squad, and waited ten minutes. By the time the police threw the eighty patrons into the waiting police vans, a crowd had gathered outside. Someone threw a bottle, and the worst race riot of the decade began.

For five days, Detroit resembled a war zone. Black rioters, acting in response to systematic police brutality, resisted an "occupying force" that was 95 percent white. After Governor Romney called for federal assistance, 4,700 army paratroopers and 8,000 national guardsmen entered the city. By the end of the month, 43 people were dead—33 of whom were Black—1,189 injured, and 7,200 arrested.

"The Vietnam war seemed to be coming home," as sociologist Todd Gitlin put it. By the end of 1967, fifteen thousand Americans had died in Vietnam, and violence had become an increasingly favored method of social resistance. That summer, nearly 170 cities experienced race-related riots. "Our nation is moving toward two societies, one Black, one white— separate and unequal," the president's National Advisory Commission on Civil Disorders later explained. "Discrimination and segregation have long permeated much of American life; they now threaten the future of every American."

Washington, the seat of power for the white government, appeared to be next. "If he can't kill you by sending you to Vietnam, he will kill you on the streets," Student Nonviolent Coordinating Committee's (SNCC) new chairman, H. Rap Brown, told a Black crowd in Washington the day after the Detroit riots. "If Washington don't turn around, you should burn Washington down. You are a majority here."

The national conference of homophile organizations was to take place in less than three weeks. "With Washington, D.C. being more than half negro, is it advisable to have our conference in the heat of mid-August?" asked Eddy Casaus, a delegate from Southern California. "Having gone through a 'Watts' in Los Angeles two years ago, I would not want to go through one in a strange city. I sincerely hope the conference will be held in the heart of an all-white section."

To consider such matters would "degrade us as individuals and would degrade our movement," responded Kameny.

Dick Leitsch and the MSNY refused to attend. "You may have noticed, if you've passed through the Washington slums recently, or read the newspapers, trying to run the world is costing us an inordinate amount of money," he wrote. "I fully intend to spend our time and money taking care of our 'own' and doing the best possible job in our own backyard."

In August, Washington avoided a major riot, and the homosexuals congregated in a basement room of George Washington University's Government Building. The delegates elected another straight minister, Reverend Robert Cromey, as the conference chairman. They elected Bob Martin, or "Stephen Donaldson," as parliamentarian, tasked with knowing and enforcing Kameny's beloved Robert's Rules of Order.

First, they discussed the matter of inclusion. Which homosexuals should be allowed in the conference?

Despite the urgings of the Credentials Committee chairman, Kameny advocated a broad tent. The conference "should be as inclusive as possible," he argued. Shirley Willer agreed with him. "Even the FBI and CIA should be included if they are sympathetic to homosexuals," she told the delegates.

Hal Call of the San Francisco Mattachine, no longer an FBI informant, urged cooperation with other minorities. Homosexuals, he argued, could not change laws and attitudes on their own.

The next morning, the delegates trekked to Capitol Hill to meet with their congressmen. After lunch, they agreed on purposes of the conference—coordinating "strategy, tactics, ideologies, philosophies, and methodologies"—and heard tales of Kameny and Gittings's Crawford battle.

Kameny urged the delegates to promote similar legal cases in their own gay communities. "We must stand up and fight," he told them.

The next day, the delegates discussed how they would execute such a national legal campaign. They decided to jumpstart their national legal defense fund with a fifteen-hundred-dollar contribution from the newly militant Daughters of Bilitis.

The delegates then passed a Unity Resolution, which called for an official "national federation or coalition of existing homophile organizations." Kameny's dream of creating a centralized, militant, ACLU-modeled network of homophile groups inched closer to reality.

The homosexuals decided to finalize the alliance's structure at their next conference, to be held in the same city—and the same month—as the 1968 Democratic National Convention in Chicago.

ON AUGUST 28, two investigators sat before twenty-two-year-old Jeffrey Migota, a stenographer for the Internal Revenue Service.

"Don't fight us," said one of the investigators. "You can make it easier on yourself and us and save time and money by talking to us now."

"I refuse to talk without representation of Counsel," said Migota.

"Who is your Counsel?"

"I refuse to say at present."

"Then I cannot let you leave this room," continued the interrogator. "What are you trying to prove by not cooperating?"

"I am not trying to prove anything, but I am a U.S. Citizen and a human being."

Two days later, the IRS chief of employee relations urged Migota to resign. The stenographer would leave with a clean record, promised the official. Plus, the investigators had photographic evidence of his behavior.

Migota had heard office rumors that the photographs depicted him in female drag. "I'm glad they are in color," he responded. "I don't like black and white."

Kameny wrote to the IRS commissioner that day. "Let it be made quite clear: Mr. Migota is NOT going to resign!" he wrote. "We may well make a 'cause celebre' out of this, if you push us," warned Kameny.

On August 31, the day after Migota's refusal to resign, the national

ACLU formally revised its policy on homosexuality. The purges were "discriminatory, unfair, and illogical," it concluded. Indeed, the threat of blackmail was the *result* of the government's own exclusionary policies. If gay employees did not fear losing their jobs, how could they be subject to blackmail?

Two weeks after the NCACLU vote, the Senate passed Ervin's bill of rights for federal employees in a 79–4 vote.

While the NCACLU prepared to sue on behalf of Migota, Kameny also prepared to retaliate via extralegal means. "We know or can find out where you, Mr. Sinai, Mr. Schaffer, Mr. Fowler, and every other IRS employee above a certain supervisory level lives," he warned. "Either by personal visits to your (pl.) neighbors, or by mass-mailings to everyone living within a certain radius of each of you, we will ask of them certain questions, such as:

"What do you know about his extra-marital affairs?

"Are you aware of adultery on his part?

"What do you know about his homosexual activities?

"When did you last see him in women's clothing?

"Do you know anything about sex orgies in his home?

"You cannot stop us," he concluded.

The IRS, still reeling from Senate investigations into prying and wiretapping the previous year, also received a more realistic threat. "We are making, and setting aside, one copy of this letter for Senator Ervin," warned Kameny. "Whether it will be sent will depend upon your reply to this."

Two days later, Kameny walked into the Pentagon for an interrogation of his own. After fourteen months, the Department of Defense had finally decided to question the astronomer about his own application for a security clearance.

"I shall expect that the interview will NOT be a 'fishing' expedition designed to dredge up some kind of 'dirt' out of my personal life, in the hope of finding something to be used against me," Kameny wrote.

Rowland Morrow, Kameny's opposing counsel for the Department of Defense in the Crawford case, questioned him. The transcript no longer exists, but the day after the interview, Kameny wrote an admonitory letter to Morrow in response to one of his questions. "In discussing fellatio, the terms 'active' role and 'passive' role are totally without meaning," he wrote. "The terms, in this usage, are passé. They force false, and usually quite factually and psychologically invalid comparison with so-called masculine and so-called feminine roles."

Six months later, Kameny received the Pentagon's statement of reasons, explaining its denial of his security clearance. Kameny had admitted to engaging in homosexual acts before his San Francisco arrest, explained the department's director of security policy. He had admitted that he *continued* to engage in those acts. He had admitted that he was an "active homosexual." And, finally, he had admitted, in the words of the Pentagon, a "strong preference to establish a sexual relationship of considerable duration with one male person."

Kameny, Schlegel, Scott, Brass, Crawford, and now Kameny again. Despite the salvo of legal challenges by these men, and despite the growing supremacy of privacy in America, the purges continued. The embattled astronomer and his cocounsel, Barbara Gittings, had one more name to add, however—a man willing to expose the federal government by exposing himself as a sexual deviant.

IN 1966, the United States sent an average of 223 warplanes to North Vietnam, killing or maiming sixty-three people, each day. John Gaffney, a twenty-year-old from New Jersey, wanted to leave the air force. He approached a chaplain with his predicament. He wanted the ability to have sex with other men, he explained.

Gaffney signed a slip of paper that authorized investigators to search his bedroom, and he received a general discharge in June 1966. In his room, investigators found a valuable item: an address book containing the contact information of other homosexuals.

One year later, thirty-two-year-old Benning Wentworth, a technical aide at Bell Telephone Labs in New Jersey, received a letter from the Department of Defense. "Available evidence indicates sexual perversion on your part," it read. "For approximately 21 months within the period 1962 to 1965, you engaged in numerous perverted acts of a homosexual nature with one John Jerry Gaffney." The Pentagon proposed to revoke his security clearance.

The short, slim, and soft-spoken Wentworth turned to the MSNY for help. The organization pointed him to Kameny and Gittings, who were, at that very moment, developing a new Pentagon strategy after the Crawford fiasco.

Yes, Wentworth told them, he would tell the world he was a homosexual.

On June 22, 1967, Wentworth responded to the department's statement of reasons with a thirteen-page document written by Kameny and Gittings. Not only did Wentworth deny engaging in perverted acts, but he also denied engaging in *any* homosexual activity with Gaffney. The openly gay air force veteran, he claimed, was lying.

Even if Wentworth *had* engaged in homosexual activity with Gaffney, he was not susceptible to blackmail. To prove this assertion, he requested that his hearing be opened to both the public and the press.

The pivot to publicity represented a two-pronged attack on the department's purges. First, it proved Wentworth had nothing to fear; if the world knew he was a homosexual, how could he possibly be blackmailed? Second, if successful, the tactic would draw public attention to the blatant invasions of privacy taking place in the Pentagon. In a post-*Griswold* America ruled by Senator Ervin, rationalized Kameny, the purges could not continue for long.

Five days before the hearing, Kameny and Gittings mailed their press release to more than one hundred outlets. "REPRESENTATIVES OF THE PRESS, RADIO, AND TELEVISION ARE INVITED BY MR. WENTWORTH, AND ARE WELCOME TO ATTEND, TO REPORT ON, AND TO BROADCAST THE HEARING. THE GENERAL PUBLIC IS ALSO INVITED."

Because Wentworth worked in New Jersey, the hearing took place at a Department of Defense office in downtown Manhattan.

Kameny, Gittings, and Wentworth arrived at the hearing room shortly before 10:00 a.m. on Friday, November 24. Two reporters—one from the Associated Press, one from *The New York Times*—spoke to Wentworth and took photographs. Yes, I am a homosexual, he admitted. Barred from the proceedings, the AP reporter waited outside the hearing room.

The examiner, Raymond F. Waldman, turned to Wentworth. Are you *sure* you do not want a real attorney?

"That's correct," responded Wentworth.

The Pentagon's attorney, Eugene F. Back, then called his first witness: John Jerry Gaffney, Wentworth's accuser.

"When and under what circumstances did you first meet Mr. Wentworth?" asked Back.

"He obtained my address from the Mattachine Society mailing list and he wrote me a letter and wanted to know if it would be possible for us to meet, and that was the first time I met him."

What happened when you met?

"We went to his bedroom, had a sex relationship."

"Did you disrobe?"

"Yes, we did."

"Can you describe the sexual relationship?

"It was fellatio."

For three months, explained Gaffney, he and Wentworth had met weekly.

"Did you in addition to fellatio have any other type of experience?"

"Yes."

"Will you tell us what that was?"

"It was rectum intercourse."

"Now in these experiences were you the active party or were you the passive party?"

"The passive."

"At all times?"

"Um hmm."

"That is, he would apply his mouth to your penis and he would insert his penis into your rectum—is that correct?"

"Um hmm."

After a short recess, Kameny began his cross-examination of the witness.

How many times, he began, did you see Mr. Wentworth?

About twelve times total, responded the witness.

"Does Mr. Wentworth have any hair on his chest?"

"Yes, he does."

"Much or little?"

"I don't know."

"Is Mr. Wentworth circumcised or uncircumcised?"

"I don't remember."

"What was the size of Mr. Wentworth's erect penis?"

"I would have no idea."

"Could you please go to the blackboard and draw us a floor plan of that apartment?"

Gaffney picked up the chalk and drew Wentworth's apartment. He depicted the living room, the bedroom, the kitchen, and the bathroom.

"Did you ever tell or indicate to Mr. Wentworth that you were going to get even with him for any reason?"

"No," responded Gaffney.

After Kameny finished, Back stood to redirect Gaffney. Is it possible, he asked, that you saw a "substantial number of men in this connection" since Wentworth? "Would you describe this as part of the reason for your not recalling some of the details?"

"Yes," said Gaffney.

"I object," exclaimed Kameny. "Objection."

"Well, yes. It is rather leading, Mr. Back," said Examiner Waldman.

Back continued. "Where he inserted his penis into your anus, did he have an emission?"

"No."

"But he definitely had an insertion, that is, his penis was inserted?"

Gaffney nodded his head, yes.

The Department of Defense rested its case.

KAMENY CALLED WENTWORTH to the stand, and the technician gave his side of the story. Two or three years ago, while sending newsletters as a volunteer in the MSNY office, he noticed the name and address of a man who appeared to live close to him, in New Jersey. Maybe this man would want to become more involved in the Mattachine, thought Wentworth.

He sent a letter, asking to have lunch or dinner to discuss the Mattachine. When they met, Gaffney arrived with a friend, and his young age startled Wentworth, especially because the MSNY had a twenty-one-year age minimum.

Wentworth felt obligated to provide them lunch, as promised, in his apartment. It soon became clear that the two high school students had no interest in the Mattachine. They seemed interested only in Wentworth.

Did any sexual activity occur?

"No, sir, there was no homosexual act at all," said Wentworth. "Not even a handshake."

What happened when it became clear you were not sexually interested?

"They were indignant," said Wentworth, "and I recall they said they would get even with me. I didn't know exactly what that meant."

Wentworth did not hear from the young men until air force investigators contacted him for an interview. They told him Gaffney wanted to leave the air force.

Finally, Kameny asked Wentworth to draw a floor plan of his apartment, next to Gaffney's own depiction. Wentworth's drawing looked nearly the same, but it exposed one major flaw in the Pentagon witness's floor plan. The layout of the bedroom, including the location of the bed, was incorrect.

In cross-examination, Back asked Wentworth about the color of his car.

Yes, he admitted, he drove a white car. Yes, he had hair on his chest. Yes, it was possible he had moved the furniture in his bedroom since 1964.

"And are you a homosexual?"

Kameny objected; the examiner overruled.

"I will answer the question," said Wentworth. "I am a homosexual."

"And during the period between 1962 and 1965 were you a homosexual?"

"Yes, I was."

"And during that period did you engage in homosexual acts with various males?"

Kameny objected. Back was engaging in a "fishing expedition," attempting to uncover *other* acts of homosexuality besides the one alleged in the department's statement of reasons.

"Objection sustained," said Waldman.

"You are sustaining my objection?" asked Kameny, surprised.

"I am sustaining your objection, Dr. Kameny."

Kameny stood to give his closing statement. Here was a man who worked in a high-demand technical industry, who only wanted to serve his country, and who, like Kameny a decade prior, faced ruin. He had stood up before the world, admitting his deviance solely to fight for his constitutional rights as a homosexual citizen. "I think he has demonstrated today a courage which is rare to the point of being beyond the experience of anyone else in the country," concluded Kameny. "Fundamentally, I feel that this is what Americanism is about."

Kameny, Gittings, and Wentworth left the Department of Defense building at 4:00 p.m., after a six-hour hearing. They felt optimistic, since at the end of the hearing, Kameny had received a good omen.

"You are making a very creditable presentation, Dr. Kameny, in view of the fact that you are not a lawyer," said Examiner Waldman. "You are very articulate, and for that I want to thank you."

"Homosexual Seeks to Save Security Role," announced the AP wire. For the first time, a security clearance holder had admitted his homosexuality to prove his immunity to the threat of blackmail.

Homosexuals across the country learned Benning Wentworth's name. The AP story appeared in no fewer than ten newspapers that Saturday, traveling as far as Chicago, Des Moines, Tampa, and Phoenix. On Sunday, *The New York Times* released its own story, which chronicled Wentworth's side of the saga.

The next day, Kameny forwarded the *Times* article to Examiner Waldman and moved to submit it as evidence. He submitted an affidavit swearing that he and Gittings had sent 102 press releases, too.

When Benning Wentworth returned to work that week, he experienced something peculiar. He overheard remarks, positive ones, about his fight against the government. Remarkably, his coworkers seemed to be going out of their way to behave *kindly*.

Two of his family members wrote to him that week. "I read about your difficulty with the government in yesterdays N.Y. Times," wrote his aunt. "I am so proud of you to be fighting it."

"Benning, dear," wrote his mother, "Good luck in all you must go thru! You are intelligent and able."

Kameny submitted the letters, plus an affidavit describing his post-*Times* workplace experience, as further evidence. How could Wentworth, now known to the entire country as a homosexual, possibly be the victim of blackmail?

KAMENY AND GITTINGS also hoped that other security clearance holders, after reading about Wentworth's fight, would feel compelled to fight the government in the same manner.

The day after the *Times* article, the MSW received a letter from a professional attorney, requesting guidance from the organization of homosexuals. His homosexual client faced a Pentagon fight nearly identical to that of Wentworth. Later that week, Barry Farber asked Kameny and Gittings to speak about their security clearance battles for two hours on his radio show. The program broadcast in thirty-eight states.

On December 4, Kameny headlined the first public event of Columbia University's Student Homophile League. He spoke before a standing-room-only audience of 350 students in the university's mammoth, neo-classical Butler Library.

After he finished explaining the morality of homosexuality, the lecture hall erupted in applause. From the podium, Kameny may have seen his mother, Rae, clapping for her son. She had journeyed from Queens to support him.

Bob Martin attended, too, revealing himself to his peers, in person, as a homosexual—no longer hiding behind the pseudonym "Stephen Donaldson"—for the first time.

When it came time for questions, Kameny witnessed something he had never seen before. When students stood to address him from the audience, many of them said it: I, too, am a homosexual.

The university was on the brink of explosion.

*Jack Nichols, center, and MSW demonstrators, bottom,
in CBS-TV's* The Homosexuals, *March 1967*

16.

THE CHAOS

In 1961, when Eva Freund first moved to Washington, she often visited the Rendezvous, a downtown lesbian club. Tiny round tables, surrounded by ice-cream-colored chairs, were crammed together in a minuscule room where smoke hung from the ceiling. The patrons identified as either butch or femme, and each night, Freund could expect a fistfight. The women would dive under the tables before the knives or guns inevitably emerged.

Every few weeks, the Rendezvous's lights abruptly turned on. As the women squinted in the brightness, police officers demanded identification from each of them. But Freund, a petite woman with short, dark hair, knew the law.

Excuse me, she once told an officer, there is no law in this country that I carry identification.

Well, then you have to come with me, said the officer.

I'll sue your ass, responded Freund.

She remained seated.

By 1964, Freund was working as a government statistician, living in Maryland, and dating a woman. She had a new group of friends, other government employees who also had college degrees. "I certainly felt more akin to their group of people," she later explained.

After Freund broke up with her girlfriend, a gay male friend wanted to distract her from her temporary state of depression. You need to meet some new people, he said. You're coming with me next week.

Where are we going? asked Freund.

To a Mattachine meeting, he answered. There's someone I want you to meet, a girl by the name of Lilli Vincenz.

At the meeting, while Kameny chaired the proceedings, Freund attempted to ask a question.

No questions, responded Kameny. Freund was not in order.

Freund laughed to herself, then decided to beat the Society's president at his own game. She went to the library for a copy of Robert's Rules of Order, studied it, and brought the book with her to the next month's meeting.

She tried to ask another question, and again, Kameny shot her down.

Actually, Freund responded, she *was* in order. She read from the relevant section in the book. Kameny had no choice but to admit defeat. He answered her question.

From then on, Kameny seemed to respect Freund. She did not gain the esteemed status of Barbara Gittings, but when the astronomer attended meetings at the Pentagon or the Civil Service Commission, he brought Freund.

She marched at the White House and in Philadelphia, and in time, she grew to respect Kameny, too. Freund was the only cosigner of his letter rebutting rumors that ECHO would transform him into a "homophile Caesar." Meanwhile, Freund and Vincenz became friends, but nothing more.

By the end of 1967, Freund was editing a new MSW newsletter, *The Insider*, and growing frustrated by the stagnation of the Society. After two years as president, Jon Swanson presided over a dwindling membership. In 1967, the Society had lost forty-six dues-paying members and gained only eleven. To combat the decline, Swanson proposed to eliminate the MSW's security protocol and open its meetings to the public, but the membership refused. They demanded secrecy.

The Society no longer picketed, Kameny and Gittings operated alone, and Nichols's Council on Religion and the Homosexual existed in name only. To the dismay of an accounting expert like Freund, in 1967, the Society received only $712 in dues and paid $1,075 for its office.

"Sorry to hear about MSW not hardly functioning," wrote one activist on November 11. "But glad Frank, at least, is still pitching. Sorry he seems to want to take center spotlight to the exclusion of all others."

A week later, Freund sent a letter to the Society's entire membership.

"An organization can flourish only when its leadership carries it toward its goals while maintaining its philosophy," she wrote. She urged the members to nominate and elect a new slate of leaders, "Frank K." for president and "Eva F." for treasurer.

Swanson may have seen the writing on the wall. He decided not to run for reelection.

On January 4, 1968, Eva Freund became the Society's treasurer, and Frank Kameny reclaimed the presidency of the organization he had founded.

FIRST, KAMENY ATTEMPTED to combat his dictatorial reputation. While working on a "State of the Society" message, he solicited ideas from members. He listed his phone number in *The Insider* and encouraged its distribution to those endangered by the CSC or the police.

For the first time, Kameny organized social events. On January 21, fifty MSW members and their friends gathered at the Golden Calf for a fund-raising party. They raised seventy-five dollars at the event, which was "quiet and dignified," *The Insider* clarified.

Kameny's greatest focus, however, remained on his government cases and writing letters to the Pentagon. "I seem to do little else these days," he explained.

On Saturday, January 13, thirty delegates attended a meeting of the Eastern Regional Homophile Conference in lecture room 517 of Columbia University's Hamilton Hall. They elected Kameny chairman, Shirley Willer assistant chairman, and Bob Martin secretary.

The delegates unanimously adopted a list of fifteen Kameny-formulated policy positions: opposing the federal purges, favoring the decriminalization of sodomy, commending New York City for employing homosexuals, protesting denial of homosexual ads in newspapers, ending entrapment, and commending the ACLU for its new policy statement on homosexuality.

In a novel initiative, the delegates agreed to "attempt to achieve greater organization of homosexuals into voting blocs." The conference authorized Kameny to write a questionnaire to be sent to candidates for president, vice president, and Congress in the upcoming 1968 election. Depending on the candidates' responses, the homosexuals would then either publicly endorse or oppose the candidates.

They would continue to march. When Gittings moved that the conference officially sponsor the fourth annual Reminder Day picket, the delegates unanimously raised their hands in favor.

Kameny's national profile continued to rise through the winter of early 1968. His appearance with Gittings on the Barry Farber radio show broadcast three more times in January. "You always lose out by interrupting your opponent, speaking too rapidly, raising your voice or losing your temper," advised his mother, upon listening to it.

On top of his work and movement obligations, Kameny had also found a love interest, another Harvard-trained astronomer.

Born on Long Island, Dr. James Pollack had a toothy grin, a round nose, and an enviable sense of humor. He had defended his dissertation, "Theoretical Studies of Venus," under the supervision of renowned astronomer Carl Sagan. By 1968, he was researching Mars alongside Sagan in Boston.

A homosexual, Pollack subscribed to the homophile movement's publications, and as a result, he learned Kameny's name and number. The last weekend of February 1968, when Pollack traveled to Washington for a scientific conference, he called Kameny. Pollack may have wanted advice on the landscape of gay Washington, or he may have wanted to meet a fellow homosexual astronomer.

"Dear Jim," wrote Kameny the following Wednesday. "I enjoyed, more than I can say, our closer moments, and can only wish that they had started sooner and had lasted very much longer."

Kameny asked Pollack about his "ideas and feelings on politics, religion, music," then tried to provoke Pollack's interest in the movement, since Boston did not yet have a homophile organization. He sent his galvanizing 1964 MSNY speech to teach him his ideology, plus a news release from the Wentworth case to illustrate his tactics.

"I hope to see you VERY soon again," concluded Kameny. "Washington is particularly lovely at Cherry Blossom time (early April)—think you might get down then, or before?"

IN NEW YORK, Craig Rodwell, the twenty-seven-year-old veteran of Wicker's 1964 picket, turned to a new cause, the development of Gay Power. In February 1968, Rodwell, disillusioned by the MSNY, published

the first edition of the *Hymnal* newsletter. "Why was the name HYM-
NAL chosen? Because HYMNAL will have a 'religious' fervor and crusading spirit in its treatment of the homosexual way of life and the
homophile movement," wrote Rodwell. "In a sense, HYMNAL is bringing Gay Power to New York."

Gay Power, Rodwell understood, already existed in pockets across
America. On the West Coast, homosexuals organized themselves to support candidates for political office, boycott discriminatory companies,
and publicize the abuses of the government and organized crime. With
numbers, West Coast homosexuals had amassed political and economic
power for themselves. The Society for Individual Rights in San Francisco
had 3,500 members, while the MSNY had only 550.

The *Hymnal*'s first edition featured an article titled "Mafia on the
Spot" as its lead story. "The Stone Wall on Christopher St. in Greenwich
Village," wrote Rodwell, "is one of the larger and more financially lucra-
tive of the Mafia's gay bars in Manhattan." He reported that the bar,
which washed its glasses in a filthy tub of old drinks, contributed to the
outbreak of hepatitis in the homosexual community. Rodwell called upon
homosexuals to wield their economic power to drive the Mafia-run bars
out of business.

While Rodwell confronted the Mafia in New York, Philadelphia lesbians confronted the local police. On March 8, authorities in trench coats
raided Rusty's, a Mafia-owned lesbian bar. The lights turned on, the music turned off, and police officers moved from table to table, demanding
identification. One woman refused to hand over her license; other patrons recalled hearing an argument, then screams. The authorities arrested
eleven women and a male bartender that night.

Two weeks later, Barbara Gittings gave a speech to the Philadelphia
DOB chapter, which had asked for her advice on its future activities. She
urged the attendees to coordinate with the ACLU and set up an emergency telephone number.

The attendees followed Gittings's advice. When two Philadelphia
DOB members demanded and then received a meeting from the police
department, they brought an ACLU observer and made a threat developed and perfected by Kameny. If the police did not respect them, there
would be publicity and protests.

"Homosexuals have been, are now, and will be treated equally with heterosexuals," announced the Philadelphia Police Department.

"You might well use this as a launching point for a general civil rights campaign," advised Kameny. "I feel that you can use this incident as an excellent opportunity to build up your own organization."

In August 1968, the DOB members unanimously agreed to dissolve their chapter; they no longer wanted to be controlled by a national organization dedicated to uplifting the lesbian. "It is our firm conviction that it is the heterosexual community which is badly in need of uplifting," they wrote. As such, they created a new group, the Homophile Action League.

The female founders opened their new group to men. The Rusty's raid had proven that all homosexuals were affected by official persecution. Men and women, they believed, fought the same enemy.

ON JANUARY 31, 1968, the first day of the Tet holiday, the Communist National Liberation Front of North Vietnam, also known as the Viet Cong, mounted a surprise attack in the south. Seventy thousand guerrillas assaulted American bases, highways, and thirty-six provincial capitals. Commandos invaded the United States Embassy, and two thousand Americans died in a single month.

The Johnson administration had repeatedly promised the war was almost won. With Tet, America saw the bitter truth. Within six weeks, public support for the war plummeted to 26 percent.

Draft-eligible homosexuals faced the choice of risking death in Vietnam or declaring their homosexuality. When Curtis C. Chambers Jr. received an induction notice from his Virginia draft board, he responded that he was a homosexual and therefore could not go to Vietnam. The draft board's clerk, dubious, wanted proof. She requested a letter from a psychiatrist and a sworn, notarized statement affirming his homosexuality.

He called several psychiatrists, but they demanded $125 (nearly one thousand in today's dollars).

Chambers called Frank Kameny, who drafted an affidavit. "I hereby affirm and certify that I, Curtis C. Chambers Jr. . . . am, and for at least 9 months have been a homosexual by tendency and inclination."

By the end of March, more than twenty thousand Americans had died in Vietnam, and requests from terrified homosexuals increasingly poured into the Society's office.

Kameny's affidavit strategy had a perfect success rate, and men like Chambers avoided Vietnam. The rest of the homophile movement followed suit, and that summer, Dick Leitsch reported that the MSNY had a file of more than four hundred men who had successfully avoided the war by declaring their homosexuality.

The war gave also gave homosexuals a strong incentive to come out of the closet, and Kameny embraced its potential. After perfecting his draft evasion strategy, Kameny wrote "Refraining from Your Induction, or, 10 Steps to Freedom."

First, "do not blow your cool. Even though you are not officially homosexual you can be in a very short time." Give your affidavit to the officer in charge. If you talk to a doctor, be honest and frank. Tell the truth.

"Be yourself. You are obvious enough."

IN 1960, when Stokely Carmichael first heard about the lunch counter sit-ins, he thought they were nothing more than a publicity stunt. Carmichael, a Black senior at New York's prestigious Bronx High School of Science, then watched the scenes on television. He saw the Greensboro students with sugar in their eyes, ketchup in their hair. "Something happened to me," he later explained. "Suddenly I was burning."

As a freshman at Howard University in Washington, he participated in the Freedom Rides, and after graduating, he joined SNCC. By the age of twenty-five, he had been arrested twenty-six times for his nonviolent activism. During one forty-nine-day sentence in Mississippi, Carmichael experienced beatings nearly every day.

On June 16, 1966, the tall, charismatic Carmichael emerged from a jail in Greenwood, Mississippi. "This is the 27th time I have been arrested," he told a crowd of six hundred people. Black Americans, he said, should stay home from Vietnam and instead fight, in America, for a new concept, Black Power.

"We have begged the president," he said. "We've begged the federal government—that's all we've been doing, begging and begging. It's time we stand up and take over. Every courthouse in Mississippi ought to be burned down tomorrow to get rid of the dirt and the mess. From now on, when they ask you what you want, you know what to tell 'em. What do you want?"

"Black power!" yelled the crowd.

After Bayard Rustin heard the slogan, he warned it would destroy the movement.

On March 28, 1968, after one of Martin Luther King Jr.'s demonstrations grew violent amidst cries of "Black Power," King reacted with despair. "Maybe we just have to admit the day of violence is here," he confided to his associates.

Three days later, on March 31, President Johnson announced a halt to bombing in North Vietnam, and to the shock of the nation, "I shall not seek, and I will not accept, the nomination of my party for another term as your President."

As April approached, Kameny, like the rest of America, felt euphoric. Jim Pollack traveled from Boston to visit him, and Kameny wrote him after the visit. "Spring has arrived! And it's lovely, as always!"

Then, on Thursday, April 4, Martin Luther King Jr. was murdered in Memphis. That night, in Washington, Stokely Carmichael demanded that Black shop owners shut their doors. "When the white man comes he is coming to kill you," he told a group of young men. "I don't want any Black blood in the street. Go home and get you a gun and then come back because I got me a gun."

The riots began, and flames consumed America. By Friday afternoon, the fires had crept to within two blocks of the White House. Over the weekend, thirteen thousand troops occupied Washington. Machine gun nests appeared on the steps of the Capitol. By Sunday night, the *Post* counted 961 injuries, 851 fires, and 4,352 arrests in the District alone. Six were confirmed dead.

"Whole blocks," recalled the *Post*'s editor, "looked as though they had been bombed into oblivion."

On Monday morning, as Washington awoke to an eerie silence punctuated by the occasional gunshot, Kameny and Gittings drove to the Pentagon. They held a press conference in the hallway outside the hearing room, but no reporters attended. The riots dominated the news.

At 10:00 a.m., the two homosexuals sat before a panel of three De-partment of Defense officials to appeal the revocation Donald Craw-ford's security clearance.

"You have just seen Washington burning," began Kameny. "You have seen the maneuverings of slimy southern demagogues with their racist dogmas, placing property interests above human interests. You need only to walk through downtown Washington to see the harvest which they are reaping." He equated the racist senators to the Pentagon bureaucrats, who were "destroying homosexuals' lives by their pettifogging legalism, and their frightened acquiescence to prejudice."

"If you choose to support morality and freedom, and if you choose to decide in consistency with the national interest, you have no choice but to give Mr. Crawford his clearance," Kameny concluded. "Common sense and the national interest demand it."

One week later, Kameny received the decision of Raymond Waldman, the Department of Defense examiner who had seemed so sympathetic during November's Wentworth security clearance hearing in New York. Yes, Wentworth had admitted his homosexuality to *The New York Times* and the rest of the world, acknowledged the examiner. "He did not also publicize the uncontroverted and established facts that he had solicited a high school boy to his apartment who he knew to be a homosexual, but that this particular one didn't appeal to him, sexually," wrote Waldman. "Thus the Applicant has not been prone to reveal more about his sexual propensities than convenient to him."

Benning Wentworth was therefore susceptible to coercion, influence, or pressure from foreign powers. It did not serve the national interest to grant him a security clearance. Kameny understood the absurdity of the logic. The Pentagon had banned the press from the hearing room—making it impossible for the world to even *hear* the allegations—yet now it blamed Wentworth for not disclosing those same allegations.

"Mr. Wentworth is becoming a minor national hero. We shall do our best to make of you a major national villain," wrote Kameny and Gittings in their response.

They did not promise violence, but they toed the line. "We intend to 'tear you to pieces', Mr. Waldman, and to 'rake you over the coals', and to do the same with our security system," they wrote.

Foster Gunnison, like Kameny's mother, had chastised Kameny for his tone on the Barry Farber radio show. "STOP BEING SO DEFENSIVE," wrote Gunnison. "The movement isnt ready for its Sap Browns [*sic*] and Hoagy Carmichaels yet—lets get a foot in the door first."

"Yes, our movement, in many ways IS ready for its Rap Browns and Carmichaels," responded Kameny, "although with far more attention to strategy and to the philosophy so dear to your heart."

With his threats to Examiner Waldman, Kameny stepped closer to embracing the fires in Stokely Carmichael's wake.

ON APRIL 18, the day after Kameny received the Wentworth determination, he sent Bob Martin a package of predrafted flyers and news releases for a new Student Homophile League campaign.

At 7:00 p.m. on Tuesday, April 23, the SHL demonstrated in front of the Alumni Auditorium at Columbia University's medical school, fifty blocks north of the undergraduate campus, to protest an antigay psychiatrist's lecture. The picketers ensured that every attendee of the panel received a copy of Kameny's flyer.

At midnight, when Martin returned home from the protest, he encountered a hostage situation. The tension had been building for years. As Columbia expanded, it bought hundreds of buildings and evicted thousands of Black and Puerto Rican residents living in its Morningside Heights neighborhood, which bordered Harlem. Then, in February 1968, the university quietly began construction of a private gymnasium on a thirty-acre public park, which had previously served as a buffer between the university and Harlem.

Columbia had agreed to build facilities for the community, but it planned to spend five times more—a total of $8.4 million—on the gym reserved for its own students. Columbia students would enter from the top of a hill, and Harlem residents would enter from the bottom. "Gym Crow," Black activists called it.

On April 23, the day of Martin's protest, four hundred students met at the center of the undergraduate campus. They listened to Cicero Wilson, the president of the Society of Afro-American Students, speak against the gymnasium. "What would you do if somebody came and took your property? Would you sit still? No. You'd use every means possible to get your property back—and this is exactly what the Black people are engaged in right now."

Another student activist suggested they occupy Hamilton Hall, the administration's headquarters and the site of Kameny's lecture the previous winter. By 2:00 p.m., hundreds of students had barricaded themselves inside the building, and they soon took hostage the acting dean of Columbia College.

Over the next four days, Martin explored the occupied buildings, interviewed students, and phoned reports to the student radio station, WKCR. He had recently decided to become a journalist rather than a politician, so he remained neutral.

At 2:30 a.m. Monday night, after six days of occupations, Martin heard the sirens. He saw bus after bus, full of officers, pull up to the university's gates. One thousand riot officers, wearing blue helmets, entered the college in military formation. They looked like Nazi stormtroopers, thought Martin.

From the stunned silence, Martin could hear students singing "We Shall Overcome." He then heard the screams of injured students as the riot police raided Low Library, then Avery Hall. In an act of passive resistance, he sat on the steps of the occupied Fayerweather Hall, joining his German professor, other faculty members, and a crowd of sympathizers. Suddenly, swinging clubs, bloody limbs, bodies in the air. Martin curled into the fetal position as police officers kicked him repeatedly. After what felt like an eternity, he found himself alone, covered in blood, and lying on the grass, thirty feet away from the steps.

Faced with criminal trespass charges, Martin spent the rest of the morning in a holding cell with forty other students. In sum, the New York Police arrested 722 people that night, including 524 students; 148 were injured.

That evening, when he spoke to Kameny on the phone, Martin told his homosexual mentor that he wanted to drop out of Columbia. How, he asked, could he remain enrolled in a university that waged war against its students? How could he not join the resistance?

Kameny urged Martin to remain at Columbia and work within the system. "Use your not inconsiderable powers of leadership and organization to assist the university to heal its wounds in a fashion which cause the least lasting harm," he wrote.

Martin stayed enrolled at Columbia, hoping to work within the system, but in the aftermath of the violence, he also watched Columbia accede to almost all of the demands of the striking students. The university dropped the charges against Martin. The occupation had been a success.

Columbia never built the gymnasium.

THE DAY AFTER the end of the Columbia occupation, Kameny lost his job. "This has nothing to do with either homosexuality or job-performance," he assured Gittings. His supervisor had been laid off, too.

Kameny initiated an "information-gathering stage" to determine his next move. He could look for a job immediately, or he could wait until he received his security clearance, which itself remained in question.

He received one hundred dollars from Benning Wentworth, still employed while fighting his case, in gratitude for Kameny's assistance. But otherwise, the astronomer had no income. "I do hope that this isn't another of the miserable summers of which I've spent so many, with no funds and no ability to do anything or go anywhere," he told Martin.

With more time on his hands, Kameny began policing the movement and propagating his brand of legal militancy. When Mattachine Midwest reported on a new series of police raids—the patrons' arrests were ultimately dismissed—he urged them to take action. "Why has no affirmative counter-action been taken by Mattachine Midwest? EVERY TIME A DISMISSAL OF CHARGES OR AN ACQUITTAL IS OBTAINED IN CASES SUCH AS THESE, CHARGES SHOULD BE BROUGHT AGAINST THE POLICE," he wrote. "Counterattack! That is what you exist for."

Kameny also considered an alluring business proposition. In 1965, three Harvard students created Operation Match, America's first computerized dating service. Each customer paid three dollars, answered more than one hundred questions in a personality survey, and mailed it to the company. Operation Match fed thousands of those surveys into an IBM 1401 computer—it filled a small room—and determined the most compatible pairings. A few weeks later, each customer received their matches, a list of fourteen names and telephone numbers. Operation Match spread from Harvard to other universities and then to the rest of the country. By the end of 1965, it had seventy-five thousand customers.

By 1968, Operation Match acquired a new IBM S/360—the size of a large refrigerator—and hoped to expand to a new clientele: homosexuals. The new service would be called Man-to-Man and offer a "discreet," computer-operated way to meet other men.

In May, after interviewing him for four days in New York, the owners of Operation Match offered the presidency of Man-to-Man to Dr. Frank Kameny. They promised him flexibility and freedom. He would be able to continue his homophile activism. Kameny was tempted, but he hesitated. How would it *look*?

"My chief concern is the image question," Gittings told him. If he took the job, she explained, he would no longer speak as the president of a civil liberties organization, but rather, as the head of a company that profited off gay men's desire for sex.

The Dowdy nightmare had occurred only five years earlier. "Imagine yourself, as head of Man-to-Man, appearing as a witness before a moderate yet not too friendly Congressional committee on a matter affecting the movement or MSW," Gittings argued.

"I'll agree with you on the image bit," wrote Foster Gunnison, Kameny's ally in the MSNY. "But Christ, if it pays—grab it."

AS HE CONTEMPLATED the decision, and as he became increasingly frustrated with the paralyzing fear that prevented homosexuals from fighting alongside him, Kameny heard a phrase that gave him an idea.

Since 1966, Black Power had become more than a purely political or economic concept. In his 1967 book, Stokely Carmichael defined it as "a call for black people in this country to unite to recognize their heritage, to build a sense of community." Black Power meant Black people leading their own organizations, defining their own goals, and not sacrificing that power to whites. It meant demanding dignity, not begging for it. It became a matter of identity and pride.

In a Philadelphia Freedom School, only a month after Carmichael's

1966 Greenwood speech, teachers developed a workbook to teach three-year-old Black students to read and write. Over and over, the children wrote, "I am black and beautiful . . . I am the greatest . . . I deserve the best . . . I want black power."

By the spring of 1967, Carmichael, while speaking before thousands of college students in the South, urged Black students to cease imitating white beauty with wigs, hair straighteners, and skin lighteners. "You must say 'our noses are broad. Our hair is nappy. We are black and beautiful.'"

That summer, in the still-burned Watts neighborhood in Los Angeles, bumper stickers began appearing. BLACK IS BEAUTIFUL, they said. Even King, aware that the concept and nonviolence were not mutually exclusive, hung a banner at one of his 1967 conventions. BLACK IS BEAUTIFUL AND IT'S SO BEAUTIFUL TO BE BLACK, it said.

In May 1968, seven hundred Black students in Newark chanted, "Black is beautiful," during a boycott of the city's high schools. On Maryland's Eastern Shore, Black college students gained an unprecedented meeting with Governor Spiro Agnew after they marched with signs that said EQUALITY, WE SHALL OVERCOME, and BLACK IS BEAUTIFUL.

Frank Kameny heard the chanting on television. Here was a minority, he realized, actively fighting the suffocating feeling of inferiority thrust upon them by American society, thus allowing them to mobilize, to fight.

It was this same feeling of inferiority that prevented homosexuals from resisting the purges, from leading their own organizations, from believing they were perfectly healthy, and from coming out of the closet. This "negativism," he explained to Gittings, saturated "every approach to the matter which one is likely to find, and colors initial assumptions, logic and reasoning, and final conclusions." Self-negativity was the confounding variable—the hidden root cause—behind the homosexual's inability to join his war.

If African Americans had a phrase that combatted a language and culture that equated Blackness with evil and ugliness, homosexuals needed their own phrase, one that counteracted the association of homosexuality with sickness and immorality.

The word *homosexual* did not roll off the tongue, and the word *gay* was still an in-group term (in speeches before heterosexuals, Kameny still had to define it). He did not want a word—like *power*—that suggested a sense of superiority, for he wanted it to appeal to heterosexuals, too.

One day in August, while eating an orange in his kitchen, Kameny discovered a solution: "Gay is Good."

The phrase was bland, but more important, it was broad. Not only did *good* connote a positive condition, but unlike other options—"Gay is Great" or "Gay is Grand"—it also connoted *moral* goodness.

The phrase served as a condensed manifestation of the novel legal argument he had developed seven years earlier. "Petitioner asserts, flatly, unequivocally, and absolutely uncompromisingly, that homosexuality, whether by mere inclination or by overt act, is not only not immoral, but that for those choosing voluntarily to engage in homosexual acts, such acts are moral in a real and positive sense, and are good, right, and desirable, socially and personally," he had written.

In 1962, Dick Schlegel had chided Kameny for writing a Supreme Court brief "long on emotion but short on law."

In 1968, as the laws remained stubbornly oppressive despite an increasingly open and militant America, perhaps homosexuals were finally ready to embrace that emotion: pride.

"THE JACKET AND TIE RULE WILL be enforced for ANY and EVERY male participating in that demonstration," wrote Kameny before the 1968 Reminder Day picket.

Yes, gay was good. But if homosexuals were to convince heterosexuals of that fact, they needed to project a certain *type* of gay. It was a matter of image, of strategy.

The day before the picket, after Kameny read a column that advised homosexuals to refrain from admitting their condition to the military, he wrote a scathing response. "I think it's time that we started saying 'Gay is Good', and following through on the positive assertion of that and of all that goes with it, instead of Mr. D.S.'s 'respectable', frightened, retiring negativism," said Kameny.

Yet respectability was exactly what Kameny commanded, a tactic reinforced by his obsession with order and uniformity. He demanded picketers' signs be *exactly* twenty-two by twenty-eight inches. He insisted the messages be identical on each side. He instructed picketers to attach each placard to its wooden post with exactly five staples, totaling ten per sign.

Yes, gay was good. But Kameny's demonstration signaled that only a certain *type* of gay was good: the man in a suit and tie, the woman in a dress. They were to look like lawyers, not drag queens. At this picket, they were all white.

Lilli Vincenz brought her video camera. Kameny, wearing an EQUALITY FOR HOMOSEXUALS button and a handwritten SPOKESMAN badge, spoke to reporters and compared the homosexual's plight to that of the African American minority.

"It's gathering momentum," added Gittings, while handing out flyers to spectators. "A movement like this takes time."

As the homosexuals prepared to leave, they heard the sound of a bugle. The melancholy sound of "Taps" played on the outdoor loudspeakers. The well-dressed homosexuals stopped and solemnly stood, motionless. They held their signs upside down, resting against the ground, in respect of the military and their country.

After the march, Clark Polak hosted a drinks reception for the picketers in his *Drum* magazine warehouse. As the marchers celebrated their fourth successful Independence Day demonstration, they did so surrounded by thousands of images of naked men.

That same week, after considering the effects on his image and the movement, Kameny rejected the presidency of Man-to-Man. He agreed to rewrite the company's personality survey for homosexual customers—he later suggested adding a question about preferred penis size—but he would not lead America's first computerized matching service for homosexuals.

Yes, gay was good, and gay was the future. Though Kameny had the opportunity, and though he helped create it, he allowed that future to progress without him. He would remain fighting, respectably, instead.

And that was that.

J. EDGAR HOOVER had ignored the homosexuals, but he had not forgotten them. In February 1968, *The Washington Post* published an exploration of the FBI director's maintenance of power for over three decades.

Hoover remained powerful—with a two-hundred-million-dollar budget, he reigned over a Bureau 50 percent larger than the Department of Labor—largely because of his secrets, the *Post* reported. His dossiers contained the "unspoken and perhaps unspeakable records and rumors of the private follies and indiscretions of the major figures, past and present, in the Washington political establishment." As one anonymous congressman told the *Post*, "Everybody on the Hill is convinced they've got a big file on all of us."

The article cited a curious exchange between Hoover and Congressman John J. Rooney during a 1966 House Committee on Appropriations hearing. Rooney had asked Hoover about the qualifications for special agents. "I notice you stressed appearance with regard to the qualifications of employees," said the congressman.

"I do," said Hoover.

"I can understand physical requirements, but why is appearance so important?"

"As regards appearance, Mr. Congressman, I certainly would not want to have any of the beatniks with long sideburns and beards as employees in the Bureau."

"How about members of the Mattachine Society?" joked Rooney.

"No member of the Mattachine Society or anyone who is a sex deviate will ever be appointed to the FBI. If I find one in the FBI he will be dismissed."

Special agents, explained Hoover, were like salesmen. To get information from people—corporate board members, laborers, longshoremen—agents had to sell themselves. When they testified before juries, they had to convince them that they were objective, impartial, and speaking without emotion. "Their personal appearance plays a great part in this."

The 1968 *Post* profile also referenced another factor behind Hoover's grip on power: his extensive network of paid informants.

The FBI had not heard from Warren Scarberry, its first MSW informant, since 1965. Kameny, on the other hand, continued to view Scarberry, the first homosexual picketer of the White House, as an annoyance. After Scarberry picketed the Tenth Precinct police station in 1965, Kameny wrote to the police chief. "We wish to make it clear that Mr. Scarberry is NOT a member of the Mattachine Society of Washington, nor has he ever been," he explained.

"Warren Scarberry is still around and lashing out here and there, now and then," Kameny told Brass later that year. "I wish he'd go away."

In March 1966, as Scarberry drifted across the country, Kameny learned that he planned to contact the Mattachine Society in San Francisco.

"He is a personable, presentable young man, outwardly sincere-seeming—who should NOT be trusted," Kameny warned Hal Call.

Hal Call, himself a former FBI informant, later received a collect call from Warren Scarberry. With Kameny's letter in hand, Call refused to answer it.

Shortly before midnight on Sunday, July 21, 1968, a woman was waiting for a bus on Monroe Avenue in Rochester, New York. She heard screaming, and when she looked across the street, she saw a young man yelling from a second-story window of an apartment building. Another man, standing outside, shouted back.

The second man was twenty-seven-year-old Paul T. Jennings, a Western Union Telegraph Company technician, originally from Buffalo. After a few moments of traded insults, he entered the apartment building. Two minutes later, he emerged, holding his shoulder, groaning, and bleeding profusely. The witness saw Jennings slump against a car outside the apartment complex.

Police officers later found a bloodied kitchen knife in the stairwell, but a jury relied on another piece of evidence to sentence the twenty-four-year-old murderer to fifteen years in Attica prison. On the side of the vehicle, before he died, the victim wrote a single incriminating word, scrawled in his own blood.

"Warren."

Frank Kameny, top; Eva Freund, center;
and Craig Rodwell, bottom, on left; Philadelphia, July 4, 1968

———

17

THE RIOTS

In 1844, New York faced a state of insurrection. Farmers in the Hudson River Valley were rioting against exorbitant rents imposed by their landlords. Local authorities, when they attempted to evict tenants, encountered angry mobs.

To avoid identification, the farmers, who called themselves "Indians," created a secret cell structure and bound themselves by oath. They wore masks and women's calico dresses, the "chiefs" of the cells wearing especially long dresses, like nightgowns.

By the end of the year, the "Indians" claimed to have ten thousand knife-wielding, cross-dressing farmers united against an unjust system. "In many a farmhouse, closemouthed wives and mothers ran up the seams of outlandish dresses for the menfolk," described historian Henry Christman.

In January 1845, New York's new governor, Silas Wright Jr., insisted that action be taken against the disguised farmers. Within days, the New York legislature passed "An act to prevent persons appearing disguised and armed." The new law deemed "every person who, having his face painted, discolored, covered or concealed, or being otherwise disguised, in a manner calculated to prevent him from being identified" a "vagrant" subject to six months in prison.

The riots only increased in scale. The state sent in its militia, which retaliated with such ruthlessness that New Yorkers, once ambivalent, flocked to the anti-rent cause. Voters demanded a constitutional convention, which, in 1846, granted significant concessions to the farmers, including an end to perpetual leases. The drag farmers disbanded, victorious.

The "disguised and armed" law remained on New York's book of statutes. By the turn of the century, the state continued enforcing it not to suppress farmers, but to persecute cross-dressers in the public spaces of New York City. Those living beyond the boundaries of gender learned that in practice, as long as you wore three gender-conforming items of clothing (if the state identified you as a "male," perhaps a tie, a men's watch, and men's underwear), you were safe. In 1968, the New York Supreme Court upheld the conviction of a cross-dressing defendant under the statute.

Yvonne Ritter of Brooklyn knew the law. When she was born in 1951, her Catholic family immediately wrapped her in blue blankets and named her "Joseph." By the age of six, Ritter knew she was female, but through high school, she tried to be male. She joined Midwood High's weight-lifting team and won third runner-up at Mr. Teenage New York State. She lifted weights in a room with a large mirror. *This isn't me*, she thought to herself, as she looked at her reflection.

By the age of seventeen, Ritter had shed her muscle and discovered the gay bars of Greenwich Village. The homosexuals she met there seemed more accepting of her femininity, of difference. She read about Christine Jorgensen, the first American woman to become famous after having gender affirming surgery in 1952, and she met trans women who had traveled to Morocco or Denmark for the operation. Ritter decided she wanted to undergo the surgery herself, but when she informed her gay friends, they were often dubious. Oh, no, you don't want to do that, they said. Have another drink.

On her eighteenth birthday, only a few days before her high school graduation, she decided to celebrate in Greenwich Village. She opened her mother's closet and chose an elegant black-and-white cocktail dress with an empire silhouette. Ritter met her friends in Brooklyn Heights, where she spent several hours applying makeup and a new partial wig. They laughed and drank cocktails. When she looked in the mirror that night, though she knew it was illegal, she felt free.

A car picked up the exuberant young women and crossed the bridge to Manhattan, headed for the Stonewall Inn.

IN THE SUMMER of 1968, Kameny felt wary about the upcoming homophile conference in Chicago, to be held only weeks before August's Democratic National Convention. "There are murmurings of civil disorders in connection with the Convention," he wrote to the DOB in Chicago. He worried not about violence, but rather about the publicity. How would the homosexuals gain the attention of the media if Chicago went up in flames?

On Monday, August 12, twenty-three accredited delegates—representing fourteen organizations—met at a gay restaurant, The Trip, in downtown Chicago. Once again, they elected Reverend Robert Cromey, a straight and married father of three, as their chairman. For three days, they met in committees.

As the weekend approached, the number of delegates and observers swelled to seventy-five. On Friday, the delegates voted to name themselves the North American Conference of Homophile Organizations (NACHO, though pronounced *nay-co*) to accommodate Canadian homophile groups. On Saturday, Kameny lost the chairmanship of NACHO to Bill Wynne, or "Marc Jeffers," of Kansas City's Phoenix Society, but the delegates elected Bob Martin as treasurer.

Despite his loss, Kameny watched his influence permeate the conference. First, delegates passed a Homosexual Bill of Rights, which codified the right to federal employment. Following Kameny's urgings, the delegates also passed the legal committee's motion "that the strongest attention should be given to the creation, indeed the manufacture, of test cases, in the hope of advancing the above listed goals through court decisions." They authorized an official NACHO candidate questionnaire for the 1968 congressional elections.

At 3:30 p.m. Saturday, Kameny won his greatest victory of the conference. He moved that the delegates adopt a resolution, seconded by Barbara Gittings.

BECAUSE homosexuals suffer from "diminished self-esteem, doubts and uncertainties as to their personal worth," and

BECAUSE homosexuals "are in need of psychological suste-
nance to bolster and to support a positive and affirmative attitude
toward themselves and their homosexuality," <u>and</u>

BECAUSE it is a function of NACHO to "replace a wishy-
washy negativism toward homosexuality with a firm, no-nonsense
positivism, to attempt to establish in the homosexual community
and its members feelings of pride, self-esteem, self-confidence,
and self-worth, in being the homosexuals that they are and have a
moral right to be (these feelings being essential to true human
dignity), <u>and</u>

BECAUSE "the Negro community has approached similar
problems and goals with some success by the adoption of the
motto or slogan: <u>Black is Beautiful</u>

RESOLVED:

<u>That it is hereby adopted as a slogan or motto for the
N.A.C.H.O. that:</u>

<u>GAY IS GOOD</u>

and that this be given the widest plausible circulation in both
the homosexual and heterosexual communities."

Only two years after the delegates had refused to affirm the mental
health of homosexuals at their first national conference in Kansas City,
the delegates unanimously passed Kameny's resolution.

News of the slogan spread across the homophile movement. Randy
Wicker, for one, disliked it. Newly prosperous from his button company
and an expert in sloganeering, he had recently returned from a month-
long tour of South America with his lover. "It's so wishy washy, I'm afraid
I'll let my competitor on the West Coast distribute it," he told Kameny.

But when Eva Freund heard the slogan, it was her "wild impulse,
upon first hearing it, to giggle somewhat hysterically," she wrote in *The
Insider*. "She sobered completely after contemplating the immense change
in laws, attitudes, social mores, religious thinking—the whole fabric of
American prejudice—implied in that single statement."

In the August edition of *Home Furnishings Daily*, the trade publication announced the homosexuals' decision. "Gay is Good: You read it here
first."

A few days after the NACHO conference, and only a week before the 1968 DNC, the Chicago Police Department's Vice Control Division raided two gay bars, arresting bartenders and patrons for "indecent behavior."

Mattachine Midwest drafted a press release and mounted a petition campaign, asserting its "moral as well as numerical strength." It planned to develop a test case and threatened to take "whatever measures are necessary to insure the equal treatment we seek."

When another NACHO delegate, Ray Hill of Houston, returned home to learn of a bar raid that had occurred during the conference, the Promethean Society similarly leapt to action. Kameny sent a sample press release. "I am most proud to report that all those arrested in this raid are vigorously fighting their twenty-five dollar fines in court," Hill later reported. "It makes one feel proud to see so many standing up where none were just last year."

Later that month, during the Democratic National Convention, Chicago became a war zone. Twelve thousand police officers, more than five thousand national guardsmen, and hundreds of FBI agents occupied the city. Six thousand army soldiers waited in the suburbs.

The masked national guard used converted flamethrowers to engulf ten thousand demonstrators in tear gas. The soldiers sprayed the substance in such vitriolic abundance that Vice President Hubert Humphrey, showering in his suite at the Hilton, could feel it.

In the aftermath of the DNC, the public sided with the police, but just as the Columbia occupation had radicalized Bob Martin, Chicago galvanized the New Left. One hundred new chapters of the Students for a Democratic Society came into being that fall.

AT 9:00 A.M. on September 9, two Department of Defense guards kept a watchful eye on Frank Kameny and Barbara Gittings as they conducted another news conference in the hallway outside room 3D-282 of the Pentagon. Before Benning Wentworth's appeals hearing, the homosexuals called for the firing of Examiner Waldman.

The embattled technical aide's renown had only grown since the unfavorable decision earlier that year. In July, *The Wall Street Journal* profiled the quiet Wentworth. "He seems anything but a crusader, and nothing in his manner evokes the stereotyped homosexual," wrote the *Journal*.

If a blackmailer ever approached Wentworth, argued Kameny, "all he has to do, we would venture to guess, is to show a copy of *The Wall Street Journal* article to a blackmailer, and the blackmailer would flee."

The Department of Defense counsel, Rowland Morrow, after experiencing Kameny and Gittings's unorthodox strategy during the 1967 Crawford-Socarides hearing, offered a forceful counterargument of his own. "There may come a day, gentlemen, when the homosexual in our society is not considered as an outcast, guilty of criminal behavior and an object of derision and humor and Broadway plays which portray him as sick, driven, and full of hatred," he declared. "But gentlemen, we submit that the Appeal Board of the Department of Defense sitting this 9th day of September must look at the world as it is, and not as it might be if the applicant's counsel's dreams were to come true. The Board must face facts, the reality of what is here and now and not what might be when the Mattachine millennia has arrived." After only five hours, the hearing concluded.

Two days later, the United States court of appeals, District of Columbia Circuit released its decision in *Scott II*. The CSC's renewed efforts to bar Bruce Scott from federal employment, it ruled in an ambiguous decision, were "unavailing."

Judge McGowan, joined in his opinion by Judge Bazelon, tore apart Chairman Macy's 1966 letter to the MSW, which the government had submitted to explain its policies. "The statement has its full share of seeming anomalies and contradictions," wrote McGowan. "Qualification for federal employment thus appears to turn not upon whether one is a law violator but whether one gets caught." The judges admitted public policy on the matter was in a "state of flux," and they called for a "clear policy line to the demarcation of appropriate disclosure requirements."

"I am not sure I grasp the meaning of this," wrote Judge Warren Burger in his dissent. "Do my colleagues now decide sub silentio that the government must employ sex deviates or that the efficiency of public service is promoted by doing so?" And what about the disposition of Bruce Scott? "What is the solution if the Commission flatly refuses to employ him?"

Scott, despite the purported victory, was left pessimistic by the decision's vagueness. The CSC, he wrote to David Carliner, appeared to be "free to try a third time to bar me from the eligible registers for which I have otherwise qualified."

Even if the CSC purged him again, more and more homosexuals were joining the fight initiated by Scott and Kameny. In September, two NACHO delegates referred a woman in the Women's Army Corps (WAC)—stationed in the nearby Fort Myer, in Virginia—to Kameny.

Her WAC company had initiated a crackdown on homosexuals, and several women found themselves under investigation. On October 1, three women sat in Kameny's living room. He had instructed them to bring anything incriminating for safekeeping at his house—address books, photo albums, letters.

Kameny wrote to the WACs' commanding officers, threatening "to take every lawful measure within our power to impede the progress of this 'purge' and to protect the interests of the women involved." He enclosed a draft of a press release, to be sent if the officers did not comply: "HOMOSEXUAL WITCH HUNT COMMENCED BY WOMEN'S ARMY CORPS."

The women, following Kameny's advice, said nothing in their interrogations. The questions about their sexuality—or their membership in the MSW—were irrelevant, they answered. By the end of the year, the three women who had taken Kameny's advice were safe, their clearances restored. Meanwhile, the WACs who had declined to fight back, as *The Ladder* later informed its lesbian readers, received dishonorable discharges.

In October, Kameny received the appeal board's determination in Crawford's case.

"Of course, homosexuality, per se, is not proscribed," began the appeal board. However, "applicant's conduct, of the nature herein alleged, is criminal, immoral and notoriously disgraceful, and is sexually perverted."

"It is abundantly clear," the determination continued, "that the applicant does not propose to correct his errors, notwithstanding their having been pointed out to him, but will continue to attempt to rationalize them away, contrary to any normal sense of responsibility to comply with the law and society's right to rely thereon."

When it came to blackmail, Crawford's admissions to the world actually *accentuated* the risk. They made him a "possible target."

Kameny and Gittings prepared to turn over Crawford's case to the NCACLU.

A few months after the Crawford decision, ACLU chapters across the country received an announcement in the Union's national bulletin. The Washington affiliate, after listening to Kameny's Pentagon tales, urged attorneys to utilize publicity in their homosexual cases against the federal government. They should encourage clients not only to fight the government, but to do so as openly gay American citizens.

AS KAMENY'S INFLUENCE spread, his financial situation—and that of his Society—became increasingly dire. Over the summer, he had written to twenty-five publishers with a proposal for a book, to be titled *The Federal Government versus the Homosexual American Citizen*. "I will need a sizable advance payment," he warned them.

No funds arrived. He became an "expert at fending off creditors," as he admitted to Shirley Willer.

"Things here are going simultaneously well and poorly," he told MSW charter member Jack Nichols, who had recently moved to New York. "MSW is going through a period of what I hope is only temporary deep decline—partly, at least, because I've been so involved in security-clearance cases that I haven't been able to to [*sic*] much else."

The telephone in the Society's office, now staffed only one night per week, played a recording that simply gave Kameny's home number. By September, after the MSW siphoned funds from its general treasury to maintain the office, the organization had barely any money at all. The executive board begged its members to pledge five dollars per month to keep the office.

Kameny's mother, deeply anxious about his unemployment, urged him to leave Washington for a city that lacked a strong connection to the federal government. "I hate to sound like the voice of doom, but this situation is a nightmare. A man with your brains, your intelligence, your ability and your qualifications can get into anything," she told him. "Even though you may have a cause which you think you should emphasize, you must face up to facts and think of your own good first."

Kameny remained too busy to look for a job. After NACHO, he drafted the homosexuals' 1968 election questionnaire and led the effort to send copies to all House and Senate candidates, 936 in total.

On October 26, the Eastern Regional Conference of Homophile Organizations (ERCHO) met in room 200 of George Washington University's Monroe Hall. The delegates unanimously reelected Kameny as its chairman, and Lilli Vincenz showed her seven-minute film of the 1968 Reminder Day picket.

The next day, the delegates analyzed the eleven responses to their political survey, and they voted to endorse four candidates, including their old friend, William F. Ryan of New York, though he had not filled out a questionnaire.

"The Conference voted to oppose the re-election of Representative John J. Rooney, incumbent Democratic candidate from the 14th District of New York," announced Kameny in a press release. Each year, he explained, Rooney asked State Department officials about how many homosexuals they had dismissed that year. He was "significantly responsible" for the purges.

Congressman Rooney received the press release, and two days after winning his election in a landslide, he wrote to Kameny. "I do want you to know that I appreciate your sending me a copy of the report of your October 26th meeting," he said. "Enclosed is a deplorable full page ad which appeared in this morning's New York Times which I am sure you all will find interesting."

Congressman Rooney had torn out the ad for a new play about homosexuals, *The Boys in the Band*, and placed it in an envelope addressed to Kameny.

"Show me a happy homosexual and I'll show you a gay corpse," said the ad.

BARBARA GITTINGS, still disillusioned after her experience on the board of the DOB, refused to become the officer of any one organization. She preferred to act as a free agent, floating between the DOB, the HAL, and the MSW. That way, she maintained control over her contributions to the movement.

Dick Leitsch pressured her to work "through MSNY, rather than dissapating them as you do, playing soliciter to his barrister in Frank's legal charades."

A loyal cocounsel, Gittings instead forwarded a copy of Leitsch's letter to Kameny.

The DOB barely resembled the group Gittings had discovered twelve years earlier. For one, the organization was bleeding members. In San Francisco, DOB cofounder Del Martin had joined the National Organization of Women in 1967. She became an officer and dedicated herself to the feminist movement, a cause that would, she believed, benefit the lesbian more than the male-dominated homophile movement.

In August 1968, only fifteen members attended the DOB's national convention in Denver. Shirley Willer hoped to use the convention as an opportunity to transform the organization into a confederation of autonomous chapters, but the delegates tabled the issue. Willer left the movement.

For DOB national president, the delegates elected Rita Laporte. "I was not only born a lesbian, but a feminist as well," she told Gittings. "My first cry was one of fury at being considered second rate because of being female."

"When you get first class citizenship, we will get full second class citizenship unless we work for women's rights," Laporte explained to Foster Gunnison. "We lesbians want first class citizenship and you homosexuals are the last to care about that. I predict that, only as women come to be accepted as fully human, will you gay guys be accepted."

By the end of the year, activists heard rumors that the DOB planned to withdraw from the male-dominated NACHO.

NACHO chairman Bill Wynne exhorted Laporte to remain in the alliance. "The younger generation is losing patience with us," he explained. "It is time to come out of the foxholes and trenches and to storm the walls of the establishment."

"We need you," he wrote.

The Daughters withdrew nonetheless.

Kameny, on the other hand, saw women's rights and lesbian rights as "TOTALLY and UTTERLY separate problems, which only interact to the detriment of both, in most cases, if mixed." An organization that fought for *all* women, Kameny argued, would inevitably leave the lesbian behind. "Women's rights organizations are a dime a dozen; Lesbian organizations are unique," he told DOB's Barbara Grier. "Don't degrade yourselves."

Gittings agreed with the astronomer. *Plenty* of women fought for the feminist movement, she reasoned. Lesbians needed dedicated groups that would fight for them. Plus, gay men and gay women certainly shared problems. One needed to look no further than Fort Myer, Virginia, where the female WACs had, with Kameny's help, successfully fought their own purge earlier that fall.

On January 2, Shirley Willer, the woman who had so adamantly opposed Kameny's tactics in 1965, sent a one-hundred-dollar donation to the Mattachine Society of Washington.

"Happy 1969," she wrote.

WITH THE COMING of the new year, Gittings worried about her cocounsel. She saw in Kameny a man who inexplicably refused to look for a temporary job despite his increasingly tall pile of unpaid bills. He risked losing his home.

She urged their mutual friend Foster Gunnison to contact Kameny before "things collapse alltogether [*sic*]," as Gunnison put it. He suggested that Kameny begin editing papers for journals. *That* wouldn't be considered menial labor unfit for a Harvard-educated astronomer, he asked, would it?

Eva Freund, meanwhile, worried about the MSW, seemingly ignored by a president who focused on his security clearance cases. As treasurer, she saw the Society collect only $420 in dues throughout all of 1968—a decrease from 1967, Jon Swanson's last year as president—and a net loss of $216. Only a year after Freund urged the Society's membership to reinstate Kameny as president, she decided to run against him.

On January 9, 1969, Kameny managed to win his reelection. Freund would continue as the MSW's treasurer.

Eleven days later, Richard Nixon became America's president, and after one week in office, he received a report from the National Commission on the Causes and Prevention of Violence. In only five years, the commission found, there had been 370 civil rights demonstrations and 239 violent urban outbursts, which resulted in 191 deaths and 8,000 injuries.

Nixon promised to spend his first hundred days in office "cooling the passions that have inflamed the country," but observers urged caution. "Those who believe in the rule of law," wrote columnists Drew Pearson and Jack Anderson, "cannot rest content with condemning those whose conscience commands them to defy the law." When Kameny read that line in the *Post*, he circled it.

Two months later, he found himself in jail.

On the night of March 14, 1969, five Baltimore Vice Squad detectives entered The Club East, a new twenty-four-hour bathhouse in Baltimore ("Run by men for men," it had advertised in the Annapolis *Capital Gazette*).

On the first and second floors of the small building, officers found men engaging in homosexual activity in cubicles, showers, and a steam bath. On the third floor, they found thirteen men inside what they later described as the "orgy room," a large space with beds.

The detectives announced themselves and began arresting the patrons. The men scrambled. Sixteen men, some wearing nothing but towels, escaped through a back door. The officers arrested fifteen men on the first two floors and all thirteen men trapped on the third floor, bringing the total to twenty-eight.

Kameny had been one of them. When the detective arrested him for participating in a "disorderly house," the astronomer panicked. What if the papers published his name?

He told an officer his name was "Frank Edward Robinson." He provided a false address and a false maiden name for his mother. And because he lied once, he continued to lie, for consistency's sake. When a judge arraigned him the next morning, he used his false name.

After paying five hundred dollars in bail, Kameny realized the gravity of the situation. He drafted a "<u>MOTION FOR ORDER TO COR-</u>

RECT RECORD OF ARREST," to explain his state of mind—"severely shaken"—and beg forgiveness from the judge.

For legal assistance, he turned to the NCACLU. Ralph Temple, its legal director, found a Baltimore attorney to represent the MSW president.

With that, the matter disappeared. There is no record of whether Kameny quietly paid the fine, if he appealed a conviction, or if prosecutors dropped the charges. The incident remained a secret shared only with his attorney and the NCACLU.

But because it was a secret, the arrest threatened his own security clearance case. A year earlier, when the Department of Defense had denied his security clearance, it mentioned nothing about blackmail.

Before his arrest, Kameny had urged the NCACLU to take his case, one devoid of secrecy. "I have spent the last ten years creating a situation in which—uniquely in a security clearance case involving homosexuality—the Statement of Reasons does NOT include the 'blackmail' allegation," he explained. "This makes for an uncluttered case in regard to the basic rationales which I am seeking—a case which you are unlikely to get again."

"I am pleased to tell you that we have decided to take your case," responded an NCACLU official. The NCACLU's lawyers panel agreed to fight Kameny's case up until the Supreme Court.

With Kameny's arrest and lies, he had created a pressure point. If the government attorneys learned about the incident, then they could make a new compelling argument.

Kameny had something to hide.

AT 11:00 A.M. on March 25, only ten days after his arrest, Kameny stood before reporters in the pressroom of the Hotel Washington. Next to him was Barbara Gittings, representing NACHO, and two MSW representatives. "Ladies and Gentlemen," Kameny began, "the American Civil Liberties Union this morning filed suit in the Federal District Court."

The case of Jeffrey Migota, the drag queen dismissed from the IRS, had given Kameny and the NCACLU an idea. One of the IRS regulations breached by Migota was his "unjustified association" with individuals engaged in "illegal, immoral, or reprehensible" activities. Did that, Kameny and the attorneys wondered, not hinder the First Amendment rights of *homosexuals* to associate with IRS employees? Did it not impinge homophile organizations' rights to acquire members, funds, and support?

"As a homosexual citizen," announced Kameny, "I claim that the IRS regulation infringes upon my right to associate freely with Internal Revenue Service employees, an infringement which belies the basis of equality which I share with all other American citizens."

The suit named the MSW, NACHO, and Frank Kameny as plaintiffs. "Homosexuals Sue," announced the next day's *Post*.

That spring, Kameny saw more evidence that his national legal strategy was spreading as intended. On May 9, the *Times* reported on the victory of the New York Civil Liberties Union after it had filed suit on behalf of two city employees. Though the city of New York hired openly gay employees, it still barred homosexuals in certain positions, like caseworkers, hospital care investigators, and children's counselors.

Two caseworkers sued, and in May, the NYCLU reached a settlement with the city. It agreed to allow homosexuals to serve as municipal caseworkers. One of those victorious plaintiffs was Ronald Brass, a founding member of the MSW and an early victim of Warren Scarberry. ("He seems to be adjusting happily to Attica Prison," Brass told Kameny.)

Kameny remained unemployed, and his Society continued to decline. In February, the MSW gave up its office. From that point forward, if someone called the Society's listed phone number, a second telephone in Kameny's home would ring.

"All of us are aware of MSW's sagging membership," wrote MSW veteran Paul Kuntzler. "In view of Washington's immense homosexual community, there is little justification for the small number of people on Society rolls."

Eva Freund, despite losing the election, attempted to save the Society. By February, she had developed a membership campaign. While Kameny's legal battles distracted him, Freund took the opportunity to explore unconventional methods of attracting homosexuals to the Society.

"A Guerrilla to Invade MSW," began the lead story in the February *Insider*. "M.S.W. IS JUST A BUNCH OF FAGGOT COMMUNISTS, ISN'T IT? WHAT HAS M.S.W. <u>EVER</u> REALLY DONE FOR HOMOSEXUALS??"

At the February 1969 meeting, Freund explained that seemingly daunting interactions—like recruiting fellow homosexuals into the MSW—were nothing more than performances. The homosexuals simply needed to rehearse those interactions, like pieces of theater, to boost their confidence and effectiveness. At each monthly meeting that spring, members rehearsed how they could "spread the word" about the Society and its goals in various scenarios—in gay bars, in workplaces, or even among family members.

After one guerrilla theater workshop, the members discussed other methods for publicizing the Society, and they settled on another provocative, less respectable idea. "If we want everybody in town to know the name Mattachine, then what better way but to put it on the bathroom walls," wrote Freund and her coeditor, Richard Schaefers, in the March *Insider*. "Graffiti is now an art and a culture in this country." In 1969, graffiti was the "in thing . . . almost as in as being a homosexual."

Paul Kuntzler, for his part, planned a Bloody Mary Brunch for the end of May (social activities, though still prohibited by the Society's constitution, were now tolerated). After all, the graffiti, the guerrilla theater, and the GAY IS GOOD buttons had done little to increase the Society's membership. Only nine members attended the May membership meeting.

"I think we all just got tired of Frank," remembered Susan Clarke.

As for Kameny, he seemed to care little about the unconstitutional brunch, the vandalizing of bathrooms, or even the decline in membership. On April 20, he wrote Randy Wicker to order five hundred lavender equal sign buttons. "I'm busy with a myriad of things," he added. "Endless speaking engagements, these days."

Meanwhile, Kameny's seven-year-old effort to infiltrate the NCACLU had not just been successful, but it had consumed him. By May 1969, of approximately one hundred cases on the NCACLU's docket, seven came from the astronomer. In two—his security clearance case and the IRS case—Kameny himself was a plaintiff.

Kameny's dream of creating a national, multipronged homosexual legal assault, the Society's primary raison d'être since 1961, had come true. The proud, openly gay plaintiff had been his invention, and now it was commonplace. But because the NCACLU fought his war so effectively, his organization became obsolete.

In the spring of 1969, instead of breathing life into his own organization, Kameny ran for a position on the executive board of the NCACLU. He received assurances of support from at least three attorneys, including Legal Director Ralph Temple.

On May 19, Kameny learned he had lost the election.

Another factor contributed to the decline of his organization. For his entire life, Kameny had relished being the expert in his field, in aluminizing telescopes, in the social world of gay Washington, and then, finally, in the homophile movement. Kameny's organization had provided him with that authority. It had been the vehicle for access to Congress, to the Pentagon and the FBI, and to the press. Now, as an integral member of the NCACLU, as the plaintiff in two major lawsuits, as the chairman of ERCHO, as a sought-after speaker, and as an aspiring author, Kameny no longer needed the Society. He had achieved authority for himself, as a homosexual, alone.

That fact did not always serve him well. Before he announced the IRS lawsuit, Kameny had failed to consult—or even inform—the chairman of NACHO's legal committee, "Austin Wade." A Harvard-educated attorney, Wade wrote Kameny to criticize his "continued unwillingness to work with others."

Kameny responded on May 23. "I shall continue to use MY methods," he wrote. "I am not interested in resting upon my laurels, but if I were, I have them, in considerable quantity, to rest upon very comfortably."

He added, "Nothing succeeds like success, Austin, and thus far I have the successes and you do not."

And that was that.

ON SATURDAY, APRIL 12, Kameny chaired a meeting of ERCHO in New York University's Loeb Student Center.

The delegates' greatest debate centered around Frank Kameny's dress code at the upcoming Philadelphia picket. Kameny provided the history of the regulations, and then, so that the delegates could *see* the power of respectability, he moved that the delegates wait to vote on the matter until they could view Lilli Vincenz's film of the 1968 demonstration.

As they watched the seven-minute film, they saw the suits and dresses, the perfectly uniform signs—ten staples each—and the picketers' solemnity as they stood in respect of the flag. A delegate moved "that dress and appearance at the 1969 demonstration be neat & in keeping with common standards of gender classification."

The motion failed 28–10. A new motion was made, one much more specific. ERCHO "formally directs dress regulations for this demonstration consisting of neat coat and trousers for males; neat dresses, skirts, or suits for females," it began. They would appoint a three-person committee to consider exceptions on a case-by-case basis.

While discussing the motion, the delegates arrived at a number of "understandings." They would not regulate hair length, and they would permit beards. They would ban blue jeans and Levi's. Pendants and beads would be subject to the committee's discretion. They would ban pantsuits and bobby socks on women.

The delegates passed the resolution unanimously.

In mid-June, Kameny suggested three members for the committee, astutely leaving himself off the list.

Carole Friedman (Homophile Action League)
Craig Rodwell (Homophile Youth Movement in Neighborhoods)
Barbara Gittings (several organizations)

Despite Kameny's concessions, MSNY executive director Dick Leitsch saw a hypocrite. How could the astronomer represent all homosexuals—how could he proclaim Gay was Good—if he barred certain types of homosexuals from his demonstrations?

"We cannot support a demonstration that pretends to reflect the feelings of all homosexuals while excluding many homosexuals from participating in the demonstration," he told Gittings. "Since our membership covers all the spectrum of gay life, we encompass drag queens, leather queens, and many, many groovy men and women whose wardrobe consists of bell-bottoms, vests and miles of gilt chains. Rather than risk the embarassment [*sic*] and insult of having some of our people rejected (as did happen a few years ago), we choose neither to participate nor support the demonstration.

"The Annual Reminder held out such promise at its inception, and I am sorry to see it become the personal property of a few who would set themselves up as an 'establishment', no less bigoted and exclusionary than the real 'Establishment' we're supposedly fighting."

On June 25, Kameny and Gittings wrote to the secretary of defense for their final appeal in the security clearance case of Donald Lee Crawford. It represented a pro forma step "to satisfy a sense of completeness" before they handed the case to the NCACLU. "Apparently, a homosexual cannot win," they concluded. "The Board is, in viciously sophisticated manner, simply implementing a class or group disqualification of all homosexuals SIMPLY BECAUSE THEY ARE HOMOSEXUALS."

The next day, the Society for Individual Rights filed suit against the Oakland and Berkeley police chiefs for their "clandestine surveillance" of public restrooms. The lawsuit had resulted from the case of Dr. Philip Caplan, a man who died of a stroke the day after officers arrested him. Two plainclothes officers had caught Caplan in Oakland's Lakeside Park, just across the water from San Francisco's East Bay train terminal, the site of Kameny's first arrest.

ON THE NIGHT of June 27, Yvonne Ritter, wearing her mother's dress and surrounded by two hundred other patrons, sat in the Stonewall. The bar itself was grim—black walls, a black ceiling, blacked-out windows, and weak drinks—but it played the Supremes and the Rolling Stones. It had go-go dancers. It felt safe.

As Ritter sat there, a group of six NYPD officers amassed outside. Two female officers already sat inside the bar, posing as lesbians, watching.

More than a year after Craig Rodwell had criticized the Mafia's ownership of gay bars, the city was finally taking action. In the last three weeks of June, it conducted five raids against purported "clubs" like the Stonewall, de facto bars that sold liquor without a license.

The raids occurred in the middle of a mayoral election campaign, when harassment of homosexuals historically spiked. Indeed, raids against gay bars looked good for those who conducted them. Officers—and the city government—could boost their arrest numbers. They were easy arrests, too; the drag queens never fought back. "Everybody behaved," the officer in charge of the raids later recalled. "It was like, 'We're going down to grab the fags.'"

At 1:20 a.m., the officers entered the Stonewall. The music turned off, and the bright white lights turned on.

Ritter, terrified, ran for the bathroom, where she thought she could escape through a window. As she reached the door, an arm grabbed her. You're not going nowhere, said the officer.

The police dragged her back to the bar and pushed her up against a wall, along with other patrons who defied gender norms. The officers demanded identification, and the policewomen began performing their second duty of the evening. They took the trans women to the bathroom, where the policewomen examined their genitalia. If patrons did not wear their three proper items of clothing, they were arrested.

Usually, the threat of an examination was sufficient to scare the suspected "transvestites," as the police called them, into confession. Usually, as the officers led them to the bathroom, they admitted it: all right, honey, I'm a man.

But it was the second raid of the Stonewall in a single week, and that night, the patrons in drag resisted the authorities. Get your hands off me, they said. Don't touch me.

Female officers examined five trans patrons, but Ritter showed her identification. "Joseph." The officers released the humiliated women and arrested Ritter. Officers told another group of detained patrons, identified by one witness as lesbian women, to stand against a back wall. Male officers pushed them, frisked them, touched them.

Meanwhile, the gay men in the bar stood in a single-file line, and one by one, after showing identification, they exited. As they waited outside for their friends to emerge—they sometimes struck a pose, eliciting applause—the crowd swelled in size. They called their friends from pay phones. The atmosphere grew festive.

The patrons arrested for improper dress then arrived. A police officer shoved one of them, and she hit him with her purse. He hit back with his club.

A *Village Voice* reporter heard boos and catcalls. Someone suggested they tip over the police wagon. An officer led Ritter to the police van, full of patrons in female clothing. When the officer turned to retrieve another one, Ritter slipped out. The officer saw her and shouted for her to stop.

Please, it's my birthday, I'm eighteen, she begged. Ritter was sobbing, her makeup running. The officer, surrounded by hundreds of increasingly angry patrons, looked the other way. Ritter ran for the anonymity of the crowd, now numbering four hundred, and the van drove away.

Officers then brought out another patron—whom they had identified as a woman—wearing cropped hair, male clothes, and handcuffs. One witness noticed a black leather suit. Another described the apparel as "fancy, go-to-bar drag for a butch dyke."

"She put up a struggle," reported the *Voice*.

"A dyke," wrote one witness, "lost her mind in the streets of the West Village—kicking, cursing, screaming, and fighting."

Twice, this patron escaped from the police car before getting caught. After the second time, an officer grabbed and violently threw the patron into the car.

A voice—a witness recalled it sounded female—shouted, "Why don't you guys do something!"

"It was at that moment," reported the *Voice*, "that the scene became explosive. Limp wrists were forgotten. Beer cans and bottles were heaved at the windows, and a rain of coins descended on the cops."

With cries of "Police brutality," "Pigs," and "Faggot cops," the insurrection began.

The officers retreated backward and bolted the door of the bar.

The mob used an uprooted parking meter as a battering ram. The door swung open, and an officer was hit by a flying object. The police grabbed a man from the crowd, dragged him into the bar, and beat him mercilessly.

A *Voice* reporter was trapped inside the bar with the officers. "The sound filtering in doesn't suggest dancing faggots any more," he later wrote. "It sounds like a powerful rage bent on vendetta."

The windows shattered. The officers, certain that the mob would storm the bar, pointed their guns outside. "We'll shoot the first motherfucker that comes through the door," said one of them.

Outside, calls of "Let's get some gas."

An arm poured lighter fluid into the room, then threw a match. A whoosh of flames. The officers prepared to shoot, and a massacre seemed imminent.

Suddenly, the sound of sirens. Fire trucks arrived, followed by two buses of riot police.

The officers escaped, and the reinforcements turned their hoses and clubs onto the crowds. For several hours, trans women, drag queens, and street youth—hustlers who worked the piers and Forty-Second Street—fought and taunted the riot police.

Facing the helmeted officers, the street youths sang "We are the Stonewall girls," chained in a chorus line, kicking their heels. Nightsticks swung at heads and backs. The rioters ran, but the officers ran faster. Witnesses saw young men, covered in blood, dragged into police cars. Craig Rodwell, the young veteran of Wicker's first New York picket, yelled, "Gay Power," while watching from a stoop.

The next evening, Saturday, the crowds grew larger. They blocked the street. Flames rose from trash cans, rioters threw bottles, and windows broke.

One Black trans woman, Marsha P. Johnson, miraculously climbed a lamppost in high heels and a tight-fitting dress. She dropped a bag full of bricks onto a police car below, shattering its windshield.

The riot police arrived again, and the street youths reprised their taunts and chorus lines. By 3:30 a.m., the crowds dispersed.

On Sunday afternoon, a sign appeared on the Stonewall's window.

WE HOMOSEXUALS PLEAD WITH
OUR PEOPLE TO PLEASE HELP
MAINTAIN PEACEFUL AND QUIET
CONDUCT ON THE STREETS OF
THE VILLAGE—MATTACHINE

The crowds, though smaller and less violent, still returned that night. Officers scattered them in a single sweep, but the Stonewall stayed open, playing rock and roll.

The poet Allen Ginsberg, a veteran of the MSNY's first picket, entered the Stonewall and danced there. "You know, the guys there were so beautiful," he said upon leaving. "They've lost that wounded look that fags all had ten years ago."

That night, Yvonne Ritter stayed in Brooklyn. She had been avoiding the Village, lying low, after taking the subway home Saturday morning.

As she graduated from high school that week, an image, a feeling, remained imprinted in her mind. After she escaped the police van full of drag queens and blended into the angry crowd, makeup streaking down her face, she, too, picked something off the ground—maybe a brick or a piece of glass, she does not know—and threw it, in anger and defiance and pride.

Christopher Street, New York City, June 28, 1969

18.

THE LIBERATION

Hours before the riots began, NASA initiated countdown procedure testing for *Apollo 11*, the mission that would take humanity to the moon. The spacecraft, atop a 281-foot-tall missile, sat on its launchpad, and Americans prepared to watch the historic event. Clifford Norton nearly had the chance to watch the mission from inside NASA, but like Frank Kameny, he could only watch from afar.

He had been a budget analyst for satellite projects at NASA, but on a Monday night in October 1963, Norton drove to Lafayette Square. At 2:00 a.m., Norton pulled up to the curb, and Madison Monroe Procter, waiting in the park, entered Norton's car.

They drove around the block. Procter later admitted that Norton touched his leg, then invited him over for a drink. "It would take an idiot," Procter later told officers, "not to be able to figure that he wanted to have sex." Norton dropped off Procter back where they had met. Procter then walked to his own car and began following Norton to his home.

Two Morals Division officers had seen everything. They pursued Norton, in a high-speed chase, through the streets of Downtown Washington until they reached Norton's apartment building in Southwest Washington. The officers arrested both men in the parking lot and took them to the Morals Division office. For two hours, the officers separately interrogated them about the incident and their sexual histories. Upon learning Norton worked at NASA, the officers followed protocol. They immediately called Bartley Fugler, the chief of NASA headquarters security operations. Fugler arrived at the Morals Division office, and for twenty minutes, he secretly observed Norton's interrogation from an adjacent room.

The Morals Division officers finally released Norton with only a traffic violation, but Fugler wanted to speak to Norton himself. Around 4:00 a.m., he brought Norton to NASA's dark offices in one of the dilapidated temporary structures near the Lincoln Memorial. Another NASA official joined Fugler and sat across from Norton.

Yes, admitted the budget analyst, he had engaged in mutual masturbation with other males in high school and college. Yes, when he drank, sometimes he experienced homosexual desires. Yes, sometimes he blacked out while drinking, and he sometimes engaged in homosexual activity when that occurred. Yes, he had experienced one of those blackouts before meeting Procter.

Fugler's interrogation ended at 6:30 a.m., and NASA promptly dismissed Norton for "immoral, indecent, and disgraceful conduct."

Norton called his old friend, Frank Kameny. They had met in the gay world of Boston, while Kameny was finishing his PhD at Harvard. After moving to Washington, Norton learned of Kameny's new organization and his legal connections. Kameny referred Norton to two NCACLU attorneys, Glenn Graves and John Karr, who agreed to take Norton's case. They filed suit against CSC chairman John Macy on October 13, 1964, only three days after both lawyers spoke at Kameny's ECHO conference in Washington.

At the time, the MSW president did not think it was a particularly good case. Norton continued to deny his homosexuality, which meant he could not attack the purges directly, as an avowed homosexual. Graves and Karr, meanwhile, made procedural arguments. Norton had not been permitted to confront his accuser, and the only evidence against him came from an illegal arrest and interrogation. Even if Norton won his case, it was unlikely to help other homosexuals.

But Norton and Kameny got lucky. After the district court upheld Norton's dismissal, *Norton v. Macy* arrived on the desks of three appeals court judges, including David Bazelon and J. Skelly Wright, two of the most liberal judges in the country. On Tuesday, July 1, 1969, nearly six years after Norton's dismissal and in the middle of the Stonewall riots, the three-judge panel released its ruling. Bazelon, joined by Wright, penned the decision.

Norton's supervisor had testified that he faced pressure to dismiss Norton because the Lafayette Square incident raised the possibility of a "public scandal." To dismiss homosexuals, he had testified, was a "custom within the agency."

Bazelon and Wright were unconvinced. "We do not doubt that NASA blushes whenever one of its own is caught in flagrante delictu [sic]," wrote Bazelon. But such embarrassment did not necessarily harm the agency. In all likelihood, NASA's explanation—its fear of embarrassment—represented no more than a "smokescreen hiding personal antipathies or moral judgments."

In a country that now acknowledged the constitutional right to privacy, homosexuals needed some semblance of due process, some protection from "arbitrary and capricious" dismissal.

"Since the record before us does not suggest any reasonable connection between the evidence against him and the efficiency of the service," decided Bazelon and Wright, "we conclude that he was unlawfully discharged."

"An agency," concluded the court, "cannot support a dismissal as promoting the efficiency of the service merely by turning its head and crying 'shame.'"

Norton learned about his victory from an article in *The New York Times*. The former NASA employee had only four dollars to his name. He had bused across the country—from Los Angeles to Cincinnati to New York—looking for a job, but he had found nothing. He was now back in Boston, "on the old scene."

"The decision gives me a new problem," Norton told Kameny. His family was "sure to pick it up—homosexual charges & all. The family have not known any of this aspect of the affair, or of my life. So— For whom are you working now? Can they use me?"

DURING THE CITY of Philadelphia's official Independence Day 1969 celebrations, astronaut Walter Cunningham, a veteran of the previous year's *Apollo 7* mission, spoke before a crowd of twenty thousand at Independence Hall. "The student problem bothers me most right now," he said, criticizing America's youth for its protests, its violent methods, and its disrespect for the military. Six times, the audience applauded the American hero's denunciations.

After the astronaut finished, the homosexuals arrived.

Kameny, when he learned of the riots, had chuckled. Following the natural progression of movements, his fellow homosexuals were finally rioting. It had been a matter of time. But this picket, *his* picket, would remain orderly and dignified.

Despite his cries of "Gay Power" a week earlier, twenty-eight-year-old Craig Rodwell tolerated Kameny's dress code. He had publicized the protest as a "vigil-type demonstration" and asked demonstrators "to observe the dignity and seriousness of the day and to dress and behave accordingly."

Threatening phone calls had followed Rodwell's picket advertisements in *The Village Voice*. Unidentified male voices threatened to follow HYMN's bus from New York, capsize it, and assault the homosexuals.

The police, for their part, worried about the newly riotous homosexuals. That afternoon, approximately twenty uniformed officers and twenty more plainclothesmen materialized across from Independence Hall.

When the bus arrived unscathed to Philadelphia with its forty occupants, longtime picketer Lilli Vincenz immediately noticed a difference in its occupants. She saw the conservatively dressed—even Rodwell wore his prescribed jacket—but, for the first time, she also saw a large contingent of New Yorkers in bell bottoms, short skirts, sandals, and beards. One interracial lesbian couple brought their child. They all seemed to be discussing the riots.

Shortly after 2:00 p.m., the fifty demonstrators—wearing Kameny's lavender GAY IS GOOD buttons—began marching, as usual, in a silent, single-file line. After thirty minutes, two women began holding hands. Kameny ran up to them. None of that, he said. Kameny broke apart their hands. His authority exerted, Kameny—he wore his SPOKESMAN badge—left with Barbara Gittings to speak to a reporter from *The Distant Drummer*, an underground newspaper based in Philadelphia.

Suddenly, the *Drummer* would later report, "one breathless young man" ran up to Kameny, Gittings, and the reporter. Craig Rodwell began "ranting and raving" about Kameny's action. "Our message is that homo-sexual love is good. Holding hands is not inappropriate," he exclaimed.

Rodwell turned to Kameny and Gittings. "If you don't change, you're going to be left behind." Then, to the reporter, "There's a generation gap among homosexuals, too." Rodwell ran back to the picket line, where he joined hands with his twenty-one-year-old lover, Fred Sargeant.

"Come on," he yelled to the picketers, "be proud homosexuals—not 'Auntie Toms.'" Two more female couples joined their hands.

One marcher, annoyed by the verbose messages on their signs—GAY IS GOOD or GAY POWER appeared nowhere—scrawled END SEXUAL FASCISM on his own sign.

Aware of the reporter's presence, and wary of risking further humili-ation, Kameny could do nothing but watch a new generation flaunt its power. Gittings attempted to perform damage control. "What we're striving for is a recognition of our rights and dignity as homosexuals," she explained to the reporter, changing the topic. Hundreds of tourists, meanwhile, watched the homosexuals. One woman, seeing dozens of ho-mosexuals inexplicably wearing suits on a hot summer day, remarked that they did not look like *real* homosexuals. Clearly, she told a reporter, some-one had paid them to protest.

A week later, Kameny wrote to Rodwell with an apology. "I am genu-inely sorry about the disagreement which surfaced at the demonstration," he wrote. "'Love-ins'—homosexual and/or heterosexual, both—have their place; so do picketing demonstrations. Neither is likely to be effec-tive, and both are more likely to be ineffective, if they are mixed.

"Particularly unfortunate," he added, "was your taking the dispute to the press. Family squabbles are best conducted in the living room, not on the front lawn, when an appearance of unity should be stressed."

Fred Sargeant, Rodwell's lover, wrote to Kameny himself. "First, why did you stop two girls from holding hands by coming up to them and knocking their hands apart? (Such stormtrooper tactics, really!)

"Secondly, why did you presume to impose your own particular brand of mores upon me after you had seen me holding hands with my lover? (Such as saying it was a question of good taste.) Correct me if I was wrong in assuming that the demonstration was an affirmation of the right of homosexuals to, among other things, hold hands in public.

"You must realize that to many of us, looking employable to the federal government is of little importance. The government is our servant, not our master.

"By dictatorialism you will only minimize the effectiveness of us all," Sargeant concluded. "I'm willing to compromise, are you?"

News of the fiasco spread across the movement. The DOB covered the scene in its newsletter, and its editor wrote to Kameny with concern that spectators had thought they were paid demonstrators. Did that not defeat the purpose of the picket?

"What the hell ever happened to the concept of freedom and equality that we espouse?" wrote Dick Michaels, editor of *The Los Angeles Advocate*. "What difference does it make whether the straights push us around directly or do it through other, uptight homosexuals. This is what the concept of 'image' eventually leads to. The image becomes more important than the goal."

Kameny penned unapologetic, defensive responses to Sargeant and Michaels. Indeed, only one person had the power—and enough respect—to change the astronomer's mind. Gittings had stood by him for years, defending his dress code and his pickets and his unorthodox methods at the Pentagon, but the incident had convinced her, too, that Kameny's rigidity was harming their cause. He stood on the precipice of allowing his movement to leave him behind.

Before speaking to Kameny on the matter, Gittings prepared herself—a necessity if she hoped to breach his stubborn mind—by drafting a list of handwritten notes.

"Frank," she wrote, "Stop being martinet, acting like a general commanding the troops." Start delegating responsibility and allow others to develop as leaders. "Younger people," she continued, are "tired of being ordered around, told what to do & how to dress, when they won't accept this in other areas." The picket, no longer newsworthy, may have outlived its purpose.

Finally, she asked, why was there no GAY IS GOOD sign?

MARTHA ALTMAN, raised by Jewish, socialist parents in Brooklyn, had always been intelligent. She attended the Bronx High School of Science and graduated in 1960, the same year as her biology class peer Stokely Carmichael.

First, she had participated in the antiwar movement, but in 1967, the curly-haired activist with glasses and a toothy grin discovered the DOB, an organization for women like her. Within a year, while working as a secretary at Barnard College, Altman became the young president of the DOB's New York chapter. For her pseudonym, she chose "Martha Shelley," a name she adopted for life.

At the 1968 ERCHO conference in Washington, she met a handsome bisexual man named Bob Martin, and though Shelley identified as a lesbian, the two began dating. Martin introduced her to the Student Homophile League, to homosexual picketing, and to LSD.

The homophile movement often frustrated Shelley. After hearing NACHO delegates discuss the resolution against tearoom sex in 1968, it seemed the movement wanted to exclude those it deemed undesirable. How, she wondered, would homosexuals gain first-class citizenship if they placed themselves above other members of their own minority, if they simply mirrored the behavior of their oppressors?

On Saturday night, June 28, Shelley walked through the East Village with two lesbian women, who were visiting New York to discuss the creation of their own DOB chapter in Boston. They stumbled upon the riots.

What's going on? asked the Boston visitors.

Oh, just a riot, responded Shelley. We have them here all the time.

The next day, she learned it had not just been a riot, but a violent uprising of homosexuals. The moment had come, she realized, to harness the anger of her kind, to march en masse against their oppression.

When she told Dick Leitsch of her idea, the MSNY's executive director told her that a march in the aftermath of the riots would be inappropriate. It would send the wrong message. Even Randy Wicker criticized the riots. "Rocks through windows don't open doors," he told an audience on July 6.

On July 9, Shelley arrived at a public meeting held by the MSNY, organized to discuss the riots. More than a hundred sat in the audience. Shelley stood and proposed a Gay Power rally in Washington Square Park, followed by a march to the Stonewall.

The attendees debated the idea for an hour until Leitsch called a vote. Who favored Shelley's march?

Nearly everyone in the audience raised their hand. Leitsch, defeated, allowed Shelley and her allies to form a planning committee in the back room. The following Saturday, while drinking beers in the Mattachine offices, the young committee members decided to create a new organization. Inspired by the Communists in Vietnam, they became the Gay Liberation Front.

On July 27, only three weeks after marching with fifty picketers in Philadelphia, Barbara Gittings stood in Washington Square Park, surrounded by five hundred homosexuals, many of whom wore lavender ribbons and armbands. Another five hundred spectators stood on the side of the park, watching.

Martha Shelley climbed onto the rim of the park's fountain. "Brothers and sisters, welcome to this city's first gay power vigil," she began. "We're tired of being harassed and persecuted. If a straight couple can hold hands in Washington Square, why can't we?

"The time has come for us to walk in the sunshine. We don't have to ask permission to do it. Here we are!"

There were "eruptions of applause, a delirium of screams," reported the *Voice*. Gittings saw people waving from their apartment windows. The crowd marched to the Stonewall in a column four abreast, stopping traffic on Sixth Avenue, cheering "Gay Power."

By early August, the GLF announced itself as an independent organization. "The society has fucked with us," its members told *RAT*, an underground newspaper, "within our families, on our jobs, in our education, in the streets, in our bedrooms; in short, it has shit all over us."

"We identify ourselves with all the oppressed: the Vietnamese struggle, the third world, the blacks, the workers . . . all those oppressed by this rotten, dirty, vile, fucked-up capitalist conspiracy," they concluded.

The GLF had no leaders, no membership list. Anyone could attend its meetings. Anyone could vote.

"Q: What does the GLF intend to do?

"A: We are relating the militancy generated by the bar bust and by increasing pig harassment to a program that allows homosexuals and sexually liberated persons to confront themselves and society through encounter groups, demonstrations, dances, a newspaper, and by just being ourselves on the street."

At first, Kameny ignored them. At the Society's first membership meeting after the riots, the day after the GLF's creation, he updated the homosexuals on the *Norton* decision, the IRS suit, and the SIR's own lawsuit in San Francisco. He mentioned the riots, but only briefly. Vincenz then showed her film of the 1968 Reminder Day picket. Eva Freund advertised an upcoming MSW-NCACLU boat ride.

On the pages of the Society's *The Insider*, however, radicalism reigned. "TO HELL WITH DYING ON YOUR KNEES," wrote coeditors Freund and Schaefers in August. "WHY SHOULD YOU continue to be oppressed?

"It appears that the structured homophile groups have failed to motivate the homosexual community. Perhaps they have not wanted to deal with the homosexual masses," they wrote.

The riots had been no "fluke," Freund and Schaefers explained. "When it becomes clear that the doors are never going to open and that door knocking is only a pacifier for the masses, then it is time to knock the doors down."

The Mattachine Society of Washington had begun to advocate violence.

IN JULY, KAMENY WROTE to the Department of Defense with a threat. "While I do not necessarily approve of violence, public disorder, and rioting," he wrote, "if—all other reasonable measured [*sic*] having failed— that turns out to be what it does take, then, by your own effective invitation, that is what you will get."

No, Kameny *himself* did not embrace violence, but as for other homosexuals, the MSW president could no longer make guarantees for them. The federal government could choose to reason with him—a logical man, making logical arguments—or it could face the wrath of Gay Power: illogical, angry, and violent.

After four years, the Department of Defense had finally identified Otto Ulrich, the man photographed by agents at the MSW's Pentagon picket. When Ulrich joined Bionetics Research in 1968, he had admitted his membership in the MSW, and he soon faced revocation of his clearance.

Kameny and Gittings flipped the switch of their publicity machine. One hundred fifty press releases introduced Ulrich as an avowed homosexual. They invited reporters to the hearing, and once again, the Department of Defense banned the media.

On July 16, Ulrich, Kameny, and Gittings strolled into the Pentagon while wearing a variety of lapel buttons—GAY IS GOOD, EQUALITY FOR HOMOSEXUALS, and an equal sign. They sat before three military officials.

Morrow began questioning Ulrich. "Would you tell the Board whether you still engage in such activities of meeting sailors in Lafayette Park and taking them to your residence?"

"He has an absolute right to meet them anywhere he wishes without reflecting in any way whatsoever on his eligibility for security clearance," responded Kameny.

"Do you continue to engage in sexual relations with other males?"

Yes, said Ulrich.

What about oral copulation? Anal copulation?

Kameny attempted to object, but Ulrich interrupted him. "The details of my sex life are none of the Government's goddamn business."

"We want that on the record," said Kameny.

How in the world, concluded Kameny, could Ulrich be blackmailed by "some petty little government in Moscow" after traveling to the heart of the United States Military while wearing homosexual lapel buttons?

"We have come in here wearing buttons saying, 'Equality for Homosexuals,'" said Kameny. "We mean it precisely and fully and by God, gentlemen, we are going to get it and you are going to give it to us willingly or you will be compelled by the courts to give it to us unwillingly to your everlasting disgrace and discredit. Let there be no mistake about that."

The homosexuals rested their case.

That same month, Richard Gayer called Kameny for assistance. An electrical engineer in San Francisco, Gayer had admitted to membership in the SIR and the Janus Society on a routine clearance form. The Department of Defense, suspicious, began interrogating him in July 1969.

Gayer's case was Kameny's first on the West Coast. The Pentagon's screening board declined to travel to San Francisco and sent a list of interrogatories, instead. "Have you ever engaged in any homosexual sexual act(s) or any act(s) of sexual perversion with (an)other male person(s)?"

A month later, for the third time, Benning Wentworth faced similar questions. In January, the appeals board had ruled that Wentworth's examiner—the relatively sympathetic Raymond Waldman—wrongfully prevented department counsel from asking additional questions about Wentworth's sex life (Kameny had objected they were a "fishing expedition"). The appeals board thus remanded the case back to Waldman for yet another trial.

On August 21, once again, Wentworth admitted his homosexuality. This time, as he sat next to Kameny and Gittings in a New York hearing room, Wentworth wore two lapel buttons, EQUALITY FOR HOMOSEXUALS and GAY IS GOOD.

"In each case, are you generally the inserter or are you generally the receptor, or is it interchangeable?" asked the Pentagon. "Do you ever attach any sexual feelings to inanimate objects?"

After Kameny and Gittings received the transcript of the hearing, they issued another press release: "<u>HOMOSEXUAL REQUIRED TO ANSWER OBSCENE QUESTIONS BY DEFENSE DEPARTMENT</u>"; "<u>PENTAGON BOARD SEEKS TITILLATION OF ITS PRURIENT INTERESTS</u>."

"What in hell," they wrote, "is the American government doing asking questions like this of ANY of its citizens under ANY circumstances, whatever?"

BOB MARTIN, working the night shift as an intern at the Associated Press, had not witnessed the riots. But neither did he *need* the riots. The Columbia occupation had already radicalized him against the system, and Martha Shelley had taught him the language of the New Left.

On July 3, Martin hosted an orgy in New York. ("Yes I've been to quite a number of orgies," said Kameny, upon hearing about it. "Don't lecture me on needing sex.") On July 4, Martin attended the Reminder Day picket in Philadelphia, and on July 5, after returning to Washington with Kameny, he tripped on LSD during a thunderstorm.

On Monday, August 25, he attended NACHO's 1969 conference in

Kansas City. Martin was the only SHL member in attendance—the GLF had not yet been accredited—but he arrived with an ambitious plan. He wanted to take over the conference on behalf of his generation of radicals.

Thirty delegates attended the conference at the Bellerive Hotel. "We are back where we started," said NACHO chairman Bill Wynne in his welcome address. "I would say that we have accomplished damn little but there were a few bright moments in the three years of darkness."

On Wednesday evening, the delegates watched *The Seasons Change*, a documentary produced by the ACLU in the aftermath of the 1968 Democratic National Convention in Chicago. Martin later described the delegates' reaction in an article for a new gay publication, *Gay Power*. "The scenes of bloody demonstrators and illegal police tactics clearly affected many delegates who had thought the homophile movement could remain unaffected by other protest," he wrote. "They had not seen Christopher Street."

That night, Martin formed the Radical Caucus, which operated under the guise of NACHO's official Youth Committee. Together, the delegates worked to articulate their beliefs in a document.

The next day, Frank Kameny moved that NACHO adopt the report of his Federal Government Committee, which recommended the continuation of his efforts against the Pentagon. Bob Martin stood in opposition to his mentor. The Youth Committee, he announced, had unanimously adopted a radical manifesto. "THE HOMOPHILE MOVEMENT MUST BE RADICALIZED!" it began.

"We see the persecution of homosexuality as part of a general attempt to oppress all minorities and keep them powerless. Our fate is linked with these minorities; if the detention camps are filled tomorrow with blacks, hippies and other radicals, we will not escape that fate, all our attempts to dissociate ourselves from them notwithstanding."

For three hours, the homosexuals debated whether Kameny's Pentagon battle indeed fed homosexuals into America's "war machine." Kameny argued that they had no choice but to fight discrimination against homosexuals everywhere, even if that fight indirectly supported a larger, unjust system.

The delegates agreed with Kameny, rebuked the radicals' motions, and ultimately approved Kameny's report. Both Kameny and his erstwhile protégé could claim victories, however. Kameny's battles remained intact, and Bob Martin could rest assured that he had begun "defining the issues and forcing delegates to think about them," as he reported in *Gay Power*.

On the last day of the conference, the homophile Phoenix Society of Kansas City hosted a farewell picnic in the city's mammoth green space, Swope Park. Some of the locals pointed out the empty public restrooms. They were padlocked, closed by the city to keep out the "local queens," they explained.

Kameny suggested they forcibly remove the locks. The local homophile group, the Phoenix Society, could mail the broken locks to the mayor.

The homosexuals, enthusiastic about his idea, promptly destroyed the locks, thus "liberating" the public restrooms.

THE CALLS HAD COME immediately after the riots. Throughout the month of July, homosexuals across the country wanted advice on how to create their own organizations. In one week alone, Kameny provided instructions to groups in Atlanta, Georgia; Norfolk, Virginia; Chapel Hill, North Carolina; and Youngstown, Ohio.

Norfolk had experienced a recent bar raid, so Kameny urged the arrested patrons to fight the charges and approach the ACLU.

"Meanwhile, organize." Find a nucleus of devoted homosexuals, create a name for the group, and write bylaws, he advised. He enclosed a set of GAY IS GOOD buttons.

"It is time that 'Gay Power' got going," he wrote.

Kameny and Gittings continued touring the East Coast, encouraging more groups to form. When they traveled to Cornell at the invitation of the university's SHL, Kameny stayed with gay astrophysicist—and former love interest—James Pollack (Kameny had been too busy "Wentworthing," as he called it, for a long-distance romance).

In print, Kameny's influence continued to spread. With his assistance, the *Harvard Law Review* published an article that concluded the government did not "offer adequate protection" to the homosexual minority.

The financial position of the MSW, now almost entirely out of

Kameny's hands, seemed to be improving. At the September member-ship meeting, Eva Freund announced the treasury had a surplus of three hundred dollars.

While Kameny occupied himself with fighting for all homosexuals, Lilli Vincenz urged the Society to help its own members. She had seen the SIR in San Francisco grow to become a political force because it rec-ognized the necessity of building a homosexual community. It sponsored not just political events, but also dances, brunches, and drag shows. In New York, the GLF had begun hosting large, successful dances. Was it not time for the MSW to start serving the needs of homosexuals in Washington?

For the first project of Vincenz's Community Service Committee, she organized a blood drive. In the 1950s, Hal Call's Mattachine Society or-ganized a blood drive to convince the straight world that homosexuals cared about the community at large, but Vincenz conceived of her blood drive to convince homosexuals that they had a family. If an organization donated enough blood, the Red Cross promised free blood to members of that group in the event of an emergency. It represented "an attempt to have lovers and roommates protected in the same way that members of the immediate family are normally protected," explained *The Insider*.

On October 13, ten Society members—they wore their GAY IS GOOD buttons—donated blood at the Red Cross. Vincenz later recalled that only one or two homosexuals were turned away, for hepatitis.

Freund and Schaefers continued publishing *The Insider*, which in-creasingly mirrored the language of Martin's Radical Caucus and the GLF. Its news stories focused on the fight against "the system" across the country: the limitation of stop-and-frisk policies in Washington, the secret files on antiwar demonstrators in New Jersey, and the entrapment of Black militants in Virginia.

Lilli Vincenz wanted a publication that would not just promote political change, but also foster community. She decided to create a new publication that would serve, as *The Insider* described it, as a "newsletter/community bulletin board/scandal sheet." Bart Wenger, an MSW member, and Nancy Tucker, a former member, agreed to serve as coeditors.

In October, *The Gay Blade*, "An Independent Publication Serving the Gay Community," appeared in gay bars across Washington. Each stack came with a collection of GAY IS GOOD buttons. The first issue, a single-sided sheet of paper, featured only eight short stories, covering the blood drive, a discussion group on "The Homosexual and the Media," a room-mate service ("Don't bother if you want to talk dirty"), an off-Broadway review, and an upcoming Kameny lecture.

The *Blade*'s editors kept Kameny away from editorial power, however. "He never saw it until it was already printed and being distributed," explained Susan Clarke, a *Blade* volunteer. "He was just impossible to work with."

"I loved him dearly, but he was like a terrible father," she added.

One of the national stories in the issue, headlined "GAY LIBERATION FRONT," had special relevance to the Society. In July, hoping to attract new members, the MSW executive board had voted to budget one hundred dollars for an advertisement in the *Post*. The newspaper, despite its editorial sympathy over the years, had refused to accept the advertisement. "No advertisement containing the words 'homosexual', 'homophile', or 'Mattachine' is acceptable," explained the paper.

The NCACLU and the MSW appealed the matter up to the publisher of the *Post*, Katharine Graham, to no avail. Kameny wrote to the national ACLU in New York, urging it to consider this "gray" area of First Amendment rights.

The GLF faced a similar problem. Though *The Village Voice* accepted its ads, the paper refused to print the words *gay* or *homosexual*. Its coverage of the "dyke" and "faggot" riots, moreover, continued to infuriate the homosexuals.

On September 12, for more than seven hours, the GLF picketed outside the offices of the *Voice*. They had no dress code, no silence, no rules. The picketers loudly chanted and distributed five thousand leaflets to passersby. Finally, the *Voice* publisher agreed to speak to three GLF representatives.

After complaining about the picket (the *Voice* was a *liberal* paper, he argued), the publisher ultimately conceded. He would allow the word *gay* to be printed, reported *The Gay Blade*.

Without a lawsuit, without much preparation, and in mere hours—using only the strength of numbers and the power of disruption—the fledgling GLF could declare victory where the MSW could not.

The GLF organized a celebratory dance while Kameny observed from Washington.

ON OCTOBER 17, the United States Court of Claims released its decision in the six-year-old case of Dick Schlegel, one of the founding members of the Society, against the Civil Service Commission. "Any schoolboy," wrote the court, "knows that a homosexual act is immoral, indecent, lewd, and obscene. Adult persons are even more conscious that this is true. If activities of this kind are allowed to be practiced in a government department, it is inevitable that the efficiency of the service will in time be adversely affected."

Despite the victory of Clifford Norton, the CSC could now argue that its purges of *active* homosexuals—federal employees who actually had sex—were entirely legal.

Schlegel wrote to the NCACLU at the suggestion of his "close friend and valued advisor," Frank Kameny, urging the Union to take his case to the Supreme Court. "Why not be open—finally—about the circumstances in my case, while still pursuing the argument for a right to privacy for Federal employees?"

The ACLU accepted Schlegel's case and began constructing a Supreme Court brief that did just that.

IN 1967, the National Institute of Mental Health selected Dr. Evelyn Hooker, a psychologist at UCLA, to lead its new Task Force on Homosexuality. At the time, the appointment provided hope for the homophile movement; for sixteen years, Hooker had conducted psychological research that proved homosexuals did not show signs of paranoia, femininity, or maladjustment. Homosexuality itself was not a mental illness, Hooker had found. The condition did not even exist as a "clinical entity."

On October 10, 1969, the Hooker committee released its report. Yes, it concluded, homosexuality *did* represent a "major problem" in American society. The problem, however, lay not in the supposed sickness of homosexuals, but in the fact that society made them suffer.

America considered homosexuality "maladaptive and opprobrious," so homosexuals experienced isolation and injustice. Legal persecution created mental health issues because of "the need for concealment and the emotional stresses arising from this need."

In October, *TIME* magazine covered the Hooker report and released its first cover story on the "Homosexual in America," intended as "atonement" for the magazine's 1966 essay that described homosexuality as a "pathetic little second-rate substitute for reality."

The *TIME* feature ended with "A Discussion: Are Homosexuals Sick?" featuring Kameny, Leitsch, Dr. Socarides, Kinsey report coauthor Dr. Wardell Pomeroy, two sociologists, an anthropologist, and an Episcopal priest.

Despite the breadth of knowledge of the panel, *TIME* opened and closed the discussion with quotes from the MSW president. "It must be declared that homosexuality is a form of emotional illness, which can be treated, that these people can be helped," said Socarides.

"With that, you will surely destroy us," responded Kameny, with the final word.

Earlier that year, Cornell astrophysicist Jim Pollack, in an attempt to assist with Kameny's nightmarish financial situation, offered him the opportunity to help with astronomical research. Using NASA facilities, Kameny would conduct microdensitometry research for Cornell. But as the months elapsed and winter of 1969 approached, Kameny had not yet finished his share of the work. He had no time because of the "inexorable tide of letters, phone calls, requests for public appearances, and the like, of an unparalleled (in my experience) magnitude," he explained to Pollack. "All the country seems to be 'at my door' to ask for aid, assistance, counsel, and authoritative comment."

With Kameny's authority as a national figure well established, building upon itself, and seemingly indestructible, he felt he could expand his purview, if only slightly, by advocating for other issues—less respectable issues—about which he felt passionately. When *Tangents*, a homophile publication, editorialized against computer dating ("satisfactory personal relationships cannot result from data processes," it argued), Kameny wrote in defense of Man-to-Man. "Does Tangents believe that a bar

pick-up, because it is face-to-face, is based upon factors any less superficial or more conducive to a successful relationship, than those included in
the Man-to-Man questionnaire?" he asked.

Faced with the new phenomenon of gay liberation, Kameny also took
steps to preserve his place in history. In late October, the same week as
the appearance of the *TIME* cover story, *The Washington Post* published a
story on the "Homosexual Revolution." Above the title sat a large repro-
duction of a GAY IS GOOD button, yet Kameny appeared nowhere in the
article.

The *Post* reported on Stonewall and the successes of the GLF's *Village
Voice* picket, which illustrated the "new openness" and "new militancy" of
the homosexual minority. As for Washington, "there is as yet no militancy
here," wrote the *Post*. "The only publications are the homophile Mattachine Society's conservative newsletter, devoted mainly to court cases,
and a nascent mimeographed sheet of somewhat the same genre called
Gay Blade."

"As the person who coined and originally publicized the slogan <u>Gay
is Good</u>, I was gratified, indeed, to see it," responded Kameny. But he had
"one cavil."

"The immediate present often tends to loom up too large and out of
proper perspective, at expense of the achievements of the past," he wrote.
The picketing demonstrations of 1965 were "at least as novel, as pioneer-
ing, as militant, as 'extreme' and as indicative of a 'new openness' as the
more recent demonstrations in New York and elsewhere, and, in fact,
prepared the groundwork without which those more recent demonstrations would have been quite impossible and simply would not have
occurred."

It was just a minor objection, he wrote. Everyone in the movement,
regardless of their methods, wanted the same thing: equality with heterosexuals "<u>as homosexuals</u>. Gay <u>IS</u> good! Sincerely yours, Franklin E.
Kameny."

EACH TIME KAMENY visited New York, for the *TIME* panel or a lecture at NYU, he attended a meeting of the Gay Liberation Front.

The new organization impressed him. He saw a group of young, dedicated activists who were willing to declare themselves as homosexuals (the name of their publication was *Come Out!*). He saw their success at *The Village Voice*, and he saw their harsh questions of candidates for mayor of New York, catching the politicians off guard and forcing them to articulate answers. "If they don't get taken over by some of the extreme-extreme radical groups (non-homophile) for their own ends, they should do well," he wrote in October.

As a student of other movements, he also saw the writing on the wall. Gay liberation was the future. "I suspect," he wrote, "this will be one of the directions taken by the Movement in the next few years. Ideologically there will be a great deal of its content which will be unpalatable—sometimes highly so; they have the advantage of numbers, enthusiasm, militancy and, above all, complete doffing of the mask and camouflage. They should be channelled into the movement."

The MSNY, on the other hand, refused to cooperate with the new organization. "I urged Dick Leitsch to work with GLF instead of against them, with the feeling that each can contribute a great deal to the other," wrote Kameny, "but he's not buying that."

On Saturday, November 1, the homosexuals of the East Coast converged in Philadelphia for another ERCHO conference. They met at My Sister's Place, a gay bar.

Only two months after the attempted coup at Kansas City, Bob Martin arrived in Philadelphia with militant reinforcements. Beside him stood Martha Shelley of the DOB; the Student Homophile Leagues of Cornell, NYU, and Columbia; and, for the first time at a homophile conference, the Gay Liberation Front.

Kameny called the meeting to order and announced that it would be his last conference as ERCHO chairman. He had too many other obligations.

That night, Martin, Shelley, and Freund met with eleven delegates in a radical caucus. They developed a plan to take over the conference.

"We wanted to *end* the homophile movement," one GLF delegate, Jim Fouratt, later explained. "We wanted them to join us in making a gay revolution."

The conservative Foster Gunnison described the next day's events: "Wild. Chaotic. Awful."

"We were a nightmare to them," admitted Fouratt.

On Sunday, Martin, Shelley, and the radicals moved a declaration of "inalienable human rights." First, "dominion over one's body," including sexual freedom, the right to birth control and abortion, and the freedom "to ingest the drugs of one's choice." The motion passed. Second, freedom from "society's attempts to define and limit human sexuality." The motion passed. Third, the freedom from persecution for all minority groups, including freedom from the "institutionalized inequities of the tax structure and the judicial system." The motion passed.

Despite Kameny's insistence that homosexuals not involve themselves in other movements, Freund's MSW delegation voted in favor of each and every radical resolution. The Society's president, a chairman without voting power, could only watch a new generation—preoccupied with oppression of all—take control of the movement he viewed as his own.

He also watched the delegates take away his pickets. Before the conference, Craig Rodwell—he voted with the radicals—developed a plan to remove the Reminder Day demonstrations from the dictatorial astronomer and to place them in the hands of the entire movement.

In October, Rodwell, Fred Sargeant, and two lesbian friends from NYU—Linda Rhodes and Ellen Broidy—had met in Rodwell's New York apartment to draft a proposal. At the conference, a delegate suggested they defer discussion of the Reminder Day pickets until the spring meeting, but twenty-three-year-old Ellen Broidy of the NYU Student Homophile League stood to introduce a resolution. She handed the proposal, already typed, to the chairman.

"RESOLVED," it began, "that the Annual Reminder, in order to be more relevant, reach a greater number of people and encompass the ideas and ideals of the larger struggle in which we are engaged—that of our fundamental human rights—be moved in time and location.

"We propose that a demonstration be held annually on the last Saturday in June in New York City to commemorate the 1969 spontaneous demonstrations on Christopher Street and this demonstration be called CHRISTOPHER STREET LIBERATION DAY."

Standing before Kameny, reminded of the fiasco of the previous picket, Broidy added a last-minute amendment. "No age or dress regulations shall be made for this demonstration," it said. Kameny called the roll. The radical delegates voted for it, including Bob Martin of the SHL and the representative of his own organization, Eva Freund.

The MSNY abstained from supporting a march that endorsed homosexual violence.

Foster Gunnison voted in favor. Barbara Gittings joined him.

With the exception of the MSNY's abstention, the delegates unanimously voted in favor of the march.

Kameny banged his gavel. His respectable demonstrations against the government's purges were dead. In their place, the homosexuals constructed a more enduring tradition, a national gay holiday, a radical insistence of pride and belonging and independence, to take place on the anniversary of the night that the despised, the least respectable elements of society, fought back.

AFTER THE VICTORIOUS Clifford Norton admitted to Kameny that his family did not know of his homosexuality, the astronomer responded with congratulations and unsolicited advice.

"You have won a major victory, not only for yourself, but for everyone," he wrote. "Your case is famous and has everyone excited in every good sense. You are something of a hero."

"I suggest that you do some re-thinking about this business of staying in the closet," he continued. "You have bearded the lion in his den. And you're still running from your family??? !!!"

Frank Kameny, a man who considered himself always right and rarely wrong, had invented the proud plaintiff. In suing the federal government, by encountering an adversary who declared him immoral, the astronomer proved the illogic and instability of that arbitrary claim by making one of his own. Homosexual activities, he had argued in his 1961 Supreme Court brief, "are moral in a real and positive sense, and are good, right, and desirable, socially and personally." What right did the government have to argue otherwise?

For eight years, Kameny continued to make that same argument, though he slowly recognized its true potential. By emulating Black Power, Kameny's claim grew from a purely legal defense, an amateur lawyer's attempt to outwit the government, to a psychological antidote. If he wanted to recruit more homosexuals to fight the government, he needed to persuade them that the psychiatrists, the laws, and the priests were wrong. Gay was good, and with that knowledge, homosexuals could think, fight, and believe for themselves.

Despite his efforts, Kameny did not have the authority to define *gay* for all who embraced that word. As more and more homosexuals *believed* Kameny's argument, they also began to believe that their individual interpretations of their gay identity—whether they declared it with suits or long hair or interlocked hands—were equally good. To conceal themselves, to conform in behavior or dress in the name of strategy and image, conflicted with that fact.

When the trans patrons and drag queens and street youth put their bodies on the line at the Stonewall, "Gay is Good" transformed from a tactic, from an antidote, to a tangible truth. The movement exploded in size because, for once, homosexuals could join the movement as themselves, as individuals who deviated from society in an infinite number of equally detested combinations. They could point to the least respectable of them all—covered in blood and tears and streaking makeup—and say, That is me.

On July 20, 1969, humankind set foot on the Moon. Eva Freund watched the news with tears in her eyes. Six days later, according to an article she wrote for *The Insider*, Freund traveled to a lesbian bar in Baltimore. She wore a GAY IS GOOD button. At midnight, the bar began playing "God Bless America." Freund, still emotional about her country's leap to the stars, gazed upward to prevent more tears. She saw a GAY IS GOOD bumper sticker on the ceiling. As she looked around, the song still playing, she noticed the stickers everywhere—on the bar, on sweatshirts, on the band's drums.

"150 stranger-friends, arms around each other, tied together by a fluke of nature and a need for companionship," wrote Freund. "One body of people, for a moment being unafraid and proud . . . with its slums and its secrecy and its sickness far removed from this bar." She concluded with utopic vision. "If the people in that crowd sometimes had doubts, sometimes wondered, they didn't on that night. All anyone had to do to be sure was to look up at the ceiling: 'Gay Is Good.'"

Fifty years later, Freund admitted that her article had been a fabrication. "Total fiction," she called it.

That moment in the Baltimore lesbian bar never happened. But did it matter? Readers of Freund's article—an astronomer watching history consume him, or a secret member of his Society, or a closeted federal employee who found it, crumpled and dirty, on the floor of a public restroom—could believe it to be true.

They could believe, at last, that to be gay was good.

Lesbian demonstrators, July 4, 1969

19.

THE PRIDE

As a child, long before she accepted her own homosexuality, Kay Tobin Lahusen knew of only one homosexual, a man she noticed at the Cincinnati Zoo's outdoor opera on warm summer evenings. He wore elegant makeup, a men's suit, and an ascot tie with a diamond stickpin. "It frightened me to pieces," she later remembered.

Lahusen moved to Boston in 1956, the year Frank Kameny graduated from Harvard. While working as a researcher for *The Christian Science Monitor*, she avoided the city's gay bars and remained alone. But in 1961, she read *Voyage from Lesbos*, a book by a psychiatrist who claimed to have cured a lesbian. Lahusen drove to New York for an appointment with the psychiatrist.

How do I meet others? she asked.

Oh, if that's what you want, that's easy, he said. The psychiatrist handed her a copy of *The Ladder*, and after only ten minutes, Lahusen walked out of the doctor's office. She immediately joined the Daughters of Bilitis.

Later that year, Lahusen received an invitation from the DOB's New York chapter. The women planned a picnic in Rhode Island to explore the potential of starting a DOB chapter in New England. At that picnic, Lahusen met its organizer, Barbara Gittings.

"She was dressed in bright, cheerful colors," Gittings recalled of Lahusen. "Red hair. Just awfully attractive."

By 1963, Lahusen and Gittings were in love, living together in Philadelphia, and working to turn the DOB into a militant organization. Lahusen, an amateur photographer, initiated Gittings's campaign to fight the prevailing image of the timid, faceless lesbian. While Gittings edited *The Ladder*, Lahusen created its covers.

When a lesbian friend complained to Lahusen about the idea of homosexual picketing ("Have you seen the kind of rabble that do this? The dirty, unwashed mobs?"), Lahusen wrote to Kameny with a request. "A good picture on our cover would be worth a thousand words in dispelling such ideas," she explained.

Lilli Vincenz soon appeared on *The Ladder*'s cover while carrying a picketing sign.

After the riots, when Lahusen and Gittings returned to New York, they discovered the Gay Liberation Front. At its meetings, Lahusen watched activists who had flocked from the New Left to the homophile movement—activists who refused to structure their meetings, denied organizational hierarchy, and engaged in endless self-criticism—and wondered whether the GLF actually represented a coordinated plot by the Communists to take over the homophile movement.

Indeed, the GLF even *supported* the police's raids of gay bars, for in theory, more homosexuals would become alienated by the authorities and join the radicals in their larger fight against America's capitalist system. As GLF treasurer Jim Owles later put it, homosexuals had become "cannon fodder for the revolution."

On November 24, 1969, Kay Lahusen joined Owles and ten others to create a new radical organization that focused solely on gay liberation. They adopted Robert's Rules of Order, the rules of debate so beloved by Kameny, and a hierarchical leadership structure. They planned to work through America's political system, not destroy it, so they created a legal committee and developed intricate plans to confront New York's political elite. They called themselves the Gay Activists Alliance (GAA), and for their logo, they chose the lambda, the symbol for wavelength in physics, to represent action.

One week later, MSW charter member Jack Nichols and his lover, former Pentagon employee Lige Clarke, published the first edition of *GAY* newspaper in New York. Lilli Vincenz, Randy Wicker, and Dick Leitsch joined *GAY*'s staff as columnists, and by April, Kay Lahusen had become its news editor. She gained the power to confront public officials not only as a GAA activist, but also as a reporter, with a camera and voice recorder in hand.

In its first issue, above a form for subscriptions lay the giant slogan, "GAY IS GOOD," and a photograph of two male models, naked and fully exposed.

AFTER THE TUMULTUOUS November 1969 ERCHO conference, six homophile organizations, including the DOB and the MSNY, voted to dissociate themselves from the GLF's resolutions. The MSNY voted to "disavow" Christopher Street Liberation Day "because we do not feel that the Stonewall riots were particularly beneficial to the homophile movement," wrote MSNY president Robert Amsel. "Although we seriously doubt that a small group of militants can destroy in a few months what it has taken us fifteen years to build up, we do not wish to support their attempt."

"My feeling was, and is, that they are a genuine threat to the movement," wrote Foster Gunnison.

Despite Kameny's personal opposition to the GLF measures, his organization—dominated by Eva Freund and a young, radical membership—refused to dissociate.

The MSW president worried more about Bob Martin. On November 15, Martin and his GLF allies distributed fourteen thousand leaflets to the half million demonstrators marching in Washington against the war. "Dear Brothers and Sisters! While the present demonstrations are quite properly focused upon the injustices perpetrated by the American government in Vietnam," it began, "the same power structure which denies justice in all these areas is also doing its best to oppress the homosexually-oriented American." The flyer declared the NACHO Youth Committee's support of other minorities and called upon straight marchers to support their cause. "To our gay and bisexual brethren: JOIN US! We need you." For those facing the draft, it provided Kameny's address and phone number.

Martin joined fifty thousand demonstrators at the Department of Justice, crying "free Bobby Seale," the Black Panther imprisoned for his participation in the 1968 DNC riots. They attempted to breach the doors of the building with a battering ram. "I got teargassed," wrote Martin. "Then we went to Georgetown and picked up two straight boys and then added a third friend of theirs and had an all-night orgy."

Kameny, because NACHO had not authorized the flyer, grew livid.

He urged NACHO delegates to repudiate Martin, the Youth Committee, and the flyer. "He is, of course, being used by more anarchistic GLF elements," Kameny lamented to Foster Gunnison. "I'm increasingly coming to consider him dangerous—certainly untrustworthy."

Martin responded with an adaptation of Bob Dylan.

Come homosexuals
Please heed the call
Don't stand in the doorway
Don't block up the hall
For he that gets hurt
Will be he who has stalled
There's a battle outside ragin'
It'll soon shake your windows
And rattle your walls
For the times they are a-changin'

Six months later, Martin informed friends and family of a deviation in his life plans. After Martin graduated from Columbia, the Associated Press fired him, and he experienced heartbreak at the hands of another boy. In a spiraling state, he made a decision. "I have resolved, through the help of a long talk session with Sharon and Phil, when all three of us were up on ½ tab acid each, my old schizophrenic illusions of being a sailor," he informed Judith Kuch, the bisexual veteran of the first White House picket. "Henceforth I will no longer wear a Navy uniform improperly, nor pretend that I am what I am not.

"In short, I've joined the Navy.

"All but Frank Kameny thought it was a good idea and might due [*sic*] me a lot of good," he told Kuch.

Martin left for basic training that summer.

ONLY DAYS AFTER Martin demonstrated against the war, MSW members received an "ANNOUNCEMENT OF SPECIAL SPEAKER(S) AT DECEMBER MEMBERSHIP MEETING."

R. D. Carter Jr., a representative of the Committee for Black Economic

Determinism, had written to the Society. "Our philosophy and struggle for liberation identifies with yours. We are fighting the same enemy, the value system. Values which are warped yield job discrimination, pressure on individuals because of their ideology, and oppression."

Article II of the Society's constitution, after the prodding of Jack Nichols in 1961, declared that the MSW would "cooperate with other minority organizations which are striving for the realization of full civil rights and liberties for all." It was a promise "we have never meaningfully put into action," admitted Kameny. The Society, after all, had always been white. From the beginning, Kameny had noticed the entirely white faces at the Society's meetings, which took place in a city with a majority Black population.

The executive board discussed how the Society could attract more Black members, and in the early years, its members even distributed a flyer at Black gay bars, titled "THE NEGRO AND THE HOMO-PHILE MOVEMENT."

"The white homosexual has only one burden. The Negro homosexual has two," it began. "Do you know that there is someone to work with you and something to work for? You are invited specifically to join the homophile movement, composed of Negroes and whites, which is trying to improve the social status of the homosexual—of all homosexuals, Black and white." It provided the Society's address and phone number, and it came attached to the group's statement of purposes.

Black homosexuals never joined the MSW. "While Blacks were struggling to obtain jobs and status, Gays were struggling to maintain jobs and status," explained one Black bisexual man who lived in Washington during the 1960s. "No one was trusting anyone for fear of losing everything or never being able to obtain anything." If African Americans risked damaging their pursuit of racial equality by attaching themselves to the homophile movement, why would they join? Black homophile activists like Ernestine Eppenger had taken that risk, and even she had abandoned the DOB for the Black freedom movement, where she saw true progress being made.

Except for the flyer, the MSW made no major effort to attract African American members, no outreach to Black organizations or civic groups, no invitations to its homophile conferences. Once, when a Black man appeared at a public MSW meeting, sitting alone among a sea of white, the other members stared at him, wondering if he was a federal agent.

With the 1969 letter from the Committee for Black Economic Determinism, a straight Black organization spurred the once-passive group of homosexuals to meet the constitutional promise it had made in 1961. "Let's open some doors far too long closed!" Kameny urged his members.

On December 4, 1969, Carter spoke on behalf of his organization in the homosexuals' St. Marks basement meeting space. "We the Committee," he wrote, "vow our support to you in any campaign you might wage in the future." Though Kameny had been emulating the Black freedom movement for nearly a decade, a formal alliance between the two minorities, two identities that often overlapped, seemed possible at last.

After the meeting, however, Carter never heard from the homosexuals again.

THAT WEEK, Kameny's friends and colleagues received a jubilant letter. "It is with a feeling of great pleasure and honor, and with a sense of deep personal satisfaction, gratification, and pride," he wrote, "that I am able to inform you that in a special election, I was just chosen, by a large majority, to membership on the Executive Board of the Washington, D.C. affiliate of the American Civil Liberties Union." The astronomer's homosexual integration of the NCACLU was complete. He had long served as the unofficial homosexual authority within the affiliate, and now his role became official.

Kameny wrote to the NCACLU legal director quickly after the election. The case of his first client, illustrator Donald Crawford, was "completely ready for the courts NOW," he said.

On January 14, 1970, Benning Wentworth received another unfavorable determination from the Pentagon's examiner. Wentworth had not *proven* he had actually sent his news releases, meaning he was still susceptible to blackmail. (The examiner was "a moral leper, a moral, emotional, and social pervert, an intellectually fossilized relic of a bygone era," responded Kameny in his official appeal.)

The MSW president had long given up hope of winning in an administrative Pentagon hearing. "We do not think that a homosexual has the chances of a snowball in hell before this Board, or in any portion of our security clearance system," explained Kameny in Wentworth's March 1970 appeal hearing. "We are here simply because we have to go through this farce in order to exhaust our administrative remedies and get this case into the courts."

Lilli Vincenz, reporting on the hearing for *GAY*, heard Kameny shouting, "More and more of our people are being radicalized!" from through the closed door. "And I was glad," she wrote. "I only wish there had been other people outside to hear it. But one day they will hear it, because there'll be a lot more people shouting than just one or two or ten."

First, Crawford; second, Wentworth; and third, picketing veteran Otto Ulrich. The Department of Defense had declined to cite blackmail as a factor in its denial of Ulrich's security clearance, and it referenced only his "criminal conduct and sexual perversion," making him unreliable and untrustworthy. "HOMOSEXUAL SECURITY CLEARANCE HOLDER FOUND NOT BLACKMAILABLE" announced Kameny and Gittings in a February press release.

Because the Pentagon assigned Ulrich's case to an examiner in California (Kameny had objected to the recycling of East Coast examiners), it opted to forgo a traditional hearing. Instead, the Department of Defense sent Ulrich a list of interrogatories. "Have you ever engaged in acts of anal copulation, sometimes referred to as sodomy or anal sodomy, with other males?"

    a. If yes, approximately how many such acts have occurred?
       (1) oral copulation (fellatio) _____
       (2) anal copulation (sodomy) _____
    b. Dates of those acts?
    c. Were they in public?
    d. With how many people?

Ulrich refused to answer, and Kameny and Gittings forwarded the questionnaire to Senator Ervin. "We consider this questionnaire to be an obscene invasion of privacy, responses to which will constitute a pornographic treatise which can only serve to titillate the prurient interest of

Defense Department officials," they wrote. They encouraged the senator to publicize the matter, including Ulrich's name.

On February 6, Kameny and Gittings disseminated another news release, "PENTAGON PERVERTS PRY PRURIENTLY," to expose the government's invasive questioning of their fourth Pentagon plaintiff, Richard Gayer. "As a healthy, unmarried male Homosexual with a sex drive of strength consistent with my 31-year age, I have engaged in, do engage in, and good luck and good health permitting, intend to continue to engage in homosexual sexual acts," Gayer had responded. The screening board was a "pack of sexual perverts," concluded the defense team. To proactively address any suspicion that he had not disseminated the news release, Kameny signed an affidavit swearing that he had sent it to ten outlets in Gayer's home city of San Francisco, to more than seventy national outlets, and to Senator Ervin.

Fifth, Frank Kameny's own security clearance case. On March 5, he arrived at the Pentagon with Gittings and NCACLU attorneys John Karr and Glenn Graves. Yes, admitted Kameny, a decade prior, he had attempted to convince Dr. Benjamin Karpman that he was a heterosexual. Yes, in 1958, he had been arrested in Lafayette Park. "They proceeded to chase me. I saw no reason to get arrested for not having done anything. I left rather hastily," he explained.

"You ran away?" asked the department counsel.

"I did, yes."

IN THE 1930S, before he founded the Mattachine, Harry Hay devoted himself to agitprop, the performance of short, five-minute Leftist propaganda plays at strikes and demonstrations. For two decades, gay political theater appeared in subtle forms, like dances in homes and bars, where homosexuals could enact a world without persecution. Homosexuals then performed respectability in the media and in picket lines. Finally, before an increasingly large audience, Kameny and his plaintiffs proclaimed and rehearsed gay pride in his lawsuits and press conferences.

But as the New Left of the 1960s borrowed and adapted the political theater of the Old Left—antiwar demonstrators burned draft cards; women's liberation activists burned bras—the homophile movement increasingly recognized the potential of a public spectacle. In Washington, months before Stonewall, Eva Freund introduced the MSW to guerrilla theater to rehearse the politicization of bar-going homosexuals. Then, one night in October 1969, Stonewall veteran and GLF member Marty Robinson began heckling New York mayoral candidates at a debate. "It's 1775, Mr. Procaccino," he yelled. "The homosexual revolution has begun." When the police ejected him and the other protesters, remarkably, the *heterosexuals* in the audience continued their line of questioning. NBC-TV and the *New York Post* reported on the confrontation.

When Marty Robinson joined Kay Lahusen and ten others to create the Gay Activists Alliance, he brought with him this political strategy of performance and confrontation, which he called a "zap." Like agitprop or guerrilla theater, a zap created a confrontational spectacle for an audience unaware of a minority group's oppression. In a public setting, those in power had no choice but to respond, and because of its novelty, the media had no choice but to cover the occasion. Homosexuals in the audience, even if they were at first dismayed by the zap, became angry and mobilized once they saw the barbaric reaction of the straight establishment.

As for the participants in the zap, the experience allowed them to act out—and come out—after years of oppression. As GAA's Arthur Evans put it, "the no-longer-closeted gays realize that assimilation into the heterosexual mainstream is no answer: gays must unite among themselves, organize their common resources for collective action, and resist."

Seven years after the spectacle of the Dowdy hearings, the GAA identified public confrontation with those in power as an invaluable tool for the gay minority. The "zap" streamlined, routinized, and weaponized it. Moreover, as one activist explained to *LIFE* magazine, participating in one good zap was worth "months on a psychiatrist's couch."

In the early months of 1970, the GAA increasingly fused traditional political activism with the zap. First, the activists developed a petition for a city council bill against homosexual employment discrimination. On January 26, at a gubernatorial campaign panel at a Village Independent Democrats event, GAA activists, strategically scattered in the audience, barraged the candidates with questions. What will you do to ensure equal employment for homosexuals in New York? they asked.

In April, while Mayor John Lindsay spoke on the steps of the Metropolitan Museum of Art, Marty Robinson ran to the podium. "When are you going to speak out on homosexual rights, Mr. Mayor?" The next week, thirty-seven GAA activists infiltrated a talk-show taping with Lindsay. GAA's Arthur Evans rushed to the stage. "What about homosexuals? Homosexuals want an end to job discrimination."

Within days of the zaps, the GAA secured meetings with the deputy mayor, Lindsay's chief counsel, and the NYPD's chief of patrol. They met with the city's top eight highest-ranking police officers and received assurances from the city's new commissioner on human rights, Eleanor Holmes Norton. On May 13, after city council member Carol Greitzer faced activists accusing her of the "crime of silence" at a public forum, she agreed to adopt the GAA petitions. Yes, she said, she would cosponsor an antidiscrimination bill in city council.

News of the confrontations spread across the country. The day after the Greitzer zap, a coalition of activists from Gay Liberation Front and women's liberation infiltrated the annual meeting of the American Psychiatric Association (APA) in San Francisco. As an Australian psychiatrist presented on "aversion therapy"—the use of unpleasant sensations, like electric shocks—to treat homosexuality, activists interrupted him with cries of "torture" and "Auschwitz." A man in white pants and an unbuttoned shirt jumped onto the stage. "The liberated meeting of the American Psychiatric Association," he announced into the microphone, "is now in session."

Meanwhile, Dick Leitsch and the MSNY, its membership dwindling, circulated a leaflet in the aftermath of yet another bar raid. "REMAIN ORDERLY," it advised.

ON MAY 1, 1970, Martha Shelley sat among three hundred women in a New York high school auditorium. Neither women's liberation nor the homophile movement clamored for lesbian activists like her. At GLF dances, complained one lesbian attendee, "Women were lost to each other in a sea of spaced-out men." In GLF meetings, lesbians seemed to be fighting "for everyone else's cause while ignoring our own," wrote Shelley in *Come Out!* magazine. Meanwhile, National Organization for Women (NOW) president Betty Friedan referred to lesbians as a "lavender menace" that threatened to delegitimize the entire women's liberation movement.

A group of GLF women began meeting separately, organizing all-women dances, and calling themselves the Radicalesbians. "A lesbian," they declared in their manifesto, "is the rage of all women condensed to the point of explosion."

To assert their place in the women's liberation movement, the Radicalesbians utilized the art of the zap. At the Congress to Unite Women meeting on May Day, at 7:15 p.m., the auditorium suddenly went dark. Attendees heard running, laughter, and rebel yells. When the lights turned back on, seventeen women stood, wearing lavender shirts with LAVENDER MENACE stenciled on them.

Shelley grabbed the microphone and urged other lesbians in the audience to stand. Twenty women, some previously closeted, joined them. To everyone's surprise, the *straight* women in the audience demanded that the lesbian issue remain on the floor.

For two hours, the women confronted each other, and the activists left with a "sense of solidarity and group identification," as a Radicalesbian reporter described it. "With that in mind you know that the LAVENDER MENACE will strike again—anywhere, anytime, anyplace."

Martha Shelley remained in the GLF, Kay Lahusen stayed in the male-dominated GAA, Lilli Vincenz continued writing for *GAY*, and Barbara Gittings kept working with her overwhelming, often overshadowing cocounsel, Frank Kameny. They did so despite the gravitational force of women's liberation, which stressed their obligation, above all else, to their fellow women. Someday, as Gittings explained to Lahusen, she would consider switching movements, but for now, "there's still an awful lot of work to do towards gay liberation."

Eva Freund, on the other hand, left the movement. In late 1969, when she departed Washington for a new job in Reading, Pennsylvania, she discovered NOW, and she never returned to the gay liberation movement, a movement dominated by men.

Del Martin, cofounder of the DOB, explained her own decision in an open letter. "Goodbye to the male chauvinists of the homophile movement," she wrote. "'Gay is good,' but not good enough—so long as it is limited to white males only. We joined with you in what we mistakenly thought was a common cause. A few of you tried, we admit. But you are still too few, and even you fall short of the mark."

STANDING BEFORE A JUDGE, Sylvia Rivera wore a purple jumpsuit, flowing auburn hair, a shoulder bag, and sunglasses in the style of Jackie Onassis.

"Name?" asked the judge.

"Ray Rivera—but call me Sylvia," she responded.

The judge glared at Rivera, then turned to her attorney. "Counsel, is your client a man or a woman?"

The lawyer hesitated before answering, "Yes, your honor."

Born in the Bronx, Rivera never knew her father. Her mother died when she was three. She began hustling on Forty-Second Street at the age of eleven or twelve, and she developed a family of fellow "street kids," many of whom were homeless, abandoned by their families.

The street kids joined with the trans patrons of Stonewall to initiate the riots, and when they fought the police, they did so with dire problems of their own. Only days after the riots, at the Mattachine meeting that led to the creation of the GLF, attendee Bob Kohler stood to describe their plight. In the days after the riots, the police were picking up young runaways and homeless youths—suspected of being homosexual—and beating them in police cars, said Kohler. He suggested that the Mattachine establish a halfway house for the children.

The other attendees ignored the suggestion and commenced planning their rally in Washington Square.

In March 1970, the eighteen-year-old Rivera learned about the GAA from an article in *Gay Power* magazine, and she became one of its most dedicated members. In a letter to the magazine, she urged her fellow "sister queens" to join GAA. "The members are all right, they don't put down no one because they act different or wear make-up," she wrote. "Girls, we are needed!"

At 7:30 p.m. on Wednesday, April 15, Rivera stood on Forty-Second Street to gather signatures for the GAA's city council petition. A police officer told her to leave, but Rivera refused, asserting that it was her right to participate in that democratic act. The officer dragged her to a police car and, according to an affidavit, Rivera screamed "discrimination against homosexuals." The officer charged her for disorderly conduct.

No lawyer agreed to represent her. On May 21, Rivera appeared for her arraignment without counsel, and thirty-five GAA and GLF members arrived to support her in the courtroom. To everyone's surprise, a young attorney noticed Rivera and, on the spot, agreed to represent her. The GAA gained a new legal ally—the attorney later handled GAA's incorporation—and because of Rivera's case, the organization reestablished its dormant legal committee.

Though Rivera's arresting officer never arrived at her hearing, the judge, disturbed by her appearance, refused to dismiss the case.

On September 20, a group of New York University students and GLF activists met to discuss the college administration's ban on gay dances in one of its dormitories, Weinstein Hall. When Martha Shelley suggested they stage a sit-in and occupy the basement of the building that same evening, the call went out. Rivera and her fellow street queens arrived first. After that night's GLF meeting, another forty activists arrived.

For five nights, the street queens and the GLF activists—including Shelley, who had built a rapport with Rivera—refused to leave the Weinstein Hall basement, and the GAA stayed away. At 2:30 Friday afternoon, the tactical police force arrived at the request of the university. The riot police, armed with guns, chained all the doors except one. Activists had only ten seconds to leave.

That night, a mob of NYU students, street queens, and GLF activists demonstrated outside Weinstein Hall. Officers attacked three demonstrators, swinging clubs at their faces, and provoked Rivera's verbal wrath. One of the officers fired his gun into the air and then pointed it at Rivera. He threatened to shoot unless the crowd disbanded.

The following week, when Rivera and her allies picketed NYU, the GAA refused to participate. According to its executive committee meeting minutes, since "the demonstrations were called by 'street people,' who are only a small segment of the gay community, it was suggested that members participate as individuals without the organization's commitment in future related actions."

Disillusioned by the GAA, Rivera partnered with Marsha P.

Johnson—the Black trans woman who, while wearing heels, managed to drop a bag of bricks from a lamppost during the Stonewall riots—to create a new organization, one that would fight. Street Transvestites for Gay Power, they called themselves. "You people run if you want to, but we're tired of running," the group announced. "We intend to fight for our rights until we get them."

Rivera and Johnson also planned to open a refuge for other homeless youth. When Rivera requested a donation toward the group's rent and clothes for the children, the GAA refused. Rivera and Johnson thus changed the name of their organization. No longer "for Gay Power," it became Street Transvestite Action Revolutionaries (STAR) instead.

WITH THE DEATH of the Reminder Day pickets, so, too, died Frank Kameny's grip on the traditional summertime demonstration of homosexuals, including the signs, the prescribed number of staples, and the dress code. Without control, and with his energy devoted to his legal cases, the NCACLU, and public lecturing, Kameny watched others manage the planning of the first Christopher Street Liberation Day.

Craig Rodwell, the young activist who had protested Kameny's dress code in 1969, ensured that no one organization controlled the event. ERCHO created a steering committee of nine delegates—they took turns chairing meetings—to share organizational power. Jon Swanson, the former MSW president, represented Washington's homosexuals.

The Christopher Street Liberation Day committee hoped to emphasize commonality. "It is *our* birthday," advertised *GAY*, "a *cause célèbre* for nearly 20,000,000 homosexuals, general male and genital female, queen and butch, femme and dyke, faggot, fairy and nance, big cock and no cock, closet and New Free."

"It is hoped that this week will promote and give further impetus to the rapid growth of gay consciousness and community which is critical to our development as a decisive power bloc," wrote Jon Swanson to MSW members. After the June MSW meeting, Swanson and Lilli Vincenz trekked across Washington with stickers that advertised the upcoming march. They stuck them on post office walls, bus stop signs, empty store fronts, Washington's new gay pornographic theater, and the fence surrounding the colossal construction site of the new FBI headquarters.

On Sunday afternoon, June 28, exactly one year after the Stonewall riots, Frank Kameny stood in Sheridan Square. He wore not a suit and tie, but a light blue short-sleeved polo shirt and slacks. "No, I would have thought a suit and tie—well, I don't think any form of dress was inappropriate, and so I simply dressed comfortably," he later explained.

It was a logically consistent decision, he reasoned. The purpose of this march was not to protest the government or its purges, per se, so Kameny saw no reason to dress as a federal employee. This march addressed a deeper problem, which Kameny had identified nearly a decade earlier. Homosexuals believed they were immoral, sick, or both, and as a result, they did not feel worthy enough to fight back.

"We are united today to affirm our pride, our life-style and our commitment to each other," explained a committee flyer distributed that day. "Despite political and social differences we may have, we are united on this common ground: For the first time in history, we are together as *The Homosexual Community*."

As the crowd gathered, the homosexuals around Kameny buzzed with apprehension. Not only did they fear exposure to the press and the crowds, but they also feared violence. Organizers instructed marchers not to wear glasses or necklaces, in case they were punched or strangled by angry onlookers.

At 2:00 p.m., amidst cheers, they began marching. The committee led the marchers with a CHRISTOPHER STREET GAY LIBERATION DAY 1970 banner and an American flag. Two hundred GAA activists followed. Randy Wicker wore a lambda shirt. Next marched the GLF and the street queens. Marsha P. Johnson wore white bell bottoms. Behind them marched Frank Kameny and his MSW contingent. One member carried a MATTACHINE SOCIETY OF WASHINGTON sign, and Kameny carried a simple, perfectly lettered sign of his own. GAY IS GOOD, it said. *The Gay Blade* editor Nancy Tucker and her girlfriend, though they looked nearly identical, wore "butch" and "femme" shirts. They swapped them throughout the day.

Lilli Vincenz arrived with a crew of six volunteers to help her film the historic event. She captured only a small portion of the signs.

RUTGERS SHL

GAY YALE

CLOSET QUEENS AND BACK ROOM BUTCHES, FEARFUL FEMS AND FRIGHTENED FRIENDS, COME OUT

I AM LESBIAN AND I AM BEAUTIFUL

LAVENDER MENACE

SMASH SEXISM: GAYS UNITE NOW

HI MOM

The marchers started as small group, less than a thousand. Hordes of nervous homosexuals watched from the sidewalk. "Half the onlookers should have been marching with us, or else why have I seen most of them cruising me in the bars on other occasions," complained one attendee.

As the masses continued up Sixth Avenue, realizing that they were safe (the city had sent three buses of riot police to protect the demonstrators), the moving crowd swelled. Spectators became demonstrators. "Come on out or I'll point you out," yelled one marcher to a friend on the sidewalk.

For three miles, in the city of his birth, Frank Kameny marched. He was surrounded, as one reporter put it, by homosexuals "in their Sunday best, their hippie best, lots of work-shirt and jeans types, a few costumes—they looked more like a peace march to whom the President had just capitulated than homosexuals."

No, they did not all look like homosexuals, but they declared themselves as such nonetheless—by holding hands, kissing, and chanting, "say it loud, gay is proud." As *The New York Times* reported on the next day's front page, "some bystanders applauded when a tall, pretty girl carrying a sign, 'I am a Lesbian,' walked by." They declared themselves as deviant beings in a state that regulated their dress and gender, in a country that drove them into Mafia-run bars or public restrooms, and in a society that told them they should not exist. Drag queens seemed to be everywhere. One large queen in a short wig and an elegant robe began walking in front of the main LIBERATION DAY sign with a simple sign of her own. GAY PRIDE, it said.

Kameny at last reached Central Park, and he followed the crowd to Sheep Meadow, a vast green lawn. There, a gay couple lay on a mattress, about to beat the world record—previously held by a straight couple—after kissing each other for nine hours. Kameny reached the southwest edge of the meadow, at the top of a gentle slope, near the granite rocks that marked the end of the march, and turned around.

Since Kameny had walked near the front of the parade, he had been unable to measure the magnitude of the march. But now, as he gazed down at Central Park, the marchers streamed into the meadow, part of a mass with no end in sight. He stood next to Jack Nichols, the man who had telephoned him only five years earlier to convince him that homosexuals, despite their fears of exposure, were prepared to march. Nichols had tears in his eyes. Others cheered. "We were on top of the world. It was pure exultation," one marcher wrote of that moment. But Kameny stood stoically, watching the meadow fill with his fellow despised. Sylvia Rivera dancing. Men and women shirtless. Hugging, kissing, oral sex.

"Tell me how you feel about being here today?" asked Vincenz.

"It feels beautiful. It's fantastic," responded a blond youth lying on the ground in a jacket and an American flag tie.

"How many years have you been a homosexual?"

"I was born homosexual. It's beautiful."

In the background, "Somebody dropped an eyelash."

"It was a truth we'd always known inwardly," Nichols wrote for the twenty-five thousand readers of *GAY*. "But now the ancient reality confirmed itself outwardly. What was it? That love's wonderfully varied expressions can break through unreal crusts of fear and misunderstanding. That love can come out of the past's dark closets."

Several months later, the MSW president sat down for a seven-hour interview with Kay Lahusen, who had decided to write a book, *The Gay Crusaders*.

"I've never been that happy," said Kameny.

"As if you were on a marijuana high?" asked Lahusen.

"Well, I don't know," he responded. But it was "a direct lineal descendant of our ten frightened little people in front of the White House, almost exactly five years before."

"Only we had ten thousand."

"No. Five thousand."

And that was that.

TWO DAYS AFTER the march, Frank Kameny and Nancy Tucker attended the first meeting of Washington's Gay Liberation Front. They sat in a large circle with forty others in an upstairs room of Grace Episcopal Church in Georgetown.

The GLF had taken nearly an entire year to arrive to Washington, which never had a Stonewall of its own. As for the social needs of homosexuals, other groups filled that void. In October 1969, a minister in Maryland created the Homophile Social League (HSL), modeled after San Francisco's SIR, to provide activities outside of bars, including dances, judo classes, theater trips, and spaghetti dinners.

The Mattachine Society of Washington had modernized itself. In the spring of 1970, the group deleted the constitutional ban against social events and the requirement for membership interviews. Kameny, consolidating his power, became the "chief executive of the organization," free to make unilateral decisions without consulting his board. The Society continued meeting throughout the spring of 1970, but it hosted only two major events, and even those focused on Kameny's legal cases.

As Gay Washington expanded, cracks had begun appearing in the detente that existed between homosexuals and their city. In April 1970, the YMCA—the site of Walter Jenkins's exposure—canceled a swimming party hosted by the Homophile Social League. That same month, the police turned their attention to Washington's new gay bathhouse, the Regency Health Club. Late one night, officers aimed giant spotlights at the front of the building, hoping to expose and frighten those inside. They inspected each floor and arrested the owner for disorderly conduct.

When antiwar activists protested Nixon's "incursion" into Cambodia and the national guard's murder of four students at Kent State, the New York GLF made its presence known in the District. On May 9, several dozen GLF activists joined one hundred thousand protesters at an antiwar rally in Washington. They carried a five-foot banner—GAY LIBERA-TION FRONT: BRING OUR BOYS HOME—and participated in a "nude-in" around the Lincoln Memorial's reflecting pool. Only one GLFer was arrested, for wandering around visibly stoned.

A few weeks later, Michael Yarr wrote a letter to the *Quicksilver Times*, an underground newspaper. Yarr, a recently out air force veteran, had noticed an article about Suharto, the anti-Communist leader of Indonesia, in the newspaper. "Suharto Sucks," it said.

"That Suharto is a fascist pig-friend of American imperialism is right on, but when you equate his fascism with sucking cocks, you put yourselves in the camp of the pig oppressors. Sucking cocks is neither ugly nor unnatural," wrote Yarr. The slur demonstrated "the necessity in Washington for gay radicals, militants and revolutionaries to get our shit together." Call this number if you want to help create a Gay Liberation Front, he advertised.

Yarr, along with friends from the Washington Peace Center, began organizing. After participating in New York's Christopher Street Liberation Day, Yarr returned to Washington galvanized.

"There was madness, chaos, anarchy," said attendee Brian Miller of that first meeting at Grace Church. They were mostly young white men in blue jeans. They wanted to talk about their emotions, revolution, or both.

MSW member Nancy Tucker was one of the few women in the room, and though she did not particularly care for the dictatorial Kameny, at least his meetings had structure, leadership, and an agenda. Mattachine meetings often had a *majority* of women present, especially when Eva Freund still lived in Washington. And unlike the GLF attendees, Society members never referred to women as "girls."

Almost immediately, however, the Washington GLF distinguished itself from its counterpart in New York. Because meetings did not have chairmen, those with the loudest voices were heard; their agendas passed. In

New York, that meant Martha Shelley or Jim Fouratt. But in Washington, the loudest attendee, the man with the most distinctive, thunderous, authoritative voice, was Frank Kameny.

To the GLF attendees, it became clear that Kameny hoped to use the GLF as a tool in his personal fight against the federal government. "Drop dead," Miller remembered attendees thinking of the forty-five-year-old MSW president, still unemployed. The GLF attendees wanted revolution—the destruction of a capitalist system—rather than meetings with police officers.

Yet Washington's Gay Liberation Front worked through the system, and it did so because of the astronomer. After the first meeting—the participants decided to liberate a "marijuana smoke-in" on Independence Day—the attendees left for the Georgetown Grill, a Washington gay bar. There, the gay bar refused to serve a lesbian GLFer who wore slacks.

"The group, with the help of Dr. Franklin Kameny of the Mattachine Society (who has also attended all GLF meetings), has also begun a civil suit against the Georgetown Grill," reported *The Advocate*. "Prosecution of the case has been taken by the Washington ACLU." Just as Kameny had once penetrated the NCACLU to ensure it worked for homosexuals, he penetrated the GLF-DC to ensure it worked with lawyers.

With the unique combination of anarchy and an embrace of the American political system, the GLF-DC grew at a rapid pace. By the end of the summer, nearly two hundred homosexuals met in the main church hall, since the upstairs meeting room had become too crowded. The GLF-DC organized itself not into cells, but committees. It established a legal committee, a political action committee, and even a ways and means committee.

While New York's gay groups competed with each other, Kameny ensured that Washington's three organizations—the MSW, the HSL, and the GLF—worked in seamless cooperation, and the MSW president established himself as the de facto spokesman of the alliance.

In August, no fewer than fifteen gay bars received a letter on official MSW letterhead. "Gentlemen: The Mattachine Society, Homophile Social League, and Gay Liberation Front of Washington, D.C. wish to extend greetings to you and to offer you our encouragement and support," began Kameny. He applauded the opening of new gay bars in Washington, but he made a warning. They were not to discriminate on the basis of race or sex.

The groups appeared to be working "in close and unmarred harmony which gives me a great deal of satisfaction," wrote Kameny.

ON THE THIRD DAY of the 1970 NACHO conference in San Francisco, in an effort to prevent the domination of the gay radicals, the national alliance voted to suspend itself.

That afternoon, the radicals invaded nonetheless. The mob, yelling, "Power to the People," and carrying a GAY POWER banner, surged into the meeting hall. They declared themselves the "liberated" NACHO. There had been whispers that one of the radicals carried a gun, so most of the original conference departed in haste. The chairman adjourned the session.

The radicals passed their own resolutions, including solidarity with women's liberation and the Black Panther Party's ten-point platform, and an immediate end to the "Amerikan [*sic*] war in Asia."

That night, State Assemblyman Willie Brown spoke to a crowd of 450 NACHO delegates and local homosexuals. Gays and African Americans "must learn to do our bickering inside our own house, must resolve our disagreements behind our own doors," he argued. Respectability, whether performed by Blacks or gays, was futile; when a racist wanted to harm a Black person, explained Brown, "he is going to find *a* Black. He is not going to look for Huey Newton. *Every* Black is a Huey Newton. And I know the Gays to be in the same category," Brown explained. Twenty-five years later, Brown became San Francisco's first Black mayor.

Kameny returned to Washington with a reinforced opinion of the radicals who were so preoccupied with self-improvement and tearing down the system. "It's much easier to say, well, we must improve ourselves before we go out to do battle simply because battle is unpleasant and they don't want to do it," Kameny explained. What was the *real* reason, he asked, for refusing to fight the government? After all, when the revolution came, when capitalism crumbled, prejudice against homosexuals would still exist. "We'll have our revolution, and when it's all over, we'll still be a lot of sick queers, and the homosexuals will be exactly where they were before," he explained. "Revolutions are divisible too."

But the MSW president was happy to use the more cooperative Washington's radicals—and the power of disruption so evident in San Francisco—as a tool in his own battles. On November 9, Kameny spoke on the first day of a weeklong "Theology and Homosexuality" seminar at Catholic University in Washington. "How dare you insult us by including homosexuality in such a program with male prostitution, child molestation and behavior therapy!" he told the audience.

The audience was "lucky," as he put it, that Washington's "more militant" gay activists were not demonstrating at the seminar. Listeners could choose to accept his logic and outreach or face the wrath of the *other*, less predictable homosexuals in the movement. When Kameny extended an olive branch at the end of his speech, the audience grabbed it. "You can learn a lot more in a few hours' tour of Washington's fine gay bars than from all the psychiatrists," he explained. "I shall be delighted to take you on a guided tour." The next evening, Kameny took a group of fifteen priests, three nuns, and five seminarians on a tour of Washington's gay bars. "The group relaxed quickly and a few even tried dancing," reported *The Advocate*.

On Wednesday afternoon, when Dr. John R. Cavanagh, the chairman of the conference, spoke on "Sexual Anomalies and Homosexualites," the GLF invaded. Twenty-five demonstrators carried a GLF flag and marched onto the stage, yelling, "Bullshit! You have no right to be talking about us."

While Cavanagh held on to the podium, a demonstrator crumpled and tossed his lecture notes. They paraded around the room several times—chanting, "Gay is Good," "Out of the closets and into the streets," and "69 is Fine"—and eventually left. Cavanagh retrieved his notes and continued speaking. Kameny remained seated, silent but content.

THREE DAYS LATER, at Kameny's suggestion, Washington's three gay organizations hosted a joint dance for the area's homosexuals. It took place at St. Mark's Episcopal Church, the home of the MSW, and attracted more than two hundred homosexuals. The organizations split the dance's $164.61 profit.

Kameny made arrangements for another dance in January. His security clearance cases, after all, were nearly out of his hands. After Benning Wentworth received his fourth unfavorable decision from the Pentagon (a "day which will live in infamy," Kameny warned the Department of Defense), Kameny wrote to Wentworth, Ulrich, and Gayer. The national ACLU, under the administration of the NCACLU chapter, had agreed to sponsor all three cases. Kameny formally withdrew as counsel for the three men, and by the end of November, an NCACLU attorney drafted their complaints.

With Crawford's case in the NCACLU pipeline, Kameny had only his own case left to argue. Otherwise, Kameny had no real job, and his personal life, in contrast to a flourishing Gay Washington, was in a free fall.

With no consistent income, he survived on speaking fees, small contributions from his mother, and by not paying his bills. He could not afford to pay his NCACLU dues, and he then lost his position on the executive board. Over the fall, Prentice Hall showed interest in contracting Kameny and Gittings to write a book, tentatively titled *The Gay Mystique*. Yet Kameny, as he continued touring the country to lecture and establish new gay liberation groups, never completed the book proposal.

Kay Lahusen penned an excoriating letter to Kameny. "I am aghast at your malaise, inability to come to grips, stage-fright, stupefaction, stultification, self-defeating tendencies, weariness, intransigence, or whatever it is that has you frozen and unable to reach out decisively for the stout rope thrown your way by P-H—a rope that could be nothing less than a life-saver to you personally, and perhaps a life-saver to our entire minority," she wrote. "I view it as a betrayal of your minority and the promise you seem to hold."

To make matters worse, that fall, Kameny began experiencing excruciating back pain and sciatica, the result of a slipped disk. In November, after falling in his bedroom, he spent four hours lying on the floor. He began wearing a therapeutic corset, which helped with the pain, but he could only walk slowly and carefully.

The Society continued functioning, and its meetings, though small, were at last open to the public. Vincenz premiered her documentary of the Christopher Street Liberation Day march. The ACLU, even without Kameny on the board, continued manufacturing gay-related cases, and that fall, it found three gay couples—including two lesbians—who volunteered to stage an act of sex in an effort to overturn Washington's sodomy laws through a test case.

The GLF, meanwhile, continued growing. It established a commune in a Dupont Circle town house, which served as its informal headquarters. With Kameny's help, it picketed a large gay-owned bar, the Plus One, for discrimination against African Americans, women, drag queens, and other "unconventionally dressed gays." Even the HSL, once a purely social organization, established a legal fund to defend homosexuals arrested for cruising in Georgetown.

Kameny had become the country's "unofficial high priest" of Gay Power, as the Philadelphia *Bulletin* termed him, yet Gay Power seemed to be progressing without him.

WASHINGTON'S SECOND MSW-GLF-HSL gay dance took place on January 16, 1971. Before it began, a group of MSW members—including Paul Kuntzler, Lilli Vincenz, Allen Hoffard, and Tony Jackubosky—approached Kameny with an idea.

A few months earlier, President Johnson had signed a bill that permitted the residents of the District of Columbia to send a nonvoting delegate to the House of Representatives. For the first time in a century, Washington would hold a local election. The MSW members sat before their president and made their pitch. Kameny should run for the House of Representatives. He would be the first openly gay man to do so. The machinery for the campaign already existed, they knew how to organize, and they had already created a campaign committee. They even showed him a premade leaflet. "Kameny for Congress," it said.

No, Kameny would not have any chance of winning, but at least he would send a clear message that homosexuals represented a significant voting bloc not just in Washington, but also across the country. His candidacy would inspire countless other gay citizens to join the movement and seek power for themselves. Most important, a campaign would give him a platform. If his name appeared on the ballot, newspapers would have no choice but to report his arguments on behalf of his minority.

Kameny reacted with cynicism. Above all, the proposal raised a daunting logistical problem. He would need at least five thousand signatures to ensure his name appeared on the ballot, and the deadline for those signatures was February 16, in exactly one month. His campaign would have to collect more than 150 signatures per day.

Dubious of his chances, aware of his precarious finances, and wary of the time commitment, Kameny said he wanted to think about it. That night, at the dance, the potential of the campaign became clear. When he talked to the attendees, not only did his own Society support the idea, but the other two organizations—including the GLF revolutionaries—supported it, too. Kameny disliked popular music, so he insisted that the disc jockey play two of his own records. Following the lead of the astronomer with a bad back, 250 gay attendees danced the polka and a Strauss waltz. Lilli Vincenz kissed him on the cheek. Come on, Frank, you've got to do this, she said.

On January 19, the NCACLU filed suit in the case of Benning Wentworth, and on January 21, it filed complaints on behalf of Richard Gayer and Otto Ulrich.

Two days later, Frank Kameny decided to run for Congress.

*Marsha P. Johnson at Sylvia Rivera's
demonstration in 1970*

20

THE CANDIDATE

In Norman, Oklahoma, a local farmer threw parties for homosexuals in his barn. At one such event, just before Halloween 1966, Michael Mc-Connell met Jack Baker. The twenty-four-year-old McConnell, a library school student, wondered whether Baker's flat-top haircut meant he was a businessman, a soldier, or a married man from the suburbs. That night, after dancing to James Brown, they slept together. He was an engineer.

In June 1967, they moved into a one-bedroom apartment, and four months later, Jack Baker received a letter from the air force. The Office of Special Investigations had interrogated another airman, who claimed that he and Baker had engaged in an act of mutual masturbation several years earlier.

The air force downgraded Baker's honorable discharge to a "General Discharge," and it notified his superior at Tinker Air Force Base. Faced with the choice of resignation or termination, Baker resigned.

"Frankly, we didn't know what to do," McConnell later recalled. To make ends meet, Baker began working at a local brewery, and after he found a job at a DuPont cellophane plant, the couple moved to Lawrence, Kansas. In the summer of 1968, at a bar near the University of Kansas, they saw a flyer advertising the North American Conference of Homophile Organizations.

During the conference, the couple stopped Kameny in the hallway. Yes, said Baker, he wanted to fight the military. "I spent a day with him, at Lawrence, immediately after the NACHO Conference left, planted a few seeds on very fertile soil, and have been cultivating the young plant ever since, via the mails," wrote Kameny, upon meeting the veteran.

On January 14, 1969, Kameny called with the news. He had persuaded the NCACLU to adopt Baker's air force case. "You are welcome to publicize this case in any manner you wish," Baker told a local homophile group. "However, I do not wish my name used publicly."

Two weeks after Stonewall, Baker arrived in Washington for his air force discharge hearing. He stayed with Kameny, who coached him through the process, and 5020 Cathedral Avenue became a laboratory for yet another activist. That fall, after deciding to become a lawyer for gay liberation, Jack Baker began his first year of law school at the University of Minnesota. He also decided to create a student homophile organization in Minneapolis.

In April 1970, Baker won his case against the air force, and the Department of Defense upgraded his discharge. With that victory, the couple realized that the United States Constitution contained a pathway to gay equality, and by fighting in the courts, they could win.

The couple embarked on their next battle: the pursuit of the right to get married. Since the 1950s, *ONE* magazine and other forward-looking elements of the homophile movement had discussed nonlegal, romantic "marriages" between homosexuals, and even Kameny had voiced support for such unions during the 1963 Dowdy hearings.

There is no known record of a gay couple attempting to get *legally* married until May 18, 1970, only one month after Baker's air force victory, when he and McConnell walked into the Minnesota's Hennepin County Courthouse. That afternoon, while wearing dark suits and surrounded by the press, the couple submitted their application for a marriage license. Technically, they argued, their marriage was perfectly legal, for Minnesota law mentioned nothing about the gender of marriage license applicants. On May 22, the county attorney denied their marriage license.

Exactly one month later, Michael McConnell received a letter from the University of Minnesota, which had recently offered him a position in its library. The university rescinded its offer of employment. His public conduct, the board of regents explained, was "not consistent with the best interest of the University." The Minnesota Civil Liberties Union filed suit against the university, and the couple filed suit against Hennepin County. Meanwhile, news of their fights spread across the country. In June, two women in Los Angeles filed suit after they attempted to apply for a marriage license. In August, two Kentucky women did the same.

That month in San Francisco, at the country's first student gay liberation conference, Charles P. Thorp climbed to the stage of SIR's auditorium. "The gay marriage is the bastard child of straight respectability," declared Thorp, a twenty-year-old with long hair. Rather than fighting for marriage, he argued, homosexuals needed to fight for those *least* respected in the homosexual community. "It will not be until what straights call 'blatant behavior' is accepted with respect that we will be in any way, any of us, free," he continued.

But for McConnell and Baker, marriage had nothing to do with behavior or respectability. They simply wanted the same legal privileges provided to straight couples: the right to share their finances, to visit each other in the hospital, to adopt children.

On January 26, only days after Kameny decided to run for Congress, *LOOK* magazine published its issue on the American family. The magazine, which had a circulation of 6.5 million readers, included a three-page feature on Baker and McConnell, "The Homosexual Couple."

"Not all homosexual life is a series of one-night stands in bathhouses, public toilets or gay bars," explained the magazine. "Some homosexuals—a minority—live together in stable, often long-lasting relationships, like Baker's and McConnell's." Readers saw *LOOK*'s images of the two men, irrefutably in love. The couple received a deluge of letters from across America and from Canada, Australia, and India. Most of all, the letter writers just wanted to know, how did you do it? How did you find love among so much hate?

"I suppose the reason it touched me so was because I knew I was the same as you," wrote one man from Louisiana. "The only difference is I am, or was, ashamed of it."

The couple continued fighting their cases in court, and Charles P. Thorp began propagating a slogan of his own, one for the deviants who had no desire to get married, a motto for the "fairies, faggots, and queens" who merely hoped to live, day to day, as themselves.

"Blatant is Beautiful."

WITH SO LITTLE TIME to acquire five thousand signatures, campaign manager Paul Kuntzler and his team worked quickly. They established a campaign office in Kameny's home, created stationery, and rented a mailbox. They recruited a press secretary, a literature officer, neighborhood coordinators, and a university coordinator. Each of Washington's gay groups had a campaign representative, including MSW's Otto Ulrich and GLF's Ted Kirkland, a Black activist who lived in the Dupont Circle commune. Lilli Vincenz became volunteer coordinator.

"Since we realistically realize that I do not have a chance in ten trillion of winning, we are not trying for that," Kameny explained to Dick Schlegel. "Our goal is to get enough votes (if I get onto the ballot) to make an impact on the politicians—a show of strength. That is all."

On Wednesday, February 3, Kameny stood on the steps of the District Building. All four local newspapers sent reporters, as did all four television networks.

"Early in the history of this country," began Kameny, "when our form of democracy was a novel experiment, Alexis de Tocqueville, writing for European readers, noted that one of the defects of the American system was what he termed the 'tyranny of the majority.' His words are still relevant to one of the most suppressed, repressed, oppressed, and persecuted of all our minority groups: our homosexual American citizens."

Prodded by the GLF, Kameny adopted the causes of other minorities. "Although I am a homosexual and the focus of my campaign will be sexual oppression," explained Kameny, "I appeal to all minority groups and to all individuals who differ from the contrived conventions of the majority, whether by desire or by circumstance, by race or by gender or by lifestyle."

"We hope that this will serve as a further spur to solidarity, activism, and a sense of brother- and sisterhood among homosexuals," he concluded.

On its front page, beneath a story about *Apollo 14*'s impending descent to the moon, hidden in a story about a different candidate, the *Star* reported on the news of Frank Kameny's announcement.

With Kuntzler and Hoffard, two political experts, running Kameny's candidacy, his campaign transformed gay Washington into a political machine. He could afford nothing less than mobilization on a massive scale—with only twenty days before the deadline, Kameny needed 250 signatures per day to qualify for the ballot.

Nancy Tucker advertised the campaign in *The Gay Blade*, now stocked in eighteen gay establishments, as an effort to spread the "'Gay is Good' message and philosophy." For the closeted bar-goers, she included reassurance. "DON'T FEEL THAT YOU ARE ADMITTING YOU ARE GAY BY SIGNING A PETITION FOR A GAY CANDIDATE."

Lilli Vincenz organized volunteers into nine neighborhood teams, and Paul Kuntzler solicited donations. "<u>WE CAN COUNT ON KAMENY, CAN WE COUNT ON YOU?</u>"

The day after Kameny's announcement, Congressman John R. Rarick of Louisiana stood on the House floor. "The Mattachine Society of Washington, a national organization of sexual perverts who strive for full equality as a matter of law now announce that they have organized a political party in Washington, D.C., and are fielding a candidate for the District of Columbia Delegate election," he warned. "There will be no return to morality in our land until our people learn the truths of God's word by reading the Holy Bible."

The congressman quoted from Leviticus. "They shall surely be put to death," he read. "Their blood shall be upon them."

KAMENY'S VOLUNTEERS stationed themselves in gay bars and bathhouses, outside grocery stores and liquor stores, and at gay thoroughfares like Thomas Circle. On Sundays, they stood outside churches. Kuntzler and Vincenz expected volunteers at straight locations to collect ten signatures per hour, and no less. They had a strict set of instructions, detailed in a leaflet, "<u>HOW TO GET THE MOST SIGNATURES THE FASTEST.</u>"

Shortly after midnight on Friday, February 19, only three days before the signature deadline, the New Yorkers arrived. Thirty-five activists traveled to Washington on a bus chartered by the GAA. The campaign matched each New York volunteer with a local host, and the next morning, they joined the Washington volunteers to collect signatures in pairs.

That night, the campaign hosted a dance for the volunteers, and Washington's two bathhouses admitted New York volunteers for free. "The dance was a blast and the Washington people were really swingers," reported GAY's Pete Fisher. "A lot of us came away with new friendships (and more)."

Plus, wrote Fisher, "Isn't it about time we began thinking about running a gay candidate for office in New York City?"

The interstate mobilization for Kameny's signatures was not an entirely grassroots effort, however. It also represented one of the country's first exertions of Gay Power in its original sense: gay economic power.

The Kameny campaign's largest donations came not from individual gay contributors, but from the commercial establishments of gay Washington—its gay bars, its two bathhouses, and most important, its pornography industry.

H. Lynn Womack, a large white man with albinism, was from Mississippi and had a PhD in philosophy. He housed his materials in a sixteen-thousand-square-foot warehouse on Capitol Hill, and each week, his Guild Press sent pornographic magazines to thousands of gay men across the country. With an industrial printing press, he could print tens of thousands of flyers and brochures in a matter of hours. Womack agreed to produce an unlimited quantity of printed materials for the MSW president's campaign.

With gay Washington's monetary donations and Womack's in-kind contributions, the Kameny campaign found itself with extra funds. In a novel instance of gay realpolitik, to ensure that Kameny received enough signatures, Paul Kuntzler struck a deal. He approached one of the Democratic candidates who had lost in the primary, and in exchange for several hundred dollars, that candidate collected 1,500 signatures for Kameny in the Black neighborhoods of Southeast Washington.

On the day of the signature deadline, Kameny stood once again on the steps of District Building. He wore a new three-piece suit, which his campaign had purchased for him. "I am here to announce the filing of a petition containing more than 7,000 signatures—well over the required 5,000—nominating me for the position of Delegate to Congress from the District of Columbia," he said.

"That more than 7,000 signatures were obtained in a mere three weeks, by a coordinated effort staged by the homosexual community—an effort involving some 400 people—indicates that this latest arrival upon the political scene will be a formidable group to be reckoned with.

"We intend to wage a vigorous and hard-hitting campaign. We intend to pull no punches.

"This is OUR country, OUR society, and OUR government—for homosexuals quite as much as for heterosexuals.

"You will be hearing much of us in the next 10 days—and long there-after," he concluded.

When Rae Beck Kameny heard the news from her son, she wrote with congratulations. "Well, I wish you luck for whatever you get out of it," she said. "One never knows—it may lead to a decent job."

With overflowing campaign coffers, Frank Kameny could finally afford a homosexual headquarters with a size representative of Washington's gay populace. His campaign acquired an entire four-story building, the former home of a restaurant, at 1307 E Street Northwest. It overlooked Pennsylvania Avenue and the sites of power on that street. To the east, the FBI; to the west, the District Building; and, only three blocks away, the White House.

The campaign hoisted three banners onto the building, covering the entirety of the top two floors: KAMENY FOR CONGRESS.

"Old J. Edgar can't miss that banner," laughed Jack Nichols.

"We are emerging openly and fully into the life of this city and of this country," announced Kameny at the grand opening. "The opening of this headquarters here on the President's Avenue symbolizes that emergence as concisely as anything can."

During his speech, Kameny's campaign strategy shifted. Indeed, the success of the signatures had raised a tantalizing possibility. If Kameny translated each of those signatures into a vote—reaching a sum of at least 7,500—then the campaign planned to register as its own party. It would automatically appear on the 1972 ballot. Kameny and his team planned to call themselves the Personal Freedom Party.

Frank Kameny and his campaign staff saw the possibility of sparking a national movement focused on a larger battle against government-mandated conformity. To accomplish this feat, just as Kameny had acquired straight signatures, he needed straight voters. Just as he had once infiltrated the ACLU, he would infiltrate mainstream Washington politics. Because only 10 percent of his future constituents were homosexual, he planned to devote only 10 percent of his time *advocating* for homosexuals, too. It was the logical and fair political move, he reasoned.

Kameny thus became only incidentally homosexual. In his speech, he compared himself to John F. Kennedy, who "served society as a citizen, not as a Catholic."

"We hope that the citizens of Washington will vote for me," he declared, "knowing that a vote for Kameny is a vote for their right to be themselves, to live their rewarding and satisfying lives, and to contribute to society and to their city, without artificial, needless barriers and obstacles—for the real freedom for which this country was founded, for which it still stands, and which is its glory."

With only three weeks until the election, Kameny threw himself into the campaign. As one of only six candidates on the ballot, he found himself automatically invited to candidate events on television, radio, and before the city's many organizations. With a professional political and speechwriting team, Kameny appeared at each and every event with a custom speech.

"He has a different, handwritten speech almost everywhere he goes," marveled the *Star* on its front page. "At a recent debate, where candidates were assigned to discuss employment, housing, schools and welfare, Kameny was the only one to do just that, while the others spent their time delivering oratorical fusillades against each other."

Kameny ran the perfect straight campaign, and he looked like the perfect straight candidate. Kay Lahusen took professional photographs of Kameny in his three-piece suit, standing stoically before the Capitol building. "Dr. Franklin E. Kameny looks like Everyman, as he hurries along a downtown street," reported the *Star*.

When the *Post* hosted a forum for the candidates, a reporter confronted Kameny about the issue. Are you just running for the homosexual minority? No, responded Kameny. "I am running on all of the issues and, in fact, I have played down the specific homosexual issue."

A week before the election, when a *Star* reporter asked to print Kuntzler's name, the campaign manager hesitated. "Well, I'd have lots of trouble at the office," he explained.

"Oh, come on. I predict that 30 to 60 days from now you'll come all the way out of the closet," said Kameny.

"I know that, I just don't want to—"

"Look. You're going to be on WTOP a week from now. On television!"

The duo continued arguing as they rushed to the next candidate event, and the *Star* refrained from printing Kuntzler's name.

HOMOSEXUALS ACROSS THE COUNTRY still saw hope in the professional campaign of a gay man. On March 7, a gay man in Pittsburgh wrote Kameny to tell him how "deliriously happy" the news of the signatures had made him. "As far as I am concerned this is the most significant development that has ever happened in the entire history of the homophile movement," he added.

For the federal government, too, despite Kameny's new image as a civil libertarian, a homosexual was a homosexual, and nothing more. On March 8, Congressman Rooney of New York conducted his annual hearings on appropriations for the State Department. The deputy assistant secretary for security, G. Marvin Gentile, sat before him.

"Is this not the place where we ask for the machinations of the Mattachine Society?" asked Rooney.

"Yes, sir," said Gentile.

"What is the score this past year?"

"Last year we had 17 employees who were removed, 16 of whom were removed as homosexual problems."

"All men?"

"Yes, sir; the 16 were."

The next day, Kameny appeared before reporters in the Pentagon's pressroom. "Kameny will provide facts and name certain high government officials who have been persecuting homosexuals for years," his campaign promised.

Kameny denounced Congressman Rooney's "annual fertility rite," the CSC, the armed forces, and the examiners of the Department of Defense.

"I have seen the inner workings of this system at first hand, as few have, and I am appalled at the fraud being perpetuated upon the American people. WE HAVE NO SECURITY SYSTEM.

"I have said twice before and I repeat: We are fed up!!" he yelled.

At noon, Kameny walked to room 3D272 of the Pentagon, where he could enter only with his NCACLU attorneys, John Karr and Glenn Graves. For the last time, in a closed Pentagon hearing, Kameny defended his right to gain a security clearance.

While arguing against the unfair standards applied to heterosexuals and homosexuals, Karr echoed the arguments of the 1961 Kameny brief. "This difference in standard was not considered when this applicant was issued a rifle in World War II and sent to Europe to defend his country in World War II," he declared. "It seems a little odd, a little strange and somehow unfair that this standard should be applied now."

Department of Defense attorney Rowland A. Morrow, Kameny's longtime foe, stood to make his final case against the congressional candidate. Kameny wanted to be considered as a single applicant rather than as a member of a minority, explained Morrow, so he urged the appeals board to do just that. "Let's concentrate on him as an individual," he said. "We find we have before us an individual who describes himself as a homosexual, who admits to having engaged in a variety of sexual practices which would include, but are not limited to, fellatio, anal sodomy, mutual masturbation and others. He is abundantly aware of the criminal nature of his act and intends indefinitely in the future to continue to engage in such acts."

Before them sat a man who, in 1956, was arrested in a San Francisco public restroom. Several years later, he was arrested again in the vicinity of a public restroom, "a notorious hangout for homosexuals," in Lafayette Park. Despite these arrests, Frank Kameny claimed that he wanted to find just one man to love. "Applicant's assertion," concluded Morrow, "that he would like to form a lasting relationship with one person is a sad and lone fact." After all, Kameny had not yet found another man, explained Morrow. "He must continue to cruise in men's rooms and homosexual bars, looking for fleeting sexual contacts with strangers.

"This is the fact of this man's existence."

ON MARCH 12, 1971, the Broadway musical *Hair*—featuring odes to sodomy, marijuana, and hippie culture—opened at Washington's National Theatre. Across the street, only a couple hundred feet away, stood the Kameny headquarters. The Catholic Legion of Decency picketed the musical on the night of its opening. While demonstrating before the theater, protesting *Hair*'s content and nudity, the anti-obscenity picketers faced a group of twenty-odd homosexual counterdemonstrators. Led by Kameny, the homosexuals held candles in silent vigil and distributed leaflets, printed by the nation's fourth-largest pornographer, to theatergoers and pedestrians. "We are firmly convinced," announced the campaign, "that if Jesus Christ were here today, he would be in the National Theatre approving and applauding and very probably participating as a member of the cast of *Hair*, knowing that this play is a truer representation of Christianity than the dour, joyless picketers out there."

The last full week of the campaign, Kameny continued traversing Washington's straight and gay worlds. Speeches, debates, and interviews during the day; gay bars at night. In each bar, while hundreds of men danced with one another, volunteers distributed literature, and Kameny walked from table to table, shaking hands and asking for votes.

Paul Kuntzler planned the climax of the campaign, a "Personal Freedom Day," for the Saturday before the election. In preparation, Womack's presses printed one hundred thousand brochures and flyers.

Is your phone tapped because you are gay?

Did you lose your job because you are gay?

Were you discharged from the military because you're gay?

Were you trapped by a plainclothesman who cruised you
right into the police station on a perjured charge?

Do you fear that one day any of these might happen to you?

**FIGHT TO END THESE VIOLATIONS OF OUR RIGHTS
AS AMERICAN CITIZENS**

VOTE KAMENY ON MARCH 23rd

The straight flyers were longer, outlining his top fourteen priorities, ranging from discrimination to freeways. "VOTE KAMENY: The Personal Freedom Candidate," they concluded.

On Friday night, the GAA bus arrived once again, and the New Yorkers joined the Frank Kameny's extended homophile network. Eva Freund came from Reading, Pennsylvania. Barbara Gittings and Kay Lahusen arrived from Philadelphia and New York. When Jack Nichols and Lige Clarke approached the capital, they heard Kameny's voice on their car radio.

Saturday morning, dozens of volunteers left to distribute the flyers at fifty Washington shopping centers. GAA volunteers slipped them under apartment doors. Beginning at 9:00 a.m., Kameny began a "walking tour" of the District, and at noon, he staged the largest press conference of his campaign. The time had come, he declared, for the president to remedy the second-class citizenship accorded to gay Americans. Kameny held a letter to Nixon, almost identical to the one he had sent in 1962 to Kennedy, a letter that had gone unanswered. It requested a meeting with the president.

While holding that letter, Kameny marched three blocks from his headquarters to the White House. Fifty homosexuals followed him, holding signs and chanting.

"Two, four, six, eight, gay is just as good as straight."

"Three, five, seven, nine, lesbians are mighty fine."

At the White House, Kameny handed the letter to an armed guard.

Kameny continued his outdoor walking tour until 6:00 p.m., and one hour later, he turned to the television. For fifteen minutes, Washington's local CBS affiliate aired an advertisement, produced and funded by the campaign, for Frank Kameny. The candidate, his staff, and thousands of local viewers witnessed the world's first paid television spot for gay rights.

Shortly thereafter, during the National Theatre's production of *Hair*, the cast members spontaneously danced across the stage while carrying KAMENY FOR CONGRESS signs. After the show, the cast joined Kameny's volunteers for a fund-raising dance at the campaign headquarters. While Lilli Vincenz and her lover sold tickets at the door, the *Hair* cast and 350 homosexuals danced beneath strobe lights and the psychedelic posters on the walls of the campaign office.

While his volunteers danced, Kameny left for Washington's two dozen gay bars. For six hours, until 3:00 a.m., Kameny—still suffering from a painful back—canvassed his community.

"That campaign was the most arduous and grueling single thing I have ever undertaken in my entire life," the World War II veteran later recalled. The next day, for the first time in his life, the exhausted Kameny canceled his speeches.

The Sunday Star gave him something invaluable that day. Writing about a man who so valued logic, the newspaper ended its front-page story not with Kameny's sexuality, but with his ideas. "If the race could be won by raising novel ideas and debating points, Kameny might well be the winner," reported the *Star*. Indeed, when the Republican and three other candidates attacked Fauntroy at a recent debate, Kameny declined to join. Instead, he suggested a novel idea: America should remove its defoliation aircraft from Vietnam use them to destroy Turkey's opium poppy fields, which contributed to Washington's heroin epidemic.

"Right on!" said the socialist candidate. The other candidates nodded with approval.

"Dr. Frank Kameny, the Harvard-educated astronomer and avowed homosexual, may not have succeeded in convincing the city that 'Gay is Good,'" added the *Daily News*, "but his straightforward advocacy of the 'right to be different,' his thoughtful examination of other important issues, his generosity in praise of his opponents, must have impressed many who met him along the way that 'Gay' is not all that bad."

On Monday, the day before the election, the campaign rented a sound truck with two powerful speakers. MSW member Tony Jackubosky sat in the back seat, speaking into a microphone, informing entire neighborhoods of Frank Kameny's qualifications.

That evening, as volunteers attempted to receive promises from gay bar-goers that they would indeed vote for Kameny, they began to notice the fear. The homosexuals of Washington seemed hesitant. Some said they wanted to vote for someone who actually had a chance, but others explained that they were closeted. They feared that the government or their employer would learn that they had voted for the gay candidate. One group of bar-goers told Kameny that they feared a "wave of oppression" if Kameny actually performed well at the polls.

At the Plus One, when a campaign staffer used the bar's microphone to solicit poll workers for the next day, the patrons froze. Nobody wanted to expose themselves as a Kameny volunteer.

The next day, Tuesday, the campaign machine switched to high gear. Each potential voter received a custom card with an assigned polling place, the date and hours for voting, and a reminder of Kameny's importance.

Volunteers compiled lists of phone numbers to double-check that their gay network voted, and the campaign's transportation committee provided a chauffeur service to carry voters to their precincts.

That day, Frank Kameny voted for himself. Then he waited. The campaign advertised an "Election Night Victory Party," featuring fifteen-cent beer, free admission, and dancing. "CASUAL DRESS," said the flyer.

As the attendees trickled into his headquarters, Kameny watched the election returns upstairs with his staff. He wore his three-piece suit and stood, as he had at Sheep Meadow, without visible emotion.

Washington voters cast 1,841 ballots for Kameny, a total of 1.6 percent of the vote. Only 25 percent of his signatures had translated to votes, but Kameny came in fourth place out of six, above the socialist and Black Nationalist candidates. ("I hope the people of the District don't think there are more homosexuals than militants who are politically active," remarked the Black Nationalist candidate, upon hearing the news.)

Kameny arrived downstairs to address the crowd. Yes, he had lost, he told them, while Lige Clarke held back tears. But it was just the beginning. "The homosexual community must be freer now because of my candidacy," said Kameny. He called on Fauntroy to appoint a congressional aide devoted to the problems of his homosexual constituents.

"We've made our impact in exactly the way we wanted to," he explained. "We gained respect and recognition for what we want."

"Kameny for President!" someone yelled.

A WEEK AFTER the election, a *Star* reporter sat in Frank Kameny's home, still only sparsely furnished. Yes, admitted the astronomer, the result had been disappointing.

"Without a job, saddled with an 'acute and dire' financial situation, Kameny still feels that the campaign for Congress was a turning point in the history of homosexuals in the United States," reported the paper. Washington's political structure would now include homosexuals, he predicted. The other candidates, including Fauntroy, had taken note of his positions.

Paul Kuntzler, meanwhile, did not intend to discard the campaign. After expenses of five thousand dollars, the Kameny machine had more than two thousand dollars in additional funds. More important, it had built a seamless operation ("one of the most cleanly run and efficient campaigns," described the *Star*).

Impressed by the GAA activists' own political coordination, Kuntzler planned an April trip to New York, funded by campaign contributions. He brought a group of campaign veterans to meet with GAA leadership, and the five men initiated the process of converting the Kameny campaign into the Gay Activists Alliance of Washington.

They did not invite Frank Kameny. The MSW president had reigned over his own organization and gay Washington for an entire decade. The new group wanted to be independent, free of domination, a truly democratic political entity.

"WE, AS HOMOSEXUAL ACTIVISTS, seeking total liberation in the eyes of society and equality under law, demand the freedom for expression of our dignity and value as human beings through confrontation with and disarmament of all mechanisms which unjustly inhibit us: economic, social, and political," began their constitution.

With the Kameny campaign and the birth of the Washington GAA, the Mattachine Society of Washington ceased to exist. Its last executive board meeting occurred in early February, just as the campaign machine came into existence. Though Kameny was determined to keep it alive—he continued using its letterhead and registering the organization with the District—the Society consisted of only one member, the same man who had founded it, hoping to create a movement around his own struggle.

Frank Kameny, once again, stood alone. He complained about his exclusion from the GAA's leadership—"I am not going to be put out to pasture!"—but the new organization remained adamant. Yes, they respected him, the founder and the face of their cause, but the movement had become too large just for one man, no matter the magnitude of his mind.

THAT MONTH, when *The Gay Blade*'s Nancy Tucker sat down to analyze the results of the election, she noticed something peculiar. If she used Kameny's own 10 percent statistic, she calculated that only 20 percent of all Washington homosexuals had voted for him.

The campaign, she decided, had failed in its initial purpose of creating a homosexual voting bloc and exerting gay political power. When the campaign pivoted to a focus on broader civil liberties, Kameny transitioned from "the" homosexual candidate to "a" homosexual candidate, thus failing to mobilize his own base, she concluded.

In *The Advocate*, Tucker criticized him for avoiding discussion of his homosexuality in his straight speeches, for his "closety" campaign staff, and for his headquarters, which contained only a single GAY IS GOOD poster.

Moreover, she argued, Kameny for Congress failed the black homosexuals of Washington. His campaign made "only a few, half-hearted, tentative, and obviously futile attempts to appeal to black Gays," she wrote. "It was a white campaign for a white candidate."

The election results supported her claim. While Kameny did well in white precincts (the same neighborhoods won by the white Republican candidate), he received only a handful of ballots in Black precincts.

"Conclusion? In a black city, any campaign for a homosexual candidate *must* be aimed at the gay black voter," wrote Tucker.

Finally, there was the problem of the drag queens. The campaign had displayed an "obvious reluctance to have drags associated in any way with the candidate," reported Tucker. His staff had even discussed banning them from the fund-raising dances. Though the campaign ultimately permitted the queens, the discussion represented an "intolerable" failure for a homosexual candidate, she wrote.

Tucker warned her readers of the implications in Washington. "If the decision to play down Kameny's homosexuality was made by his campaign committee (and there is good reason to think that it was) and not by Kameny himself, then the man is easily manipulated and was on a giant ego trip, and I caution the gay community should he ever decide to run for the presidency—which I think he will."

ON APRIL 8, Walter Cronkite announced the news to more than twenty-five million American viewers. "In Minneapolis, an admitted homosexual, Jack Baker, has been elected president of the University of Minnesota Student Association," he reported.

Baker, while still fighting for his right to marry another man, had won 2,766 votes, or 46 percent, in a field of five candidates. Because of his galvanizing candidacy, the university witnessed the highest voter turnout in its history.

Baker had run as a blatantly gay candidate. In his posters, Baker sat on the ground, staring contemplatively at the camera, wearing perfectly groomed hair, a button-down shirt, jeans, and—closest to the viewer— high-heeled shoes.

"PUT YOURSELF IN JACK BAKER'S SHOES!" it proclaimed.

When Baker and McConnell noticed the posters were disappearing from dormitory hallways, they caught someone in the act of ripping one down.

I was going to put it in my room, explained the student.

LESS THAN a month later, on a Monday evening, May 3, 1971, Frank Kameny sat in the front row of Washington's Shoreham Hotel ballroom. Next to him sat Lilli Vincenz and Jack Baker, and behind them sat 2,500 psychiatrists, who had flown from across the country to attend the 1971 annual meeting of the American Psychiatric Association.

Following the GLF invasion of their 1970 San Francisco meeting, the psychiatrists had made a concession. They had agreed to allow Kameny, Vincenz, and Baker to speak on an unprecedented panel, titled "Lifestyles of Non-Patient Homosexuals," alongside DOB cofounder Del Martin.

The APA permitted the homosexuals to attend the Convocation of Fellows, its awards ceremony on the first night of the conference. A row of elderly psychiatrists sat on the stage, wearing medals in recognition of their professional achievements. Also in the ballroom sat Ramsey Clark, the United States attorney general, scheduled to give the APA's convocation address later in the program.

Security had never been so tight. In addition to the protection measures for the attorney general, the APA had hired a special security consultant to ensure that its annual meeting proceeded without incident. The Washington police, however, were distracted that day. Thirty thousand demonstrators had streamed into the District over the May Day weekend. Demanding an immediate end to the Vietnam War, they planned to shut down the American government by disrupting traffic and preventing federal employees from entering their offices.

President Nixon authorized the execution of Operation Garden Plot, a secret protocol later exposed by Senator Sam Ervin. Ten thousand federal troops worked in coordination with all 5,100 Metropolitan Police officers to detain anyone remotely suspected of participating in the civil disturbance. Tear gas wafted into the cars and buses of government workers. "Dozens of employees were seen hurrying to their offices with tears streaming down their faces," reported *The New York Times*.

On May 3, the government arrested seven thousand suspected demonstrators, the most ever arrested in a single day of the capital's history. The military bussed the demonstrators to a temporary outdoor detention facility on the practice field of the Washington Redskins, where they were detained without attorneys or proper facilities.

That night, as Frank Kameny sat in the audience, he prepared to target the "root of the abscess," as he referred to the field of psychiatry. In collaboration with the GLF and GAA of Washington, he had studied the blueprint of the hotel and developed intricate contingency plans. The night prior, his colleagues scouted the hotel and managed to wedge open the fire doors that connected the Regency Ballroom to the hotel garage.

Shortly before Attorney General Clark's speech, the APA's Task Force on Aggression and Violence began presenting the awards for its essay contest. At that moment, a Volkswagen van and several cars appeared in front of the hotel's garage. Thirty activists from Washington and New York emerged from the vehicles. They carried signs and flags, and half of them wore drag: obscenely bright makeup, sparkling lamé dresses, giant wigs, and violently high heels. They flew through the ballroom's fire doors and charged for the stage. Members of the APA's Radical Caucus stood from their chairs and joined them. Hordes of psychiatrists resisted the gay offensive, resulting in a brawl. Two gay demonstrators and one APA official were thrown from the stage.

"The noise coming from the Regency Room was like out of the Inferno," reported one GLF attendee, trapped outside by a psychiatrist who had barricaded the fire door. Six GAA members carried identical copies of a speech. According to their plans, whoever managed to reach the microphone would deliver it. But the 2,500 psychiatrists outnumbered the homosexuals. None of them could make it to the podium.

Frank Kameny leapt onto the stage and lunged for the microphone.

He did not have a script. "Psychiatry is the enemy incarnate," he yelled. "Psychiatry has waged a relentless war of extermination against us." One of the elderly psychiatrists unplugged the microphone, but Kameny grew louder. "You may take this as a declaration of war against you," he screamed. The GLF activists stared at him, stunned by the gall and the fury of the forty-seven-year-old astronomer. Standing on the stage, Kameny gazed at his audience, thousands of psychiatrists still shouting "faggots" and "drag queens" and "Nazis" and "go fuck yourself," and then the members of his minority, blatant and beautiful, part of a kinship he had not chosen but to whom he now surrendered.

Amidst the chaos, he was free.

The Washington Shoreham Hotel's Regency Ballroom, May 3, 1971

THE WHITE HOUSE

Frank Kameny, wearing an ill-fitting suit and an old, faded tie, slowly entered the Oval Office. He stood next to the vice president, a gay congressman, and a lesbian congresswoman. The president sat in front of him. Kameny, seemingly emotionless, looked down, over the president's shoulder as the president signed the executive order. The president capped his pen and handed it to the former astronomer. The room smiled and clapped, but Kameny remained stoic until he shook the president's hand, whereupon he allowed himself a grin. He stuck the pen in his pocket.

The victories had come, at first, with breathtaking speed. In September 1971, a district court judge ordered the restoration of Otto Ulrich and Richard Gayer's security clearances. Benning Wentworth won his case the following year.

After the 1971 zap of the APA in Washington, the psychiatrists capitulated to the homosexuals' demands. Kameny, after allying with sympathetic APA officials, received the news on December 15, 1973. At 8:30 a.m., the APA's board of trustees had unanimously voted to remove homosexuality from the *Diagnostic and Statistical Manual of Mental Disorders*, thus "curing us all, instantaneously, en masse, in one fell swoop, by semantics and by vote, instead of by therapy," explained Kameny.

"So we are permanently healthy!!!" he told Gittings.

Kameny joined efforts to inform the public of a *new* sickness, one that referred not to the benign condition of homosexuality but to the pathology of bigotry, an illness called *homophobia*.

Meanwhile, the number of groups devoted to the rights of the sexual deviant exploded in number. The GAA-DC, for one, soon realized that it needed the dictatorial astronomer. Frank Kameny submitted the GAA-DC's articles of incorporation, Kameny's house became its first headquarters, and Kameny served as its first legal committee chairman.

The GLF faded from Washington with the rise of the GAA and after an exodus of women from the organization. "You are committing suicide by your deprecation of the opposite sex," Nancy Tucker had admonished the overwhelmingly male GLF.

The days of the Mattachine Society of Washington, when men and women could work equally under Kameny's reign, were over. The Society remained alive only because Kameny deemed it alive, though he continued to list the one-man organization in the local directory of services, promising assistance and counseling for homosexuals in need. If you found yourself arrested or sick or homeless or simply wanted to learn about the District's gay bars, you could always call Frank Kameny.

He continued marching in New York's Pride parades, and in 1973, for the first time, Rae Beck Kameny marched beside her son, holding his hand. After experiencing the march, she joined the recently formed Parents and Friends of Lesbians and Gays (PFLAG). "So, at 77, she's joining the Gay Liberation Movement," Kameny told Gittings. She would continue to support her son and the movement until she passed away at the age of one hundred.

The Pentagon, despite the victories of Wentworth, Ulrich, and Gayer, continued to revoke the security clearances of suspected homosexuals. In July 1974, after a successful ACLU lawsuit, the press witnessed the inner workings of the American security system for the first time. During the four-day hearing, reporters heard Otis Francis Tabler's mother testify about her knowledge of her son's sexual practices, "including but not limited to acts of oral copulation and anal sodomy in both the inserter and insertee roles," as she explained to the examiner. Five months later, the Department of Defense granted him a clearance. "PENTAGON SURRENDERS," announced Kameny in a press release.

That year, the District of Columbia finally won home rule, and the homosexual citizens of Washington gained the ability to vote for their own city government. When the GAA learned that Mayor Walter E.

Washington planned to appoint members to the District's new Commission on Human Rights, the organization demanded that he appoint a homosexual.

On March 25, 1975, Kameny stood next to his mother and the mayor. He raised his right hand and swore to uphold the human rights of the District's residents. The audience, full of GAA members and other gay Washingtonians, applauded for the District's openly gay human rights commissioner.

As commissioner, Kameny became a hearing examiner, tasked with judging violations of the District's Human Rights Act. For the first time, he wielded governmental power over his own oppressors. As he explained to his friends, "I AM the law, and I can assure you that as far as this Commissioner is concerned, NO one is going to be discriminated against for ANYthing in the District of Columbia."

Two months later, the city council abolished the Morals Division of the Metropolitan Police Department.

The Civil Service Commission continued to terminate suspected homosexuals, but with mounting pressure in the courts, it began showing signs of surrender. Immediately after his campaign, Kameny had initiated direct negotiations with the general counsel of the Civil Service Commission, and in August 1973, almost exactly ten years after his first request for a meeting, Kameny met with the chairman of the CSC himself.

On July 3, 1975, the general counsel of the CSC called Frank Kameny with the news. Later that day, the CSC would announce that homosexual conduct no longer disqualified Americans citizens from federal employment.

"The war, which they have fought against the Gay Community since 1950, and against me personally since 1957, is over," Kameny told Gittings and Lahusen.

"We have won."

WARREN SCARBERRY, the former FBI informant, continued his activism from within Attica Prison. The warden had prohibited Scarberry from writing to or receiving mail from the Mattachine Society of New York, so in 1969, the inmate partnered with the organization to sue the state's Department of Correctional Services.

On the morning of September 13, 1971, state troopers invaded Attica. Prisoners, protesting squalid conditions and mail censorship, had rebelled, taken hostages, and occupied the facility for four days. In retaliation, the troopers opened fire indiscriminately, killing twenty-nine prisoners and ten hostages. In total, state authorities fired at least 450 rounds and shot 128 people.

Warren Scarberry was one of them. He survived his bullet wounds, however, and seven years later, a District Court judge ruled that Attica Prison could no longer ban gay political literature.

Only months after Attica, on April 27, 1972, J. Edgar Hoover appeared once more to testify before Congressman John J. Rooney's appropriations committee.

Does the FBI allow gay activists to become agents? asked Rooney.

"We don't allow any types of activists in the FBI, gay or otherwise," answered the seventy-seven-year-old Hoover. "We permit no hippies in the bureau. I can guarantee that."

Four days later, Hoover died in his sleep. Upon hearing the news, his personal secretary immediately began shredding the director's secret files, and later, all 330,000 pages of his Sex Deviates file.

Around this time, Richard Socarides, the son of antigay psychiatrist Dr. Charles Socarides, fell in love with a boy at his New York private school. While his father continued his attempts to cure homosexuals in the downstairs office of their Upper East Side home, Richard began secretly meeting with his boyfriend on the upper floors of the town house. He later became President Clinton's liaison to the gay community.

For Kameny, perhaps the most satisfying turn of events occurred on Monday, January 28, 1974. That day, Congressman John Dowdy reported to the front gate of a jail in Missouri. In 1965, the year after his anti-Mattachine bill overwhelmingly passed in the House of Representatives, Dowdy had accepted a briefcase containing twenty-five thousand dollars at the Atlanta airport. In return, according to an FBI informant strapped with a hidden tape recorder, Dowdy had blocked the investigation of a Maryland construction company. A jury convicted the congressman of eight counts of bribery, conspiracy, and perjury. After resigning from Congress, Dowdy served six months in prison.

THE COMMISSION ON HUMAN RIGHTS did not provide Kameny a salary, and he remained unemployed. He relied on help from his mother and on modest fees for his appearances; in 1973, he narrated a pornographic film. Though he gave approximately 150 speeches per year throughout the 1970s, they brought hardly enough income to pay rent. MSW veteran Nancy Tucker, disturbed by the lack of food in Kameny's house, anonymously left bags of food on his doorstep.

How could he distract himself with a real job when he still saw injustice everywhere?

In 1971, the navy discovered Bob Martin's sexuality, and Kameny helped his homophile protégé conduct a publicity campaign against the navy. Though Senator Sam Ervin sent three letters to the secretary of the navy on behalf of the bisexual sailor, Martin still received a less-than-honorable discharge.

Meanwhile, Kameny guided the legal crusade of air force sergeant Leonard Matlovich, a three-tour Vietnam veteran and the recipient of a Purple Heart. In 1975, while Matlovich fought the air force in court (he eventually received a $160,000 settlement), he also came out before the world on the cover of *TIME* magazine, declaring, "I Am a Homosexual."

After Democrat Jimmy Carter won the 1976 election, Bob Martin applied to the Carter administration's special discharge review program, intended to extend mercy to Vietnam-era discharges. On September 22, 1977, a five-officer navy review board unanimously revised his less-than-honorable discharge to "Honorable."

The military's ban on homosexuals remained in place, however, and the purges continued unhindered in the State Department, the CIA, the NSA, the FBI, and the Foreign Service. But by the late 1970s, Americans had elected openly gay public officials in Michigan, Massachusetts, and California. In Washington, after witnessing the mobilizing power of the District's new gay political organization, the Gertrude Stein Democratic Club, Mayor Marion Barry attributed his 1978 election to the gay vote.

In 1979, after the assassination of Harvey Milk, seventy-nine thousand homosexuals marched in Washington.

By the end of the decade, Frank Kameny could read a gay newspaper, shop in a mostly gay grocery store, have lunch in a gay steak house, purchase books in a gay bookstore, pray in a gay church service, strategize in a gay political meeting, and then head to a gay bar, gay bathhouse, or gay cinema. Gay Washington, as one homosexual told *The Washington Post*, had become "utopia."

IN 1981, MAYOR BARRY declared April 9 to be "Franklin E. Kameny Day" in the District of Columbia. Three months later, an article appeared on page twenty of *The New York Times*. "RARE CANCER SEEN IN 41 HOMOSEXUALS," it announced. The Centers for Disease Control and Prevention first called it GRID, gay-related immunodeficiency, and then AIDS, acquired immunodeficiency syndrome. When a reporter asked for a comment from the Reagan White House, the press secretary laughed. "I don't have it. Do you?"

Homosexuals, once purged from their government jobs, faced a purge from existence. By December 1983, playwright Larry Kramer of New York had a green notebook with the names of thirty-seven dead friends. "I heard about Vinny on Saturday," he told Maureen Dowd. "Ron is a black actor I know. Paul, a pianist. Gayle went to Yale with me. Ron Doud, the designer of Studio 54. Mark, I was involved with a long time ago. Peter, an architect."

Lesbians, many still disenchanted by the misogyny of the male-dominated gay movement, took care of the dying. In 1985, Lilli Vincenz created People Living with AIDS (PLA), a gay-affirmative empowerment group at Washington's Whitman-Walker clinic. To educate the public about the epidemic, participants created a newsletter, appeared on television, and spoke at universities. She modeled the effort after the Mattachine Society of Washington.

By 1986, twelve thousand Americans, mostly men who had sex with men, were dead. The government seemed preoccupied with *testing* gay men, but not with preventing the disease. What, asked activists, would authorities do with the infected?

The Prevent AIDS Now Initiative Committee (PANIC) began advocating for a mass quarantine. Conservative commentator William F. Buckley Jr. called for mandatory tattoos on the buttocks of homosexuals with AIDS. In November 1986, two million Californians voted to make AIDS patients subject to "quarantine and isolation," and the possibility of homosexual detention camps became increasingly real. Hospitals put dead gay men in trash bags.

For the 1987 New York pride march, a new organization, the AIDS Coalition to Unleash Power (ACT UP), built a parade float with barbed wire, hospital masks, and badges with pink triangles—the Nazi symbol for homosexuals during the Holocaust. ACT UP adopted that symbol, defiantly rotated upside down, and a motto, "Silence = Death." GAA cofounder Marty Robinson brought his perfected zap technique, and the group organized "die-ins." Police officers used stretchers to carry away the protesters who lay prone on the ground.

Kameny, for his part, maintained faith in medical research and the scientific process. "We'll look back on it and it will be a nasty vile glitch or blip in history," he predicted. Even after a cure, he explained, prejudice would remain, so he continued what he did best, lecturing on homosexuality and counseling those who faced government purges.

In 1986, while the Reagan administration refused to fund further AIDS research, the United States Supreme Court upheld Georgia's anti-sodomy law. In response, activists organized the Second National March on Washington for Lesbian and Gay Rights.

On October 11, 1987, marchers with AIDS led the procession. They walked or rode wheelchairs, and the weakest occupied two Metrobuses. Five had to be taken to George Washington University Hospital for emergency treatment during the march.

Behind the people with AIDS marched no fewer than two hundred thousand additional demonstrators. Frank Kameny marched with them, and the following Tuesday, he joined activisits on the steps of the Supreme Court. The demonstrators, numbering several thousand, wore armbands to commemorate loved ones who had died, and they faced dozens of police officers in riot gear.

They chanted "shame" and scattered confetti, tiny pink triangles, on the steps of the court. In small groups, the demonstrators breached the line of police officers and sat motionless on the court's plaza. Police officers in white surgical gloves handcuffed and dragged away the sixty-two-year-old astronomer. Authorities bussed nearly six hundred demonstrators to jail, the District's largest mass arrest since the May Day protests of 1971.

"Your gloves don't match your shoes," shouted the activists.

The militant tactics, just as they had forced change upon the field of psychiatry, revolutionized America's medical–industrial complex. Burroughs Wellcome, the drugmaker whose AIDS drug, AZT, was the most expensive prescription drug in history, cut its price by 20 percent after experiencing the wrath of ACT UP.

The next year, to commemorate the mammoth 1987 demonstration, and to encourage gay Americans to combat the stigma attached to homosexuality and AIDS, activists established a new annual holiday, National Coming Out Day, for the anniversary of the march, October 11.

The partnership between AIDS activists and researchers contributed to the development of highly active antiretroviral therapy (HAART), the "cocktail" of medications that brought the virus to undetectable levels. After July 1996, when researchers announced their astounding findings at the Eleventh International AIDS Conference in Vancouver, it became possible for patients with HIV to live long and healthy lives.

The discovery of HAART, slowed by a government that laughed at the idea of a gay plague, came too late for three hundred thousand Americans. On average, for an entire decade after 1985, two people disappeared from the District of Columbia each day.

AIDS decimated the gay rights movement. It killed Ron Balin, charter member of the MSW; Marty Robinson, the creator of the zap; and Jim Owles, the first president of the GAA. Before Leonard Matlovich died, he designed his own gravestone, featuring two pink triangles, for Washington's Congressional Cemetery.

WHEN I WAS IN THE MILITARY
THEY GAVE ME A MEDAL FOR KILLING TWO MEN
AND A DISCHARGE FOR LOVING ONE

Bob Martin had been teaching at Columbia University and working on an encyclopedia of homosexuality. He had planned to attend the thirtieth anniversary celebration of Columbia's Student Homophile League. He died on July 19, 1996, one week after the pivotal Vancouver AIDS conference and one week before his fiftieth birthday.

DURING HIS 1992 CAMPAIGN, President Clinton promised to remove the ban on homosexuals in the military, and his compromise legislation, known as "Don't Ask, Don't Tell," indeed prevented the military from asking about inductees' sexual orientation. Despite its enactment, however, if the armed forces *learned* about homosexual activity, service members still faced a discharge. The military had once forced homosexuals to lie, and now it forced them to remain in the closet.

A greater victory arrived on August 2, 1995, when Clinton signed Executive Order 12968, prohibiting the denial of security clearances on the basis of sexual orientation. The American government—including the State Department, the Department of Defense, and the CIA—could no longer discriminate against gay civilians in the name of security. "The Government has gone beyond simply ceasing to be a hostile and vicious adversary and has now become an ally," marveled Kameny.

Marriage equality simultaneously edged closer to reality. In 1990, when two lesbians attempted to marry each other in Hawaii, not a single gay rights group agreed to take their case. The couple hired a straight attorney, and on May 5, 1993, the Hawaii Supreme Court ruled in the couple's favor. Lambda Legal, founded two decades earlier by a GAA attorney, joined the fight.

Hawaiian voters overwhelmingly amended the state's constitution to reestablish a gay marriage ban, and Clinton signed the Defense of Marriage Act, which prohibited the federal government from recognizing gay marriages.

More and more plaintiffs sued for gay rights, and in 2003, the Supreme Court struck down America's sodomy laws. The next year, the Massachusetts Supreme Court legalized gay marriage. In 2008, the California and Connecticut Supreme Courts followed suit.

On December 15, 2009, Mayor Adrian Fenty signed a bill that legalized gay marriage in the District of Columbia. In 2011, New York. Three states in 2012. Seven states in 2013. Nineteen in 2014.

An Ohio ACLU case, *Obergefell v. Hodges*, ultimately reached the Supreme Court. On June 26, 2015, in a 5–4 decision, the court ruled that "Baker v. Nelson must be and now is overruled," referring to the failed marriage case of Jack Baker and Michael McConnell. Gay marriage became legal across the country.

For many couples, the marriage fight had taken too long. Bayard Rustin, before he died in 1987, formalized his relationship by the only means available: adoption.

Barbara Gittings had shifted her energies to the American Library Association's Task Force on Gay Liberation. Her lover, Kay Tobin Lahusen, published her book, *The Gay Crusaders*, only after her publisher forced her to list a man (she chose Randy Wicker) as a coauthor. Gittings and Lahusen remained together for forty-six years—they came out to the residents of their assisted living facility through a newsletter article—until Gittings passed away in 2007. A memorial bench in Washington's Congressional Cemetery features both of their names and an epitaph: "Partners in life, Married in our hearts."

On June 16, 2008, the mayor of San Francisco officiated the wedding ceremony between DOB founders Del Martin, eighty-seven, and Phyllis Lyon, eighty-three, after fifty-five years together. Martin died two months later.

In 2013, Eva Freund, the MSW official responsible for its shift to radicalism, married her lover of twenty-one years. Lilli Vincenz, the first lesbian marcher at the White House, promised herself to her lover, Nancy Davis, three times over three decades, but never legally married.

Jack Baker and Michael McConnell did not see the need to marry again, since they maintained that their 1971 marriage had always been legal. But even after marriage equality, American courts refused to recognize their license. At last, on February 16, 2019, the Social Security Administration informed Baker and McConnell, still living together in Minneapolis, that the government now recognized their five decades of marriage.

IN THE 1990s, as gay rights activists pivoted to the fight for marriage equality, Sylvia Rivera slipped in and out of homelessness. Rivera, the founder of Street Transvestite Action Revolutionaries (STAR), had long been exiled from the movement she had helped create.

She had single-handedly regenerated the legal efforts of the New York GAA, which itself had given birth to Lambda Legal, the first organization to battle for marriage equality. But Rivera's own organization for the trans youth of New York, without the help of other gay organizations, soon collapsed. Some lesbian activists repeatedly referred to Rivera as a man in a dress. The GAA refused to fight for trans people or the homeless youth who had fought at Stonewall. In 1973, Rivera left the movement.

That year, Randy Wicker met Marsha P. Johnson, the Black trans veteran of Stonewall and the cofounder of STAR. At the time, Wicker still identified drag queens and trans women as an obstacle to the gay movement. "The drag queen is something we've been stuck with," he explained to one television audience.

In the 1970s, Wicker opened a new antique shop in Greenwich Village, and Johnson became a minor celebrity, modeling for Andy Warhol and performing with a drag group. By 1980, Johnson and Wicker had become friends, and after she became homeless once more, she moved into Wicker's apartment.

For twelve years, they lived together, and Johnson became the house mother of Wicker's extended gay family. When Wicker's lover of eighteen years, David Combs, fell ill with AIDS, Johnson took care of him. She was by Combs's side when he died in 1990.

On July 6, 1992, the NYPD pulled Johnson's body from the Hudson River. Without an investigation, officials quickly ruled her death a suicide. Wicker believed it to be a murder, and he protested the police's declaration. To this day, the case remains open. At Johnson's funeral procession, Randy Wicker and Sylvia Rivera walked side by side, and he apologized for his lifetime of transphobia. He had been, as he later called himself, a "male chauvinist pig."

Before Rivera died of liver cancer in 2002, she called for the destruction of the Human Rights Campaign, a national gay rights organization that had excluded trans rights from its proposed Employment Non-Discrimination Act. Even without trans protections, Congress still refused to pass the bill. President George W. Bush still threatened to veto it.

Randy Wicker, after closing his antique shop in 2003, transformed his high-rise Hoboken apartment into a shrine to Marsha P. Johnson, whom he deemed a saint. Today, his walls are covered with her image, trans flags, and a poster of Saint Bayard Rustin. At the age of eighty-one, he continues to march in his wheelchair, wearing Marsha P. Johnson buttons, at trans protests and vigils across New York City. As a member of the Reclaim Pride Coalition, he avoided the 2019 Pride Parade, which now travels south from Madison Square Park. Instead, he marched as he did in 1970—from the Village to Central Park—in a large mass of demonstrators, without the participation of corporations or police departments and in the original spirit of pride, the emotion of resistance.

That weekend, Stonewall veteran Yvonne Ritter, a retired nurse and a volunteer at the New York LGBT Community Center, celebrated her sixty-eighth birthday in Brooklyn.

In twenty-eight states, it is still legal for private companies to discriminate against LGBTQ+ Americans. Under the Trump administration, transgender citizens are still barred from serving in the United States military.

KAMENY'S OWN WAR, the personal war waged against him by the United States federal government, ended during the Obama administration. Kameny was happy to attend his friends' weddings, but he no longer had an interest in the institution himself. Despite his wishes, he had not found a long-term love interest since Keith, the undergraduate who had first helped Kameny come out of the closet in Tucson, Arizona, six decades earlier.

On April 23, 2009, the director of the Office of Personnel Management (OPM), the agency that had replaced the Civil Service Commission in 1979, took his oath of office. With Obama's appointment, John Berry became the highest-ranking gay official in American history. Michelle Obama and Frank Kameny, eighty-three, attended his swearing-in ceremony.

Two months later, on June 17, Kameny stood in the Oval Office, peering over the president's shoulder as he expanded the health benefits for the partners of gay federal employees.

The next week, on June 24, Kameny returned to the OPM headquarters. While Kameny sat on a stage, flanked by a row of American flags, Berry presented him with one last letter from the federal government.

"Dear Dr. Kameny: In what we know today was a shameful action, the United States Civil Service Commission in 1957 upheld your dismissal from your job solely on the basis of your sexual orientation," it began.

"With the fervent passion of a true patriot, you did not resign yourself to your fate or quietly endure this wrong. With courage and strength, you fought back.

"Please accept our apology for the consequences of the previous policy of the United States government."

After Berry finished reading the letter, Kameny stood. "Apology accepted," he said.

The purges continued in the military. Since the implementation of "Don't Ask, Don't Tell," over thirteen thousand service members had been discharged from the United States Armed Forces because of their sexual orientation.

On December 22, 2010, Obama signed the repeal of the ban before an audience of five hundred people. He thanked the politicians and the military leaders who had enabled the reform. "And finally," he said, "I want to express my gratitude to the men and women in this room who have worn the uniform of the United States Armed Services."

As the room applauded, Kameny sat in the front row of the audience, wearing his Combat Infantryman Badge.

A few months later, on July 21, 2011, the space shuttle *Atlantis* landed on a Florida runway. After 135 shuttle missions, it marked the end of NASA's human spaceflight program. A crowd of NASA employees met the shuttle's crew on the runway, where they wept for the end of an era.

Frank Kameny had wanted to be one of them. Every now and then, he still wondered what life would have been like if his government had accepted him for being gay—where he would have traveled, what systems he would have invented, what stars he would have seen.

At the age of eighty-six, Kameny remained proudest of just one thing:

his formulation of the simple, logical assertion, once unfathomable, that homosexuality was morally good.

"Here you are a national hero on a small scale," he had told Clifford Norton, the victorious yet closeted former NASA employee, in 1969. "You have fought the very Government of the United States itself, and won."

"If I were you, just now, impoverishment and all," he continued, "I'd be holding my head up in pride and looking ANYone straight in the eye and saying: I'm a Homosexual and so what. Accept me on MY terms or you don't get me, and you'll lose more than I will. And that includes your family."

"The closet is getting very stuffy. Come out. The fresh air and the sunshine are invigorating."

Kameny died in his sleep on October 11, 2011, a sensible day to die, since it was National Coming Out Day.

"*Gay is good*. It is."

And that is that.

The Oval Office, June 17, 2009

SOURCES AND ACKNOWLEDGMENTS

The history of this book begins in Frank Kameny's attic. In 2005, at the age of eighty, he was living in near destitution. He owned only his house and his personal papers: tens of thousands of pages of letters, transcripts, and other documents from the cases of countless men and women whom he had assisted in their fights against the federal government. Kameny described himself as a "pack rat" and almost never discarded the letters he received—or copies of letters he sent—for the entirety of his life as a gay activist. In his attic and throughout the rest of his house, his papers had acquired a disconcertingly thick layer of dust and mold.

Unable to pay his bills, Kameny sometimes called a friend, Charles Francis, for financial assistance. After one of these calls, Francis had an idea. The historically significant papers were worth something, he reasoned; perhaps Kameny could sell them. Francis and another volunteer, Bob Witeck, cofounded the Kameny Papers Project, which hired an appraiser and raised enough money to buy the papers from Kameny. In 2006, the Kameny Papers Project donated the collection to the Library of Congress. By 2008, the Library had completed processing the papers, a collection so large that if you stacked its contents one on top of another, the pile would rise taller than a six-story building. Because of Francis and Witeck's effort, future generations of scholars gained the ability to access a crucial part of our history, and Kameny himself gained a source of income for the next five years, until his death in 2011.

I discovered Kameny's name in the spring of 2013, just more than a year later. I was in need of a topic for a research paper in an undergraduate urban history seminar, and after searching for "Harvey Milk," the only gay activist I knew, Harvard's library database suggested Kameny's name. I was surprised to learn that although historians had long identified Kameny as the grandfather of the gay rights movement, no one had written a book about him. With the help and encouragement of my instructors, Professor Samuel Zipp and teaching fellow Claire Dunning, I traveled to the Manuscript Division of the Library of Congress for the first time.

I quickly realized that I was staring at the hidden history of the American gay rights movement, and I became obsessed with telling the story of the MSW. That summer, with funding from the Harvard-Cambridge Summer Scholarship, I researched the FBI's surveillance of Kameny's organization. I did so under the supervision of Peter Martland at the University of Cambridge; he had immediately predicted J. Edgar Hoover's preoccupation with the homosexuals and guided me to the organization's 900-page FBI file. Since that summer, Peter has become an invaluable mentor and a remarkable friend.

The following year, my seminar paper on the Mattachine Society of Washington evolved into my senior thesis, with the help and encouragement of other brilliant scholars at Harvard: Brett Flehinger, Summer Shafer, Ari Hoffman, Heidi Tworek, Tomiko Brown-Nagin, and Vincent Brown.

After completing my thesis, I decided I couldn't abandon the story. Frank Kameny deserved a book. On a whim, I sent my thesis to several literary agents, and only one replied: Dan Lazar at Writers House. He responded with helpful notes (my thesis sounded too much like a thesis), and four years later, I emailed him again with a book proposal. Since then, he has been the world's greatest champion of both my book and my career, and I can't thank him enough.

I returned to Cambridge in 2014 with the naïve hope of writing a book in a year, over the course of an MPhil degree program. Under the supervision of Peter Martland and with gracious funding from the Harvard-Cambridge Scholarship, I was able to spend several weeks in the Library of Congress, where I digitized tens of thousands of documents from Kameny's collection. I'm grateful to the staff of the Manuscript Division, including Ryan Reft, for putting up with me during this process.

I soon understood that I needed significantly more time to tell the

MSW's story in the context of the 1960s. I am grateful to the Gates Cambridge Trust and my doctoral supervisor, Gary Gerstle, for enabling me to spend the next four years tracing the connections between the MSW and the homophile and other movements. I am indebted to the staff of the New York Public Library's Manuscripts Division, the US National Archives, the ONE Archives at the University of Southern California, the W. R. Poage Legislative Library at Baylor University, and the Seeley G. Mudd Manuscript Library at Princeton University for assisting me with my archival research.

At Cambridge, in addition to Gary and Peter, I am grateful to the administration and fellows of Emmanuel College, including Dame Fiona Reynolds, Jeremy Caddick, Helen Waterson, Chris Whitton, and the entirety of the porters' lodge for supporting and tolerating a sometimes disruptive and often confused American. Moreover, Andrew Preston and Jonathan Bell offered exceedingly helpful questions and critiques during my PhD defense.

This book would not have been possible without the activists and allies who shared their remarkable stories with me in dozens of hours of interviews. They include, in roughly chronological order, Randy Wicker, Bob Hardgrave, Christopher Kaufman, Paul Kuntzler, Richard Rosendall, Zona Hostetler, Eva Freund, Martha Shelley, Nancy Tucker, R. D. Carter Jr., Michael McConnell, Richard Mulvey, Bob Witeck, Susan Clarke, Joel Martin, Michael Bedwell, Yvonne Ritter, Kay Tobin Lahusen, and Lou Chibbaro Jr. Through email correspondence, Deborah Carliner and her son, Jacob Remes, provided me with valuable descriptions of David Carliner, the heroic NCACLU attorney. I am particularly grateful to Charles Francis and Pate Felts for their help throughout the research process.

Because many of the characters in this book passed away before I had the chance to speak with them, I am indebted to the scholars who were gracious enough to share their own interviews: David K. Johnson, Genny Beemyn, Eric Marcus, and Adam Nagourney. Douglas Charles generously shared several extraordinary FBI files, which I had been unable to acquire from the federal bureaucracy. Several other historians provided advice and insight while I wrote this book, including John D'Emilio, Lillian Faderman, William Eskridge Jr., and Michael G. Long. Jeff Donahoe and Philip Clark of the Rainbow History Project provided me other essential sources. I am also grateful to Matthew Riemer for his comments on my manuscript during the editing process.

I am thankful for those at Farrar, Straus and Giroux who believed in and guided this project to publication, including my editor, Colin Dickerman, and the others on the *Deviant's* team: Jeff Seroy, Ian Van Wye, and June Park, not to mention the many others who worked behind the scenes.

A humbling number of friends also made this book possible. Amy Alemu supported, prodded, and inspired me from day one, and I can't describe a better historian or friend. Month after month, Jimmy Biblarz shared access to online historical resources that became invaluable after the Cambridge University Library refused, despite student pressure, to invest in essential LGBTQ+ databases. Courtney Froehlig, Ruth Lawlor, and Hana Le provided wise comments after reading my manuscript, and I am also grateful for their friendship. Caroline McKay constantly reminded me to write this book; she also gave me moral support and champagne. Nick Cion and Elizabeth Holden helped me through the daunting beginnings of the publication process. David Manella shared his own access to source materials and offered his legal prowess before I signed a book contract. Johnathon Davis, Megan Edwards, Jen Zhu, Brennen Cain, and Melissa Mullins helped me access periodicals or archival materials while I lived abroad. In Los Angeles, Gregory Lehrmann, Jack Dodge, Nate McLeod, and Nate Makuch helped me navigate the world of podcasts and publicity. I am overwhelmingly thankful for all of these people.

Adam Powell, my boyfriend, often introduces himself as my manager. Not only is he my greatest day-to-day advocate and advisor, but he never fails to make me laugh at the absurdity of the human condition. For that, I am grateful, and I love him deeply.

Last and most important is my mother, Lynn Cervini. She raised me singlehandedly, and my interest in social justice began with her. When I was a child, long before I knew I was gay, she brought me to antiwar marches and AIDS memorial services. She took me to conferences to strategize for the legalization of gay marriage. The first wedding I recall attending was between two women. She has sacrificed an immeasurable amount for me, and she has never failed to support me, even when I inexplicably spurned other opportunities so that I could continue working on this project. And, in a more literal sense, this book would not be possible without her: she served as an indefatigable research assistant, helping me transcribe dozens of hours of interviews over the past seven years. In the process, she became the world's leading expert on many of the characters in this book, intimately familiar with their stories and voices. I will never be able to properly express my gratitude to my mother for all she has done for me, but as part of that larger effort, I have dedicated this book to her.

Christopher Street Liberation Day, June 28, 1970

NOTES

INTRODUCTION: THE RITUAL

3 *For ten years . . . of the men*: John F. Galliher, Wayne Brekhus, and David P. Keys, *Laud Humphreys: Prophet of Homosexuality and Sociology* (Madison, WI: University of Wisconsin Press, 2006), 16–17.

3 *As always, the . . . looking, touching, fellatio*: Laud Humphreys, "Chapter Four: Patterns of Collective Action," in *Tearoom Trade: Impersonal Sex in Public Places* (New Brunswick: Aldine Transaction, 1970), 59–80.

3 *"Like the smell . . . of the interaction"*: Ibid., 84.

3 *But if all . . . hurt, nobody offended*: Ibid., 78.

3 *In 1966, as . . . public park restrooms*: Ibid., 31.

3 *Married with two children*: Galliher, Brekhus, and Keys, *Laud Humphreys*, 16.

3 *He adopted the . . . he nodded*: Humphreys, *Tearoom Trade*, 26–28.

3 *"By passing as . . . hidden tape recorder*: Ibid., 178.

3 *The next step . . . of the men*: Ibid., 37–38.

4 *He waited a . . . their lives*: Ibid., 42, 114.

4 *Over half of . . . women*: Ibid., 105.

4 *The rest . . . as safe havens*: Ibid., 122–29.

4 *gay bars were . . . were watching*: Genny Beemyn, *A Queer Capital: a History of Gay Life in Washington, D.C.* (New York: Routledge, 2015), 117.

4 *Sometimes, police officers . . . conduct*: See, for example, "6 Arrested in Perversion Case Here," *San Francisco Chronicle*, June 22, 1956, 3.

4 *The names, addresses . . . Laurel Street*: Ibid.

4 *After World War . . . sexual deviation*: This estimate can be found in William N. Eskridge Jr., *Gaylaw: Challenging the Apartheid of the Closet* (Cambridge, MA: Harvard University Press, 1999), 60.

4 *Men unable to . . . hands and disappeared*: Humphreys, *Tearoom Trade*, 80.

4 *Laud Humphreys ultimately . . . incentivizing blackmailers*: Ibid., 89.

5 *He estimated that . . . the tearoom*: Ibid., 9.

5 *"What the covert . . . such a device"*: Ibid., 154.

5 *The sociologist also . . . of the tearoom*: Humphreys, "Chapter Seven: The Breastplate of Righteousness," in *Tearoom Trade*, 131–48.

5 *With the publication . . . teaching contract*: Ibid., 128; Galliher, Brekhus, and Keys, *Laud Humphreys*, 27; Myron Glazer, *The Research Adventure: Promise and Problems of Field Work* (New York: Random House, 1972), 107–24.

5 *Humphreys eventually repudiated . . . of his methodology*: Galliher, Brekhus, and Keys, *Laud Humphreys*, 45.

5 *at a 1974 . . . gay man*: Ibid., 78.

5 *Sociology professors now . . . of propriety*: For a survey of Humphreys's appearance in sociology textbooks, see ibid., 43–47.

5 *A young Harvard-educated . . . in the ritual*: In dozens of hours of interviews in the 1970s and his later years, Kameny (hereafter, "FEK") avoided discussion of his 1956 arrest. See for example, FEK, interviewed by Kay Tobin Lahusen, Washington, D.C., 1971 (hereafter, "Lahusen interview"); Barbara Gittings and Kay Tobin Lahusen Papers, New York Public Library, New York, New York (hereafter, "Gittings Papers"); FEK, interviewed by Dudley Clendinen, telephone, 1993.

5 *That summer evening, as . . . the restroom*: "The People of California vs. Franklin Edward Kameny," Box 45, Folder 3, Franklin Edward Kameny Papers, Library of Congress, Washington, D.C. (hereafter, "FEK Papers"); Kameny, "Statement Regarding Arrest," November 2, 1958, Box 44, Folder 7, FEK Papers.

1. THE ASTRONOMER

7 *As a teenager . . . emigrating from Poland*: Lahusen interview.
7 *Rae Beck Kameny . . . in southeastern Queens*: Rae Beck Kameny, interviewed by David K. Johnson, New York, NY, 1992 (hereafter, "Rae Beck Kameny interview"). I am indebted to Professor Johnson for sharing the audio file of this interview. For more on Richmond Hill, see Kenneth T. Jackson, *The Encyclopedia of New York City* (New Haven: Yale University Press, 2011), 5716.
7 *Franklin's parents quickly . . . "that was that"*: Lahusen interview.
8 *The short, hazel-eyed . . . he would obey*: Rae Beck Kameny interview.
8 *In school, he . . . age of twelve*: Lahusen interview.
8 *A rational boy . . . girls*: Ibid.
8 *As the years . . . reject society itself*: Ibid.
8 *If society and . . . that was that*: Ibid.
8 *At Richmond Hill . . . in sports*: Ibid.
9 *He claimed to . . . recall meeting them*: Rae Beck Kameny interview.
9 *He went on . . . the skies*: Lahusen interview.
9 *He founded an . . . York City planetarium*: Rae Beck Kameny interview.
9 *His mother bought . . . the stars, alone*: Frank E. Kameny, "An Informal, Condensed Autobiography," Box 43, Folder 11, FEK Papers.
9 *"His work in . . . work too seriously"*: Letter from Lyndon D. Burton, March 23, 1943, Box 157, Folder 2, FEK Papers.
9 *He felt at . . . explained*: Lahusen interview.
9 *"He has a . . . of true Americanism"*: Letter from Irene D. Casey, March 18, 1943, Box 157, Folder 2, FEK Papers.
9 *Frank Kameny enrolled . . . a few weeks*: Lahusen interview.
9 *when hundreds of . . . December 7, 1941*: "Japan Wars on U.S. and Britain," *The New York Times*, December 8, 1941, 1.
9 *When America entered . . . age was twenty-one*: David T. Zabecki, *World War II in Europe: An Encyclopedia* (New York: Garland, 1999), 55.
9 *Kameny continued his . . . continue unbroken*: FEK, "An Informal, Condensed Autobiography," Box 43, Folder 11, FEK Papers.
9 *But in November . . . six months*: Dorit Geva, *Conscription, Family, and the Modern State: A Comparative Study of France and the United States* (Cambridge: Cambridge University Press, 2013), 180.
9 *His family scrambled . . . linguists in training*: Lahusen interview; Robert R. Palmer, Bell I. Wiley, and William R. Keast, *The Army Ground Forces: The Procurement and Training of Ground Combat Troops* (Washington, D.C.: Army Ground Forces Historical Division, Department of the Army, 1948), 31.
10 *The ASTP required . . . enroll in courses*: Ibid., 36.
10 *So on May . . . joined the army*: Letter from Rae B. Kameny and Emil Kameny, May 14, 1943, Box 157, Folder 2, FEK Papers; FEK, interviewed by Lara Ballard, Washington, D.C., January 8, 2003, Veterans History Project, Library of Congress (hereafter, "Ballard interview").
10 *At the induction . . . and a questionnaire*: For more on the induction process, see Harold J. Harris, "The Cornell Selectee Index: An Aid in Psychiatric Diagnosis," *Annals of the New York Academy of Sciences* 46, no. 7 (July 1946), 593–608.
10 *As he completed . . . unpleasant to you?"*: In later years, Kameny remembered answering the question in a written form. It is possible that he was one of the first men to take the Cornell Selectee Index, which was first used and evaluated in New York City, 1943. See Ballard interview; Harry Grant, "A Rapid Personality Evaluation Based on the Minnesota Multiphasic Personality Inventory and the Cornell Selectee Index," *The American Journal of Psychiatry* 103, no. 1 (July 1946), 33–41; Arthur Weider et al., "The Cornell Selectee Index," *The Journal of the American Medical Association* 124, no. 4 (January 1944), 224–28.
10 *eighteen million other inductees*: Allan Bérubé, *Coming Out Under Fire: The History of Gay Men and Women in World War II* (Chapel Hill: University of North Carolina Press, 1990), 33.
10 *had to prove . . . society," as psychiatrists*: Weider et al., "The Cornell Selectee Index," 225.
10 *Since early 1942 . . . a "patulous rectum"*: Bérubé, *Coming Out Under Fire*, 19–20.
10 *But as examiners . . . professional psychiatrist*: Ibid.; Weider et al., "The Cornell Selectee Index," 227.
10 *Like the vast . . . Kameny checked "no"*: Ballard interview.
10 *At basic training . . . of early 1944*: Ibid.
10 *In February, only . . . ASTP*: Marshall noted an "outstanding deficiency" of noncommissioned officers with "satisfactory standards of intelligence and qualities of leadership." Officers in the Army Ground Forces

considered the ASTP wasteful, especially since it removed men of high intelligence from the essential units that needed them most: headquarters, topographical, and radio intelligence signal companies. See Palmer, Wiley, and Keast, *The Army Ground Forces*, 38–39.

10 *"The rug was . . . eighty-one-millimeter mortar*: Ballard interview.

11 *In November 1944 . . . the terrified men*: Ibid.

11 *The ASTP fiasco . . . onto the battlefield*: Indeed, if he had not participated in the program, Kameny could have enrolled in an officer candidate school, thereby avoiding combat at such a low rank. See Palmer, Wiley, and Keast, *The Army Ground Forces*, 39.

11 *Kameny had placed . . . dirty deal"*: Rae Beck Kameny interview.

11 *Kameny's ship slowly . . . the weapons*: Ballard interview.

11 *the first man-made . . . travel into space*: Chris Forrester, *High Above: The Untold Story of Astra, Europe's Leading Satellite Company* (London: Springer, 2010), 130.

11 *They looked like . . . the sky*: Ballard interview.

11 *By the time . . . Netherlands, he fought*: Ibid.

11 *As part of . . . would feast*: Lahusen interview.

12 *"We lost quite . . . the subject*: Ballard interview.

12 *Kameny was in . . . unit*: Ibid.

12 *It was a . . . ever seen*: Lahusen interview.

12 *On March 24 . . . of his mind*: Ballard interview.

12 *Historians have described . . . in battle*: John D'Emilio, *Sexual Politics, Sexual Communities: The Making of a Homosexual Minority in the United States, 1940–1970* (Chicago: University of Chicago, 1983), 24. See also Bérubé, *Coming Out Under Fire.*

12 *Kameny, however, had . . . so many"*: Ballard interview.

12 *Kameny returned to . . . in astronomy*: Lahusen interview.

12 *During Kameny's first . . . not yet*: Ibid.

13 *By 1949, he . . . miles away*: "New 61-Inch Telescope Installed at Oak Ridge," *The Harvard Crimson*, December 18, 1933; Adam M. Guren, "Historic Telescope Takes Last Gaze Skyward," *The Harvard Crimson*, August 5, 2005; "Oak Ridge," Smithsonian National Air and Space Museum, n.d., https://airandspace.si.edu/exhibitions/explore-the-universe/online/kiosks/whatsnew/overview.cfm.

13 *Every few years . . . glass*: Ibid.; John Strong, "The Evaporation Process and Its Application to the Aluminizing of Large Telescope Mirrors," *The Astrophysical Journal* 83, no. 5 (June 1936), 401; Richard J. Wainscoat, "University of Hawaii 2.2-Meter Telescope Primary Mirror Aluminization," University of Hawaii Institute for Astronomy (2005), https://www.ifa.hawaii.edu/88inch/aluminizing.htm.

13 *Not only did . . . astronomy library*: See Franklin E. Kameny and Harlan J. Smith, *A Manual for Aluminization at the Agassiz Station of the Harvard College Observatory* (Cambridge, MA: Harvard University Observatory, 1952). The Harvard library catalog entry is available at http://id.lib.harvard.edu/aleph/005687531/catalog.

13 *He taught Harvard . . . men of Yale*: FEK, "An Informal, Condensed Autobiography," FEK Papers; John M. Broder, "Edward M. Kennedy, Senate Stalwart, Is Dead at 77," *New York Times*, August 26, 2009, https://www.nytimes.com/2009/08/27/us/politics/27kennedy.html; "Stevenson, Adlai Ewing III," *Biographical Directory of the United States Congress*, http://bioguide.congress.gov/scripts/biodisplay.pl?index=s000890.

13 *As Kameny became . . . a year there*: Lahusen interview.

14 *In Tucson, Kameny . . . stars above him?*: Ibid.

14 *That summer, the . . . the observatory*: Ibid.

14 *Kameny and Keith . . . two decades*: Ibid. See also Jose Antonio Vargas, "Signs of Progress," *The Washington Post*, July 23, 2005, C1.

15 *Kameny returned to . . . fall of 1955*: E. M. Lindsay, "Report of Proceedings of Armagh Observatory," *Monthly Notices of the Royal Astronomical Society* 116, no. 2 (1956), 171.

15 *Bars that attracted . . . 1950s*: John D'Emilio and Estelle B. Freedman, *Intimate Matters: A History of Sexuality in America* (Chicago: University of Chicago Press, 1988), 291.

15 *Scollay Square had . . . men foregathered"*: Joseph P. Kahn, "Harvard Square's Club Casablanca Closes for Good," *The Boston Globe*, December 30, 2012; Douglass Shand-Tucci, *The Crimson Letter: Harvard, Homosexuality, and the Shaping of American Culture* (New York: St. Martin's Press, 2003), 93–98; Joan Ilacqua and Andrew Elder, "LGBTQ Freedom Trail," *Boston Pride 2015* (Boston: New Boston Pride Committee, 2015), 95–96.

15 *Faced with such . . . elaboration*: Lahusen interview.

15 *Kameny completed and . . . that June*: FEK, "An Informal, Condensed Autobiography," FEK Papers.

16 *The junior senator . . . and intellectuals"*: John F. Kennedy, "Harvard Commencement Speech," June 14, 1956, Series 11, Papers of John F. Kennedy, Harvard University.

16 *On the evening . . . train terminal*: E. F. Carpenter, "The Berkeley Joint Meeting of the Astronomical Society of the Pacific and the American Astronomical Society," *Publications of the Astronomical Society of the Pacific* 68, no. 405 (1956), 562; Kameny, "An Informal, Condensed Autobiography," FEK Papers.

16 *It had been . . . government*: Ibid., 564.

16   *by 12:45 a.m. . . . parts of KAMENY"*: "The People of California vs. Franklin Edward Kameny," Box 45, Folder 3, FEK Papers; Kameny, "Statement Regarding Arrest," November 2, 1958, Box 44, Folder 7, FEK Papers.

16   *Kameny later claimed . . . seconds*: Kameny, "Statement Regarding Arrest," November 2, 1958, Box 44, Folder 7, FEK Papers.

16   *"When questioned both . . . the officers*: "The People of California vs. Franklin Edward Kameny," Box 45, Folder 3, FEK Papers.

17   *Kameny spent the . . . and loitering*: His first violation was Section 215 of the municipal police code, which prohibited engaging in or soliciting any "lewd, indecent, or obscene act or conduct." Second was Section 647.5 of the California Penal Code, which specifically defined "every lewd or dissolute person, or every person who loiters in or about public toilets in public parks" as "a vagrant" facing punishment of up to six months in prison. See ibid.

17   *The next morning . . . of reassuring news*: Kameny, "Statement Regarding Arrest," November 2, 1958, Box 44, Folder 7, FEK Papers.

17   *If he complied . . . Guilty, Case Dismissed"*: "The People of California vs. Franklin Edward Kameny," FEK Papers.

2. THE LETTER

18   *In 1916, Dr. . . . Boston*: James H. Jones, *Alfred C. Kinsey: A Life* (New York: W. W. Norton, 2004), 129, 138–40, 169.

18   *He remained quiet . . . later described him*: Wardell B. Pomeroy, *Dr. Kinsey and the Institute for Sex Research* (New Haven: Yale University Press, 1982), 37.

18   *The blue-eyed, bow-tied . . . new marriage course*: Jones, *Alfred C. Kinsey*, 326.

18   *Scientists, Kinsey observed . . . about farm animals*: Alfred C. Kinsey, Wardell B. Pomeroy, and Clyde E. Martin, *Sexual Behavior in the Human Male* (Bloomington: Indiana University Press, 1948), 3.

18   *He paid no . . . only—bars for homosexuals*: Regina Markell Morantz, "The Scientist as Sex Crusader: Alfred C. Kinsey and American Culture," *American Quarterly* 29, no. 5 (1977), 569.

18   *Sexual Behavior in . . . only five thousand copies*: "Dr. Kinsey Is Dead; Sex Researcher, 62," *The New York Times*, August 26, 1956, 1.

18   *The New York . . . million copies*: Morantz, "The Scientist as Sex Crusader," 564.

18   *Kinsey admitted he . . . of the country"*: Kinsey, Pomeroy, and Martin, *Sexual Behavior in the Human Male*, 625.

19   *Kinsey also found . . . sexual activity*: D'Emilio, *Sexual Politics, Sexual Communities*, 34.

19   *His downfall began . . . to female pleasure*: Alfred C. Kinsey, *Sexual Behavior in the Human Female* (Philadelphia: Saunders, 1953), 468.

19   *Accused of "hurling . . . lost his funding*: Morantz, "The Scientist as Sex Crusader," 575.

19   *By 1956 . . . Sex Research*: "Dr. Kinsey Is Dead," *The New York Times*, April 26, 1956, 1.

19   *"No single event"*: "Medicine: 5,940 Women," *TIME*, August 24, 1953, 53.

19   *In 1950, a . . . the various states"*: Hugh M. Hefner, "The *Playboy* Philosophy," *Playboy* 12, no. 11, November 1965, 69.

19   *The student, Hugh . . . three years later*: See *Playboy* 1, no. 1, December 1953.

19   *On August 25 . . . California, Berkeley*: Kinsey died at 8:00 a.m. ET, while the opening scientific session of the AAS began at 9:00 a.m. PST. "Activities of the Society," *Publications of the Astronomical Society of the Pacific* 68, no. 402, June 1956, 283; Jones, *Alfred C. Kinsey*, 768.

19   *Because of the . . . 37 percent*: D'Emilio, *Sexual Politics, Sexual Communities*, 35.

20   *Kameny arrived in . . . of his own*: Lahusen interview.

20   *In the early . . . contained slave pens*: Carol W. Gelderman, *A Free Man of Color and His Hotel: Race, Reconstruction, and the Role of the Federal Government* (Washington, D.C.: Potomac Books, 2012), 8.

20   *in 1885, after . . . trees for cover*: Beemyn, *A Queer Capital*, 21–22. See also Jeb Alexander and Ina Russell, *Jeb and Dash: A Diary of Gay Life, 1918–1945* (Boston: Faber and Faber, 1994).

20   *Washington did not . . . 1930 and 1950*: David K. Johnson, *The Lavender Scare: The Cold War Persecution of Gays and Lesbians in the Federal Government* (Chicago: University of Chicago Press, 2004), 43.

20   *The city scrambled . . . living together*: Beemyn, *A Queer Capital*, 33.

20   *The gay bars . . . Sundays*: Ibid., 102.

21   *The gay bars . . . workers*: Jack Nichols, interviewed by Genny Beemyn, telephone, May 20, 1995.

21   *But at night . . . God have mercy on such as we"*: Jack Nichols, "Chapter Two," in *Memoirs of Jack Nichols: Unfinished and Unedited*, Jack Nichols Photographs and Papers, Rainbow History Project, https://archives.rainbowhistory.org/items/show/119.

21   *On the next . . . to be everywhere*: Beemyn, *A Queer Capital*, 130; Johnson, *The Lavender Scare*, 164.

21   *Though Washington did . . . for them*: Beemyn, *A Queer Capital*, 105–6.

21   *In total, by . . . bars, was white*: Ibid., 102.

21   *Fear of persecution . . . homosexuals*: Ibid., 22, 138, 143.

21 *"Never a week . . . 1947*: Ibid., 140, 144.

22 *The Washington police . . . kill her*: Ibid., 112.

22 *Saturdays at midnight . . . later recalled*: Lahusen interview; Frank Kameny, interviewed by Genny Beemyn, Washington, D.C., March 20, 1994.

22 *Kameny's network expanded . . . two mammoth cottages*: Lahusen interview.

22 *Acting as a . . . later remarked*: Ibid.

23 *Hundreds, perhaps thousands . . . came with it*: Ibid.

23 *Georgetown University did . . . later told investigators*: "Report of Special Interview," November 26, 1957, *Kameny v. Brucker* (1959), Case 1628–59, Accession #021–74A-6269, Box 122, National Archives (Kansas City).

23 *Before fear, there . . . from the new"*: Paul Dickson, *Sputnik: The Shock of the Century* (Lincoln: University of Nebraska Press, 2019), 1.

23 *"Red 'Moon' Flies . . . page*: "Red 'Moon' Flies 18,000 M.P.H.," *The Washington Evening Star*, October 5, 1957, 1.

23 *"Soviets Fire Earth . . . own eyes*: William J. Jorden, "Soviets Fire Earth Satellite Into Space," *The New York Times*, October 5, 1957, 1.

23 *In the days . . . wrote*: "Red 'Moon' Flies 18,000 M.P.H.," 1.

24 *Not only did . . . development*: "Device Is 8 Times Heavier Than One Planned by U.S.," *The New York Times*, October 5, 1957, 1.

24 *The public contemplated . . . LIFE magazine*: Walter A. McDougall, *The Heavens and the Earth: A Political History of the Space Age* (New York: Basic Books, 1985), 141–42.

24 *Technology and its . . . concluded LIFE magazine*: Ibid., 145.

24 *If America wanted . . . important citizens*: There were only 150 attendees at the 1950 meeting of the American Astronomical Society, a number that grew to five hundred in 1960. See Ronald E. Doel, *Solar System Astronomy in America: Communities, Patronage, and Interdisciplinary Science, 1920–1960* (Cambridge: Cambridge University Press, 1996), 188.

24 *Frank Kameny had . . . Army Map Service*: Lahusen interview.

24 *To send a . . . scientists like Kameny*: Ibid.

24 *He explained his . . . that distance*: Ibid.

25 *Nine days after . . . years away"*: L. Edgar Prina, "'Operation Moon' Becomes New Goal for the World's Space Scientists," *The Washington Evening Star*, October 13, 1957, A29.

25 *America's only successful ballistic missiles*: Martin L. Gross, "Nickerson Sees U.S. Losing Missile Race," *The Washington Evening Star*, September 8, 1957, 1; Dickson, *Sputnik*, 124.

25 *had been publicly . . . technology, since 1952*: See Wernher von Braun, "Crossing the Last Frontier," *Collier's*, March 22, 1952, 24.

25 *In the . . . told the Star*: L. Edgar Prina, "Longer Range Missiles Called Infantry Need," *The Washington Evening Star*, October 27, 1957, 7.

25 *When America created . . . to volunteer*: Lahusen interview.

25 *The letter arrived . . . Island of Hawaii*: "Memo Routing Slip," October 24, 1957, Box 43, Folder 12, FEK Papers.

25 *"It is necessary . . . and classifying employees*: B. D. Hull to Franklin E. Kameny, October 15, 1957, Box 43, Folder 12, FEK Papers.

25 *A mistake had . . . himself*: Lahusen interview.

26 *"It is hoped . . . personnel officer*: B. D. Hull to Franklin E. Kameny, October 15, 1957, Box 43, Folder 12, FEK Papers.

26 *He watched the . . . was imminent*: Dickson, *Sputnik*, 141.

26 *On November 7 . . . said Eisenhower*: Dwight D. Eisenhower, *Public Papers of the Presidents of the United States: Dwight D. Eisenhower, 1957* (Washington, D.C.: United States Government Printing Office, 1999), 799. See also McDougall, *The Heavens and the Earth*, 150.

26 *On Tuesday, November . . . care to make?"*: "Report of Special Interview," November 26, 1957, *Kameny v. Brucker* (1959), Case 1628–59, Accession #021–74A-6269, Box 122, National Archives (Kansas City).

26 *Four months earlier . . . Charge Dismissed"*: "Application for Federal Employment," Franklin E. Kameny Personnel File, National Personnel Records Center, Annex, NARA (Valmeyer, Illinois).

27 *Despite his disclosure . . . three days later*: "Notification of Personnel Action: Temporary Appointment," Franklin E. Kameny Personnel File, National Personnel Records Center, Annex, NARA (Valmeyer, Illinois).

27 *"I do not . . . nor did I"*: "Report of Special Interview," November 26, 1957, *Kameny v. Brucker* (1959), Case 1628–59, Accession #021–74A-6269, Box 122, National Archives (Kansas City).

27 *Then, the allegation . . . the interview ended*: Ibid.

27 *On December 6 . . . inferno*: McDougall, *The Heavens and the Earth*, 155.

27 *By then, Kameny . . . for the AMS*: FEK to Commanding Officer, Army Map Service, n.d., Box 43, Folder 12, FEK Papers.

27   *"Dr. Kameny," asked . . . USA," he argued*: "Report of Special Interview," December 5, 1957, *Kameny v. Brucker* (1959), Case 1628–59, Accession #021–74A-6269, Box 122, National Archives (Kansas City).
28   *Four days after . . . to respond*: B. D. Hull to Franklin E. Kameny, December 10, 1957, FEK Personnel File, National Personnel Records Center, Annex, NARA (Valmeyer, Illinois).
28   *"I wish to . . . government is concerned"*: We do not know if Kameny truly made a mistake or if he lied in his Form 57 application. He may have been telling the truth, since in the court order that "set aside" his verdict, there was no mention of the charge's title: only "215 MPC." In San Francisco, Kameny may have panicked, focusing on the arrest itself rather than the exact charges. He had spent a year trying to forget the matter, and in Washington, homosexuals usually faced charges of disorderly conduct, not lewd conduct. See "The People of the State of California vs. Franklin Edward Kameny," March 1, 1957, FEK Personnel File, National Personnel Records Center, Annex, NARA (Valmeyer, Illinois). See FEK to Commanding Officer, Army Map Service, n.d., Box 43, Folder 12, FEK Papers; FEK to Commanding Officer, Army Map Service, December 11, 1957, FEK Personnel File, National Personnel Records Center, Annex, NARA (Valmeyer, Illinois).
28   *Kameny submitted the . . . you needed"*: Lahusen interview.
28   *Four days after . . . a "hit"*: Michael J. Neufeld, *Von Braun: Dreamer of Space, Engineer of War* (New York: Alfred A. Knopf, 2007), 317; McDougall, *The Heavens and the Earth*, 155.
29   *Von Braun, meanwhile . . . city of London*: Lahusen interview; Neufeld, *Von Braun*, 163.
29   *The AMS formally . . . States government*: "Notification of Personnel Action: Removal," December 20, 1957, FEK Personnel File, National Personnel Records Center, Annex, NARA (Valmeyer, Illinois).

3. THE PANIC

30   *According to the . . . spoke "sugar-sweetly, softly"*: John R. Schindler, "Redl—Spy of the Century?," *International Journal of Intelligence and Counterintelligence* 18, no. 3, 2005, 490.
30   *Beginning in 1901 . . . in the empire*: Ibid., 488.
30   *In Vienna . . . army officer*: Ibid., 488–89.
30   *Redl closely guarded . . . in return*: Ibid., 492.
30   *He then began . . . the military*: Ibid., 484–87.
31   *Three years later . . . for the empire*: Allen W. Dulles, *The Craft of Intelligence* (New York: Harper & Row, 1963), 123–24. For more on the Redl affair, including outdated versions of the story, see Johnson, *The Lavender Scare*, 108–9; Robert Asprey, *The Panther's Feast* (London: Jonathan Cape, 1959); Richard Rowan, *Secret Service: Thirty-Three Centuries of Espionage* (New York: Hawthorne Books, 1967); Fitzroy Maclean, *Take Nine Spies* (London: Weidenfeld & Nicolson, 1978).
31   *In 1945, only . . . Activities Committee (HUAC)*: Robert Griffith, *The Politics of Fear: Joseph R. McCarthy and the Senate* (Lexington: University Press of Kentucky, 1970), 34.
31   *In the 1946 . . . sixteen years*: Ibid., 38.
31   *In March 1947 . . . loyalty*: Douglas M. Charles, *Hoover's War on Gays: Exposing the FBI's "Sex Deviates" Program* (Lawrence: University Press of Kansas, 2015), 71.
31   *Three months later . . . national security*: Johnson, *The Lavender Scare*, 21.
31   *In September 1949 . . . State Department"*: Griffith, *The Politics of Fear*, 47–49.
32   *Nobody else had . . . his baggage*: Ibid., 50.
32   *His number . . . abjectly"*: "Sewer Politics," *The Washington Post*, February 14, 1950, 10. For more on press coverage of McCarthy, see Edwin R. Bayley, *Joe McCarthy and the Press* (Madison: University of Wisconsin Press, 1981).
32   *On the evening . . . Griffith*: Griffith, *The Politics of Fear*, 57.
32   *Two of the . . . own sexuality*: Senator McCarthy, February 20, 1950, 81st Cong., 2d Sess., Congressional Record, 1978–1979; Johnson, *The Lavender Scare*, 4, 15–16.
32   *Other Republicans took . . . loyalty program*: U.S. Congress, Senate, Subcommittee of the Committee on Appropriations, Departments of State, Justice, Commerce, and the Judiciary Appropriations for 1951, 81st Cong., 2d Sess., February 28, 1950, 603. See also Robert Dean, *Imperial Brotherhood: Gender and the Making of Cold War Foreign Policy* (Amherst: University of Massachusetts Press, 2001), 77; Johnson, *The Lavender Scare*, 18.
32   *And with that . . . the Potomac" began*: "The Washington Sex Story," *New York Post*, July 10, 1950, 4.
32   *And with that . . . Administration"*: Dean, *Imperial Brotherhood*, 77; Johnson, *The Lavender Scare*, 18.
33   *The chief of . . . "emergency condition"*: Johnson, *The Lavender Scare*, 79–80.
33   *The Senate committee . . . security risk"*: U.S. Congress, Senate, Committee on Expenditures in Executive Departments, Investigations Subcommittee, Hearings Pursuant to S. Res. 280, Executive Session, 81st Cong., 2d Sess., July 14, 1950, 2089 (hereafter, "Hoey Hearings").
33   *Of all the . . . violence*: Ibid., 2092.
33   *in fact, a . . . of women"*: Schindler, "Redl—Spy of the Century?," 490.
33   *became the primary . . . come*: Hoey Hearings, 2100. Hillenkoetter cited other cases, but he did so off the record. The committee's final report states that the senators heard how "Nazi and Communist agents have at-

tempted to obtain information from employees of our Government by threatening to expose their abnormal sex activities." The Communists, Hillenkoetter claimed, were successful "in a number of such approaches." See Hoey Hearings, 2102; U.S. Congress, Senate, Committee on Expenditures in the Executive Departments, "Employment of Homosexuals and Other Sex Perverts in Government," Senate Doc. 241, 81st Cong., 2d Sess., 1950, 5 (hereafter, "Hoey Report"). See also Johnson, *The Lavender Scare*, 114.

33 *1. Homosexuals experience . . . of the moment*": Hoey Hearings, 2094–99.

34 *The testimony of . . . the CIA director*: None of the witnesses could provide evidence of blackmail, but the assistant director of the FBI testified that his Bureau had "unquestionable" evidence that "orders have been issued by high Russian intelligence officials" to investigate the private lives of American government officials "to find a clink [*sic*] in their armor and a weakness upon which they might capitalize, at the appropriate time." Ibid., 2125, 2133, 2145, 2155.

34 *the Hoey committee's . . . only example*: Homosexuals were, first and foremost, unsuitable because their homosexuality caused them to lack "emotional stability" and "moral fiber." They attempted to recruit their coworkers into homosexuality and elevate their own: even "one homosexual can pollute a Government office." In its report, the Hoey committee called for an end to the "head-in-the-sand attitude toward the problem of sex perversion" and the full enforcement of regulations that already prohibited immoral conduct. It applauded steps that agencies had taken in response to congressional pressure: the FBI now collected police records of perversion charges from Washington and across the nation, which it then disseminated to the Civil Service Commission. The CSC, in turn, forwarded the arrest information to the relevant agency and ensured that action was taken. The new system worked well; while civilian agencies purged only 192 homosexuals in the three years before April 1950, they purged 382 in the seven months since then—nearly two perverts per day. See Hoey Report, 4, 5, 8.

35 *Hillenkoetter's thirteen principles*: Johnson, *The Lavender Scare*, 115.

35 *David Johnson*: In 2004, Johnson argued that the Lavender Scare, by creating a large number of disillusioned ex–federal employees with little to lose, sparked militant homophile activism. In his chapter on the MSW, Johnson suggested that state persecution contributed to the identity formation of the homosexual minority. This book, on the other hand, examines 1) the ideological implications of that phenomenon within a minority group and 2) the significance of the primary arena (i.e., the courts) in which it took place. This study also suggests that the state-ideological dialectic did not only occur in the MSW, the sole subject of Johnson's chapter, but also across a national homophile network, which allowed the ideological project of gay pride to spread to other regions at a rapid pace. In 2009, moreover, Margot Canaday argued that the federal government's exclusionary policies directly contributed not just to the rise of activism, but also to the formulation of homosexual identity itself. However, unlike the state-focused histories of Johnson and Canaday or the grassroots histories of D'Emilio and Chauncey, this book places emphasis on the conversation *between* the state and a minority group. Gay pride as a self-conscious political strategy emerged in a dialectical process that took place not just in government buildings, picket lines, or homophile meetings, but also in another crucial forum: the courts. What Margot Canaday terms the "Straight State," then, gave rise to the Proud Plaintiff. See Johnson, *The Lavender Scare*, 9–10, 214, Chapter 8; Margot Canaday, *The Straight State: Sexuality and Citizenship in Twentieth-Century America* (Princeton: Princeton University Press, 2009). For other studies that emphasize the role of the state in the construction of gay identity, see Dean, *Imperial Brotherhood*, and Anna Lvovsky, "Queer Expertise: Urban Policing and the Construction of Public Knowledge About Homosexuality, 1920–1970" (PhD dissertation, Harvard University, 2018).

35 *Dwight D. Eisenhower . . . a year*: Johnson, *The Lavender Scare*, 121–23, 134.

35 *McCarthy's downfall came . . . caliber rifle*: Rick Ewig, "McCarthy Era Politics: The Ordeal of Senator Lester Hunt," *Annals of Wyoming* 55, no. 1 (Spring 1983), 9–21. See also Johnson, *The Lavender Scare*, 140–42.

35 *Two days before . . . security clearance*: "Appeal from Removal," Box 44, Folder 1, FEK Papers.

36 *The officials clarified . . . were tied*: FEK to MSNY, May 5, 1960, Box 44, Folder 1, FEK Papers.

36 *First, he wrote . . . truthfulness*": FEK to Philip, n.d., Box 44, Folder 6, FEK Papers.

36 *Yale professor Harlan . . . character*": Harlan J. Smith, "Affidavit," December 31, 1957, Box 44, Folder 6, FEK Papers.

36 *The former director . . . character*": Harlow Shapley, January 1, 1958, Box 44, Folder 6, FEK Papers.

36 *An army friend . . . your plans*": Philip to FEK, n.d., Box 44, Folder 6, FEK Papers.

36 *Yet Kameny's twelve-page . . . his life*: "Appeal from Removal," Box 44, Folder 1, FEK Papers.

37 *Kameny demanded that . . . on totalitarianism*: Ibid.

37 *He twisted the . . . American ones*": Ibid.

37 *In the late . . . lapse in evolution?*: John D'Emilio, *Sexual Politics, Sexual Communities*, 15. See also George Chauncey Jr., "From Sexual Inversion to Homosexuality: Medicine and the Changing Conceptualization of Female 'Deviance,'" in *Passion and Power: Sexuality in History*, ed. Kathy Lee Peiss and Christina Simmons (Philadelphia: Temple University Press, 1989), 98.

37 *In 1909, Dr. . . . . it a sickness*: Benjamin B. Wolman and John Money, *Handbook of Human Sexuality* (Northvale: Jason Aronson, 1980), 306; D'Emilio, *Sexual Politics, Sexual Communities*, 16. For more on the rise and

fall of the medical model of homosexuality, see Ronald Bayer, *Homosexuality and American Psychiatry: The Politics of Diagnosis* (New York: Basic Books, 1987); Jack Drescher and Joseph P. Merlino, *American Psychiatry and Homosexuality: An Oral History* (Hoboken: Taylor and Francis, 2012); Henry L. Minton, *Departing From Deviance: A History of Homosexual Rights and Emancipatory Science in America* (Chicago: University of Chicago Press, 2002); Jennifer Terry, *An American Obsession: Science, Medicine, and Homosexuality in Modern Society* (Chicago: University of Chicago Press, 1999); Kenneth Lewes, *Psychoanalysis and Male Homosexuality* (Lanham, MD: Aronson, 2009).

37 *The "burly, gruff... 1907*: Thelma Z. Lavine, "Benjamin Karpman, M.D. 1888–1962," *Proceedings and Addresses of the American Philosophical Association*, vol. 36 (1962–1963), 116.

37 *He joined the... Washington, in 1920*: Centennial Commission, Centennial Papers, St. Elizabeths Hospital, 1855–1955 (Washington, D.C.: St. Elizabeths Hospital, 1956), 47; Frank Rives Millikan, "Wards of the Nation: The Making of St. Elizabeths Hospital, 1852–1920" (PhD dissertation, The George Washington University, 1990), vi; "To study criminals and help these unfortunates," recalled Karpman, "was my secret hope in going to St. Elizabeths." See Lavine, "Benjamin Karpman, M.D. 1888–1962."

37 *Karpman believed that... desire it*: Benjamin Karpman, quoted in Beemyn, *A Queer Capital*, 137.

37 *Even in the... not incarceration*: Benjamin Karpman, "The Sexual Psychopath," *The Journal of Criminal Law, Criminology, and Police Science* 42, no. 2 (1951), 197. Karpman distanced himself from this definition, believing that anyone who was abnormal qualified as a psychopath, but he recognized that the law defined it in this way. See Benjamin Karpman, "H.R. 2937-H.R. 5264 Criminal Sexual Psychopaths," Committee on the District of Columbia, U.S. House of Representatives, February 20, 1948.

38 *Karpman predicted a... common*: "Era of Sexual Looseness Is Predicted," *The Washington Post*, September 17, 1945, 1.

38 *He made these... nation*: Beemyn, *A Queer Capital*, 135. "Although the shooting is over," one army psychiatrist wrote, "the public interest in the profession of mental health and illness and the challenge of that interest to professional psychiatry is at an all-time high, as a result of the war. See D'Emilio, *Sexual Politics, Sexual Communities*, 18.

38 *Dr. Karpman became... Elizabeths in 1948*: "Dr. Benjamin Karpman, 75, Psychiatrist, Crime Expert," *The Washington Evening Star*, May 18, 1962, 30.

38 *(a local synagogue... report)*: "Adas Israel Club to Hear Karpman on Kinsey Report," *The Washington Evening Star*, November 14, 1948, 4. Karpman's own 1948 book, *The Alcoholic Woman*, attracted November headlines for the sexual experiences described in its case histories. Like the Kinsey report, Karpman's study of alcoholism was intended for professionals. But an anti-obscenity crusader reported the book to the Washington police, describing it as "the filthiest, most obscene, pornographic, libidinous and licentious piece of trash that ever polluted the reading public." Authorities searched newsstands for copies of the text, but there were none to be found. The publicity from the ordeal had, according to the distributor, "caused a sellout of all available copies and numerous requests for more." See Leo Grove, "Chief Barrett Orders Probe of Book Sale," *The Washington Post*, November 13, 1948, 1; "Book Called Obscene and Sellout Follows," *The Washington Evening Star*, November 13, 1948, 3.

38 *During that year's... sexual psychopath law*: For a discussion of the Washington sodomy law's common law predecessor, see Beemyn, *A Queer Capital*, 134.

38 *Republican congressman Arthur... Elizabeths*: Edward F. Ryan, "400% Sex Offense Jump Here in 7 Years Is Cited at Hearing," *The Washington Post*, February 21, 1948, B1.

38 *The Miller Act... crime*: "Report to Accompany H.R. 6071," U.S. House of Representatives, 80th Cong., 2d Sess., May 21, 1948, 10.

38 *In February 1948... in June*: Karpman testified in February 1948 with the superintendent of St. Elizabeths, who saw the law "as progressive, as practical, as indicating a closer union of the law with medicine." An early draft of the law, however, defined a sexual psychopath as anyone who had "criminal propensities to the commission of sex offenses." But as Kinsey had informed the country only one month earlier, nine in ten Americans technically qualified as sex offenders. So although Karpman testified in favor of the law, he warned against the "criminal" component of the definition. If a husband engages in an illegal sexual act with his wife, Karpman asked, "are you going to send him to St. Elizabeths?" Congress took his point: the final bill allowed only a psychiatrist—not an archaic, unenforceable law—to deem a patient "dangerous to other persons" and therefore a sexual psychopath. See ibid.; Benjamin Karpman, "H.R. 2937-H.R. 5264 Criminal Sexual Psychopaths," Committee on the District of Columbia, U.S. House of Representatives, February 20, 1948, 97, 112–14.

38 *Authorities arrested the... summer*: Johnson, *The Lavender Scare*, 59.

38 *They arrested forty... of solicitation*: Beemyn, *A Queer Capital*, 137.

38 *Twenty-nine states enacted... 1957*: Eskridge, *Gaylaw*, 60–61.

38 *In only a... and lobotomies*: Ibid., 62; D'Emilio, *Sexual Politics, Sexual Communities*, 17.

39 *Despite his involvement... way*: George Beveridge, "Hospital Can't Provide Care Sex Offenders Need, Doctors Told," *The Washington Evening Star*, June 4, 1950, 1. See also Johnson, *The Lavender Scare*, 88.

39 *Karpman retired from . . . Frank Kameny*: By the time Kameny was preparing his defense package, the astronomer may have already been familiar with Karpman; that year the doctor had published a new book on alcoholism, *The Hangover*, and had been a guest on the Steve Allison radio show in November. "Dr. Benjamin Karpman, 75, Psychiatrist, Crime Expert," *The Washington Evening Star*, May 18, 1962, 30; Eve Edstrom, "New Book Calls Hangover Key to Alcoholic's Entire Problem," *The Washington Post*, October 6, 1957, B8; "Highlights on Radio," *The Washington Post*, November 9, 1957, C14.

39 *One morning in . . . Karpman*: FEK to Benjamin Karpman, n.d., Box 44, Folder 4, FEK Papers.

39 *"I have examined . . . a homosexual"*: "I," n.d., Box 44, Folder 4, FEK Papers.

39 *When Karpman read . . . and exited*: "II," n.d., Box 44, Folder 4, FEK Papers.

40 *During their sessions . . . in this case"*: "III," FEK to Karpman, n.d., Box 44, Folder 4, FEK Papers.

40 *Perhaps worried that . . . you make"*: Ibid.

40 *Kameny lied in . . . your miseries."*: FEK to "Dr. K," n.d., Box 44, Folder 4, FEK Papers.

40 *The letter that . . . Karpman, M.D."*: Benjamin Karpman to Joseph Fanelli, January 27 1958, Franklin E. Kameny Personnel File, National Personnel Records Center, Annex, NARA (Valmeyer, Illinois).

41 *Kameny signed . . . Frank."*: FEK to "Dr. K," No Date, Box 44, Folder 4, FEK Papers.

41 *In January, while . . . conduct"*: "Petition for a Writ of Certiorari," *Kameny v. Brucker*, October Term, 1960, Box 44, Folder 8, FEK Papers, 11.

41 *Kameny now faced . . . do so*: The AMS was under jurisdiction of the CSC because it was a civilian agency. FEK to MSNY, May 5, 1960, Box 44, Folder 1, FEK Papers.

41 *His interrogators, responded . . . he added*: "Sworn Appeal by Dr. Franklin E. Kameny," February 14, 1958, Box 43, Folder 12, FEK Papers.

41 *Once again, Kameny . . . for him*: Ibid.

41 *After reviewing Kameny's . . . unsurprising outcome*: "Summary of Relevant Facts Regarding My Case Against the Government," n.d., Box 44, Folder 7, FEK Papers; "Petition for a Writ of Certiorari," *Kameny v. Brucker*, 44–45.

41 *As Kameny saw . . . appeals court*: FEK to MSNY, May 5, 1960, Box 44, Folder 1, FEK Papers.

42 *Their reasoning, however . . . to dismiss homosexuals*: "Petition for a Writ of Certiorari," *Kameny v. Brucker*, 44–45.

42 *Kameny soon appeared . . . were tied*: FEK to MSNY, May 5, 1960, Box 44, Folder 1, FEK Papers.

42 *On March 27 . . . headquarters*: FEK to Harris Ellsworth, n.d., Box 44, Folder 1, FEK Papers.

42 *He insisted on . . . guilt*: FEK to MSNY, May 5, 1960, Box 44, Folder 1, FEK Papers.

42 *On March 30 . . . Harris Ellsworth*: "Summary of Relevant Facts Regarding My Case Against the Government," n.d., Box 44, Folder 7, FEK Papers.

42 *Six weeks later . . . responded Castle*: Ibid.; FEK to MSNY, May 5, 1960, Box 44, Folder 1, FEK Papers.

43 *The astronomer returned . . . country*: In this letter, Kameny also included a new argument: he had a right to privacy. During his discussion with officials, he gathered that the CSC took "amiss the attitude expressed by me at one point, that a man's personal life is not his employer's affair." FEK to Harris Ellsworth, n.d., Box 44, Folder 1, FEK Papers.

43 *On June 12 . . . final appeal*: "Summary of Relevant Facts Regarding My Case Against the Government," n.d., Box 44, Folder 7, FEK Papers.

43 *Kameny's father . . . weeks later*: "Emil Kameny," *The New York Times*, June 27, 1958, 25; Rae Beck Kameny interview.

43 *At the beginning . . . clearance*: FEK to MSNY, May 5, 1960, Box 44, Folder 1, FEK Papers.

43 *Kameny knew that . . . he later wrote*: Ibid.

43 *If Kameny wanted . . . to the president*: FEK to Dwight D. Eisenhower, n.d., Box 44, Folder 1, FEK Papers.

44 *"They did not . . . the White House*: The White House did not completely ignore him: a sympathetic administration official contacted Ellsworth to inquire about Kameny's case, but that was the extent of the White House's intervention. Lahusen interview; FEK to MSNY, May 5, 1960, Box 44, Folder 1, FEK Papers.

44 *After Eisenhower, Kameny . . . Committee*: "Summary of Relevant Facts Regarding My Case Against the Government," n.d., Box 44, Folder 7, FEK Papers.

44 *At least two . . . he wrote*: "Dr. Kameny is aware of all of the circumstances of his case and of the reasons why it was determined by the Commission that he should be barred from Federal Civil Service employment," responded Ellsworth. See FEK to Ellsworth, n.d., Box 44, Folder 3, FEK Papers.

44 *After Ellsworth's insinuations . . . astronomer*: After Ellsworth's insinuations, the politicians did no more for the astronomer. See "Summary of Relevant Facts Regarding My Case Against the Government," n.d., Box 44, Folder 7, FEK Papers.

44 *On September 28 . . . Lafayette Park*: The only official record of the arrest is a 1961 letter from the commissioner of the District of Columbia confirming that his arrest had been expunged. It is this document that confirms that the arrest occurred in 1958 rather than 1957, the year provided in several past histories. See, for example, Dudley Clendinen and Adam Nagourney, *Out for Good: The Struggle to Build a Gay Rights Movement in America* (New York: Simon & Schuster, 1999), 112; Walter N. Tobriner to FEK, December 18, 1961, Box 44, Folder 12, FEK Papers.

44 *He wrote to . . . and non-specific nature*": FEK to Ellsworth, 1958, Box 44, Folder 3, FEK Papers.
44 *His CSC interrogations . . . unethical conduct*": Ibid.
45 *He also made . . . the Constitution*": Ibid.
45 *The purges . . . utter chaos?*": For the first time, Kameny invoked his military service. "I can tell you, Mr. Ells-worth, that if I had known, in 1943, '44, and '45, when I put my life into jeopardy to help fight a war against the enemies of this country, that this was the kind of government for which I was fighting, that this sort of thing could possibly happen in the United States, that all of our pretensions of personal liberty, human freedom, and justice which we loudly proclaim before the world, are a sham, a fraud, a flimsy facade, and a gross deception—if I had known this during World War II, I would have thought hard, and hesitated long before undertaking to fight for this country—and I might well not have fought at all." See ibid.
45 *The commission, wrote . . . Kameny's case*: FEK to Ellsworth, 1958, Box 44, Folder 3, FEK Papers.
45 *Johns Hopkins University . . . later*: John C. Burke to FEK, November 12, 1958, Box 43, Folder 12, FEK Papers.
45 *Kameny's unemployment compensation . . . two questions*": FEK to Ellsworth, 1958, Box 44, Folder 3, FEK Papers.
45 *"In two weeks . . . an executioner*": Ibid.
46 *Throughout Kameny's ordeal . . . astronomers like him*: Ibid.

4. THE UNION

48 *Former schoolteacher . . . unimportant*": Robert W. McChesney, *Telecommunications, Mass Media, & Democracy: The Battle for Control of U.S. Broadcasting, 1928–35* (New York: Oxford University Press, 1995), 237.
48 *After Scott faced . . . in 1938*: Scott was arrested—then acquitted—for driving under the influence in 1935. And though he was reelected in 1936, he lost his 1938 election by only 342 votes; Scott made allegations of election fraud, but his opponent kept the seat. When Scott ran again in 1940, he lost by more than thirteen thousand votes. See "Scott Freed of Charges," *Los Angeles Times*, October 8, 1935, 1; "Scott Trial Postponed," *Los Angeles Times*, October 3, 1935, A3; "State Votes Tabulated: Official Returns on Races for Congress Announced by Peek," *Los Angeles Times*, December 13, 1940, 22.
48 *He decided to . . . of McCarthyism*: "Scott, Byron Nicholson," Biographical Directory of the United States Congress, http://bioguide.congress.gov/scripts/biodisplay.pl?index=S000165.
48 *calm, slow-speaking Scott*: For Scott's diction, "Barr v. Matteo," Oyez, https://www.oyez.org/cases/1958/350.
48 *defended a Berkeley . . . to avoid self-incrimination*: "Young Scientist Acquitted of Contempt of Congress," *The Washington Evening Star*, June 30, 1951, 23; Kevin Starr, *Embattled Dreams: California in War and Peace, 1940–1950* (New York: Oxford University Press, 2003), 327.
48 *In 1955, William . . . of Congress*: When Elizabeth Bentley listed the members of an espionage ring for HUAC in 1948, Taylor was on her list. He had declared his innocence from the beginning, and because he worked for an international organization rather than the federal government, he retained his job. But the federal government exerted tremendous pressure on both Taylor and his employer. The attorney general had testified against him in Congress, and two treasury secretaries had urged the IMF to terminate him. Taylor himself had been interrogated nineteen times. And in 1953, an International Organizations Employees Loyalty Board was established. It charged Taylor that same year. See Murrey Marder, "Fund Official Seeks Bentley Confrontation," *The Washington Post*, May 22, 1955, E1.
48 *Byron Scott began . . . accusers*: "Taylor Wants to Quiz Witness," *The Washington Evening Star*, April 19, 1955, 3.
48 *Scott mounted a . . . called it*: Ralph S. Brown Jr., "Book Review: Ex-Communist Witnesses: Four Studies in Fact Finding," *Faculty Scholarship Series* (New Haven: Yale University, 1963), 409.
49 *and the . . . attorney general*: "Apology Asked from Brownell," *The Washington Evening Star*, January 10, 1956, 4.
49 *Scott continued taking . . . the crusades*: L. Edgar Prina, "Old Tax Job Demanded by 'Risk' Suspended in '54," *The Washington Evening Star*, June 27, 1956, A24.
49 *On April 12 . . . two federal employees*: William A. Millen, "Flemming Is Accused of Repudiating Board in Leave Pay Cases," *The Washington Evening Star*, April 12, 1953, 19.
49 *Oral arguments took . . . bono work*: Scott ultimately lost *Barr v. Matteo* in a 5–4 decision (the court found that federal officials had "absolute immunity" against libel claims). See "Libel Protection Given to U.S. Aides," *The New York Times*, June 30, 1959, 23; *Barr v. Matteo*, 360 U.S. 564 (1959).
49 *Kameny had chosen . . . at all*: FEK to MSNY, May 5, 1960, Box 44, Folder 1, FEK Papers; Lahusen interview.
49 *Only Kameny and . . . he wrote*: Ibid.
49 *But he told . . . for money*: Lahusen interview.
50 *On December 15 . . . ACLU's Washington office*: FEK to Penelope L. Wright, December 15, 1958, Box 43, Folder 12, FEK Papers.

50 *It was unlikely . . . protection*: In 1951, when a woman facing expulsion from the air force asked the ACLU for assistance, it advised her to seek medical treatment and to "abandon homosexual relations." Three years later, when a homosexual publication, *ONE* magazine, sued the U.S. Postal Service for censorship, the ACLU of Southern California refused to take the case. In 1956, Spencer Coxe, the executive director of the Philadelphia ACLU, stumbled upon a copy of *ONE*. The magazine's allegations startled him: homosexuals were being purged from the military, facing unconstitutional searches and seizures, and being sent to jail under vague "sexual psychopath" laws. He wrote to the ACLU headquarters in New York. "Have you seen this magazine? Have the allegations of denial of civil liberties against this group of our population ever been investigated by ACLU?" "We have not seen this and should," an official responded. "Please help us to broaden our sense of diversity in life." Coxe forwarded the magazine to headquarters, and the ACLU began investigating the magazine's claims. The Union did not speak to homosexuals; instead, it interviewed a minister who was "somewhat of an expert on the matter of due process for homosexuals." Within three months, the ACLU adopted an official policy on homosexuality. See Allan Bérubé and John D'Emilio, "The Military and Lesbians during the McCarthy Years," *Signs* 9, no. 4 (1984), 775; Eskridge, *Gaylaw*, 91; Lillian Faderman, *The Gay Revolution: The Story of the Struggle* (New York: Simon & Schuster Paperbacks, 2016), 95; S. Coxe to L. J., May 3, 1956, Box 1127, Folder 6, American Civil Liberties Union Papers, Seeley G. Mudd Manuscript Library, Princeton University (hereafter, "ACLU Papers"); "Greater Phila.," May 7, 1956, Box 1127, Folder 6, ACLU Papers; L. Golden to S. C., October 4, 1956, Box 1127, Folder 6, ACLU Papers.
50 *In a policy . . . of homosexuals"*: "ACLU Position on Homosexuality," January 7, 1957, Box 1127, Folder 7, ACLU Papers.
50 *As for the . . . due process*: Ibid.
50 *Shortly after the . . . about "minority problems"*: Gonzalo Segura Jr. to B. W. Huebsch, November 21, 1957, Box 1127, Folder 7, ACLU Papers.
50 *"While we appreciate . . . this issue"*: Alan Reitman to Gonzalo Segura Jr., November 29, 1957, Box 1127, Folder 7, ACLU Papers.
50 *The Washington ACLU . . . Kameny's case*: Patrick Murphy Malin to Nelson Stone, November 8, 1957, Box 1127, Folder 7, ACLU Papers. For Kameny's own conflicting accounts on whether the ACLU assigned an attorney, see Jeff Kisseloff, *Generation on Fire: Voices of Protest from the 1960s: An Oral History* (Lexington: University Press of Kentucky, 2007), 186, and Lahusen interview.
50 *Not only did . . . to maintain*: Anthony Marro, "F.B.I. Files Disclose '50s Tie to A.C.L.U.," *The New York Times*, August 4, 1977, 39.
50 *In April 1959 . . . if he won*: Lahusen interview.
50 *That same month . . . called it*: Ibid.
51 *Kameny contacted an . . . loan*: FEK to MSNY, May 5, 1960, Box 44, Folder 1, FEK Papers.
51 *With the senator's fall . . . too far*: Lavender-tinted rumors, so important to McCarthy's rise, had contributed to his fall. They centered around G. David Schine, a wealthy, blond, twenty-five-year-old Harvard graduate who worked as an unpaid "chief consultant" for the senator's committee. See Robert Shogan, *No Sense of Decency: The Army–McCarthy Hearings* (Chicago: Ivan R. Dee, 2009), 12, 118; Arthur Herman, *Joseph McCarthy: Reexamining the Life and Legacy of America's Most Hated Senator* (New York: Free Press, 2000), 271; Ted Morgan, *Reds: McCarthyism in Twentieth-Century America* (New York: Random House, 2004), 467–68; "National Affairs: The Case of Private Schine," *TIME*, March 22, 1954; Griffith, *The Politics of Fear*, 249; Dean, *Imperial Brotherhood*, 151; Edwin R. Bayley, *Joe McCarthy and the Press* (Madison: University of Wisconsin Press, 1981), 167, 208.
51 *Democrats regained control . . . the government*: Administration officials concluded that the country had lost faith in its security program; one official warned the White House that the security program was "undermining the source of American scientific leadership." Johnson, *The Lavender Scare*, 142–43.
51 *On the legal . . . harm others*: Frank R. Kent Jr., "Sex Offenses Weighed for New Moral Code," *The Washington Post*, May 20, 1955, 44.
51 *"This area of . . . authorities"*: Eskridge, *Gaylaw*, 84.
51 *The ALI acknowledged . . . the ALI vote*: Phil Yeager and John Stark, "Revision of Sex Laws Arouses Controversy," *The Washington Evening Star*, June 12, 1955, 27.
51 *In 1957, the . . . the mail*: *Roth v. United States*, 354 U.S. 476 (1957); *ONE Inc. v. Olesen*, 355 U.S. 371 (1958); Eskridge, *Gaylaw*, 95–96.
52 *One case . . . his job*: Additionally, when the Food and Drug Administration terminated one of its inspectors, Kendrick Cole, for "close association with individuals reliably reported to be Communists," he sued. What, he asked, did food inspection have to do with national security? In its 1956 decision, the court ruled that Eisenhower's Executive Order 10450, allowing agencies to terminate national security risks, applied only if the employee occupied a "sensitive" position. But Cole left ample room for the gay purges to continue: an agency simply had to determine that a targeted employee indeed occupied a sensitive position. See *Cole v. Young*, 351 U.S. 536 (1956).
52 *One case involved . . . 1959*: *Greene v. McElroy*, 360 U.S. 474 (1959); "Greene v. McElroy," Oyez, https://www.oyez.org/cases/1958/180.

52 *Five days later . . . the good"*: The Supreme Court's clerk, in a terse response, informed Kameny that the Greene case had already been argued and was now under consideration by the court. See FEK to Earl Warren, April 6, 1959, Box 43, Folder 12, FEK Papers; R. J. Blanchard to FEK, April 14, 1959, Box 43, Folder 12, FEK Papers.

52 *Kameny lost his . . . needed him*: Lahusen interview.

52 *After his experiences*: FEK to Neil McElroy, June 1, 1959, Box 43, Folder 12, FEK Papers.

52 *The next day . . . the matter*: FEK to MSNY, May 5, 1960, Box 44, Folder 1, FEK Papers.

53 *On June 3 . . . mammoth headquarters*: FEK to H. C. Anderson, July 10, 1959, Box 43, Folder 12, FEK Papers.

53 *Applegate and two . . . got it!"*: FEK to MSNY, May 5, 1960, Box 44, Folder 1, FEK Papers.

53 *On June 17 . . . due process*: "Petition for a Writ of Certiorari," *Kameny v. Brucker*, October Term, 1960, Box 44, Folder 8, FEK Papers, 12.

53 *The complaint raised . . . a hearing*: Lahusen interview.

53 *On June 29 . . . cross-examined"*: *Greene v. McElroy*, 360 U.S. 474 (1959).

53 *The next day . . . clearance"*: R. L. Applegate to FEK, June 30, 1959, Box 45, Folder 1, FEK Papers.

54 *Kameny, disappointed that . . . once again*: FEK to MSNY, May 5, 1960, Box 44, Folder 1, FEK Papers.

54 *Applegate admitted that . . . clear response*: Ibid.

54 *With Applegate's letter . . . of Defense*: Ibid.

54 *He wrote to . . . for one"*: FEK to H. C. Anderson, July 10, 1959, Box 43, Folder 12, FEK Papers.

54 *At least one . . . replied*: FEK to MSNY, May 5, 1960, Box 44, Folder 1, FEK Papers.

55 *Kameny's analysis of . . . toward themselves"*: FEK to R. L. Applegate, July 21, 1959, Box 45, Folder 1, FEK Papers.

55 *Yes, society was . . . word* homosexual.*)*: Ibid.

55 *Kameny began to . . . security problems"*: Joseph H. Engel to FEK, September 3, 1959, Box 43, Folder 12, FEK Papers.

55 *NASA, formed only . . . the astronomer*: Robert J. Lacklen to FEK, July 30, 1959, Box 43, Folder 12, FEK Papers.

55 *In early September . . . in his case*: Lahusen interview.

55 *Standing before Judge . . . dismissal*: "Petition for a Writ of Certiorari," *Kameny v. Brucker*, 20.

56 *While Kameny waited . . . few days later*: Lahusen interview.

56 *an intimidating figure. . . . eye*: "Roy E. Blick, 72, Dies; Ex-Vice Squad Chief," *The Washington Evening Star*, June 19, 1972, 39.

56 *As Kameny sat . . . gay bars"*: Frank Kameny, interviewed by Genny Beemyn, Washington, D.C., March 20, 1994; Lahusen interview.

57 *On December 22 . . . case*: FEK to MSNY, May 5, 1960, Box 44, Folder 1, FEK Papers.

57 *He had lost the first round*: She found "no genuine issue of material fact. See "Petition for a Writ of Certiorari," *Kameny v. Brucker*, 1A.

57 *Byron Scott appealed . . . bite"*: FEK to *ONE*, August 27, 1960, Box 44, Folder 1, FEK Papers.

57 *Scott filed the . . . explained Kameny*: FEK to MSNY, May 5, 1960, Box 44, Folder 1, FEK Papers.

57 *Kameny had done . . . retain a clearance"*: Ibid.

57 *Though the civil . . . and in writing"*: Ibid.

58 *Kameny and Scott . . . positive sense"*: Ibid.

58 *Emboldened with a . . . will be fought"*: Ibid.

58 *After a court of appeals . . . to win"*: FEK to Joseph H. Engel, June 1, 1960, Box 44, Folder 1, FEK Papers.

58 *On June 6 . . . therefore "unnecessary"*: *Kameny v. Brucker*, 282 F.2d 823 (1960).

58 *Scott and Kameny . . . factual grounds"*: FEK to *ONE*, August 27, 1960, Box 44, Folder 1, FEK Papers.

59 *The court of appeals . . . racial grounds"*: "Petition for a Writ of Certiorari," *Kameny v. Brucker*, 12.

59 *It was no . . . moral authority?*: Marissa Chappell, Jenny Hutchinson, and Brian Ward, "Dress modestly, neatly . . . as if you were going to church: Respectability, Class and Gender in the Montgomery Bus Boycott and the Early Civil Rights Movement," in *Gender and the Civil Rights Movement*, ed. Peter J. Ling and Sharon Monteith (New York: Garland, 1999), 69. For additional discussion of protesters' dress in the Greensboro sit-ins, see Rebekah J. Kowal, "Staging the Greensboro Sit-Ins," *TDR: The Drama Review* 48, no. 4 (2004): 135–54.

59 *In August, Washington's . . . the act"*: *Rittenour v. District of Columbia*, August 19, 1960, Box 8, Folder 5, Mattachine Society, Inc. of New York Records, New York Public Library, New York, NY (hereafter, "MSNY Papers").

59 *The decision "rendered . . . than disgusting"*: "Morality and Crime," *The Washington Post*, August 28, 1960, E4. In July, Kameny had also read a *Washington Post* editorial about the debate in the aftermath of the United Kingdom's Wolfenden report, which had recommended the legalization of homosexual behavior. "However offensive it may be to the mores of the majority, homosexuality is a fact of life," the *Post* declared. America needed a discussion like the one taking place in England: after all, "ancient taboos can be overthrown only

by patient persuasion." See FEK to Albert J. de Dion, August 30, 1960, Series III, Reel 18, MSNY Papers; "Where Light Is Needed," *The Washington Post*, July 10, 1960. For more on Wolfenden, see Jeffrey Weeks, *Coming Out: Homosexual Politics in Britain from the Nineteenth Century to the Present* (London: Quartet Books, 1977); Patrick Higgins, *Heterosexual Dictatorship: Male Homosexuality in Postwar Britain* (London: Fourth Estate, 1996); Derek McGhee, *Homosexuality, Law and Resistance* (Abingdon: Taylor & Francis, 2001); Matt Houlbrook, *Queer London: Perils and Pleasures in the Sexual Metropolis, 1918–1957* (Chicago: University of Chicago Press, 2006).

59 *On August 31 . . . Supreme Court*: "Petition for a Writ of Certiorari," *Kameny v. Brucker*, 1.

60 *clean-cut fellows who . . . typical all-American boys*: "How the Reds Blackmailed Homosexuals into Spying for Them!," *Top Secret*, February 1961, 14.

60 *sat on an . . . spying on allies*: "Two U.S. Code Clerks Turn Up in Moscow," *The Washington Evening Star*, September 6, 1960, 3; James Bamford, *The Puzzle Palace: A Report on America's Most Secret Agency* (New York: Penguin, 1983), 190.

60 *"Investigators also . . . War II"*: Jack Anderson, "Those Missing Security Experts Contacted Soviet Embassy in U.S.," *The Atlanta Journal-Constitution*, September 4, 1960, 18A.

60 *Congress planned hearings . . . weeks*: The partisan tables had turned. The Democratic HUAC chairman also claimed that more than a thousand "security risks" currently held government jobs and claimed that Eisenhower was refusing to release their names. See ibid.; "President Says Turncoat Case Shows Laxity," *The Washington Evening Star*, September 7, 1960, 1.

60 *The NSA investigated . . . weeks*: Johnson, *The Lavender Scare*, 145.

60 *"Nothing has stirred . . . one columnist*: Robert Spivach, "The Ghost of the Late Senator McCarthy Rides Again!," *The Philadelphia Tribune*, September 13, 1960, 4.

60 *Despite the duo's . . . the Pentagon*: "President Says Turncoat Case Shows Laxity" *The Washington Evening Star*, September 7, 1960, 1.

60 *Mitchell's own father . . . he said*: Bamford, *The Puzzle Palace*, 191.

60 *After thirteen months . . . the defection"*: Ibid.

60 *"Is it not . . . own country"*: George E. Sokolsky, "These Days. . . . The Traitors," *The Washington Post*, September 14, 1960, A21.

61 *"The Reds are . . . by using—homosexuals!"*: "How the Reds Blackmailed Homosexuals into Spying for Them!," *Top Secret*, February 1961, 14.

61 *That fall, Byron . . . it alone*: Lahusen interview.

61 *"If I'd gone . . . a brief*: Ibid.

61 *With the petition . . . may end."*: FEK to *ONE*, August 27, 1960, Box 44, Folder 1, FEK Papers.

61 *Jack Nichols was . . . rights of homosexuals*: Nichols, "Chapter Two," *Memoirs of Jack Nichols*.

61 *"We are a . . . had written*: Donald Webster Cory, *The Homosexual in America: A Subjective Approach* (New York: Greenberg, 1951), 13.

62 *Nichols stood from . . . to replace Scott*: Nichols, "Chapter Two," *Memoirs of Jack Nichols*.

62 *One evening, a . . . Metropolitan Policemen"*: Leslie H. Whitten, "Well-Patrolled Park Leads to Police Fight," *The Washington Post*, November 13, 1960, A3.

63 *"In a town . . . the Post*: "Lafayette, Here We Come," *The Washington Post*, November 16, 1960, A16.

63 *President Kennedy swore . . . his life*: "Kennedy Inaugural Speech: 'We Will Defend Liberty,'" *The Washington Evening Star*, January 20, 1961, Box 137, Folder 13, FEK Papers.

63 *"This court is . . . of its aspects"*: "Petition for a Writ of Certiorari," *Kameny v. Brucker*, 17.

63 *Kameny wrote for . . . an impartial hearing"*: Ibid., 14.

63 *He had . . . an impartial hearing"*: Ibid., 16.

63 *Kameny also wrote . . . is uninformed"*: Ibid., 18.

64 *Unlike his early . . . immoral conduct"*: Ibid., 20.

64 *The Civil Service . . . and capricious"*: Ibid., 28.

64 *Plus, argued Kameny . . . Amendment*: Ibid., 30. Just as the American Law Institute and Britain's Wolfenden report had drawn from Mill to conclude that the government should differentiate between law and morality when considering sodomy, Kameny drew from Mill to advocate for the homosexual's right to federal employment. See Eskridge, "January 27, 1961," 40.

64 *He called upon . . . to racial integration"*: Ibid., 51.

64 *Just like the . . . nation stands for"*: Ibid., 58–59.

65 *And if the . . . personally"*: Ibid., 26.

65 *gay pride*: In this book, I make two broad claims of continuity. First, the Mattachine Society of Washington was, from day one, primarily a *legal* organization that responded to the discriminatory employment policies of the United States federal government. After the failed lawsuit of its founder, Frank Kameny, the Society systematically endeavored to recruit other plaintiffs to emulate his efforts. With the ACLU's assistance, it was successful. The organization's lobbying efforts, demonstrations, and other initiatives were secondary in importance to the court cases that the MSW sponsored and encouraged. Second, our contemporary conception

of gay pride originated as an embedded legal argument in response to the logic of the federal government's purges, and homophile activists consistently and increasingly deployed it as a political strategy throughout the 1960s. But what, exactly, is gay pride? The *New Oxford American Dictionary* defines it as "a sense of dignity and satisfaction in connection with the public acknowledgment of one's own homosexuality." For the purposes of this exploration, I bisect this definition into two criteria. First, gay pride requires an assertion that one's homosexuality contributes positively to society, or, in other words, that it is a moral good. Second, this declaration must be made openly and without concealment; homosexuals must declare their pride visibly and as their authentic selves. (It is this second criterion that distinguishes the pride examined in this book from other expressions of pride, no less valid, in militant publications like *ONE*. Almost invariably, these declarations were made by authors writing under a pseudonym, a necessity for writers hoping to avoid exposure to their employers, their families, or federal investigators.) This brand of gay pride, as this book reveals, is an inherently political act, not dissimilar to the rite of "coming out." Though it is possible to proclaim gay pride in an apolitical context—one can be proud of his or her homosexuality without publicly declaring it—this book concerns itself with gay pride in its public and political form, the proclamation deemed so crucial by post-Stonewall gay liberationists. I refer to this specific iteration when I use the term "gay pride." See *New Oxford American Dictionary*, 2nd ed., s.v. "Gay Pride" (New York: Oxford University Press, 2005). For examples of pride in *ONE*, see Frank Golovitz [Jim Kepner], "Gay Beach," OM Volume 6, Number 7 (July 1958), 7; Hollister Barnes [Dorr Legg], "I Am Glad to Be Homosexual", *ONE* 6, no. 8 (August 1958), 7. A notable exception, however, is the pseudonym-free writing of the defiant homosexual defendant Dale Jennings. For an account of how *ONE* magazine "seeded the intellectual climate" for gay pride, see John Dennett Master, "'A Part of Our Liberation': *ONE Magazine and the Cultivation of Gay Liberation, 1953–1963* (PhD dissertation, University of California, Riverside, 2006), 55, 341. For an exploration of the importance of coming out and pride to gay liberationists, see D'Emilio, *Sexual Politics, Sexual Communities*, 235; George Chauncey, *Why Marriage?: The History Shaping Today's Debate over Gay Equality* (New York: Basic Books, 2004), 33–34.

65   *"In World War . . . in that battle"*: "Petition for a Writ of Certiorari," *Kameny v. Brucker*, 18–19.

5. THE MATTACHINE

67   *In 153 B.C. . . . their slaves*: Max Harris, "Claiming Pagan Origins for Carnival: Bacchanalia, Saturnalia, and Kalends," *European Medieval Drama* 10 (2006), 81–82.

67   *The early Christians . . . grew in popularity*: Enid Welsford, *The Fool: His Social and Literary History* (New York: Doubleday, 1961), 199.

67   *When the empire . . . a woman*: Harris, "Claiming Pagan Origins for Carnival," 87.

67   *By the thirteenth . . . as women*: Max Harris, *Sacred Folly: A New History of the Feast of Fools* (Ithaca, NY: Cornell University Press, 2011), 67; Harris, "Claiming Pagan Origins for Carnival," 106.

68   *The church banned . . . their masks*: Harris, *Sacred Folly*, 200, 279; Welsford, *The Fool*, 204.

68   *One of their . . . death*: Julia Sutton, Elizabeth Kurtz, César Delgado Martínez, and John Forrest, "Matachins," in *The International Encyclopedia of Dance*, ed. Selma Jeanne Cohen (Oxford: Oxford University Press, 1998).

68   *Though the Sociétés . . . survived*: Harris, *Sacred Folly*, 280.

68   *Spanish colonists brought . . . the audience*: Sutton, Kurtz, and Martínez, "Matachins," *The International Encyclopedia of Dance*; "'El Viejo', peregrino con labor de demonio," *ABC Noticias*, November 11, 2013, https://abcnoticias.mx/el-viejo-peregrino-con-labor-de-demonio/17704.

68   *Harry Hay discovered . . . the proletariat*: Stuart Timmons, *The Trouble with Harry Hay: Founder of the Modern Gay Movement* (Boston: Alyson, 1990), xiv, 127.

68   *Hay was . . . homosexual house parties*: Ibid., 98, 132.

68   *In 1948, Kinsey's . . . potential power*: D'Emilio, *Sexual Politics, Sexual Communities*, 65.

68   *Homosexuals could pool . . . do just that*: Timmons, *The Trouble with Harry Hay*, 136.

69   *The idea died . . . with Marxist foundations?*: Ibid., 141.

69   *The couple proceeded . . . "imperative"*: Hay and Roscoe, *Radically Gay*, 140.

69   *When Hay taught . . . settled on homophile*: Timmons, *The Trouble with Harry Hay*, 149–50.

69   *The Mattachine Society's . . . a brotherhood*: The new organization also drew its structure from Hay's class. In the eighteenth century, composers Mozart and Haydn had been members of the Freemasons, an outlawed, clandestine brotherhood. Its template for secrecy was especially helpful as the gay Communists began planning their organization in the midst of the gay panic and McCarthyism; Senator Hoey released his sensational report within weeks of the group's first meeting. Second Order members were responsible for forming and maintaining their own discussion groups, which allowed for horizontal expansion. The seven founders constituted the Fifth Order, which set organizational policy from above. The Third and Fourth Orders never materialized. See D'Emilio, *Sexual Politics, Sexual Communities*, 63, 65; Timmons, *The Trouble with Harry Hay*, 152.

70 *As the discussion . . . coworker explained*: Ibid., 158.

70 *In February 1952 . . . police officer*: Dale Jennings, "To Be Accused, Is to Be Guilty," *ONE*, January 1, 1953, 12.

70 *The next morning . . . risky defense strategy*: Timmons, *The Trouble with Harry Hay*, 164–65.

70 *To publicize the . . . Hollywood*: D'Emilio, *Sexual Politics, Sexual Communities*, 70.

70 *Yes, Dale Jennings . . . declared victory*: Faderman, *The Gay Revolution*, 65.

70 *Never before had*: Ibid.

70 *"Were heterosexuals to . . . admitting homosexuality"*: Jennings, "To Be Accused, Is to Be Guilty," 12.

71 *Because of the . . . first editor*: D'Emilio, *Sexual Politics, Sexual Communities*, 71.

71 *ONE magazine's inaugural . . . story*: Jennings, "To Be Accused, Is to Be Guilty," 12.

71 *and it was . . . copies per month*: D'Emilio, *Sexual Politics, Sexual Communities*, 71–72.

71 *The Mattachine continued . . . additional entrapment cases*: See The Mattachine Foundation, Inc., to George E. Shibley, January 5, 1953, Homophile Organizations Mattachine Foundation Correspondence, Donald Stewart Lucas Papers, GLBT Historical Society, San Francisco, CA (hereafter, "Don Lucas Papers").

71 *it moved into . . . entrapping homosexuals?*: "Request for Information," April 7, 1953, FBI File #100–45888–5.

71 *The questionnaire marked . . . 'I'd worry'*: Paul V. Coates, "Well, Medium and Rare," *Los Angeles Mirror*, March 12, 1953, clipping in FBI File #100–45888–4.

71 *It was, after . . . American loyalty oath*: D'Emilio, *Sexual Politics, Sexual Communities*, 76.

71 *On May 23 . . . homosexuality and homosexuals"*: Marilyn P. Rieger to Delegates of the Convention, May 23, 1953, Box 2, Folder 21, Don Lucas Papers. At an earlier session of the conference, Fifth Order member Chuck Rowland had defended the founders' vision of a homosexual minority. "The time will come when we will march down Hollywood Boulevard arm in arm, proclaiming our pride in our homosexuality," he had predicted. "I say with pride, 'I am a homosexual!'" See Faderman, *The Gay Revolution*, 70.

72 *The next day . . . ending his life*: Timmons, *The Trouble with Harry Hay*, 179–80.

72 *proud homosexual minority*: As the story goes, a respectability-focused homophile movement replaced the Marxist-inspired militancy of the Mattachine, and Chuck Rowland's vision of pride went dormant for fifteen years. As John D'Emilio put it in his seminal 1983 account of the homophile movement, "For almost twenty years that vision was lost, until a new generation of gay radicals built a liberation movement motivated by similar goals of pride, openness, and community." This narrative of lost pride—re-discovered in the final years of the Sixties—has continued through more recent accounts, including Robert Self's 2012 description of the significance of Gay Liberation: "Post-1968 gay activists, under the mantle of liberation, set forth a compelling project based on pride, power, sexual freedom, and the moral legitimacy of same-sex love. Gay is not just acceptable, they insisted. Gay is *good*. Far more than the Stonewall uprising or any other single event, this idea marked the boundary between the homophile politics of the 1960s and what many called the liberationist politics of the early 1970s." This book seeks to determine whether gay pride truly disappeared until, abruptly, it re-emerged in the zeitgeist of the late sixties. It searches for articulations of pride in America's courts, a forum largely overlooked by social historians. It examines whether, as the story of Dale Jennings's case suggests, spectacles of defiant homosexuals served as radicalizing moments for the movement. By focusing on the legal alliance between a single homophile organization, the Mattachine Society of Washington (MSW), and a single civil liberties organization, the ACLU, this book reevaluates the rise of gay pride, the deployment of respectability, and the decline of the homophile movement. See John D'Emilio, *Sexual Politics, Sexual Communities*, 250; and Robert O. Self, *All in the Family: The Realignment of American Democracy since the 1960s* (New York: Hill and Wang, 2012), 220.

72 *According to the . . . the nobility"*: Hay and Roscoe, *Radically Gay*, 140.

72 *Talk of a . . . sexual deviant*: D'Emilio, *Sexual Politics, Sexual Communities*, 81–82.

72 *"We do not . . . the truth"*: Ken Burns to Dale Jennings, March 1, 1954, Box 2, Folder 8, Don Lucas Papers.

73 *Women, especially, felt . . . campaign*: Marilyn P. Rieger to Ken Burns, November 24, 1953, Box 2, Folder 3, Don Lucas Papers. See also Faderman, *The Gay Revolution*, 72; D'Emilio, *Sexual Politics, Sexual Communities*, 92.

73 *At the May . . . Dwight Huggins*: Sign-in sheet, May 14, 1955, Box 3, Folder 2, Don Lucas Papers. For Huggins's age, see "Buell Dwight Huggins," *U.S., Social Security Applications and Claims Index, 1936-2007* (Provo, UT: Ancestry.com, 2015).

73 *Originally from Illinois . . . room*: In 1947, Huggins had begun working as a typist in the Post Office Department. After almost eight years, he noticed he was not getting promoted. He had a suspicion the government knew what had happened in college, and he believed his employers were holding him back. So on the last day of 1954, he quit his job. Huggins moved to Los Angeles, found a clerical position at the Internal Revenue Service, and joined the Mattachine. He kept his IRS job for only six weeks; he resigned on May 13, 1955, and the next day, he was the last attendee to arrive at the 1955 annual Mattachine convention in Los Angeles. See ibid.; Buell Dwight Huggins to Alan Reitman, September 18, 1964, Box 1063, Folder 16, American Civil Liberties Union Papers, Mudd Library, Princeton University, Princeton, NJ (hereafter, "ACLU Papers"); "The Mattachine Society, Inc. Information Concerning (Internal Security)," April 12, 1957, FBI File #100–132065;

SAC [Special Agent in Charge], St. Louis, to Director, FBI, April 22, 1957, FBI File #100–403320–49. For a study of FBI surveillance of Huggins, see Charles, *Hoover's War on Gays*, 227–35. I am deeply grateful to Professor Charles for his willingness to share these and other FBI files.

73 *After the Mattachine . . . of homosexuals*: SAC, St. Louis, to Director, FBI, April 22, 1957, FBI File #100–403320–49.

73 *On June 28 . . . Society*: B. D. Huggins to Ken Burns, June 28, 1956, Box 3, Folder 21, Don Lucas Papers.

73 *He penned a . . . organization*: No, the Society was "unalterably opposed to Communism," and it did not exist to blackmail homosexuals, wrote Huggins. No, it did not intend to establish a homosexual "mecca." No, they would not "indulge in marijuana cigarettes at chapter meetings." The Mattachine Society, Inc., *Washington Newsletter* 1, no. 1, July 16, 1956, GLBT Historical Society.

73 *"The risks that . . . and bars"*: Huggins's newsletter announced that the chapter would fight employment discrimination and antihomosexual laws. It would work to gain the support of legislators. By August, Huggins referred to the chapter by a new name, the Council for Repeal of Unjust Laws. The Mattachine Society, Inc., *Washington Newsletter* 1, no. 2, August 16, 1956, GLBT Historical Society.

73 *An official . . . valor," he wrote*: Toby Marotta, *The Politics of Homosexuality* (Boston: Houghton Mifflin, 1981), 14–15.

73 *sixteen newsletter subscribers*: Dwight Huggins to Curtis Dewees, November 27, 1957, Box 1, Folder 8, MSNY Papers.

73 *thirteen members*: The majority of these likely never paid their dues, resulting in an even lower official membership count. By December 1957, the national Mattachine had not received dues from anyone in Washington, let alone from Huggins. The two checks it had received from him, including the chapter's filing fee, had bounced. Thus, technically, there was no Washington Mattachine at all. Huggins eventually left Washington, and under new leadership, the group experienced a period of rejuvenation in 1958: the organization even welcomed Dr. Benjamin Karpman as a guest speaker. The FBI learned that the Mattachine's meetings welcomed as many as forty attendees, but by November 1958, the national Mattachine reported only nine official members in its Washington chapter. By 1959, the Washington Mattachine had disappeared entirely. See The Mattachine Society, Inc., *Washington Newsletter* 1, no. 2, August 16, 1956, GLBT Historical Society; Don Lucas to Curtis Dewees, December 2, 1957, Box 4, Folder 12, Don Lucas Papers; The Mattachine Society, Inc., Washington Newsletter 3 no. 1, January 1958, Box 8, Folder 6, MSNY Papers; SAC, WFO, to Director, FBI, August 14, 1958, FBI File #100–33796–20; Hal Call to Al de Dion, November 12, 1958, Box 7, Folder 26, MSNY Papers.

73 *Kameny never joined the group*: Kameny denied any "sense of community" in Washington and never mentioned his membership in subsequent interviews. See Lahusen interview.

73 *The dangers, after . . . opening proceedings*: D'Emilio, *Sexual Politics, Sexual Communities*, 120–21.

74 *They were morals . . . its existence*: Ibid.

74 *The national Mattachine . . . its money?*: Rolland Howard, "A House Divided," *Interim*, October 25, 1960, GLBT Historical Society.

74 *On March 15 . . . name*: Mattachine Society, Inc., to All Area Councils and Members, March 15, 1961, Box 68, Folder 1, Gittings Papers.

74 *Chapters across the . . . altogether*: D'Emilio, *Sexual Politics, Sexual Communities*, 123.

74 *The astronomer had . . . request reemployment*: FEK to William Lambert, July 26, 1961, Box 70, Folder 8, FEK Papers.

74 *He then sent . . . the New Frontier!"*: FEK to JFK, May 15, 1961, Box 125, Folder 4, FEK Papers.

74 *He heard only . . . proper rights"*: FEK to John W. Macy, June 5, 1961, Box 41, Folder 12, FEK Papers.

75 *"The winds of change . . . coordinated fashion*: Despite the disintegration of the Mattachine, pockets of the homophile movement were ready for a fight. *ONE* magazine, after spinning off from one of the original Mattachine discussion groups in Los Angeles, had maintained its militancy for nearly a decade. In its battles with the government, it had won. When the Los Angeles postmaster seized copies of the "obscene, lewd, lascivious and filthy" magazine in 1954, *ONE* took him to court. Four years later, after a series of failed appeals, the Supreme Court ruled in the homosexual magazine's favor. And in January 1961, the theme of the magazine's Midwinter Institute was "A Homosexual Bill of Rights," which horrified its more conservative attendees. ("One cannot demand or legislate attitudes," argued one homophile leader.) Though the conference failed to ratify a final document, it represented a discussion that was shifting from education and research to the demanding of rights. See *ONE Inc. v. Olesen*, 355 U.S. 371 (1958); W. Dorr Legg, "*ONE* Midwinter Institute," *ONE* 9, no. 4, April 1961, 5; D'Emilio, *Sexual Politics, Sexual Communities*, 114.

75 *Since 1960, Kameny . . . Dion, its chairman*: See FEK to MSNY, May 5, 1960, Box 44, Folder 1, FEK Papers.

75 *De Dion and . . . brothers, not a couple*: According to Dewees, "de Dion" was a pseudonym. See Curtis Dewees, *Memoirs of a Gay Rights Maverick* (New York: Self-Published, 2010), 106–7; Vern L. Bullough, *Before Stonewall: Activists for Gay and Lesbian Rights in Historical Context* (New York: Harrington Park, 2002), 225.

75 *Since the disappearance . . . the nation's capital*: Albert J. de Dion to Clayton D. Laughran, August 3, 1960, Box 2, Folder 4, MSNY Papers; Curtis Dewees to Dwight Huggins, n.d., Box 1, Folder 8, MSNY Papers.

75 *In the middle . . . legal battle*: FEK to MSNY, May 5, 1960, Box 44, Folder 1, FEK Papers.

75 *fifty-dollar contribution*: Albert J. de Dion to FEK, September 19, 1960, Box 8, Folder 5, MSNY Papers.

75 *By the end . . . bank account*: Mattachine Society New York Area Council, "Treasurer's Report September 1960," Box 9, Folder 4, MSNY Papers.

75 *With the 1961 . . . of human-sexuality-and-society"*: MSNY to Members and Friends, March 27, 1961, Box 68, Folder 1, Gittings Papers.

75 *Kameny wanted to . . . a decent beginning"*: Albert J. de Dion to FEK, May 24, 1961, Box 8, Folder 5, MSNY Papers; FEK to Albert J. de Dion, June 27, 1961, Box 8, Folder 5, MSNY Papers.

75 *On the night . . . drag show*: "Vice Squad Sees Dance 3 Times Then Arrests 5," May 21, 1961, Box 137, Folder 12, FEK Papers.

75 *In high school . . . a professional dancer*: "Louis Anthony Fochett," Eastern High School 1941 Yearbook, *U.S., School Yearbooks, 1900–1999* (Provo, UT: Ancestry.com, 2010).

75 *now, for the . . . indecent performance*: "Vice Squad Sees Dance 3 Times Then Arrests 5," press clipping, May 21, 1961, Box 137, Folder 12, FEK Papers.

76 *On June 22 . . . employment"*: John W. Macy Jr. to FEK, June 22, 1961, Box 41, Folder 12, FEK Papers.

76 *Gardner Laboratories laid . . . month*: "Application for Federal Employment," February 11, 1966, Box 136, Folder 8, FEK Papers.

76 *He responded to . . . unemployment"*: FEK to John W. Macy Jr., July 22, 1961, Box 41, Folder 12, FEK Papers.

76 *Earlier that year . . . sit-ins*: Lahusen interview; "Supreme Court to Rule on Sit-Ins," *The Washington Evening Star*, March 20, 1961, 1.

76 *To his relief . . . of his case*: Lahusen interview.

76 *on July 10 . . . immediately to ONE*: FEK to William Lambert, July 26, 1961, Box 70, Folder 8, FEK Papers.

76 *its editor reassured . . . committed supporters*: William Lambert to FEK, July 18, 1961, Box 44, Folder 1, FEK Papers.

76 *It had referred . . . only as "PETITIONER"*: "That it should have taken these many thousands of years of man's history," wrote *ONE*, "for a single individual to have so forthrightly proclaimed this irrefutable logic seems well-nigh incredible. In spite of which, it is quite likely that his very audacity will take away the breath of the majority of homosexuals, brain-washed as they so long have been by the condemnation which a hostile society vents upon their affectational preferences." See "To the Friends of *ONE*," *ONE Confidential* 6, no. 5, May 1961, 1.

76 *The correspondent had . . . Law Week*: FEK to "Mr. Seitz," July 19, 1961, Box 44, Folder 1, FEK Papers.

77 *The last week . . . your community"*: Albert J. de Dion to Friend, July 25, 1961, Box 78, Folder 6, FEK Papers.

77 *On August 1 . . . executive meeting room*: SAC, WFO, to Director, FBI, August 8, 1961, FBI File #100–403320.

77 *De Dion and . . . is operating*: Lahusen interview.

6. THE BUREAU

80 *In 1933, a . . . virile masculinity"*: Curt Gentry, *J. Edgar Hoover: The Man and the Secrets* (New York: W. W. Norton, 1991), 158–59.

80 *Despite the rumors . . . and eight presidents*: Ibid., 27.

80 *In 1935, the*: Charles, *Hoover's War on Gays*, 32; D'Emilio and Freedman, *Intimate Matters*, 206.

80 *The "sex fiend . . . in 1937*: That year, when the State Department initiated its own gay purges, and when the U.S. Park Police launched its Pervert Elimination Campaign, the FBI was not yet an integral part of the purges' machinery. But it was inching closer: President Truman ordered the FBI to start conducting loyalty investigations of federal employees, and the Bureau continued adding to its Sex Offenders file. See Beemyn, *A Queer Capital*, 131; Johnson, *The Lavender Scare*, 59; Charles, *Hoover's War on Gays*, 32.

80 *On April 10 . . . ranks*: Charles, *Hoover's War on Gays*, 83. The Senate's December 1950 Hoey report lauded this new system, but it urged vigilance; to "pussyfoot" would only "allow some known perverts to remain in Government." See Hoey Report, 13, 20.

81 *Hoover's Sex Deviates . . . within days*: Charles, *Hoover's War on Gays*, 103–5.

81 *The Bureau kept . . . collection of secrets*: Ibid.

81 *Hoover also used . . . press*: Gentry, *J. Edgar Hoover*, 402.

81 *Sometimes, if the . . . the government*: Ibid., 413.

81 *When Hoover . . . control the Mattachine*: SAC, Los Angeles, to Director, December 31, 1953, FBI File #100–403320. The FBI first learned of Harry Hay's Mattachine Society only at the beginning of the Fifth Order's downfall, with the publication of Paul Coates's March 1953 article on the organization's political activity. In May, after the first Mattachine convention, an informant within the Society forwarded a copy of *ONE* magazine

to the FBI. One of the convention speakers, warned the informant, seemed to be "pro-communist," and the magazine landed on Hoover's desk within two days. On May 28, 1953, four days after the openness faction's victory, an informant, referred to only as "T-1" in heavily redacted records, warned the FBI that the chairman of the Bay Area chapter had refused to sign an American loyalty oath while teaching at Berkeley. Over the next three months, T-1 became an eager source. He provided the name and description of the suspicious Mattachine chairman, the names of several members of the San Francisco chapter, descriptions of meeting attendees who appeared to be members of the military, and a copy of the Mattachine constitution. Another Mattachine informant, referred to as "T-3," verified T-1's information. The new Mattachine became complicit in Hoover's maintenance of the gay purges. In August, the FBI director forwarded the informants' information to the Department of Justice so it could investigate whether the Mattachine members were federal employees. Meanwhile, Hoover ordered the San Francisco Field Office to forward the names to the appropriate military intelligence agencies—and chastised the special agent for not doing so earlier—so they could conduct their own purges. Who was informant T-1? Two weeks after his victory as part of Marilyn Rieger's openness faction, David Finn of the San Francisco Mattachine wrote to Ken Burns, the Society's new president. Finn had been talking to the FBI, he admitted, and he had given the Bureau a copy of the Society's constitution. Then, at a November 1953 Mattachine convention, he threatened to hand the attendees' names to the FBI if they did not finish cleansing the Society's constitution of the Fifth Order's "communistic" principles. See SAC, San Diego, to Director, FBI, May 21, 1953, FBI File #100–403320; John A. Chase, "Mattachine Foundation," July 14, 1953, FBI File #100–403320; Director, FBI, to Assistant Attorney General Warren Olney III, August 19, 1953, FBI File #100–403320; Director, FBI, to SAC, San Francisco, August 6, 1943, FBI File #100–403320; D'Emilio, *Sexual Politics, Sexual Communities*, 84–85.

82 *But the Bureau's . . . who had donated*: H. Rawlins Overton, "The Mattachine Society," FBI File #100–403320, 10.

82 *Over the next . . . agencies*: Ibid. In 1960, the U.S. Army's Counterintelligence Corps initiated "Project 220," an effort to determine whether 220 men arrested for homosexual activity in San Francisco had connections to the United States military. The army identified fifteen men, and the following year, when the initiative expanded to include five cities, it became "Project 440." When the FBI learned of the army's initiative, the Bureau decided to begin a project of its own. In May 1961, FBI agents contacted the San Francisco Police and learned that a new homosexual organization had recently materialized in the Bay Area. Two SFPD officers had recently attended an organizational meeting of the League for Civil Education (LCE). The chairmen, Guy Strait and José Sarria—the latter a prominent drag queen at the Black Cat Tavern—recognized the officers and welcomed them to the meeting. Somehow, the FBI acquired Strait's handwritten meeting notes. "Homosexual Activity in the San Francisco Division; Information Concerning," June 2, 1961, FBI File #100–37394; "League for Civil Education," June 5, 1961, FBI File #100–37394.

82 *On July 28 . . . faction in 1953*: We know that the agents spoke with Call and another Mattachine official—and we know what Call told the agents—because, in its classified report, the Bureau failed to redact Call's name on three separate occasions. To this day, we do not know the identity of "Informant T-3," the member of the San Francisco Mattachine who verified the information that Informant T-1, David Finn, handed to the Bureau back in 1953. But Call had been a prominent member of that chapter and the one to recruit Finn into the Mattachine. Now, when he spoke to the agents, Call told them Strait's company was a "front." See SA [Redacted] to SAC, "Homosexual Activities in San Francisco," July 28, 1961, FBI File #100–37394. For more on Call, see D'Emilio, *Sexual Politics, Sexual Communities*, 79; James T. Sears, *Behind the Mask of the Mattachine: The Hal Call Chronicles and the Early Movement for Homosexual Emancipation* (New York: Harrington Park, 2006).

82 *Hours before the . . . meeting room*: SUPV [Supervisor] [Redacted] to SAC, WFO, August 1, 1961, FBI File #100–33796.

82 *Deputy Chief Roy . . . defect, too*: Ibid.

83 *The FBI's Washington . . . homosexuals and Communists*: Ibid.

83 *When an FBI . . . on the homosexuals*: SAC, WFO, to Director, FBI, August 8, 1961, FBI File #100–403320.

83 *During the meeting . . . few blocks away*: Ibid.

83 *Al de Dion . . . understand," he wrote*: Albert J. de Dion to FEK, October 4, 1961, Box 8, Folder 5, MSNY Papers. Indeed, the MSNY had problems of its own. Only days before its annual conference, Hal Call's Mattachine sent letters to the MSNY's convention speakers to inform them that, as another homophile leader warned de Dion, "the group they are going to address is NOT the Mattachine Society and that you are, in essence, imposters." Call also wrote to the New York secretary of state, hoping to prompt a state investigation of the MSNY. De Dion successfully reassured the speakers, and Karpman spoke on "Unconscious Homosexuality," which, he argued, "pervades our entire lives . . . without exception!" But the looming threat of Hal Call—who now threatened a lawsuit—and the daunting task of forming an independent, legitimate homosexual corporation may have indicated that it was no time for territorial expansion. See Del Martin to Albert J. de Dion, August 30, 1961, Box 54, Folder 8, Gittings Papers; "Current Research Trends," *The Ladder* 6, no. 2, November 1961, 6.

83 *on November 7 . . . another meeting*: Albert J. de Dion to Friend, November 7, 1961, Box 3, Folder 32, MSNY Papers.

84 *On Wednesday, November . . . Washington*: Ibid.

84 *The attendees voted . . . that name*: Lahusen interview.

84 *The MSNY's articles . . . word homosexual*: "Certificate of Incorporation of the Mattachine Society, Inc., of New York," Box 3, Folder 3, MSNY Papers.

84 *"It is the . . . knew discrimination existed?*: "Constitution of the Mattachine Society of Washington," n.d., FBI File #100–33796.

84 *The Society's constitution . . . MSW constitution*: Ibid.

85 *The attendees agreed . . . for all"*: Ibid.; for Nichols's involvement, see Bullough, *Before Stonewall*, 226.

85 *Otherwise, the Mattachine . . . meetings*: "By-Laws of the Mattachine Society of Washington," n.d., Box 80, Folder 11, FEK Papers.

85 *As a homosexual . . . membership*: Ibid.

85 *Meanwhile, the Society . . . the membership*: "Constitution of the Mattachine Society of Washington," n.d., FBI File #100–33796.

85 *On November 29 . . . Washington*: FEK to Albert J. de Dion, November 24, Box 8, Folder 5, MSNY Papers.

85 *Just as he . . . Washington*: Lahusen interview.

86 *Although gay Washington . . . spring of 1962*: Paul Kuntzler, in "50th Anniversary of the Mattachine Society of Washington Panel Discussion," Rainbow History Project, October 13, 2011.

86 *The MSW's board . . . Society officer*: "Minutes of Meeting of the Executive Board," February 5, 1962, Box 85, Folder 9, FEK Papers.

86 *Board member Paul . . . after former lovers*: Paul Kuntzler, in "50th Anniversary of the Mattachine Society of Washington Panel Discussion," Rainbow History Project, October 13, 2011.

86 *Kameny himself did . . . against blackmail*: Lahusen interview.

86 *If something went . . . formation meeting*: Ibid.

86 *Kameny did not . . . NCACLU*: Ibid. Kameny had reason to believe that attorneys, rather than psychiatrists, would be the most effective allies in his war: earlier that summer, the Illinois state legislature had adopted the recommendations of the American Law Institute, the group of eminent jurists who had been preparing its Model Penal Code for nearly ten years. Thus, in January 1962, Illinois would become the first state in America to legalize private, consensual homosexual acts. See "Experts Laud Revised Criminal Code: But Overnight Results Aren't Expected," *Chicago Daily Tribune*, July 10, 1961, 10; "Model Penal Code Is Approved by the American Law Institute," *The New York Times*, May 25, 1962, 1. For a discussion of the political maneuvering behind the adoption of the MPC in Illinois, see Eskridge, *Gaylaw*, 84.

87 *Kameny entered that . . . that feat*: In his efforts to receive a response from CSC Chairman John Macy Jr.— four months after accusing him of perpetuating a homosexual genocide—Kameny began making a new argument for why he deserved a response. "I, uniquely in this country, by virtue of my Supreme Court case, and the efforts connected with it, have earned that right, beyond other citizens," he wrote. Kameny, bolstered by his new leadership position and by the praise he had received from the homophile movement, was beginning to see himself—and beginning to force others to see him—as the homosexual authority. See FEK to John W. Macy Jr., September 24, 1961, Box 41, Folder 12, FEK Papers; John W. Macy Jr. to FEK, October 10, 1961, Box 41, Folder 12, FEK Papers.

87 *He faced an . . . however*: In May 1962, when he learned that another ACLU chapter was defending a homosexual against deportation by arguing that there was no proof of homosexuality—rather than arguing against the policy of deportation itself—he contacted the Union's national headquarters in New York. "I wish to ask why this devious means of approach to the question was adopted," he wrote. Indeed, the constitutionality of homosexual laws was an area "ripe for action" by civil liberties groups, and he requested an update on current ACLU policy. Associate Director Alan Reitman responded by directing Kameny to the Union's 1957 statement on homosexuality, which explicitly condoned the purges. But Reitman alluded to the possibility of change. "I expect that the Union in the coming years will be more actively involved in this area," he said. Kameny responded by calling the 1957 statement "disappointing," but he was "encouraged" by Reitman's prediction that the ACLU would become more active in the field of homosexuality. See FEK to the American Civil Liberties Union, May 15, 1962, Box 80, Folder 12, FEK Papers; ACLU Position on Homosexuality," January 7, 1957, Box 1127, Folder 7, ACLU Papers; Alan Reitman to FEK, May 28, 1962, Box 80, Folder 12, FEK Papers; FEK to Alan Reitman, June 18, 1962, Box 80, Folder 12, FEK Papers.

87 *When Kameny asked . . . court context"*: James H. Heller to FEK, Jul 10, 1962, Box 75, Folder 6, FEK Papers.

87 *Bruce Scott was . . . would eventually come*: Interview with Bruce Scott, 1978, Gregory Sprague Collection, Chicago Historical Society, tape 3.

87 *In February 1956 . . . him to resign*: Ibid.

87 *For five years . . . a letter*: Ibid.

88 *Six weeks later . . . "Bruce Schuyler"*: Ibid., tape 1.

88 *In October, he . . . Examination*: CSC to Bruce Chardon Scott, February 14, 1962, Box 32, Folder 4, FEK Papers.

88　*on April 27 . . . was that*: "Brief for Appellant," Bruce C. Scott v. John W. Macy Jr. et al., Box 8, Folder 4, Gittings Papers.

88　*Kameny's second legal . . . Penn State"*: Richard Schlegel, interview with Marc Stein, May 10–11, 1993, Philadelphia LGBT History Project.

88　*On July 31 . . . sue the government*: Ibid.; *Richard L. Schlegel v. the United States*, 416 F.2d 1372 (Ct. Cl. 1969).

88　*In October 1961 . . . legal advisor*: FEK to Harold L. Call, December 1, 1962, Box 81, Folder 2, FEK Papers; Richard Schlegel to FEK, n.d., Box 9, Folder 3, FEK Papers.

88　*Kameny later denied . . . the federal government*: Lahusen interview.

89　*On Sunday, May . . . MANAGING SOCIETY"*: [Redacted] Clerk to SAC, WFO, May 27, 1962, FBI File #100–33796.

89　*A nineteen-year-old from . . . sometimes, he lied*: Don McCardle, interviewed by Eric Cervini, telephone, June 16, 2019.

89　*At the Bureau . . . with them"*: SA [Redacted] to SAC, WFO, June 5, 1962, FBI File #100–33796.

90　*Scarberry knew of . . . to him"*: Ibid.

90　*The MSW meeting . . . the Society*: Ibid.

90　*Six days after . . . "gay crowd"*: These quotes originate from Brass's signed statement, which likely summarized admissions that he made to the agents the previous day. See "In the Matter of the Suspension and Proposed Removal of Ronald Bertram Brass, Statement of Charges," April 11, 1963, Box 15, Folder 4, FEK Papers.

91　*The Department of . . . to his fate*: Ibid.; Ronald B. Brass, "Statement Concerning FBI Attempt to Procure Mattachine Society Membership List," n.d., Box 15, Folder 4, FEK Papers.

91　*The Bureau followed . . . within its ranks*: Redacted Letterhead Memo, June 18, 1962, FBI File #100–33796.

92　*When Brass told . . . the ACLU*: FEK to Harold L. Call, June 17, 1963, Box 81, Folder 2, FEK Papers.

92　*The FBI agents' . . . of purposes*: FEK to Robert F. Kennedy, June 28, 1962, FBI File #100–33796. Kameny's letter confused the Department of Justice. Robert Kennedy forwarded it to Hoover, and by July 9, his top officials concluded that they did not know what Kameny was talking about. Maybe he was writing about a recent murder in Virginia—or another redacted crime—that had been committed by "sex deviates," they speculated. FBI headquarters did not know about the investigation of Ronald Brass because it did not need to know; indeed, by 1961, the Bureau's Sex Deviates program was so routinized, and so vast, that there was no reason for the director to know the details of every case. Subsequently, Hoover provided verifiably false information to Robert Kennedy, and he may have done so knowingly. Despite Hal Call's description of the national Society's dissolution the year prior, and despite Hoover's receipt of an updated Mattachine constitution in 1956, the director quoted from the outdated constitution of the Fifth Order. Kameny's group, he informed Kennedy, was a chapter of a "California corporation founded in 1953," working to integrate a "highly ethical homosexual culture" into society. Hoover also described the Bureau's practice of interrogating homosexuals in cases that involved sexual deviants: "Members of Dr. Kameny's group logically are considered as possible suspects in investigations of this type. Certainly, this Bureau has not engaged in harassment or intimidation of this or any other group. In view of the tenor of Dr. Kameny's letter, his malicious and unfounded charges and background information concerning him, it is suggested that you not acknowledge his communication," concluded Hoover. See D. C. Morrell to Mr. DeLoach, July 9, 1962, FBI File #100-HQ-403320; SAC, Los Angeles, to Director, FBI, August 23, 1956, FBI File #100-HQ-403320; D. C. Morrell to Mr. DeLoach, July 9, 1962, FBI File #100-HQ-403320; Director, FBI, to the Attorney General, July 9, 1962, FBI File #100-HQ-403320.

92　*Kameny never received . . . from Robert Kennedy*: See Box 82, Folder 2, FEK Papers.

92　*Warren Scarberry continued . . . informant (CI)*: After Scarberry handed over his list of eighty-five homosexuals, his special agent handler had made a recommendation to the head of the Washington Field Office: "In view of [REDACTED] desire to cooperate with the Bureau and inasmuch as he apparently has an extended knowledge of the homosexual element in the Metropolitan area, [REDACTED]." See SA [Redacted] to SAC, WFO, June 5, 1962, FBI File #100–33796.

92　*The FBI destroyed . . . program in 1978*: FBI to Eric Cervini, November 3, 2017, Author's Collection.

92　*But on August . . . meeting*: "Mattachine Society of Washington," August 20, 1962, FBI File #100–33796.

92　*The next day . . . was Frank Kameny*: [Redacted] to WFO [Redacted], August 21, 1962, FBI File #100–33796.

93　*After meeting . . . Bureau like it?*: "Mattachine Society of Washington," August 20, 1962, FBI File #100–33796.

93　*Within a few . . . the astronomer*: "Photo of Franklin [Redacted]," August 17, 1962, FBI File #100–33796.

7. THE CRUSADER

94　*Yes, he enjoyed . . . State Police*: Randy Wicker, interviewed by Eric Cervini, July 28, 2017, Hoboken, NJ.

94　*When Charlie returned . . . local Parent-Teacher Association*: Maurice Olian, "Petition Signers Rise," *The Daily Texan*, n.d., clipping in Personal Papers of Randy Wicker, Hoboken, NJ.

94　*Charlie drafted a . . . and local figures*: Ibid.; E. Ernest Goldstein, "The Facts, Ma'am." *The Daily Texan*, n.d., clipping in Personal Papers of Randy Wicker, Hoboken, NJ.

94 *The PTA retreated . . . students' newsstands*: Larry Hurwitz, "Students Find *Playboy* Back on Newsstands," n.d., clipping in Personal Papers of Randy Wicker, Hoboken, NJ.

94 *"Hayden plans Capitol . . . risk alienating legislators?"*: "Hayden Plans Capitol March to Protest House 'Fees Bill,'" *The Daily Texan*, May 6, 1959, 1.

95 *At one o'clock . . . the fountain"*: Ray Hanson, "Arise!!," *Texas Ranger*, April 1960, 19.

95 *Cognizant of the . . . Everyone laughed*: Ibid.

95 *"March Fails: Hayden's . . .* Texan: Leo Cardenas, "March Fails," *The Daily Texan*, n.d., clipping in Personal Papers of Randy Wicker, Hoboken, NJ.

95 *But the humiliation . . . claim success"*: "The Firing Line: Hayden Defended," *The Daily Texan*, n.d., clipping in Personal Papers of Randy Wicker, Hoboken, NJ.

95 *Newspapers across the . . . the bill stalled*: Hanson, "Arise!!," 19.

95 *"You are a . . . and upward!"*: Nancy Aldrich et al. to Charlie Hayden, n.d., Personal Papers of Randy Wicker, Hoboken, NJ.

95 *Charlie spent the . . . hard work*: Randy Wicker, interviewed by Eric Cervini, July 28, 2017, Hoboken, NJ.

96 *But he still . . . the university*: Ibid.

96 *He heard the . . . scandal*: Ibid.

96 *On election day . . . votes*: "Unofficial Election Returns," *The Daily Texan*, n.d., clipping in Personal Papers of Randy Wicker, Hoboken, NJ.

96 *Five months later . . . real political office*: Randy Wicker, interviewed by Eric Cervini, July 28, 2017, Hoboken, NJ.

96 *His battles, however . . . it concluded)*: Hanson, "Arise!!," 19.

96 *Because of Charlie . . . many enemies"*: Ibid.

96 *Charlie had another . . . to "wicked"*: Bullough, *Before Stonewall*, 278.

97 *On visits to . . . wrong about homosexuals?*: Randy Wicker, interviewed by Eric Cervini, July 28, 2017, Hoboken, NJ.

97 *He moved to . . . building demolition company*: Ibid.

97 *Wicker began developing*: Randolfe Wicker, "Adventures of a Homosexual Organizer," n.d., Personal Papers of Randy Wicker, Hoboken, NJ.

97 *And in April . . . hours of therapy*: Randy Wicker, "Memories of gay activism, 1959 to 1970," September 13, 2007, The Tangent Group; Milton Bracker, "Homosexuals Air Their Views Here," *The New York Times*, July 16, 1962, 36.

97 *Wicker promptly marched . . . time to respond*: "Subscriber's Program Folio," WBAI-FM, July 9–July 22, 1962, Box 2, Printed Ephemera 1958–1962, Randy Wicker Papers, New York Public Library, New York, NY (hereafter, "Wicker Papers").

97 *The station acquiesced . . . everything they said*: "Minority Listening," *Newsweek*, July 30, 1962, 48.

97 *When WBAI started . . . to "WSICK"*: Jack O'Brian, "Swing & Sway—With H.V.K.," *New York Journal-American*, July 9, 1962, 18.

97 *Wicker had a . . . Texan drawl*: "Live and Let Live," WBAI, digital audio recording, July 17, 1962, in the possession of the author.

97 *After explaining the . . . only one"*: "Live and Let Live," *The Realist*, no. 36, August 1962, 1.

98 *For the next . . . said another homosexual*: Ibid.

98 *With that, the . . . the air*: Randy Wicker, "Live & Let Live," *LCE News* 1, no. 22, August 6, 1962, 3. The WBAI broadcast was not entirely unprecedented. As early as 1954, a member of the Los Angeles Mattachine had appeared on a televised program, *The Sex Variant in Southern California*, as an acknowledged homosexual (he promptly lost his job after his boss recognized him). And only two months before the WBAI broadcast, Hal Call and Jaye Bell, the president of the Daughters of Bilitis, had appeared on another televised panel discussion in Los Angeles. See Edward Alwood, "A Gift of Gab: How Independent Broadcasters Gave Gay Rights Pioneers a Chance to Be Heard," in *Media Q: Media/Queered*, ed. Kevin G. Barnhurst (New York: Peter Lang, 2007), 29; Sten Russell, "KTTV Presents 'Argument'-Society and the Homosexual," *The Ladder* 6, no. 9, June 1962, 9.

98 *The next day . . . critic*: Milton Bracker, "Homosexuals Air Their Views Here," *The New York Times*, July 16, 1962, 36; Jack Gould, "Radio: Taboo Is Broken," *The New York Times*, July 16, 1962, 35.

98 *Stations rebroadcast the . . . transcript*: See "Live and Let Live," *The Realist*, no. 36, August 1962, 1; Elsa Knight Thompson to Randolfe Wicker, July 16, 1962, Box 1, "Correspondence" Folder, Wicker Papers; Randy Wicker, "Wicker Report," 1962, Box 1, "Miscellaneous Papers" Folder, Wicker Papers.

98 *Reveling in the . . . spokesman*: After condensing the impressive collection of articles on the broadcast into a single broadsheet, he made hundreds of copies. See Randolfe Wicker, "Progress Report," 1962, Box 10, Folder 12, FEK Papers.

98 *On August 5 . . . date*: "Social Series II: The Homosexual," *New York Chapter Humanist Newsletter* 1, no. 3, August 1962, Box 2, "Printed Ephemera 1958–1962" Folder, Wicker Papers; Randolfe Wicker, "Adventures of a Homosexual Organizer," n.d., Personal Papers of Randy Wicker, Hoboken, NJ.

98 *Wicker's efforts sent . . . and plodding"*: Robert R. Liechti to Randy Wicker, July 17, 1962, Box 1, "Correspondence (Misc)" Folder, Wicker Papers.

98 *To de Dion . . . disorganized and tactless*: Curtis Dewees, interviewed by John D'Emilio, January 24, 1979, New York, NY, OutHistory.org.

98 *ONE magazine, meanwhile . . . subject," it wrote*: Del McIntire, "Tangents," *ONE* 10, no. 10, October 1962, 19.

99 *Wicker still sent . . . publicist for gay rights*: FEK to Randolfe Wicker, August 2, 1962, Box 81, Folder 7, FEK Papers.

99 *In August 1962 . . . prostitute"*: SUPV to SAC, August 16, 1962, FBI File #100–37394, 69.

99 *The Bureau deployed . . . convention*: Ibid.

99 *It acquired a . . . of Washington*: SA [special agent] to SAC, San Francisco, October 1, 1962, FBI File #100–37394, 75.

99 *Schlegel spoke as . . . the Homophile Movement"*: "Mattachine Society, Inc.," August 21, 1962, FBI File #100–37394, 68; Del McIntire, "Tangents," *ONE*, October 1962.

99 *The United States . . . on law"*: Richard L. Schlegel, "Homosexuals in Government," *Mattachine Review* 8, no. 11, November 1962, 13.

99 *The FBI . . . if necessary*: SA to SAC, San Francisco, October 1, 1962, FBI File #100–37394, 75.

100 *After the "fiery" . . . legal war*: See Richard L. Schlegel, "Homosexuals in Government," *Mattachine Review* 8, no. 11, November 1962, 13; "A Decade of Progress in the Homophile Movement," *The Ladder* 7, no. 2, November 1962, 7.

100 *The remnants of . . . for that"*: Harold L. Call to FEK, November 27, 1962, Box 81, Folder 2, FEK Papers.

100 *Kameny refused to . . . his organization's name*: FEK to W. Dorr Legg, December 30, 1962, Box 82, Folder 3, FEK Papers.

100 *but if he . . . of Defense*: SA [Redacted] to SAC, San Francisco, November 26, 1962, FBI File #100–37394, 78.

100 *In the summer . . . world*: "News Release," August 28, 1962, FBI File #100–33796, 15; FEK to Randolfe Wicker, August 21, 1962, Box 1, "Correspondence" Folder, Wicker Papers.

100 *With media coverage . . . for reform*: For early drafts of letter to Congress referencing the proposed ad and the press release, see Box 85, Folder 5, FEK Papers.

100 *"A formation of . . . security clearance system*: "News Release," August 28, 1962, FBI File #100–33796, 15.

100 *The Society sent . . . release in mid-August*: FEK to Randolfe Wicker, August 21, 1962, Box 1, "Correspondence" Folder, Wicker Papers.

100 *"I HOPE TO . . . HIGH PLACES"*: Randolfe Wicker to FEK, August 17, 1962, Box 81, Folder 7, FEK Papers.

101 *"Dear Mr. Wicker . . . the press release*: FEK to Randolfe Wicker, August 21, 1962, Box 1, "Correspondence" Folder, Wicker Papers.

101 *Kameny remained optimistic . . . had closed?*: Ibid.

101 *On August 28 . . . E. Kameny*: "Congress," Box 85, Folder 5, FEK Papers.

101 *The Society had . . . letters each official*: Lahusen interview.

101 *In each envelope . . . each recipient*: See, for example, FEK to Raymond F. Farrell, August 28, 1962, Box 81, Folder 4, FEK Papers; FEK to Cyrus R. Vance, August 28, 1962, Box 85, Folder 5, FEK Papers.

101 *Because of Warren . . . would be prepared*: SAC, WFO, to Director, FBI, "Mattachine Society of Washington, Information Concerning," August 20, 1962, FBI File #100–403320, 612.

102 *In the weeks . . . the Bureau*: See FEK to William C. Cramer, August 28, 1962, FBI File #100-HQ-403320, 621; Joe M. Kilgore to J. Edgar Hoover, September 17, 1962, FBI File #100-HQ-403320, 623.

102 *The vast majority . . . hoax"*: Kilgore knew that each member of Congress had received copies, suggesting that the officials had discussed the letters among themselves. See ibid.

102 *The Department of Defense . . . a crank"*: SAC, Baltimore, to Director, FBI, October 5, 1962, FBI File #100-HQ-403320, 627.

102 *Within the Civil . . . rather quickly*: L. V. Meloy to John W. Macy, Jr., September 21, 1962, Homosexuals and Suitability, Legal Advisory Files, Office of the General Counsel, Records of the U.S. Civil Service Commission and the Office of Personnel Management, RG 146, National Archives (College Park, MD). I am grateful to Charles Francis and Pate Felts for calling my attention to this document.

102 *Chairman Macy responded . . . your society."*: John W. Macy Jr. to Bruce Schuyler, September 28, 1962, Box 85, Folder 5, FEK Papers.

102 *From members . . . a revolting communication"*: Charles E. Chamberlain to FEK, August 30, 1962, Box 85, Folder 5, FEK Papers.

102 *Democratic congressman Paul . . . filthy trash"*: FEK to Paul E. Jones, August 28, 1962, Box 85, Folder 5, FEK Papers.

103 *On September 8 . . . NIX, M.C."*: Robert N. C. Nix to FEK, September 8, 1962, Box 82, Folder 6, FEK Papers.

103 *Congressman Nix of . . . a former slave*: "Robert N. C. Nix Sr., 88, Dies," *The Washington Post*, June 23, 1987, B4; "NIX, Robert Nelson Cornelius, Sr.," History, Art & Archives, United States House of Representatives, http://history.house.gov/People/Detail?id=18971.

103 *Kameny walked into . . . rotunda*: "Cannon House Office Building," https://www.aoc.gov/capitol-buildings
/cannon-house-office-building.

103 *Nix told Kameny . . . any way possible*: FEK to The Janus Society, September 15, 1962, Box 82, Folder 1, FEK
Papers.

103 *and he even . . . MSW*: Board Meeting Agenda, September 19, 1962, Box 85, Folder 1, FEK Papers.

103 *Kameny quickly wrote . . . upcoming election*: FEK to The Janus Society, September 15, 1962, Box 82, Folder 1,
FEK Papers.

103 *Congressman William Fitts . . . forty-year-old Princeton man*: "William F. Ryan," *The Harvard Crimson*,
December 6, 1962, http://www.thecrimson.com/article/1962/12/6/william-f-ryan-pnew-yorks-only.

103 *"I hope that . . . said*: William F. Ryan to FEK, September 10, 1962, Box 83, Folder 1, FEK Papers.

103 *By the end . . . their congressman*: FEK to Albert J. de Dion, September 15, 1962, Box 81, Folder 3, FEK
Papers.

103 *For the first . . . national security"*: "Annual Report for the Year 1962," House Un-American Activities Committee, January 2, 1963, 64.

104 *Kameny wrote to . . . private industry"*: FEK to William F. Ryan, September 18, 1962, Box 83, Folder 1, FEK
Papers.

104 *On September 19 . . . H.R. 11363*: "Protection of Classified Information," September 19, 1962, 87th Cong.,
2d sess., *Congressional Record*, 19943.

104 *which ultimately failed . . . only six votes*: The bill, after a motion to pass it via suspension of the rules, failed to
achieve the requisite two-thirds majority of the House. "Annual Report for the Year 1962," House Un-
American Activities Committee, January 2, 1963, 102. In Kameny's letter, he urged the congressmen to vote
against two HUAC bills that involved security clearances. The second bill, however, dealt less with the industrial security system than with the National Security Administration's internal employee security measures,
implemented after the Martin and Mitchell defections. While Ryan voted against the bill, Nix voted for it.
H.R. 12082 passed in the House by an overwhelming 352–23 vote. See FEK to William F. Ryan, September
18, 1962, Box 83, Folder 1, FEK Papers; "Internal Security Act of 1950," *Congressional Record*, 87th Congress, 2d session, September 19, 1962, 19944.

104 *Yes, Congressman Ryan . . . first homosexual lobby*: William F. Ryan to FEK, September 21, 1962, Box 83,
Folder 1, FEK Papers.

104 *On September 5 . . . charity's legitimacy*: C. N. Cardano to FEK, September 5, 1962, Box 82, Folder 3, FEK
Papers.

104 *On September 10 . . . Society's homosexuals*: FEK to The Mattachine Society, October 15, 1962, Box 82, Folder
4, FEK Papers.

104 *Kameny asked the . . . therefore be revoked*: Ibid.

104 *First, the Society . . . with Kameny*: Julian P. Green to FEK, September 13, 1962, Box 82, Folder 3, FEK
Papers.

105 *"Group Aiding Deviates . . . story, a scandal*: "Group Aiding Deviates Issued Charity License," *The Washington
Evening Star*, September 16, 1962, A22.

105 *The superintendent of . . . records for examination"*: Ibid.

105 *The Society had . . . newspaper complied*: Ibid.

105 *Unlike Wicker, Kameny . . . publicity*: Although a local news station interviewed him in early October—
Kameny simply listed his organization's purposes—the Society's executive board remained entirely preoccu-
pied by its communications with Congress. See FEK to Wicker, November 18, 1962, Box 81, Folder 7, FEK
Papers; Board Meeting Agenda, September 19, 1962, Box 85, Folder 1, FEK Papers.

105 *The congressional meetings . . . involved"*: FEK to The Mattachine Society, October 15, 1962, Box 82, Folder 4,
FEK Papers.

105 *As Kameny's authority . . . of Washington*: R. L. Applegate to Bruce Schuyler, October 15, 1962, Box 80, Folder
12, FEK Papers.

106 *For three months . . . security policy*: FEK to Walter P. Skallerup, July 31, 1962, Box 45, Folder 1, FEK Papers;
Bruce Schuyler to Walter T. Skallerup Jr., August 28, 1962, Box 85, Folder 5, FEK Papers.

106 *Though it would . . . process*: FEK to Walter T. Skallerup Jr., October 11, 1962, Box 45, Folder 1, FEK
Papers.

106 *When Bruce Scott . . . particular issues"*: Bruce Schuyler to Robert L. Applegate, October 5, 1962, Box 80,
Folder 12, FEK Papers.

106 *the Pentagon official finally agreed*: R. L. Applegate to Bruce Schuyler, October 15, 1962, Box 80, Folder 12,
FEK Papers.

106 *twenty-two-year-old*: "Allen Duncan," Coolidge High School 1956 Yearbook, *U.S., School Yearbooks, 1900–
1999* (Provo, UT: Ancestry.com, 2010); "Allen S. Duncan," *Connecticut Department of Health, Connecticut
Death Index, 1949–2012* (Provo, UT: Ancestry.com, 2003).

106 *The young man's . . . in the area*: Marvin J. Duncan, "Announcement," *The Washington Evening Star*, June 28,
1952, 34.

106 *his mother, Marie . . . recipe book*: Pillsbury, *Best of the Bake-Off Cookies and Bars* (Minneapolis, MN: General Mills, 2012), 66.

106 *mother of five*: "Congratulations, Mrs. Duncan," *The Washington Evening Star*, December 6, 1951, 51.

106 *walked into the . . . of homosexuals*: FEK to Mrs. Marvin Duncan, October 27, 1962, Box 81, Folder 3, FEK Papers.

107 *"Tell us exactly . . . the Hay-Adams meeting*: Marie Duncan captured the entirety of the meeting in her transcription, which included the nonverbal interactions (e.g., laughter) that are described in these paragraphs. "Meeting October 23, 1962," Box 85, Folder 10, FEK Papers, 1.

107 *The security clearance . . . admitted Applegate*: Ibid.

107 *Bruce Scott then . . . job*: Ibid., 2.

107 *But this solution . . . responded Kameny*: Ibid., 4.

107 *Throughout the discussion . . . responded Kameny*: Ibid., 16.

108 *"A homosexual is . . . Lewis*: Ibid., 12.

108 *Halfway through the . . . endorse homosexuality"*: Ibid., 11.

108 *The officials argued . . . responded Lewis*: Ibid., 22.

109 *But what* evidence *. . . to help*: Ibid., 26.

109 *During the three-hour . . . to fight*: Bruce Schuyler to Robert L. Applegate, November 2, 1962, Box 80, Folder 12, FEK Papers.

109 *Kameny followed through . . . country*: See FEK to Charles Hayden, November 18, 1962, Box 1, Correspondence, Wicker Papers, NYPL; FEK to The Mattachine Society, November 22, 1962, Box 82, Folder 4, FEK Papers; and FEK to Demophil Center, November 22, 1962, Box 81, Folder 3, FEK Papers.

109 *Homosexuals facing the . . . he advised*: FEK to ONE Inc., November 14, 1962, Box 82, Folder 6, FEK Papers.

109 *On the West . . . aside"*: "We Must Fight Now," *LCE News*, October 15, 1962, 1.

110 *Two weeks later . . . of Congress"*: "Now We Are Fighting," *LCE News*, October 29, 1962, 1. As in Washington, the homosexual's logical legal ally in San Francisco was the American Civil Liberties Union. But in November, when Strait wrote to the ACLU headquarters in New York, he was dismayed by Associate Director Alan Reitman's response. As usual, Reitman sent a copy of the Union's five-year-old, pro-purge policy statement. "It is true that we have not yet tackled the basic question," admitted Reitman, "only for the reason that we thought it necessary to have the Supreme Court's thinking in this area before considering the matter." Before the ACLU could argue for the right to homosexual activity, it first needed to wait for the court to decide on the right to heterosexual activity: specifically, the right to use birth control, which was still banned in several states. Once the Supreme Court ruled on that matter, perhaps in a year or two, the Union would be able to reconsider homosexuality. "This may sound like a long time to wait," wrote Reitman, "but in a field as sensitive as this it is wiser to have the Court's thinking before plunging into a case which might set us back considerably." "I have concluded that it is not in my interest to continue as a member of the ACLU," responded Strait. "I am accordingly returning my membership card which is attached." Kameny, however, was more understanding: "If the Court's decision is unfortunately such as to indicate that the states do have complete control of private, consenting sexual behavior, then there is nothing that the ACLU can do in this field," he explained to *ONE*. But he also understood that his cases, those fighting the purges, dealt less with the privacy of the bedroom and more with other constitutional issues: due process and equal protection under the law. See "Help from ACLU?," *LCE News*, November 12, 1962, 2; FEK to W. Dorr Legg, December 30, 1962, Box 82, Folder 3, FEK Papers.

110 *In Washington, the . . . his job*: James H. Heller to FEK, July 10, 1962, Box 75, Folder 6, FEK Papers.

110 *The MSW also . . . Washington chapter*: Interview with Bruce Scott, 1978, Gregory Sprague Collection, Chicago Historical Society, Tape 2; FEK to W. Dorr Legg, March 10, 1963, Box 82, Folder 3, FEK Papers.

110 *Kameny, meanwhile, worked . . . and Loyalty Committee*: FEK to Demophil Center, November 22, 1962, Box 81, Folder 3, FEK Papers.

110 *In the fall . . . about it?*: Lahusen interview.

111 *Kameny drafted the press release*: National Capital Area Civil Liberties Union, Press Release, December 3, 1962, Box 132, Folder 2, FEK Papers.

111 *His speech to . . . Beaux-Arts Russian compound*: Doris Kanter, "Labor's New Houses," *The Sunday Star Magazine*, May 25, 1958, 7; Norman Polmar and Thomas B. Allen, *Merchants of Treason: America's Secrets for Sale* (New York: Delacorte, 1988), 24; "President's Limousines to Moscow," *Independent Press-Telegram* (Long Beach, CA), July 9, 1972, 147.

111 *"First, the number . . . could even point*: Ibid.

111 *Kameny's speech was . . . hunting down Jews"*: Ibid.

112 *Kameny admitted that . . . just begun"*: Ibid.

112 *Three weeks earlier . . . serious trouble"*: Ronald Brass to Franklin Kameny, November 22, 1962, Box 15, Folder 4, FEK Papers.

112 *Two months earlier . . . noon*: "Prayer," on October 10, 1962, 87th Cong., 2d Sess., *Congressional Record*, 22931.

112 *The missile situation . . . the embargo?*: "Association of Greek Shipowners Honors Recommendation to Halt Shipping to Cuba," on October 10, 1962, 87th Cong., 2d Sess., *Congressional Record*, 23012.

113 *A Democratic congressman . . . correct this situation"*: "Charitable Solicitations in the District of Columbia," on October 10, 1962, 87th Cong., 2d Sess., *Congressional Record*, 23012.

8. THE ALLIANCE

114 *But where were . . . the female homosexuals?*: Del Martin and Phyllis Lyon, interviewed by Kay Tobin Lahusen, 1970–1971, Box 122, Folder 7, Gittings Papers; D'Emilio, *Sexual Politics, Sexual Communities*, 102.

114 *She had married . . . only child*: Del Martin and Phyllis Lyon, interviewed by Kay Tobin Lahusen, 1970–1971, Box 122, Folder 7, Gittings Papers.

114 *In 1949 . . . a briefcase*: Faderman, *The Gay Revolution*, 74.

114 *Phyllis Lyon had . . . painless. Fun, even*: Del Martin and Phyllis Lyon, interviewed by Kay Tobin Lahusen, 1970–1971, Box 122, Folder 7, Gittings Papers.

114 *She had been . . . lipstick*: Faderman, *The Gay Revolution*, 74–75.

114 *After two years . . . by death*: Ibid.; Del Martin and Phyllis Lyon, interviewed by Kay Tobin Lahusen, 1970–1971, Box 122, Folder 7, Gittings Papers.

115 *In 1953, the . . . zoo animals*: Ibid.

115 *On September 21 . . . sexual deviants?*: D'Emilio, *Sexual Politics, Sexual Communities*, 102.

115 *The eight women . . . later recalled*: Del Martin and Phyllis Lyon, interviewed by Kay Tobin Lahusen, 1970–1971, Box 122, Folder 7, Gittings Papers.

115 *A year later . . . of social acceptance*: Faderman, *The Gay Revolution*, 78.

115 *Society made lesbians . . . government?*: Del Martin and Phyllis Lyon, interviewed by Kay Tobin Lahusen, 1970–1971, Box 122, Folder 7, Gittings Papers.

115 *Martin and Lyon . . . identities*: Ibid.; D'Emilio, *Sexual Politics, Sexual Communities*, 103.

115 *By recruiting women . . . York chapter*: Barbara Gittings, interviewed by Kay Tobin Lahusen, 1969–1971, Box 122, Folder 4, Gittings Papers.

116 *Although those groups . . . and their materials*: Del Martin and Phyllis Lyon, interviewed by Kay Tobin Lahusen, 1970–1971, Box 122, Folder 7, Gittings Papers.

116 *they did not . . . their unique concerns—seriously*: Ibid.; D'Emilio, *Sexual Politics, Sexual Communities*, 105.

116 *At the 1959 . . . about Lesbians?"*: "Mattachine Breaks Through the Conspiracy of Silence," *The Ladder* 4, no. 1 (October 1959): 19.

116 *The next year . . . joining other organizations*: Daughters of Bilitis, "Amendments to the Constitution," May 29, 1960, Box 1, Folder 2, Phyllis Lyon, Del Martin and the Daughters of Bilitis collection, GLBT Historical Society, San Francisco, CA.

116 *As one DOB . . . "Up yours"*: D'Emilio, *Sexual Politics, Sexual Communities*, 105.

116 *Daughters of Bilitis? . . . absurd name?*: Barbara Gittings, interviewed by Jonathan Ned Katz, July 19, 1974, Philadelphia, PA, OutHistory.org; also published in Jonathan Ned Katz, *Gay American History: Lesbians and Gay Men in the U.S.A.* (New York: Thomas Y. Crowell, 1976).

116 *As a child . . . discussed only men*: Barbara Gittings, interviewed by Kay Tobin Lahusen, 1969–1971, Box 122, Folder 4, Gittings Papers; Bullough, *Before Stonewall*, 242.

117 *Her obsession with . . . freshman year*: Ibid.

117 *Gittings moved to . . . the rocks*: Ibid.

117 *In the summer . . . lesbian organization*: Kay Tobin and Randy Wicker, *The Gay Crusaders* (New York: Arno Press, 1972), 206.

117 *The Village Voice . . . names*: Ibid., 211–12.

117 *Lesbians could meet . . . was enough*: Barbara Gittings, interviewed by Jonathan Ned Katz, July 19, 1974, Philadelphia, PA, OutHistory.org.

117 *In February 1963 . . . interim replacement*: Barbara Gittings, interviewed by Kay Tobin Lahusen, 1969–1971, Box 122, Folder 4, Gittings Papers.

117 *For her first . . . lesbian wedding*: Jody Shotwell, "Gay Wedding," *The Ladder* 7, no. 5 (February 1963): 4.

117 *That same month . . . Frank Kameny*: Barbara Gittings, Handwritten Notes, The Mattachine Society of Washington, February 23, 1963, Box 64, Folder 3, Gittings Papers.

118 *The MSW's unprecedented . . . document*: Jack Ervin to The Mattachine Society of Washington, September 22, 1962, Box 82, Folder 1, FEK Papers.

118 ONE *invited Kameny . . . that coming January*: W. Dorr Legg to FEK, November 8, 1962, Box 82, Folder 6, FEK Papers.

118 *"I didn't suspect," . . . mailings to congressmen"*: J. C. Thorne to FEK, October 8, 1962, Box 78, Folder 6, FEK Papers.

118 *In December 1962 . . . coordinate activities?*: FEK to Richard Inman, July 13, 1965, Box 5, Folder 11, FEK Papers.

118 *Representatives of four . . . that summer*: The Mattachine Society of Washington, January 26, 1963, Box 64, Folder 3, Gittings Papers; "Dear Barbara & Kay," n.d., Box 63, Folder 8, Gittings Papers.

118 *At a second . . . she wrote*: Barbara Gittings, Handwritten Notes, The Mattachine Society of Washington, February 23, 1963, Box 64, Folder 3, Gittings Papers.

118 *At first, Gittings . . . and professional contacts?*: Barbara Gittings to Jaye Bell et al., April 1963, Box 63, Folder 8, Gittings Papers.

118 *But later . . . with heterosexuals"*: Barbara Gittings, interviewed by Kay Tobin Lahusen, 1969–1971, Box 122, Folder 4, Gittings Papers.

119 *At the March . . . damn please"*: Randy Wicker to Barbara Gittings, 1963, Box 1, "Correspondence 63, 65" Folder, Wicker Papers.

119 *"Thank yo ufo . . . were together"*: FEK to Charlie Hayden, March 30, 1963, Box 8, Folder 5, MSNY Papers.

119 *Kameny had taken . . . seriously*: When Scarberry revealed that CSC investigators had visited Ronald Brass's home, the embattled Department of Commerce employee wrote a summary of Scarberry's allegations for Kameny. Not only had CSC investigators talked to Scarberry, but so had army investigators. See Ronald Brass to Franklin Kameny, November 22, 1962, Box 15, Folder 4, FEK Papers.

119 *According to the . . . years old*: Ibid.

119 *Kameny himself knew . . . sounded accurate*: "Security Board Hearing in the Matter of the Suspension and Proposed Removal of Ronald B. Brass," Transcript, n.d., Box 15, Folder 5, FEK Papers.

119 *Kameny turned to . . . such "slander"*: The Union managed to prevent Brass's termination, but because investigators had been "overzealous" in confronting Scarberry, the NCACLU stepped in. With the attorneys' assistance, wrote Kameny, "a criminal complaint (assault, trespassing, defamation, slander, etc.) was made before the U.S. attorney, against the investigators, and a hearing held." There are no surviving records of what happened in that hearing. See FEK to W. Dorr Legg, March 10, 1963, Box 82, Folder 3, FEK Papers.

119 *The relationship between . . . homosexual"*: In the early months of 1963, Kameny had continued attending meetings of the NCACLU's Discrimination Committee. At one of them, the attorneys mentioned an upcoming conference to be held by the advisory committee for the U.S. Commission on Civil Rights, and on February 28, Kameny submitted an eight-page statement, a replica of his NCACLU speech, to the commission. The idea for the white paper, meanwhile, had come from the very top: NCACLU chairman David Carliner had suggested it, and the head of the discrimination committee, a local Quaker attorney named Hal Witt, led the operation. Kameny had reason to believe the white paper would be "completely favorable" to his minority. As Witt began his research, he immediately turned to Kameny, asking the MSW president for a list of books on the homosexual's employment problems and for information about the underlying logic of the purges—blackmail, psychological stability, and morality. See FEK to Segal, January 13, 1962, Box 83, Folder 2, FEK Papers; The Mattachine Society of Washington, "Discrimination Against the Employment of Homosexuals," February 28, 1963, Box 8, Folder 5, MSNY Papers; FEK to Curtis Dewees, March 20, 1963, Box 78, Folder 6, FEK Papers.

119 *Kameny's greatest NCACLU . . . earlier*: H. C. Bolton to Bruce Chardon Scott, May 16, 1962, Box 32, Folder 4, FEK Papers; "Brief for Appellant and Joint Appendix," *Bruce C. Scott v. John W. Macy Jr. et al.*, Box 8, Folder 4, Gittings Papers, 4.

120 *In September 1962 . . . from federal employment?*: Bruce C. Scott to John W. Macy Jr., September 11, 1962, in "Brief for Defendant and Joint Appendix," *Bruce C. Scott v. John W. Macy Jr. et al.*, Box 8, Folder 4, Gittings Papers, 38.

120 *In December . . . of Bruce Scott*: FEK to W. Dorr Legg, December 30, 1962, Box 82, Folder 3, FEK Papers.

120 *In March, Scott . . . the purges*: FEK to Clark Polak, March 31, 1963, Box 82, Folder 7, FEK Papers. For a physical description of Carliner, see Jacob Remes to Eric Cervini, email correspondence, June 21, 2019; Deborah Carliner to Eric Cervini, email correspondence, June 24, 2019.

120 *On April 23 . . . Civil Service Commission*: "Brief for Appellant and Joint Appendix," *Bruce C. Scott v. John W. Macy Jr. et al.*, Box 8, Folder 4, Gittings Papers, A2.

120 *First and foremost . . . or immoral?*: Ibid.

121 *According to* The *. . . in Virginia*: "Homosexuality as Bar to U.S. Job Challenged," *The Washington Evening Star*, April 24, 1963, 2. See also "Ex-Worker Sues U.S. for New Job," *The Washington Post*, April 24, 1963, B11.

121 *Scott's lawsuit represented . . . Gayety Buffet*: Walter William Goldstein, "Affidavit," June 26, 1963, Box 113, Folder 7, FEK Papers.

121 *The restaurant, located . . . clientele*: Beemyn, *A Queer Capital*, 119.

121 *Goldstein wore makeup*: Walter William Goldstein, "Affidavit," June 26, 1963, Box 113, Folder 7, FEK Papers.

121 *Washington still required . . . into unconsciousness*: Ibid.

121 *Kameny vaulted to . . . in her establishment*: FEK to David Carliner, June 4, 1963, Box 81, Folder 2, FEK Papers.

122 *In only a . . . Kameny*: Ibid.

122 *The MSW president . . . demanded a meeting*: FEK to Robert V. Murray, June 26, 1963, Box 113, Folder 7, FEK Papers.

122 *Chief Murray . . . about the incident*: Franklin E. Kameny, "Civil Liberties: A Progress Report," July 22, 1964, *New York Mattachine Newsletter*, Box 68, Folder 2, Gittings Papers.

122 *Blick ultimately agreed . . . police department*: FEK to Robert V. Murray, June 26, 1963, Box 113, Folder 7, FEK Papers.

122 *Three weeks after . . . of Commerce headquarters*: John H. Harmon III to FEK, June 15, 1963, Box 15, Folder 4, FEK Papers.

122 *The ax had . . . without pay*: FEK to David Carliner, April 5, 1963, Box 81, Folder 2, FEK Papers.

123 *One month later . . . one Warren Scarberry"*: "Statement of Charges," April 11, 1963, Box 15, Folder 4, FEK Papers.

123 *The department had . . . or pressure"*: Ibid.

123 *John H. Harmon III*: Harmon was an especially good fit, since he had experienced an eerily similar nightmare one decade earlier. One morning in May 1953, Harmon was woken by five armed men and told to get dressed. He was a twenty-one-year-old Black man from the Bronx, drafted by the army only six months earlier, and the men were from the Counterintelligence Corps. Harmon was suspected of subversion, they said. They put him in a room with a single light and no ventilation, and for five hours, they questioned him. How long had he been a Communist? How many cells had he organized? The army had no proof Harmon was a Communist, but the investigators were suspicious. Before he was drafted, Harmon had associated with groups sympathetic to the Communist cause, like the Detroit Urban League and the American Labor Party. At the end of the investigation, the army deemed him a security risk and, despite his excellent service record, promptly gave him an undesirable discharge. Harmon, now labeled a disloyal American, took a number of menial jobs—bellhop, shipping clerk, waiter, and temporary postal clerk. But when the Post Office Department learned about his discharge, it fired him. Harmon turned to the ACLU, which agreed to take his case against the army. After lower courts decided against him, on March 3, 1958, the Supreme Court released its 8–1 decision in *Harmon v. Brucker*. The army had no right to discharge the disgraced soldier based solely on his pre-induction activities. Three years later, in 1961, the court refused to hear *Kameny v. Brucker*. But by then, John H. Harmon had a law degree from Washington's Howard University. He had won a case in the Supreme Court. When he joined the fledgling NCACLU, and when he learned of the many parallels in Ronald Brass's case, he took it. See *John H. Harmon, III, Appellant, v. Wilber M. Brucker, Individually and As Secretary of the Department of the Army, Appellee*, 243 F.2d 613 (D.C. Cir. 1957); "Court May Get New Discharge for GI," *Indiana Evening Gazette*, March 4, 1958, 7; "Service Record Ruled Only Discharge Basis," *The Washington Post*, March 4, 1958, A15; *Harmon v. Brucker*, 355 U.S. 579 (1958); "'It's Not Legal—But We Did It,' Army to Harmon," *New York Amsterdam News*, January 25, 1958, 1.

123 *Instead, he would . . . pressure, or blackmail?"*: Ronald Brass to FEK, May 1, 1963, Box 15, Folder 4, FEK Papers.

123 *Kameny wrote to . . . PROMPTLY"*: FEK to Curtis Dewees, May 5, 1963, Box 81, Folder 3, FEK Papers; FEK to President, Los Angeles Mattachine Society, Inc., May 5, 1963, Box 81, Folder 3, FEK Papers; FEK to President, The Mattachine Society, May 5, 1963, Box 81, Folder 4, FEK Papers.

123 *Armed with these letters*: See Harold L. Call to FEK, May 8, 1963, Box 15, Folder 4, FEK Papers; Hal Call to FEK, May 8, 1963, Box 81, Folder 2, FEK Papers.

123 *on June 18 . . . said Kameny*: Untitled Transcript, June 18, 1963, Box 15, Folder 5, FEK Papers.

125 *When he returned . . . pay it*: W. L. Whitsett to FEK, June 24, 1963, Box 15, Folder 4, FEK Papers.

125 *On June 5 . . . across it*: "Lecture," June 11, 1963, FBI File #100–403320, 647.

125 *The Society had . . . Pentagon*: FEK to Robert L. Applegate, June 4, 1963, Box 45, Folder 1, FEK Papers.

126 *Why, he began . . . him nowhere?*: In February, Hoover and Attorney General Robert Kennedy received a warning. Bruce Scott, writing as "Bruce Schuyler," informed the officials that despite the Department of Justice's silence, the homosexuals were not going anywhere. Their grievances, he wrote, "will not vanish if you look the other way long enough; when you look back, they will be right there awaiting your proper attention to them." Hoover forwarded the letter to seven top FBI officials, who duly investigated Scott's pseudonym, "Bruce Schuyler," and otherwise ignored him. See Bruce Schuyler to J. Edgar Hoover, February 16, 1963, FBI File FBI File #100–403320, 640.

126 *So when the . . . mention Kameny's name*: Mattachine Society of Washington *Gazette* 1, no. 1 (May 1963), Box 86, Folder 2, FEK Papers.

126 *The first issue . . . and the Homosexual"*: Ibid.

126 *The answer to . . . own organizations*: Ibid. See also Chapters Six, Nine.

126 *Donald Webster Cory . . . down*: J. C. Einbinder to FEK, May 9, 1963, Box 81, Folder 5, FEK Papers; James Reeb to FEK, May 24, 1963, Box 83, Folder 1, FEK Papers; FEK to Reverend Cosby, April 26, 1963, Box 81, Folder 2, FEK Papers; William Jaffe to FEK, April 29, 1963, Box 82, Folder 1, FEK Papers.

126 *When one board . . . publication refused*: FEK to Frank Gatewood, May 31, 1963, Box 82, Folder 7, FEK Papers.

126 *He provided complimentary . . . Hoover*: Bruce Schuyler to Richard N. C. Nix, June 4, 1963, Box 82, Folder 6, FEK Papers; Bruce Schuyler to William F. Ryan, June 4, 1963, Box 83, Folder 1, FEK Papers; Bruce Schuyler

to Robert F. Kennedy, June 4, 1963, Box 82, Folder 2, FEK Papers; Bruce Schuyler to Lyndon B. Johnson, June 4, 1963, Box 82, Folder 1, FEK Papers; Bruce Schuyler to Justice Douglas, June 4, 1963, Box 81, Folder 3, FEK Papers; Bruce Schuyler to R. L. Applegate, June 4, 1963, Box 80, Folder 12, FEK Papers; Bruce Schuyler to John W. Macy Jr., June 4, 1963, Box 82, Folder 4, FEK Papers; Bruce Schuyler to J. Edgar Hoover, June 4, 1963, Box 81, Folder 7, FEK Papers.

127   *Within hours of . . . the lecture*: SAC, WFO, to Director, FBI, June 10, 1963, FBI File #100–403320, 650.

127   *By now, in . . . of the lecture*: Ibid. This individual may have been the same PCI who provided an MSW application to the FBI in October 1962. See SA [Redacted] to SAC, WFO, October 11, 1962, FBI File #100–33796, 68.

127   *On June 7 . . . scrawled Hoover*: D. C. Morrell to DeLoach, June 7, 1963, FBI File #100–403320, 649.

127   *Three days later . . . the White House*: TIME magazine asked to attend after receiving the Society's *Gazette*. See Joseph J. Kane to MSW, May 21, 1963, Box 83, Folder 4, FEK Papers; FEK to Curtis Dewees, June 3, 1963, Box 81, Folder 3, FEK Papers.

127   *The Washington Post . . . two officials*: FEK to John Schaffer, July 5, 1963, Box 31, Folder 8, FEK Papers.

127   *In the audience . . . homophile movement*: Scarberry also provided a copy of the Kameny's Civil Rights Commission statement. See SA [Redacted] to SAC, WFO, July 11, 1963, FBI File #100–33796, 127.

127   *No, he had . . . their full identity"*: Ibid.

127   *Five weeks after . . . July 22*: SA [Redacted] to SAC, WFO, July 23, 1963, FBI File #100–33796, 120.

127   *The FBI director . . . President, presiding"*: Kameny likely did not use this pseudonym during the event itself, since the transcript shows he did not introduce himself at all. See "Proceedings," FBI File #100–33796, 79.

128   *Rae Beck Kameny . . . her son*: Lahusen interview. The month before the lecture, when Kameny collected statements from homophile leaders for the Brass hearing, Hal Call had made a surprising admission. "I have never officially admitted by letter or from a platform or on radio or television or in a newspaper or magazine that I am homosexual," he said. It was "no one's business except my own." "I am in full agreement with you (as apparently also, with Curtis Dewees, in New York) about a public declaration of homosexuality," responded Kameny. See Harold L. Call to FEK May 8, 1963, Box 81, Folder 2, FEK Papers; FEK to Harold L. Call, June 17, 1963, Box 81, Folder 2, FEK Papers.

128   *By the time . . . was named "RANDY."*: SAC, WFO, to Director, FBI, June 10, 1963, FBI File #100–403320, 650.

128   *"Jackson, Miss.— . . . nightly horrors*: "Freedom Riders Sexually Abused," *The Washington Afro American*, June 11, 1963, 1.

128   *If* Washington Afro-American . . . *SCOTT ROOM GRAMERCY INN*: Ibid., 6.

129   *Though* The Washington . . . *it*: Ronald Lockwood to Viola May Warf, June 6, 1963, Box 80, Folder 12, FEK Papers.

129   *national newspaper . . . a former slave*: Cary D. Wintz, "Baltimore Afro-American," in *Encyclopedia of African American History: 1896 to the Present* (Oxford, U.K.: Oxford University Press, 2009), 234.

129   *"Homosexual's Civil Rights . . . Society's file*: "Homosexual's Civil Rights Discussed in Lecture Here," *The Washington Afro American*, June 15, 1963, 24, clipping in FBI File #100–33796, 76.

129   *Randy Wicker, meanwhile . . . to jail*: Foster Hailey, "500 Are Arrested in Negro Protest in Birmingham," *The New York Times*, May 3, 1963, 1.

129   *He saw the . . . surrender*: "The Birmingham Truce Agreement," in *Eyes on the Prize: a Reader and Guide*, ed. Clayborne Carson, (New York: Penguin, 1987), 119.

129   *That same day . . . upon it"*: "Negro Workers Plan March on D.C. in Fall," *The Washington Evening Star*, May 10, 1963, 21.

130   *A month later . . . on Washington*: Gould Lincoln, "JFK on Peace at Home and Abroad," *The Washington Evening Star*, June 11, 1963, 10.

130   *America faced "a . . . rights bill*: Taylor Branch, *Parting the Waters: America in the King Years 1954–63* (New York: Simon and Schuster, 2007), 822.

130   *By June . . . wrote Levin*: In two articles, a product of a Wicker-guided tour of gay New York, Levin portrayed homosexuals not only as victims of outdated sex laws—resulting in police entrapment, blackmail, and government purges—but also as defiant citizens willing to fight back. He described MSNY's center of operations (a "pale-green, cluttered cubicle"), the MSW's Pentagon meeting, and Wicker's "several recent trips to Washington to keep abreast of developments in what he calls a 'crucial case,'" referring to *Scott v. Macy*. See Alan Levin, "Sex and Laws," *New York Post Magazine*, June 19, 1963, 39; Alan Levin, "Sex and Laws," *New York Post Magazine*, June 20, 1963.

130   *That month, the . . . publicity campaign?"*: Dan Wakefield, "The Gay Crusader," *Nugget*, June 1963, 51; Karen Wells, "The Gay Crusader—A Review," *The Ladder* 7, no. 9 (May 1963): 19.

130   *Wicker seemed to . . . Randolfe Wicker"*: Wakefield, "The Gay Crusader."

130   *Yet Wicker was . . . to its core*: Kennedy and King had been in contact since June 23, 1960. See Branch, *Parting the Waters*, 314, 838.

131   *In the ten . . . arrests—in 186 cities*: Ibid., 825.

131   *A. Philip . . . the day*: Ibid., 817.

131 *The FBI learned . . . from 'RANDY.'*": SAC, WFO, to Director, FBI, June 10, 1963, FBI File #100–403320, 650.

131 *On June 12 . . . Secret Service updated*: "Homosexuals Planning to Picket White House," June 12, 1963, FBI File #100–403320, 652.

131 *"I haven't died," . . . having fun*": "Charlie" to FEK, July 1963, Box 81, Folder 6, FEK Papers.

131 *Kameny was not . . . learned elsewhere*": FEK to Theodore C. Sorensen, June 21, 1963, Box 83, Folder 3, FEK Papers.

132 *That month, the . . . Washington Now*": SA [Redacted] to SAC, WFO, July 11, 1963, FBI File #100–33796, 127.

132 *a protest organized . . . of Racial Equality*: "Negroes Stage D.C. Protest for Rights," *The Washington Evening Star*, June 14, 1963, 1.

132 *Scarberry, though unaffiliated . . . FOR ALL*": SA [Redacted] to SAC, WFO, July 11, 1963, FBI File #100–33796, 127.

132 *In late 1962 . . . northwest Washington*: "Dr. Franklin E. Kameny Residence," National Register of Historic Places Registration Form, September 23, 2011, National Park Service, United States Department of the Interior.

132 *With income from . . . District's stoplights*: Nichols, "Chapter Six," *Memoirs of Jack Nichols*.

133 *Kameny lost his . . . the first dismissed*: Lahusen interview.

133 *Kameny began collecting . . . once more*: Franklin E. Kameny, United States Employment Service, June 20, 1963, Box 136, Folder 14, FEK Papers.

133 *On July 5 . . . changed forthwith*": John Dowdy, "The Mattachine Society of Washington," July 5, 1963, in U.S. Congress, House of Representatives, Committee on the District of Columbia, Subcommittee no. 4, Amending District of Columbia Charitable Solicitation Act, 88th Cong., 1st Sess., August 8, 1963 (hereafter, "Dowdy Hearings"), 2.

133 *Dowdy's proposed bill . . . is revoked*": Dowdy Hearings, 1.

134 *Kameny had not . . . any suggestions*": FEK to David Carliner, July 10, 1963, Box 80, Folder 7, FEK Papers.

134 *At an emergency . . . board*: The President to the Executive Board, July 10, 1963, Box 85, Folder 1, FEK Papers; FEK to Walter N. Tobriner, July 17, 1963, Box 80, Folder 7, FEK Papers.

134 *On July 31 . . . to testify*": FEK to David Carliner, July 31, 1963, Box 85, Folder 1, FEK Papers.

134 *On August 6 . . . you so desire*": James T. Clark to FEK, August 5, 1963, Box 80, Folder 7, FEK Papers.

9. THE CONGRESSMAN

136 *A stout, bespectacled . . . a ruddy complexion*: Dowdy interview, February 4, 1970, FBI File WFO 58–1177, Box 502, Folder 1, John V. Dowdy, Sr. Papers, W. R. Poage Legislative Library, Baylor University (hereafter, "Dowdy Papers"), 10.

136 *Dowdy was a . . . border*: "Not Guilty, Rep. Dowdy Tells Court," *The Washington Evening Star*, April 11, 1970, 1.

136 *He worked as . . . the state*: David R. Boldt, "They Love Dowdy," *The Washington Post*, May 4, 1970, A1.

136 *In 1944, though . . . of Representatives*: Ibid.

136 *A few months . . . later wrote*: Dowdy to Everett E. Kersey, February 24, 1966, Box 366, Folder 16, Dowdy Papers.

136 *Appointed to the . . . crusade*: "Name Rep. Robeson to House Subgroup," *Daily Press* (Newport News), July 31, 1955, 9C; "'Chatterley' Movie Decision Called 'Shock' in Congress," *Catholic Chronicle*, July 17, 1959, 2.

136 *In March 1956 . . . mail-worthiness*: "Curbs Placed on Flow of Obscene Printed Matter," *Denton Record-Chronicle*, May 24, 1956, 4; "Late News Briefs," *The Catholic Advance*, May 4, 1956, 4.

137 *Only four months . . . into law*: "Detention of Mail for Temporary Periods in Certain Cases," H.R.9842, July 11, 1956, 84th Cong., 2d Sess., *Congressional Record*, 12290; "Senate Approves Bill to Crack Down on Obscene Literature," *The Word and Way* (Kansas City), August 2, 1956, 2.

137 *The Supreme Court . . . importance*"?: *Roth v. United States*, 354 U.S. 476 (1957).

137 *The decision marked . . . legally enjoy*: Commission on Obscenity and Pornography, *The Report of the Commission on Obscenity and Pornography* (New York: Bantam Books, 1970) quoted in D'Emilio, *Sexual Politics, Sexual Communities*, 133.

137 *Dowdy doubled his . . . yearlong jail sentence*: Roy E. Blick to John Dowdy, April 1, 1958, Box 361, Folder 3, Dowdy Papers.

137 *For five years . . . bill through Congress*: "We have been unable to get Congress to pass other laws or resolutions to protect the people," complained Dowdy to a constituent in 1961. See John Dowdy to Jane Allen, September 28, 1961, Box 139, Folder 15, Dowdy Papers.

137 *And for five . . . homosexual pornography itself*: D'Emilio, *Sexual Politics, Sexual Communities*, 132.

137 *That year, Dowdy*: "Solon Leads Closest Race," *Austin American-Statesman*, May 8, 1962, 1; "John, Don Get Busy for June 2 Runoff," *Austin American-Statesman*, May 9, 1962, 13; "Dowdy Certified as Demo Winner," *The Bonham Daily Favorite*, May 16, 1962, 1.

137   *On October 3 . . . Kennedy's desk*: U.S. Congress, House of Representatives, Indecent Publications in the District
      of Columbia: Conference Report, 87th Cong., 2d Sess., October 3, 1962. Two vocal adversaries—the NCA-
      CLU and the Washington press—rose against the Texas congressman. Dowdy's bill allowed police officers
      "untrammeled authority," as the NCACLU put it, to seize any property involved in the creation of obscene
      materials. "If you had a copy of Chaucer's 'Canterbury Tales,'" warned the Washington *Daily News*, "the District
      could proceed to seize your furniture, your car, your lawn mower." Entire newspapers could be shut down. "It
      would be just about as sensible and just about as efficacious to put blinders and earmuffs on everyone in the
      community and forbid them to read or see or hear anything," wrote *The Washington Post*. "May the President
      preserve us by veto from a pseudo-sanctity so insufferable!" See Felton West, "JFK Regretfully Vetoes Obscene
      Publications Bill," *The Houston Post*, n.d., Box 362, Folder 28, Dowdy Papers; "Dangerous Bill," *Daily News*
      (Washington), October 6, 1962, 12; "Imprisoning the Press," *The Washington Post*, October 5, 1962, A16.
137   *Less than a . . . Mississippi*: "Texas Congressman Asks JFK About Marshals 'Riot Action,'" *The Greenwood
      Commonwealth*, October 9, 1962, 1.
138   *three days before . . . Eighty-Eigth Congress adjourned*: "Session Dates of Congress," History, Art, & Archives,
      United States House of Representatives, https://history.house.gov/Institution/Session-Dates/All.
138   *Dowdy began his . . . of Washington*: John Dowdy, "Charitable Solicitations in the District of Columbia," on
      October 10, 1962, 87th Cong., 2d Sess., *Congressional Record*, 23012.
138   *"Of course, no . . . a constituent*: John Dowdy to Bill Kellogg, October 11, 1962, Box 366, Folder 16, Dowdy
      Papers.
138   *Kennedy indeed vetoed . . . "grave" constitutional concerns*: John F. Kennedy, "Memorandum of Disapproval,"
      October 19, 1962, Box 362, Folder 28, Dowdy Papers.
138   *but the congressman's . . . the vote*: "Connally Slates Press Conference for Today," *Corpus Christi Caller Times*,
      November 8, 1962, 1.
138   *First, in May, his obscenity bill*: U.S. Congress, House of Representatives, "H.R. 5989," 88th Cong., 1st Sess.,
      May 1, 1963.
138   *in July, H.R. . . . homosexuals"*: John Dowdy to Bill Kellogg, October 11, 1962, Box 366, Folder 16, Dowdy
      Papers.
138   *As one Texan . . . that's unbeatable"*: David R. Boldt, "They Love Dowdy," *The Washington Post*, May 4, 1970,
      A1.
138   *On the morning . . . "Unpopular Causes"*: "Unpopular Causes," *The Washington Post*, August 8, 1963, A14.
138   *"A House District . . . "promote homosexual activity"*: Ibid.
138   *Not only did . . . Kameny's name*: Ibid.
139   *At 10:25 a.m. . . . Corporation Counsel's Office"*: Dowdy Hearings, 7.
139   *Kneipp sat at . . . government, he began*: Ibid., 10.
139   *The District of . . . immorality," accused Dowdy*: Ibid., 8
139   *Kneipp explained that . . . obscenity bill*: Ibid., 11.
139   *C. T. Nottingham . . . use," added Nottingham*: Ibid., 17.
140   *"We have the . . . have to say"*: Ibid., 21.
140   *Kameny sat at . . . of food*: Ibid., 22–23.
140   *"Let me ask . . . the next morning*: Ibid., 24.
141   *"D.C. Fights Bill . . . it reported*: The *Star* also reported that the subcommittee placed into the record a letter
      from the District Republican Committee, which supported the commissioners' position against the bill. See
      "D.C. Fights Bill Cutting Help for Homosexuals," *The Washington Evening Star*, August 8, 1963, 22.
141   *At 10:10 the . . . the Society's Gazette*: Dowdy Hearings, 25–26.
141   *Indeed, at that . . . every word*: Lahusen interview.
141   *"Are you part . . . asked Dowdy, skeptically*: Dowdy Hearings, 26.
142   *"I have here . . . to blackmail"*: Ibid., 27.
142   *"How large a . . . the MSW, too*: Ibid., 29.
143   *"Can you name . . . asked Horton*: Ibid., 30–32.
143   *What is the . . . bleaching the Negro"*: Ibid., 33–35.
143   *"You do condone . . . of criminal law"*: Ibid., 36.
143   *How does the . . . the Society received?*: Ibid., 36–40.
144   *"Some twenty or . . . losing their jobs"*: Ibid., 40–41.
144   *"If you are . . . a membership list*: Ibid., 42.
144   *He had . . . jail sentence*: Ibid., 43–45.
145   *"I think maybe . . . to this proceeding"*: Ibid., 46.
146   *Three times, Kameny . . . the individual involved?"*: Ibid., 47.
146   *"I have not . . . the question"*: Ibid., 48–49.
147   *Horton continued probing . . . its fund-raising activities*: Ibid., 49–56.
147   *"As the president . . . he read*: Ibid., 56–59.
147   *Dowdy interrupted. Is . . . District of Columbia*: Ibid., 60–62.

148 *What about bestiality? asked Huddleston*: Ibid., 63.
148 *What about homosexual . . . about," retorted Dowdy*: Ibid., 70–71.
149 *"Are you trying . . . to elevate yourselves?"*: Ibid., 79.
149 *In total, Kameny . . . he could breathe*: Ibid., 90.
149 *"Mr. Kameny, will . . . course you can"*: Ibid., 92–93.
150 *Dowdy instead decided . . . around," said Huddleston*: Ibid., 94.
150 *Her real name . . . committed suicide*: Paul Kuntzler, in "50th Anniversary of the Mattachine Society of Washington Panel Discussion," Rainbow History Project, October 13, 2011.
150 *"Are you married?" . . . approximately two hours*: Dowdy Hearings, 94–95.
151 *What do they . . . Monroe H. Freedman*: Ibid., 96–100.
151 *Freedman introduced himself . . . Freedman added*: Ibid., 100–1.
152 *First, he explained . . . could conceive of "*: Ibid., 106–7.
152 *Second, the bill . . . could conceive of "*: Ibid., 109.
152 *"It is not . . . enterprise," answered Dowdy*: Ibid., 112.
152 *It is the . . . against those things"*: Ibid., 114–15.
152 *Horton wanted a . . . forget about it "*: Ibid., 116.
152 *Dowdy wanted to . . . that was that*: Ibid., 118–19.
153 *On August 15 . . . Society's permit*: John Dowdy to Walter N. Tobriner, August 15, 1963, Box 366, Folder 16, Dowdy Papers.
154 *The same day . . . Employment of Homosexuals"*: The Washington Field Office did not mention where it acquired the statement, though it may have come from Dowdy's investigators; at least six other top Bureau officials also received a copy. SAC, WFO, to Director, FBI, August 7, 1963, FBI File #100–403320, 664.
154 *And as the . . . the* Star: See "Group Defends Fund Collecting Role," *Daily News* (Washington), August 9, 1963, and "Bill on Homosexuals Held Unconstitutional," *The Washington Post*, August 10, 1963, clippings in FBI File #100–403320, 662–63.
154 *Four days after . . . Warren Scarberry*: J. Edgar Hoover to SAC, WFO, August 13, 1963, FBI File #100–403320, 655; "Mattachine Society of Wash., D.C. Identification Matters," Federal Bureau of Investigation Latent Fingerprint Section Work Sheet, August 12, 1963, FBI File #100–403320, 656–61.
154 *The District of . . . had committed fraud*: J. J. Ilgenfritz to FEK, September 10, 1963, Box 82, Folder 3, FEK Papers.

10. THE MARCH

156 *On August 13 . . . a homosexual*: Senator Thurmond, "Washington Post Article on Bayard Rustin, Leader of March on Washington," on August 13, 1963, 88th Cong., 1st Sess., *Congressional Record*, 14837.
156 *Bayard Rustin had . . . general unmanliness"*: Bayard Rustin and Michael G. Long, *Bayard Rustin's Life in Letters* (San Francisco: City Lights Books, 2012), 44.
156 *Over the next . . . nonviolent, Gandhi-inspired activism*: Ibid., 468.
156 *On January 21 . . . peace organization*: John D'Emilio, *Lost Prophet: The Life and Times of Bayard Rustin* (New York: Simon & Schuster, 2010), 190–91.
156 *By then, he . . . the United States*: Eric Pace, "Bayard Rustin Is Dead at 75; Pacifist and a Rights Activist," *The New York Times*, August 25, 1987, 1.
157 *After Rustin's Pasadena . . . whole cause"*: D'Emilio, *Lost Prophet*, 190–91.
157 *Undaunted, in February . . . bombs, and fear*: Ibid., 230.
157 *Montgomery's reporters became . . . of a car*: Branch, *Parting the Waters*, 180.
157 *the movement exiled the gay pacifist*: Ibid., 314.
157 *But because of . . . of nonviolent protest*: D'Emilio, *Lost Prophet*, 230–34.
157 *In December 1962 . . . moment altogether*: Ibid., 327–28.
157 *In May, King's . . . cosponsor*: Ibid., 338.
157 *and that summer . . . J. Edgar Hoover*: Ibid., 348.
157 *Standing before the . . . of "sex perversion"*: Thurmond, "Washington Post Article on Bayard Rustin, Leader of March on Washington," 14837.
158 *Rustin prepared for . . . Bayard Rustin's character"*: D'Emilio, *Lost Prophet*, 348.
158 *"My task is . . . Rustin himself*: "Capital March Goal Outlined," *Billings Gazette*, August 15, 1963, 18.
158 *No fewer than . . . attended Rustin's March*: D'Emilio, *Lost Prophet*, 354; Pace, "Bayard Rustin Is Dead at 75; Pacifist and a Rights Activist."
158 *Frank Kameny marched . . . seven Mattachine members*: Ronald Lockwood to Bill of Rights Award Committee, NCACLU Office, September 15, 1963, Box 75, Folder 6, FEK Papers.
158 *including Jack Nichols . . . recalled Nichols*: Nichols, "Chapter Six," *Memoirs of Jack Nichols*.
158 *Randy Wicker's threatened . . . any participants*: SAC, WFO, to Director, FBI, September 3, 1963, FBI File #100–403320, 676.

158   *A special agent . . . homosexual demonstration*: Director, FBI, to the Attorney General, September 11, 1963, FBI File #100–403320, 677.

159   *The "hostile" subcommittee . . . an ally*: MSW to Homophile Organizations, September 4, 1963, Box 81, Folder 7, FEK Papers.

159   *In the August . . . in the magazine*: Sidney Bronstein, "Pencil Sketches," *ONE* 11, no. 8, August 1963, 16.

159   *After Kameny . . . unnatural lusts!"*: Bruce Schuyler to *ONE*, September 14, 1963, Box 82, Folder 6, FEK Papers.

159   *As for picketing . . . he wrote*: FEK to Charlie Hayden, n.d., Box 1, "Correspondence 63, 65" Folder, Randy Wicker Papers.

159   *Thus, while Wicker . . . Day weekend*: The organizers, including Kameny, had spent the summer inviting psychiatrists, attorneys, religious figures—anyone—who would speak at their conference. See Robert King to Walter T. Skallerup Jr., July 10, 1963, Box 84, Folder 7, FEK Papers; Robert King to David Carliner, July 10, 1963, Box 84, Folder 7, FEK Papers; Robert King to Kimbell Johnson, July 10, 1963, Box 84, Folder 7, FEK Papers; Robert King to Alan Barth Jr., July 10, 1963, Box 84, Folder 7, FEK Papers; Robert King to John W. Macy Jr., July 10, 1963, Box 84, Folder 7, FEK Papers; L. V. Meloy to Robert King, July 17, 1963, Box 41, Folder 12, FEK Papers.

159   *Only days . . . hotel capitulated*: Ken Travis, "Confidential Reporter Attends First Homosexual Convention in U.S. History," *Confidential* 12, no. 1 (January 1964), 26.

160   *The organizers, including . . . same hotel*: There were signs the press would be interested: for two hours Friday afternoon, radio talk show host Ed Harvey discussed homosexuality with two psychiatrists on the ECHO program. Radio host Frank Ford even interviewed two pseudonymous homosexuals: Robert King of the MSW and DOB national president Jaye Bell, who had driven from San Francisco to attend. See ibid.; Jody Shotwell, "East Coast Homophile Organizations," *The Ladder* 8, no. 5, December 1963, 8.

160   *On Friday evening . . . brochure-folding orgy!"*: Ibid.

160   *"Deadly respectability . . . here, thank you*: Travis, "Confidential Reporter Attends First Homosexual Convention in U.S. History."

160   *Donald Webster Cory . . . Cory*: Ibid.

160   *In the next . . . quarter?"*: Ibid.

160   *The conference only . . . homosexual psychologists*: Edward L. Lee Jr., "The Church and Homosexuality," August 31, 1963, Box 64, Folder 3, Gittings Papers; Press Release, National Psychological Association for Psychoanalysis, Inc., August 31, 1963, Box 64, Folder 3, Gittings Papers.

160   *The Saturday-night . . . the attendees*: Shotwell, "East Coast Homophile Organizations."

160   *As Ellis began . . . homosexual*: "Ellis Address: A Summary," Mattachine Society of Washington *Gazette* 2, no. 1, Spring 1964, Box 86, Folder 2, FEK Papers, 6.

161   *For an "interminable" . . . was deafening*: J. Seeley, "Ellis and the Chestnuts," *The Ladder* 8, no. 2, November 1963, 15; Transcript: 50th Anniversary of the Mattachine Society of Washington Panel Discussion, Rainbow History Project, October 13, 2011.

161   *The next day . . . the congressman*: Shotwell, "East Coast Homophile Organizations." Kameny's speech impressed many within the movement. A few months later, Donald Webster Cory, the man most responsible for popularizing the concept of a homosexual minority, lauded Kameny for his concrete, short-term goals. The homophile movement's "development of an action program," he wrote Kameny, "can be attributed to your leadership." The Washington Mattachine, said Cory, "speaks for all of us." See D. W. Cory to FEK, December 11, 1963, Box 9, Folder 2, FEK Papers.

161   *"Dear Mr. Dowdy," . . . convention in Philadelphia"*: FEK to John Dowdy, September 6, 1963, Box 81, Folder 3, FEK Papers.

161   *Four days later . . . not be revoked*: J. J. Ilgenfritz to FEK, September 10, 1963, Box 82, Folder 3, FEK Papers.

161   *After NCACLU attorney . . . tendencies"*: Monroe H. Freedman to FEK, September 10, 1963, Box 81, Folder 4, FEK Papers.

162   *That same day . . . solicitation license*: J. J. Ilgenfritz to FEK, September 10, 1963, Box 82, Folder 3, FEK Papers.

162   *The District's Department of Licenses . . . September 24*: "D.C. Hearing to Challenge Homosexuals," FBI File #100–403320, 680.

162   *as Freedman began . . . in 1962*: U.S. Congress, House of Representatives, Committee on the District of Columbia, Subcommittee no. 4, Amending District of Columbia Charitable Solicitation Act, 88th Cong., 2d Sess., January 10, 1964 (hereafter, "Second Dowdy Hearing"), 122–23.

162   *Freedman met with . . . a license?*: Monroe H. Freedman to The Mattachine Society of Washington, October 14, 1963, Box 81, Folder 4, FEK Papers.

162   *"Mattachine Unit Loses . . . the hearing*: "Mattachine Unit Loses Its Permit to Solicit Funds," *The Washington Evening Star*, October 4, 1963, 7. The *Daily News* and *Post* carried similar pieces. Kameny wrote to all three Washington papers to clarify the situation. They had "apparently misled some of your readers into believing that the Mattachine Society of Washington has surrendered part of its right to carry on its activities," he

wrote. "Quite the contrary is true." Dowdy had not won. The Society could still raise funds, and it welcomed contributions. See FEK to Washington *Daily News*, October 5, 1963, Box 82, Folder 6, FEK Papers.

162 *One week later ... the regulations*": The same day the District notified the Society of its intention to revoke its license, a commissioner wrote Dowdy with a proposed amendment to H.R. 5990, which would require the "true name" of each organization's officer. But since the District was already moving to revoke the license on those same grounds, the commissioner predicted that the Society's counsel "will make capital thereof— perhaps with undesirable effect." As such, "the Corporation Counsel and I feel strongly that this amendment should not be presently introduced." Second Dowdy Hearing, 123–24.

162 *The District scheduled ... Society was safe*: "Mattachine Society Harassment Charged," *The Washington Evening Star*, November 9, 1963, 15; Zona Hostetler, interviewed by Eric Cervini, January 5, 2018, Washington, D.C.

162 *Monroe Freedman charged ... his services*: Monroe H. Freedman to MSW, October 14, 1963, Box 81, Folder 4, FEK Papers.

162 *To pay that ... is $1499.99*": "Dear Friend," November 1963, FBI File #100–403320, 688.

163 *Since the anonymous ... his name*: "Homosexual Group Asks Understanding," *The New York Times*, October 18, 1963, 28, clipping in FBI File #100–132065, 112.

163 *Four days later ... the demonstration*: SAC, New York, to Director, FBI, October 22, 1963, FBI File #100– 33796, 149.

163 *According to another ... New York Mattachine*: SA [Redacted] to SAC, New York, October 30, 1963, FBI File #100–132065, 113.

163 *Yet the Bureau ... radio show*: SAC, WFO, to Director, FBI, October 24, 1963, FBI File #100–403320, 679.

163 *"This is the ... his own name*: "Homosexuality Aired on Radio Show," n.d., Box 85, Folder 14, FEK Papers.

163 *"It is with ... Geophysicist*": David K. Langstaff to FEK, November 11, 1963, Box 136, Folder 5, FEK Papers.

163 *President Kennedy was ... Earl Warren complained*: Gentry, *J. Edgar Hoover*, 553.

164 *As summarized in ... from government*": Jones to DeLoach, December 19, 1963, FBI File #100–403320, 685.

164 *J. Edgar Hoover ... this?*": Ibid.

164 *In reply, an ... had written*: Jones to DeLoach, December 23, 1963, FBI File #100–403320, 684.

164 *"Someone should re-check ... on December 23*: Ibid.

164 *Officials rushed to ... he wrote*: D. J. Brennan Jr., to W. C. Sullivan, December 24, 1963, FBI File #100– 403320, 683.

164 *Bruce Scott had ... to hesitate*": Bruce Scott to FEK, December 24, 1963, Box 9, Folder 5, FEK Papers.

164 *On January 15 ... of the service*": "Brief for Appellant and Joint Appendix," *Scott v. Macy*, United States Court of Appeals for the District of Columbia Circuit, Box 8, Folder 4, Gittings Papers, 40.

164 *"Maybe it shouldn't ... it is*": "Attack on U.S. Job Bar to Homosexuals Slowed," *The Washington Post*, January 15, 1964, B6.

164 *Judge Hart agreed ... of the service*": "Brief for Appellant and Joint Appendix," *Scott v. Macy*, United States Court of Appeals for the District of Columbia Circuit, Box 8, Folder 4, Gittings Papers, 40.

164 *Despite David Carliner's ... first round*: "Attack on U.S. Job Bar to Homosexuals Slowed," *The Washington Post*, January 15, 1964, B6.

165 *The next week ... and unjust*": "Misplaced Morality," *The Washington Post*, January 21, 1964, A12.

165 *"The editorial in ... said Scott*: Bruce Scott to FEK, January 24, 1964, Box 9, Folder 5, FEK Papers.

165 *Kameny, meanwhile, wrote ... careful re-consideration*": FEK to Judge George L. Hart Jr., January 24, 1964, Box 32, Folder 4, FEK Papers.

165 *In January 1964 ... a physicist*: FEK to District Unemployment Compensation Board, January 24, 1964, Box 136, Folder 5, FEK Papers; FEK to James F. Greene, March 31, 1964, Box 136, Folder 9, FEK Papers.

165 *Kameny caught up ... Cathedral Avenue*: FEK to Charlie Hayden, May 24, 1964, Box 10, Folder 12, FEK Papers.

165 *But Kameny grew ... his motion*: East Coast Homophile Organizations, "Minutes," February 8, 1964, Box 64, Folder 3, Gittings Papers.

165 *The previous December ... discussion series*: Temple Sinai, "Brotherhood News & Notes," November 22, 1963, Box 129, Folder 8, FEK Papers. In February, he delivered a speech in Philadelphia, hosted by Clark Polak's Janus Society. "Be sure to attend this excellent lecture by one of the country's most famous and influential homophile leaders," advertised a Janus flyer. See Janus Society, "Homosexuality and Civil Liberties," Box 129, Folder 8, FEK Papers.

165 *In March 1964*: That month, on March 6, the House District Committee reported H.R. 5990 to the full House of Representatives. The final version of the bill, as Kameny explained to his executive board, was "much more innocuous, as far as we are concerned." It no longer explicitly revoked the Society's certificate; it did not require true names or remove the $1,500 exemption. The bill simply required organizations to prove they would "benefit or assist in promoting the health, welfare, and morals of the District of Columbia." Kameny knew it was still dangerous. According to the committee's report, H.R. 5990 would allow the District to revoke exemptions, too. If enacted into law, it was entirely possible Dowdy's bill would prevent the

Society from raising any money at all. "The bill is directed simply and ONLY at our organization," Kameny warned his board. The Society and the NCACLU leapt to action. "We wish to direct your attention to HR 5990 up for a vote on Monday," wrote Mattachine member Lilli Vincenz to congressmen Nix and Ryan. It was unnecessary and discriminatory, she wrote. "We would appreciate any action you can exert to defeat it." One hundred other congressmen received telegrams signed by NCACLU chairman David Carliner, urging them to vote against Dowdy's bill. On March 9, *The Washington Post* attacked the bill once again: H.R. 5990 was an "oddly inept little bill introduced by that master of morality, Rep. John Dowdy of Texas, and sent to the floor with slapdash indifference by the House District Committee." The bill would allow the commissioners to ban any group they disliked, warned the *Post*; it urged the House to "consign it promptly to oblivion." Ten days later, nine members of the House Committee on the District of Columbia released a strongly worded minority report: "In our judgment H.R. 5990 is an ill-considered, unnecessary, unwise, and unconstitutional measure. It is a danger to the people of the District of Columbia, and should be rejected." "The bill is so poorly drafted," it continued, "even for its ostensible purpose, that it would forbid hundreds of charitable and benevolent organizations from conducting legitimate money-raising activities in the District of Columbia." The commissioners had no right to evaluate the morality of private organizations. "We, the undersigned members of the House District Committee," concluded the report, "urge that the House of Representatives reject the bill." While Kameny waited for the House to schedule a vote for the bill, he helped the NCACLU with its latest endeavor: the drafting of a policy statement regarding the federal employment of homosexuals, an outgrowth of the previous year's white paper on the subject. "Whether it would have risen to the top of the pile without Frank, I'm not sure," remembered NCACLU attorney Zona Hostetler, five decades later. "He was always lecturing us," she laughed. The NCACLU's Discrimination Committee finished an early draft in June: "It is widely recognized that the homosexual in the United States is the target for prejudice, discrimination and abuse in many areas of life," began the statement. The federal government's exclusion of homosexuals inevitably led to "demoralizing, degrading and oppressive inquiries and methods, including entrapment." Claims of homosexuality's immorality, argued the NCACLU, were "matters of personal opinion and individual ethical and often religious belief," a repetition of Kameny's primary contention since his first CSC interrogation. The blackmail rationale, meanwhile, was illogical: "History is replete with instances where heterosexual behavior has led to serious difficulties, yet heterosexuals are not barred from government employment." "The NCACLU calls upon the United States Civil Service Commission to reconsider its policies under which homosexuals are considered to be unsuitable," it concluded. The Discrimination Committee, after witnessing the injustices of the Dowdy hearings and the *Scott* decision, adopted the arguments of Frank Kameny and the Mattachine Society of Washington nearly verbatim. The Society's infiltration of the Union nearly complete, the two organizations prepared to take their fight to the national stage. See U.S. Congress, House of Representatives, Amending District of Columbia Charitable Solicitation Act: Report, 88th Cong., 2d Sess., March 6, 1964; The President to the Executive Board, February 15, 1964, Box 85, Folder 1, FEK Papers; Lily Hansen to Robert Nix et al., March 5, 1964, Box 81, Folder 1, FEK Papers; "Fund Raising Bill Target for ACLU," *The Washington Post*, March 9, 1964, A15; Paul A. Schuette, "Dowdy Bill Attacked by 9 in House," *The Washington Post*, March 21, 1964, B2; U.S. Congress, House of Representatives, Amending District of Columbia Charitable Solicitation Act: Minority Report, 88th Cong., 2d Sess., March 19, 1964; Zona Hostetler, interviewed by Eric Cervini, January 5, 2018, Washington, D.C.; "First Revised Draft Statement: Federal Employment of Homosexuals," June 8, 1964, Box 75, Folder 6, FEK Papers; Chairman, Committee on Discrimination to Members of the Executive Board, June 12, 1964, Box 75, Folder 6, FEK Papers.

165   *he contacted* LIFE . . . *he wrote*: FEK to George Hunt, March 15, 1964, Box 82, Folder 3, FEK Papers.
166   *In April, he . . . added Kameny*: "Off the Cuff," Transcript, Box 3, Folder 14, FEK Papers.
166   *Their claims sparked . . . indeed an illness"*: "Deviants Proud, Doctors Report," *The New York Times*, May 19, 1964, 1.
166   *The LIFE feature . . . flaunting, their deviation"*: "Homosexuality in America," *LIFE*, June 26, 1964, 66.
166   *Kameny himself had . . . since early 1963*: The Mattachine Society of Washington, "Discrimination Against the Employment of Homosexuals," February 28, 1963, Box 8, Folder 5, MSNY Papers.
166   *That October, after . . . agonizing cry"*: Jack Nichols to the Executive Board, October 14, 1963, Box 85, Folder 1, FEK Papers.
166   *Kameny pressed their . . . do so"*: FEK, "Our President Speaks," Mattachine Society of Washington *Gazette* 2, no. 1 (Spring 1964), in Box 86, Folder 2, FEK Papers, 2.
167   *Nichols, a Unitarian . . . he predicted*: Jack Nichols to Donald Webster Cory, February 3, 1964, Box 2, Folder 5, MSNY Papers.
167   *By April, the . . . first chairman*: "Committee on Religious Concerns," Mattachine Society of Washington *Gazette* 2, no. 2 (Winter 1964), in Box 8, Folder 6, MSNY Papers, 7.
167   *On July 22 . . . and social action*: FEK, "Civil Liberties: A Progress Report," July 22, 1964, *New York Mattachine Newsletter*, Box 68, Folder 2, Gittings Papers.

167 *"Any movement which . . . his goals thereby"*: Ibid.

168 *Federal policies and . . . fight accordingly*: Ibid.

168 *On July . . . sickness question*: Envelope addressed to J. Edgar Hoover, stamped July 16, 1964, FBI File #100–403320, 697.

168 *"The above Society . . . Cathedral Ave."*: Jones to DeLoach, July 20, 1964, FBI File #100–403320, 690.

168 *At last, the agents . . . Kameny by telephone*: Jones to DeLoach, August 7, 1964, FBI File #100–403320, 694.

168 *The FBI hoped . . . later explained.)*: Lahusen interview.

169 *Kameny arrived at . . . list," it said*: Jones to DeLoach, August 7, 1964, FBI File #100–403320, 694.

169 *Kameny and Belanger . . . immediately declined"*: Ibid.

169 *In late July . . . to the NCACLU*: The Society's alliance with the Union was stronger than ever. On August 7, the day of Kameny's FBI meeting, the NCACLU voted to adopt its Kameny-inspired policy statement, concluding "homosexual behavior per se is irrelevant to Federal employment." That week, NCACLU chairman David Carliner contacted his source on the District of Columbia Committee, Congressman B. F. Sisk of California. No one was sure when the bill would come up for a vote, Sisk told him, because the bill's proponents were keeping quiet. See "First Revised Draft Statement: Federal Employment of Homosexuals," June 8, 1964, Box 75, Folder 6, FEK Papers; FEK to Julian Hodges, August 1, 1964, Box 8, Folder 5, MSNY Papers, NYPL.

169 *"ACLU Asks Solicitation . . . NCACLU chairman*: "ACLU Asks Solicitation Bill's Defeat," *The Washington Post*, August 10, 1964, C1.

170 *On August 11 . . . for other purposes"*: "Amending District of Columbia Charitable Solicitation Act," H.R. 5990, on August 11, 1964, 88th Cong., 2d Sess., *Congressional Record*, 18943.

170 *Dowdy had made . . . language, became passable*: Ibid., 18943–944.

170 *William F. Ryan . . . of Columbia"*: Ibid., 18945–946.

170 *Congressman Gene Snyder . . . of Washington*: Ibid.

170 *"I would suggest . . . homosexuals in Washington"*: Ibid., 18946–947.

171 *The debate lasted . . . in a landslide*: Ibid., 18948–949.

171 *But the following . . . the paper reported*: "House Passes Teachers' Fire, Police Pay Hike," *Daily News* (Washington), August 12, 1964, 10. Indeed, the Senate committee's chairman was Senator Alan Bible of Nevada. He may have known President Johnson, following in President Kennedy's footsteps, was unlikely to sign yet another Dowdy bill of questionable constitutionality. Bible's state of Nevada, moreover, had a burgeoning casino industry. Long a defender of gambling in Congress, Bible may not have wished to expand the federal government's power to prohibit organizations based upon vague notions of morality. If the government went after the homosexuals, would it come after his state's casinos next? See Mary Ellen Glass, *Nevada's Turbulent '50s: Decade of Political and Economic Change* (Reno, NV: University of Nevada Press, 1981), 32.

171 *Congress was scheduled . . . of Representatives*: The *Post* and the NCACLU, for example, agreed that the bill would not affect the MSW's exemption, despite the claims of Dowdy. See "ACLU Asks Solicitation Bill's Defeat," *The Washington Post*, August 10, 1964, C1; "D.C. Renewal Bills Remain Stalled as House Group Cancels Meeting," *The Washington Post*, August 13, 1964, F9; "Capitol Hill Is on the Move," *The Washington Evening Star*, November 6, 1964, 4.

171 *"The whole thing . . . dead, dead"*: Lilli Vincenz to Barbara Gittings, October 27, 1964, Box 64, Folder 4, Gittings Papers.

171 *In New York . . . "Miss Mattachine"*: Randy Wicker, interviewed by Eric Cervini, July 28, 2017, Hoboken, NJ.

172 *Wicker walked away . . . for Sexual Freedom*: Ibid.

172 *a new . . . love" advocate*: David Allyn, *Make Love, Not War: The Sexual Revolution, an Unfettered History* (New York: Little, Brown and Company, 2000), 41–42.

172 *At weekly meetings . . . obscenity statutes*: After an undercover police officer arrested Jonas Mekas, an avant-garde filmmaker and film critic for *The Village Voice*, at his showing of a homosexual film, the League for Sexual Freedom picketed the district attorney's office. In April, after comedian Lenny Bruce was arrested upon leaving the stage at a Greenwich Village club, the League coordinated a committee for his defense. See Allyn, *Make Love, Not War*, 45–47; Mel Heimer, "My New York," *The Logan Daily News*, July 2, 1964, 10.

172 *The League did . . . same issue*: "News," *Drum* 4, no. 9 (November 1964), 5.

172 *so at club . . . next*: Randy Wicker, interviewed by Eric Cervini, July 28, 2017, Hoboken, NJ.

172 *On the League . . . recruit*: Jefferson Poland to East Coast Homophile Organizations, September 1964, Box 100, Folder 7, FEK Papers.

172 *16,263 U.S. military . . . 1963*: Robert D. Ramsey, Advising indigenous forces: American advisors in Korea, Vietnam, and El Salvador (Fort Leavenworth, KS: Combat Studies Institute Press, 2006), 28.

172 *"I hope that . . . in May 1964*: Arnold F. Norden to FEK, May 28, 1964, Box 82, Folder 6, FEK Papers. "Influx of Deviates and Addicts Linked to City Draft Rejections," *The New York Times* had reported in January 1964. In less than a decade, the number of men rejected from military service for psychiatric reasons had tripled; the *Times* blamed the "homosexuals and narcotics addicts who come here from other parts of the country."

Homosexuals already in the military, meanwhile, continued to face dishonorable discharges if they were discovered. See Farnsworth Fowle, "Influx of Deviates and Addicts Linked to City Draft Rejections," *The New York Times*, January 6, 1964, 10.

173   *In early 1964 . . . States Army*: FEK to Charlie Hayden, May 24, 1964, Box 10, Folder 12, FEK Papers.

173   *"The boy who . . . DOCUMENTED," he wrote*: Charlie Hayden to FEK, n.d., Box 10, Folder 12, FEK Papers.

173   *Kameny drafted letters . . . and the army*: "Organization" to Stephen Ailes, September 1964, Box 100, Folder 7, FEK Papers.

173   *plus a flyer . . . the army*: Untitled Flyer Draft, September 1964, Box 100, Folder 7, FEK Papers.

173   *Wicker adopted Kameny's . . . in Times Square*: Randolfe Wicker to Robert S. McNamara, September 20, 1964, Box 100, Folder 7, FEK Papers; Randolfe Wicker to Stephen Ailes, September 20, 1964, Box 100, Folder 7, FEK Papers.

173   *almost all of . . . VERSUS SEX*: Former MSW member Ronald Brass, unemployed and now living in New York, wrote Kameny to inform him of Wicker's scheme. Unaware of the MSW president's involvement, Brass enclosed the final version of Kameny's own flyer. See Ronald Brass to FEK, September 17, 1964, Box 15, Folder 4, FEK Papers.

173   *On September 16 . . . Whitehall Street*: Ibid.

173   *On that rainy . . . former ballet dancer*: Faderman, *The Gay Revolution*, 126.

174   *and two young . . . Garden*: Tobin and Wicker, *The Gay Crusaders*, 65.

174   *Wicker brought his . . . her infant child*: Martin B. Duberman, *Stonewall* (New York: Penguin, 1993), 81.

174   *The cameras and . . . circle*: Tobin and Wicker, *The Gay Crusaders*, 68.

174   *The men wore . . . Nancy Garden*: Nancy Garden, email correspondence with Betsy Kuhn, n.d. https://www.betsykuhn.net/bonus-features.html.

174   *ARMY INVADES SEXUAL . . . leaflets*: "Randy Wicker and Craig Rodwell picketing," photographed September 19, 1964, New York Public Library Digital Collections, https://digitalcollections.nypl.org/items/510d47e3%E2%80%9393cc-a3d9-e040-e00a18064a99.

174   *HOMOSEXUALS DIED FOR . . . said Cafiero's sign*: Randy Wicker, "Renee Cafiero," photographed September 19, 1964, available at https://www.flickr.com/photos/randywicker/5319413138/in/album-72157625735060922.

174   *"LOVE AND . . . Jack Diether's*: Randy Wicker, "Jack Diether, HLNY & LSF 1t public demo for homosexual civil rights," photographed September 19, 1964, available at https://www.flickr.com/photos/randywicker/5319414566/in/album-72157625735060922.

174   *Afterward, the wet . . . uneventful," remembered Garden*: Nancy Garden, email correspondence with Betsy Kuhn.

174   *"Dr. Kameny—Demonstration was . . . no press"*: Jefferson Poland to East Coast Homophile Organizations, September 1964, Box 100, Folder 7, FEK Papers.

174   *Despite the gloom . . . harassment or injury*: Nancy Garden, email correspondence with Betsy Kuhn.

174   *Wicker resolved to . . . a larger one*: Randy Wicker, interviewed by Eric Cervini, July 28, 2017, Hoboken, NJ.

174   *In October 1964 . . . Nichols laughed*: Jack Nichols, "Chapter Six," *Memoirs of Jack Nichols*.

174   *Johnson attended every subsequent Society meeting*: "Warren Adkins" to Dick Leitsch, February 9, 1965, Box 8, Folder 5, MSNY Papers.

175   *The executive board . . . materials, instead?*: Gail Johnson to [Redacted] Special Agent, October 1, 1964, FBI File #100–403320, 708.

175   *"This letter is . . . wrote Hoover*: Jones to DeLoach, October 9, 1964, FBI File #100–403320, 707. Though this incident would mark the end of the Bureau's direct communication with the Society, it continued to keep a close eye on the group. See FBI File #100–403320, 709.

175   *Barbara Gittings did . . . some soul-searching"*: Barbara Gittings to Lilli Vincenz, August 21, 1964, Box 3, Folder 1, Lilli Vincenz Papers, Library of Congress, Washington, D.C. (hereafter, "Vincenz Papers").

176   *Despite Gittings's enthusiasm . . . my business"*: Agatha Mathys to Barbara Gittings et al., September 2, 1964, Box 54, Folder 5, Gittings Papers.

176   *three separate Washington . . . Northwest Washington*: Del Martin to DOB Governing Board, August 26, 1964, Box 54, Folder 5, Gittings Papers; "ECHO," *Drum* 4, no. 9 (November 1964), 14; FEK, "Hotel Pays ECHO Homosexuals," n.d., Box 126, Folder 7, FEK Papers.

176   *Meanwhile, attorney Monroe . . . out-of-court settlement*: "ECHO Report '64," *The Ladder* 9, no. 4 (January 1965), 4.

176   *"Homosexuality: Social . . . a phone number*: "1964 E.C.H.O. Conference," *The Village Voice*, October 8, 1964, clipping in Box 64, Folder 2, Gittings Papers.

176   *Followers of George . . . they warned*: Lilli Vincenz to Barbara Gittings, October 27, 1964, Box 64, Folder 4, Gittings Papers.

176   *The MSW notified . . . actually appeared*: "ECHO Report '64," *The Ladder* 9, no. 4 (January 1965), 4.

176   *On the morning . . . HOMOSEXUALS*: Ibid.

176 *Kameny detested their . . . he admonished Wicker*: FEK to Charlie Hayden, n.d., Box 1, "Correspondence 63, 65" Folder, Wicker Papers.

176 *The attendees included . . . Division*: "ECHO," *Drum* 4, no. 9 (November 1964), 14.

177 *News of the . . . noted*: "ECHO Report '64," *The Ladder* 9, no. 4 (January 1965), 4.

177 *Robert Belanger, speaking . . . will be discovered"*: Robert King, "Keynote Address," October 10, 1964, Box 3, Folder 24, MSNY Papers.

177 *bespectacled, dark-haired ECHO . . . originally from Massachusetts*: See "Robert Joseph Belanger," https://www .findagrave.com/memorial/143139436; for a photograph of Belanger, see Doug Hinckle, 1986 MSW Reunion photograph, *Washington Blade*, reproduced in Johnson, *The Lavender Scare*, photograph insert.

177 *"We want to . . . to stir"*: King, "Keynote Address."

177 *Julian Hodges, the . . . summer*: D'Emilio, *Sexual Politics, Sexual Communities*, 164.

177 *"Let us learn . . . in politics?"*: Julian C. Hodges, "Politics is Everybody's Business," October 10, 1964, Box 3, Folder 24, MSNY Papers.

177 *Monroe Freedman spoke . . . a closetful"*: Monroe H. Freedman, "Official Discrimination Against the Homosexual: The Broader Context," October 10, 1964, Box 3, Folder 24, MSNY Papers. Four more NCACLU attorneys, one after another, spoke after Freedman: Hal Witt on recognizing the homosexual's solidarity with other minority groups, Sidney Sachs on the Miller Sexual Psychopath Law, John Karr on the history of sodomy laws, and Glenn Graves on the homosexual's litigation strategy. See Sidney S. Sachs, "A Short Discussion of the Miller Act," Box 3, Folder 24, MSNY Papers; John W. Karr, "Criminal Sanction Upon Homosexuality and Homosexual Behavior," Box 3, Folder 24, MSNY Papers; Glenn R. Graves, "What are the Civil Rights of the Homosexual in America?," Box 3, Folder 24, MSNY Papers.

177 *At 3:15 p.m. . . . they concluded*: "Homosexuality and the Law: A Prognosis," October 10, 1964, Box 63, Folder 9, Gittings Papers.

178 *At that night's . . . was grateful*: "E.C.H.O. Conference 1964," October 10, 1964, Box 63, Folder 10, Gittings Papers, 94.

178 *The next afternoon . . . legal battles*: Ibid., 129.

178 *Yes, the movement . . . The audience applauded*: Ibid., 141.

178 *By 3:00 p.m. . . . four other ministers*: Nichols, "Chapter Seven," *Memoirs of Jack Nichols*.

179 *More of the audience joined . . . arrested the Nazi*: This retelling of the incident primarily relies on Kay Tobin Lahusen's transcription of the audio recording from the incident. See Kay Tobin, "Part Three: A Nazi Stunt Fails," *The Ladder* 9, no. 4 (January 1965), 20. For the audio itself, see "1964 Conference: Part 7," Audio File, in Box 63, Folder 9, Gittings Papers.

179 *The room could . . . Connecticut Avenue"*: Jack Nichols, "Chapter Seven."

179 *As Officer Graham . . . audience clapped*: Kay Tobin, "Part Three: A Nazi Stunt Fails."

11. THE BOUQUET

181 *On the evening . . . administration officials*: John McMullan, "The Homosexual Problem in the Nation's Capital," *New York Post*, October 20, 1964; David Wise, "'O, No, Not Walter!'—LBJ," *The Boston Globe*, October 18, 1964, 1.

181 *The guest list . . . and dubious finances*: James Reston, "Setback for Johnson," *The New York Times*, October 15, 1964, 31.

181 *"If Lyndon Johnson . . . Moyers*: Bill Moyers quoted in Al Weisel, "LBJ's Gay Sex Scandal," *Out* 8, no. 6 (December 1999), 76.

181 *The last staffer . . . classified secrets*: "The Nation," *TIME* 84, no. 17, October 23, 1964, 19. See also Charles, *Hoover's War on Gays*, 269; Weisel, "LBJ's Gay Sex Scandal."

181 *Three weeks before . . . House," wrote* TIME: Ibid.

181 *Jenkins arrived at . . . White House*: Ibid.

182 *Near 8:30 p.m. . . . for a decade*: Ibid.

182 *Officer Robert Graham . . . and watch*: Ibid.

182 *"Who was . . . taking it"*: Charles, *Hoover's War on Gays*, 273.

182 *Officer Graham and . . . until midnight*: "The Nation," *TIME* 84, no. 17, October 23, 1964, 19.

182 *One week later . . . tip*: Ibid.

182 *The White House . . . himself*: Weisel, "LBJ's Gay Sex Scandal."

182 *Fortas took him . . . twenty-four-hour suicide watch*: "The Nation," *TIME* 84, no. 17, October 23, 1964, 19.

183 *At 8:09 p.m. . . . unprecedented scandal*: Ibid.

183 *Walter Jenkins became . . . name*: Reston, "Setback for Johnson."

183 *Johnson requested and . . . national security?*: "Johnson Denies Jenkins Cover-Up; Sets F.B.I. Inquiry," *The New York Times*, October 16, 1964, 1.

183 *Television stations described . . . months earlier*: Harriet Van Horne, "3 Big Stories Throw TV Into Tizzy," *New York Telegraph and Sun*, October 16, 1964.

183   *"Mr. Jenkins is . . . president"*: "Johnson Denies Jenkins Cover-Up; Sets F.B.I. Inquiry," *The New York Times*, October 16, 1964, 1.

183   *Johnson's opponent, Senator . . .* New York Times: "The Jenkins Case," *The New York Times*, October 16, 1964, 38.

183   *To the media's . . . didn't care"*: Rowland Evans and Robert Novak, "Johnson Standing Unhurt by Jenkins?," *The Miami Herald*, October 20, 1964, 14A.

183   *As the election . . . the White House"*: "No Evidence Found by FBI That Jenkins Compromised U.S. Security or Interests," *The Washington Post*, October 23, 1964, 1. See also Charles, *Hoover's War on Gays*, 274–76.

184   *On October 22 . . . not a threat*: Ibid.

184   *"The FBI report . . . Hoover and Associates"*: "The Nation," *TIME* 84, no. 18, October 30, 1964, 34.

184   *"The Jenkins affair . . . the government"*: Dick Leitsch to FEK, October 20, 1964, Box 8, Folder 5, MSNY Papers.

184   *After the FBI . . . so with haste*: FEK to Washington *Daily News*, October 25, 1964, Box 128, Folder 11, FEK Papers.

184   *On December 7 . . . restroom*: "Test Refused in Restroom Mirrors Case," *The Washington Evening Star*, December 7, 1964, 8.

185   *A few days . . . of privacy"*: A search of one large periodicals database for the Postmaster General's statement yields thirty-six results in December 1964 alone. See https://www.newspapers.com/search/#ym=1964 -12&query=%22unfortunate+invasion+of+privacy%22. See also "Spyholes in Postal Rest Rooms Banned," *The Washington Post*, December 12, 1964, A20.

185   *On December 23 . . . tantalizing glimpse*: David Carliner to Walter N. Tobriner, December 23, 1964, Box 75, Folder 6, FEK Papers; "National Capital Area Civil Liberties Union Statement on Jenkins Case," Box 97, Folder 7, Gittings Papers. The NCACLU's solution, a "re-examination" of criminal laws relating to sexual offenses, was identical to the phrasing Kameny had long been using in his own statements. See, for example, The Mattachine Society of Washington, "Discrimination Against the Employment of Homosexuals," February 28, 1963, Box 8, Folder 5, MSNY Papers.

185   *"D.C. Asked to . . .* Post: "D.C. Asked to Bar Use of Police Peepholes," *The Washington Post*, December 28, 1964, D3.

185   *While Kameny basked . . . articulating lesbian defiance*: Faderman, *The Gay Revolution*, 86.

185   Ladder *covers . . . from Indonesia*: Ger van B, "Notes from Abroad," *The Ladder* 9, no. 2 (November 1964), 9.

185   *"I do think . . . and wonderful"*: "Readers Respond," *The Ladder* 9, no. 3 (December 1964), 26.

185   *In New York . . . "Homosexuality, A Disease"*: "The Division of Adult Education of the Cooper Union," Box 102, Folder 15, Gittings Papers.

185   *WE REQUEST 10 . . . their signs*: "'Expert' Challenged," *The Ladder* 9, no. 5–6 (February–March 1965), 18.

185   *The lecture's organizers . . .* The Ladder: Ibid. See also Faderman, *The Gay Revolution*, 87.

186   *"I just tore . . . years later*: Randy Wicker, interviewed by Eric Cervini, July 28, 2017, Hoboken, NJ.

186   *The day after . . . a radical"*: Randolfe Wicker to FEK, December 26, 1964, Box 10, Folder 12, FEK Papers.

186   *REPEAL MARIHUANA PROHIBITION!!! . . . Tompkins Square*: "Marihuana March," December 27, 1964, Personal Collection of Randy Wicker, Hoboken, NJ.

186   *"For three hours . . . and marijuana"*: "Demonstration Held to Protest the Law Against Marijuana," *The New York Times*, December 28, 1964, clipping in the personal collection of Randy Wicker, Hoboken, NJ.

186   The Village Voice *. . . J. EDGAR HOOVER*: Mary Perot Nichols, "Pickets for Pot Push Legalization," *The Village Voice*, December 31, 1964, 3.

186   *Ronald Brass, upon . . . an idiot"*: Ronald Brass to FEK, December 2, 1964, Box 15, Folder 4, FEK Papers.

186   *In 1963, Bruce Scott*: interview with Bruce Scott, 1978, Gregory Sprague Collection, Chicago Historical Society.

186   *and in 1964, Ron Balin*: Lilli Vincenz, interviewed by Genny Beemyn, Arlington, VA, June 6, 1998.

186   *Kameny had won . . . explained*: Eva Freund, interviewed by Mark Meinke, November 3, 2002, Rainbow History Project, Washington, D.C.

187   *"Frank was impossible . . . gave up"*: Susan Clarke, interviewed by Eric Cervini, telephone, October 11, 2019.

187   *Then the Society's . . . he asked*: FEK to John Schaffer, July 5, 1963, Box 31, Folder 8, FEK Papers.

187   *In December 1964 . . . KAMENY HALL"*: David L. et al. to MSW, December 1964, Box 68, Folder 5, Gittings Papers.

187   *Kameny's allies struck . . . YOUR FIGHTS"*: "Make It Safe to Be Gay, with F.E.K.," December 1964, Box 80, Folder 6, FEK Papers. On Christmas Day, Kameny penned his own defense. "We are engaged in a struggle for the minds of men," he wrote, "an enterprise designed to raise millions of people from the level of despised near-subhumans to their full dignity as full human beings." Yes, he may have offended some members in that fight; "if so, I am genuinely sorry." "A vote for Robert for President," he concluded, "will represent a repudiation of much of the good that we have accomplished thus far, a repudiation of the concept of a vigorous, energetic, active, outward-directed organization, dedicated, wholly and whole heartedly, to the improvement of the status and position of the homosexual American citizen." See FEK to MSW, December 25, 1964, Box 68, Folder 5, Gittings Papers.

187   *When MSNY board . . . of a hint"*: Dick Leitsch to Robert King, December 28, 1964, Box 6, Folder 11, FEK Papers.

188   *"To remove him . . . pro-Belanger MSW member*: Dick Leitsch to Lilli Vincenz, December 28, 1964, Box 6, Folder 11, FEK Papers.

188   *In January, by . . . for him"*: Paul Kuntzler, in "50th Anniversary of the Mattachine Society of Washington Panel Discussion," Rainbow History Project, October 13, 2011.

188   *"Allow me to . . . Mattachine Society"*: Ronald Brass to FEK, January 21, 1965, Box 15, Folder 4, FEK Papers.

188   *"This series of . . . Outlook section*: Jean M. White, "Those Others: A Report on Homosexuality," *The Washington Post*, January 31, 1965, E1.

188   *White, a World . . . March on Washington*: Adam Bernstein, "Jean M. White, Post journalist who covered civil rights and reviewed mysteries, dies at 87," *The Washington Post*, July 17, 2012.

188   *one year later . . . Organizations*: Jean White, "Homophile Groups Argue Civil Liberties," *The Washington Post*, October 11, 1964, B10.

188   *White's first article*: White, "Those Others: A Report on Homosexuality."

188   *"Scientists Disagree on*: Jean M. White, "Scientists Disagree on Basic Nature of Homosexuality, Chance of Cure," *The Washington Post*, February 1, 1965, A1.

188   *"Homosexuals Are in . . . of Society"*: Jean M. White, "Homosexuals Are in All Kinds of Jobs, Find Place in Many Levels of Society," *The Washington Post*, February 2, 1965, A1.

188   *The "obviously sick" . . . wanted equality*: Ibid.

189   *"The public response . . . its midst"*: Jean M. White, "Homosexuals' Militancy Reflected in Attacks on Ouster From U.S. Jobs," *The Washington Post*, February 4, 1965, A1.

189   *The series represented . . . those same facts*: Franklin E. Kameny, "Homosexuality in the News," *Eastern Mattachine Magazine* 10, no. 3, March 1965, 17.

189   *"Congratulations to you . . . own eyes"*: Jefferson Keith to FEK, February 3, 1965, Box 82, Folder 2, FEK Papers.

189   *The series rippled . . . "Militant Minority"*: Jean M. White, "Those Others: A Report on Homosexuality in America," *The Providence Sunday Journal*, February 7, 1965, H3; Bob Whearley, "'Militant Minority' Poses Serious Problem for Society,' *The Denver Post*, February 14, 1965, 25.

189   *Hugh Hefner's* Playboy *. . . affair*: See search of "homosexual" or "homosexuality" in *Playboy*'s online archives at https://www.iplayboy.com/search?query=homosexuality&sort=date&order=asc&page=4.

189   *The MSW's new . . . homophile movement??"*: Lilli Vincenz to Dick Leitsch, January 8, 1965, Box 8, Folder 5, MSNY Papers.

190   *"The statement," Kameny . . . kind from, heterosexuality.'"*: FEK to Jean White, January 17, 1965, Box 134, Folder 1, FEK Papers.

190   *The matter grew . . . it announced*: "Therapy Is Found Curing Deviates," *The New York Times*, January 31, 1965, 61.

190   *Though Kameny had . . . passages highlighted*: Warren D. Adkins to Dick Leitsch, January 24, 1965, Box 8, Folder 5, MSNY Papers; Nichols, "Chapter Seven," *Memoirs of Jack Nichols*.

190   *Well, I know . . . with one another*: Paul Kuntzler, in "50th Anniversary of the Mattachine Society of Washington Panel Discussion," Rainbow History Project, October 13, 2011.

190   *"We cannot play . . . own fate"*: "Positive Policy," *Eastern Mattachine Magazine* 10, no. 4, May 1965, 23.

191   *On March 4 . . . 27–5 vote*: Paul Kuntzler, in "50th Anniversary of the Mattachine Society of Washington Panel Discussion," Rainbow History Project, October 13, 2011.

191   *the Mattachine Society . . . for "sickness"*: FEK to Barbara Gittings, March 13, 1965, Box 6, Folder 11, Gittings Papers.

191   *"With his passion . . . Kameny joked*: Nichols, "Chapter Seven," *Memoirs of Jack Nichols*.

191   *While the MSW . . . against homosexual sin*: The MSW had heard whispers of new alliances on the West Coast. In May 1964, San Francisco's Glide Memorial Methodist Church, led by Cecil Williams, a Black minister, partnered with Guy Strait's League for Civil Education to organize a "Church and the Homosexual" conference, which featured a clergy tour of the city's gay bars. The event represented a "re-birth of Christian fellowship," reported Del Martin in *The Ladder*. In December 1964, the ministers and the homosexuals formed a joint Council on Religion and the Homosexual, which planned a New Year's Eve costume ball for its first event. The ministers, after hearing tales of police harassment, won promises from authorities that the homosexuals' event could occur without disruption. When the ministers and the homosexuals—six hundred in total—arrived to the event, they found a line of police cars at the entrance. The attendees faced the flashes of police photographers as they entered the hall, fully aware of the authorities' message: if you were a homosexual or supported the cause, the police would remember your face. Fifteen officers invaded the hall. When three volunteer attorneys and a straight housewife—she was collecting tickets at the entrance—blocked the officers' entrance and demanded a warrant, the four were arrested. Ministers escorted the terrified homosexuals to their cars, hoping to shield them from arrest or further incriminating photographs; the officers threatened to arrest them, too. "Angry Ministers Rip Police," announced the *San Francisco Chronicle*. In a January 2 press conference, seven ministers, three of whom stood in cassocks, accused the SFPD of "intimidation,

broken promises and obvious hostility." Six weeks later, a crowd of ministers, homosexuals, and supporters packed into a courtroom. When the judge asked a Sex Detail officer why so many officers had arrived at the ball, the officer pled ignorance: "We went just to inspect the premises," he said. The courtroom laughed. On February 11, to the courtroom's shock, the judge interrupted the proceedings and directed the jury to return a Not Guilty verdict. "Complaining officers sat with mouths agape," reported the *Chronicle*. See D'Emilio, *Sexual Politics, Sexual Communities*, 193; Del Martin, "The Church and the Homosexual: A New Rapport," *The Ladder* 8, no. 12 (September 1964), 9; "Trial Halted on Technicality," *San Francisco Chronicle*, February 12, 1965.

191   *On February 14 . . . Among Us*": "Church Applauds MSW," *Eastern Mattachine Magazine* (May 1965), 22.
191   *"The bar to . . . straight congregants*: Ibid.
191   *On March 22 . . . religious community*: "Homosexuals Confer with Clergy," Press Release, March 22, 1965, Box 68, Folder 6, Gittings Papers.
191   *The sympathetic Unitarian . . . Dr. King*: Maude McGovern, "UUCR 60th Anniversary History," Unitarian Universalist Congregation of Rockville, October 2016, 17.
191   *In October 1964 . . . men*: Allyn, *Make Love, Not War*, 150.
192   *Kameny agreed to . . . still 50 percent clothed*: *Drum* 4, no. 8, October 1964.
192   *In the December . . . nonetheless*: *Drum* 4, no. 10, December 1964.
192   *(It appealed to . . . thinking homosexual.")*: Dick Leitsch to Lilli Vincenz, January 12, 1965, Box 8, Folder 5, MSNY Papers.
192   *That issue represented . . . a semipornographic publication?*: FEK to Marjorie L. McCann, January 30, 1965, Box 79, Folder 5, FEK Papers.
192   *By February, ECHO . . . from its ranks*: East Coast Homophile Organizations, Meeting Minutes, February 6, 1965, Box 3, Folder 23, MSNY Papers.
192   *Kameny's name disappeared from* Drum's *masthead*: *Drum* 5, no. 1, March 1965, 3.
192   *And in Janus's . . . of Philadelphia*: The Mattachine Society of Philadelphia, Press Release, March 2, 1965, Box 68, Folder 4, Gittings Papers.
192   *On November 24 . . . it began*: "Federal Job Corps to Exclude Youths Having Police Records," *The New York Times*, November 21, 1964, 30.
192   *Kameny had long . . . that is wrong*": FEK to Charlie Hayden, n.d., Box 1, "Correspondence 63, 65" Folder, Randy Wicker Papers.
192   *"Genocide is an . . . Sargent Shriver*: FEK to Sargent Shriver, November 28, 1964, Box 106, Folder 7, FEK Papers.
193   *If the OEO . . . Washington and elsewhere*": Ibid.
193   *Over the next . . . disobedience*: FEK to Barbara Gittings, March 13, 1965, Box 6, Folder 11, Gittings Papers.
193   *On February 1 . . . right to vote*: "Dr. King, 300 Negroes Arrested in Selma," *International Herald Tribune*, February 2, 1965.
193   *Five days later . . . Village sidewalk*: "NYCLU Docket of Current Cases," *Civil Liberties in New York*, April 1965, 4.
193   *On February 18 . . . his honor*: Taylor Branch, *At Canaan's Edge* (New York: Simon & Schuster, 2007), 8–9.
193   *On Sunday, March . . . broken limbs*: Ibid., 56.
193   *Five days later . . . Cole, in Selma*: McGovern, "UUCR 60th Anniversary History," 11.
194   *On March 15*: "President Johnson Speaks on Tolerance and Brotherhood," *Eastern Mattachine Magazine* (May 1965), 2.
194   *On March 17 . . . a permit*: "Ministers Held in Selma Stage Courtroom Sit-In," *The Washington Evening Star*, March 18, 1965, 4.
194   *The next day . . . he warned*: FEK to Sheldon S. Cohen, March 18, 1965, Box 6, Folder 11, Gittings Papers.
194   *The IRS responded . . . when due*": Matthew Riedl to FEK, April 12, 1965, Box 106, Folder 6, FEK Papers.
194   *Kameny buckled within . . . for $575.95*: FEK to Sheldon S. Cohen, April 15, 1965, Box 6, Folder 11, Gittings Papers; Robert Good to FEK, April 19, 1965, Box 137, Folder 3, FEK Papers.
194   *On April 1 . . . 1:00 p.m.*: SAC, WFO, to Director, FBI, April 1, 1965, FBI File #100–403320, 784.
195   *The FBI again . . . attorney general*: Ibid., Director, FBI, to the Attorney General, April 2, 1965, FBI File #100–403320, 783.
195   *That Saturday, for . . . homosexual? responded Scarberry*: Warren Scarberry, *American Homosexual Activities* 1, no. 1 (May 15, 1965), 3, quoted in Frank Kameny and Michael G. Long, *Gay Is Good: The Life and Letters of Gay Rights Pioneer Franklin Kameny* (Syracuse, NY: Syracuse University Press, 2014), 123–24.
195   *Two hours after . . . ECHO convention*: ECHO Minutes, April 3, 1965, Box 64, Folder 4, Gittings Papers.
195   *On April 7 . . . we shouldn't*": Dick Leitsch to FEK, April 7, 1965, Box 8, Folder 5, MSNY Papers.
195   *a feat that . . . for himself*: Randy Wicker, interviewed by Eric Cervini, July 28, 2017, Hoboken, NJ.
195   *On April 15 . . . labor camps*": "Cuban Government Is Alarmed by Increase in Homosexuality," *The New York Times*, April 16, 1965, 2.
195   *That night, Kameny . . . to march*: Lahusen interview, Nichols, "Chapter Seven," *Memoirs of Jack Nichols*.

196 *Kameny first reacted . . . through Switzerland*: Lahusen interview.

196 *Nichols had struck . . . USSR*": See "Report of Special Interview," *Kameny v. Brucker* (1959), Case 1628–59, Accession #021–74A-6269, Box 122, National Archives (Kansas City).

196 *"We could,' admitted . . . ordered Kameny*: Nichols, "Chapter Seven," *Memoirs of Jack Nichols*.

12. THE PICKET

197 *Born in Nazi . . . school within weeks*: Lilli Vincenz, interviewed by Genny Beemyn, Arlington, VA, June 6, 1998. See also Lilli Vincenz, interviewed by David K. Johnson, Arlington, VA, 1992.

197 *In 1962, she . . . Vincenz's homosexual activity*: Ibid.

197 *Her straight roommate . . . the major*: Ibid.

198 *Vincenz signed the . . . later explained*: Lilli Vincenz to Hans Rosenhaupt, January 25, 1966, Box 5, Folder 1, Vincenz Papers.

198 *"Dear Mr. Kameny,". . . Society's board*: Lilli Vincenz to FEK, September 24, 1963, Box 18, Folder 5, Vincenz Papers.

198 *"Upon their recommendation . . . first lesbian member*: Bruce Schuyler to Lilli Vincenz, November 1, 1963, Box 18, Folder 5, Vincenz Papers.

198 *Within four months . . . against H.R.5990*: Lily Hansen to Robert Nix et al., March 5, 1964, Box 81, Folder 1, FEK Papers.

198 *Though she grew . . . the sickness debate*: Lilli Vincenz to Dick Leitsch, January 8, 1965, Box 8, Folder 5, MSNY Papers; Nichols, "Chapter Seven," *Memoirs of Jack Nichols*.

198 *In April 1965 . . . to march*: Lilli Vincenz to Phil Devin, April 8, 1965, Box 3, Folder 2, Vincenz Papers.

198 *That Friday night . . . not attend*: Nichols, "Chapter Seven," *Memoirs of Jack Nichols*.

198 *Kameny disseminated the . . . advance*": FEK to Guy Strait, April 30, 1965, Box 9, Folder 8, FEK Papers.

199 *Kameny's reasoning for . . . look employable*: Nichols, "Chapter Seven," *Memoirs of Jack Nichols*.

199 *With only hours . . . White House*: "News Bulletin," Box 85, Folder 14, FEK Papers; FEK to Barbara Gittings, April 17, 1965, Box 6, Folder 11, Gittings Papers.

199 *"The demonstration started . . . their signs*: "Viet-Nam War Protest is Staged by 16,000," *The Washington Post*, April 18, 1965, 1; "Thousands Picket Here for Peace," April 17, 1965, *The Washington Evening Star*, 1.

199 *In February, Johnson . . . Nang*: "The U.S. in Vietnam: A Chronology," *Miami Herald*, April 28, 1985, 6D.

199 *On April 17 . . . President Johnson*: "Jets Bomb North Viet Highway," *The Washington Post*, April 18, 1965, A13.

199 *That day's "March . . . in American history*: Todd Gitlin, *The Sixties: Years of Hope, Days of Rage* (New York: Bantam Books, 1993), 183.

199 *Pacifists like Bayard . . . for civil disobedience*: Fulton Lewis Jr., "Leftists Aim to Thwart Efforts in Viet Nam," *Standard-Speaker* (Hazleton, PA), April 12, 1965, 8.

199 *at the march . . . record player*: "Thousands Picket Here for Peace," April 17, 1965, *The Washington Evening Star*, 1.

200 *Lige Clarke drove . . . Staff*: Nichols, "Chapter Seven," *Memoirs of Jack Nichols*. See also Johnson, *The Lavender Scare*, 185.

200 *Kameny immediately began . . . would follow him*: Ibid.

200 *First, Nichols carried . . . U.S. MUCH BETTER!*: "News Bulletin," Box 85, Folder 14, FEK Papers.

201 *At 4:20 p.m. . . . House fence*: Ibid.

201 *Tourists seemed to . . . the Secret Service?*: Lahusen interview.

201 *For an hour . . . in silence*: Ibid.; "News Bulletin," Box 85, Folder 14, FEK Papers.

201 *"Only a very . . . never appeared*: Ibid.

201 *One newspaper reported . . . said Kameny*: "10 Oppose Gov't on Homosexuals," *The Washington Afro American*, April 20, 1965, 18.

201 *"HISTORY IN THE . . . a homosexual organization*: Kameny admitted that Warren Scarberry had picketed the White House before—in fact, he revealed, Scarberry had picketed the White House twice, including one time in 1964—but that day's march constituted the first White House picket organized by a group of homosexuals. FEK to Barbara Gittings, April 17, 1965, Box 6, Folder 11, Gittings Papers.

201 *They pledged to . . . put it*: Nichols, "Chapter Seven," *Memoirs of Jack Nichols*.

201 *"We were going . . . remembered Vincenz*: Lilli Vincenz, interviewed by Genny Beemyn, Arlington, VA, June 6, 1998.

201 *Gail Green, the . . . high heels*: Lahusen interview.

201 *"Americans! Civil libertarians! . . . they said*: Untitled Leaflet!, April 16, 1965, Box 3, Folder 21, MSNY Papers; Warren D. Adkins and Dennis Livingstone, "We're on the Move Now . . . ," *Eastern Mattachine Magazine* 10, no. 5 (June 1965), 4.

202 *On a cloudy . . . Freedom—Si! Persecution—No!*": Adkins and Livingstone, "We're on the Move Now . . ."; Lahusen interview.

202   *"Sex in Any Form is Good"*: Duberman, *Stonewall*, 289.

202   *"Let all good . . . homosexual victims"*: "Stop Crimes Against Humanity," April 18, 1965, Box 3, Folder 21, MSNY Papers.

202   *In New York . . . walked away"*: Adkins and Livingstone, "We're on the Move Now . . ."

202   *Kameny received Warren . . . Brass*: FEK to Ronald Brass, April 29, 1965, Box 15, Folder 4, FEK Papers.

202   *When Ronald Brass . . . picketing*: Ronald Brass to FEK, May 3, 1965, Box 15, Folder 4, FEK Papers.

203   *"He is under . . . added Brass*: Ibid. The same night as Scarberry's police station picket, three teenagers refused to leave Dewey's, an all-night restaurant in Philadelphia. The restaurant had refused to serve more than 150 young, "camping" homosexuals and those wearing "non-conformist clothing," as *Drum* described them. The three youths were arrested and found guilty on disorderly conduct charges. For the next five days, the homosexuals of the Janus Society—wearing suits and perfectly parted hair, distinguishing them from the patrons they defended—demonstrated outside of Dewey's, distributing 1,500 flyers that warned potential patrons of the restaurant's discriminatory practices. Dewey's soon reversed its policy, a result of America's first gay sit-in. See "News," *Drum* 5, no. 6, August 1965, 5; see also Marc Stein, *City of Sisterly and Brotherly Loves: Lesbian and Gay Philadelphia, 1945–1972* (Chicago: University of Chicago Press, 2000), 245–46.

203   *Despite Brass's objections . . . Demonstrations*: "I have a good core group of enthusiastic, determined people (Lilli is one of my best)," Kameny wrote Gittings. "It should be an interesting summer. Want to picket Independence Hall in Philly, with us?" FEK to Barbara Gittings, April 30, 1965, Box 6, Folder 11, Gittings Papers.

203   *He wrote—and Belanger . . . to picket*: Robert King to John W. Macy Jr., April 24, 1965, Box 41, Folder 12, FEK Papers.

203   *"No useful purpose . . . responded Macy*: John W. Macy Jr. to Robert King, May 13, 1965, Box 41, Folder 12, FEK Papers.

203   *In the aftermath . . . a little.'"*: "Federal Interrogation," *Eastern Mattachine Magazine* 10, no. 3, March 1965, 7.

203   *The TAKE ONE . . . Department*: FEK to Dick Leitsch, May 4, 1965, Box 8, Folder 5, MSNY Papers.

203   *Over the next . . . North Carolina*: Newark SAC to FBI Director, May 6, 1965, FBI File #100–403320, 785; Louisville SAC to FBI Director, June 4, 1965, FBI File #100–403320, 791; Birmingham SAC to FBI Director, June 6, 1965, FBI File #100–403320, 831; Charlotte SAC to FBI Director, June 21, 1965, FBI File #100–403320, 813.

203   *In a July . . . Klux Klan*: FBI Director to the Attorney General, July 6, 1965, FBI File #100–403320, 842; Jones to DeLoach, June 29, 1965, FBI File #100–403320, 818.

204   *Meanwhile, in May . . . his release"*: "Homosexuals to Picket White House," May 29, 1965, Box 68, Folder 6, Gittings Papers.

204   *On the afternoon . . . of it"*: "Warren Adkins" to Dick Leitsch, June 2, 1965, Box 8, Folder 5, MSNY Papers.

204   *That Saturday, from . . . OF US?*: FEK to Barbara Gittings, May 30, 1965, Box 6, Folder 11, Gittings Papers.

204   *The Associated Press . . . day*: Ibid.

204   *Larry Littlejohn of . . . conspiracy of silence"*: Larry Littlejohn to The Mattachine Society, May 29, 1965, Box 82, Folder 3, FEK Papers.

204   *"Protest Subject Is . . . York*: "Protest Subject Is Deviants," *Press & Sun-Bulletin* (Binghamton, NY), May 30, 1965, 1.

204   *At least a . . . march*: See query for *homosexual* and *picket* at https://www.newspapers.com/search/#query =homosexual&ymd=1965%E2%80%9305%E2%80%9330.

205   *"The neatly dressed . . . the AP*: "Protest Subject Is Deviants," *Press & Sun-Bulletin* (Binghamton, NY), May 30, 1965, 1.

205   *The "well dressed . . . UPI*: "Homosexuals Protest Federal Treatment," *Star Tribune* (Minneapolis), May 30, 1965, 2.

205   *That Sunday, the . . . name or face*: Jean M. White, "Those Others: A Report on Homosexuality," *The Washington Post*, January 31, 1965, E1.

205   *But . . . Lilli Vincenz*: Jean M. White, "A Moral-Medical Dilemma," *Chicago Sun-Times*, V23.

205   *In May, David . . . constitutional principles"*: "Brief for Appellant and Joint Appendix," *Scott v. Macy*, United States Court of Appeals for the District of Columbia Circuit, Box 8, Folder 4, Gittings Papers, 10.

205   *On June 7 . . . Rights*: Griswold v. Connecticut, 381 U.S. 479 (1965). Scott, Carliner, and Kameny saw other signs that legal thought was indeed shifting in their favor. In October 1964, after the Supreme Court agreed to hear the case of a married man fired from his job in the Federal Aviation Administration—it learned of homosexual acts in his past—the FAA withdrew its defense and reinstated him. The government did not want to risk losing in a precedent-setting Supreme Court case. The employee had simply made a "youthful mistake," explained the FAA administrator. He was now "fully rehabilitated." In May 1965, both the New York State Legislature and the British Parliament reconsidered the criminalization of homosexual acts. "Nothing and nobody is going to change a man's basic desires, his erotic makeup. If he is basically homosexual he will continue homosexual," argued the Earl of Arran in the House of Lords. "To punish in such circumstances is to persecute a minority as others have persecuted Jews and Negroes." The bill passed the House

NOTES

of Lords before the House of Commons narrowly refused to consider it. In New York, meanwhile, the state legislature voted for a new penal code that removed sodomy from its provisions—until a last-minute amendment ensured it remained illegal. The *Eastern Mattachine Magazine* covered both efforts as its lead stories. Meanwhile, even elements of the Catholic Church supported the *Griswold* decision. "It does not seem reasonable to me to forbid in civil law a practice that can be considered a matter of private morality," Cardinal Cushing of Boston argued. Because the decision suggested that other immoral acts—adultery, fornication, homosexuality—could soon fall under the protected realm of morality and privacy, it gave the homophile movement "a renewed sense of hope and optimism," as the *Eastern Mattachine Magazine* reported. See *Dew v. Halaby*, 317 F.2d 582, 583 (D.C. Cir. 1963); "FAA Rehires Employee Fired in Morals Case," *The Washington Post*, October 3, 1964, B2; "Ex-Homosexual Got U.S. Job Back," *The New York Times*, October 18, 1964, 54; "Bishop on Moral Issue," *San Francisco Examiner*, May 13, 1965, 7; "General News," *Eastern Mattachine Magazine* 10, no. 6, July 1965, 26; "Lords Vote to Ease Homosexual Ban," *The New York Times*, May 25, 1965, 1.

205 *Because the decision . . .* Mattachine Magazine *reported*: Michael Kotis, "New York Penal Code Falters," *Eastern Mattachine Magazine* 10, no. 6, July 1965, 7.

205 *Nine days later . . . of due process*: *Scott v. Macy*, 349 F.2d 182 (D.C. Cir. 1965).

206 *Scott had won . . . 'immoral conduct' here*: Bazelon also introduced the "nexus" argument that would later be accepted by the court in its Norton decision. The CSC, he wrote in Scott, must "state why that conduct related to 'occupational competence or fitness.'" Because Judge McGowan only concurred with his specificity argument, this rule did not become legally binding. See ibid.

206 *"The walls of . . . release*: Press Release, n.d., Box 126, Folder 7, FEK Papers.

206 *"No Federal court . . . day's* Post: "Unspecific Charge of Homosexuality Held No Bar to Federal Employment," *The Washington Post*, June 17, 1965, A3.

206 *The day after . . . GREAT SERVICE"*: Bruce Scott to FEK, June 17, 1965, Box 32, Folder 4, FEK Papers.

206 *Drum* magazine began . . . *of thousands*: *Drum* 5, no. 7, September 1965, 26. For circulation numbers of homophile publications, see Dick Leitsch to Robert S. Walker, January 6, 1965, Box 2, Folder 6, MSNY Papers.

206 *The MSW, meanwhile . . . Supreme Court*: FEK to Barbara Gittings, June 23, 1965, Box 6, Folder 11, Gittings Papers.

206 *A picket risked . . . unemployed*: Ibid.

206 *Two days after . . . he complained*: FEK to John W. Macy Jr., June 18, 1965, Box 152, Folder 6, FEK Papers.

206 *Bruce Scott favored . . . he told Kameny*: Bruce Scott to FEK, June 26, 1965, Box 32, Folder 4, FEK Papers.

206 *On June 21 . . . press release, enclosed*: FEK to John W. Macy Jr., June 21, 1965, Box 41, Folder 12, FEK Papers.

206 *"We consider that . . . meeting," responded Macy*: John W. Macy Jr. to FEK, June 23, 1965, Box 41, Folder 12, FEK Papers.

206 *The press releases . . . newsrooms across Washington*: "Information Bulletin," June 26, 1965, Box 85, Folder 13, FEK Papers.

206 *on June 26 . . . Civil Service Commission*: "Information Bulletin," June 26, 1965, Box 85, Folder 13, FEK Papers.

207 CIVIL SERVICE COMMISSION . . . GOVERNOR WALLACE: Ibid. The group included a clergyman in his cassock, likely recruited at a meeting of the Council on Religion and the Homosexual at American University the day prior. See "Revised Notice of Meeting," Box 104, Folder 12, FEK Papers.

207 *The picketers saw . . . Macy himself*: Lahusen interview.

207 *He donated one hundred dollars—nearly . . . the Dowdy affair*: Clark P. Polak to MSW, December 2, 1963, Box 82, Folder 7, FEK Papers.

207 *the two leaders . . . Washington and Philadelphia*: Janus Society, "Homosexuality and Civil Liberties," Box 129, Folder 8, FEK Papers.

207 *Polak sent an . . . to Frank's leadership*: Clark P. Polak to FEK, January 5, 1965, Box 8, Folder 8, FEK Papers.

207 *Polak's magazine, however . . . demonstrations*: Stein, *City of Sisterly and Brotherly Loves*, 236.

207 *In April, Polak . . . Cruising"*: *Drum* 5, no. 2, April 1965.

207 *in his July . . . they were called*: *Drum* 5, no. 5, July 1965.

207 *Kameny could not . . . is publishing?*: "These magazines, which may sometimes have the best intentions, can easily bolster the public's erroneous image of the homosexual as a child-molesting sex fiend," he explained in the *Eastern Mattachine Magazine*. Kameny saw nothing wrong with pornography per se—indeed, he admitted to enjoying pornography—but he wanted it to remain wholly separate from the homophile movement. See FEK, "Washington Editorial," *Eastern Mattachine Magazine* 10, no. 10–11, November/December 1965, 19.

207 *On June 3 . . . regular basis"*: "Policies of the Mattachine Society of Washington," Box 80, Folder 11, FEK Papers.

208 *In May, he . . . he wrote*: Committee on Picketing and Lawful Demonstrations, "Rules for Picketing," Box 3, Folder 21, MSNY Papers; a reference to the May regulations appears in FEK to Hendrick Ruitenbeek and Richard McConchie, July 7, 1965, Box 107, Folder 17, FEK Papers.

208   *Onlookers, he explained . . . a political tool*: Ibid.
208   *History provided evidence . . . organizers told marchers*: Chappell, Hutchinson, and Ward, "Dress modestly, neatly . . . as if you were going to church," 71.
208   *Kameny thus required . . . absolutely necessary*: "Regulations for Picketing," Box 80, Folder 9, FEK Papers.
208   *"I'm all in . . . in summer?"*: Ronald Brass to FEK, June 11, 1965, Box 15, Folder 4, FEK Papers.
208   *ninety degrees*: "History: Philadelphia International Airport, Pennsylvania," *Weather Underground*, https://www.wunderground.com/history/daily/us/pa/philadelphia/KPHL/date/1965-7-4.
209   *thirty-nine picketers—thirty-two . . . Independence Hall*: "Information Bulletin," July 4, 1965, Box 68, Folder 6, Gittings Papers.
209   *Their signs spoke . . . FOR HOMOSEXUALS*: Ibid.
209   *To Kameny's dismay . . . pair to participate*: FEK to Hendrick Ruitenbeek and Richard McConchie, July 7, 1965, Box 107, Folder 17, FEK Papers.
209   *"Frank, since I . . . has been reached*: Dick Leitsch to FEK, July 5, 1965, Box 6, Folder 11, FEK Papers.
209   *"The more I . . . the middle-class"*: Ibid.
209   *Kameny refused to apologize*: FEK to Hendrick Ruitenbeek and Richard McConchie, July 7, 1965, Box 107, Folder 17, FEK Papers.
209   *"First, I will . . . become so"*: FEK to Dick Leitsch, July 12, 1965, Box 8, Folder 5, MSNY Papers.
210   *On Friday, July . . . forces, it announced*: FEK, "Homosexuals Picket in Washington and Philadelphia," *Eastern Mattachine Magazine* 10, no. 8/9, (September/October 1965), 19.
210   *Since May, Kameny . . . threaten a demonstration*: "Why Are Homosexual American Citizens Picketing the Pentagon?" July 31, 1965, Box 102, Folder 13, Gittings Papers.
210   *The Pentagon ignored . . . the homosexual picketers*: SA [Redacted] to SAC, WFO, August 24, 1965, FBI File #100–33796, 169.
210   *Shortly before 2:00 p.m. . . . his telephoto lens*: Ibid.
210   *Kameny arrived in . . . of each picketer*: Ibid.
210   *IF YOU DON'T*: "Information Bulletin," July 31, 1965, Box 68, Folder 6, Gittings Papers.
210   *Three weeks later . . . Government agency"*: SA [Redacted] to SAC, WFO, August 24, 1965, FBI File #100–33796, 169.
211   *Around this time . . . his identity*: Lahusen interview. "Handled," concluded a handwritten note at the bottom of the FBI memorandum. "Not gov't." See ibid.
211   *In* The Ladder *. . . homosexual scientific research*: FEK, "Does Research into Homosexuality Matter?," *The Ladder* 9, no. 8 (May 1965), 14. At the same time, Gittings gave a platform to those excluded from the respectable world of Kameny's homophile movement: "Come on, honey! Who told you women are slaves today? Women run the world and you know it!" wrote Susanna Valenti, a trans woman, only a few pages after Kameny's article. "It makes me, as a TV, indignant to see the fabulous amount of freedom a girl (born a girl) enjoys in our present society." "The transvestites," Valenti continued, "are the only ones who are rebelling against this artificial definition of what man is and wants, and we feel proud of being able to show the world an honest inner self—who adores frills, loves to walk on high heels, and is happy to sign an article like this with her real 'real' name." See Susanna Valenti, "I Hate Men," *The Ladder* 9, no. 8 (May 1965), 24.
211   *Meanwhile, the DOB's . . . 9–3 vote*: Marjorie McCann to DOB Governing Board, June 13, 1965, Box 54, Folder 6, Gittings Papers.
211   *The DOB delegates . . . organizations*: Ibid.
211   *"Unilateral picketing by . . . larger community"*: "Statement of DOB Policy," June 7, 1965, Box 54, Folder 6, Gittings Papers.
211   *Gittings urged the . . . well-planned picketing project"*: Barbara Gittings to DOB Governing Board, June 18, 1965, Box 54, Folder 6, Gittings Papers.
211   *Kameny himself wrote . . . the Negro movement*: FEK to DOB President and Governing Board, June 8, 1965, Box 69, Folder 5, FEK Papers.
211   *"With the kindest . . . at stake"*: Ibid.
212   *Willer, as Lilli . . . of lesbians"*: Lilli Vincenz, interviewed by Jack Nichols, *GayToday*, 1997.
212   *During the meeting . . . mind," she recalled*: Lilli Vincenz to Kay Tobin Lahusen, August 20, 1965, Box 60, Folder 4, Gittings Papers.
212   *Willer . . . the room*: Ibid.
212   *Rumors of the . . . slapped her"*: Jody Shotwell to FEK, August 18, 1965, Box 9, Folder 6, FEK Papers.
212   *Kameny sent Willer . . . to you"*: FEK to Shirley Willer, August 12, 1965, Box 10, Folder 14, FEK Papers.
212   *Barbara Gittings, meanwhile . . . Daughters of Bilitis"*: Kay Tobin Lahusen to FEK, July 17, 1965, Box 6, Folder 12, Gittings Papers.
212   *Her October 1965 . . . Service Commission*: *The Ladder* 10, no. 1 (October 1965).
212   *"wild-eyed, dungareed radicals"*: Joan Fraser to Cleo Glenn et al., June 6, 1965, Box 54, Folder 6, Gittings Papers.

212 *In Washington, Vincenz . . . his mind"*: Lilli Vincenz to Kay Tobin Lahusen, August 20, 1965, Box 60, Folder 4, Gittings Papers.

213 *Secretary of State . . . not happen"*: Bernard Gwertzman, "Rusk Says U.S. Seeks Hanoi Signal for Talks," *The Washington Evening Star*, August 28, 1965, 1.

213 *"Mr. Secretary," began . . . discharge them"*: For footage of the exchange, see "CBS Remembers Gay Rights Pioneer Frank Kameny," CBS News, https://www.youtube.com/watch?v=zbU_lcVzJ0I.

213 *Kameny was ecstatic. . . . their demonstrations*: FEK to Barbara Gittings, August 29, 1965, Box 6, Folder 12, Gittings Papers.

213 *The next day . . . BURY IT*: "Information Bulletin," August 28, 1965, Box 102, Folder 13, Gittings Papers.

213 *The CBS reporters . . . an individual"*: "CBS Remembers Gay Rights Pioneer Frank Kameny," CBS News.

213 *While Kameny talked . . . provide it*: Lahusen interview.

214 *"Those picketing were . . . the camera, grinning*: SAC, WFO, to Director, FBI, September 3, 1965, FBI File #100–403320, 837. For surveillance photographs of the picket, see Box 158, Folder 7, FEK Papers.

214 *Before they started . . . with the MSW*: FEK to Barbara Gittings, August 29, 1965, Box 6, Folder 12, Gittings Papers.

13. THE STUDENT

215 *In December 1964 . . . becoming either?"*: Robert A. Martin Jr. to J. Edgar Hoover, December 15, 1964, FBI File #100–434516–146.

215 *Hoover responded by . . . Communism"*: J. Edgar Hoover to Robert A. Martin Jr., December 22, 1964, FBI File #100–434516–146.

215 *and promptly opened . . . file on Martin*: Ibid.

215 *The son of . . . Delaware, perhaps*: Wilson Barto, "He's an All 'Go-Bo' Guy," clipping in Box 17, Folder 2, Stephen Donaldson Papers, New York Public Library, New York, NY (hereafter, "Donaldson Papers").

215 *Martin was attracted . . . he later explained.)*: Robert A. Martin to Gay People at Columbia-Barnard, March 6, 1982, Box 2, Folder 8, Donaldson Papers.

215 *During the summer . . . homeless*: David Eisenbach, *Gay Power: An American Revolution* (New York: Carroll & Graf, 2006), 53.

216 *As he entered . . . Village apartment*: Robert A. Martin to Gay People at Columbia-Barnard, March 6, 1982, Box 2, Folder 8, Donaldson Papers.

216 *MSNY planned to . . . his guest*: Ibid.

216 *On the evening . . . Personnel Investigations*: Nicholas J. Oganovic to FEK, August 27, 1965, Box 41, Folder 12, FEK Papers; FEK to Richard Inman, September 2, 1965, Box 5, Folder 12, FEK Papers.

216 *The homosexuals did . . . THAT ALL?"*: Lilli Vincenz, "A Statement from a Member of the Mattachine Society of Washington," 1965, Box 18, Folder 5, Vincenz Papers.

217 *The officials requested . . . indefensible" purges*: Mattachine Society of Washington, "Federal Employment of Homosexual American Citizens," November 15, 1965, Box 8, Folder 5, MSNY Papers.

217 *Then, only days . . . v. Macy decision*: FEK to Barbara Gittings, October 10, 1965, Box 98, Folder 5, Gittings Papers.

217 *In early October . . . federal employment*: Bruce Scott to FEK, October 6, 1965, Box 9, Folder 5, FEK Papers.

217 *Lilli Vincenz had . . . once more*: Lilli Vincenz, interviewed by Genny Beemyn, Arlington, VA, June 6, 1998.

217 *In the summer . . . know about"*: FEK to Barbara Gittings and Kay Tobin Lahusen, November 27, 1965, Box 6, Folder 12, Gittings Papers.

217 *The membership replaced . . . White House picket*: For a photograph of Swanson, see *Eastern Mattachine Magazine* 11, no. 1 (January 1966), 6.

217 *Restrained from power . . . in other states*: FEK to Richard Inman, September 2, 1965, Box 5, Folder 12, FEK Papers.

217 *When the MSW's . . . Executive Director"*: John Marshall et al., "Strengthen ECHO Properly!," September 4, 1965, Box 64, Folder 1, Gittings Papers. Kameny responded by defending ECHO and the concept of a national organization: "You have just received a most unfortunate letter, filled with non-factual allegations and some old-wives tales, implying the existence of a completely fictitious conspiracy," he wrote. "Where would the ACLU be, were it the CLU of Chicago," he asked. "Certainly not the respected organization that it now is, carrying the weight that it does." ECHO coordinator Dick Leitsch of New York grew equally angry: "I have received three telephone calls this afternoon from members of your organization. All of them were incensed at a letter they received from your organization," he wrote Marshall. "It seems you have chosen this time, three weeks before the Conference, to undermine support for ECHO!" See FEK and Eva Friend to Fellow Members, September 7, 1965, Box 64, Folder 1, Gittings Papers; Dick Leitsch to John Marshall, September 7, 1965, Box 8, Folder 5, MSNY Papers.

218 *Despite the suspicions . . . 1965 ECHO conference*: John Marshall et al. to Fellow Member, September 23, 1965, Box 3, Folder 23, MSNY Papers.

218   *to be held . . . to accommodate them*: "The Homosexual Citizen in the Great Society," *Eastern Mattachine Magazine* 11, no. 1 (January 1966), 2.

218   *The Friday night . . . they explained*: Jody Shotwell to Barbara Gittings, November 5, 1965, Box 63, Folder 9, Gittings Papers.

218   *The next morning . . . San Francisco*: "ECHO Conference a Success," *Eastern Mattachine Magazine* 10, no. 8/9 (September/October 1965), 13.

218   *In Kameny's address . . . the convention*: "The Homosexual Citizen in the Great Society," *Eastern Mattachine Magazine* 11, no. 1 (January 1966), 3.

218   *Before that night's . . . homosexuality*: Ibid.

218   *Under the lights . . . way*": "Madison Ave. Queens and the PTA," *The Ladder* 10, no. 6 (March 1966), 7.

219   *After the banquet . . . reported*: "ECHO Conference a Success," *Eastern Mattachine Magazine* 10, no. 8/9 (September/October 1965), 13.

219   *There had been . . . February 1966*: Warren D. Adkins and Michael Fox, "ECHO 1965," *The Homosexual Citizen* 1, no. 1 (January 1966), 5; FEK to Dorr Legg, January 21, 1966, Box 70, Folder 8, FEK Papers.

219   *In the December . . . and money*": Clark Polak, "The Homophile Puzzle," *Drum* 5, no. 10 (December 1965), 17.

219   *Bruce Scott received . . . for employment*": Bruce Scott to FEK, October 21, 1965, Box 9, Folder 5, FEK Papers.

219   *The CSC had . . . over again*": Bruce Scott to David Carliner, October 21, 1965, Box 32, Folder 4, FEK Papers.

219   *David Carliner and . . . another lawsuit*: "U.S. Government Clings to Prejudice," n.d., Box 98, Folder 5, Gittings Papers.

219   *When Ernestine Eppenger . . . Black freedom movement*: Ernestine Eppenger, interviewed by Barbara Gittings, March 15, 1966, New York, NY, transcribed from audio file in box 62, Folder 4, Gittings Papers (hereafter, "Eppenger interview").

220   *She had already . . . own lesbian organization*: Ibid.

220   *But she had . . . for the homosexual*": Ibid.

220   *When Eppenger learned . . . march there, too*: Ibid.

220   *It marked the . . . in tactics*: Lahusen interview.

221   *On October 16 . . . in Vietnam*: "Thousands Hit Viet Nam War Across Nation," *The Washington Evening Star*, October 16, 1965, 1.

221   *On October 23 . . . fifteen women—marched*: "Information Bulletin," October 23, 1965, Box 102, Folder 14, Gittings Papers.

221   *marched in a . . . FEDERAL EMPLOYMENT*: See Kay Tobin Lahusen, "Barbara Gittings in Picket Line," October 23, 1965, The New York Public Library Digital Collections, http://digitalcollections.nypl.org/items /510d47e3-b64c-a3d9-e040-e00a18064a99.

221   *CBS, still shooting . . . agents*: SAC, WFO, to Director, FBI, October 25, 1965, FBI File #100–403320, 867.

221   *And, for the . . . GET SERIOUS*: Ibid.

221   *After the march . . . drank*: "Buffet Dinner," October 23, 1965, Box 102, Folder 13, Gittings Papers.

221   *The next month . . . ticket*: FEK to Ernestine D. Eppenger, March 2, 1966, Box 69, Folder 5, FEK Papers; D'Emilio, *Sexual Politics, Sexual Communities*, 172.

221   *She immediately invited . . . homophile movement*": Ernestine Eppenger to FEK, February 12, 1966, Box 69, Folder 5, FEK Papers.

221   *In November, after . . . Space Flight Center)*: FEK to William Nordberg, January 19, 1966, Box 136, Folder 8, FEK Papers.

222   *The new Mattachine . . . a projector*: Terry Grand to FEK, November 5, 1965, Box 77, Folder 6, FEK Papers; "Big Weekend Report," *Mattachine Midwest Newsletter* 1, no. 6, (December 1965), 5.

222   *The MSW, on . . . bar*: "A Cocktail Party," November 20, 1965, Box 85, Folder 11, FEK Papers.

222   *In December, Kameny . . . strategy*": FEK to Fellow Member, December 19, 1965, Box 68, Folder 6, Gittings Papers.

222   *In January, the . . . from the presidency*: John Marshall to Clark Polak, February 8, 1966, Box 82, Folder 7, FEK Papers.

222   *That month, Kameny . . . NASA.)*: William Nordberg to FEK, January 27, 1966, Box 136, Folder 8, FEK Papers.

222   *Then, on Wednesday . . . Kameny's door*: Bob Martin, Diary, January 26, 1966, Box 7, Folder 18, Donaldson Papers.

222   *It had been . . . persecuted and followed*": Bob Martin, Diary, January 11, 1966, Box 7, Folder 18, Donaldson Papers.

222   *He moved out . . . months later*: Bob Martin, Diary, January 26, 1966, Box 7, Folder 18, Donaldson Papers.

223   *Washington's first homosexual*: FEK to Larry Littlejohn, January 20, 1966, Box 6, Folder 12, FEK Papers; "We Are Proud to Announce," *The Homosexual Citizen* 1, no. 3 (March 1966), 20; Nancy Tucker, telephone interview with Eric Cervini, February 26, 2019.

223 *It contained a . . . trouble, help*: "Office Staff Dwindling," *The Insider*, June 1967, Box 86, Folder 2, FEK Papers.
223 *That month, Lilli . . . Calf*: *The Homosexual Citizen* 1, no. 1 (January 1966).
223 *Kameny worried that . . . large?*: FEK to Barbara Gittings, March 3, 1966, Box 6, Folder 13, Gittings Papers.
223 *On January 21 . . . 1965*: FEK to Barbara Gittings and Kay Tobin Lahusen, November 27, 1965, Box 6, Folder 12, Gittings Papers.
223 *"Hopefully an enlightened . . . a good piece"*: Philip Mandelkorn to FEK, November 16, 1965, Box 83, Folder 4, FEK Papers.
223 *Homosexuality*, TIME *concluded . . . pernicious sickness"*: "The Homosexual in America," *TIME*, January 21, 1966, 40.
223 *The homophile movement . . . he wrote*: John Marshall, "Our President Speaks," *The Homosexual Citizen* 1, no. 1 (January 1966), 11.
224 *On February 6 . . . Washington*: J. B. Adams to Mr. Callahan, February 14, 1966, FBI File #100-403320-138. I am grateful to Professor Douglas M. Charles for uncovering this document and sharing it with me. A full account of the Nichols-FBI saga can be found in Douglas M. Charles, "'A Source of Great Embarrassment to The Bureau': Gay Activist Jack Nichols, his FBI Agent Father, and the Mattachine Society of Washington," *The Historian* 79, no. 3 (Fall 2017), 504–22.
224 *Special Agent . . . one week earlier*: J. Edgar Hoover to J. Richard Nichols, January 31, 1966, FBI File #67-HQ-87294.
224 *But four days . . . homosexual organization*: J. B. Adams to Mr. Callahan, February 14, 1966, FBI File #100-403320-138.
224 *Agent Nichols requested . . . "inexcusable."*: Ibid.
224 *Despite Nichols Sr.'s offer . . . his career*: Charles, "'A Source of Great Embarrassment to The Bureau,'" 518.
224 *Jack Nichols never . . . again*: Nichols, "Chap. Seven," *Memoirs of Jack Nichols*.
224 *On Tuesday, February . . . in Kansas City*: FEK to Robert Martin, February 27, 1966, Box 7, Folder 3, FEK Papers.
224 *"The 'gathering of . . . told Bob Martin*: Ibid.
224 *Jack Nichols and . . . fourteen organizations*: "Persons in Attendance," Box 75, Folder 2, Gittings Papers; John Marshall to Clark P. Polak, February 8, 1966, Box 82, Folder 7, FEK Papers. Dick Leitsch of the MSNY had telegrammed from New York: "Cannot make it to the meeting. Please take good care of it. I have a surprise weekend meeting with two state senators to discuss at their invitation reintroduction of penal code change." As a member of its board, Kameny would therefore represent the MSNY. See Dick Leitsch to Clark Polak, February 19, 1966, Box 68, Folder 2, FEK Papers.
224 *The meeting began . . . their chairman*: "Minutes of the National Planning Conference of Homophile Organizations," February 19, 1966, Box 75, Folder 2, Gittings Papers.
224 *Clark Polak of . . . to be homosexual"*: Clark P. Polak, Bill of Rights Proposal, n.d., Box 68, Folder 2, FEK Papers; FEK, Bill of Rights Proposal, Box 68, Folder 2, FEK Papers.
225 *The West Coast . . . homophile movement*: "Minutes of the National Planning Conference of Homophile Organizations," February 19, 1966, Box 75, Folder 2, Gittings Papers.
225 *Kameny responded that . . . motion failed*: Ibid.
225 *"The meeting was . . . mass intellectual mediocrity"*: FEK to Robert Martin, February 27, 1966, Box 7, Folder 3, FEK Papers.
225 *By the end . . . or organizational "superstructure"*: "Minutes of the National Planning Conference of Homophile Organizations," February 19, 1966, Box 75, Folder 2, Gittings Papers.
225 *There had been . . . draft*: Ibid.
225 *They decided on . . . San Francisco*: Ibid.
225 *Kameny and Gittings . . . treatment," gloated Kameny*: FEK to Robert Martin, February 27, 1966, Box 7, Folder 3, FEK Papers.
226 *"The upshot," Kameny . . . February 25*: Ibid.
226 *That day, CSC . . . a minority group*: John W. Macy Jr. to The Mattachine Society of Washington, February 25, 1966, Box 67, Folder 5, Gittings Papers.
226 *Macy claimed that . . . be safe*: Ibid.
226 *"In point of . . . Kameny wrote*: FEK to John W. Macy Jr., Draft, n.d., Box 41, Folder 12, FEK Papers.
227 *Macy's letter had . . . of illogic"*: FEK, "Immoral Mores," *The Ladder* 10, no. 9 (June 1966), 17.
227 *He had been . . . Drum magazine)*: FEK to Clark P. Polak, March 21, 1966, Box 8, Folder 8, FEK Papers.
227 *He was . . . of Defense*: FEK to NCACLU, March 2, 1966, Box 75 Folder 6, FEK Papers.
227 *NASA, Johns Hopkins . . . for the astronomer*: Samuel D. Falbo to FEK, May 9, 1966, Box 136, Folder 8, FEK Papers; William S. Kirby to FEK, March 23, 1966, Box 136, Folder 8, FEK Papers; R. S. Ayres to FEK, March 19, 1966, Box 136, Folder 8, FEK Papers; A. Labita to FEK, March 21, 1966, Box 136, Folder 8, FEK Papers.

227 *"It thus seems . . . his case?"*: FEK to NCACLU, March 2, 1966, Box 75 Folder 6, FEK Papers.

227 *At this moment . . . their mother*: Lahusen interview.

227 *Rae sent her . . . like being Jewish*: FEK to Rae Beck Kameny, March 2, 1966, in possession of the author. I am grateful to Charles Francis for sharing copies of these letters.

228 *"I wish that . . . my love, always."*: Rae Beck Kameny to FEK, March 13, 1966, in possession of the author.

228 *Kameny received . . . he told Bob Martin*: FEK to Robert A. Martin Jr., March 21, 1966, Box 7, Folder 3, FEK Papers.

228 *A member of . . . a security clearance*: FEK to Barbara Gittings and Kay Tobin Lahusen, March 22, 1966, Box 6, Folder 13, Gittings Papers.

228 *"I will have . . . just wonder"*: Ibid.

228 *He asked Clark . . . first paycheck*: FEK to Clark P. Polak, March 21, 1966, Box 8, Folder 8, FEK Papers.

228 *After sending the . . . Scott case*: FEK to Barbara Gittings and Kay Tobin Lahusen, March 22, 1966, Box 6, Folder 13, Gittings Papers.

228 *"The daffodil buds . . . of leisure"*: FEK to Robert A. Martin Jr., March 21, 1966, Box 7, Folder 3, FEK Papers.

228 *On Armed Forces . . . terms*: Randy Wicker refused to participate in the demonstration: "We will have NOTHING to do with a demonstration calling for the drafting of homosexuals," he wrote. The MSNY also declined to participate in the demonstrations, since it had local problems of its own. Mayor John Lindsay of New York had failed in his effort to clean up Greenwich Village of its homosexuals, drug users, and other undesirables. On Friday evening, March 18, 1966, the NYPD erected barricades around a fourteen-block area to prevent their entrance. "The barricades attracted a howling, chanting mob of 1500 'assorted undesirables' who forced the police to retreat and remove their barricades," reported Jack Nichols in *The Homosexual Citizen*. The MSNY began distributing Kameny's "If You Are Arrested" pamphlet to the Village's weekend crowds. The incident, an embarrassment for the police and Mayor Lindsay, prompted a neighborhood meeting at Judson Memorial Church, which featured a panel of NYPD officials. Randy Wicker stood to blame the police for closing gay bars, which drove homosexuals to Mafia-run underground bars or the streets. In response, an NYPD official blamed the New York State Liquor Authority for a ban on serving alcohol to homosexuals. MSNY's Dick Leitsch decided to force the State Liquor Authority (SLA) to explain its policies. "It was a Greek scene in more ways than one," reported *The Village Voice* of the MSNY's April 21 effort. "The actors in the odyssey were three homosexuals, with four reporters and a photographer as supporting players. The three men were determined to force the State Liquor Authority to clarify its regulations concerning the serving of homosexuals in places of public accommodation." Dick Leitsch led the crusade, "conservatively dressed in a well cut gray suit with narrow blue stripes and a light blue shirt. With a black attache case in hand, he was the picture of a Madison Avenue executive." With him was twenty-one-year-old John Timmons and twenty-five-year-old Craig Rodwell. Two bars permitted the homosexuals, after announcing themselves as such, to order a drink. Finally, the trio tried a third establishment: Julius', a gay bar on West Tenth Street (uninvited, Wicker joined them). At Julius', the manager refused to serve the homosexuals. Leitsch announced a lawsuit. Four days later, the SLA's chairman told the *Times* that the state had never outlawed the serving of homosexuals. The MSNY thus confirmed the homosexuals' legal right to be served; if the NYPD raided or closed bars in the future, the homosexuals would know whom to blame. See Randolfe Wicker to FEK, April 20, 1966, Box 10, Folder 12, FEK Papers; Warren D. Adkins, "Newsfronts," *The Homosexual Citizen* 1, no. 5 (May 1966), 12; "Farelik Urges Public to Report Police Trapping of Homosexuals," *The New York Times*, April 2, 1966, 1; "Meeting on Village Cleanup," *New York Mattachine Newsletter* 11, no. 3 (April 1966), 1; Lucy Komisar, "Three Homosexuals in Search of a Drink," *The Village Voice*, May 5, 1966, 15; "S.L.A. Won't Act Against Bars Refusing Service to Deviates," *The New York Times*, April 26, 1966, 55. See also David Carter, *Stonewall: The Riots That Sparked the Gay Revolution* (New York: St. Martin's Press, 2005), 48–51.

229 *For one, he . . . code*: "Picketers Needed," May 21, 1966, Box 68, Folder 6, Gittings Papers.

229 *"You may be . . . in turn"*: Don Slater to FEK, May 3, 1966, Box 9, Folder 7, FEK Papers.

229 *On 3:00 p.m. . . . signs*: "News Release," May 19, 1966, Box 102, Folder 13, Gittings Papers.

229 *After picketing from . . . Bilitis*: FEK to Robert Martin Jr., May 15, 1966, Box 7, Folder 3, FEK Papers.

229 *Even Kameny's DOB . . . the event*: FEK to Shirley Willer, May 8, 1966, Box 10, Folder 14, FEK Papers.

229 *Only West . . . Los Angeles*: "Deviates Demand the Right to Serve," May 22, 1966, *San Francisco Chronicle*, 3; Faderman, *The Gay Revolution*, 111.

229 *At the end . . . be you"*: Dick Leitsch to FEK, May 27, 1966, Box 6, Folder 11, FEK Papers.

229 *But in . . . had changed*: Foster Gunnison Jr. to FEK, May 28, 1966, Box 4, Folder 10, Gittings Papers.

229 *One week after . . . newly employed astronomer's home*: Bob Martin, Diary, June 5, 1966, Box 7, Folder 18, Donaldson Papers.

14. THE ILLUSTRATOR

231 *On October 18 . . . a statement*: Crawford Statement, October 18, 1965, Box 17, Folder 6, FEK Papers.

231 *Six months later . . . to his employer*: Ibid.

231 *The Pentagon had . . . national interest"*: "Statement of Reasons," April 21, 1966, Box 17, Folder 6, FEK Papers.

231 *In May, the Pentagon . . . 5. Untrustworthiness*: Donald Lee Crawford to Director, Office of Industrial Personnel Access Authorization Review, May 12, 1966, Box 17, Folder 6, FEK Papers.

232 *After their first . . . (were you??)"*: FEK to Robert Martin, February 10, 1966, Box 7, Folder 3, FEK Papers.

232 *Martin kept Kameny . . . Marks Baths*: Robert Martin to FEK, March 1, 1966, Box 7, Folder 3, FEK Papers.

232 *"I decided to . . . the process"*: Robert Martin to FEK, February 25, 1966, Box 7, Folder 3, FEK Papers.

232 *Their correspondence became . . . it astrology??)"*: Robert Martin to FEK, April 27, 1966, Box 7, Folder 3, FEK Papers.

232 *That summer, Martin . . . from Georgia*: Wilson Barto, "He's an All 'Go-Bo' Guy," Newspaper clipping in Box 17, Folder 2, Donaldson Papers.

233 *On July 2 . . . Hut*: Bob Martin, Diary, July 2–4, 1966, Box 7, Folder 18, Donaldson Papers. Schlegel, Martin learned, was still fighting his case against his former employer, the army, in the United States Court of Claims. In 1963, after filing his suit in Washington, Schlegel found a job in Harrisburg, Pennsylvania, as the director of finance for the state's Department of Highways. In 1965, however, two postal inspectors informed his boss, the secretary of highways, that Schlegel was subscribed to a homosexual magazine. He was asked to resign immediately. By 1966, Schlegel moved to Washington, where he met Martin. See Richard Schlegel, interview with Marc Stein, May 10–11, 1993, Philadelphia LGBT History Project.

233 *Kameny was in . . . America's birth*: Duberman, *Stonewall*, 113.

233 *"Let me assure . . . homosexual citizens"*: Craig Rodwell to John Marshall, June 2, 1966, Box 107, Folder 17, FEK Papers.

233 *The young organizer . . . off—yet")*: FEK to Craig Rodwell, June 24, 1966, Box 78, Folder 6, FEK Papers.

233 *informed Philadelphia authorities . . . 4:00 p.m.*: FEK to Mr. Colbert, June 11, 1966, Box 2, Folder 6, MSNY Papers.

233 *On the Fourth—at . . . were arrested*: John P. Corr and Alfred P. Klimcke, "Hottest July 4 on Record—103 Degrees," *The Philadelphia Inquirer*, July 5, 1966, 1; David Jewell, "37 Seized at Rally," *The Philadelphia Inquirer*, July 5, 1966, 1.

233 *Rodwell's bus left . . . are marching on*: "Now We Are Marching On," Box 3, Folder 21, MSNY Papers; Denny, "Homophile Freedom Song," *The Homosexual Citizen* 1, no. 9 (September 1966), 14–15.

234 *A visibly sweating . . . a police barricade*: Kay Tobin Lahusen, "Barbara Gittings and Randy Wicker Picketing," July 4, 1966, The New York Public Library Digital Collections, http://digitalcollections.nypl.org/items /510d47e3-b6a4-a3d9-e040-e00a18064a99.

234 *Kameny returned to . . . over party guests"*: Bob Martin, Diary, July 5–18, 1966, Box 7, Folder 18, Donaldson Papers.

234 *For Martin's birthday . . . to Fire Island*: FEK to Robert Anthony Martin Jr., July 17, 1966, Box 7, Folder 3, FEK Papers.

234 *Aug 14—"Crisis with . . . rectum, maybe gonorrhea"*: Bob Martin, Diary, August 14–16, 1966, Box 7, Folder 18, Donaldson Papers.

234 *Martin recovered by . . . in Cherry Grove*: FEK to the Beach Hotel and Club, August 14, 1966, Box 122, Folder 3, FEK Papers.

234 *After a series . . . arrested homosexuals*: "Good Deeds," *The Homosexual Citizen* 1, no. 11 (November 1966), 19.

234 *Kameny and Martin . . . a family*: Robert A. Martin to Gay People at Columbia-Barnard, March 6, 1982, Box 2, Folder 8, Donaldson Papers.

234 *For two years . . . size*: Barbara Gittings, interviewed by Kay Tobin Lahusen, 1969–1971, Box 122, Folder 4, Gittings Papers; Faderman, *The Gay Revolution*, 87.

234 *including a smiling . . . at the CSC*: *The Ladder* 10 no. 1 (October 1965), 1.

234 *another close-up of Vincenz*: *The Ladder* 10, no. 4 (January 1966), 1.

234 *close-up of Dinesline . . . In June 1966*: *The Ladder* 10, no. 9 (June 1966), 1.

235 *That same month . . . choosing*: Barbara Gittings, interviewed by Kay Tobin Lahusen, 1969–1971, Box 122, Folder 4, Gittings Papers.

235 *Ernestine Eppenger, frustrated . . . that month, too*: D'Emilio, *Sexual Politics, Sexual Communities*, 172.

235 *Randy Wicker, equally . . . were dead*: Leroy F. Aarons, "Bull Market in Buttons," *The Washington Post*, November 27, 1966, K1; "Buttons," *Newsday*, August 6, 1966, 3.

235 *On Thursday morning . . . of Homophile Organizations*: Foster Gunnison to Richard Inman, September 19, 1966, Box 4, Folder 10, Gittings Papers.

235 *The delegates elected . . . opportunity"*: Franklin E. Kameny, "What Concrete Steps I Believe I Can and Must Be Taken to Further the Homophile Movement," August 25, 1966, Box 75, Folder 2, FEK Papers.

236   *Shirley Willer, recently . . . too*: Shirley Willer, "What Further Steps Can Be Taken to Further the Homophile Movement?," n.d., Box 75, Folder 2, Gittings Papers; Shirley Willer, "What Concrete Steps?," *The Ladder* 11, no. 2 (November 1966), 17.

236   *The call from . . . the delegates*: "Further Actions and Reactions," *ONE Confidential* 11, no. 9 (September 1966), Box 71, Folder 3, 17.

236   *The delegates spent . . . one delegate*: Foster Gunnison to Richard Inman, September 19, 1966, Box 4, Folder 10, Gittings Papers.

236   *It was "a . . . put it*: Jean-Paul Marat, "The Daily Blab," August 25, 1966, Box 68, Folder 3, FEK Papers.

236   *On Saturday, the . . . in the title?*: Foster Gunnison to Richard Inman, September 19, 1966, Box 4, Folder 10, Gittings Papers.

236   *The most spirited . . . by Kameny*: Ibid.

236   *Vanguard, an organization . . . other organizations*: Jean-Paul Marat, "Statement," n.d., Box 68, Folder 3, FEK Papers.

236   *The delegates defeated . . . 35–23 vote*: Foster Gunnison to Richard Inman, September 19, 1966, Box 4, Folder 10, Gittings Papers.

236   *On Sunday, the . . . "this respect"*: Ibid.

237   *Two delegates, for . . . seventeen years earlier*: Ibid.; "Preliminary Summary of Substantive Actions Approved by the National Planning Conference of Homophile Organizations," August 25–27, 1966, Box 75, Folder 2, Gittings Papers.

237   *A month later . . . of its own*: Bob Martin, Diary, September 27, 1966, Box 7, Folder 18, Donaldson Papers; Robert A. Martin to Gay People at Columbia-Barnard, March 6, 1982, Box 2, Folder 8, Donaldson Papers.

237   *On October 2 . . . Kameny admonished*: FEK to Robert A. Martin Jr., October 2, 1966, Box 7, Folder 3, FEK Papers.

237   *Kameny had become . . . from you"*: FEK to Robert A. Martin Jr., October 9, 1966, Box 7, Folder 3, FEK Papers.

237   *The Episcopal chaplain . . . the new organization*: Robert A. Martin to Gay People at Columbia-Barnard, March 6, 1982, Box 2, Folder 8, Donaldson Papers.

238   *Martin joined the . . . cooperation*: Bob Martin, Diary, October 9, 1966, Box 7, Folder 18, Donaldson Papers.

238   *For his pseudonym . . . "Stephen Donaldson"*: Robert A. Martin to Gay People at Columbia-Barnard, March 6, 1982, Box 2, Folder 8, Donaldson Papers.

238   *On October 27 . . . new campus group*: FEK and Barbara Gittings to MSNY Board of Directors, November 6, 1966, Box 86, Folder 9, Gittings Papers.

238   *MSNY president Dick . . . build*: Dick Leitsch to FEK, May 14, 1967, Box 6, Folder 11, FEK Papers.

238   *In November, Martin . . . Student Homophile League*: Bob Martin, Diary, November 14, 1966, Box 7, Folder 18, Donaldson Papers.

238   *To gain recognition . . . hands*: Steven Donaldson to Wardell B. Pomeroy, November 20, 1966, Box 105, Folder 6, FEK Papers.

238   *Until Columbia relaxed . . . Inn, dancing*: Robert A. Martin Jr. to FEK, January 3, 1967, Box 7, Folder 3, FEK Papers. Because Martin visited the Stonewall on the night of January 2, 1967, his letter indicates that the bar had opened as early as December 1966.

238   *Kameny, proud of . . . you danced?"*: FEK to Robert A. Martin Jr., January 7, 1967, Box 7, Folder 3, FEK Papers.

238   *On October 7 . . . court*: "ACLU Testing Eligibility for Federal Job," *The Washington Post*, October 7, 1966, C7.

238   *This time, the . . . homosexual acts?"*: In 1947, he was arrested for loitering in a Lafayette Square restroom. In 1951, he was arrested—but not charged—at a Greyhound bus station. His former employer admitted that although Scott was not necessarily "effeminate," his thinking ran "across lines which are not common in a man." His job performance was fine, but "he generally had dirty clothes and his fingernails were always dirty." "I would not recommend him for a position of responsibility and trust in the Federal Service because he is a homosexual," he concluded. Scott's neighbor accused him of being a homosexual, too. See United States Civil Service Commission, "Information Disclosed by Investigation in the Case of Bruce Chardon Scott," December 3, 1965, Box 32, Folder 4, FEK Papers.

238   *David Carliner of . . . once again*: Bruce C. Scott to Woodrow L. Browne, April 16, 1966, Box 7, Folder 5, Gittings Papers; United States Civil Service Commission, "Information Disclosed by Investigation in the Case of Bruce Chardon Scott," December 3, 1965, Box 32, Folder 4, FEK Papers. Through the rest of 1966, Carliner continued to propagate the concept of homosexuality as a civil liberties issue within the nationwide ACLU. After Clive Boutilier, a thirty-two-year-old building maintenance man from Canada, was ordered deported from America for being a homosexual, the immigrant sued. After losing in the court of appeals, Boutilier appealed to the Supreme Court, and he did so with the financial support of Clark Polak's Janus Society. Carliner, meanwhile, agreed to write an amicus brief for Boutilier on behalf of the ACLU, teaming with three other attorneys from the New York Civil Liberties Union. The law barring immigrants with "psychopathic" personalities, wrote Carliner and his NYCLU team, was unconstitutionally vague; how could

Boutilier have possibly known that homosexual activity would get him deported for being a psychopath? See Clark Polak to FEK, December 1, 1966, Box 8, Folder 8, FEK Papers; Brief of American Civil Liberties Union and New York Civil Liberties Union, *Boutilier v. INS*, 387 U.S. 118 (1967).

238 *Meanwhile, Kameny's arguments . . . the committee*: The Office to Due Process Committee, American Civil Liberties Union, October 6, 1966, Box 58, Folder 2, Gittings Papers; The Office to the Board, American Civil Liberties Union, November 10, 1966, Box 76, Folder 2, FEK Papers.

239 *On January 6 . . . for the government*: "CSC's Right to Bar Deviate Upheld," *The Washington Post*, January 7, 1967, B1. The next day, *The New York Times* reported that New York's municipal Civil Service Commission had quietly changed its policies a full year earlier; without any public announcement, it now allowed homosexuals, parolees, and unwed mothers to work for the city (female applicants for city jobs were previously asked for their marriage date and the age of their oldest child). "There are some questions we just don't ask any more," said the city's CSC chairman. "Society's attitudes have changed considerably." Kameny sent letters to the *Post* and the *Star* within hours of hearing the news. The stories from Washington and New York provided an "interesting contrast," he wrote. "It would appear that our benighted, barbaric, backward Washington officialdom, in both the executive and judicial branches, has a great deal to learn from our more enlightened, civilized, progressive neighbors to the north." For the first time, both newspapers published a letter from the angry homosexual. See "City Hires Paroleees in Change of Policy," *The New York Times*, January 7, 1967, 1; Franklin E. Kameny, "'Officialdom' Assailed," *The Washington Evening Star*, February 5, 1967, C1; Franklin E. Kameny, "Policy of Exclusion?," January 18, 1967, A20.

239 *"Every civil rights . . . have Bruce"*: "Bruce Scott Case," *New York Mattachine Newsletter* 12, no. 1, January/February 1967, 3.

239 *Two weeks later . . . Franz Kafka"*: FEK to David H. Henretta Jr., January 21, 1967, Box 17, Folder 6, FEK Papers.

239 *For months, Kameny . . . explained Kameny*: FEK To Rowland A. Morrow, February 14, 1967, Box 57, Folder 7, FEK Papers.

239 *As amateur attorneys . . . the Kafka*: The book depicted "the rather nightmarish ordeal of a citizen pitted against, and at the mercy of an all-powerful, unreachable, impersonal, unseen, arbitrarily-acting government which cannot be brought to account or even to explanation for its acts," wrote Kameny. "It should be required reading for all government officials." See FEK to David H. Henretta Jr., January 21, 1967, Box 17, Folder 6, FEK Papers.

239 *"We are busily . . . they warned*: FEK to Rowland A. Morrow, January 10, 1967, Box 17, Folder 6, FEK Papers.

240 *In 1918, the . . . their hallways crooked*: Jerry Landauer, "'Tempo' Built in First World War Still Used as 'Munitions Building,'" *The Washington Post*, April 26, 1960, A7; "Main Navy and Munitions Buildings," Naval History and Heritage Command, United States Navy, https://www.history.navy.mil/our-collections/photography/places/washington-dc/main-navy---munitions-buildings.html; Liza Mundy, *Code Girls: The Untold Story of the American Women Code Breakers of World War II* (New York: Hachette, 2017), 84.

240 *At 10:00 a.m. . . . entire proceeding*: Department of Defense Office of the Assistant Secretary of Defense, "Hearing: Donald Lee Crawford," February 23, 1967, Box 18, Folder 1, FEK Papers.

240 *"All letters, motions . . . said Crawford*: Ibid., 4.

240 *In his opening . . . applicant," he continued*: Ibid., 18.

240 *The security clearance . . . unconstitutional*: Ibid., 28.

240 *By appealing to . . . Donald Crawford*: Ibid., 32.

240 *Thomas Nugent, assistant . . . homosexual activity*: Ibid., 41–48.

240 *The department lawyers . . . for lunch*: Ibid., 63–74.

241 *"I would like . . . Psychoanalytic Study*: Ibid., 76–79.

241 *There were two . . . certainly is diagnosable"*: Ibid., 86, 100.

242 *"Doctor, I would . . . disorders, sociopathic type"*: Ibid., 87.

242 *Is mutual masturbation . . . said Socarides*: Ibid., 97.

242 *"In homosexuality, ironically . . . of homosexuality"*: Ibid., 100.

242 *"Doctor, do you . . . "Yes, very sick"*: Ibid., 102.

242 *So an obligatory . . . intensity with anyone"*: Ibid., 112.

242 *"You have referred . . . thoroughly skewed sampling"*: Ibid., 123–24.

243 *For three additional . . . he reminded Kameny*: Ibid., 168–70.

243 *They recessed at . . . Munitions Building*: Ibid., 188.

243 *Kameny and Gittings . . . Dr. Socarides"*: FEK to Robert A Martin Jr., February 26, 1967, Box 7, Folder 3, FEK Papers; Department of Defense Office of the Assistant Secretary of Defense, "Hearing: Donald Lee Crawford," February 24, 1967, Box 18, Folder 1, FEK Papers, 195.

243 *They had prepared . . . Gittings*: "Experts re Crawford," December 1966, Box 7, Folder 5, Gittings Papers.

243 *Will you write . . . security risk?*: See, for example, Barbara Gittings to Isadore Rubin, December 16, 1966, Box 8, Folder 6, Gittings Papers.

243 *At 2:00 p.m. . . . to homosexuals*: Department of Defense Office of the Assistant Secretary of Defense, "Hearing: Donald Lee Crawford," February 24, 1967, Box 18, Folder 1, FEK Papers, 270–82.

244 *"It is indeed . . . Hooker's letter*: Evelyn Hooker to FEK, September 28, 1966, Box 17, Folder 9, FEK Papers.

244 *At 3:10 p.m. . . . hearing concluded*: Department of Defense Office of the Assistant Secretary of Defense, "Hearing: Donald Lee Crawford," February 24, 1967, Box 18, Folder 1, FEK Papers, 295.

244 *Though Kameny and . . . they felt confident*: FEK to Robert A. Martin, Jr., February 26, 1967, Box 7, Folder 3, FEK Papers

244 *After that day . . . of the Pentagon*: See Chapter Sixteen.

244 *Before Kameny and . . . seemed fair*: "Notice of Intent to Appeal from Examiner's Determination," July 30, 1967, Box 17, Folder 7, FEK Papers.

15. THE FLOOR PLAN

245 *In a debate . . . whites' civil liberties*: "Rights Bill is Tagged Blueprint for Tyranny," *The Oshkosh Northwestern*, April 11, 1964, 3; Karl E. Campbell, *Senator Sam Ervin: Last of the Founding Fathers* (Chapel Hill: University of North Carolina Press, 2014), 134.

245 *After the bill's . . . South*: Campbell, *Senator Sam Ervin*, 151.

245 *Chairman Macy claimed . . . computers*: Alfred Friendly, "Protection for Whom? . . . : Ervin's 'Bill of Rights,'" *The Washington Post*, August 11, 1966, A25.

245 *But for Ervin . . . to privacy*: Campbell, *Senator Sam Ervin*, 205.

245 *In December, Ervin . . . sex*: Phil Casey, "Psychology Test Shocks Sen. Ervin," *The Washington Post*, December 9, 1964, A39.

245 *Such questions were . . . he claimed*: Campbell, *Senator Sam Ervin*, 202.

246 *After the Supreme . . . African Americans?*: The press seized upon Ervin's war. "There's a Dossier on You," announced the *Post* in a May 1966 exposé of the federal surveillance state. The government employed more investigators than doctors, it reported. The CSC, which spent more than half its budget probing into American citizens' private lives, held eight million secret dossiers on the personal lives of federal applicants and jobholders. The Federal Housing Administration, meanwhile, collected reports on the "marital stability" of prospective home buyers (higher chances of a divorce meant higher chances of foreclosure) at the rate of four thousand per day. The homosexual experience was becoming universalized: Americans were learning that their lives, their secrets, were under investigation, too. "For millions of us there are extensive life histories with intimate details of our sexual habits, friendships, financial affairs, oddities and political and religious beliefs," concluded the *Post*. "The dossiers continue to pile up in the offices of Government and industry. What will become of them, nobody knows." The MSW's *Homosexual Citizen* reprinted the entire exposé as the lead story of its August 1966 issue, and that month, Senator Ervin introduced his bill of rights for federal employees. The bill banned the race-related questionnaires as only one of ten provisions: among others, Ervin also proposed to bar the federal government from asking employees about their religion, personal relationships, or "sexual attitudes" via interviews, psychological tests, or polygraphs. Perplexed liberals, including those within the ACLU and the AFL-CIO, endorsed the bill, and their lobbyists worked with Ervin to pass it. See Richard Harwood, "There's a Dossier on You," *The Washington Post*, May 29, 1966, E1; "There's a Dossier on You," *The Homosexual Citizen* 1, no. 8 (September 1966), 3; Friendly, "Protection for Whom?"; Campbell, *Senator Sam Ervin*, 207.

246 *On February 21 . . . bill of rights*: Senator Ervin, "Protection of Constitutional Rights of Government Employees and to Prevent Un-Warranted Invasions of Their Privacy—Protection of the Rights of the Military," on February 21, 1967, 90th Cong., 1st Sess., *Congressional Record*, 4039–75.

246 *To support his . . . in homosexual conduct?*: Ibid.; Robert G. Sherrill, "U.S. Civil Service: Washington's Bland Bondage," *The Nation*, February 20, 1967, 239.

246 *The senator from . . . rights*: Ibid.

246 *Ervin, who would . . . Supreme Court justice*: Campbell, *Senator Sam Ervin*, 154.

246 *In January 1967 . . . attended its meetings*: Richard Inman to Lilli Vincenz, January 28, 1967, Box 18, Folder 1, Vincenz Papers.

246 *other homophile groups . . . in Washington?*: Richard Inman to Lilli Vincenz, October 1, 1966, Box 18, Folder 1, Vincenz Papers.

246 *On March 7 . . . corporate sponsor*: David Wayne, "The Homosexuals Viewed Through the Big Eye," *The Homosexual Citizen* 2, no. 4 (April 1967), 3.

247 *That same week . . . dormancy*: The homosexuals and their allies in the clergy discussed recent events, including an October 1966 seminar organized by the ecumenical National Council of Churches of Christ. Approximately forty attended that church-led conference, held in White Plains, New York, including psychiatrists, attorneys, and three homosexuals: Kameny, Gittings, and Leitsch. While Kameny denounced the "basic immorality" or the government's policies toward homosexuals, Gittings spoke on the morality of homosexuality itself: "I note that the name tags we are wearing do not give our credentials," began Gittings. "Lest

anyone here be uncertain, my credential for being at this seminar is that I am a homosexual." Most homosexuals, she explained, knew that "there is absolutely nothing wrong with their homosexuality per se." While the American government behaved immorally, homosexuals knew they had the "moral right" to be homosexual. See "Notice to Members," March 6, 1967, Box 104, Folder 12, FEK Papers; FEK, "National Council of Churches Sponsors Three-Day Seminar on Homosexuality," n.d., Box 126, Folder 6, FEK Papers; FEK to Barbara Gittings, n.d., Box 104, Folder 5, FEK Papers.

247 *Afterward, Nichols planned . . . Hut for themselves*: The Washington Area Council on Religion and the Homosexual, "Membership Meeting," May 8, 1967, Box 104, Folder 12, FEK Papers.

247 *By July . . . FBI surveillance*: Nancy Tucker, in "50th Anniversary of the Mattachine Society of Washington Panel Discussion," Rainbow History Project, June 7, 2014; Nancy Tucker, interviewed by Eric Cervini, telephone, February 26, 2019.

247 *In New York*: Bob Martin, Diary, March 1967, Box 7, Folder 18, Donaldson Papers.

247 *The university refused . . . the group*: Robert A. Martin to Gay People at Columbia-Barnard, March 6, 1982, Box 2, Folder 8, Donaldson Papers.

247 *In April, the . . . the country*: SHL News Release, April 26, 1967, Box 86, Folder 9, Gittings Papers.

247 *"Columbia Charters Homosexual . . . university*: Murray Schumach, "Columbia Charters Homosexual Group," *The New York Times*, May 3, 1967, 1.

247 *Outraged calls flooded . . . said the dean*: Peter Greene, "Truman Questions Homophile Group's Place at Columbia," *Columbia Daily Spectator*, May 5, 1967, 1. Columbia's director of university relations, meanwhile, wrote to the *Times* for damage control, explaining the university did not actually "charter" the organization; it had simply registered it. See Wesley First, "Homophile League at Columbia," *The New York Times*, June 3, 1967, 30.

247 *Administration officials initiated . . . sodomy laws*: SHL News Release, May 7, 1967, Box 105, Folder 7, FEK Papers.

248 *"I was speaking . . . New York"*: Dick Leitsch to FEK, May 14, 1967, Box 6, Folder 11, FEK Papers.

248 *A few weeks . . . the astronomer*: FEK, "Rules and Regulations for Rent-Free Guests in Extended Residence," June 26, 1967, Box 7, Folder 4, FEK Papers.

248 *On July 4 . . . outside Independence Hall*: "Barricade War Protesters at Independence Hall Fete," *The Des Moines Register*, July 5, 1967, 10.

248 *Nearly half a . . . ground in Vietnam*: Gitlin, *The Sixties*, 220.

248 *As she . . . North Vietnamese*: "Barricade War Protesters at Independence Hall Fete," *The Des Moines Register*, July 5, 1967, 10.

248 *By 3:30 p.m. . . . . The Philadelphia Inquirer*: Rose DeWolf, "Another Minority Bids for Equality," *The Philadelphia Inquirer*, July 6, 1967, 33; "Information Bulletin," July 4, 1967, Box 85, Folder 13, FEK Papers.

249 *Six days later . . . coitus," it said*: "Determination of Examiner David H. Henretta, Jr.," July 10, 1967, Box 17, Folder 7, FEK Papers.

249 *Crawford, wrote Henretta . . . and untrustworthiness"*: Ibid.

249 *It was not . . . remained suspended*: Ibid.

249 *"What a shabby . . . of (their) life."*: Franklin E. Kameny and Barbara Gittings, "Notice of Intent to Appeal from Examiner's Determination," July 30, 1967, Box 17, Folder 7, FEK Papers.

250 *Similarly, he continued . . . of Donald Crawford?*: Ibid.

250 *The hearing . . . of meaning*: Ibid.

250 *At 3:45 a.m. . . . . the decade began*: Malcolm McLaughlin, *The Long, Hot Summer of 1967: Urban Rebellion in America* (New York: Macmillan, 2014), xii; DeNeen L. Brown, "In Detroit, 'the rage of oppression.' For five days in 1967, riots consumed a city," *The Washington Post*, July 23, https://www.washingtonpost.com/news/retropolis/wp/2017/07/23/in-detroit-the-rage-of-oppression-for-five-days-in-1967-riots-consumed-a-city.

250 *"The Vietnam war . . . every American"*: Gitlin, *The Sixties*, 242–45.

250 *Washington, the seat . . . majority here"*: Ben A. Franklin, "S.N.C.C. Head Advises Negroes in Washington to Get Guns," *The New York Times*, July 28, 1967, 14.

251 *The national conference . . . section"*: Eddy Casaus to FEK, August 1, 1967, Box 68, Folder 4, FEK Papers.

251 *To consider such . . . responded Kameny*: FEK to Eddy Casaus, August 11, 1967, Box 68, Folder 4, FEK Papers.

251 *Dick Leitsch and . . . own backyard"*: Dick Leitsch to FEK, August 15, 1967, Box 6, Folder 11, FEK Papers.

251 *In August, Washington . . . Building*: "National Planning Conference of Homophile Organizations," August 17, 1967, Box 75, Folder 3, Gittings Papers.

251 *The delegates elected . . . possible," he argued*: Meeting Minutes, North American Homophile Conference, August 16–18, 1967, Box 68, Folder 4, FEK Papers. Kameny's embrace of inclusion had limits, however. The concept of a Credentials Committee itself—and the potential of excluding groups—most threatened the West Coast, which placed less emphasis on political organizing in favor of social services and community building. When the West Coast groups met in April 1967, they released a statement titled "ON PREJUDICE WITHIN

THE MOVEMENT." "Since the homosexual community is composed of all types of persons, we feel that the movement ought not be constricted by any limiting concept of public image," it said. "We do not feel that drag, sado-masochism and other aspects of sexual behavior can be summarily dismissed as necessarily invalid expressions of human love." Kameny, infuriated, thought the statement represented the low point of the movement, an inflammatory document written by "the kooks and the cultists." It should have been titled, as he told Don Slater of Los Angeles, "How to Lose Friends and Ensure Being Ingored [*sic*] by People." See "Resolution: On Prejudice within the Movement," April 23, 1967, Box 75, Folder 4, Gittings Papers; FEK to Foster Gunnison Jr., May 21, 1967, Box 67, Folder 7, FEK Papers; FEK to Don Slater, May 22, 1967, Box 9, Folder 7, FEK Papers.

251 *Shirley Willer agreed . . . methodologies*: Meeting Minutes, North American Homophile Conference, August 16–18, 1967, Box 68, Folder 4, FEK Papers.

251 *heard tales . . . told them*: Kameny quotes himself in FEK to William J. Scanlon, September 2, 1967, Box 17, Folder 7, FEK Papers.

252 *The next day . . . Daughters of Bilitis*: Meeting Minutes, North American Homophile Conference, August 16–18, 1967, Box 68, Folder 4, FEK Papers. For the history of the NAACP's LDF, see "History," *LDF*, http://naacpldf.org/aubout-us/history.

252 *The delegates then . . . Convention in Chicago*: Ibid.; Resolution, "SAME-PHOENIX-MMW-COF," n.d., Box 75, Folder 3, Gittings Papers.

252 *On August 28 . . . and white*": Transcript, August 28, 1967, Box 27, Folder 10, FEK Papers.

252 *Kameny wrote to . . . warned Kameny*: FEK to Sheldon S. Cohen, August 30, 1967, Box 27, Folder 10, FEK Papers.

252 *On August 31 . . . to blackmail?*: Layered on top of the NCACLU's 1964 policy was a new emphasis on privacy. "The right of privacy should extend to all private sexual conduct, heterosexual or homosexual, of consenting adults," it began. Harassment of gay bars violated the freedom of assembly; police entrapment and the use of peep holes in restrooms were "reprehensible." The NCACLU's policy statement ended with a caveat, however. "Conceivably in certain jobs," it concluded, "there may be a relevancy between that job and a person's private sexual conduct, including homosexuality." The national ACLU office immediately forwarded the statement to Kameny and Gittings, requesting their feedback. "In what conceivable jobs could homosexuality, or a person's private sexual conduct, generally, legitimately be a factor?" responded Kameny. "I can think of none." See "ACLU Statement on Homosexuality," n.d., Box 78, Folder 10, FEK Papers; Alan Reitman to Barbara Gittings, August 29, 1967, Box 78, Folder 10, Gittings Papers; FEK to Lynn Rosner, September 17, 1967, Box 76, Folder 2, FEK Papers.

253 *Two weeks after . . . 79–4 vote*: Mike Causey, "Detector Ban Bill Advances," *Austin American-Statesman*, September 14, 1967, 28.

253 *While the NCACLU . . . us," he concluded*: FEK to Sheldon S. Cohen, October 3, 1967, Box 27, Folder 10, FEK Papers.

253 *The IRS, still . . . the previous year*: Samuel Walker, *Presidents and Civil Liberties from Wilson to Obama* (Cambridge: Cambridge University Press, 2014), 261.

253 *"We are making . . . to this"*: FEK to Sheldon S. Cohen, October 3, 1967, Box 27, Folder 10, FEK Papers.

253 *Two days later . . . me," Kameny wrote*: FEK to William J. Scanlon, September 24, 1967, Box 44, Folder 12, FEK Papers.

253 *Rowland Morrow, Kameny's . . . feminine roles*": FEK to Rowland A. Morrow, October 6, 1967, Box 44, Folder 12, FEK Papers.

254 *Six months later . . . one male person*": Joseph J. Liebling to FEK, April 3, 1968, Box 44, Folder 12, FEK Papers.

254 *In 1966, the . . . each day*: "Operation Rolling Thunder: 1966," in Michael Clodfelter, *Warfare and Armed Conflicts: A Statistical Encyclopedia of Casualty and Other Figures, 1492–2015* (Jefferson, NC: McFarland, 2017), 697.

254 *John Gaffney, a . . . he explained*: "I was upset and disturbed because I couldn't have any [homosexual] acts while I was in service," Gaffney later testified. See Department of Defense, "In the Matter of: Benning Wentworth," November 24, 1967, 36.

254 *Gaffney signed a . . . of other homosexuals*: Ibid., 86.

254 *One year later . . . clearance*: "Statement of Reasons," May 2, 1967, Box 37, Folder 4, FEK Papers.

255 *The short, slim . . . was a homosexual*: Will Lissner, "Homosexual Fights Rule in Security Clearance," *The New York Times*, November 26, 1967, 70; Charles Alverson, "A Minority's Plea: U.S. Homosexuals Gain in Trying to Persuade Society to Accept Them," *The Wall Street Journal*, July 17, 1968, 1.

255 *On June 22 . . . the press*: Benning Wentworth, "Statement in Reply to Statement of Reasons," June 22, 1967, Box 37, Folder 4, FEK Papers.

255 *Five days before . . . ALSO INVITED*": "News Release," November 20, 1967, Box 8, Folder 10, Gittings Papers.

255 *Kameny, Gittings, and . . . hearing room*: FEK to Don Slater, December 9, 1967, Box 9, Folder 7, FEK Papers.

255 *The examiner, Raymond . . . responded Wentworth*: Department of Defense, Transcript, "In the Matter of: Benning Wentworth," November 24, 1967, 4–5.

256 *The Pentagon's attorney . . . , Wentworth's accuser*: Ibid., 19.

256 *"When and under . . . met him"*: Ibid., 23.

256 *What happened when . . . "Um hmm"*: Ibid., 27.

256 *After a short . . . of that apartment?"*: Ibid., 29–33.

257 *Gaffney picked up . . . "No," responded Gaffney*: Ibid., 33–36.

257 *After Kameny finished . . . rested its case*: Ibid., 37 39.

257 *Kameny called Wentworth . . . the air force*: Ibid., 47–53.

258 *Finally, Kameny asked . . . bed, was incorrect*: Ibid., 55–59.

258 *In cross-examination . . . Dr. Kameny"*: Ibid., 60–63, 70–72.

259 *Kameny stood to . . . Americanism is about"*: Ibid., 127–34.

259 *Kameny, Gittings, and . . . to thank you"*: Ibid., 126.

259 *"Homosexual Seeks to . . . threat of blackmail*: "Homosexual Seeks to Save Security Role," *Chicago Tribune*, November 25, 1967.

259 *Homosexuals across the . . . Tampa, and Phoenix*: See periodicals database query for "Benning Wentworth" in November 1967, https://www.newspapers.com/search/#ym=1967–11&query=%22benning+wentworth%22 &oquery=11%2F1967+%22benning+wentworth%22.

259 *On Sunday, . . . the saga*: Will Lissner, "Homosexual Fights Rule in Security Clearance," *The New York Times*, November 26, 1967, 70.

259 *The next day . . . press releases, too*: FEK and Barbara Gittings, "Motion for Admission of Evidence," November 27, 1967, Box 9, Folder 2, Gittings Papers; Franklin Edward Kameny, "Affidavit," November 1967, Box 9, Folder 2, Gittings Papers.

259 *When Benning Wentworth . . . behave kindly*: Benning Wentworth, "Affidavit," December 1967, Box 9, Folder 2, Gittings Papers.

259 *"I read about . . . be fighting it"*: Benning Wentworth, "Motion for Admission of Three Items of Evidence," December 5, 1967, Box 37, Folder 4, FEK Papers.

259 *"Benning, dear," wrote . . . and able"*: Ibid.

259 *Kameny submitted the . . . victim of blackmail?*: Ibid.

260 *The day after . . . of Wentworth*: Earl I. Rosenthal to Mattachine Society of Washington, November 27, 1967, Box 41, Folder 1, FEK Papers.

260 *Later that week . . . in thirty-eight states*: Hearing Transcript, "In the Matter of Benning Wentworth," August 19, 1969, Box 38, Folder 1, FEK Papers, 350.

260 *On December 4 . . . neoclassical Butler Library*: Jan Steenblik, "Homophile Speaker Asserts Homosexuality Not a Disease," *Columbia Daily Spectator*, December 5, 1967.

260 *After he finished . . . erupted in applause*: Robert Martin to Lige Clarke, December 6, 1967, Box 1, Folder 18, Donaldson Papers.

260 *From the podium . . . to support him*: Rae Beck Kameny to FEK, December 15, 1967, Box 153, Folder 7, FEK Papers.

260 *Bob Martin attended . . . the first time*: Robert Martin to "Henry," December 6, 1967, Box 2, Folder 17, Donaldson Papers.

260 *When it came . . . am a homosexual*: FEK to Don Slater, December 9, 1967, Box 9, Folder 7, FEK Papers.

16. THE CHAOS

262 *In 1961, when . . . remained seated*: Eva Freund, interviewed by Mark Meinke, November 3, 2002, Rainbow History Project, Washington, D.C.

262 *By 1964, Freund . . . of Lilli Vincenz*: Ibid.

263 *At the meeting . . . Kameny, too*: Eva Freund, interviewed by Eric Cervini, telephone, December 14, 2018.

263 *Freund was the . . . Caesar"*: Eva Friend to Fellow Members, September 7, 1965, Box 64, Folder 1, Gittings Papers.

263 *Meanwhile, Freund and . . . but nothing more*: Eva Freund, interviewed by Eric Cervini, telephone, December 14, 2018.

263 *By the end . . . newsletter*, The Insider: *The Insider* (October 1967), Box 86, Folder 2, FEK Papers.

263 *After two years . . . eleven*: Eva Friend to Membership, November 20, 1967, Box 68, Folder 6, Gittings Papers.

263 *To combat the . . . demanded secrecy*: Jon Swanson, interviewed by David K. Johnson, July 1992.

263 *To the dismay . . . its office*: "Statement of Income & Expense," December 31, 1967, Box 86, Folder 2, FEK Papers.

263 *"Sorry to hear . . . all others"*: Richard Inman to Lilli Vincenz, January 12, 1968, Box 18, Folder 1, Vincenz Papers.

263 *A week later . . . for treasurer*: Eva Friend to Membership, November 20, 1967, Box 68, Folder 6, Gittings Papers.

264   *Swanson may have . . . for reelection*: Jon Swanson, interviewed by David K. Johnson, July 1992.

264   *On January 4 . . . founded*: "Election Results," *The Insider* (January 1968), Box 86, Folder 2, FEK Papers.

264   *First, Kameny attempted . . . the police*: "President's Statement," *The Insider* (January 1968), Box 86, Folder 2, FEK Papers.

264   *For the first . . . clarified*: "Mattachine Fund-Raising Cocktail Party Provides Fellowship and Chatter and Money Too!," *The Insider* (January 1968), Box 86, Folder 2, FEK Papers.

264   *Kameny's greatest focus . . . he explained*: FEK to Florence Jaffy, March 1, 1968, Box 6, Folder 2, FEK Papers. With the exception of the federal government, the rest of the country seemed to move forward without the Society's help; on January 4, the day of Kameny's election, newspapers across the country reported on a Episcopalian symposium that decided to label homosexuality "morally neutral." Almost simultaneously, thousands of congregations across the country received booklets—written by the social action departments of the Presbyterian Church and the United Church of Christ—outlining the moral obligation of churches to change society's attitude toward homosexuals. If churches denied that homosexual activity was immoral, how could the government still logically make that claim? "It is obvious that 'generally accepted standards of morality' are by no means any longer fixed and determined and generally accepted—if they ever were," wrote Kameny to David Shapiro, an NCACLU attorney, in an effort to bring the Migota IRS case to court. Given the *Scott II* decision and the "theological and sociological ferment" of the time, he wrote, "I cannot conceive of a better time to bring such a case as this one just now." Migota, moreover, was prepared to announce his homosexuality in the process. See Louis Cassels, "Churchmen Try to Change Attitudes on Homosexuals," *The Brownsville Herald*, January 4, 1968, 8; FEK to David I. Shapiro, January 7, 1968, Box 27, Folder 10, FEK Papers.

264   *On Saturday, January . . . Martin secretary*: "Minutes of the Second Session of the Eastern Regional Homophile Conference," January 13–14, 1968, Box 64, Folder 6, Gittings Papers.

264   *The delegates unanimously : . . statement on homosexuality*: Ibid.; "Unanimously Adopted," January 1968, Box 64, Folder 6, Gittings Papers.

264   *In a novel . . . the candidates*: Ibid.

265   *They would continue . . . in favor*: Ibid.

265   *His appearance with . . . January*: FEK to Jerry Joachim, January 27, 1968, Box 73, Folder 2, FEK Papers.

265   *"You always lose . . . to it*: Rae Beck Kameny to FEK, January 9, 1968, Box 153, Folder 7, FEK Papers.

265   *Born on Long . . . humor*: Jeffrey N. Cuzzi, "James B. Pollack, 1938–1994," *Bulletin of the American Astronomical Society* 26, no. 4 (1994), 1606–8.

265   *He had defended . . . Carl Sagan*: Ibid.; James B. Pollack, "Theoretical Studies of Venus: An Application of Planetary Astro-physics" (PhD dissertation, Harvard University, 1965).

265   *By 1968, he . . . in Boston*: William Sheehan, *The Planet Mars: A History of Observation & Discovery* (Tucson: University of Arizona Press, 1996), 171.

265   *A homosexual, Pollack . . . homosexual astronomer*: FEK to Dick Leitsch, May 26, 1968, Box 6, Folder 11, FEK Papers.

265   *"Dear Jim," wrote . . . or before?"*: FEK to James Pollack, February 28, 1968, Box 8, Folder 9, FEK Papers.

265   *In February 1968 . . . to New York*: "*Hymnal* Makes Bow," *Hymnal* 1, no. 1 (February 1968), Box 240, Folder 2, LGBT Periodicals Collection, New York Public Library, New York, NY (hereafter, "LGBT Periodicals"), 1. See also Carter, *Stonewall*, 51–52, 109.

266   *Gay Power, Rodwell . . . only 550*: Ibid.

266   *The* Hymnal's *first . . . of business*: "Mafia on the Spot," *Hymnal* 1, no. 1 (February 1968), Box 240, Folder 2, LGBT Periodicals, 1.

266   *Philadelphia lesbians confronted . . . night*: Stein, *City of Sisterly and Brotherly Loves*, 275–76.

266   *Two weeks later . . . emergency telephone number*: Ibid.; Barbara Gittings to FEK, March 19, 1968, Box 3, Folder 14, FEK Papers.

266   *The attendees followed . . . Philadelphia Police Department*: Ibid.

267   *"You might well . . . own organization"*: FEK to Daughters of Bilitis, June 5, 1968, Box 69, Folder 5, FEK Papers.

267   *In August 1968 . . . same enemy*: Stein, *City of Sisterly and Brotherly Loves*, 277–78.

267   *On January 31 . . . 26 percent*: Gitlin, *The Sixties*, 300; Branch, *At Canaan's Edge*, 681.

267   *When Curtis C. . . . inclination"*: Curtis Chambers to Draft Board #3, March 4, 1968, Box 16, Folder 10, FEK Papers; Curtis C. Chambers Jr. to Lucille M. Scates, March 5, 1968, Box 16, Folder 10, FEK Papers.

268   *By the end . . . died in Vietnam*: "U.S. Dead Pass 20,000 in Vietnam," *The Record* (Hackensack), March 21, 1968, 24.

268   *requests from terrified . . . avoided Vietnam*: FEK to Ralph Temple, March 24, 1968, Box 75, Folder 6, FEK Papers.

268   *The rest of . . . their homosexuality*: Dick Leitsch to FEK, July 16, 1968, Box 6, Folder 11, FEK Papers.

268   *The war gave . . . obvious enough"*: "Refraining from your Induction, or, 10 Steps to Freedom," n.d., Box 26, Folder 5, FEK Papers.

268   *In 1960, when ... every day*: Michael T. Kaufman, "Stokely Carmichael, Rights Leader Who Coined 'Black Power,' Dies at 57," *The New York Times*, November 16, 1988, B10.

268   *On June 16 ... the crowd*: Branch, *At Canaan's Edge*, 486.

269   *After Bayard Rustin ... the movement*: D'Emilio, *Lost Prophet*, 428.

269   *On March 28 ... his associates*: Branch, *At Canaan's Edge*, 731–34.

269   *Three days later ... your President"*: Charles Kaiser, *1968 in America: Music, Politics, Chaos, Counterculture, and the Shaping of a Generation* (New York: Grove Press, 1988), 128.

269   *As April approached ... as always!"*: FEK to James B. Pollack, March 30, 1968, Box 8, Folder 9, FEK Papers.

269   *Then, on Thursday ... a gun"*: "New Violence Erupts in District," *The Washington Evening Star*, April 5, 1968, 1.

269   *The riots began ... Capitol*: Kaiser, *1968 in America*, 146.

269   *By Sunday night ... confirmed dead*: Willard Clopton Jr. and Robert G. Kaiser, "Fires Dying Out, Arrests Decline, Curfew Continues," *The Washington Post*, April 8, 1968, A1.

269   *"Whole blocks," recalled ... into oblivion"*: J. Samuel Walker, *Most of 14th Street Is Gone: The Washington, DC Riots of 1968* (Oxford: Oxford University Press, 2018), 3.

269   *On Monday morning ... the occasional gunshot*: Willard Clopton Jr. and Carl W. Sims, "Washington Turns to Relief Effort," *The Washington Post*, April 9, 1968, A1.

269   *Kameny and Gittings ... dominated the news*: FEK to Clark P. Polak, April 11, 1968, Box 8, Folder 8, FEK Papers.

270   *"You have ... to prejudice*: Department of Defense, "In the Matter of: Donald Lee Crawford," April 8, 1968, 25–26.

270   *"If you choose ... interest demand it"*: Ibid., 28.

270   *One week later ... of the logic*: "Determination of Examiner Raymond A. Waldman," April 16, 1968, Box 37, Folder 4, FEK Papers.

270   *The Pentagon had ... same allegations*: As the homosexuals contemplated the conundrum, they looked to Senator Sam Ervin of North Carolina. That spring, Ervin was still pushing his bill of rights for federal employees by exposing governmental invasions of privacy. Kameny clipped one particularly compelling article in the *Star*, which reported that the Pentagon was asking female heterosexual security clearance holders a series of inappropriate questions, and Ervin exposed them. Have you participated in political demonstrations? Have you ever had an abortion? Do you take birth control? Does your boyfriend visit often? Homosexuals, concluded Kameny, could similarly publicize the inappropriate questions, allegations, and innuendos that they were facing. The public could then see that the Department of Defense—rather than the homosexual clearance holder—was guilty of obscenity. See "Security Quiz Is Attacked," *The Washington Evening Star*, May 3, 1968, Box 138, Folder 3, FEK Papers, 1. Kameny compared his strategy to Ervin's and explained his reasoning in an earlier letter to the Pentagon, suggesting he was developing the tactic as early as March. See FEK to William J. Scanlon, March 20, 1968, Box 17, Folder 7, FEK Papers.

270   *"Mr. Wentworth ... they wrote*: FEK and Barbara Gittings to Raymond A. Waldman, May 26, 1968, Box 9, Folder 2, Gittings Papers.

271   *Foster Gunnison, like ... door first"*: Foster Gunnison to FEK and Barbara Gittings, December 30, 1967, Box 4, Folder 11, Gittings Papers.

271   *"Yes, our movement ... your heart"*: FEK to Foster Gunnison Jr., January 3, 1968, Box 4, Folder 11, Gittings Papers.

271   *On April 18 ... Homophile League campaign*: The Physicians and Surgeons Club at Columbia Medical School planned to host a panel of psychiatrists, speaking on "CURRENT CONCEPTS: HOMOSEXUALITY," the following week. Moderated by the director of the New York Psychiatric Institute, the panel of psychiatrists would include Irving Bieber, a psychoanalyst who labeled homosexuality a harmful pathology caused by overbearing mothers and distant fathers. Because the panel included not a single homosexual—the organizers had refused the SHL's requests—the homosexuals, at Kameny's suggestion, planned to protest. See FEK to Robert A. Martin Jr., April 18, 1968, Box 105, Folder 6, FEK Papers.

271   *At 7:00 p.m. ... Kameny's flyer*: "News Release," April 23, 1968, Box 97, Folder 5, Gittings Papers; "We Protest the Kolb Panel," April 23, 1968, Box 97, Folder 5, Gittings Papers.

271   *The tension had ... called it*: Kaiser, *1968 in America*, 155–56.

271   *On April 23 ... Columbia College*: Ibid., 159–60.

272   *Over the next ... remained neutral*: Bob Martin, "Occupied, but Liberated Columbia University," May 12, 1968, Box 7, Folder 4, FEK Papers.

272   *At 2:30 a.m. ... other students*: Ibid.

272   *In sum, the ... were injured*: Kaiser, *1968 in America*, 162.

272   *That evening, when ... the resistance?*: FEK to Robert A. Martin Jr., May 8, 1968, Box 7, Folder 4, FEK Papers.

272   *Kameny urged Martin ... wrote*: Ibid.

273   *Martin stayed enrolled . . . within the system*: Bob Martin to JD Kuch, June 3, 1968, Box 2, Folder 24, Donaldson Papers.

273   *Columbia accede to . . . the gymnasium*: Kaiser, *1968 in America*, 165.

273   *The day after . . . in question*: FEK to Barbara Gittings, May 6, 1968, Box 6, Folder 14, Gittings Papers.

273   *He received one hundred dollars . . . for Kameny's assistance*: Benning Wentworth to FEK, May 17, 1968, Box 37, Folder 7, FEK Papers.

273   *"I do hope . . . told Martin*: FEK to Robert A. Martin Jr., May 13, 1968, Box 7, Folder 4, FEK Papers.

273   *When Mattachine Midwest . . . exist for"*: FEK to Mattachine Midwest, May 18, 1968, Box 77, Folder 6, FEK Papers. When the West Side Discussion Group in New York publicized a discussion about the views of psychiatrists and novelists on homosexuality, he berated them for not discussing the views of homosexuals on homosexuality, instead. "When are we going to gain enough confidence in ourselves as meaningful human beings to realize that WE—alone—are THE authorities upon homosexuality?!" And when the editors of *The Los Angeles Advocate*, a new homophile publication in Los Angeles, argued that some arrest victims could not afford the publicity of a trial—they had jobs to maintain—the unemployed astronomer replied with loftiness. "As one who indeed has starved," he wrote, "I feel that I have earned the right to say that if you truly believe in a principle it is well worth it." See FEK to West Side Discussion Group, May 7, 1968, Box 100, Folder 14, FEK Papers; FEK to *The Los Angeles Advocate*, June 8, 1968, Box 128, Folder 5, FEK Papers.

273   *Kameny also considered . . . seventy-five thousand customers*: T. Jay Mathews, "Operation Match," *The Harvard Crimson*, November 3, 1965; Jane Hinde, "Operation Match's Computer Mix-Up Has Vassar Dating Pembroke, Wellesley," *The Miscellany News* (Vassar College), December 15, 1966, 3.

274   *By 1968, Operation . . . meet other men*: Douglas Wood to MSNY Mailing List, n.d., Box 123, Folder 12, FEK Papers.

274   *In May, after . . . would it look?*: Steve Milgrim to FEK, May 24, 1968, Box 123, Folder 12, FEK Papers; FEK to Foster Gunnison Jr., June 25, 1968, Box 4, Folder 9, FEK Papers.

274   *"My chief concern . . . MSW," Gittings argued*: Barbara Gittings to FEK, June 22, 1968, Box 3, Folder 14, FEK Papers.

274   *"I'll agree with . . . grab it"*: Foster Gunnison to FEK, June 28, 1968, Box 4, Folder 10, Gittings Papers.

274   *Since 1966, Black . . . and pride*: Stokely Carmichael and Charles V. Hamilton, *Black Power: The Politics of Liberation in America* (New York: Random House, 1967), 44; Michael T. Kaufman, "Stokely Carmichael, Rights Leader Who Coined 'Black Power,' Dies at 57," *The New York Times*, November 16, 1988, B10; "Young Blacks Walking Taller in Watts, With a New Pride," *Pittsburgh Courier*, May 18, 1968, 16.

274   *In a Philadelphia . . . black power"*: "Negroes in North Organize to Fight Slums," *Star Tribune* (Minneapolis), July 17, 1966, 33.

275   *By the spring . . . and beautiful"*: "Carmichael Chides Negro Audience," *Orlando Evening Star*, April 18, 1967, 7.

275   *That summer, in . . . they said*: "Watts' Festival Offers Displays for Everybody," *Lancaster Eagle-Gazette*, August 12, 1967, 1.

275   *Even King, aware . . . it said*: "March Complete in Dixie's Rain," *Dayton Daily News*, August 20, 1967, 3.

275   *In May 1968 . . . schools*: "Newark Student Boycott Enters Third Day," *The Daily Home News* (Central New Jersey), May 15, 1968, 50.

275   *On Maryland's Eastern . . . is BEAUTIFUL*: "Agnew to Meet Protesters," *The Evening Sun* (Baltimore), May 21, 1968, C3.

275   *Frank Kameny heard . . . mobilize, to fight*: Kameny later remembered hearing the phrase during coverage of student protests on the Eastern Shore, which most likely referred to this demonstration. See FEK, interview by David K. Johnson, January 26, 1992, Washington, D.C.

275   *It was this . . . his war*: FEK to Barbara Gittings, August 4, 1968, Box 6, Folder 14, Gittings Papers.

275   *The word homosexual . . . to heterosexuals, too*: FEK, interview by David K. Johnson, January 26, 1992, Washington, D.C.

276   *One day in . . . is Good"*: FEK to Barbara Gittings, August 4, 1968, Box 6, Folder 14, Gittings Papers.

276   *The phrase was . . . moral goodness*: FEK, interview by David K. Johnson, January 26, 1992, Washington, D.C.

276   *The phrase served . . . written*: "Petition for a Writ of Certiorari," *Kameny v. Brucker*, 26.

276   *In 1962, Dick . . . short on law"*: Richard L. Schlegel, "Homosexuals in Government," *Mattachine Review* 8, no. 11, November 1962, 13.

276   *"The jacket . . . Reminder Day picket*: FEK to Edward Trust, June 15, 1968, Box 79, Folder 2, FEK Papers. "While we are in general agreement with the principle of good grooming and appearance," responded Trust, "we do not feel that a strict jacket and tie policy will present a realistic picture of the average homosexual nor will it encourage attendance on the part of our members." Trust informed Kameny that the MSNY had applied for its own demonstration permit; his organization would picket separately from the other groups. "Please do not consider this as a rebuff or a 'holier-than-thou' attitude," added Trust, "but as Polonius says to Laertes, 'To thine own self be true.'" See Ed Trust to FEK June 20, 1965, Box 78, Folder 7, FEK Papers.

276   *The day before . . . said Kameny*: FEK to Mattachine Midwest, July 3, 1968, Box 77, Folder 6, FEK Papers.

276   *He demanded picketers' . . . per sign*: FEK to Daughters of Bilitis, June 20, 1968, Box 69, Folder 5, FEK Papers.

277   *At this picket . . . African American minority*: Lilli Vincenz, "The Second Largest Minority," 1968, The National Audio-Visual Conservation Center, Library of Congress, https://blogs.loc.gov/now-see-hear/2014 /06/lilli-vincenz.

277   *"It's gathering momentum," . . . their country*: Ibid.

277   *After the march . . . naked men*: FEK to Herman Slade, June 15, 1968, Box 78, Folder 7, FEK Papers.

277   *That same week . . . for homosexuals*: Handwritten Notes, n.d., Box 123, Folder 12, FEK Papers; FEK to Steven Milgrim, August 10, 1968, Box 123, Folder 12, FEK Papers; FEK to Foster Gunnison Jr., June 25, 1968, Box 4, Folder 9, FEK Papers.

277   *J. Edgar Hoover . . . Appropriations hearing*: Richard Harwood, "J. Edgar Hoover: A Librarian with a Lifetime Lease," *The Washington Post*, February 25, 1968, D1.

278   *Rooney had asked . . . in this"*: U.S. Congress, House, Committee on Appropriations, Departments of State, Justice, and Commerce, the Judiciary, and Related Agencies Appropriation Bill, Fiscal Year 1967 (to Accompany H.R. 18119), 89th Cong., 2d Sess., 1968, 293–96.

278   *The 1968 Post . . . of paid informants*: Harwood, "J. Edgar Hoover."

278   *Kameny, on the . . . he explained*: FEK to John B. Layton, June 18, 1965, Box 80, Folder 8, FEK Papers.

278   *"Warren Scarberry is . . . go away"*: FEK to Ronald Brass, December 22, 1965, Box 15, Folder 4, FEK Papers.

279   *In March 1966 . . . warned Hal Call*: FEK to Hal Call, March 30, 1966, Box 78, Folder 2, FEK Papers.

279   *Hal Call, himself . . . answer it*: Hal Call to FEK, April 1, 1966, Box 78, Folder 2, FEK Papers.

279   *Shortly before midnight . . . own blood. "Warren"*: "'Writes' Name of Suspect," *The Ithaca Journal*, July 22, 1968, 11; "Man Arraigned in Murder," *Democrat and Chronicle* (Rochester, NY), July 23, 1968, 14; "Name in Blood on Car Door Key Exhibit in Slaying Case," *Democrat and Chronicle* (Rochester), December 11, 1968, 21.

17. THE RIOTS

281   *In 1844, New . . . Henry Christman*: David Murray, ed., *Delaware County, New York: History of the Century, 1797–1897* (Delhi, NY: William Clark, 1898), 246; Henry Christman, *Tin Horns and Calico: A Decisive Episode in the Emergence of Democracy* (Cornwallville, NY: Hope Farm Press, 1978), 92.

281   *In January 1845 . . . in prison*: Charles W. McCurdy, *The Anti-Rent Era in New York Law and Politics, 1839–1865* (Chapel Hill: University of North Carolina Press, 2003), 175; "An Act to Prevent Persons Appearing Disguised and Armed," January 28, 1845, ed. John Worth Edmonds, *Statutes at Large of the State of New York* (Albany, NY: W.C. Little, 1863), 279.

281   *The riots only . . . disbanded, victorious*: Thomas Summerhill, "Anti-Rent Wars (New York)," *Encyclopedia of U.S. Labor and Working-class History*, ed. Eric Arnesen, vol. 1 (New York: Taylor & Francis, 2007), 118–19.

282   *"disguised and . . . City*: George Chauncey, *Gay New York: Gender, Urban Culture, and the Makings of the Gay Male World, 1890–1940* (New York: Basic Books, 1994), 294–95.

282   *Those who did . . . safe*: Yvonne Ritter, interviewed by Kate Davis, WGBH Media Library & Archives, 2011, http://openvault.wgbh.org/catalog/V_C771C1F47D7547BAAE5D3912B4AB3E77 (hereafter, "Ritter interview"). See also Leslie Feinberg, *Transgender Warriors: Making History from Joan of Arc to Dennis Rodman* (Boston, MA: Beacon Press, 1997), 3.

282   *In 1968, the . . . statute*: People v. Archibald, 58 Misc.2d 862 (1968). With New York's 1967 penal reform, the law was reworded to ban "unnatural attire or facial alteration," defining the crime as loitering rather than vagrancy. See Edward Thompson Co., *McKinney's Consolidated Laws of New York, Annotated* (New York: West Publishing Company, 1967), 139.

282   *Yvonne Ritter of . . . her reflection*: Ritter interview.

282   *By the age . . . another drink*: Ibid.

282   *On her eighteenth . . . Stonewall Inn*: Ibid.; Carter, *Stonewall*, 130.

283   *In the summer . . . flames?*: FEK to DOB, February 22, 1968, Box 69, Folder 5, FEK Papers.

283   *On Monday, August . . . met in committees*: Meeting Minutes, Fourth Meeting, North American Conference of Homophile Organizations, August 17, 1968, Box 75, Folder 6, Gittings Papers; Foster Gunnison to Steve Donaldson, August 2, 1968, Box 76, Folder 3, Gittings Papers; "Homosexuals Ask Candidates' Ideas," *The New York Times*, August 19, 1968, 29.

283   *As the weekend . . . Martin as treasurer*: Meeting Minutes, Fourth Meeting, North American Conference of Homophile Organizations, August 17, 1968, Box 75, Folder 6, Gittings Papers.

283   *Despite his loss . . . congressional elections*: The Bill of rights had five planks: first, legalizing sodomy; second, legalizing solicitation for sexual activity; and third through fifth, Kameny's three governmental targets—ending homosexual discrimination in the armed forces, in the granting of security clearances, and in federal employment. See ibid.

283   *BECAUSE homosexuals suffer . . . and heterosexual communities"*: "Resolution Passed by the N.A.C.H.O., August 1968," Box 1, Folder 16, MSNY Papers.

284   *Only two years . . . Kameny's resolution*: The delegates then adopted another Kameny resolution, declaring that homosexuals had the "moral right to be a homosexual," free of "arrogant and insolent pressures to convert to

the prevailing heterosexuality, and free of penalty, disability or disadvantage of any kind, public or private, official or unofficial for his non-conformity." See Meeting Minutes, Fourth Meeting, North American Conference of Homophile Organizations, August 17, 1968, Box 75, Folder 6, Gittings Papers.

284 *News of the . . . he told Kameny*: Randy Wicker to FEK, October 2, 1968, Box 10, Folder 12, FEK Papers.

284 *But when Eva . . . single statement*": Eva Freund, "NACHO Meets in Chicago," *The Insider*, September 1968, Box 86, Folder 2, FEK Papers.

284 *In the August . . . here first*": "FYI," *Home Furnishings Daily*, August 28, 1968, 2.

285 *A few days . . . we seek*": Jim Bradford et al. to James B. Conlisk Jr., August 21, 1968, Box 67, Folder 10, Gittings Papers; "Chicago Police Harass Homosexual Bars," August 21, 1968, Box 67, Folder 10, Gittings Papers; "Petition Campaign Mounted to Protest Police Harassment of Homosexuals," August 23, Box 67, Folder 10, Gittings Papers.

285 *When another NACHO . . . last year*": Ray Hill to FEK, September 11, 1968, Box 100, Folder 8, FEK Papers.

285 *Later that month . . . the suburbs*: Gitlin, *The Sixties*, 323.

285 *The masked national . . . feel it*: Ibid., 332.

285 *In the aftermath . . . fall*: Ibid., 335–36.

285 *At 9:00 a.m. . . . Examiner Waldman*: FEK to Ray Hill, September 16, 1968, Box 100, Folder 8, FEK Papers; "News Release," August 26, 1968, Box 8, Folder 10, Gittings Papers; "Invitation," September 3, 1968, Box 8, Folder 10, Gittings Papers.

285 *The embattled technical . . . wrote the* Journal: Charles Alverson, "A Minority's Plea: U.S. Homosexuals Gain in Trying to Persuade Society to Accept Them," *The Wall Street Journal*, July 17, 1968, 1.

286 *If a blackmailer . . . would flee*": Department of Defense, "In the Matter of: Benning Wentworth," September 9, 1968, Box 37, Folder 9, FEK Papers, 50.

286 *"There may come . . . arrived*": Ibid., 73.

286 *Two days . . . appropriate disclosure requirements*": *Scott v. Macy*, 402 F.2d 644 (1968).

286 *"I am not . . . employ him?*": Ibid.

287 *Scott, despite the . . . otherwise qualified*": Bruce Scott to David Carliner, September 1968, Box 9, Folder 5, FEK Papers.

287 *Even if the . . . albums, letters*: FEK to Barbara Gittings, October 1, 1968, Box 4, Folder 1, FEK Papers.

287 *Kameny wrote to . . . ARMY CORPS*": "News Release," October 1968, Box 68, Folder 6, Gittings Papers; FEK to Nelda Cade, October 3, 1968, Box 68, Folder 6, Gittings Papers; FEK to Captain Riedel, October 3, 1968, Box 68, Folder 6, Gittings Papers.

287 *The women, following . . . dishonorable discharges*: FEK, "WACS Prevail over Army," *The Ladder* 13, no. 11/12 (August/September 1969), 3.

287 *In October, Kameny . . . "possible target*": The determination contained a glimmer of hope. One of the three appeal board members, though he agreed Crawford did not deserve a security clearance, dissented on the blackmail matter. When he heard Crawford declare, "I have no feeling of shame, fear, guilt, wrongdoing," this examiner believed him. "I do not believe on the information of record in this case that the applicant could be coerced or pressured," he concluded. See Joseph J. Liebling to FEK, October 25, 1968, Box 17, Folder 7, FEK Papers; "Memorandum of Reasons," Box 17, Folder 7, FEK Papers.

288 *A few months . . . American citizens*: "National Board Meets Feb. 15–16; Agenda" *Inside ACLU* 1, no. 19, February 3, 1969, Box 1127, Folder 26, ACLU Papers. The relationship between the NCACLU and the MSW had never been stronger. Kameny continued to attend meetings of the NCACLU's Subcommittee on Discrimination, and in September 1968, the subcommittee met to discuss the use of "non-legalistic tools" to fight security clearance cases. By the end of the meeting, Kameny had convinced the attorneys that the press release method—publicly declaring one's homosexuality—was "exceedingly effective," as it concluded in a report. The attorneys agreed that since there was "an overlap in both areas of interest and personnel, between the committee and the Society, closer cooperation would seem to be reasonable." And since there existed so much overlap between the two organizations, it made sense for the NCACLU and the MSW to raise funds together. In August, Kameny proposed cosponsoring a cocktail party with the NCACLU. The executive board established an ad hoc committee, chaired by Eva Freund, to explore the possibility. Freund wrote to members in early October, explaining the purpose of the event was "to give ACLU an opportunity to recruit new members, thereby enabling them to have more money to provide us with more lawyers enabling us to get closer to being first class citizens." In early 1969, the NCACLU would return the favor. The Society would be able to talk about its cause and recruit members from within the ranks of the NCACLU. That night, at the Parkside Hotel, the attorneys explained everything the NCACLU was doing for the homosexuals, like the Scott case, the Dowdy affair, their assistance in the security clearance hearings. And the homosexuals were grateful. As Clark Polak explained to *The Wall Street Journal* earlier that year, "Volunteer heterosexual lawyers are the backbone of our movement. It's very similar to the early days of the civil rights movement when the strongest supporters were the whites." See NCACLU Invitation, October 26, 1968, Box 68, Folder 6, Gittings Papers; Frank Kameny, "Forcing the Doors of the Star Chamber," Box 9, Folder 7, FEK Papers; Franklin E. Kameny, "Government Employment Committee, Subcommittee on Discrimina-

tion, Homosexuality," Box 75, Folder 6, FEK Papers; Eva Freund to MSW, October 3, 1968, Box 85, Folder 3, FEK Papers; Charles Alverson, "A Minority's Plea: U.S. Homosexuals Gain in Trying to Persuade Society to Accept Them," *The Wall Street Journal*, July 17, 1968, 1.

288 *Over the summer . . . he warned them*: FEK to John R. Nichols, September 14, 1968, Box 7, Folder 10, FEK Papers; FEK to Harper & Row, September 1, 1968, Box 97, Folder 1, Gittings Papers.

288 *No funds arrived. . . . Shirley Willer*: FEK to Shirley Willer, September 20, 1968, Box 10, Folder 14, FEK Papers.

288 *"Things here are . . . much else"*: FEK to John R. Nichols, September 14, 1968, Box 7, Folder 10, FEK Papers.

288 *The telephone in . . . number*: "MSW Needs You!," *The Insider*, September 1968, Box 86, Folder 2, FEK Papers.

288 *By September, after . . . keep the office*: Martha B. and John Marshall to MSW Member, September 5, 1968, Box 85, Folder 9, FEK Papers.

288 *Kameny's mother, deeply . . . good first"*: Rae Beck Kameny to FEK, November 28, 1968, Box 153, Folder 7, FEK Papers.

289 *Kameny remained too . . . in total*: FEK to Marc Jeffers, October 6, 1968, Box 68, Folder 8, FEK Papers. Candidates received the surveys less than a month before the election, so Kameny received only eleven completed questionnaires and six more letters in response. Compared to the responses from the MSW's 1962 campaign, however, the initiative was a success: nearly all the respondents agreed that homosexuals should be allowed to work for the government and that sodomy laws needed reform. "I think your cause a just one but an even more difficult one than the black man's," wrote one candidate, a Democrat from Wisconsin. "Where I can help to eliminate homosexual discrimination, I will," promised another candidate, a Democrat from California. Both candidates ultimately lost. See "Report on National Political Questionnaire," 1968, Box 75, Folder 6, Gittings Papers.

289 *On October 26 . . . Day picket*: Meeting Minutes, Fourth Session of the Eastern Regional Conference of Homophile Organizations, October 26, 1968, Box 64, Folder 6, Gittings Papers.

289 *The next day . . . questionnaire*: Ibid.; "Report on National Political Questionnaire," 1968, Box 75, Folder 6, Gittings Papers.

289 *"The Conference voted . . . the purges*: "Homosexual Endorse, Oppose Congressional Candidates," October 31, 1968, Box 64, Folder 6, Gittings Papers. Not only did ERCHO function smoothly, but the national organization conceived to spread Kameny's ideology and tactics, NACHO, grew despite the discord at Chicago. In December, the board of the MSNY voted to join the confederation. See Arthur Warner to Marc Jeffers, December 25, 1968, Box 77, Folder 2, Gittings Papers.

289 *winning his election in a landslide*: Myron D. Hartman, ed., *The New York Red Book, 1969–1970* (Albany: Williams Press, 1970), 1096.

289 *"I do want . . . will find interesting"*: John J. Rooney to ERCHO, November 7, 1968, Box 122, Folder 6, FEK Papers.

289 *Congressman Rooney had . . . the ad*: *The Boys in the Band* advertisement, November 1968, Box 138, Folder 3, FEK Papers. Kameny thanked Rooney for the ad, a symbol of America's newfound ability to discuss homosexuality. "I might say that I, too, find the advertisement somewhat deplorable," he added. "I found it deplorable because it makes homosexuality seem to be a sickness." See FEK to John J. Rooney, November 8, 1968, Box 122, Folder 6, FEK Papers.

289 *Barbara Gittings, still . . . to Kameny*: Dick Leitsch to Barbara Gittings, August 10, 1968, Box 6, Folder 11, FEK Papers.

290 *The DOB barely . . . movement*: D'Emilio, *Sexual Politics, Sexual Communities*, 228.

290 *In August 1968 . . . the movement*: Marcia M. Gallo, *Different Daughters: A History of the Daughters of Bilitis and the Rise of the Lesbian Rights Movement* (Emeryville, CA: Seal Press, 2007), 142–43.

290 *For DOB national . . . being female"*: Rita Laporte, quote in D'Emilio, *Sexual Politics, Sexual Communities*, 229.

290 *"When you get . . . be accepted"*: Rita Laporte to Foster Gunnison, October 23, 1968, Box 4, Folder 11, Gittings Papers. *The Ladder*, under the editorship of Barbara Grier, transformed into a publication far more radical than even Gittings had imagined. By November, *The Ladder* contained articles attacking the institution of marriage—why should homosexuals "bind themselves together for life" because heterosexuals do it?—and urging readers to fight for the feminist cause from within NOW. See Martha Shelley, "On Marriage," *The Ladder* 13, no. 1/2 (October/November 1968), 46; Dorothy L. Martin, "The Lesbian's Other Identity," *The Ladder* 13, no. 3/4 (December 1968/January 1969), 16.

290 *By the end . . . wrote*: Marc Jeffers to Rita Laporte, January 8, 1969, Box 77, Folder 2, Gittings Papers.

290 *The Daughters withdrew nonetheless*: They were joined by three San Francisco organizations: the Society for Individual Rights, the Tavern Guild, and the Council on Religion and the Homosexual. See Del Martin, "Gay is Good—So What?," *The Ladder* 13, no. 7/8 (April/May 1969), 24.

291 *Kameny, on the . . . degrade yourselves"*: FEK to Barbara Grier, April 25, 1969, Box 4, Folder 7, FEK Papers.

291 *Gittings agreed with . . . that fall*: Barbara Gittings, interviewed by Kay Tobin Lahusen, 1969–1971, Box 122, Folder 4, Gittings Papers; Interrogation Summary, December 9, 1968, Box 96, Folder 8, Gittings Papers.

291 *On January 2 . . . she wrote*: Shirley E. Willer to MSW, January 2, 1969, Box 83, Folder 5, FEK Papers.

291   *With the coming . . . would it?*: Foster Gunnison to FEK, December 8, 1968, Box 4, Folder 10, Gittings
      Papers.
291   *Eva Freund, meanwhile . . . loss of $216*: "MSW Statement of Income and Expenses," *The Insider*, February
      1969, Box 86, Folder 2, FEK Papers.
291   *Only a year . . . against him*: MSW Ballot, January 9, 1969, Box 80, Folder 6, FEK Papers.
291   *On January 9 . . . the MSW's treasurer*: "The Orderly Change of Power," *The Insider*, February 1969, Box 86,
      Folder 2, FEK Papers.
292   *Eleven days later . . . he circled it*: Drew Pearson and Jack Anderson, "Report Shows Violence Gripping U.S.,"
      The Washington Post, January 28, 1969, D23, clipping in Box 138, Folder 4, FEK Papers.
292   *On the night . . . in Baltimore*: "Steam Bath Raid Nets 30 Men," *The Baltimore Sun*, March 15, 1969, 20; "Vice
      Squad Detective Tells of Raid on Steam Bath," *The Baltimore Sun*, March 25, 1969, 13.
292   *"Run by men for men"*: "Now Open," *Capital Gazette* (Annapolis), December 30, 1968, 18.
292   *On the first . . . to twenty-eight*: "Steam Bath Raid Nets 30 Men," 20; "Vice Squad Detective Tells of Raid on
      Steam Bath," 13.
292   *Kameny had been . . . from the judge*: FEK, "Motion for Order to Correct the Record of Arrest," March 21,
      1969, Box 137, Folder 4, FEK Papers.
293   *For legal assistance . . . MSW president*: Elsbeth Levy Bothe to FEK, April 14, 1969, Box 137, Folder 4, FEK
      Papers.
293   *With that, the . . . and the NCACLU*: On March 31, Kameny's attorney informed him that the judge had ruled
      that anyone not "accidentally present" at the bathhouse would automatically be found guilty. If Kameny was
      convicted, they would appeal. Kameny received a $250 invoice from his attorney, Elsbeth Levy Bothe, with a
      note: she did not expect payment "as a courtesy to Ralph Temple, Esq. who requested that I secure represen-
      tation for you without charge." See ibid.; Elsbeth Levy Bothe to FEK, March 31, 1969, Box 137, Folder 4,
      FEK Papers.
293   *"I have spent . . . get again"*: "My Own Case Against the Defense Department," n.d., Box 45, Folder 1, FEK
      Papers; FEK to Ralph J. Temple, January 4, 1969, Box 45, Folder 1, FEK Papers.
293   *"I am pleased . . . official*: Sylvia Lewis to FEK, February 18, 1969, Box 45, Folder 1, FEK Papers.
293   *The NCACLU's lawyers . . . Court*: FEK to Thomas C. Nugent, February 12, 1969, Box 8, Folder 2, Gittings
      Papers.
293   *At 11:00 a.m. . . . Federal District Court"*: "Taxation Without Association," *The Insider*, May 1969, Box 80,
      Folder 26, FEK Papers; FEK, "Statement to the Press," March 25, 1969, Box 68, Folder 6, Gittings Papers.
293   *The case of . . . funds, and support?*: Ibid.
294   *"As a homosexual . . . other American citizens"*: FEK, "Statement to the Press," March 25, 1969, Box 68, Folder
      6, Gittings Papers.
294   *The suit named . . . plaintiffs*: "ACLU Charges IRS Chief with Creating 'American Apartheid' Directed at
      Homosexuals—Press Conference Held," March 25, 1969, Box 68, Folder 6, Gittings Papers; Franklin E.
      Kameny, "Statement to the Press," March 25, 1969, Box 68, Folder 6, Gittings Papers; "Complaint," *Franklin
      E. Kameny et al. v. William H. Smith*, March 25, 1969, Box 9, Folder 7, Gittings Papers.
294   *"Homosexuals Sue," announced . . . Post*: "Homosexuals Sue," *The Washington Post*, March 26, 1969, C8.
294   *That spring, Kameny . . . Warren Scarberry*: "City Lifts Job Curb For Homosexuals," *The New York Times*, May
      9, 1969, 1.
294   *"He seems to . . . to Attica Prison"*: Ronald Brass to FEK, June 4, 1969, Box 15, Folder 5, FEK Papers.
294   *Kameny remained unemployed . . . office*: "The Orderly Change of Power," *The Insider*, February 1969, Box 86,
      Folder 2, FEK Papers.
294   *From that point . . . would ring*: "Let's Do It," *The Insider*, April 1969, Box 86, Folder 2, FEK Papers.
294   *"All of us . . . Society rolls"*: Paul Lemay to MSW Membership, April 15, 1969, Box 85, Folder 3, FEK Papers.
      The Society's members understood the group still had potential. When *The Insider* coeditors Eva Freund and
      Dick Schaefers brought Society brochures and GAY IS GOOD buttons to distribute at gay bars, to their sur-
      prise, the bar owners accepted the paraphernalia with enthusiasm. "As the homophile community is more
      open about itself, Mattachine is seen less as a threatening force trying to rock the boat," they wrote. Then, a
      March lecture by an NCACLU attorney on "Homosexuals and the Law"—he urged the MSW to lobby for
      the repeal of sodomy statutes—attracted the Society's largest crowd since its founding. See "Who's Afraid of
      the Big Bad Bar Owners?," *The Insider*, April 1969, Box 86, Folder 2, FEK Papers; "Victims of a Holy Mis-
      sion," *The Insider*, May 1969, Box 86, Folder 2, FEK Papers.
295   *"A Guerrilla to . . . FOR HOMOSEXUALS??"*: "A Guerrilla to Invade MSW," *The Insider*, February 1969, Box
      86, Folder 2, FEK Papers.
295   *At the February . . . family members*: "Guerrilla Came, Saw and Conquered The February Meeting," *The Insider*,
      March 1969, Box 86, Folder 2, FEK Papers; "It's What's Up Front That Counts," *The Insider*, May 1969, Box
      86, Folder 2, FEK Papers.
295   *After one guerrilla . . . a homosexual"*: Ibid. Freund and her coeditor, Dick Schaefers, also brought the new
      concept of Gay Power—focused on consolidating economic and political strength—to the Society. They

reported on the Society's acquisition of a hundred lavender buttons emblazoned with GAY IS GOOD, a slogan that gave "support to the so-called 'gay power' approach to reform." They began publishing a list of gay-friendly companies to "consolidate gay 'buying' power in Washington." And after Freund learned that the Black Panthers, the radical Black Power group, used their newsletter to provoke discussion and mobilization of its members, she attempted to do the same. She reported on a series of raided gay bars in Richmond, Virginia, which led to the formation of a Homophile League of Richmond. Homosexuals in San Francisco, she reported, were picketing a steamship line for its discriminatory practices. See "Market Place," *The Insider*, February 1969, Box 86, Folder 2, FEK Papers; Eva Freund, interviewed by Eric Cervini, telephone, December 14, 2018; Meeting Minutes, May 1, 1969, Box 85, Folder 9, FEK Papers.

295 *Paul Kuntzler, for . . . tolerated)*: Paul Lemay to "Fellow Member," May 14, 1969, Box 85, Folder 3, FEK Papers.

295 *Only nine members . . . membership meeting*: Meeting Minutes, May 1, 1969, Box 85, Folder 9, FEK Papers.

295 *"I think we . . . tired of Frank"*: Susan Clarke, interviewed by Eric Cervini, telephone, October 11, 2019.

295 *As for Kameny, he seemed to . . . these days"*: FEK to Randolfe Wicker, April 20, 1969, Box 10, Folder 12, FEK Papers.

295 *Meanwhile, Kameny's seven-year-old . . . a plaintiff*: The Union had accepted MSW member Perrin Shaffer's security clearance case. Then there were three additional cases, all Kameny referrals: a security clearance case, a CSC case, and an air force discharge case. Benning Wentworth, once his case was ready, would be the plaintiff in a seventh case. See FEK to Austin Wade, May 23, 1969, Box 75, Folder 8, Gittings Papers; FEK to Scanlon, n.d., Box 37, Folder 7, FEK Papers.

296 *In the spring . . . the election*: He remained welcome at the NCACLU's board meetings. "We sincerely hope," wrote Executive Director Irma Thexton, "that we may invite you to join the Executive Board as vacancies occur." See Irma Thexton to Candidate, May 19, 1969, Box 75, Folder 6, FEK Papers.

296 *Before he announced . . . others"*: Austin Wade to FEK, April 28, 1969, Box 15, Folder 9, Gittings Papers.

296 *Kameny responded on . . . do not"*: FEK to Austin Wade, May 23, 1969, Box 75, Folder 8, Gittings Papers.

296 *On Saturday, April . . . Student Center*: FEK, "Eastern Regional Conference of Homophile Organizations," April 12, 1969, Box 64, Folder 7, Gittings Papers.

296 *The delegates' greatest . . . gender classification"*: In her notes, Gittings did not mention who introduced this proposal. See Barbara Gittings, ERCHO Meeting Notes, April 12–13, 1969, Box 64, Folder 7, Gittings Papers.

297 *The motion failed 28–10*: Craig Rodwell's HYMN, Philadelphia's Homophile Action League, and even Foster Gunnison's one-man organization, the Institute for Social Equality, voted against it. See ibid.

297 *A new motion . . . the resolution unanimously*: "Resolution Passed at ERCHO Conference," April 12–13, 1969, Box 64, Folder 7, Gittings Papers.

297 *In mid-June, Kameny . . . several organizations*: Chairman, ERCHO, to the Executive Committee, ERCHO, June 13, 1969, Box 102, Folder 16, Gittings Papers.

297 *"We cannot support . . . supposedly fighting"*: Dick Leitsch to Barbara Gittings, June 24, 1969, Box 6, Folder 11, FEK Papers.

298 *On June 25 . . . ARE HOMOSEXUALS"*: FEK and Barbara Gittings to Melvin R. Laird, June 25, 1969, Box 7, Folder 6, Gittings Papers.

298 *The next day . . . first arrest*: "Cross Currents," *The Ladder* 14, no. 1/2 (October/November 1969), 35.

298 *On the night . . . lesbians, watching*: Carter, *Stonewall*, 134.

298 *More than a . . . a license*: Ibid., 123.

298 *The raids occurred . . . numbers*: Ibid., 102.

299 *They were easy . . . the fags."*: Lincoln Anderson, "'I'm Sorry,' Says Inspector Who Led Stonewall Raid," *The Villager*, June 22, 2004, https://www.thevillager.com/2004/06/im-sorry-says-inspector-who-led-stonewall -raid. See also Faderman, *The Gay Revolution*, 172.

299 *At 1:20 a.m. . . . lights turned on*: Carter, *Stonewall*, 137.

299 *Ritter, terrified, ran . . . said the officer*: Ritter interview.

299 *The police dragged . . . Don't touch me*: Ibid., 140.

299 *Female officers examined . . . to be women*: Howard Smith, "Full Moon over Stonewall," *The Village Voice*, July 3, 1969, 29.

299 *Officers told another . . . album, identified them*: Carter, *Stonewall*, 140–41.

299 *Meanwhile, the gay . . . atmosphere grew festive*: Ibid.; Lucian Truscott, "Gay Power Comes to Sheridan Square," *The Village Voice*, July 3, 1969, 1.

299 *The patrons arrested . . . with his club*: Carter, *Stonewall*, 148.

300 *A Village Voice . . . the police wagon*: Truscott, "Gay Power Comes to Sheridan Square."

300 *An officer led . . . way*: Carter, *Stonewall*, 149; Ritter interview.

300 *now numbering four hundred*: "4 Policemen Hurt in 'Village' Raid," *The New York Times*, June 29, 1969, 33.

300 *Officers then brought . . . a butch dyke"*: Carter, *Stonewall*, 150.

300 *"She put up . . . reported the Voice*: Truscott, "Gay Power Comes to Sheridan Square."

300 *"A dyke," wrote . . . screaming, and fighting"*: Carter, *Stonewall*, 150.

300   *Twice, this patron . . . do something!":* Ibid.
300   *"It was at . . . the cops":* Truscott, "Gay Power Comes to Sheridan Square."
300   *With cries of . . . him mercilessly:* Smith, "Full Moon over Stonewall."
300   *A* Voice *reporter . . . one of them:* Ibid.
301   *Outside, calls of . . . some gas":* Truscott, "Gay Power Comes to Sheridan Square."
301   *An arm poured . . . massacre seemed imminent:* Smith, "Full Moon over Stonewall."
301   *The officers escaped . . . a stoop:* Carter, *Stonewall,* 177–78.
301   *The next evening . . . shattering its windshield:* Ibid., 188; Duberman, *Stonewall,* 204.
301   *The riot police . . . the crowds dispersed:* Truscott, "Gay Power Comes to Sheridan Square."
301   *On Sunday afternoon . . . OF THE VILLAGE—MATTACHINE:* Carter, *Stonewall,* 196–97.
301   *The crowds, though . . . years ago":* Truscott, "Gay Power Comes to Sheridan Square."
302   *That night, Yvonne . . . Saturday morning:* Yvonne Ritter, interviewed by Eric Cervini, telephone, February 10, 2019.
302   *As she graduated . . . defiance and pride:* Ritter interview.

18. THE LIBERATION

303   *Hours before the . . . historic event:* David M. Harland, *The First Men on the Moon: The Story of Apollo 11* (Berlin, Germany: Springer, 2007), 93; C. E. Wright, "Rooms with View of Moon Shot," *The New York Times,* June 29, 1969, 29.
303   *He had been . . . to his home:* Norton v. Macy, 417 F.2d 1161 (1969).
303   *Two Morals Division . . . an adjacent room:* Ibid.
304   *in one of . . . the Lincoln Memorial:* Ibid.; Elizabeth Suckow, "'L' Building," in "Hidden Headquarters," NASA Headquarters Operations, March 24, 2009, https://hqoperations.hq.nasa.gov/docs/Hidden_Headquarters _March_24_2009.pdf.
304   *Another NASA official . . . and disgraceful conduct":* Norton v. Macy, 417 F.2d 1161 (1969); "Complaint for Declaratory Judgment and Other Relief," October 13, 1964, *Norton v. Macy,* Box 29, Folder 5, FEK Papers.
304   *Norton called his . . . his legal connections:* FEK to John R. Nichols, July 12, 1969, Box 7, Folder 10, FEK Papers.
304   *They filed suit . . . in Washington:* Glenn R. Graves to FEK, October 14, 1964, Box 29, Folder 5, FEK Papers.
304   *At the time . . . help other homosexuals:* "Complaint for Declaratory Judgment and Other Relief," October 13, 1964, *Norton v. Macy,* Box 29, Folder 5, FEK Papers; FEK to Douglas E. Decker, July 11, 1969, Box 19, Folder 13, FEK Papers.
304   *David Bazelon and . . . in the country:* In Bruce Scott's case, Bazelon had argued that the government needed to prove the connection between Scott's immoral conduct and his "occupational fitness." Bazelon wanted evidence that Scott's homosexuality harmed the "efficiency of the service," as the law put it. But in 1965, none of Bazelon's fellow judges joined him in that aspect of his opinion, and the court only required the CSC to be more specific about its charges of immorality. See *Scott v. Macy,* 349 F.2d 182 (D.C. Cir. 1965). For Bazelon and Wright's liberal reputations, see Marilyn Berger, "David Bazelon Dies at 83; Jurist Had Wide Influence," *The New York Times,* February 21, 1993, 38; Marjorie Hunter, "Judge Skelly Wright, Segregation Foe, Dies at 77," *The New York Times,* August 8, 1988, 10.
304   *On Tuesday, July . . . and crying 'shame.'":* Norton v. Macy, 417 F.2d 1161 (1969).
305   *Norton learned about . . . they use me?":* Clifford Norton to FEK, July 6, 1969, Box 29, Folder 5, FEK Papers.
305   *During the city . . . American hero's denunciations:* James Eady, "Astronaut Decries Dissent on Campus at July 4th Rites," *The Philadelphia Inquirer,* July 5, 1969, 1.
306   *Kameny, when he . . . orderly and dignified:* "While I do not necessarily approve of violence, public disorder, and rioting, I could not repress a satisfied and sympathetic chuckle at seeing the members of my community finally refusing any longer to be 'shoved around', and at the picture of the police cowering (as indeed they did) in terror from massed 'Gay Power' (It is just a pity that it apparently takes that to bring you people into line, but apparently that is what it does take. If—all other reasonable measured [*sic*] having failed—that turns out to be what it does take, then, by your own effective invitation, that is what you will get)." See FEK to the Screening Board, July 20, 1969, Box 8, Folder 8, Gittings Papers.
306   *Despite his cries . . . and behave accordingly":* "5th Annual Reminder," 1969, Box 64, Folder 7, Gittings Papers.
306   *Threatening phone calls . . . the homosexuals:* Duberman, *Stonewall,* 209.
306   *The police, for . . . Independence Hall:* "The Last Peaceful?? Demonstration," *The Insider,* August 1969, Box 86, Folder 2, FEK Papers.
306   *When the bus . . . sandals, and beards:* Ibid.
306   *One interracial lesbian . . . the riots:* Lilli Vincenz, interviewed by Genny Beemyn, Arlington, VA, June 6, 1998.
306   *Shortly after 2:00 p.m. . . . silent, single-file line:* Bill Wingell, "Great to Be Gay: A Time for Holding Hands," *The Distant Drummer,* July 10, 1969, 8.
306   *After thirty minutes . . . hands:* Duberman, *Stonewall,* 210.

306 *His authority exerted . . . the reporter*: Wingell, "Great to Be Gay."

307 *"ranting and raving"*: Duberman, *Stonewall*, 210.

307 *"Our message is . . . inappropriate," he exclaimed*: Wingell, "Great to Be Gay."

307 *Rodwell turned to . . . his own sign*: Ibid.

307 *Aware of the . . . to protest*: Ibid.

307 *"I am genuinely . . . should be stressed"*: FEK to Craig Rodwell, July 11, 1969, Box 67, Folder 3, FEK Papers.

307 *Fred Sargeant, Rodwell's . . . you?"*: Frederic A. Sargeant to FEK, September 27, 1969, Box 105, Folder 1, FEK Papers.

308 *News of the . . . the picket?*: Barbara Grier to FEK, August 8, 1969, Box 4 Folder 7, FEK Papers.

308 *"What the hell . . . the goal"*: Richard Michaels to FEK, August 3, 1969, Box 1, Folder 9, FEK Papers.

308 *Kameny penned unapologetic . . . Sargeant and Michaels*: FEK to Frederic A. Sargeant, October 24, 1969, Box 105, Folder 1, FEK Papers; FEK to Barbara Grier, August 13, 1969, Box 4, Folder 7, FEK Papers; FEK to Richard Michaels, August 6, 1969, Box 1, Folder 9, FEK Papers.

308 *Before speaking to . . . sign?*: "Frank," Handwritten Notes, n.d., Box 6, Folder 14, Gittings Papers.

308 *Martha Altman, raised . . . Stokely Carmichael*: Martha Shelley, interviewed by Eric Cervini, telephone, February 8, 2019.

309 *First, she had . . . for life*: Martha Shelley, interviewed by Kelly Anderson, San Francisco, CA, October 12, 2003, Voices of Feminism Oral History Project, Sophia Smith Collection, Smith College, Northampton, MA.

309 *At the 1968 . . . to LSD*: Ibid.; Bob Martin to Henry, April 2, 1969, Box 2, Folder 18, Donaldson Papers; Bob Martin to JD, November 24, 1968, Box 2, Folder 24, Donaldson Papers.

309 *The homophile movement . . . their oppressors?*: Martha Shelley, "Respectability," *The Ladder* 14, no. 1/2 (October/November 1969), 24.

309 *On Saturday night . . . against their oppression*: Carter, *Stonewall*, 211.

309 *When she told . . . message*: Martha Shelley, interviewed by Kelly Anderson, San Francisco, CA, October 12, 2003.

309 *Even Randy Wicker . . . July 6*: Carter, *Stonewall*, 213.

309 *On July 9 . . . audience*: Duberman, *Stonewall*, 125.

309 *Shelley stood and . . . favored Shelley's march?*: "Gay Liberation Meetings," *The Ladder* 14, no. 1/2 (October/November 1969), 40.

310 *Nearly everyone in . . . Liberation Front*: Martha Shelley to Eric Cervini, email correspondence, October 28, 2019; see also Faderman, *The Gay Revolution*, 194.

310 *On July 27 . . . armbands*: Barbara Gittings, "Rally," Handwritten Notes, n.d., Box 67, Folder 3, Gittings Papers.

310 *Another five hundred . . . park, watching*: "Gay Power in New York City," *The Ladder* 14, no. 1/2 (October/November 1969), 41.

310 *Martha Shelley climbed . . . Here we are!"*: Jonathan Black, "Gay Power Hits Back," *The Village Voice* 14, no. 42, July 31, 1969.

310 *There were "eruptions . . . Voice*: Ibid.

310 *Gittings saw people . . . windows*: Barbara Gittings, "Rally," Handwritten Notes, n.d., Box 67, Folder 3, Gittings Papers.

310 *The crowd marched . . . "Gay Power"*: "On Target," *The Insider*, September 1969, Box 86, Folder 2, FEK Papers.

310 *By early August . . . capitalist conspiracy"*: Martha Shelley, interviewed by Kelly Anderson, San Francisco, CA, October 12, 2003; "Gay Revolution Comes Out," RAT, August 12–26, 1969, Box 138, Folder 4, FEK Papers.

310 *The GLF had . . . the street"*: Ibid.

311 *At first, Kameny . . . boat ride*: "Board Actions for July 8, 1969," July 8, 1969, Box 68, Folder 6, Gittings Papers.

311 *On the pages . . . be oppressed?"*: "To Hell With Dying on Your Knees," *The Insider*, August 1969, Box 86, Folder 2, FEK Papers.

311 *"It appears that . . . the doors down"*: Ibid.

311 *In July, Kameny . . . you will get"*: FEK to the Screening Board, July 20, 1969, Box 8, Folder 8, Gittings Papers.

311 *After four years . . . his clearance*: Sanford J. Ungar, "Suit Backs Jobs in Defense for 4 Homosexuals," *The Washington Post*, January 27, 1971, A6; Barry Kalb, "4 Homosexuals Sue U.S. In Denial of Security OK," *The Washington Evening Star*, January 26, 1971, B3.

312 *Kameny and Gittings . . . banned the media*: FEK, "Affidavit," July 11, 1969, Box 8, Folder 8, Gittings Papers.

312 *On July 16 . . . rested their case*: Department of Defense, "Interview with Otto H. Ulrich, Jr.," July 16, 1969, Box 8, Folder 9, Gittings Papers.

312 *That same month . . . July 1969*: "Complaint for Declaratory Judgment and Injunction," *Richard L. Gayer v.*

Melvin L. Laird and Robert F. Froehlke, November 30, 1970, Box 22, Folder 8, FEK Papers; Richard Gayer, Interview with Marc Stein, Philadelphia LGBT History Project, January 11, 1994.

312   *Gayer's case was . . . male person(s)?"*: Richard Lee Gayer, "Direct Interrogatories," n.d., Box 7, Folder 9, Gittings Papers.

313   *A month later . . . another trial*: The appeals board required a re-hearing to determine the "probability that Mr. Wentworth will in future engage in conduct of the nature alleged." William J. Scanlon to FEK, January 18, 1969, Box 9, Folder 1, Gittings Papers.

313   *On August 21 . . . IS GOOD*: Charlayne Hunter, "Homosexual Seeks to Retain Security Clearance," *The New York Times*, August 20, 1969, 38.

313   *"In each case . . . inanimate objects?"*: At this hearing, Kameny brought two additional witnesses to testify: Wardell Pomeroy, coauthor of the Kinsey report, and Warren R. Johnson, a professor of health education at the University of Maryland. Both testified that the Department of Defense's use of the term *sexual perversion* was, ultimately, meaningless. See Hearing Transcript, "In the Matter of Benning Wentworth," August 19, 1969, Box 38, Folder 1, FEK Papers.

313   *After Kameny and . . . circumstances, whatever?"*: "News Release," November 17, 1969, Box 335, Folder 4, ACLU Papers.

313   *Bob Martin, working . . . the riots*: Bob Martin to "Elaine," July 3, 1969, Box 2, Folder 12, Donaldson Papers.

313   *But neither did . . . New Left*: Faderman, *The Gay Revolution*, 192.

313   *On July 3 . . . New York*: Foster Gunnison to FEK, July 31, 1969, Box 5, Folder 1, FEK Papers.

313   *"Yes I've been . . . on needing sex"*: FEK to Foster Gunnison, August 4, 1969, Box 5, Folder 1, FEK Papers.

313   *On July 4 . . . a thunderstorm*: Bob Martin to "Frank," October 27, 1969, Box 1, Folder 16, Donaldson Papers.

314   *Thirty delegates . . . the Bellerive Hotel*: "Panel on Homosexuality Notes Burdens Changes," *The Kansas City Times*, August 26, 1969, clipping in Box 75, Folder 7, Gittings Papers.

314   *"We are back . . . of darkness"*: Marc Jeffers, "The Chairman's Report," August 25–30, 1969, Box 75, Folder 7, Gittings Papers.

314   *On Wednesday evening . . . seen Christopher Street"*: Stephen Donaldson, "NACHO 69," Box 75, Folder 7, Donaldson Papers.

314   *That night, Martin . . . in a document*: Ibid.

314   *The next day . . . radical manifesto* Ibid.

314   *"THE HOMOPHILE MOVEMENT . . . RADICALIZED!" it began*: "A Radical Manifesto," August 28, 1969, Box 75, Folder 7, Gittings Papers.

314   *"We see the . . . them notwithstanding"*: Ibid.

314   *For three hours . . . larger, unjust system*: Donaldson, "NACHO 69."

314   *The delegates agreed . . . Gay Power*: Ibid.

315   *On the last . . . the public restrooms*: Ibid.

315   *The calls had . . . Youngstown, Ohio*: FEK to Larry Jackson, July 20, 1969, Box 82, Folder 1, FEK Papers; FEK to Norman Goodwin, July 26, 1969, Box 81, Folder 5, FEK Papers; FEK to David Brutan, July 20, 1969, Box 81, Folder 1, FEK Papers; FEK to John B., July 11, 1969, Box 83, Folder 6, FEK Papers.

315   *"Meanwhile, organize." Find . . . he wrote*: FEK to Norman Goodwin, July 26, 1969, Box 81, Folder 5, FEK Papers.

315   *Kameny and Gittings . . . long-distance romance)*: FEK to Barbara Gittings, September 29, 1969, Box 6, Folder 14, Gittings Papers; FEK to Louis Crompton, October 9, 1969, Box 2, Folder 12, FEK Papers. "An avowed lesbian, Barbara Gittings, said that homosexuality is not a sickness," reported *The Cornell Daily Sun* in October. She spoke before a crowd of two hundred students. They also attended a new class at New York University titled "The Homosexual in Society." And in Washington, Kameny spoke before an audience at American University, where he found the students more "uptight." See Richard L. Neubauer, "Lesbian Discusses Homosexuality," *The Cornell Daily Sun*, October 24, 1969; Barbara Gittings to Roger Bernhardt, October 1, 1969, Box 129, Folder 9, FEK Papers.

315   *In print, Kameny's . . . homosexual minority*: The author recommended a "program of graduated liberalization" that would first employ homosexuals in positions "least offensive to relevant segments of the public." See "Government-Created Employment Disabilities of the Homosexual," *Harvard Law Review* 82, no. 8, June 1969, 1738–51; Christopher Kaufman to FEK, January 8, 1969, Box 5, Folder 7, FEK Papers. In March, *Playboy* published Kameny's response to a published reader's letter that recommended behavior therapy for homosexuals. Rather than curing homosexuality, Kameny argued for the magazine's 5.5 million readers, therapy should consist of "instilling in him a sense of confident self-acceptance so he could say with pride, 'Gay is good.'" (In response, *Playboy*'s editors agreed homosexuals were not sick. Rather, they suffered from "compulsion based on phobic reactions to heterosexual stimuli." To claim homosexuals represented a minority group, they added, was "inaccurate.") *Playboy*'s discussion of Kameny's "Gay is Good" letter continued throughout the summer. "Dr. Kameny was right and *Playboy* was wrong," wrote one Los Angeles reader, in

August. "You cannot produce one jot of real evidence that homosexual acts are any less desirable or less natural than heterosexual acts." Despite the magazine's antagonism, between March and September, Kameny received no fewer than ten calls from individuals who heard about the MSW from Hugh Hefner's magazine. See FEK, "Gay is Good," *Playboy* 16, no. 3, March 1969, 46; William Edward Glover, "The Nature of Homosexuality," *Playboy* 16, no. 8, August 1969, 50; MSW Office Call Log, February 27, 1969 to August 29, 1969, Box 86, Folder 4, FEK Papers. For *Playboy* circulation numbers, see Jeffrey A. Harris, *Transformative Entrepreneurs: How Walt Disney, Steve Jobs, Muhammad Yunus, and Other Innovators Succeeded* (New York: Springer, 2012), 24. In September, the *New York Post* reported on Kameny and Gittings's fight against the Department of Defense, concluding the military was "on the retreat in the face of growing militancy" within the homophile movement. And in October, the United Church of Christ published *The Same Sex: An Appraisal of Homosexuality*, a book intended for both its clergy and the public. It featured chapters from psychiatrists, theologians, attorneys, and for "equal time," homosexuals including Gittings, Kameny, and Leitsch. See Warren Hoge, "Federal Job Barriers on Homosexuals Falling," *New York Post*, September 10, 1969; United Church Press, "Scope and Specifications for a Symposium on the Issue of Homosexuality," Box 97, Folder 1, Gittings Papers; Ralph W. Weltge, ed., *The Same Sex: An Appraisal of Homosexuality* (Philadelphia: United Church Press, 1969).

315   *The financial position . . . surplus of three hundred dollars*: Meeting Minutes, September 4, 1969, Box 68, Folder 6, Gittings Papers.

316   *She had seen . . . shows*: D'Emilio, *Sexual Politics, Sexual Communities*, 190.

316   *In New York . . . successful dances*: Faderman, *The Gay Revolution*, 201.

316   *In the 1950s . . . community at large*: D'Emilio, *Sexual Politics, Sexual Communities*, 87.

316   *Vincenz conceived of . . .* The Insider: "Dropping the Middle Class Bag," *The Insider*, October 1969, Box 86, Folder 2, FEK Papers.

316   *On October 13 . . . Red Cross*: "On the Streets/Into the World," *The Insider*, November 1969, Box 86, Folder 2, FEK Papers.

316   *they wore their . . . away, for hepatitis*: Lilli Vincenz, interviewed by Genny Beemyn, Arlington, VA, June 6, 1998. That fall, the Society took another measure to protect Washington's homosexual community: a blackmailer was targeting homosexuals who cruised Dupont Circle. He looked up their license plates and then called his victims, pretending to be a police officer and demanding cash. The Society urged its members, if contacted in such a manner, to go to the police, since cruising—simply being in a public place—was legal; homosexuals were "morally and legally entitled to police protection," *The Insider* explained. By the end of the year, the Society negotiated with the Morals Division to invite an officer to address Washington's homosexuals on the "blackmail problem." See "Homosexuals and the Law," *The Insider*, November 1969, Box 86, Folder 2, FEK Papers; "It's What's Up Front that Counts," *The Insider*, December 1969, Box 86, Folder 2, FEK Papers.

316   *Freund and Schaffers . . . in Virginia*: "How's the Old Establishment Doing?," *The Insider*, October 1969, Box 86, Folder 2, FEK Papers.

316   *Lilli Vincenz and . . . community bulletin board/scandal sheet*": "Dropping the Middle Class Bag," *The Insider*, October 1969, Box 86, Folder 2, FEK Papers.

316   *In October,* The *. . . upcoming Kameny lecture*: *The Gay Blade* 1, no. 1, October 1969. Early editions of *The Gay Blade* are available at https://digdc.dclibrary.org/islandora/object/dcplislandora%3A2841.

317   *The Blade's editors . . . she added*: Susan Clarke, interviewed by Eric Cervini, telephone, October 11, 2019.

317   *One of the . . . explained the paper*: "Gay Liberation Front," *The Gay Blade* 1, no. 1 (October 1969); "Board Actions for July 8, 1969," July 8, 1969, Box 68, Folder 6, Gittings Papers.

317   *The NCACLU and . . . Amendment rights*: FEK to Board of Directors, ACLU, July 26, 1969, Box 76, Folder 2, FEK Papers.

317   *The GLF . . . infuriate the homosexuals*: Michael Brown, Michael Tallman, and Leo Martello, "The Summer of Gay Power, and the *Village Voice* Exposed!," *Come Out!* 1, no. 1, November 14, 1969. See also Carter, *Stonewall*, 226–27.

317   *On September 12 . . . conceded*: Ibid.

317   *He would allow . . . to be printed*: "Gay Liberation Front," *The Gay Blade* 1, no. 1, October 1969.

317   *Without a lawsuit . . . observed from Washington* Carter, *Stonewall*, 227.

318   *On October 17 . . . sex—were entirely legal*: The Court argued that unlike Clifford Norton, who merely touched another man's leg, Dick Schlegel "committed four acts on three different males on four different occasions." Schlegel's dismissal was justified, and thus, despite the victory of Norton, the CSC could argue that its purges of active homosexuals—federal employees who actually had sex—were entirely legal. See *Richard L. Schlegel v. the United States*, 416 F.2d 1372 (Ct. Cl. 1969).

318   *Schlegel wrote to . . . Federal employees?*": Richard L. Schlegel to Ralph Temple, October 27, 1969, Box 1680, "*Schlegel v. U.S.*" *Folder*, ACLU Papers; Richard L. Schlegel to Melvin Wulf, November 20, 1969, Box 1680, "*Schlegel v. U.S.*" *Folder*, ACLU Papers.

318   *The ACLU accepted . . . just that*: Melvin L. Wulf to Carl L. Shipley, December 15, 1969, Box 1680, "*Schlegel*

v. U.S." Folder, ACLU Papers; "Petition for a Writ of Certiorari to the United States Court of Claims," *Richard L. Schlegel v. the United States*, October Term 1969, Box 1680, "*Schlegel v. U.S.*" Folder, ACLU Papers. Kameny, meanwhile, continued funneling other cases to the Union. Two days after the Schlegel decision, he forwarded the cases of three women facing purges in the Women's Army Corps (his previous two WAC clients, "Miss X" and "Miss Y," were still safe). Four days later, he forwarded a novel case, that of two drag queens. The teenagers—one Black, one white—were walking downtown, dressed as women, when a police officer offered to pay them for sex. They declined, the officer insisted, and then he arrested them for solicitation. When the officer learned they were men, he changed the charge to lewd and immoral activity, and the drag queens called Kameny from jail at 3:00 a.m. Washington, unlike New York, did not criminalize drag. Kameny thus recommended that the NCACLU take their case. He wanted a lawsuit against the officer and an injunction against the police department; he had already filed an official complaint. And, no matter what, he wanted the NCACLU to represent the queens in their criminal trial. The astronomer promised to leave all matters of "tactics and strategy," however, to the attorneys. See FEK to Ralph Temple, October 19, 1969, Box 75, Folder 6, FEK Papers; FEK to Barbara Grier, October 17, 1969, Box 4, Folder 7, FEK Papers; FEK to Ralph Temple, October 23, 1969, Box 75, Folder 6, FEK Papers.

318 *In 1967, the . . . Force on Homosexuality*: Robert O. Self, *All in the Family: The Realignment of American Democracy Since the 1960s* (New York: Hill and Wang, 2012), 92.

318 *At the time . . . "clinical entity"*: David W. Dunlap, "Psychologist, Defied Orthodoxy on Homosexuals," *Pittsburgh Post-Gazette*, November 23, 1996, 27; Faderman, *The Gay Revolution*, 101; D'Emilio, *Sexual Politics, Sexual Communities*, 141.

318 *On October 10 . . . this need"*: "Final Report of the Task Force on Homosexuality," October 10, 1969, Box 18, Folder 5, Vincenz Papers.

319 *In October . . . for reality"*: *TIME* invited Gittings—then Kameny when she proved unavailable—to a closed symposium on homosexuality, intended to educate its reporters and staff on the topic in preparation for the story. At the symposium, *TIME* staff members confided that the article would serve as "atonement" for the magazine's 1966 essay that described homosexuality as a "pathetic little second-rate substitute for reality." The cover story described the significance of Stonewall, the homophile movement, the GLF, the *Norton* decision, and *The Boys in the Band*. The magazine called for "greater tolerance" but remained ambivalent on the medical nature of the condition. See "The Homosexual: Newly Visible, Newly Understood," *TIME*, October 31, 1969, 56; FEK to Louis Crompton, October 9, 1969, Box 2, Folder 12, FEK Papers; FEK to Barbara Grier, October 17, 1969, Box 4, Folder 7, FEK Papers.

319 *The TIME feature . . . the final word*: "A Discussion: Are Homosexuals Sick?," *TIME*, October 31, 1969, 66.

319 *Earlier that year . . . Cornell*: FEK to Louis Crompton, October 9, 1969, Box 2, Folder 12, FEK Papers.

319 *But as the . . . authoritative comment"*: FEK to James Pollack, December 7, 1969, Box 8, Folder 9, FEK Papers.

319 *With Kameny's . . . he asked*: FEK to *Tangents*, September 15, 1969, Box 74, Folder 1, FEK Papers.

320 *The Post reported . . . Gay Blade"*: Nancy L. Ross, "Homosexual Revolution," *The Washington Post*, October 25, 1969, C1.

320 *"As the person . . . E. Kameny"*: FEK to *The Washington Post*, November 3, 1969, Box 129, Folder 1, FEK Papers.

320 *Each time Kameny . . . wrote in October*: FEK to Louis Crompton, October 17, 1969, Box 2, Folder 12, FEK Papers.

321 *As a student . . . into the movement"*: Ibid.

321 *The MSNY, on . . . buying that"*: Ibid.

321 *On Saturday, November . . . obligations*: "Minutes of the Eastern Regional Conference of Homophile Organizations," November 1–2, 1969, Box 64, Folder 7, Gittings Papers; Bob Martin to Foster Gunnison, November 18, 1969, Box 7, Folder 5, FEK Papers.

321 *That night, Martin . . . admitted Fourat*: Duberman, *Stonewall*, 228–29.

322 *On Sunday, Martin . . . The motion passed*: "Minutes of the Eastern Regional Conference of Homophile Organizations," November 1–2, 1969, Box 64, Folder 7, Gittings Papers.

322 *Despite Kameny's insistence . . . radical resolution*: Ibid.

322 *Before the conference . . . a proposal*: Ibid.; Carter, *Stonewall*, 230.

322 *At the conference . . . the chairman*: Resolution Draft, Eastern Regional Conference of Homophile Organizations, n.d., Box 64, Folder 7, Gittings Papers. Earlier, Kameny introduced a letter from Philadelphia Police commissioner Frank L. Rizzo. The previous July, Kameny had commended Rizzo's Civil Disobedience Squad for its "courteous and helpful presence during our protest." Kameny began reading Rizzo's response, when, suddenly, the GLF interrupted. They moved that Kameny stop reading the letter. "We all know where police departments stand on homosexuality." The motion was defeated 42–18, and Kameny read the commissioner's letter. "I am personally very proud of the members of our department, but it is especially gratifying when someone like you expresses satisfaction with their performance," said Rizzo. The GLF moved that the delegates censure the commissioner. Amidst protests, they withdrew the motion. See FEK to Frank L. Rizzo, July 25, 1969, Box 64, Folder 7, Gittings Papers; Barbara Gittings, "ERCHO-Nov. 1–2, 1969," Handwritten

Notes, Box 64, Folder 7, Gittings Papers; Frank L. Rizzo to FEK, August 20, 1969, Box 67, Folder 3, Gittings Papers; "Minutes of the Eastern Regional Conference of Homophile Organizations," November 1–2, 1969, Box 64, Folder 7, Gittings Papers.

322   *"RESOLVED," it began . . . LIBERATION DAY"*: Ibid.

322   *Standing before Kameny . . . it said*: Barbara Gittings, "ERCHO-Nov. 1–2, 1969," Handwritten Notes, Box 64, Folder 7, Gittings Papers.

322   *Kameny called the . . . the march*: Ibid.

323   *"I suggest that . . . family??? !!!"*: FEK to Clifford Norton, July 11, 1969, Box 29, Folder 5, FEK Papers.

323   *"are moral . . . personally"*: FEK, "Petition for a Writ of Certiorari," *Kameny v. Brucker*, 26.

324   *On July 20 . . . the band's drums*: Eva Freund, "Gay Is," *The Insider*, September 1969, Box 86, Folder 2, FEK Papers.

324   *"150 stranger-friends, arms . . . 'Gay Is Good.'"*: Ibid.

324   *Fifty years later . . . called it*: Eva Freund to Eric Cervini, email correspondence, December 19, 2018.

19. THE PRIDE

326   *As a child . . . later remembered*: Kay Lahusen, interviewed by Marc Stein, Philadelphia, PA, September 29, 1993, OutHistory.org.

326   *Lahusen moved to . . . of Bilitis*: Eric Marcus, *Making Gay History: The Half-Century Fight for Lesbian and Gay Equal Rights* (New York: HarperCollins, 2009), 85–86.

326   *Later that year . . . awfully attractive"*: Ibid.

326   *By 1963, Lahusen . . . its covers*: Barbara Gittings, interviewed by Kay Tobin Lahusen, 1969–1971, Box 122, Folder 4, Gittings Papers.

327   *When a lesbian . . . she explained*: Kay Tobin Lahusen to FEK, July 17, 1965, Box 6, Folder 12, Gittings Papers.

327   *Lilli Vincenz soon . . . picketing sign*: *The Ladder* 10, no. 1 (October 1965), 1.

327   *After the riots . . . homophile movement*: Marcus, *Making Gay History*, 136. See also Marotta, *The Politics of Homosexuality*, 142–43.

327   *Indeed, the GLF . . . the revolution"*: Donn Teal, *The Gay Militants* (New York: Stein and Day, 1971), 89–90. For one moderate GLF faction, the last straw came in November 1969, when the organization considered a proposal to donate five hundred dollars to the Black Panthers. Its proponents argued that homosexuals had a moral obligation to support the Black radicals: where would homosexuals be without the Black freedom movement? The proposal's opponents pointed to the Panthers' tendency to refer to their enemies as "faggots." ("Homosexuality is a sickness, just as are baby-rape or wanting to be head of General Motors," wrote Eldridge Cleaver, a protégé of Stokely Carmichael, in *Soul on Ice*.) Plus, if the GLF spent all its money on other movements, what would be left for the homosexuals? Even Martha Shelley opposed the measure, but after three interminable meetings, the GLF passed it. Shelley remained, but the moderates walked out, and Jim Owles resigned as GLF treasurer. See Faderman, *The Gay Revolution*, 210; Peniel E. Joseph, *Stokely: A Life* (New York: Basic Civitas Books, 2016), 177, 181; Marotta, *The Politics of Homosexuality*, 135, 142–43; Marcus, *Making Gay History*, 137–38.

327   *On November 24 . . . on gay liberation*: Arthur Bell, *Dancing the Gay Lib Blues: A Year in the Homosexual Liberation Movement* (New York: Simon and Schuster, 1971), 17.

327   *They adopted Robert's . . . elite*: For early activities of the Legal Committee, see Hal Weiner to Ken Burdick, January 13, 1970, Box 16, Folder 17, Gay Activists Alliance Collection, New York Public Library, New York, NY (hereafter, "GAA Papers").

327   *They called themselves . . . represent action*: Bell, *Dancing the Gay Lib Blues*, 18–19; Marotta, *The Politics of Homosexuality*, 145.

327   *One week later . . . staff as columnists*: Masthead, *GAY*, December 1, 1969, 2.

327   *by April . . . recorder in hand*: Masthead, *GAY*, April 13, 1970, 2; Marcus, *Making Gay History*, 139.

328   *In its . . . fully exposed*: "Gay is Good!," *GAY*, December 1, 1969, 18.

328   *After the tumultuous . . . resolutions*: Robert Angell, "Dissociation from ERCHO Resolutions," January 1970, Box 64, Folder 8, Gittings Papers.

328   *The MSNY voted . . . their attempt"*: Robert Amsel to ERCHO Secretary, December 1, 1969, Box 68, Folder 2, Gittings Papers.

328   *"My feeling was . . . Foster Gunnison*: Foster Gunnison to ISE Associates & Correspondents, November 12, 1969, Box 5, Folder 1, FEK Papers.

328   *Despite Kameny's personal . . . membership—refused to dissociate*: Robert Angell, "Dissociation from ERCHO Resolutions," January 1970, Box 64, Folder 8, Gittings Papers.

328   *On November 15 . . . phone number*: Bob Martin, "Radicalism and Homosexuality," November 1969, Box 75, Folder 7, Gittings Papers.

328   *Martin joined fifty thousand . . . ram*: Teal, *The Gay Militants*, 82.

328 *"I got teargassed," . . . all-night orgy"*: Bob Martin to "Ralph," December 12, 1969, Box 1, Folder 7, Donaldson Papers.

328 *Kameny, because NACHO . . . and the flyer*: FEK to NACHO, Draft, n.d., Box 76, Folder 1, Gittings Papers.

329 *"He is, of . . . Gunnison*: FEK to Foster Gunnison, November 18, 1969, Box 5, Folder 1, FEK Papers.

329 *"I'm increasingly coming . . . certainly untrustworthy"*: FEK to Foster Gunnison, November 14, 1969, Box 5, Folder 1, FEK Papers.

329 Come homosexuals . . . are a-changin': Bob Martin to Foster Gunnison, November 18, 1969, Box 7, Folder 5, FEK Papers.

329 *Six months later . . . joined the Navy"*: Bob Martin to "JD and Don," June 9, 1970, Box 2, Folder 24, Donaldson Papers.

329 *"All but Frank . . . training that summer*: Ibid.

329 *Only days after . . . DECEMBER MEMBERSHIP MEETING"*: FEK, "Announcement of Special Speaker(s) at December Membership Meeting," December 4, 1969, Box 68, Folder 6, Gittings Papers.

329 *R. D. Carter Jr. . . . ideology, and oppression"*: Ibid.

330 *Article II of . . . for all"*: See Chapter Six.

330 *It was a . . . admitted Kameny*: FEK, "Announcement of Special Speaker(s) at December Membership Meeting," December 4, 1969, Box 68, Folder 6, Gittings Papers.

330 *The Society, after . . . population*: Rebecca C. Dolinsky, "Lesbian and Gay DC: Identity, Emotion, and Experience in Washington, DC's Social and Activist Communities (1961–1986)" (PhD dissertation, University of California, Santa Cruz, 2010), 103.

330 *The executive board . . . THE HOMOPHILE MOVEMENT"*: "The Negro and the Homophile Movement," n.d., Box 85, Folder 3, FEK Papers. The flyer is undated, but it refers to two phone numbers with telephone exchange names, which were replaced by all-digit numbers by 1965. See, for example, *The Insider*, September 1965, Box 8, Folder 6, MSNY Papers. For more on the flyer and the topic of race in the MSW, see Kent W. Peacock, "Race, the Homosexual, and the Mattachine Society of Washington, 1961–1970," *Journal of the History of Sexuality* 25 no. 2 (2016), 267–96.

330 *"The white homosexual . . . statement of purposes*: Ibid.

330 *Black homosexuals never . . . join?*: A. Billy S. Jones-Hennin, quoted in Dolinsky, "Lesbian and Gay DC," 7–8.

330 *Black homophile activists . . . progress being made*: See Chapter Fourteen.

330 *Once, when a . . . federal agent*: Peacock, "Race, the Homosexual, and the Mattachine Society of Washington, 1961–1970," 269.

331 *"Let's open some . . . his members*: "The Negro and the Homophile Movement," n.d., Box 85, Folder 3, FEK Papers.

331 *On December 4 . . . future"*: Ibid.

331 *After the meeting . . . homosexuals again*: RD Carter Jr., interviewed by Eric Cervini, telephone, March 1, 2019.

331 *That week, Kameny's . . . Union"*: FEK to Friends, December 1, 1969, Box 6, Folder 14, Gittings Papers.

331 *The astronomer's homosexual . . . became official*: "About when will the Ulrich and Wentworth cases be ready for court? Are we going to handle them here?" asked Legal Director Ralph Temple later that month. ("Please confine your answer to ten lines," he added.) See Ralph J. Temple to FEK, December 17, 1969, Box 75, Folder 6, FEK Papers.

331 *Kameny wrote to . . . he said*: FEK to Ralph J. Temple, December 18, 1969, Box 75, Folder 6, FEK Papers. Kameny's fight against the Pentagon had acquired new urgency. On December 12, the District of Columbia Circuit released its decision in the case of Robert Adams, a friend of Kameny and an engineer at a private defense firm. In 1964, during a security clearance investigation, Adams admitted homosexual activity. "His case would have gone rather differently if either I had not had to work the day of his interrogation, or if he had followed the advice and coaching which I gave him at great length before his interrogation," Kameny later complained. The MSW president referred him to NCACLU attorneys, who took his case and represented him—instead of Kameny—in Adams's internal Pentagon hearings. In a 2–1 decision, a federal appeals court upheld the revocation of his security clearance. The Pentagon afforded Adams sufficient due process, concluded the majority, partially because his NCACLU lawyers failed to use the administrative hearings to explore "the relationship between the conduct with which he was charged and his capacity to protect classified information." If homosexuals were to win against the Pentagon, they needed to make the "nexus" argument from the beginning, not just in court. Kameny's involvement became all the more crucial, since he established the record for judges' later consideration. The *Adams* decision also provided hope: in liberal judge Skelly Wright's dissent, he identified publicity as an antidote to the security risk. "Certainly after the publicity surrounding this court suit, his alleged homosexuality is no longer a basis for blackmail, if indeed it ever was." Wright also provided a helpful term for the Pentagon's policies of exclusion, a label familiar to the MSW: "the Board's ruling is in effect a bill of attainder against all homosexuals," he concluded. See FEK to James Kepner, December 21, 1969, Box 1, Folder 9, FEK Papers; *Adams v. Laird*, 420 F.2d 230 (D.C. Circ. 1969).

331　*On January 14 . . . to blackmail*: "Supplemental Determination of Examiner Raymond A. Waldman," January 14, 1970, Box 8, Folder 10, Gittings Papers.

331　*The examiner was . . . his official appeal*: FEK and Barbara Gittings, "Notice of Appeal," January 17, 1970, Box 8, Folder 10, Gittings Papers.

331　*"We do not . . . the courts"*: Department of Defense, "In the Matter of Benning Wentworth," March 30, 1970, Box 37, Folder 10, FEK Papers.

332　*Lilli Vincenz, reporting . . . or ten"*: Lily Hansen, "Pitch Forks in the Pentagon," *GAY*, April 27, 1970, 7.

332　*The Department of Defense . . . release*: "News Release," February 2, 1970, Box 8, Folder 10, Gittings Papers. By labeling Ulrich safe from blackmail, the Pentagon had taken the case and "gold-plated it, studded it with diamonds, and handed it back to us on a silver platter as a superbly-fashioned test case," wrote Kameny. See FEK to Richard L. Gayer, December 1, 1969, Box 7, Folder 9, Gittings Papers.

332　*Because the Pentagon . . . hearing*: FEK to Richard L. Gayer, February 27, 1970, Box 22, Folder 7, FEK Papers.

332　*Instead, the Department . . . how many people?*: Department of Defense, "Interrogatories to Applicant," 1970, Box 8, Folder 2, Gittings Papers.

332　*Ulrich refused to . . . Ulrich's name*: FEK to Sam J. Ervin Jr., April 18, 1970, Box 8, Folder 8, Gittings Papers.

333　*On February 6 . . . defense team*: "News Release," February 6, 1970, Box 7, Folder 9, Gittings Papers. Gayer later confirmed that the language attributed to him was likely drafted by Kameny himself. See Richard Gayer, interviewed by Eric Cervini, telephone, October 10, 2019.

333　*To proactively address . . . Senator Ervin*: FEK, "Affidavit," February 6, 1970, Box 7, Folder 9, Gittings Papers.

333　*On March 5 . . . Graves*: FEK to Alfred Rosran, March 7, 1970, Box 16, Folder 15, FEK Papers. Kameny had reason to believe his attorneys, the same men who had represented Clifford Norton after his dismissal from NASA, would eventually win. Only days earlier, the United States Solicitor General decided against appealing the Norton, thus avoiding a potential loss for the CSC in the Supreme Court. Norton prepared to resume his job at NASA and receive over one hundred thousand dollars (today, more than half a million dollars) in back pay. After the victories of Norton and Scott, however, the state of Kameny's second battle—against the Civil Service Commission—still remained in flux. On April 21, the Supreme Court rejected the petitions for writs of certiorari filed by the NCACLU on behalf of MSW charter member Dick Schlegel. See NACHO Committee on the Federal Government, "Memorandum," February 20, 1970, Box 97, Folder 6, Gittings Papers; Norman Dorsen to Carter Durden, January 7, 1971, Box 335, Folder 1, ACLU Papers.

333　*Yes, admitted Kameny . . . did, yes"*: The transcript of this hearing is not found in Kameny's papers, but Examiner Klyde makes reference to these admissions in his determination. See Department of Defense, "Determination of Examiner Charles J. Kylde," August 13, 1970, Box 44, Folder 14, FEK Papers.

334　*In Washington, months . . . homosexuals*: See Chapter Eighteen.

334　*Then, one night . . . the confrontation*: Carter, *Stonewall*, 228; Eisenbach, *Gay Power* (New York: Carroll & Graf, 2006), 131.

334　*When Marty Robinson joined . . . straight establishment*: Larry P. Gross, *Up from Invisibility: Lesbians, Gay Men, and the Media in America* (New York: Columbia University Press, 2001), 46.

334　*As for the . . . and resist"*: Ibid.

334　*"months on a psychiatrist's couch"*: Eisenbach, *Gay Power*, 130.

334　*First, the activists . . . they asked*: Kay Tobin, "Gay Activists Confront Politicos," *GAY*, March 1, 1970 3. See also Teal, *The Gay Militants*, 114.

334　*In April*: The turning point occurred on the evening of Saturday, March 7. The Snake Pit was an illegal after-hours gay bar—open from midnight to 8:00 a.m.—in a small basement. It had a capacity for fifty patrons, but at 5:00 Sunday morning, it held more than two hundred. Inspector Seymour Pine, the same man who led the Stonewall raid, arrived at the Snake Pit to serve liquor violation papers. Fearing another riot, Pine and his plainclothesmen officers arrested 163 patrons and confined them to a large room at the police station. Nobody knew their charges; nobody was told their rights. "Suddenly, I hear a sound, like something falling, then screams," recalled one patron. Diego Vinales, an immigrant from Argentina, feared being deported after a homosexual arrest. He ran up a flight of stairs and attempted to escape out a window. He fell, landing on the police station's iron picket fence. Six fourteen-inch spikes pierced his body. Firemen used a blowtorch to sever the fence and bring the still-impaled victim to the hospital, where, miraculously, he survived. The next day, the GAA distributed three thousand flyers to announce a rally that night: "Any way you look at it—that boy was PUSHED!! We are ALL being pushed." The GAA activists invited their peers in the GLF, who then invited their straight peers in the New Left. Five hundred demonstrators marched to the police station to demand an end to gay bar raids. Despite differences in strategy and ideology, solidarity prevailed. "Shouts and chants of *GAY* POWER! filled the air," reported *GAY*. The homosexuals then solemnly marched to St. Vincent's Hospital, where Vinales remained in critical condition. Within days, Congressman Ed Koch, the future mayor of New York, wrote to the police commissioner to protest the harassment of homosexuals. Meanwhile, zaps began occurring at an increasing rate. See Jonathan Black, "The Boys in the Snake Pit: Games 'Straights' Play," *The Village Voice*, March 19, 1970, 1; "500 Angry Homosexuals Protest Raid," *GAY*,

April 13, 1970, 3; "Political Club Acts to Halt Raids," *GAY*, April 13, 1970, 10; GAA, "Koch Issues Statement on Homosexual Rights," September 12, 1970, Box 87, Folder 4, FEK Papers. See also Teal, *The Gay Militants*, 102; Marotta, *The Politics of Homosexuality*, 154.

334   *while Mayor John . . . Mayor?"*: Faderman, *The Gay Revolution*, 244; Teal, *The Gay Militants*, 121.

335   *The next week . . . job discrimination"*: Though WNEW-TV edited the homosexuals out of that night's show, the zaps still seemed to be working. Not only did the straight members of the television studio audience join the homosexuals' chants after they were escorted away ("Answer the questions!"), but the GAA began receiving concessions from officials fearful of disruption. See Sandra Vaughn, "Lindsay & Homosexuals: An Edited Encounter," *The Village Voice*, April 23, 1970, 8.

335   *Within days of . . . Eleanor Holmes Norton*: "GAA Meets with City Brass," *GAY*, May 25, 1970, 3; "N.Y. Rights Commissioner Backs Employment Demands," *GAY*, May 18, 1970, 20.

335   *On May 13 . . . city council*: "Councilman Greitzer Yields to Gay Activists," *GAY*, June 1, 1970, 3.

335   *News of the . . . "Auschwitz"*: Bayer, *Homosexuality and American Psychiatry*, 103.

335   *A man in . . . in session"*: "GLF and Women's Lib Zap Shrinks," *GAY*, June 8, 1970, 3.

335   *Meanwhile, Dick Leitsch . . . it advised*: MSNY, "If You Are in a Raid," 1970, Box 78, Folder 10, FEK Papers.

335   *On May 1 . . . auditorium*: "The Lavender Menace Strikes," *Come Out!* 1, no. 4 (June/July 1970), 14.

335   *Neither women's liberation . . . men"*: Clendinen and Nagourney, *Out for Good*, 85.

335   *In GLF meetings . . . magazine*: Martha Shelley, quoted in Faderman, *The Gay Revolution*, 228.

335   *Meanwhile, National Organization . . . liberation movement*: Ibid., 253.

336   *A group of . . . Radicalesbians*: Ibid., 233.

336   *"A lesbian," they . . . of explosion"*: Radicalesbians, "The Woman Identified Woman," n.d., Folder 15230, Lesbian Herstory Archives, New York, NY.

336   *To assert their . . . on them*: "The Lavender Menace Strikes," *Come Out!* 1, no. 4 (June/July 1970), 14.

336   *Shelley grabbed the . . . the floor*: Martha Shelley, interviewed by Kelly Anderson, San Francisco, CA, October 12, 2003, Voices of Feminism Oral History Project, Sophia Smith Collection, Smith College, Northampton, MA. See also Clendinen and Nagourney, *Out for Good*, 90–91.

336   *For two hours . . . anytime, anyplace"*: "The Lavender Menace Strikes," *Come Out!* 1, no. 4 (June/July 1970), 14.

336   *Someday, as Gittings . . . gay liberation"*: Barbara Gittings, interviewed by Kay Tobin Lahusen, 1969–1971, Box 122, Folder 4, Gittings Papers.

336   *Eva Freund, on . . . by men*: Eva Freund, interviewed by Eric Cervini, telephone, December 14, 2018.

336   *"Goodbye to the . . . the mark"*: Del Martin, "Female Gay Blasts Men, Leaves Movement," *The Advocate* 4, no. 18 (October 28–November 10, 1970), 21.

337   *Standing before a . . . your honor"*: Harold M. Weiner, "Oscar Wilde Died for Our Sins," *Juris Doctor*, November 1971, 56, clipping in Box 16, Folder 8, GAA Papers.

337   *Born in the . . . by their families*: Duberman, *Stonewall*, 27–28, 80.

337   *The street kids . . . of their own*: See Chapter Seventeen.

337   *Only days after . . . Washington Square*: "Gay Liberation Meetings," *The Ladder* 14, no. 1/2 (October/November 1969), 40. See also Carter, *Stonewall*, 213–14.

337   *In March 1970 . . . are needed!"*: Bell, *Dancing the Gay Lib Blues*, 64–65. In New York, no organization yet existed to help trans women—let alone frequently homeless trans women—like Rivera. There was the Erickson Educational Foundation, an organization funded by trans millionaire Reed Erickson, but it concentrated on trans research and education. And a few months after Rivera joined GAA, a group of fifteen trans women split from the Los Angeles GLF to create the Transvestite-Transsexual Action Organization. "I'd had my fill," wrote founder Angela Douglas, "of insults from gays, all demanding I be a man and stop dressing as a woman." Drag queens, too, felt excluded. As Lee Brewster complained in December 1969, "The organizations really do look down on the drag queen. They say they don't, but they do." See "Reed Erickson and the Erickson Educational Foundation," Transgender Archives, University of Victoria, https://www.uvic.ca /transgenderarchives/collections/reed-erickson/index.php; "TV's and Transsexuals Organize," *GAY*, June 22, 1970, 12; "Drag Queens to Form Their Own Organization," *GAY*, December 1, 1969, 10.

337   *At 7:30 p.m. . . . democratic act*: Criminal Court of the City of New York, "*The People of the State of New York v. Rey Rivera*," July 6, 1970, Box 16, Folder 8, GAA Papers.

337   *The officer dragged . . . disorderly conduct*: Ibid. See also Bell, *Dancing the Gay Lib Blues*, 62–63.

338   *No lawyer agreed to represent her*: GAA Legal Action Committee, "A Report to GAA," July 8, 1971, Box 16, Folder 7, GAA Papers.

338   *On May 21 . . . courtroom*: GAA Meeting Minutes, May 21, 1970, Box 19, Folder 1, GAA Papers.

338   *To everyone's surprise . . . legal committee*: GAA Meeting Minutes, June 11, 1970, Box 19, Folder 1, GAA Papers; GAA Legal Action Committee, "A Report to GAA," July 8, 1971, Box 16, Folder 7, GAA Papers.

338   *Though Rivera's arresting . . . the case*: Over the course of three months and five aborted hearings, Rivera fought the charges while facing a new one: in July, she was arrested once again, this time for "female impersonation." The GAA collected fifty dollars for her bail fund, and in August, a new judge finally dismissed the disorderly

conduct charges. See GAA Meeting Minutes, May 21, 1970, Box 19, Folder 1, GAA Papers; GAA Meeting Minutes, May 28, 1970, Box 19, Folder 1, GAA Papers; GAA Meeting Minutes, June 4, 1970, Box 19, Folder 1, GAA Papers; GAA Meeting Minutes, June 11, 1970, Box 19, Folder 1, GAA Papers; GAA Meeting Minutes, June 18, 1970, Box 19, Folder 1, GAA Papers; GAA Meeting Minutes, June 25, 1970, Box 19, Folder 1, GAA Papers; GAA Meeting Minutes, July 2, 1970, Box 19, Folder 1, GAA Papers; GAA Meeting Minutes, July 9, 1970, Box 19, Folder 1, GAA Papers; GAA Meeting Minutes, July 30, 1970, Box 19, Folder 1, GAA Papers.

338 *On September 20 . . . activists arrived*: Arthur Bell, "Sylvia Goes to College: 'Gay Is Proud' at NYU," *The Village Voice*, October 15, 1970, 61. See also Bell, *Dancing the Gay Lib Blues*, 112.

338 *For five nights . . . GAA stayed away*: Marcus, *Making Gay History*, 151–52. According to Arthur Bell, the GLF activists worried the GAA members would take over their action; meanwhile, though the GAA executive committee endorsed the sit-in, it refrained from officially joining the action until a full membership meeting. See Bell, *Dancing the Gay Lib Blues*, 116; GAA Executive Committee, Emergency Meeting Minutes, September 21, 1970, Box 15, Folder 15, GAA Papers.

338 *At 2:30 Friday . . . crowd disbanded*: Bell, *Dancing the Gay Lib Blues*, 117–18. "Pandemonium followed," reported Arthur Bell for *The Village Voice*. Rivera and her fellow street queens led the demonstrators in a march. "We took to the center of the street, holding hands, gays, straights, street people, transvestites, middle-class people, college kids, chanting, dancing, stomping, 'Power to the people,'" wrote Bell. See Bell, "Sylvia Goes to College: 'Gay Is Proud' at NYU."

338 *The following week . . . refused to participate*: Ibid., 120.

338 *According to its . . . related actions"*: GAA Executive Committee Meeting Minutes, October 4, 1970, Box 15, Folder 15, GAA Papers.

338 *Disillusioned by the . . . (STAR), instead*: Bell, *Dancing the Gay Lib Blues*, 120–21.

339 *Craig Rodwell, the . . . Washington's homosexuals*: Foster Gunnison to ERCHO Executive Committee, February 9, 1970, Box 64, Folder 8, Gittings Papers.

339 *"It is . . . New Free"*: John Francis Hunter, "Gay Pride on Parade," *GAY*, June 29, 1970, 10.

339 *"It is hoped . . . to MSW members*: John Marshall to MSW Members, May 28, 1970, Box 68, Folder 7, Gittings Papers.

339 *After the June . . . FBI headquarters*: Lilli Vincenz, "Fertility Rites for Lesbians: And Other Matters," *GAY*, July 27, 1970, 6.

340 *On Sunday afternoon, June 28*: The day before the march, Kameny and thirty-one other activists met at Central Commercial High School for the 1970 ERCHO conference. The meeting was a shadow of the alliance the MSW president had once imagined: in February, the ERCHO executive committee had voted to suspend the alliance's bylaws to test an "alternative structure." The strategic move, intended to prevent further domination by the GLF, prevented ERCHO from adopting resolutions or participating in official actions. It was, as the conservative Foster Gunnison complained, "a curious move akin to shooting oneself in the head to prevent the next guy from doing it for you." For a single day, the delegates discussed political action and confrontation, religion, organizational mechanics, self-liberation, the law. The low attendance caused the groups to lose nearly one hundred dollars on the event. ERCHO never met again. See Foster Gunnison to *Playboy* Forum, April 15, 1970, Box 64, Folder 8, Gittings Papers; Craig Schoonmaker, "Homosexual Conference," June 27, 1970, Box 67, Folder 4, Gittings Papers; "Special Accounting ERCHO Spring Conference," July 1, 1970, Box 67, Folder 1, Gittings Papers.

340 *Frank Kameny stood . . . later explained*: Lahusen interview.

340 *It was a . . . to fight back*: Ibid.

340 *"We are united . . . Homosexual Community"*: Kay Tobin, "Thousands Take Part in Gay Marches," *GAY*, July 20, 1970, 12.

340 *As the crowd . . . angry onlookers*: Carter, *Stonewall*, 253.

340 *At 2:00 p.m. . . . followed*: Ibid.; Lacey Fosburgh, "Thousands of Homosexuals Hold a Protest Rally in Central Park," *The New York Times*, June 29, 1970, 1.

340 *Randy Wicker wore a lambda shirt*: Kay Tobin, "Peter Ogren, Prescott Townsend, Tom Doerr, Mark Golderman, and Randy Wicker in Sheep Meadow," June 28, 1970, New York Public Library Digital Collections, https://digitalcollections.nypl.org/items/510d47e3-af4d-a3d9-e040-e00a18064a99.

340 *Next marched the . . . bell bottoms*: Diana Davies, "Christopher Street Liberation Day, 1970, contact sheet 5," June 28, 1970, New York Public Library Digital Collections, https://digitalcollections.nypl.org/items/8c73c0e3-b1d3-22b7-e040-e00a18061874.

340 *Behind them marched . . . it said*: Kay Tobin, "Frank Kameny and Mattachine Society of Washington Members Marching," June 28, 1970, New York Public Library Digital Collections, https://digitalcollections.nypl.org/items/510d47e3-af4c-a3d9-e040-e00a18064a99.

340 The Gay Blade *editor . . . the day*: Nancy Tucker, interviewed by Eric Cervini, telephone, February 26, 2019.

341 *Lilli Vincenz arrived . . . HI MOM*: Lilli Vincenz, "Gay and Proud," 1970, The National Audio-Visual Conservation Center, Library of Congress, https://www.loc.gov/item/mbrs01991430.

341   *The marchers started . . . one attendee*: Jason Gould, "Homosexual Liberation Day 1970," *GAY*, July 20, 1970, 4; Carter, *Stonewall*, 253.

341   *As the masses . . . the sidewalk*: Ibid.

341   *He was surrounded . . . than homosexuals"*: Suzannah Lessard, "Gay Is Good for Us All," *Washington Monthly*, December 1970, 39.

341   *No, they did . . . by"*: Fosburgh, "Thousands of Homosexuals Hold a Protest Rally in Central Park."

342   *Drag queens seemed . . . it said*: Diana Davies, "Christopher Street Liberation Day, 1970, contact sheet 5," June 28, 1970, New York Public Library Digital Collections, https://digitalcollections.nypl.org/items/8c73c0e3 -b1d3-22b7-e040-e00a18061874.

342   *There, a gay . . . nine hours*: Gould, "Homosexual Liberation Day 1970."

342   *Kameny reached the . . . Others cheered*: Lahusen interview; Nichols, "Chapter Ten," *Memoirs of Jack Nichols*.

342   *"We were . . . was pure exultation"*: Gould, "Homosexual Liberation Day 1970."

342   *But Kameny stood . . . his fellow despised*: Lahusen interview; Nichols, "Chapter Ten," *Memoirs of Jack Nichols*.

342   *Sylvia Rivera dancing. . . . women shirtless*: Vincenz, "Gay and Proud."

342   *Hugging, kissing, oral sex*: Gould, "Homosexual Liberation Day 1970."

342   *"Tell me how . . . dropped an eyelash"*: Vincenz, "Gay and Proud."

342   *"It was a . . . dark closets"*: Jack Nichols and Lige Clarke, "Love's Coming of Age: June 28, 1970," *GAY*, July 20, 1970, 2.

342   *That night, after . . . Is Born*: Gould, "Homosexual Liberation Day 1970."

342   *Several months later . . . Five thousand"*: Lahusen interview.

343   *Two days after . . . in Georgetown*: "Gay Liberation Front," *The Gay Blade* 1, no. 10 (July 1970), 1; Nancy Tucker, "Washington File: Gay Activities Multiply," *The Advocate*, September 2–15, 1970, 17; Nancy Tucker, interviewed by Eric Cervini, telephone, February 26, 2019.

343   *In October 1969 . . . spaghetti dinners*: "Homosexual Social League forms in D.C.," *The Advocate*, April 29– May 12, 1970, 6; *The Gay Blade* 1, no. 5 (February 1970), 1; *The Gay Blade* 1, no. 6 (March 1970), 1.

343   *In the spring . . . interviews*: They also removed the twenty-one-year-old minimum age, the requirement for non-members to acquire invitations to attend meetings, and the cap of two sets of membership records. See "Interior Decorating for Mattachine," *The Gay Blade* 1, no. 5 (February 1970), 2.

343   *Kameny, consolidating his . . . board*: MSW, "Meeting Notice and Ballot," June 11, 1970, Box 68, Folder 7, Gittings Papers.

343   *The Society continued . . . legal cases*: In February, a lieutenant from the Metropolitan Police's Morals Division lectured on "Blackmail and Homosexuality," an event to assure homosexuals that they could report instances of blackmail, without fear of exposure, to the police (Kameny promptly cited the lieutenant's promises in Ulrich's security clearance appeal). In March, the Society featured a Dallas-based attorney, who talked about his efforts to overturn Texas's sodomy statute. Only nine members attended. See MSW, "Meeting Notice," February 5, 1970, Box 85, FEK Papers; "Bulletin," February 3, 1970, Box 85, Folder 13, FEK Papers; FEK, "Affidavit," in Otto H. Ulrich Jr., "Statement in Response to Statement of Reasons," February 6, 1970, Box 8, Folder 8, Gittings Papers; Handwritten Meeting Minutes, February 1970, Box 85, Folder 9, FEK Papers; "Meeting Notice," March 5, 1970, Box 85, Folder 9, FEK Papers.

343   *In April 1970 . . . League*: *The Gay Blade* 1, no. 7 (April 1970), 1.

343   *That same month . . . disorderly conduct*: Nancy Tucker, "Washington File," *The Advocate*, July 8–21, 1970, 24.

344   *When antiwar activists protested . . . at Kent State*: Gitlin, *The Sixties*, 410.

344   *On May 9 . . . visibly stoned*: "N.Y. Gays Join in Washington War Protest," *The Advocate*, June 10–23, 1970, 4; *The Gay Blade* 1, no. 8 (May 1970), 1.

344   *A few weeks . . . said*: Michael Yarr, in "50th Anniversary of the Mattachine Society of Washington Panel Discussion," Rainbow History Project, June 7, 2014.

344   *"That Suharto is . . . Front, he advertised*: Mike Yarr, "Letters," June 9–19, 1970, *Quicksilver Times*, 2.

344   *Yarr, along with . . . Washington galvanized*: Michael Yarr, in "50th Anniversary of the Mattachine Society of Washington Panel Discussion," Rainbow History Project, June 7, 2014.

344   *"There was madness . . . or both*: Brian Miller, in "50th Anniversary of the Mattachine Society of Washington Panel Discussion," Rainbow History Project, June 7, 2014.

344   *MSW member Nancy . . . as "girls"*: Nancy Tucker, interviewed by Eric Cervini, telephone, February 26, 2019.

344   *Because meetings did . . . Frank Kameny*: Ibid.

345   *To the GLF . . . police officers*: Brian Miller, in "50th Anniversary of the Mattachine Society of Washington Panel Discussion," Rainbow History Project, June 7, 2014.

345   *Yet Washington's Gay . . . GLFer, who wore slacks*: Tucker, "Washington File: Gay Activities Multiply"; *The Advocate* 1, no. 10 (July 1970), 1.

345   *"The group, with . . . ACLU"*: Ibid.; "A Letter to Bar Owners," *The Gay Blade* 1, no. 11 (August 1970), 1.

345   *With the unique . . . means committee*: Ibid.

345   *In August, no . . . or sex*: He had uncovered evidence that bars were unfairly applying age checks, drink minimums, and dress codes to Black and female patrons. He threatened to take "necessary steps to bring these

discriminatory patterns to an end" and requested a meeting; he suggested a cooperative of bar owners like the San Francisco Tavern Guild. To reach any of the groups, bar owners could write to his address on Cathedral Avenue. FEK to the 1832 Club, August 21, 1970, Box 92, Folder 4, FEK Papers.

346 *The groups appeared . . . satisfaction," wrote Kameny*: FEK to Kay Lahusen, October 28, 1970, Box 119, Folder 9, Gittings Papers. Nancy Tucker's *Gay Blade* served as a community newsletter for all three groups, all of which worked through the courts. When *the Gay Blade* learned of plainclothes police officers arresting gay men who cruised in Georgetown, Tucker published a warning and advertisement: "*The Gay Blade* and all 3 organizations urge you to avoid Georgetown for the time being unless you want to help challenge the police on this matter. If you want to act as a test case, contact GLF at 265–2181, HSL at 779–5725 or MSW at 363–3881." See "Uglies in Georgetown," *The Gay Blade* 2, no. 2 (November 1970), 1.

346 *On the third . . . suspend itself*: Later, it was replaced by a "panel" on the federal government, and the delegates still planned to meet in 1971. See Rob Cole, "NACHO 'Liberated' on Final Day," *The Advocate*, October 14–27, 1970, 8.

346 *That afternoon, the . . . session*: Ibid.; "N.A.C.H.O. 70'—San Francisco," *New York Mattachine Times*, September 1970, 9.

346 *The radicals passed . . . Asia"*: NACHO Meeting Minutes, August 27, 1970, Box 68, Folder 8, FEK Papers.

346 *That night, State . . . Black mayor*: "Brown Urges Gays Join with Other Minorities," *The Advocate*, September 30–October 13, 1970, 5.

346 *Kameny returned to . . . divisible too"*: Lahusen interview.

347 *On November 9 . . . told the audience*: "Homosexual Leader Hits Church," *Daily News* (Washington), November 10, 1970, clipping in Box 92, Folder 4, FEK Papers; "A Seminar on Theology and Homosexuality," *The Washington Evening Star*, October 18, 1970, B7.

347 *The audience was . . . tour"*: Ibid.

347 *The next . . . Advocate*: "Gays Tell It Like It Is at Catholic Seminar," *The Advocate*, December 9, 1970, 7.

347 *On Wednesday afternoon . . . talking about us"*: Ibid.

347 *While Cavanagh held . . . but content*: Ibid.

347 *Three days later . . . homosexuals*: FEK to James R. Adams, November 15, 1970, Box 158, Folder 8, FEK Papers. Securing the venue had been a feat in itself. "As you might suspect, a great many members of the Vestry (including myself) are somewhat nervous and upset by the idea of 'gay' dances," admitted the church's priest. But St. Mark's ultimately permitted the dance. See James R. Adams to FEK, September 23, 1970, Box 158, Folder 8, FEK Papers.

348 *The organizations split . . . $164.61 profit*: "Statement of Receipts and Expenses for Joint MSW-HSL-GLF Dance," November 14, 1970, Box 158, Folder 8, FEK Papers.

348 *Kameny made arrangements . . . in January*: FEK, "Check No. 322, Jan 16 Dance, Liquor License," January 4, 1970, Box 85, Folder 2, FEK Papers.

348 *"day which will live in infamy"*: FEK to Joseph J. Liebling, July 20, 1970, Box 37, Folder 5, FEK Papers.

348 *Kameny wrote to . . . all three cases*: FEK to Richard L. Gayer, Otto H. Ulrich, and Benning Wentworth, July 25, 1970, Box 22, Folder 7, FEK Papers.

348 *Kameny formally withdrew . . . the three men*: FEK to Joseph J. Liebling, August 21, 1970, Box 37, Folder 5, FEK Papers.

348 *by the end . . . their complaints*: "Complaint for Declaratory Judgment and Injunction," *Wentworth v. Laird*, November 30, 1970, Box 38, Folder 2, FEK Papers; "Complaint for Declaratory Judgment and Injunction," *Gayer v. Laird*, November 30, 1970, Box 22, Folder 8, FEK Papers; "Complaint for Declaratory Judgment and Injunction," *Ulrich v. Laird*, November 3, 1970, Box 35, Folder 9, FEK Papers.

348 *With Crawford's case . . . the NCACLU pipeline*: FEK to Ralph J. Temple, January 3, 1971, Box 17, Folder 8, FEK Papers.

348 *Kameny had only . . . left to argue*: "Determination of Examiner Charles J. Klyde," August 13, 1970, Box 44, Folder 14, FEK Papers.

348 *He could not . . . his NCACLU dues*: Florence Robin to FEK, May 5, 1970, Box 75, Folder 7, FEK Papers.

348 *he then lost . . . the executive board*: In February 1971, Kameny referred to himself as a "former member of the Washington-area executive board." See "Kameny Announces Candidacy for D.C. Delegate," February 3, 1971, Box 17, Folder 1, Vincenz Papers.

348 *Over the fall . . . Gay Mystique*: Dorothy Ruth Crouch to Barbara Gittings, August 11, 1970, Box 119, Box 8, Gittings Papers.

348 *"I am aghast . . . to hold"*: Kay Tobin Lahusen to FEK, November 26, 1970, Box 6, Folder 16, Gittings Papers.

348 *To make matters . . . slowly and carefully*: FEK to Robert A. Martin, January 7, 1971, Box 26, Folder 15, FEK Papers.

348 *The Society continued . . . Liberation Day march*: "Gay and Proud," *The Gay Blade* 2, no. 4 (January 1971), 1.

349 *The ACLU, even . . . sodomy laws*: *The Gay Blade* 1, no. 12 (September 1970), 2.

349   *The GLF, meanwhile . . . its informal headquarters*: Brian Miller, in "50th Anniversary of the Mattachine Society of Washington Panel Discussion," Rainbow History Project, June 7, 2014.

349   *With Kameny's help . . . gays"*: "Gay Liberation," *The Gay Blade* 2, no. 5 (February 1971), 2; Nancy Tucker, "Washington File: Plus One Gets Zapped," *The Advocate*, February 17–March 2, 1971, 13. Meanwhile, in late November, twelve GLF-NY members—they became known as the "DC 12"—were arrested for trashing a straight bar that refused to serve them. See Ned Scharff, "The New Radicals," *The Washington Evening Star*, January 24, 1971, D1.

349   *Even the HSL . . . in Georgetown*: *The Gay Blade* 2, no. 3 (December 1970), 2.

349   *Kameny had become . . . Bulletin termed him*: "'Other Society' Wants Equality," *Bulletin* (Philadelphia), July 19, 1970, clipping in Box 67, Folder 5, Gittings Papers.

349   *Washington's second MSW-GLF-HSL . . . an idea*: FEK to Thomas W. Parker, January 26, 1971, Box 8, Folder 6, FEK Papers; Lilli Vincenz, interviewed by Genny Beemyn, Arlington, VA, June 6, 1998.

349   *A few months . . . Congress," it said*: Ibid.

349   *No, Kameny would . . . of his minority*: Ibid.

350   *Kameny reacted with . . . signatures per day*: Ibid.

350   *Dubious of his . . . it, too*: Ibid.

350   *Kameny disliked popular . . . waltz*: Lahusen interview.

350   *Lilli Vincenz kissed . . . she said*: Lilli Vincenz, interviewed by Genny Beemyn, Arlington, VA, June 6, 1998.

350   *On January 19 . . . Otto Ulrich*: FEK to Thomas W. Parker, January 26, 1971, Box 8, Folder 6, FEK Papers.

350   *Two days later . . . for Congress*: Ibid.

20. THE CANDIDATE

352   *In Norman, Oklahoma . . . an engineer*: Michael McConnell, Jack Baker, and Gail Langer Karwoski, *The Wedding Heard 'Round the World* (Minneapolis: University of Minnesota Press, 2016), 1–2.

352   *In June 1967 . . . a one-bedroom apartment*: Ibid., 22.

352   *The Office of . . . years earlier*: Richard J. Baker to Ralph Temple, September 26, 1968, Box 143, Folder 6, FEK Papers; Richard J. Baker to Stuart Land, February 11, 1969, Box 143, Folder 6, FEK Papers.

352   *The air force . . . Baker resigned*: McConnell, Baker, and Karwoski, *The Wedding Heard 'Round the World*, 27.

352   *"Frankly, we didn't . . . what to do"*: Michael McConnell, interviewed by Eric Cervini, telephone, March 13, 2019.

352   *To make ends . . . Homophile Organizations*: McConnell, Baker, and Karwoski, *The Wedding Heard 'Round the World*, 41.

352   *During the conference . . . fight the military*: Ibid.

352   *"I spent a . . . the mails"*: FEK to Marc Jeffers, November 7, 1969, Box 68, Folder 6, FEK Papers.

353   *On January . . . used publicly"*: Richard J. Baker to Chris Gordon, January 30, 1969, Box 143, Folder 6, FEK Papers.

353   *Two weeks after . . . the process*: McConnell, Baker, and Karwoski, *The Wedding Heard 'Round the World*, 44.

353   *That fall, after . . . Minnesota*: FEK to Marc Jeffers, November 7, 1969, Box 68, Folder 6, FEK Papers.

353   *He also decided . . . could win*: Michael McConnell, interviewed by Eric Cervini, telephone, March 13, 2019.

353   *Since the 1950s . . . Dowdy hearings*: For an early discussion of *legalized* gay marriage, see E. B. Saunders, "Reformer's Choice," *ONE* 1, no. 8 (August 1953), 10. For a discussion of romantic, non-legal marriage, see Randy Lloyd, "Let's Push Homophile Marriage," *ONE* 11, no. 6 (June 1963), 5. For other examples of discussions about marriage within the homophile movement, see Stephen Vider, "Lesbian and Gay Marriage and Romantic Adjustment in the 1950s and 1960s United States," *Gender & History* 29, no. 3 (November 2017), 693–715. For Kameny's response to Dowdy, see Chapter Nine.

353   *No gay couple . . . their marriage license*: McConnell, Baker, and Karwoski, *The Wedding Heard 'Round the World*, 66–71.

353   *Exactly one month . . . University"*: Ibid., 76.

353   *The Minnesota Civil . . . County*: "U. of Mich. Refuses Gay Job—ACLU to Protest," *GAY*, August 3, 1970, 3.

353   *Meanwhile, news of . . . across the country*: See "His and His Wedding Plans," *Daily News* (Washington), May 20, 1970, clipping in Box 16, Folder 3, Vincenz Papers; "Two Men Ask Minnesota License for First Legal U.S. Gay Marriage," *The Advocate*, June 10–23, 1970, 1; "Two Men Apply for Marriage License," *GAY*, June 15, 1970, 12.

353   *In June, two . . . the same*: Erik Larsson, "Kentucky Lesbians Apply for Marriage License," *GAY*, August 10, 1970, 3.

354   *"The gay marriage . . . of us, free"*: Donovan Bess, "Homosexual Call for Militancy," *San Francisco Chronicle*, August 22, 1970, clipping in Box 119, Folder 9, Gittings Papers.

354   *But for McConnell . . . adopt children*: Michael McConnell, interviewed by Eric Cervini, telephone, March 13, 2019.

354   *On January 26 . . . Homosexual Couple"*: Jack Star, "The Homosexual Couple," *LOOK*, January 26, 1971, 69.

354 *6.5 million*: "Cowles Closing Look Magazine After 34 Years," *New York Times*, September 17, 1971, 1.

354 *"Not all homosexual . . . in love*: Star, "The Homosexual Couple."

354 *The couple received . . . much hate?*: McConnell, Baker, and Karwoski, *The Wedding Heard 'Round the World*, 99.

354 *"I suppose . . . of it"*: Ibid., 101.

354 *The couple continued . . . cases in court*: Michael McConnell, interviewed by Eric Cervini, telephone, March 13, 2019.

354 *and Charles P. . . . themselves "Blatant is Beautiful"*: Bess, "Homosexual Call for Militancy."

354 *They established . . . became volunteer coordinator*: "Kameny Campaign Volunteers," n.d., Box 14, Folder 1, Vincenz Papers. For more on Ted Kirkland, see "Collective Living," Rainbow History Project Digital Collections, https://archives.rainbowhistory.org/exhibits/show/glf/organization/glf-houses.

355 *"Since we realistically . . . is all"*: FEK to Richard L. Schlegel, January 29, 1971, Box 9, Folder 3, FEK Papers.

355 *On Wednesday, February . . . television networks*: FEK to Barbara Gittings, February 7, 1971, Box 119, Folder 8, Gittings Papers. The week had begun favorably. The day prior, Kameny awoke to an editorial in the *Post*, titled "Fairness for Homosexuals," about his Pentagon cases. The ACLU "has served the cause of decency as well as fairness by going to court on behalf of a man denied industrial security clearance solely because he is a homosexual," wrote the *Post*. "Persecution of homosexuals is as senseless as it is unjust." See "Fairness for Homosexuals," *The Washington Post*, February 2, 1971, A14.

355 *"Early in the . . . American citizens"*: FEK, "Statement of Dr. Franklin E. Kameny, Candidate for Congress," February 3, 1971, Box 17, Folder 1, Vincenz Papers.

355 *"Although I am . . . among homosexuals"*: Ibid.

355 *On its front . . . Kameny's announcement*: Michael Anders, "Socialist May Be on D.C. Ballot," *The Washington Evening Star*, February 3, 1971, 1.

355 *Nancy Tucker advertised . . . GAY CANDIDATE*: "Kameny for Congress!!!," *The Gay Blade* 2, no. 5 (February 1971), 1.

356 *"The Mattachine Society . . . be upon them"*: John R. Rarick, "Homosexuality—The Holy Bible Versus the Washington Post," on February 3, 1971, 92nd Cong., 1st Sess., *Congressional Record*, 1831–1832.

356 *Kameny's volunteers stationed . . . churches*: Kameny for Congress, "Guide for Petition Circulators," n.d., Box 9, Folder 6, Gittings Papers; "5,000 Signatures Needed," Kameny Bulletin no. 1, n.d., Box 9, Folder 6, Gittings Papers.

356 *Kuntzler and Vincenz . . . THE FASTEST"*: "How to Get the Most Signatures the Fastest," n.d., Box 9, Folder 6, Gittings Papers.

356 *Shortly after midnight . . . in pairs*: Pete Fisher, "Personal Account: The Kameny Campaign," *GAY*, March 29, 1971, 1.

356 *That night, the . . . York City?"*: Ibid.

357 *H. Lynn Womack . . . country*: When Womack was arrested on obscenity charges in 1960, he fought his case to the Supreme Court; the justices decided in a 6–1 decision that though his magazines were "dismally unpleasant, uncouth, and tawdry," they were not obscene. See David K. Johnson, *Buying Gay: How Physique Entrepreneurs Sparked a Movement* (New York: Columbia University Press, 2019), 154–55, 169.

357 *With an industrial . . . president's campaign*: Clendinen and Nagourney, *Out for Good*, 123.

357 *With gay Washington's . . . him*: Ibid., 120–21.

357 *"I am here . . . of Columbia"*: FEK Statement, February 22, 1971, Box 17, Folder 1, Vincenz Papers.

357 *"That more than . . . long thereafter"*: Ibid.

358 *"Well, I wish . . . decent job"*: Rae Beck Kameny to FEK, March 6, 1971, Box 153, Folder 8, FEK Papers.

358 *With overflowing campaign . . . White House*: Lige Clarke and Jack Nichols, "Congress Keeps the Closet Closed," *Screw*, April 12, 1971, 19.

358 *The campaign hoisted . . . Jack Nichols*: Ibid.

358 *"We are emerging . . . anything can"*: Nancy Tucker, "Campaign Center Opened by Kameny," *The Advocate*, March 31–April 13, 1971, 3.

358 *During his speech . . . Freedom Party*: FEK to Thomas W. Parker, January 26, 1971, Box 8, Folder 6, FEK Papers.

358 *Because only 10 . . . move, he reasoned*: Nancy Tucker, "Kameny Campaign: A Funny Thing Happened on Our Way to Congress," *The Advocate*, April 28–May 11, 1971, 2.

358 *Kameny thus became . . . as a Catholic"*: FEK Statement, February 22, 1971, Box 17, Folder 1, Vincenz Papers.

359 *"We hope that . . . its glory"*: Ibid.

359 *With only three . . . custom speech*: When he spoke before the Metropolitan Washington Board of Trade on Consumer Protection, he advocated for the Rosenthal-Dwyer bills for an independent consumer protection agency; when he spoke before the Far Southeast Civic Association, he cited the District's education statistics. He developed detailed positions on crime, federal revenue, transportation, drugs, and the economy. See FEK, "Metropolitan Washington Board of Trade on Consumer Protection," March 2, 1971, Box 9, Folder 6, Gittings

Papers; FEK, "Education in the District of Columbia," March 10, 1971, Box 9, Folder 6, Gittings Papers; Kameny for Congress, "The Issues," n.d., Box 9, Folder 6, Gittings Papers.

359   *"He has a . . . each other"*: "Kameny Pegs Campaign on Honesty," *The Washington Evening Star*, March 16, 1971, 25.

359   *Kay Lahusen took . . . the Capitol building*: Kay Tobin, "Frank Kameny with Briefcase on Capitol Hill #2," 1971, New York Public Library Digital Collections, https://digitalcollections.nypl.org/items/510d47e3-afc6 -a3d9-e040-e00a18064a99.

359   *"Dr. Franklin E. . . . reported the* Star: John Fialka, "Kameny Pegs Campaign on Honesty," 25.

359   *When the* Post *. . . homosexual issue"*: "Text of D.C. Delegate Candidates' Opinions," *The Washington Post*, March 18, 1971, B1.

359   *A week before . . . Kuntzler's name*: Fialka, "Kameny Pegs Campaign on Honesty," 25.

360   *On March 7 . . . he added*: Chuck Yoder to FEK, March 7, 1971, Box 152, Folder 8, FEK Papers.

360   *On March 8 . . . 16 were"*: U.S. Congress, House of Representatives, Departments of State, Justice, and Commerce, the Judiciary, and Related Agencies Appropriations for 1972, Part 2, Department of State, 92nd Cong., 1st Sess., March 8, 1971, 371.

360   *The next day . . . campaign promised*: Kameny for Congress Committee, "Kameny to Criticize Federal Security Clearance and Civil Service Hiring Policies," March 6, 1971, Box 9, Folder 6, Gittings Papers.

360   *Kameny denounced Congressman . . . he yelled*: Kameny for Congress Committee, "Speech by Dr. Franklin E. Kameny," March 9, 1971, Box 9, Folder 6, Gittings Papers.

360   *At noon, Kameny . . . a security clearance*: Department of Defense, "In the Matter of: Dr. Franklin Edward Kameny," March 9, 1971, Box 44, Folder 14, FEK Papers.

361   *"This difference in . . . applied now"*: Ibid., 22.

361   *"Let's concentrate on . . . man's existence"*: Ibid., 34.

361   *On March 12 . . . Washington's National Theatre*: "Hair: The Dawning of the Age of Aquarius," *The Washington Evening Star*, February 14, 1971, 87.

361   *Across the street . . . pedestrians*: Kameny for Congress Committee, "Kameny to Hold Candlelit Vigil in Support of 'Hair,'" March 12, 1971, Box 9, Folder 6, Gittings Papers. On "fourth-largest pornographer," see James Lardner, "A Pornographer's Rise, Fall," *The Washington Post*, January 12, 1978, 1.

362   *"We are firmly . . . out there"*: Clarke and Nichols, "Congress Keeps the Closet Closed," 19.

362   *The last full . . . for votes*: Bart Barnes, "The Candidates: Kameny Stresses Personal Freedom," *The Washington Post*, March 13, 1971, B1.

362   *Paul Kuntzler planned . . . and flyers*: Kameny for Congress Committee, "Saturday, March 20, Designated as 'Personal Freedom Day' in Washington," March 13, 1971, Box 9, Folder 6, Gittings Papers.

362   *"Is your phone . . . MARCH 23rd"*: Kameny for Congress, "Is Your Phone Tapped . . . ," n.d., Box 9, Folder 6, Gittings Papers.

362   *The straight flyers . . . they concluded*: Kameny for Congress, "The Issues," n.d., Box 9, Folder 6, Gittings Papers.

362   *On Friday night . . . car radio*: Clarke and Nichols, "Congress Keeps the Closet Closed."

363   *Saturday morning, dozens . . . Washington shopping centers*: Kameny for Congress Committee, "Saturday, March 20, Designated as 'Personal Freedom Day' in Washington."

363   *GAA volunteers slipped . . . doors*: Richard C. Wandel, "The Last Lap: Kameny Campaign Ends," *GAY*, April 26, 1971, 2.

363   *Beginning at 9:00 a.m. . . . District*: Bart Barnes, "Candidates Enter Stretch Drive in District Delegate Race," *The Washington Post*, March 21, 1971, D1.

363   *at noon, he . . . Americans*: William Holland, "Kameny Calls for Nixon to Aid Homosexuals," *The Washington Evening Star*, March 20, 1971, 15.

363   *Kameny held a . . . the president*: FEK to the President, March 13, 1971, Box 125, Folder 4, FEK Papers.

363   *While holding that . . . armed guard*: Barnes, "Candidates Enter Stretch Drive in District Delegate Race."

363   *Kameny continued his . . . gay rights*: Kameny for Congress Committee, "Saturday, March 20, Designated as 'Personal Freedom Day' in Washington."

363   *Shortly thereafter, during . . . office*: Clarke and Nichols, "Congress Keeps the Closet Closed."

363   *While his volunteers . . . his community*: Kameny for Congress Committee, "Saturday, March 20, Designated as 'Personal Freedom Day' in Washington."

363   *"That campaign was . . . his speeches"*: FEK, interviewed by Dudley Clendinen, telephone, 1993.

364   *The Sunday Star . . . reported the* Star: Michael Anders and Duncan Spencer, "Candidates Step Up Campaign Pace as Election Day Nears," *The Washington Evening Star*, March 21, 1971, 1.

364   *Indeed, when the . . . with approval*: Alma Robinson, "4 Foes Hit Fauntroy in TV Debate," *The Washington Evening Star*, March 16, 1971, 25.

364   *"Dr. Frank Kameny . . . that bad"*: Washington *Daily News* quoted in Lige Clarke and Jack Nichols, "A Campaign to Remember," *GAY*, April 26, 1971, 6.

364   *On Monday, the . . . Kameny's qualifications*: Wandel, "The Last Lap: Kameny Campaign Ends."

364 *That evening, as . . . Kameny volunteer*: Ibid.

364 *The next day . . . their precincts*: Paul Kuntzler to "All Kameny Supporters," March 12, 1971, Box 9, Folder 6, Gittings Papers.

365 *That day, Frank . . . said the flyer*: "Election Night Victory Party," March 23, 1971, Box 9, Folder 6, Gittings Papers.

365 *As the attendees . . . visible emotion*: "Fauntroy Elected D.C. Delegate," *The Washington Post*, March 24, 1971, A10.

365 *Washington voters cast . . . hearing the news*: Jacqueline Trescott, "Gospel Tunes and Tears," *The Washington Evening Star*, March 24, 1971, F1.

365 *Kameny arrived downstairs . . . tears*: Clarke and Nichols, "A Campaign to Remember," 6.

365 *But it was . . . homosexual constituents*: "Fauntroy Elected D.C. Delegate," *The Washington Post*, March 24, 1971, A10.

365 *"We've made our . . . want"*: Alma Robinson and Timothy Hutchens, "Fauntroy Hailed—'It's Nation Time,'" *The Washington Evening Star*, March 24, 1971, 1.

365 *"Kameny for President!" someone yelled*: Clarke and Nichols, "A Campaign to Remember," 6.

365 *A week after . . . the Star)*: Duncan Spencer, "Kameny Happy Despite Low Vote," *The Washington Evening Star*, March 29, 1971, 20.

366 *Impressed by the . . . of Washington*: Paul Kuntzler, "The Early Days in Washington, DC," Gay and Lesbian Activist Alliance of Washington, D.C., 1971–2010, OutHistory.org; Joel Martin, interviewed by Eric Cervini, telephone, April 3, 2019.

366 *They did not . . . democratic political entity*: Ibid.

366 *"WE, AS HOMOSEXUAL . . . their constitution*: "Constitution and Bylaws of the Gay Activists Alliance of Washington, D.C.," April 20, 1971, Box 87, Folder 9, FEK Papers.

366 *Its last executive . . . existence*: Otto U. to MSW Members, July 10, 1971, Box 18, Folder 5, Vincenz Papers.

366 *he continued using . . . with the District*: See, for example, MSW, Inc., "Gay Activist Appointed to D.C. Human Rights Commission," March 31, 1975, Box 85, Folder 14, FEK Papers.

366 *"I am not . . . out to pasture!"*: Kameny verifies this phrasing in an interview with Mark Meinke, quoted in "Gay and Lesbian Activists Alliance," Box 157, Folder 17, FEK Papers.

366 *Yes, they respected . . . his mind*: Kuntzler, "The Early Days in Washington, DC"; Joel Martin, interviewed by Eric Cervini, telephone, April 3, 2019.

366 *That month, when . . . base, she concluded*: Tucker, "Kameny Campaign: A Funny Thing Happened on Our Way to Congress."

367 *In The Advocate . . . white candidate"*: Ibid.

367 *The election results . . . wrote Tucker*: Ibid. Jack Nichols of *GAY* concluded that gay Black voters "had to choose between their loyalty to a black or a homosexual candidate," but Tucker had seen no effort to capture their vote. In an election with assured victory for the Black candidate, the campaign lost an opportunity to reach the Black homosexuals of Washington. See Clarke and Nichols, "A Campaign to Remember."

367 *Finally, there was . . . she wrote*: Ibid. The exclusion may have been a political failure, too, since Kameny's campaign was not entirely unprecedented. In 1961, two weeks before the founding of the Mattachine Society of Washington, a drag queen ran for office in San Francisco. José Sarria, the beloved performer at the Black Cat Tavern, ran for the city's board of supervisors, and the League for Civil Education encouraged the city's gay citizens to vote for their effeminate icon. In a city with almost exactly the same population as Washington, years before Stonewall and an entire decade before Kameny's campaign, the drag queen won a total of 5,613 votes, three times the astronomer's tally. San Francisco voters had the option of choosing five candidates for the board of supervisors, which partially explains his large vote count. The assured victory of Walter Fauntroy in 1971, however, suggests that the comparison is apt. See D'Emilio, *Sexual Politics, Sexual Communities*, 188; "Jose Julio Sarria," Declarations of Candidacy, City and County of San Francisco, November 7, 1961, 26; "Final S.F. Vote," *San Francisco Chronicle*, November 8, 1961, 1.

367 *"If the decision . . . he will"*: Ibid.

367 *more than . . . viewers*: For Cronkite viewership numbers, see John J. O'Connor, "TV News: Backstage at C.B.S.," *The New York Times*, October 21, 1971, 93.

367 *"In Minneapolis, an . . . he reported*: Walter Cronkite quoted in Tobin and Wicker, *The Gay Crusaders*, 135–36.

367 *Baker, while still . . . its history*: Ibid.

368 *Baker had run . . . explained the student*: McConnell, Baker, and Karwoski, *The Wedding Heard 'Round the World*, 110.

368 *Less than a . . . and Jack Baker*: Lahusen interview. Barbara Gittings, in her interview for *The Gay Crusaders*, confirmed that she arrived to Washington after the zap. See Barbara Gittings, interviewed by Kay Tobin Lahusen, 1969–1971, Box 122, Folder 4, Gittings Papers.

368 *behind them sat . . . Psychiatric Association*: Herbert M. Gant, "Annual Meeting Runs Smoothly While Protests Hit Washington," *Psychiatric News* 6, no. 11 (June 2, 1971), 1.

368   *Following the GLF . . . Del Martin*: The panel also included SIR's Larry Littlejohn. See Thomas R. Dunn,
      "Dr. H[omosexual] Anonymous, Gay Liberation Activism, and the American Psychiatric Association,
      1963–1973," in *Social Controversy and Public Address in the 1960s and Early 1970s*, ed. Richard J. Jensen
      (East Lansing: Michigan State University Press, 2017), 198; Bayer, *Homosexuality and American Psychiatry*,
      105.

368   *The APA permitted . . . their professional achievements*: Dunn, "Dr. H[omosexual] Anonymous, Gay Liberation
      Activism, and the American Psychiatric Association, 1963–1973," 199.

368   *Also in . . . in the program*: Gant, "Annual Meeting Runs Smoothly While Protests Hit Washington."

368   *Security had never . . . incident*: "Five Days in May," *Psychiatric News* 6, no. 11 (June 2, 1971), 2.

368   *The Washington police . . . entering their offices*: Richard Halloran, "7,000 Arrested in Capital War Protest,"
      The New York Times, May 3, 1971, 1.

369   *President Nixon authorized . . . Senator Sam Ervin*: J. Michael Botts, "Operation Garden Plot," in *The Social
      History of Crime and Punishment in America*, ed. Wilbur R. Miller (Thousand Oaks, CA: Sage Publications,
      2012), 749.

369   *Ten thousand federal troops . . . proper facilities*: York Times: Halloran, "7,000 Arrested in Capital War Protest."

369   *On May 3 . . . proper facilities*: Ibid.

369   *"root of [the] abscess"*: Lahusen interview.

369   *collaboration with the . . . plans*: Bayer, *Homosexuality and American Psychiatry*, 105.

369   *The night prior . . . hotel garage*: Mark Meinke, "Zapping the Shrinks," Rainbow History Project.

369   *Shortly before Attorney . . . essay contest*: Gant, "Annual Meeting Runs Smoothly While Protests Hit
      Washington."

369   *At that moment . . . them wore drag*: Perry Brass, "Gay May Day," *Come Out!* 2, no. 7b (Spring/Summer 1971),
      6.

369   *obscenely bright makeup . . . violently high heels*: Faderman, *The Gay Revolution*, 280.

369   *They flew through . . . a brawl*: Brass, "Gay May Day."

369   *Two gay demonstrators . . . the stage*: Editor's note in response to FEK, "Homosexuality," *Psychiatric News* 6,
      no. 13 (July 7, 1971), 2.

369   *"The noise coming . . . to the podium*: Brass, "Gay May Day."

369   *Frank Kameny leapt . . . he screamed*: Bayer, *Homosexuality and American Psychiatry*, 105.

370   *The GLF activists . . . astronomer*: Brass, "Gay May Day."

370   *"faggots" and "drag queens"*: Ibid.

370   *"Nazis"*: Bayer, *Homosexuality and American Psychiatry*, 105.

370   *"go fuck yourself"*: Lahusen interview.

EPILOGUE: THE WHITE HOUSE

371   *Frank Kameny, wearing . . . his pocket*: Andy Sullivan, "Obama Extends Benefits, Promises More for Gays," *Reu-
      ters*, June 16, 2009, https://www.reuters.com/article/us-obama-rights-benefits-idUSTRE55G0OR20090617.
      For video of the scene, see Obama White House, "President Obama Announces Benefits for Gay Partners of
      Federal Employees," June 17, 2009, https://vimeo.com/5210003.

371   *In September 1971 . . . clearances*: Security clearance holders had the "right under the First Amendment, for
      an individual to keep private the details of his sex life," the judge explained. Moreover, in an echo of the
      Norton decision, he required "proof of a nexus between that condition and his ability to protect classified
      information." See FEK, "Gays Win Major Court Victory: Security Clearances Restored," September 13,
      1971, Box 128, Folder 1, FEK Papers.

371   *Benning Wentworth won . . . the following year*: FEK to Elver Barker, June 2, 1972, Box 2, Folder 1, FEK
      Papers; John H. Pratt, "Order," *Wentworth v. Laird*, May 26, 1972, Box 8, Folder 5, Gittings Papers. In 1973,
      an appeals court upheld Wentworth and Ulrich's victory, while remanding Gayer's case back to the adminis-
      trative level. See *Gayer, Ulrich, and Wentworth v. Schlesinger*, 490 F.2d 740 (D.C. Cir. 1973).

371   *After the 1971 . . . demands*: They invited Kameny and Gittings to the APA's 1972 convention in Dallas, which
      featured a booth titled "Gay, Proud and Healthy." During a panel discussion, a gay psychiatrist, fearful of
      exposing his identity to his colleagues, announced his condition from behind a rubber mask. See John P.
      LeRoy, "Shrinks Asked to Join Gay Liberation," *GAY*, June 12, 1972, 1; "Gay, Proud and Healthy," 1972, Box
      6, Folder 16, Gittings Papers.

371   *Kameny, after allying . . . explained Kameny*: FEK to Friends, December 15, 1973, Box 122, Folder 9 FEK
      Papers. For more on the APA fight, see Bayer, *Homosexuality and American Psychiatry*; "Chapter Sixteen:
      How Gays and Lesbians Stopped Being Crazies," in Faderman, *The Gay Revolution*, 279–98.

371   *"So we are . . . told Gittings*: The decision did not become truly permanent until an April 1974 APA referen-
      dum, which upheld the decision with the support of 58.4 percent of all voting APA members. See FEK to
      Barbara Gittings, April 8, 1974, Box 6, Folder 16, FEK Papers; FEK to Jack Nichols, February 2, 1974, Box
      7, Folder 10, FEK Papers.

371 *Kameny joined efforts . . . called* homophobia: FEK, "'Defining' Homosexuals into Sickness," *The Washington Post*, January 28, 1978, 17.

372 *Frank Kameny submitted . . . incorporation*: FEK to Office of the Recorder of Deeds, Corporation Division, February 1972, Box 87, Folder 10, FEK Papers.

372 *Kameny's house became its first headquarters*: Ibid.

372 *Kameny served as . . . legal committee chairman*: Bill Bricker to Ralph Temple, July 18, 1972, Box 87, Folder 10, FEK Papers.

372 *"You are committing . . . overwhelmingly male GLF*: Nancy Tucker, "Fuck You, 'Brothers'! or Yet Another Woman Leaves the Gay Liberation Movement," *The Ladder* 15, no. 11/12 (August/September 1971), 52. Meanwhile, Lilli Vincenz, after receiving countless calls from lesbian women during the Kameny campaign, created a Gay Women's Open House in her Arlington home. Each Wednesday, dozens of women could meet each other and socialize in a safe environment, a tradition that continued uninterrupted for seven years. See Lilli Vincenz, interviewed by Genny Beemyn, Arlington, VA, June 6, 1998; Lilli Vincenz, in "50th Anniversary of the Mattachine Society of Washington Panel Discussion," Rainbow History Project, October 13, 2011; Robert Mott, "Homosexual Lives as Varied as Those of Any Other Group," *The Washington Post*, April 24, 1973, C1. Additionally, in May 1971, ten women created a lesbian separatist collective, modeled after a Bolshevik cell, in Adams Morgan. They called themselves "the Furies" and published a newspaper. Lesbianism, they argued, was not just compatible with women's liberation, but a prerequisite: "You can't build a strong movement if your sisters are out there fucking with the oppressor," explained cofounder Rita Mae Brown. See Beemyn, *A Queer Capital*, 198; Faderman, *The Gay Revolution*, 238.

372 *The days of . . . Frank Kameny*: Maryland Directory of Community Services, "Mattachine Society of Washington, Inc.," December 13, 1977, Box 85, Folder 11, FEK Papers.

372 *He continued marching . . . told Gittings*: FEK to Barbara Gittings, July 16, 1973, Box 6, Folder 16, Gittings Papers.

372 *She would continue . . . age of one hundred*: "Rae B. Kameny," *U.S., Social Security Death Index, 1935–2014* (Provo, UT: Ancestry.com, 2014).

372 *The Pentagon, despite . . . first time*: NCACLU, "Homosexual Sues for Public Defense Department Hearing," November 30, 1973, Box 159, Folder 13, FEK Papers; William J. Scanlon to FEK, December 27, 1973, Box 34, Folder 14, FEK Papers; Inderjit Badhwar, "Gays Fight Back Openly," *Federal Times*, August 14, 1974, clipping in Box 42, Folder 1, FEK Papers.

372 *During the four-day . . . the examiner*: Department of Defense, "In the Matter of: Otis Francis Tabler, Jr.," July 30, 1974, Box 35, Folder 1, 157.

372 *Five months later . . . clearance*: Office of the Assistant Secretary of Defense, "Determination of Examiner Richard S. Farr," Otis Francis Tabler Jr., December 17, 1974, Box 68, Folder 7, Gittings Papers.

372 *"PENTAGON SURRENDERS," . . . press release*: The final victory had come on July 31, 1975, after the Department of Defense dropped its appeal of the examiner's determination in the Tabler case. Kameny was also "authoritatively informed that there has been a de facto reversal of the Defense Department's policy of automatic denial of security clearances to Homosexuals" in clearance cases, he announced. With still "much 'dust to settle,' it is clear that the persistently-denied but nonetheless real per se denial of clearances to Homosexuals is at an end." See MSW, "Pentagon Surrenders on Security Clearances," August 4, 1975, Box 68, Folder 7, Gittings Papers; "Homosexual Gets Security Clearance," *The Washington Post*, February 2, 1975, 3; Vernon A. Guidry Jr., "Pentagon Easing Gay Curbs," *The Washington Evening Star*, August 15, 1975, 14. For more on the Tabler case, see Ryan Reft, "Sexual Equality: Los Angeles, the Military Industrial Complex, and the Gay Liberation Movement," KCET, December 11, 2015, https://www.kcet.org/history-society/sexual-equality-los-angeles-the-military-industrial-complex-and-the-gay-liberation.

372 *That year, the . . . city government*: After his congressional campaign, Kameny's political profile in the District continued to grow. He ran for delegate to the 1972 Democratic National Convention, and though he also lost that race, he persuaded the District's delegation to lobby for a party position against homosexual discrimination. The Republicans invited him to testify at their national convention. And after Nixon ultimately won reelection, Kameny spoke before more than thirty-five thousand demonstrators on the day of the inauguration. "We are here as American citizens to join with our fellow American citizens of every kind and from every walk of life, in raising our voices against this endless, interminable, wanton, useless war," he yelled. Five months later, on June 6, Kameny was elected the executive secretary of the NCACLU. By the end of the year, Kameny and the GAA machine convinced the Washington city council to include gay rights in the creation of the District's new civil rights law. The law, which prohibited antigay discrimination in housing and employment, became the most comprehensive human rights statute in the country; as one city council staff member put it, the homosexuals of Washington did "a hell of a job of lobbying." See "D.C. Home Rule," Council of the District of Columbia, 2016, https://dccouncil.us/dc-home-rule; Stephen Green, "Del. Fauntroy, Wife of POW to Second," *The Washington Post*, July 12, 1972, A16; FEK to *The Advocate*, September 19, 1972, Box 128, Folder 5, FEK Papers; FEK to James Foster, August 25, 1972, Box 124, Folder 7, FEK Papers; FEK to Clifton R. Witt, August 25, 1972, Box 124, Folder 7, FEK Papers; FEK, "Remarks Delivered,"

January 20, 1973, Box 131, Folder 4, FEK Papers; David Holmberg, "Demonstrators Stage Anti-War Protests," *The Washington Evening Star*, January 21, 1973, 1; Rima Z. Parkhurst to FEK, June 12, 1973, Box 75, Folder 7, FEK Papers; FEK to Florence Isbell, June 13, 1973, Box 75, Folder 7, FEK Papers; FEK, "The Durfee Award: Background Information in Support of the Nomination of Franklin Edward Kameny," Box 135, Folder 7, 10; FEK, "Civil Rights in D.C.," *The Washington Post*, November 13, 1973, A15; Cynthia Gorney, "District's Gays Gain Power After Shedding Secrecy," *The Washington Post*, May 23, 1977, C1.

372   *When the GAA . . . a homosexual*: In its list of six potential nominees, the GAA also nominated Paul Kuntzler and Nancy Tucker. See GAA, "Open Gay Washingtonians Proposed for Membership in the District of Columbia Human Rights Commission," Box 87, Folder 10, FEK Papers; Gorney, "District's Gays Gain Power After Shedding Secrecy," October 1974.

373   *On March 25 . . . rights commissioner*: "Washington Names Kameny," Contact, May 7, 1975, clipping in Box 111, Folder 4, FEK Papers; MSW, "Gay Activist Appointed to D.C. Human Rights Commission," March 31, 1975, Box 85, Folder 14, FEK Papers. For additional photographs of the event, see Box 111, Folder 3, FEK Papers.

373   *As commissioner, Kameny . . . of Columbia"*: FEK to Morty Manford, May 19, 1975, Box 7, Folder 2, FEK Papers.

373   *Two months later . . . Police Department*: FEK to Peter Lewis, June 13, 1975, Box 40, Folder 12, FEK Papers.

373   *The Civil Service . . . terminate suspected homosexuals*: In light of the *Norton* victory, the CSC cited the conflicting Schlegel decision, instead. In December 1971, however, the NCACLU filed the country's first class action lawsuit against the CSC's purges, and the Society for Individual Rights filed a similar lawsuit on the West Coast. See FEK to Richard L. Schlegel, June 22, 1971, Box 9, Folder 3, FEK Papers; NCACLU, "ACLU Fund Sues on Homosexuals," December 17, 1971, Box 122, Folder 6, FEK Papers; Society for Individual Rights, "Gay Employment Rights Victory," November 3, 1973, Box 42, Folder 2, FEK Papers.

373   *Immediately after his . . . Civil Service Commission*: FEK to Richard L. Schlegel, June 22, 1971, Box 9, Folder 3, FEK Papers.

373   *in August 1973 . . . himself*: An official change in policy was imminent, promised the chairman. Meanwhile, more and more gay federal applicants found themselves receiving federal jobs: in 1973, the CSC accepted Richard Schlegel's application for employment. See FEK to Robert E. Hampton, September 2, 1972, Box 41, Folder 13, FEK Papers; James J. Kilpatrick, "Surveillance Report Has Orwellian Parallels," *The Washington Evening Star*, September 5, 1972, A9; Thomas P. Sandow to Richard Lamar Schlegel, April 27, 1973, Box 31, Folder 10, FEK Papers; FEK to David C. Moon, June 11, 1973, Box 42, Folder 2, FEK Papers.

373   *On July 3 . . . news*: FEK, "The Durfee Award," 3.

373   *Later that day . . . federal employment*: News Release, Civil Service News, July 3, 1975, Box 7, Folder 5, Gittings Papers; Joseph Young, "Homosexuals Given Equal Job Rights," *The Washington Evening Star*, July 3, 1975, 1.

373   *"The war, which . . . have won"*: FEK to Barbara Gittings and Kay Tobin Lahusen, July 8, 1975, Box 6, Folder 16, Gittings Papers.

373   *Warren Scarberry . . . Correctional Services*: "Mattachine New York Suing Prison Establishment," 1969, Box 5, Folder 13, MSNY Papers; *Jackson v. Ward*, 458 F. Supp. 546 (W.D.N.Y. 1978).

374   *On the morning . . . 128 people*: Heather Ann Thompson, *Blood in the Water: The Attica Prison Uprising of 1971 and Its Legacy* (New York: Pantheon, 2016), 177; Tom Robbins, "The Attica Turkey Shoot," *The Marshall Project*, May 26, 2015, https://www.themarshallproject.org/2015/05/26/the-attica-turkey-shoot.

374   *Warren Scarberry was . . . bullet wounds*: "9 of Wounded from Here," *Rochester Democrat and Chronicle*, September 17, 1971, 9A.

374   *seven years later . . . political literature*: *Jackson v. Ward*, 458 F. Supp. 546 (W.D.N.Y. 1978). Scarberry was released from prison after serving only six years. By 1974, he was serving as the chairman of the MSNY's Penal Reform Committee. The *Mattachine Times* heralded him as "lean, handsome, with the personal intensity of a genuine crusaders and all the right reasons for being one." See "Gay Penal Crusade," *Mattachine Times*, 1974, clipping in Box 4, Folder 16, MSNY Papers.

374   *on April 27 . . . can guarantee that"*: "Hoover Tells of Rise in Vice Convictions," *The Washington Post*, April 28, 1972, A3.

374   *Four days later . . . Deviates file*: The FBI continued tracking the gay movement's political activities; it received a copy of Kameny and Gittings's 1972 "Gay, Proud and Healthy" leaflet and a list of gay delegates to the DNC and RNC conventions. See Gentry, *J. Edgar Hoover*, 31; Charles, *Hoover's War on Gays*, 109–10; SAC, Miami, to Acting Director, FBI, June 19, 1972, FBI File #100–469170, in Box 157, Folder 16, FEK Papers.

374   *Around this time . . . gay community*: Chris Bull, "His Public Domain, His Private Pain," *The Washington Post Magazine*, July 11, 1999, 19.

374   *on Monday, January . . . Missouri*: "Dowdy Begins Serving 'Death Sentence' Jail Term," *The Morning Herald* (Hagerstown, MD), January 23, 1974, 7.

374   *In 1965, the . . . Maryland construction company*: Joy Aschenbach, "Dowdy, Witnesses Accused of Lying," *The Washington Evening Star*, December 28, 1971, 17.

374   *A jury convicted . . . months in prison*: An appeals court had thrown out all but three perjury counts. See "Ex-Congressman Ordered to Prison," *The Weirton Daily Times*, January 23, 1974, 1.

375   *The Commission on Human Rights . . . for his appearances*: Friends urged him to become a lawyer, thus allowing him to monetize his legal knowledge. But Kameny resisted; becoming a real lawyer would hinder his strategy. "Having never been 'embarred', I cannot be disbarred, and so, in the interest of the advancement of justice and human dignity, can ignore the Canons of Legal Ethics with impunity, to good effect," he later explained. See FEK, "The Durfee Award," 2.

375   *in 1973, he . . . a pornographic film*: Jerry Oppenheimer, "Film Tells All About D.C. Sex," *The Washington Evening Star*, May 31, 1973, D1.

375   *Though he gave . . . throughout the 1970s*: FEK to David Rinckey, October 4, 1972, Box 8, Folder 14, FEK Papers.

375   *MSW veteran Nancy . . . his doorstep*: Nancy Tucker, interviewed by Eric Cervini, telephone, February 26, 2019.

375   *In 1971 . . . the navy*: FEK to Robert A. Martin Jr., August 6, 1971, Box 26, Folder 15, FEK Papers.

375   *Though Senator Sam . . . of the sailor*: Sam J. Ervin Jr. to John H. Chafee, February 11, 1972, Box 2, Folder 3, Donaldson Papers; Sam J. Ervin Jr. to R. A. Martin, April 5, 1972, Box 2, Folder 3, Donaldson Papers; Sam J. Ervin Jr. to James E. Johnson, April 5, 1972, Box 2, Folder 3, Donaldson Papers.

375   *Martin still received . . . less-than-honorable discharge*: Bob Martin to FEK, March 24, 1972, Box 26, Folder 15, FEK Papers.

375   *Meanwhile, Kameny guided . . . a Homosexual"*: Jay Mathews, "Air Force Begins Homosexuality Case," *The Washington Post*, September 16, 1975, 3; Lesley Oelsner, "Homosexual Fights the Military," *The Washington Evening Star*, May 26, 1975, 2; *TIME*, September 8, 1975; Faderman, *The Gay Revolution*, 348, 478.

375   *After Democrat . . . "Honorable"*: Bob Martin, "Gay Vet Wins Honorable Discharge," n.d., Box 7, Folder 6, FEK Papers. There had been indications that the new administration would take pity on the disgraced sailor. On the afternoon of March 26, 1977, only two months after Carter's inauguration, Kameny entered the White House for the first time. One of fourteen delegates invited to confer with an aide about the problems of gay and lesbian Americans, Kameny spoke for five minutes on the remnants of employment discrimination in the federal government. Carter later demoted the aide who had organized that meeting. See Margaret Costanza to National Gay Task Force, February 8, 1977, Box 125, Folder 5, FEK Papers; National Gay Task Force, "Agenda," March 26, 1977, Box 125, Folder 5, FEK Papers; Robert W. Merry, "Gays Find an Open White House Door," *National Observer*, April 9, 1977, clipping in Box 125, Folder 5, FEK Papers; Bill Peterson, "Brown's Support for Gays Brings Cheers," *The Washington Post*, November 28, 1979, 2.

375   *The military's ban . . . the Foreign Service*: FEK, Statement on Federal Employment, n.d., Box 42, Folder 4, FEK Papers.

375   *But by the . . . and California*: Faderman, *The Gay Revolution*, 394–97.

375   *In Washington, after . . . gay vote*: Milton Coleman, "Washington's Gay Vote: Homosexuals a Force in May Election District Gays Believed Factor in Council Race," *The Washington Post*, April 21, 1979, 1.

376   *In 1979, after . . . in Washington*: Lena Williams, "200,000 March in Capital to Seek Gay Rights and Money for AIDS," *The New York Times*, October 12, 1987, 1.

376   *By the end . . . become "utopia"*: Cynthia Gorney, "District's Gays Gain Power After Shedding Secrecy," *The Washington Post*, May 23, 1977, C1.

376   *In 1981, Mayor . . . District of Columbia*: FEK, "The Durfee Award," 14. In July 1980, Kameny forced the hypersecretive National Security Agency to reinstate one of his clients, a gay linguist. He continued serving as human rights commissioner, and the NCACLU reelected him to its board. See Bamford, *The Puzzle Palace*, 82–83; FEK, "Human Rights that Are 'Unambiguously Clear,'" *The Washington Post*, May 8, 1980, 18; Marilyn T. Welles to FEK, June 3, 1980, Box 75, Folder 8, FEK Papers.

376   *"RARE CANCER SEEN IN 41 HOMOSEXUALS"*: Lawrence K. Altman, "Rare Cancer Seen in 41 Homosexuals," *The New York Times*, July 3, 1981, 20.

376   *The Centers for . . . Do you?"*: Tim Fitzsimons, "LGBTQ History Month: The Early Days of America's AIDS Crisis," NBC News, October 15, 2018, https://www.nbcnews.com/feature/nbc-out/lgbtq-history-month-early-days-america-s-aids-crisis-n919701.

376   *"I heard about . . . an architect"*: Maureen Dowd, "For Victims of AIDS, Support in a Lonely Siege," *The New York Times*, December 5, 1983, B1.

376   *Lesbians, many still . . . of Washington*: Lilli M. Vincenz, "Empowerment Groups for People Living with AIDS," *The Community Psychologist* 21, no. 2 (Spring 1988), 27–28; Linda Rapp, "Vincenz, Lilli," 2013, GLBTQ Archives, http://www.glbtqarchive.com/ssh/vincenz_lilli_S.pdf.

376   *By 1986, twelve thousand . . . with the infected?*: Faderman, *The Gay Revolution*, 426.

376   *The Prevent AIDS . . . quarantine*: David L. Kirp, "LaRouche Turns to AIDS Politics," *The New York Times*, September 11, 1986, 27.

377   *Conservative commentator William . . . AIDS*: William F. Buckley, "Crucial Steps in Combatting the AIDS Epidemic: Identify All Carriers," *The New York Times*, March 18, 1986, 27.

377 *In November 1986 . . . isolation*: "November 4, 1986 Election," California Ballot Propositions 1980–1989, LA Law Library, http://www.lalawlibrary.org/research/ballots/1980/1986.aspx; Faderman, *The Gay Revolution*, 424.

377 *Hospitals put dead . . . trash bags*: Barbara Starrett, in *How to Survive a Plague*, dir. David France (New York: Mongrel Media, 2012).

377 *For the 1987 . . . Holocaust*: Faderman, *The Gay Revolution*, 428.

377 *ACT UP adopted . . . Death"*: Ibid.

377 *Inspired by the . . . ground*: Ronald Sullivan, "AIDS Overtakes Disease of Heart as No. 2 Worry," *The New York Times*, March 25, 1987, B2.

377 *"We'll look back . . . blip in history"*: Jack Nichols, "The Father of the Movement Speaks,"TWN, April 12, 1995, 24.

377 *Even after a . . . faced government purges*: Ibid.

377 *In 1986, while . . . the march*: Lisa M. Keen, "The National March Takes Washington by Surprise," *Washington Blade* 18, no. 42 (October 16, 1987), 1.

377 *Behind the people . . . two hundred thousand additional demonstrators*: Lisa M. Keen, "How Many People Were There?," *Washington Blade* 18, no. 42 (October 16, 1987), 14.

377 *Frank Kameny marched . . . of 1971*: Karlyn Barker and Linda Wheeler, "Gay Activists Arrested at High Court: Peaceful Civil Disobedience by 572 Culminates Week's Events," *The Washington Post*, October 14, 1987, 1; Jack Nichols, "The Father of the Movement Speaks,"TWN, April 12, 1995, 24; Lena Williams, "600 in Gay Demonstration Arrested at Supreme Court," *The New York Times*, October 14, 1987, B8; Lou Chibbaro Jr., "Large Arrest Protest at Supreme Court," *Washington Blade* 18, no. 42 (October 16, 1987), 1.

378 *"Your gloves don't . . . the activists*: Williams, "600 in Gay Demonstration Arrested at Supreme Court."

378 *The militant tactics . . . ACT UP*: Ibid. "Did Act-Up play a significant role in the whole idea of expanded access to experimental drugs?" asked the official responsible for studying AIDS at the National Institutes of Health. "The answer is yes." See Philip J. Hilts, "AIDS Drug's Maker Cuts Price by 20%," *The New York Times*, September 19, 1989, 1; Jason Deparle, "Rude, Rash, Effective, Act-Up Shifts AIDS Policy," *The New York Times*, January 3, 1990, B1.

378 *The next year . . . October 11*: Faderman, *The Gay Revolution*, 430–31. By then, Kameny was distraught by the lack of mobilization to respond to the increasingly deadly epidemic. When he learned that the government was delaying testing of a new drug, Ribavirin, he wrote to the President's Commission on the HIV Epidemic: "For heavens sake get the drug tested—properly—once and for all! NOW!!! Pronto!!" And why, he asked, was there not a "Manhattan Project" initiative to find a cure? See FEK to James D. Watkins, April 8, 1988, Box 122, Folder 7, FEK Papers.

378 *The partnership between . . . healthy lives*: "One World, One Hope: Vancouver 1996," in *20 Years of the International AIDS Society*, Lars Kallings and Craig McClure (Geneva: International AIDS Society, 2008), 28.

378 *The discovery of . . . for three hundred thousand Americans*: "First 500,000 AIDS Cases—United States, 1995," *Morbidity and Mortality Weekly Report* 44, no. 46 (November 24, 1995), 849–53.

378 *On average, for . . . each day*: Amy Goldstein, "Gay Social Club in D.C. Raises Health Concerns," *The Washington Post*, April 17, 1995, 1. In 1985, the death toll in Washington was 104. See James Schwartz, "AIDS: Now a Number 1 Killer," *The Washington Post*, July 28, 1985, B5.

378 *Ron Balin*: "Ronald Balin," *The Washington Post*, August 4, 1988, D5.

378 *Marty Robinson*: Bruce Lambert, "Martin Robinson, 49, Organizer of Demonstrations for Gay Rights," *The New York Times*, March 24, 1992, 22.

378 *Jim Owles*: David W. Dunlap, "James W. Owles Is Dead at 46; Was Founder of Gay Rights Group," *The New York Times*, August 8, 1993, 46.

378 *Leonard Matlovich*: "Gay Activist Leonard Matlovich, 44, Is Buried with Full Military Honors," *Chicago Tribune*, July 3, 1988, https://www.chicagotribune.com/news/ct-xpm-1988-07-03-8801120440-story.html.

378 *Bob Martin had . . . fiftieth birthday*: Ray Smith, "SHL Founder Stephen 'Donnie' Donaldson," *GABLES Community News* 5, no. 1 (September 1996), http://www.columbia.edu/cu/gables/hiv/mem/donaldson.html.

379 *During his 1992 . . . in the military*: Susan Baer, "Clinton Reaffirms His Promise to End Military's Ban on Gays," *The Baltimore Sun*, November 12, 1992, https://www.chicagotribune.com/news/ct-xpm-1988-07-03-8801120440-story.html.

379 *his compromise legislation . . . the closet*: Joyce Murdoch, "Sailor Who Disclosed Homosexuality Now Finds Himself in Legal Limbo: At Least 100 in Military Are Affected by Clinton Compromise," *The Washington Post*, February 8, 1993, 6.

379 *A greater victory . . . of security*: Todd S. Purdam, "Clinton Ends Ban on Security Clearance for Gay Workers," *The New York Times*, August 5, 1995, 9. Three years later, Clinton signed Executive Order 13087, which added sexual orientation to the list of classifications protected from discrimination in federal employment. See FEK, "Government v. Gays: Two Sad Stories with Two Happy Endings, Civil Service Employment and Security Clearances," 1998–1999, Box 160, Folder 1, FEK Papers.

379 *"The Government has . . . become an ally"*: FEK, "Government v. Gays: Two Sad Stories with Two Happy Endings, Civil Service Employment and Security Clearances," 1998–1999, Box 160, Folder 1, FEK Papers.

379 *In 1990, when . . . a straight attorney*: Molly Ball, "How Gay Marriage Became a Constitutional Right," *The*

Atlantic, July 1, 2015, https://www.theatlantic.com/politics/archive/2015/07/gay-marriage-supreme-court -politics-activism/397052.

379 *on May 5 . . . gay marriage ban*: Previously, Lambda Legal's Evan Wolfson was only permitted to submit an amicus brief in favor of the couple's right to marry. See ibid.; Faderman, *The Gay Revolution*, 586–87.

379 *Clinton signed the . . . gay marriages*: Bull, "His Public Domain, His Private Pain."

379 *More and more . . . America's sodomy laws*: *Lawrence v. Texas*, 539 U.S. 558 (2003). See also Faderman, *The Gay Revolution*, 551.

379 *The next year . . . suit*: "Connecticut Supreme Court legalizes same-sex marriage," *The Boston Globe*, October 10, 2008, https://web.archive.org/web/20081013010832/http://www.boston.com/news/local/breaking _news/2008/10/connecticut_sup.html.

379 *On December 15 . . . District of Columbia*: Stefanie Dazio, "Same-Sex Marriage in D.C: A Timeline," *The Washington Post*, February 24, 2012, https://www.washingtonpost.com/blogs/the-buzz/post/same-sex -marriage-in-dc-a-timeline/2012/02/24/gIQAZoFTYR_blog.html.

379 *In 2011, New . . . in 2014*: Meanwhile, California voters amended the state constitution to ban gay marriage. In 2009, the Iowa Supreme Court overturned the state's gay marriage ban; legislatures in Vermont, Maine, and New Hampshire voted in favor of gay marriage. See "A Timeline of the Legalization of Same-Sex Marriage in the U.S.," Georgetown Law Library, August 6, 2019, http://guides.ll.georgetown.edu/c.php?g =592919&p=4182201.

380 *An Ohio ACLU . . . the country*: *Obergefell v. Hodges*, 576 U.S. ___ (2015); "*Obergefell, et al. v. Hodges*, Freedom to Marry in Ohio," ACLU, June 26, 2015, https://www.aclu.org/cases/obergefell-et-al-v-hodges-freedom -marry-ohio.

380 *For many couples . . . available: adoption*: "Long Before Same-Sex Marriage, 'Adopted Son' Could Mean 'Life Partner,'" NPR, June 28, 2015, https://www.npr.org/2015/06/28/418187875/long-before-same-sex -marriage-adopted-son-could-mean-life-partner; Koa Beck, "How Marriage Inequality Prompts Gay Partners to Adopt One Another," *The Atlantic*, November 27, 2013, https://www.theatlantic.com/national /archive/2013/11/how-marriage-inequality-prompts-gay-partners-to-adopt-one-another/281546.

380 *Barbara Gittings had . . . away in 2007*: Margalit Fox, "Barbara Gittings, 74, Prominent Gay Rights Activist Since '50s, Dies," *The New York Times*, March 15, 2007, https://www.nytimes.com/2007/03/15/obituaries /15gittings.html.

380 *A memorial bench . . . our hearts*": Kay Tobin Lahusen, interviewed by Eric Cervini, telephone, October 11, 2019; "Barbara Gittings," Find a Grave, February 18, 2007, https://www.findagrave.com/memorial /18047727/barbara-gittings.

380 *On June 16 . . . fifty-five years together*: Rachel Gordon, "Couple of 55 Years Tie the Knot—Again," *San Francisco Chronicle*, June 17, 2008, https://www.sfgate.com/news/article/Couple-of-55-years-tie-the-knot -again-3208710.php.

380 *Martin died two months later*: William Grimes, "Del Martin, Lesbian Activist, Dies at 87," *The New York Times*, August 27, 2008, https://www.nytimes.com/2008/08/28/us/28martin.html.

380 *In 2013, Eva . . . twenty-one years*: Eva Freund, email correspondence with Eric Cervini, March 30, 2019.

380 *Lilli Vincenz, the . . . married*: Kris McLaughlin, email correspondence with Lou Chibbaro Jr., March 3, 2020.

380 *Jack Baker and . . . fact, valid*: Erik Eckholm, "The Same-Sex Couple Who Got a Marriage License in 1971," *The New York Times*, May 16, 2015, https://www.nytimes.com/2015/05/17/us/the-same-sex-couple-who -got-a-marriage-license-in-1971.html; Matt Baume, "Meet the Gay Men Whose 1971 Marriage Was Finally Recognized," *The Advocate*, March 1, 2019, https://www.advocate.com/people/2019/3/01/meet-gay -men-whose-1971-marriage-was-finally-recognized.

380 *In the 1990s . . . the movement*: Michael Bronski, Z, April 1, 2002, https://zcomm.org/zmagazine/sylvia-rivera -1951-2002-by-michael-bronski; Clendinen and Nagourney, *Out for Good*, 171–72.

381 *That year, Randy . . . audience*: Randy Wicker in Michael Kasino, "TRANSforming Randy Wicker," September 22, 2016, https://www.youtube.com/watch?v=7my2TObmmDo. See also Randy Wicker, interviewed by Eric Cervini, July 28, 2017, Hoboken, NJ.

381 *In the 1970s . . . into Wicker's apartment*: Sewell Chan, "Marsha P. Johnson," *The New York Times*, March 8, 2018, https://www.nytimes.com/interactive/2018/obituaries/overlooked-marsha-p-johnson.html.

381 *For twelve years . . . in 1990*: Randy Wicker, interviewed by Eric Cervini, July 28, 2017, Hoboken, NJ.

381 *On July 6 . . . open*: Chan, "Marsha P. Johnson."

381 *At Johnson's funeral . . . chauvinist pig*": Randy Wicker in Michael Kasino, "TRANSforming Randy Wicker," September 22, 2016, https://www.youtube.com/watch?v=7my2TObmmDo. See also Randy Wicker, interviewed by Eric Cervini, July 28, 2017, Hoboken, NJ.

381 *Before Rivera died . . . Act*: Bronski, "Sylvia Rivera: 1951–2002."

381 *Even without trans . . . veto it*: Andrew Sullivan, "Bush's ENDA Veto," *The Atlantic*, October 24, 2007, https:// www.theatlantic.com/daily-dish/archive/2007/10/bushs-enda-veto/224244/.

382 *Randy Wicker, after . . . of resistance*: Randy Wicker, interviewed by Eric Cervini, telephone, April 1, 2019.

382 *That weekend, Stonewall . . . in Brooklyn*: Erin Faith Wilson and Trudy Ring, "What Came of the Stonewall

Rebels," *The Advocate*, June 28, 2015, https://www.advocate.com/stonewall/2015/06/28/what-came
-stonewall-rebels.

382 *In thirty states . . . their LGBTQ+ employees*: Ryan Thoreson, "Why the US needs the Equality Act," *The Hill*,
March 16, 2019, https://thehill.com/opinion/civil-rights/434287-why-the-us-needs-the-equality-act.

382 *Under the Trump . . . States military*: Ariane de Vogue and Zachary Cohen, "Supreme Court Allows Transgender Military Ban to Go into Effect," *CNN*, January 22, 2019, https://www-m.cnn.com/2019/01/22
/politics/scotus-transgender-ban/index.html.

382 *Kameny did not . . . decades earlier*: By no means was he a "compulsive coupler," as he called it. See FEK to
Paul Varnell, September 10, 1997, Box 153, Folder 2, FEK Papers. Michael McConnell confirmed Kameny's
views on marriage: Michael McConnell, interviewed by Eric Cervini, telephone, March 13, 2019. See also
Jose Antonio Vargas, "Signs of Progress," *Washington Post*, July 23, 2005, C1.

382 *On April 23 . . . in American history*: Lisa Rein, "John Berry, Head of OPM and Openly Gay, Helps Obama
Reach Out to Gay Community," *The Washington Post*, September 18, 2012, https://www.washingtonpost
.com/politics/john-berry-head-of-opm-and-openly-gay-helps-obama-reach-out-to-gay-community/2012
/09/18/3f0b8316-a453-11e1-9e73-f4e3879b34a3_story.html.

382 *Michelle Obama and . . . swearing-in ceremony*: Ed O'Keefe, "Michelle Obama Visits, John Berry Sworn In at
OPM," *The Washington Post*, April 23, 2009, http://voices.washingtonpost.com/federal-eye/2009/04/michelle
_obama_visits_opm.html.

382 *Two months later . . . federal employees*: Sullivan, "Obama Extends Benefits, Promises More for Gays."

383 *"Dear Dr. Kameny: . . . States government"*: Kevin Naff, "Gov't Apologizes to Kameny," *Washington Blade*, July
5, 2009, http://www.washblade.com/blog/blog.cfm?blog_id=25888+.

383 *"Apology accepted"*: Joe Davison, "Kameny's Fight for Gay Rights Made Federal Workforce Better for Us All,"
The Washington Post, October 12, 2011, https://www.washingtonpost.com/politics/kamenys-fight-for-gay
-rights-made-federal-workforce-better-for-us-all/2011/10/12/gIQAqL8AgL_story.html.

383 *The purges continued . . . sexual orientation*: The Williams Institute, "Discharges Under the Don't Ask/Don't
Tell Policy," September 2010, https://williamsinstitute.law.ucla.edu/wp-content/uploads/Gates-Discharges2009
-Military-Sept-2010.pdf.

383 *On December 22 . . . Infantryman Badge*: Matt Negrin, "Obama Signs 'Don't Ask' Repeal," *Politico*, December
22, 2010, https://www.politico.com/story/2010/12/obama-signs-dont-ask-repeal-046715; Sheryl Gay Stol-
berg, "Obama Signs Away 'Don't Ask, Don't Tell,'" *The New York Times*, December 22, 2010, https://www
.nytimes.com/2010/12/23/us/politics/23military.html; David Carter, "Pioneer Fighter for Gay Rights,"
CNN, December 24, 2010, http://www.cnn.com/2010/OPINION/12/24/carter.gay.rights.kameny/index
.html.

383 *A few months . . . an era*: Richard Luscombe, "Space Shuttle Atlantis Touches Down, Ending an Era of Adventure in Space," *The Guardian*, July 21, 2011, https://www.theguardian.com/science/2011/jul/21/space
-shuttle-atlantis-touches-down; Sarah Loff, "Space Shuttle Era," NASA, August 3, 2017, https://www.nasa
.gov/mission_pages/shuttle/flyout/index.html.

383 *Frank Kameny had . . . have seen*: Cindy Loose, "Gay Activists Summon Their Hopes, Resolve: March Comes
at Crucial Time, Leaders Say," *The Washington Post*, April 18, 1993, 1.

383 *At the age . . . morally good*: Bob Roehr, "Remember Me for 'Gay is Good,'" *PrideSource*, September 13, 2007,
https://pridesource.com/article/remember-me-for-gay-is-good.

384 *"Here you are . . . are invigorating"*: FEK to Clifford Norton, July 11, 1969, Box 29, Folder 5, FEK Papers.

384 *Kameny died in . . . Coming Out Day*: David W. Dunlap, "Franklin Kameny, Gay Rights Pioneer, Dies at 86,"
The New York Times, October 12, 2011, https://www.nytimes.com/2011/10/13/us/franklin-kameny-gay
-rights-pioneer-dies-at-86.html.

384 *"Gay is good. It is."*: FEK in *The Same Sex*, ed. Ralph W. Weltge, 145.

INDEX

Page numbers in *italics* refer to photographs.

ILLUSTRATION CREDITS

page 6: from Laud Humphreys, *Tearoom Trade: Impersonal Sex in Public Places* (New Brunswick: AldineTransaction, 1970), 35. Reproduced with permission of Taylor & Francis Group LLC.

page 17: Courtesy of Eric Marcus and the *Making Gay History* podcast. Reproduced with permission of the Franklin Edward Kameny estate.

page 29: Library of Congress Prints and Photographs Division, Washington, D.C.

page 47: from J. Edgar Hoover, "How Safe Is Your Daughter?" *American Magazine* 144 (July 1947), 33.

page 66: from James Shawcross, "How the Reds Blackmailed Homosexuals into Spying for Them!" *Top Secret* (February 1961), 14.

page 79: from *Mattachine Review* 3 (May-June 1955). Reproduced with the permission of the New York Public Library.

page 93: SAC, WFO, to Director, FBI, August 8, 1961, FBI File #100-403320.

page 113: from Ray Hanson, "Arise!!," *Texas Ranger* (April 1960), 19. Courtesy of Randy Wicker. Reproduced by permission of Texas Student Media.

page 135: "Barbara Gittings Eating, 1960-65." Photograph by Kay Tobin Lahusen. New York Public Library Digital Collections. Reproduced with the permission of the New York Public Library.

page 155: Photograph of John Dowdy, Box 451A, Folder 74, John V. Dowdy Sr. Papers, Baylor Collections of Political Materials, W. R. Poage Legislative Library, Baylor University. Reproduced with the permission of Baylor University.

page 180: Renee Cafiero at the Whitehall Induction Center, September 19, 1964. Courtesy of Randy Wicker.

page 196: Mondadori Portfolio / Getty Images.

page 214: MSW Surveillance Photograph, Box 158, Folder 2, FEK Papers. Reproduced with the permission of the Library of Congress.

page 230: "Barbara Gittings in Picket Line, 1965." Photograph by Kay Tobin Lahusen. New York Public Library Digital Collections. Reproduced with the permission of the New York Public Library.

page 244: Frank Kameny and Bob Martin on Fire Island, September 1966, Box 122, Folder 3, FEK Papers. Reproduced with the permission of the Library of Congress.

page 261: CBS Reports, "The Homosexuals," March 1967. Reprinted with the permission of CBS News, a Division of CBS Inc.

page 280: "The Second Largest Minority," 1968. Photograph by Lilli Vincenz. The National Audio-Visual Conservation Center, Library of Congress. Reproduced with the permission of the Library of Congress and the Vincenz estate.

page 302: "Stonewall Celebrations, 1969," June 28, 1969. Fred W. McDarrah / Getty Images.

page 325: "Women Picketing While Holding Hands." Photograph by Nancy Tucker. New York